THE MOVEMENT

DOCUMENTARY OF A STRUGGLE FOR EQUALITY

TEXT BY **LORRAINE HANSBERRY**

SIMON AND SCHUSTER · NEW YORK · 1964

*This book was prepared with the cooperation and assistance
of the Student Nonviolent Coordinating Committee.*

It is a terrible, an inexorable law that one cannot deny the humanity of another without diminishing one's own. —JAMES BALDWIN

This is the road from Jackson to Yazoo City, leading into the Mississippi Delta country, the heart of the Deep South.

In the countryside, between the towns, familiar images of the
Old South are conjured up . . .

... all of them.

The New South slams up against the Old, but the coming of industry into the Southland has not changed the problems of many of its people—white or black —for the better.

That is why, for a long time, one of the South's chief exports has been people. Their destination: the ghettos of the North.

The Negro baby born in America today, regardless of the section or the state in which he is born, has about one-half as much chance of completing a high school as a white baby born in the same place, on the same day; one-third as much chance of completing college; one-third as much chance of becoming a professional man; twice as much chance of becoming unemployed; about one-seventh as much chance of earning $10,000 a year; a life expectancy which is seven years shorter, and the prospects of earning only half as much.

—JOHN F. KENNEDY, in his broadcast to the nation, June 11, 1963.

In both North and South, joblessness and decrepitude. But in the South there is something else too: being treated as a joke, as local color, as part of "a charming way of life."

Not that people don't create things to sustain themselves. Not that people don't find things to smile about. Not, certainly, that they do not know how to endure. . . .

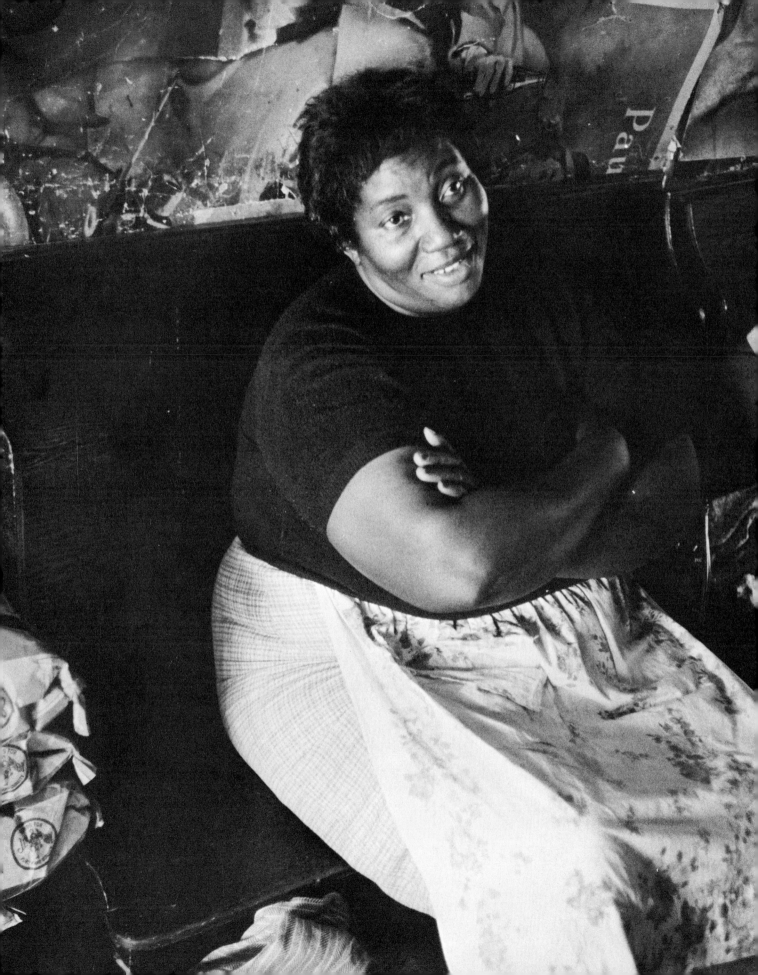

There's a great deal to endure. This man earns about $2.50 a day.

And if a man's family is hungry, he may steal, and if he steals he can be sentenced to years of hard labor. In some states, convict labor has long been commonplace.

The sentences inflicted are cruel and excessive. Twenty-five per cent of the convicts are condemned for life and sixty per cent for ten years or more.... The fortunes of many a prominent white Georgia family are red with the blood of black men justly and unjustly held to labor in Georgia prison camps....—William E. B. DuBois, 1906

And then there is all the complicated silliness that a system took so much trouble to create. The silly . . .

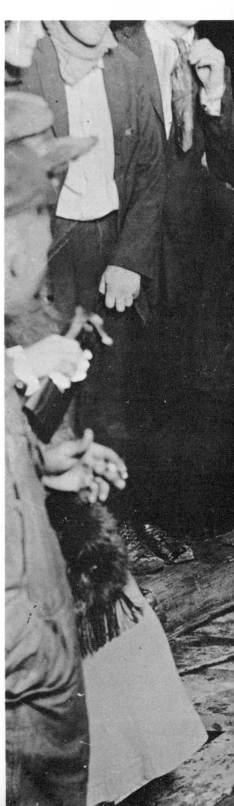

. . . and the unspeakable.

The laws which enforce segregation do not presume the inferiority of a people; they assume an inherent equalness. It is the logic of the lawmakers that if a society does not erect artificial barriers between the people at every point of contact, the people might fraternize and give their attention to the genuine, shared problems of the community.

The results prevail everywhere.

Who can look upon the turbulence in men's eyes and pretend
he has witnessed contentment—or even resignation?

On February 1, 1960, four Negro students sat down at the "white only" lunch counter of the Woolworth store in Greensboro, North Carolina. What followed is changing the entire nation.

I woke up this morning with my mind
Stayed on freedom,
I woke up this morning with my mind
Stayed on freedom,
I woke up this morning with my mind
Stayed on freedom,
Hallelu, Hallelu, Hallelujah!

Everywhere across the Southern landscape young Negroes picked up the aspiration of their fathers, re-kindled it, and started marching.

TODAY'S OBJECTIVE: before she is an adult, FREEDOM

NOW!

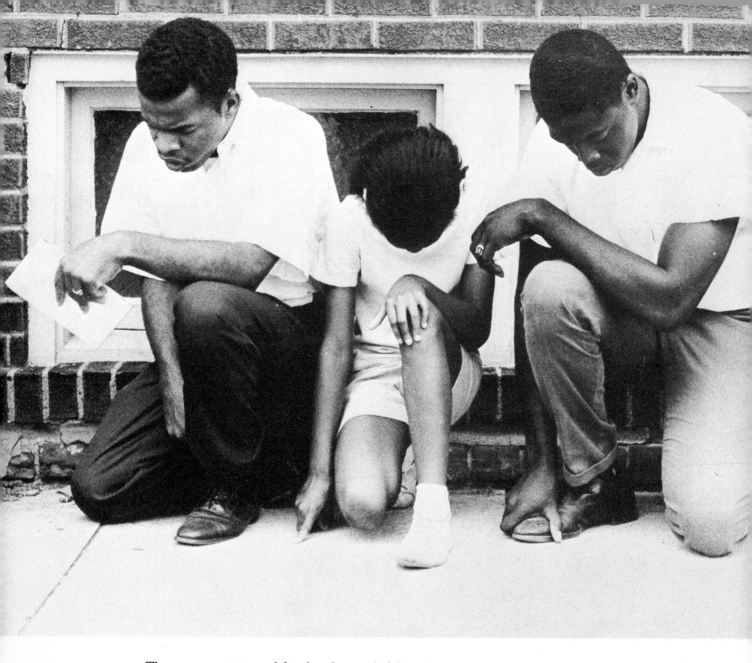

The movement toward freedom has varied faces.
It draws on the devotions of our culture—traditional Christianity . . .

. . . and more recently, Islam:
We believe in the One God Whose proper Name is Allah. . . . We believe this is the time in history for the separation of the so-called Negroes and the so-called white Americans. . . . We believe that the offer of integration is hypocritical and is made by those who are trying to deceive the black peoples into believing that their 400-year-old open enemies of freedom, justice and equality are, all of a sudden, their 'friends.' . . .
—Muhammad Speaks

The Black Muslim movement represents a pot-luck nationalism that looks backward, not to the wonders of black African civilization of medieval and antique periods, but to Arabic cultures. Muslim "separation" is not a program, but an accommodation to American racism. It is, nonetheless, an important indicator of the anguished frustrations of a people who find "eleven o'clock on Sunday morning the most segregated hour in America." And its followers are dedicated, disciplined, intimidating.

The main burden of Negro aspiration remains what it has always been: total integration into the fabric of a nation which our slave fathers helped to create. EQUALITY: economic, political, social, civil.

The Movement is very old. It began in the seventeenth century when Africans being transported to the New World mutinied on the high seas. Under slavery, it took the form of sabotage, escape and insurrection. It came to a climax in the Civil War, when thousands of black men and women fought for freedom—as spies, in service units and, above all, as fighting troops of Abraham Lincoln's Grand Army of the Republic. In stunning contradiction to the myth of Negro passivity, there has been virtually no institution of Negro life, from the churches to the blues, which has not had a fundamental preoccupation with freedom. The "new Negro" has merely brought to the Movement new methods and fresh determination.

We have got about five hundred guns, aplenty of lead, but not much powder. I hope you have made a good collection of powder and ball, and will hold yourself in readiness to strike whenever called for and never be out of the way. It will not be long before it will take place.
    —Note from a Negro slave insurrectionist, Yorktown, Virginia, circa 1793

I began to direct my attention to this great object, to fulfill the purpose for which, by this time, I felt assured I was intended.
—NAT TURNER, leader of slave insurrection, Southampton County, Virginia, 1831

By every consideration which binds you to your enslaved fellow countrymen, and the peace and welfare of your country; by every aspiration which you cherish for the freedom and equality of yourselves and your children; by all the ties of blood and identity which make us one with the brave black men now fighting our battles in Louisiana and in South Carolina, I urge you to fly to arms and smite with death the power that would bury the government and your liberty in this same hopeless grave.
    —FREDERICK DOUGLASS, 1863

We want to live in peace with all mankind, and especially with the whites of the South. Our interests are identical. But we do not want the peace of the lamb with the lion. . . . Give us our rights! Will you do this or force us away from you?
    —Negro minister, Selma, Alabama, 1887

TODAY: James Baldwin

WE SHALL OVERCOME!

But the ways of the *old* order have not changed.

What the dogs and guns and hoses have proved is that the entire power structure of the South must be altered. The original demand for equal treatment on buses and at lunch counters has had to broaden and sharpen, to strike at the political base of Negro oppression...

. . . by demanding the vote.
In doing so, the Negro has tried to gain the protection of the Federal Government. For the most part, it has been a futile effort.

These young men are standing on United States Government property in Selma, Alabama.

Moving in to arrest them are "local authority" in the person of Sheriff Jim Clarke and his men.

Officials of the U. S. Department of Justice and agents of the Federal Bureau of Investigation were mere yards away. They took no action.

Assistant Attorney General Burke Marshall:
I'm not running a police force.

Theron Lynd, Registrar of Forrest County, Mississippi.

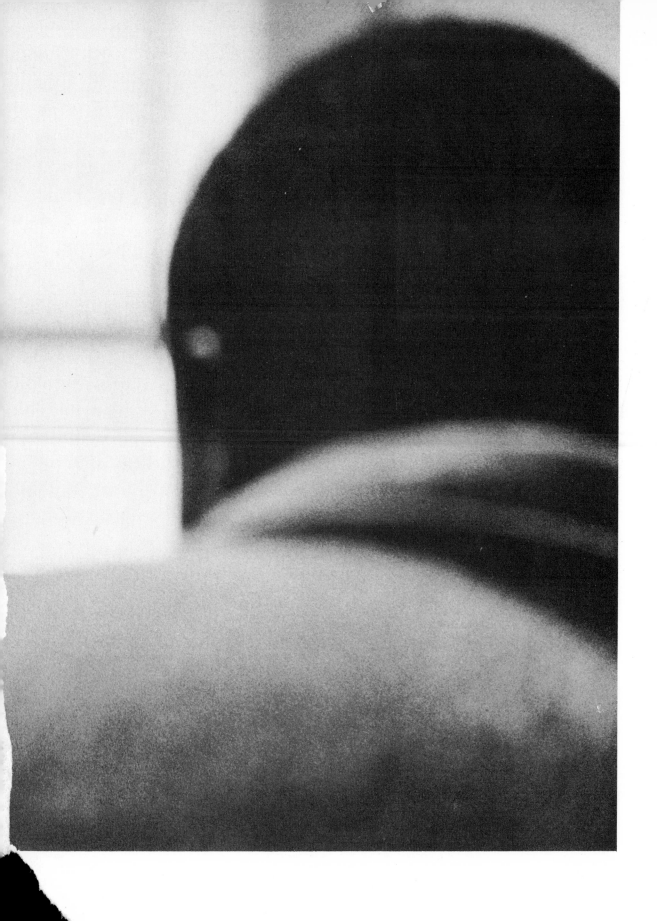

The men in helmets are from a class of Southerners who are themselves victims of a system that has used them and their fathers before them for generations.

In the South the great planters form proportionately a quite small class, but they have, singularly enough, at their command some five million poor whites; that is, there were actually more white people to police the slaves than there were slaves. Considering the economic rivalry of the black and white worker, it would have seemed natural that the poor white would have refused to police the slave. But two considerations led him in the opposite direction. First of all, it gave him work and some authority as overseer, slave driver and member of the patrol system. But above and beyond this, it fed his vanity because it associated him with the masters. To these Negroes he transferred all the dislike and hatred he had for the whole slave system. The result was the system was held stable and intact by the poor white.

—WILLIAM E. B. DuBois, 1935

"Are you a nigger
    or a white man?"

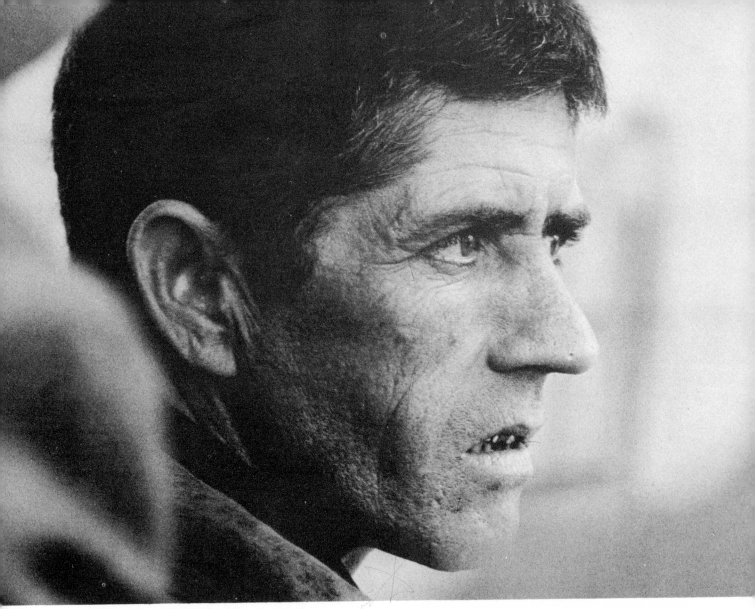

Whites across the South observe and react in their different ways: Alabama, Georgia and, above, Ole Miss at the time of James Meredith's admission . . .

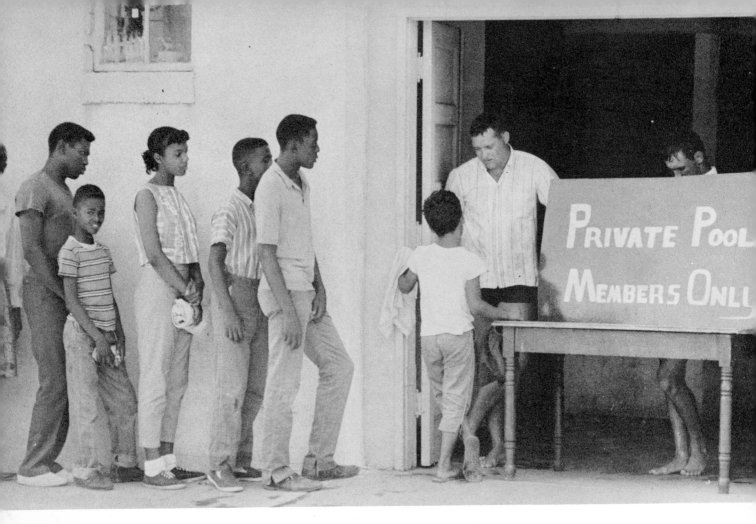

. . . while the Movement keeps on growing and spreading, East, West, North. Above, a swimming pool in Cairo, Illinois.

Allies crop up in meaningful places. This Atlanta woman stepped forward to defend the demonstrators against the mob, crying out, "Leave them alone! What do you know about what it is to be black?" They turned upon her after that, and she began to cry and then sat down in the street with the demonstrators.

But always the legacy of the past holds.
North and South...

...the old order, which must be protected from these new giants.

The jails fill, empty, fill again. From Alabama...

. . . to New York. But many testify that the experience of being behind bars can transcend the immediate realities of imprisonment.

We are smuggling this note from the drunk tank of the county jail in Magnolia, Mississippi. Twelve of us are here, sprawled out along the concrete bunker; Curtis Hayes, Hollis Watkins, Ike Lewis, and Robert Talbert, four veterans of the bunker, are sitting up talking—mostly about girls; Charles McDew ("Tell the story") is curled into the concrete and the wall; Harold Robinson, Stephen Ashley, James Wells, Lee Chester Vick, Leotus Eubanks, and Ivory Diggs lay cramped on the cold bunker; I'm sitting with smuggled pen and paper, thinking a little, writing a little; Myrtis Bennett and Janie Campbell are across the way wedded to a different icy cubicle.

Later on Hollis will lead out with a clear tenor into a freedom song; Talbert and Lewis will supply jokes; and McDew will discourse on the history of the black man and the Jew. McDew—a black by birth, a Jew by choice and a revolutionary by necessity—has taken on the deep hates and deep loves which America, and the world, reserve for those who dare to stand in a strong sun and cast a sharp shadow.

In the words of Judge Brumfield, who sentenced us, we are "cold calculators" who design to disrupt the racial harmony . . . of McComb into racial strife and rioting; we, he said, are the leaders who are causing young children to be led like sheep to the pen to be slaughtered (in a legal manner). "Robert," he was addressing me, "haven't some of the people from your school been able to go down and register without violence here in Pike County?" I thought to myself that Southerners are most exposed when they boast.

It's mealtime now: we have rice and gravy in a flat pan, dry bread and a "big town cake"; we lack eating and drinking utensils. Water comes from a faucet and goes into a hole.

This is Mississippi, the middle of the iceberg. Hollis is leading off with his tenor, "Michael, row the boat ashore, Alleluia; Christian brothers don't be slow, Alleluia; Mississippi's next to go, Alleluia." This is a tremor in the middle of the iceberg.

—Bob Moses, November 1, 1961

The stockade was about a mile out of town. The car pulled up to the side of the building. The boys went around the front and kept "Pop," the guard, busy by talking to him. I crawled around the back and shot through the bars in the rear. All the girls had been arrested in demonstrations in Americus. Some had been in the stockade a few days, others had been there for three weeks; they had no furniture, blankets or clothing other than what they had been arrested in. The toilet was clogged and gave off a smell strong enough to be sickening outside the building. The only source of water for washing or drinking was a dripping shower head. It was just one long room with bars on the windows. I reached through the broken glass to the girls. They all reached out. "Freedom." They wanted to know my name. Their daily food consisted of four cold hamburgers each in the morning. When I saw them they were in good spirits.   —DANNY LYON, 1964

Freedom fighters have believed that if there is anything at all to America's much touted sense of fair play, then the airing of the Negro's grievances and aspirations should have some meaningful effect. It was this lingering hope that led us, by the hundreds of thousands, to the nation's capital on August 28th, 1963 . . .

. . . to sing and listen and let the whole world see, as Langston Hughes said decades ago, "How beautiful I am!"

Different rallies, different faces...

. . . And three weeks
after the March
on Washington,
this was Birmingham's
answer:

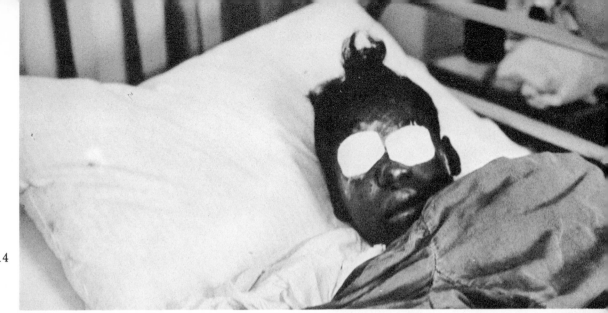

Addie Mae Collins, 14
Denise McNair, 11
Carol Robertson, 14
Cynthia Wesley, 14

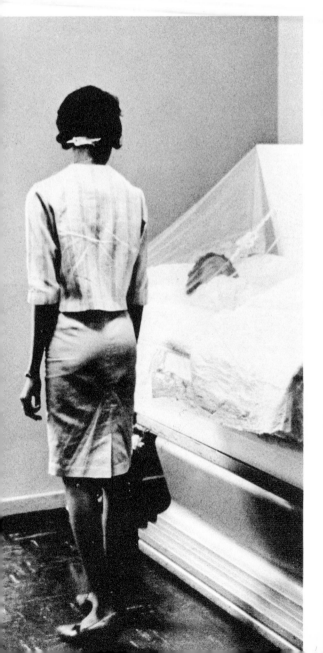

In the aftermath of the Sunday school bombing, twenty million people began to ask with a new urgency: Is nonviolence the way?

The responsibility for an answer lies heavy on the hearts and shoulders of the men who lead.

Why come ye hither, redcoat?
Your mind what madness fills?
In our valleys there is danger!
And there's dangers in our hills!
—"The Riflemen of Bennington," an American Revolutionary broadside

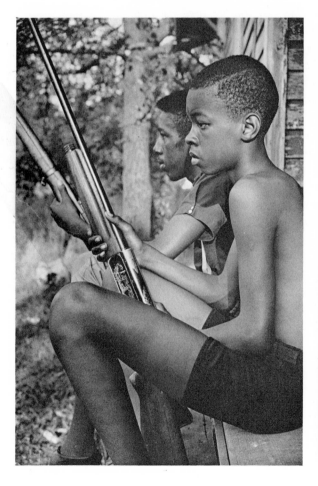

I have in my church black men, fugitive slaves. They are the crown of my apostleship, the seal of my ministry. It becomes me to look after their bodies in order to save their souls. I have had to arm myself. I have written my sermons with a pistol on my desk, loaded . . . ready for action. Yes, with a drawn sword within reach of my right hand. . . . You know I do not like fighting; it is no small matter which will compel me to shed human blood. But what could I do? I was born in the little town where the fight and the bloodshed of the Revolution began. My grandfather fired the first shot in the Revolution. The blood that flowed there was kindred to this which courses in my veins today. . . . With these things before me . . . when a fugitive, pursued by kidnappers, came to my house, what could I do but defend her to the last? Oh, my brothers . . . I should not dare to violate the eternal law of God!
—THE REVEREND THEODORE PARKER, Boston abolitionist, 1850

We must use nonviolence as a means as long as this is feasible but . . . there are those who pretend to be horrified by the idea that a black veteran who shouldered arms for the United States would willingly take up weapons to defend his wife, his children, his home and his life. . . . We use and approve nonviolent resistance. But we also believe that a man cannot have human dignity if he allows himself to be abused on the basis that he is so pious, so self-righteous, that it would demean his personality if he fought back.
—ROBERT WILLIAMS, former Monroe, North Carolina, NAACP chapter head

It is an error to think of Negro citizens as beggars at The Golden Door, waiting to see if their countrymen will somehow "accept" them. The demands of the Negro Movement are far more audacious than that. We are "old stock" Americans in every sense: by blood, culture and temperament. We were here when the great European migrations came in the mid- and late eighteen hundreds. That is why we bristle when the grandsons and even the sons of the new ones lean back in their chairs and say that they think they will find it permissible for one of us to be President in another half-century. *We are old stock Americans, that arrogant, that certain of the rightness of our American cause.* That's why we borrow as freely from Patrick Henry as from contemporary slang.

And because we are also, strangely enough under the circumstances, patriotic Americans, most of us would prefer *not* to see this country torn with violence. We are still willing, despite the dogs and the hoses and the police, to set forth the message of our discontent by walking and talking ...

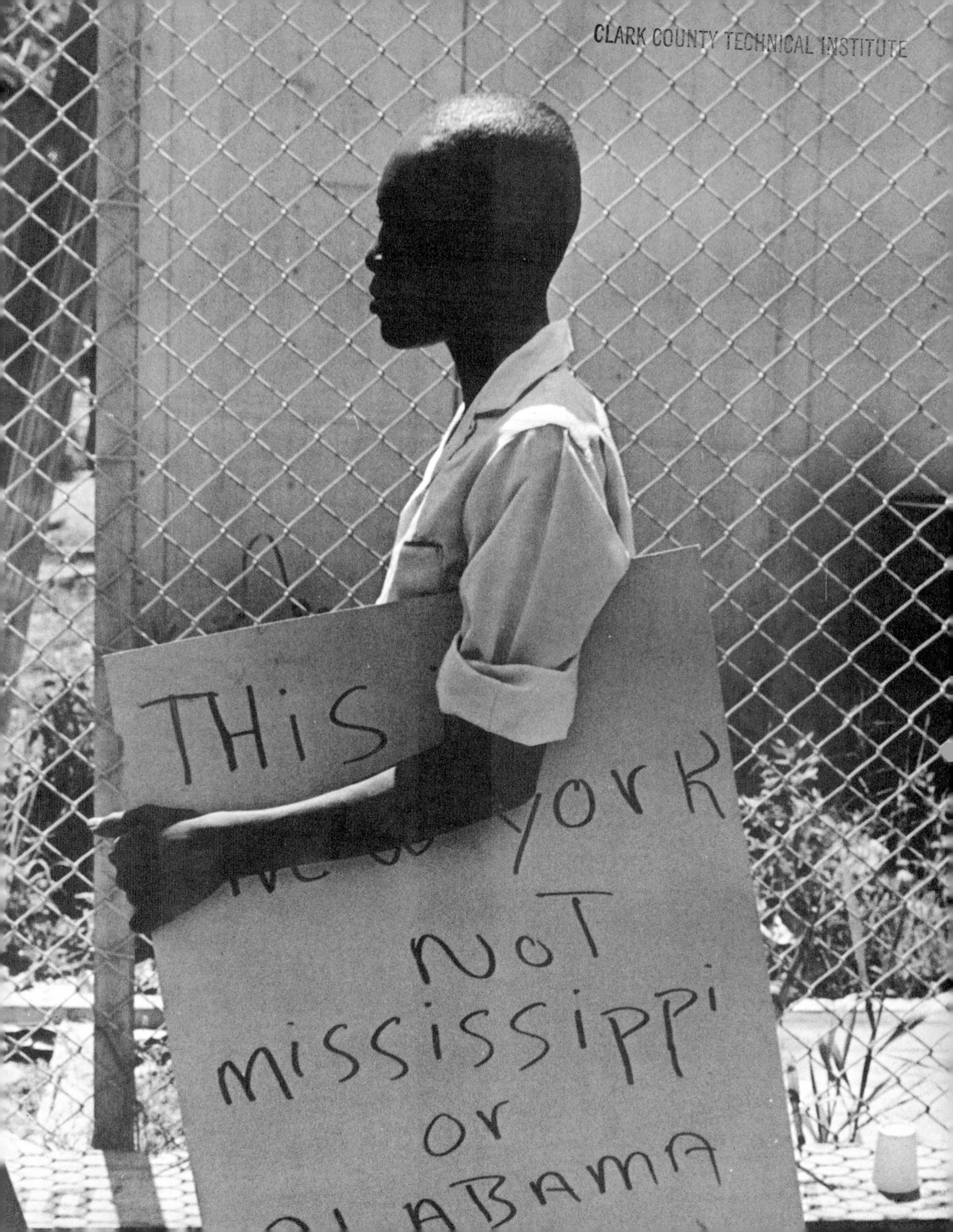
THIS
YORK
NOT
MISSISSIPPI
OR

...and sitting on pavements...

. . . and filling the air with freedom songs. The next time you pass a demonstration, hum a little or clap your hands, pick up the words. Perhaps the time after that you will join in and sing—for my freedom and for yours. You, I mean you, my countryman, reading this.

For it's not a threat but a fact that there are meaningful voices which ridicule the belief that the American vision can be made to work. Symbols of this point of view: the berets and dark shirts of Black Nationalists . . .

. . . or simply the assertion of a newfound West African past.

This, some of our people would now say, is fraternization with "white devils."
They do not laugh when they say it.

Others still find it in themselves to continue to work at voter registration and the teaching of nonviolent tactics.

Leaders for many years: (seated) A. Philip Randolph; Roy Wilkins; Bayard Rustin. And in New York, below, the actor-playwright Ossie Davis.

The man in Mississippi: Robert Moses, educated at Hamilton and at Harvard, who went South for the Student Nonviolent Coordinating Committee (SNCC) in 1961; who directed the Mississippi Summer Project in 1964; who has narrowly escaped assassination and been brutally beaten.

All ages, every manner of action. Comedian Dick Gregory . . . SNCC worker Doris Latner of Jackson, Mississippi . . . Mrs. Fannie Lou Hamer of Ruleville, Mississippi. When Mrs. Hamer tried to register to vote, she lost her job as a plantation worker; in 1964 she ran for Congress in Senator Eastland's district.

In community after community, the Movement thrusts up new, energetic leadership. Two of the leading theorists and strategists of the Student Nonviolent Coordinating Committee are James Forman (seated) and John Lewis. The leader of the movement in Cambridge, Maryland: Mrs. Gloria Richardson (below and at right).

The Movement has been influenced by the spirit of Frederick Douglass, who associated the abolition of slavery with human rights everywhere. Today, leaders such as Bayard Rustin (above) and James Farmer (below center) insist that the achievement of Negro rights must carry with it genuine first-class status for Puerto Ricans, Mexicans and Indian Americans.

Malcolm X. Sometimes his volatile words sound like an easier way to freedom than . . .

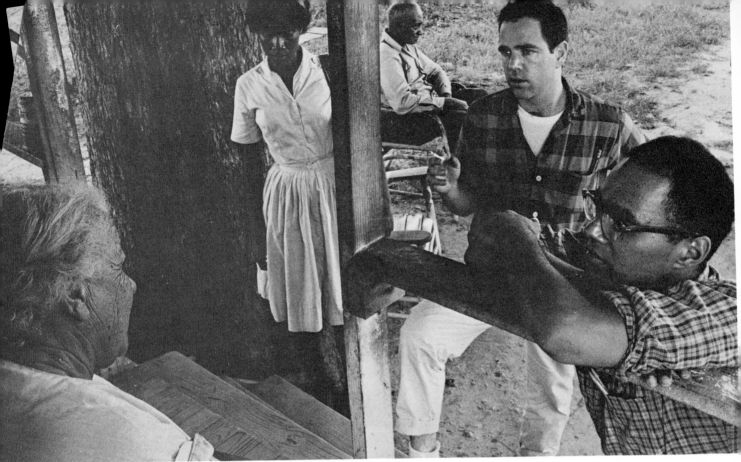

. . . working, talking, persuading: "Come down and try to register. You may lose your job, you may even lose your house. You may be beaten . . . but join us, come on down and register to vote."

NOTICE

Applications for Registration must be completely filled out without any assistance or suggestions of any person or memorandum.

After 10 days applicants names and addresses are published for two consecutive weeks in the newspaper. They cannot be ruled on until 14 days after the second publication. Therefore it can take as long as 33 days before we can give you an answer as to your application being accepted or rejected.

Your indulgence is appreciated.

The REGISTRAR

The SNCC office in Greenwood is like a front company headquarters during war-time. . . . I was greeted by Annelle Ponder, whose younger sister I taught at Spelman College. . . . The Ponder girls are all tall, black-skinned and beautiful. Annelle has been in Greenwood this past year handling the Southern Christian Leadership Conference's part of the voter registration project. She has been beaten by police in Winona, Mississippi. When friends went to the jail one day, they found her sitting there, her face swollen and marked, barely able to speak. She looked up at them, and just managed to whisper one word: "Freedom." —HOWARD ZINN, *The Nation*

People do not always need poets and playwrights to state their case. This woman has just said:
I worked for three dollars a day. I want freedom. All my life I want freedom. We all cry for freedom!

Everyone who had demonstrated lined up in the parking lot nearby. A pickup truck came tearing down the street and drove straight into the crowd. We all scattered except this girl, who wouldn't move. The truck slammed on its brakes, then hit her. She got up after that. She wasn't hurt too badly. —DANNY LYON

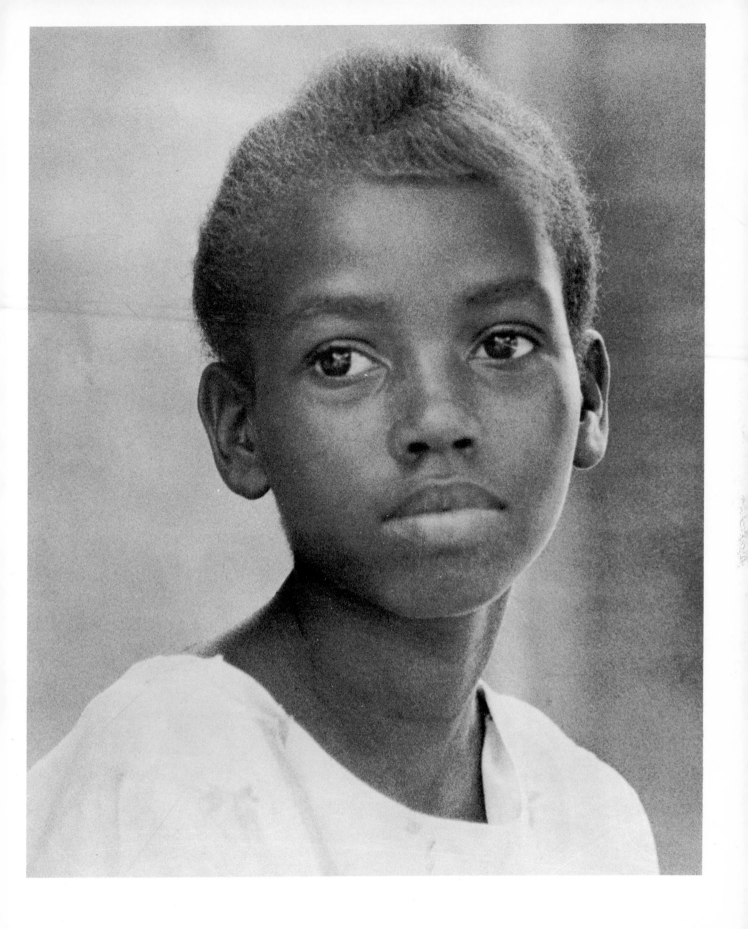

COME...TOGETHER
Let Us Build A
Non-Violent World

They stand in the hose fire at Birmingham; they stand in the rain at Hattiesburg.
They are young, they are beautiful, they are determined.
It is for us to create, now, an America that deserves them.

THE PHOTOGRAPHS: Credits and Comments

frontispiece DECLAN HAUN, Black Star.

PAGE

7 DANNY LYON.

8 MATT HERRON. Windsor, a famous Mississippi plantation mansion, burned shortly after the Civil War. This area of the Grand Gulf was never rebuilt.

9 NORRIS McNAMARA. In the Delta, overlooking the Mississippi River.

10–11 UNKNOWN PHOTOGRAPHER.

12 *top*—DANNY LYON. Phenix City, Alabama.
bottom—DANNY LYON. In the Delta, just south of Greenville, Mississippi.

13 DANNY LYON. Panama City, Florida.

14 ROY DE CARAVA. New York City.

15 DON CHARLES. New York City.

16–18 ROY DE CARAVA. New York City.

19 DANNY LYON. The French Quarter of New Orleans.

20 DANNY LYON. Greenwood, Mississippi.

21 NORRIS McNAMARA. A woman in her own store at Boquechille, Alabama.

22 DANNY LYON. Ruleville, Mississippi.

23 DANNY LYON. Arkansas State Prison Farm.

24 DANNY LYON. Dougherty County Courthouse, Albany, Georgia.

25 BROWN BROTHERS. Omaha, Nebraska, 1919.

26 *top*—DANNY LYON. Jackson, Mississippi.
bottom—DANNY LYON. Atlanta, Georgia.

27 *top*—TONY ROLLO, Newsweek.
bottom—DANNY LYON. Moscow, Fayette County, Tennessee.

28 UPI. Detroit, 1943.

29 ROBERT FRANK. New Orleans.

30 LEROY McLUCAS. New York City.

31 *top*—DANNY LYON. Selma, Alabama.
bottom—DON CHARLES. New York City.

32 DANNY LYON. Ruleville, Mississippi.

33 DANNY LYON. Near Pine Bluff, Arkansas.

34–35 DAVID HEATH. From his book *A Dialogue with Solitude,* published by The Community Press, Culpeper, Virginia.

PAGE

37 NORRIS McNAMARA. Albany, Georgia. "One night this appeared on stop signs all over the city."

38 DANNY LYON. Atlanta, Georgia.

39 DANNY LYON. Washington, D. C.

40 KENNETH THOMPSON. Savannah, Georgia.

41 DANNY LYON. Hattiesburg, Mississippi.

42 DANNY LYON. Atlanta, Georgia.

43 ROY DE CARAVA. New York City.

44 DANNY LYON. Danville, Virginia. "Three days after 'bloody Monday,' a night when forty demonstrators were sent to the hospital with billy-club wounds and busted heads, the demonstrators returned to City Hall. They wanted to see the mayor. He wouldn't see them so they sat down and waited. They waited till twelve midnight. Then police and two fire trucks scattered them."

45 ENRICO SARSINI. Chicago, Illinois.

46 DANNY LYON. Cairo, Illinois, August 1962. "On the left is John Lewis. He had been active in the Freedom Rides and the Nashville Movement. Soon he would become Chairman of SNCC. He led about fifty people to the small city hall of Cairo, where they knelt in prayer in protest against segregation in Cairo and in sympathy with the struggle in Albany, Georgia."

47 DON CHARLES. Malcolm X (upper right) and Muslims.

48 DON CHARLES. Muslim FOI (Fruit of Islam) members are guarding the cars in which The Honorable Elijah Muhammad and his entourage will ride. Harlem.

49 DON CHARLES.

50 *top*—DANNY LYON. Greenwood, Mississippi, March 1963. "This was a big mass meeting for Greenwood. A year before there weren't twenty people who dared come to a mass meeting in the Delta."
bottom—BOB ADELMAN. New York City.

51 KENNETH THOMPSON. Savannah, Georgia.

53 DANNY LYON. Selma, Alabama. "It was the evening after Selma's Freedom Day. In a town famous for its lynchings, 350 people had stood at the courthouse for eight hours waiting to be registered. Five were. Some SNCC members were arrested. Two were beaten in the streets. James Baldwin, for the first time in his life, had seen the South in operation."

54 *top*—DANNY LYON. Atlanta, Georgia.

bottom—DANNY LYON. "On the steps of the Movement church, in defiance of the police and posse across the street, high school students came out to sing. They had been the backbone of the Selma Movement and only after a month of marches and sit-ins would their parents dare to join them at the courthouse."

55 DANNY LYON. Selma, Alabama. A sixteen-year-old high school student active in the Movement.

56 DANNY LYON. Atlanta, Georgia. "This is seventeen-year-old Taylor Washington, militant teenager in the Atlanta Movement. An honor student in high school. It was Taylor's eighth arrest in Atlanta."

57 DANNY LYON. Birmingham, Alabama. Early Monday morning, the day after the bombing of the Sixteenth Street Baptist Church, a state trooper eyes the ruins.

58 *top*—DANNY LYON. Danville, Virginia.

bottom—FRANK DANDRIDGE. Cambridge, Maryland.

59 *top* — FRANK DANDRIDGE. Cambridge, Maryland.

bottom—DANNY LYON. Hattiesburg, Mississippi.

60 *top*—DANNY LYON. Oxford, Mississippi. A Mississippi highway patrolman awaiting the arrival of James Meredith.

bottom — BOB ADELMAN. Birmingham, Alabama.

61 NORRIS McNAMARA. Selma, Alabama.

62–63 DANNY LYON. Selma, Alabama. "Freedom Day: a line of 350 Negroes stands at the courthouse across the street

when two SNCC workers suddenly emerge from the old postoffice building with picket signs."

64–65 MATT HERRON. Hattiesburg, Mississippi. An injunction ordering Theron Lynd to cease discrimination against Negroes was issued by a Federal court more than a year ago. He refused to comply and was cited for contempt. Despite this citation, no fines or imprisonment have been imposed on him.

66 NORRIS McNAMARA. Selma, Alabama. Sheriff Jim Clarke tells James Forman of SNCC to move on.

67 *top*—DANNY LYON. Birmingham, Alabama, the day after the bombing of the Sixteenth Street Baptist Church.

bottom—DANNY LYON. Clarksdale, Mississippi. "That day, members of the church had come from the North to meet with Clarksdale ministers about the situation there. These officers stood guard across the street."

68 DANNY LYON. Danville, Virginia.

69 DANNY LYON. Atlanta, Georgia.

70 *top*—DANNY LYON. Selma, Alabama.

bottom—DANNY LYON. Savannah, Georgia.

71 DANNY LYON. Oxford, Mississippi. These students at "Ole Miss" were photographed a short while before the riots began.

72 *top*—DANNY LYON. Cairo, Illinois. "When the town's only swimming pool was declared public by the Illinois State Attorney General, the town put up a 'private club' sign. Eventually, the pool was closed."

bottom—BOB ADELMAN.

73 DANNY LYON.

74 *top* — DANNY LYON. Selma, Alabama. "State troopers converged on Negroes as they approached the courthouse in what was to be an attempt to picket for voter registration."

bottom—DANNY LYON. New York World's Fair.

75 DANNY LYON. James Forman (bottom) and others being arrested in Atlanta, Georgia.

76 BOB ADELMAN. Birmingham, Alabama.

77 DANNY LYON. Savannah, Georgia.

ENGLISH / FRENCH

ANGLAIS / FRANÇAIS

OXFORD
PICTURE
DICTIONARY

SECOND EDITION

Jayme Adelson-Goldstein

Norma Shapiro

OXFORD
UNIVERSITY PRESS

198 Madison Avenue
New York, NY 10016 USA

Great Clarendon Street, Oxford OX2 6DP UK

Oxford University Press is a department of the University of Oxford.
It furthers the University's objective of excellence in research, scholarship,
and education by publishing worldwide in

Oxford New York

Auckland Cape Town Dar es Salaam Hong Kong Karachi
Kuala Lumpur Madrid Melbourne Mexico City Nairobi
New Delhi Shanghai Taipei Toronto

With offices in

Argentina Austria Brazil Chile Czech Republic France Greece
Guatemala Hungary Italy Japan Poland Portugal Singapore
South Korea Switzerland Thailand Turkey Ukraine Vietnam

OXFORD and OXFORD ENGLISH are registered trademarks of
Oxford University Press.

© Oxford University Press 2009

Library of Congress Cataloging-in-Publication Data

Adelson-Goldstein, Jayme.
    The Oxford picture dictionary. Monolingual /
    Jayme Adelson-Goldstein and Norma Shapiro.– 2nd ed.
        p. cm.
    Includes index.
    ISBN: 978-0-19-474013-5

    1. Picture dictionaries, English. 2. English
language–Textbooks for foreign speakers.
I. Shapiro, Norma. II. Title.
PE1629.S52 2008
423'.1–dc22

                    2007041017

Database right Oxford University Press (maker)

Executive Publishing Manager: Stephanie Karras
Managing Editor: Sharon Sargent
Development Editors: Glenn Mathes II, Bruce Myint, Katie La Storia
Associate Development Editors: Olga Christopoulos, Hannah Ryu, Meredith Stoll
Design Manager: Maj-Britt Hagsted
Project Manager: Allison Harm
Senior Designers: Stacy Merlin, Michael Steinhofer
Designer: Jaclyn Smith
Senior Production Artist: Julie Armstrong
Production Layout Artist: Colleen Ho
Cover Design: Stacy Merlin
Senior Image Editor: Justine Eun
Image Editors: Robin Fadool, Fran Newman, Jenny Vainisi
Manufacturing Manager: Shanta Persaud
Manufacturing Controller: Faye Wang
Translated by: Techno-Graphics & Translations, Inc.

ISBN: 978 0 19 474013 5

Printed in China

10 9 8 7 6

This book is printed on paper from certified and well-managed sources.

The OPD team thanks the following artists for their storyboarding and sketches:
Cecilia Aranovich, Chris Brandt, Giacomo Ghiazza, Gary Goldstein, Gordan Kljucec,
Vincent Lucido, and Glenn Urieta

Illustrations by: Lori Anzalone: 13, 70-71, 76-77; Joe "Fearless" Arenella/Will Sumpter:
178; Argosy Publishing: 66-67 (call-outs), 98-99, 108-109, 112-113 (call-outs), 152, 178,
193, 194-195, 196, 197, 205; Barbara Bastian: 4, 15, 17, 20-21, 162 (map), 198, 216-217
(map), 220-221; Philip Batini/AA Reps: 50; Thomas Bayley/Sparks Literary Agency:
158-159; Sally Bensusen: 211, 214; Annie Bissett: 112; Peter Bollinger/Shannon
Associates: 14-15; Higgens Bond/Anita Grien: 226; Molly Borman-Pullman: 116,
117; Jim Fanning/Ravenhill Represents: 80-81; Mike Gardner: 10, 12, 17, 22, 132,
114-115, 142-143, 174, 219, 228-229; Garth Glazier/AA Reps: 106, 118-119; Dennis
Godfrey/Mike Wepplo: 204; Steve Graham: 124-125, 224; Graphic Map & Chart Co.:
200-201, 202-203; Julia Green/Mendola Art: 225; Glenn Gustafson: 9, 27, 48, 76,
100, 101, 117, 132, 133, 136, 155, 161, 179, 196; Barbara Harmon: 212-213, 215; Ben
Hasler/NB Illustration: 94-95, 101, 148-149, 172, 182, 186-187; Betsy Hayes: 134,
138-139; Matthew Holmes: 75; Stewart Holmes/Illustration Ltd.: 192; Janos Jantner/
Beehive Illustration: 5, 13, 82-83, 122-123, 130-131, 146-147, 164-165, 184, 185; Ken
Joudrey/Munro Campagna: 52, 68-69, 177, 208-209; Bob Kaganich/Deborah Wolfe:
10, 40-41, 121; Steve Karp: 230, 231; Mike Kasun/Munro Campagna: 218; Graham
Kennedy: 27; Marcel Laverdet/AA Reps: 23; Jeffrey Lindberg: 33, 42-43, 92-93, 133,
160-161, 170-171, 176; Dennis Lyall/Artworks: 198; Chris Lyons:/Lindgren & Smith:
173, 191; Alan Male/Artworks: 210, 211; Jeff Mangiat/Mendola Art: 53, 54, 55, 56, 57,
58, 59, 66-67; Adrian Mateescu/The Studio: 188-189, 232-233; Karen Minot: 28-29;
Paul Mirocha/The Wiley Group: 194, 216-217; Peter Miserendino/P.T. Pie Illustrations:
198; Lee Montgomery/Illustration Ltd.: 4; Roger Motzkus: 229; Laurie O'Keefe: 111,
216-217; Daniel O'Leary/Illustration Ltd.: 8-9, 26, 34-35, 78, 135, 136-137, 238; Vilma
Ortiz-Dillon: 16, 20-21, 60, 98-99, 100, 211; Terry Pazcko: 46-47, 144-145, 152, 180,
227; David Preiss/Munro Campagna: 5; Pronk & Associates: 192-193; Tony Randazzo/
AA Reps: 156, 234-235; Mike Renwick/Creative Eye: 126-127; Mark Riedy/Scott Hull
Associates: 48-49, 79, 140, 153; Jon Rogers/AA Reps: 112; Jeff Sanson/Schumann &
Co.: 84-85, 240-241; David Schweitzer/Munro Campagna: 162-163; Ben Shannon/
Magnet Reps: 11, 64-65, 90, 91, 96, 97, 166-167, 168-169, 179, 239; Reed Sprunger/
Jae Wagoner Artists Rep.: 18-19, 232-233; Studio Liddell/AA Reps: 27; Angelo Tillary:
108-109; Ralph Voltz/Deborah Wolfe: 50-51, 128-129, 141, 154, 175, 236-237;
Jeff Wack/Mendola Art: 24, 25, 86-87, 102-103, 134-135, 231; Brad Walker: 104-105,
150-151, 157, 206-207; Wendy Wassink: 110-111; John White/The Neis Group: 199;
Eric Wilkerson: 32, 138; Simon Williams/Illustration Ltd.: 2-3, 6-7, 30-31, 36, 38-39,
44-45, 72-73; Lee Woodgate/Eye Candy Illustration: 222-223; Andy Zito: 62-23; Craig
Zuckerman: 14, 88-89, 112-113, 120-121, 194-195.

Chapter icons designed by Von Glitschka/Scott Hull Associates

Cover Art by CUBE/Illustration Ltd (hummingbird, branch); Paul Mirocha/The Wiley
Group (cherry); Mark Riedy/Scott Hull Associates (stamp); 9 Surf Studios (lettering).

Studio photography for Oxford University Press done by Dennis Kitchen Studio: 37,
61, 72, 73, 74, 75, 95, 96, 100, 180, 181, 183, 226.

Stock Photography: Age FotoStock: 238 (flute; clarinet; bassoon; saxophone; violin; cello;
bass; guitar; trombone; trumpet; xylophone; harmonica); Comstock, 61 (window);
Morales, 221 (bat); Franco Pizzochero, 98 (cashmere); Thinkstock, 61 (sink); Alamy:
Corbis, 61 (table); Gary Crabbe, 220 (park ranger); The Associated Press: 198 (strike;
soldiers in trench); Joe Rosenthal, 198 (Iwo Jima); Neil Armstrong, 198 (Buzz Aldrin
on Moon); CORBIS: Philip Gould, 198 (Civil War); Photo Library, 220 (Yosemite Falls);
Danita Delimont: Greg Johnston, 220 (snorkeling); Jamie & Judy Wild, 220 (El Capitan);
Getty Images: 198 (Martin Luther King, Jr.); Amana Images, 61 (soapy plates), The
Granger Collection: 198 (Jazz Age); The Image Works: Kelly Spranger, 220 (sea turtle);
Inmagine: 238 (oboe; tuba; French horn; piano; drums; tambourine; accordion);
istockphoto: 61 (oven), 98 (silk), 99 (suede; lace; velvet); Jupiter Images: 61 (tiles); 98
(wool); 99 (corduroy); Foodpix: 98 (linen); Rob Melnychuk/Brand X Pictures, 61 (glass
shower door); Jupiter Unlimited: 220 (seagulls); 238 (electric keyboard); Comstock, 99
(denim); Mary Evans Picture Library: 198 (women in factory); NPS Photo: Peter Jones, 221
(Carlsbad Cavern entrance; tour; cavern; spelunker); OceanwideImages.com: Gary Bell,
220 (coral); Photo Edit, Inc: David Young-Wolff, 220 (trail); Picture History: 198 (Hiram
Rhodes); Robertstock: 198 (Great Depression); Punchstock: 98 (t-shirt), Robert Glusic,
31 (Monument Valley); Roland Corporation: 238 (organ); SuperStock: 99 (leather); 198
(Daniel Boone); Shutterstock: Marek Szumlas, 94 (watch); United States Mint: 126;
Veer: Brand X Pictures, 220 (deer); Photodisc, 220 (black bear); Yankee Fleet, Inc.: 220
(Fort Jefferson; Yankee Freedom Ferry), Emil von Maltitz/Lime Photo, 37 (baby carrier).

This second edition of
the Oxford Picture Dictionary
is lovingly dedicated to
the memory of Norma Shapiro.

Her ideas, her pictures, and
her stories continue to teach,
inspire, and delight.

Acknowledgments

The publisher and authors would like to acknowledge the following individuals for their invaluable feedback during the development of this program:

Dr. Macarena Aguilar, Cy-Fair College, Houston, TX

Joseph F. Anselme, Atlantic Technical Center, Coconut Creek, FL

Stacy Antonopoulos, Monterey Trail High School, Elk Grove, CA

Carol Antunano, The English Center, Miami, FL

Irma Arencibia, Thomas A. Edison School, Union City, NJ

Suzi Austin, Alexandria City Public School Adult Program, Alexandria, FL

Patricia S. Bell, Lake Technical Center, Eustis, FL

Jim Brice, San Diego Community College District, San Diego, CA

Phil Cackley, Arlington Education and Employment Program (REEP), Arlington, VA

Frieda Caldwell, Metropolitan Adult Education Program, San Jose, CA

Sandra Cancel, Robert Waters School, Union City, NJ

Anne Marie Caney, Chula Vista Adult School, Chula Vista, CA

Patricia Castro, Harvest English Institute, Newark, NJ

Paohui Lola Chen, Milpitas Adult School, Milpitas, CA

Lori Cisneros, Atlantic Vo-Tech, Ft. Lauderdale, FL

Joyce Clapp, Hayward Adult School, Hayward, CA

Stacy Clark, Arlington Education and Employment Program (REEP), Arlington, VA

Nancy B. Crowell, Southside Programs for Adults in Continuing Education, Prince George, VA

Doroti da Cunha, Hialeah-Miami Lakes Adult Education Center, Miami, FL

Paula Da Silva-Michelin, La Guardia Community College, Long Island City, NY

Cynthia L. Davies, Humble I.S.D., Humble, TX

Christopher Davis, Overfelt Adult Center, San Jose, CA

Beverly De Nicola, Capistrano Unified School District, San Juan Capistrano, CA

Beatriz Diaz, Miami-Dade County Public Schools, Miami, FL

Druci J. Diaz, Hillsborough County Public Schools, Tampa, FL

Marion Donahue, San Dieguito Adult School, Encinitas, CA

Nick Doorn, International Education Services, South Lyon, MI

Mercedes Douglass, Seminole Community College, Sanford, FL

Jenny Elliott, Montgomery College, Rockville, MD

Paige Endo, Mt. Diablo Adult Education, Concord, CA

Megan Ernst, Glendale Community College, Glendale, CA

Elizabeth Escobar, Robert Waters School, Union City, NJ

Joanne Everett, Dave Thomas Education Center, Pompano Beach, FL

Jennifer Fadden, Arlington Education and Employment Program (REEP), Arlington, VA

Judy Farron, Fort Myers Language Center, Fort Myers, FL

Sharyl Ferguson, Montwood High School, El Paso, TX

Dr. Monica Fishkin, University of Central Florida, Orlando, FL

Nancy Frampton, Reedley College, Reedley, CA

Lynn A. Freeland, San Dieguito Union High School District, Encinitas, CA

Cathy Gample, San Leandro Adult School, San Leandro, CA

Hillary Gardner, Center for Immigrant Education and Training, Long Island City, NY

Martha C. Giffen, Alhambra Unified School District, Alhambra, CA

Jill Gluck, Hollywood Community Adult School, Los Angeles, CA

Carolyn Grimaldi, LaGuardia Community College, Long Island City, NY

William Gruenholz, USD Adult School, Concord, CA

Sandra G. Gutierrez, Hialeah-Miami Lakes Adult Education Center, Miami, FL

Conte Gúzman-Hoffman, Triton College, River Grove, IL

Amanda Harllee, Palmetto High School, Palmetto, FL

Mercedes Hearn, Tampa Bay Technical Center, Tampa, FL

Robert Hearst, Truman College, Chicago, IL

Patty Heiser, University of Washington, Seattle, WA

Joyce Hettiger, Metropolitan Education District, San Jose, CA

Karen Hirsimaki, Napa Valley Adult School, Napa, CA

Marvina Hooper, Lake Technical Center, Eustis, FL

Katie Hurter, North Harris College, Houston, TX

Nuchamon James, Miami Dade College, Miami, FL

Linda Jennings, Montgomery College, Rockville, MD

Bonnie Boyd Johnson, Chapman Education Center, Garden Grove, CA

Fayne B. Johnson, Broward County Public Schools, Fort Lauderdale, FL

Stavroula Katseyeanis, Robert Waters School, Union City, NJ

Dale Keith, Broadbase Consulting, Inc. at Kidworks USA, Miami, FL

Blanche Kellawon, Bronx Community College, Bronx, NY

Mary Kernel, Migrant Education Regional Office, Northwest Educational Service District, Anacortes, WA

Karen Kipke, Antioch High School Freshman Academy, Antioch, TN

Jody Kirkwood, ABC Adult School, Cerritos, CA

Matthew Kogan, Evans Community Adult School, Los Angeles, CA

Ineza Kuceba, Renton Technical College, Renton, WA

John Kuntz, California State University, San Bernadino, San Bernadino, CA

Claudia Kupiec, DePaul University, Chicago, IL

E.C. Land, Southside Programs for Adult Continuing Education, Prince George, VA

Betty Lau, Franklin High School, Seattle, WA

Patt Lemonie, Thomas A. Edison School, Union City, NJ

Lia Lerner, Burbank Adult School, Burbank, CA

Krystyna Lett, Metropolitan Education District, San Jose, CA

Renata Lima, TALK International School of Languages, Fort Lauderdale, FL

Luz M. Lopez, Sweetwater Union High School District, Chula Vista, CA

Osmara Lopez, Bronx Community College, Bronx, NY

Heather Lozano, North Lake College, Irving, TX

Betty Lynch, Arlington Education and Employment Program (REEP), Arlington, VA

Meera Madan, REID Park Elementary School, Charlotte, NC

Ivanna Mann Thrower, Charlotte Mecklenburg Schools, Charlotte, NC

Michael R. Mason, Loma Vista Adult Center, Concord, CA

Holley Mayville, Charlotte Mecklenburg Schools, Charlotte, NC

Margaret McCabe, United Methodist Cooperative Ministries, Clearwater, FL

Todd McDonald, Hillsborough Adult Education, Tampa, FL

Nancy A. McKeand, ESL Consultant, St. Benedict, LA

Rebecca L. McLain, Gaston College, Dallas, NC

John M. Mendoza, Redlands Adult School, Redlands, CA

Bet Messmer, Santa Clara Adult Education Center, Santa Clara, CA

Christina Morales, BEGIN Managed Programs, New York, NY

Lisa Munoz, Metropolitan Education District, San Jose, CA

Mary Murphy-Clagett, Sweetwater Union High School District, Chula Vista, CA

Jonetta Myles, Rockdale County High School, Conyers, GA

Marwan Nabi, Troy High School, Fullerton, CA

Dr. Christine L. Nelsen, Salvation Army Community Center, Tampa, FL

Michael W. Newman, Arlington Education and Employment Program (REEP), Arlington, VA

Rehana Nusrat, Huntington Beach Adult School, Huntington Beach, CA

Cindy Oakley-Paulik, Embry-Riddle Aeronautical University, Daytona Beach, FL

Acknowledgments

Janet Ochi-Fontanott, Sweetwater Union High School District, Chula Vista, CA

Lorraine Pedretti, Metropolitan Education District, San Jose, CA

Isabel Pena, BE/ESL Programs, Garland, TX

Margaret Perry, Everett Public Schools, Everett, WA

Dale Pesmen, PhD, Chicago, IL

Cathleen Petersen, Chapman Education Center, Garden Grove, CA

Allison Pickering, Escondido Adult School, Escondido, CA

Ellen Quish, LaGuardia Community College, Long Island City, NY

Teresa Reen, Independence Adult Center, San Jose, CA

Kathleen Reynolds, Albany Park Community Center, Chicago, IL

Melba I. Rillen, Palmetto High School, Palmetto, FL

Lorraine Romero, Houston Community College, Houston, TX

Eric Rosenbaum, BEGIN Managed Programs, New York, NY

Blair Roy, Chapman Education Center, Garden Grove, CA

Arlene R. Schwartz, Broward Community Schools, Fort Lauderdale, FL

Geraldyne Blake Scott, Truman College, Chicago, IL

Sharada Sekar, Antioch High School Freshman Academy, Antioch, TN

Dr. Cheryl J. Serrano, Lynn University, Boca Raton, FL

Janet Setzekorn, United Methodist Cooperative Ministries, Clearwater, FL

Terry Shearer, EDUCALL Learning Services, Houston, TX

Elisabeth Sklar, Township High School District 113, Highland Park, IL

Robert Stein, BEGIN Managed Programs, New York, NY

Ruth Sutton, Township High School District 113, Highland Park, IL

Alisa Takeuchi, Chapman Education Center, Garden Grove, CA

Grace Tanaka, Santa Ana College School of Continuing Education, Santa Ana, CA

Annalisa Te, Overfelt Adult Center, San Jose, CA

Don Torluemke, South Bay Adult School, Redondo Beach, CA

Maliheh Vafai, Overfelt Adult Center, San Jose, CA

Tara Vasquez, Robert Waters School, Union City, NJ

Nina Velasco, Naples Language Center, Naples, FL

Theresa Warren, East Side Adult Center, San Jose, CA

Lucie Gates Watel, Truman College, Chicago, IL

Wendy Weil, Arnold Middle School, Cypress, TX

Patricia Weist, TALK International School of Languages, Fort Lauderdale, FL

Dr. Carole Lynn Weisz, Lehman College, Bronx, NY

Desiree Wesner, Robert Waters School, Union City, NJ

David Wexler, Napa Valley Adult School, Napa, CA

Cynthia Wiseman, Borough of Manhattan Community College, New York, NY

Debbie Cullinane Wood, Lincoln Education Center, Garden Grove, CA

Banu Yaylali, Miami Dade College, Miami, FL

Hongyan Zheng, Milpitas Adult Education, Milpitas, CA

Arlene Zivitz, ESOL Teacher, Jupiter, FL

The publisher, authors, and editors would like to thank the following people for their expertise in reviewing specific content areas:

Ross Feldberg, Tufts University, Medford, MA

William J. Hall, M.D. FACP/FRSM (UK), Cumberland Foreside, ME

Jill A. Horohoe, Arizona State University, Tempe, AZ

Phoebe B. Rouse, Louisiana State University, Baton Rouge, LA

Dr. Susan Rouse, Southern Wesleyan University, Central, SC

Dr. Ira M. Sheskin, University of Miami, Coral Gables, FL

Maiko Tomizawa, D.D.S., New York, NY

The publisher would like to thank the following for their permission to reproduce copyrighted material:

p. 26: Penny, nickel, dime, quarter-dollar, half-dollar, and dollar coin images from the United States Mint.

pp. 125, 134–135: U.S. Postal Service Priority Mail Logo, Express Mail Logo, Certified Mail, Ready Pack Packaging, Letter Carrier Uniform, Postal Clerk Uniform, Automated Postal Center, Round Top Collection Mailbox, and Lady Liberty Stamp Image are trademarks and copyrighted material of the United States Postal Service and are used with permission.

p. 152: Metrocard is an MTA trademark and is used with permission.

p. 152: Metro token for L.A.'s bus and rail system used with permission.

p. 229: Little League used courtesy of Little League® Baseball and Softball.

p. 231: Frisbee®, a registered trademark of Wham-O, Inc.

Table of Contents Table des matières

Introduction Introduction . . . . .ix–xi

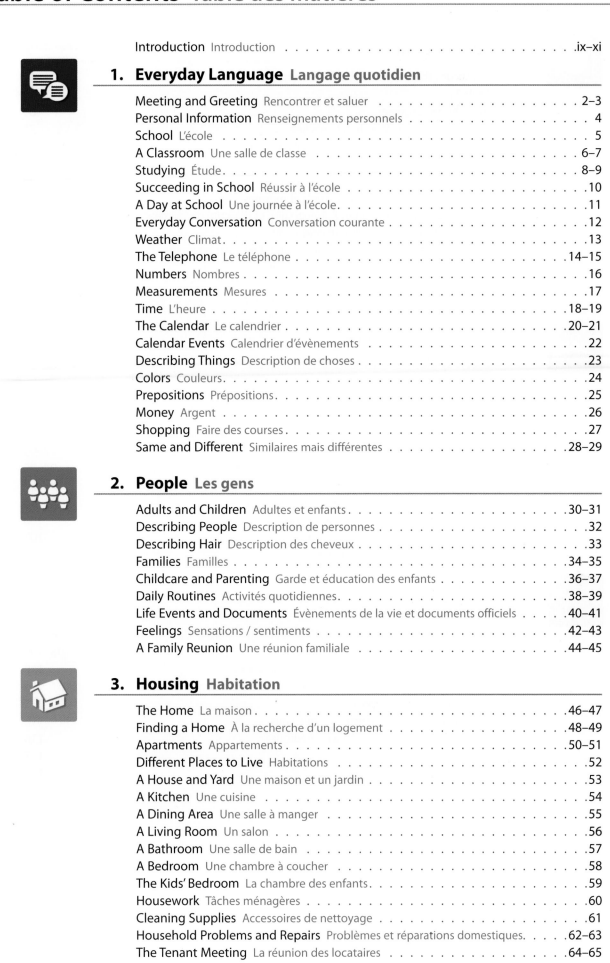

1. Everyday Language Langage quotidien

Meeting and Greeting Rencontrer et saluer 2–3
Personal Information Renseignements personnels 4
School L'école 5
A Classroom Une salle de classe 6–7
Studying Étude. 8–9
Succeeding in School Réussir à l'école 10
A Day at School Une journée à l'école. 11
Everyday Conversation Conversation courante 12
Weather Climat. 13
The Telephone Le téléphone 14–15
Numbers Nombres .16
Measurements Mesures 17
Time L'heure 18–19
The Calendar Le calendrier 20–21
Calendar Events Calendrier d'évènements 22
Describing Things Description de choses 23
Colors Couleurs. 24
Prepositions Prépositions. 25
Money Argent 26
Shopping Faire des courses. 27
Same and Different Similaires mais différentes 28–29

2. People Les gens

Adults and Children Adultes et enfants. 30–31
Describing People Description de personnes 32
Describing Hair Description des cheveux 33
Families Familles .34–35
Childcare and Parenting Garde et éducation des enfants 36–37
Daily Routines Activités quotidiennes. 38–39
Life Events and Documents Évènements de la vie et documents officiels 40–41
Feelings Sensations / sentiments 42–43
A Family Reunion Une réunion familiale 44–45

3. Housing Habitation

The Home La maison. 46–47
Finding a Home À la recherche d'un logement 48–49
Apartments Appartements. 50–51
Different Places to Live Habitations 52
A House and Yard Une maison et un jardin 53
A Kitchen Une cuisine 54
A Dining Area Une salle à manger 55
A Living Room Un salon 56
A Bathroom Une salle de bain 57
A Bedroom Une chambre à coucher 58
The Kids' Bedroom La chambre des enfants. 59
Housework Tâches ménagères 60
Cleaning Supplies Accessoires de nettoyage 61
Household Problems and Repairs Problèmes et réparations domestiques. . . .62–63
The Tenant Meeting La réunion des locataires 64–65

Contents Contenu

4. Food Nourriture

Back from the Market Revenir du marché 66–67
Fruit Fruits 68
Vegetables Légumes 69
Meat and Poultry Viandes et volailles 70
Seafood and Deli Charcuterie et fruits de mer .71
A Grocery Store Une épicerie 72–73
Containers and Packaging Récipients et emballage 74
Weights and Measurements Poids et mesures 75
Food Preparation and Safety Préparation et salubrité des aliments 76–77
Kitchen Utensils Ustensiles de cuisine 78
Fast Food Restaurant Restaurant minute / Restauration rapide 79
A Coffee Shop Menu Un menu de cafétéria .80–81
A Restaurant Un restaurant 82–83
The Farmers' Market Le marché des producteurs 84–85

5. Clothing Vêtements

Everyday Clothes Vêtements de tous les jours 86–87
Casual, Work, and Formal Clothes Vêtements décontractés,
    de travail et de soirée 88–89
Seasonal Clothing Vêtements saisonniers 90
Underwear and Sleepwear Sous-vêtements et vêtements de nuit 91
Workplace Clothing Vêtements de travail 92–93
Shoes and Accessories Chaussures et accessoires 94–95
Describing Clothes Description de vêtements 96–97
Making Clothes Fabriquer des vêtements 98–99
Making Alterations Faire des retouches 100
Doing the Laundry Faire la lessive 101
A Garage Sale Un vente-débarras 102–103

6. Health Santé

The Body Le corps 104–105
Inside and Outside the Body À l'intérieur et à l'extérieur du corps 106–107
Personal Hygiene Hygiène personnelle 108–109
Symptoms and Injuries Symptômes et blessures 110
Illnesses and Medical Conditions Maladies et affections médicales 111
A Pharmacy Une pharmacie 112–113
Taking Care of Your Health Soignez-vous 114–115
Medical Emergencies Urgences médicales 116
First Aid Premiers soins 117
Medical Care Soins médicaux 118
Dental Care Soins dentaires 119
Hospital Hôpital 120–121
A Health Fair Foire sur la santé 122–123

7. **Community** Communauté

Downtown Centre-ville. 124–125
City Streets Rues en ville 126–127
An Intersection Une intersection 128–129
A Mall Un centre commercial 130–131
The Bank La banque 132
The Library La bibliothèque. 133
The Post Office La poste 134–135
Department of Motor Vehicles (DMV) Préfecture (service des cartes grises). . 136–137
Government and Military Service Service militaire et organismes
    gouvernementaux 138–139
Civic Rights and Responsibilities Droits et responsabilités civiques 140
The Legal System Le système juridique 141
Crime Criminalité / Délinquance. 142
Public Safety Sécurité publique. 143
Emergencies and Natural Disasters Urgences et désastres naturels 144–145
Emergency Procedures Procédures d'urgence 146–147
Community Cleanup Nettoyage collectif 148–149

8. **Transportation** Transport

Basic Transportation Moyens de transport 150–151
Public Transportation Transport public 152
Prepositions of Motion Prépositions / expressions indiquant le mouvement 153
Traffic Signs Panneaux de signalisation 154
Directions and Maps Directions et cartes 155
Cars and Trucks Voitures et camions 156
Buying and Maintaining a Car Acheter et entretenir une voiture 157
Parts of a Car Pièces d'une voiture 158–159
An Airport Un aéroport. 160–161
Taking a Trip Partir en voyage. 162–163

9. **Work** Travail

The Workplace Le lieu de travail 164–165
Jobs and Occupations A-C Emplois et professions A-C 166
Jobs and Occupations C-H Emplois et professions C-H 167
Jobs and Occupations H-P Emplois et professions H-P 168
Jobs and Occupations P-W Emplois et professions P-W 169
Job Skills Compétences professionnelles 170
Office Skills Compétences en travail de bureau 171
Career Planning Planification de carrière 172
Job Search Recherche d'emploi 173
Interview Skills Compétences en matière d'entrevue 174
A Factory Une usine 175
Landscaping and Gardening Aménagement du paysage et jardinage. . . . 176
Farming and Ranching A la ferme et au ranch 177
Construction Construction 178
Job Safety La sécurité au travail. 179
Tools and Building Supplies Outils et fournitures pour le bâtiment 180–181
An Office Un bureau 182–183
A Hotel Un hôtel 184
Food Service Service alimentaire 185
A Bad Day at Work Une mauvaise journée au travail. 186–187

Contents Contenu

10. Areas of Study Champs d'étude

Schools and Subjects Écoles et sujets 188–189
English Composition Composition anglaise. 190–191
Mathematics Mathématiques. 192–193
Science Science 194–195
Computers Ordinateurs. 196
The Internet L'Internet 197
U.S. History Histoire des États-Unis 198
World History Histoire du monde. 199
North America and Central America Amérique du Nord et Amérique centrale . . 200–201
World Map Carte du monde 202–203
Geography and Habitats Géographie et habitats 204
The Universe L'univers 205
A Graduation Obtention d'un diplôme 206–207

11. Plants and Animals Plantes et animaux

Nature Center Centre d'initiation à la nature 208–209
Trees and Plants Arbres et plantes 210
Flowers Fleurs 211
Marine Life, Amphibians, and Reptiles Faune marine, amphibiens, et reptiles . . 212–213
Birds, Insects, and Arachnids Oiseaux, insectes, et arachnides. . . . 214
Domestic Animals and Rodents Animaux domestiques et rongeurs 215
Mammals Mammifères. 216–217
Energy and Conservation Énergie et conservation 218–219
U.S. National Parks Parcs nationaux des États-Unis 220–221

12. Recreation Loisirs

Places to Go Endroits où aller. 222–223
The Park and Playground Le parc et le terrain de jeux. 224
The Beach La plage. 225
Outdoor Recreation Activités de plein air. 226
Winter and Water Sports Sports d'hiver et nautiques 227
Individual Sports Sports individuels 228
Team Sports Sports d'équipe 229
Sports Verbs Verbes se rapportant à des sports 230
Sports Equipment Articles de sport. 231
Hobbies and Games Passe-temps et jeux. 232–233
Electronics and Photography Électronique et photographie 234–235
Entertainment Divertissements. 236–237
Music Musique 238
Holidays Jours fériés 239
A Birthday Party Une fête d'anniversaire 240–241

Verb Guide Guide des verbes. 242–244
How to Use the Index Utilisation de l'index. 245
English Index Index anglais. 246–281
Geographical Index Index géographique 282–284
French Index Index français. 285–304
Research Bibliography Bibliographie de recherche 305

Teaching with the *Oxford Picture Dictionary* Program

The following general guidelines will help you prepare single and multilevel lessons using the OPD program. For step-by-step, topic-specific lesson plans, see *OPD Lesson Plans*.

1. Use Students' Needs to Identify Lesson Objectives

- Create communicative objectives based on your learners' needs assessments (*see OPD 2e Assessment Program*).
- Make sure objectives state what students will be able to do at the end of the lesson. For example: *Students will be able to respond to basic classroom commands and requests for classroom objects.* (pp. 6–7, A Classroom)
- For multilevel classes, identify a low-beginning, high-beginning, and low-intermediate objective for each topic.

2. Preview the Topic

Identify what your students already know about the topic.

- Ask general questions related to the topic.
- Have students list words they know from the topic.
- Ask questions about the picture(s) on the page.

3. Present the New Vocabulary

Research shows that it is best to present no more than 5–7 new words at a time. Here are a few presentation techniques:

- Say each new word and describe it within the context of the picture. Have volunteers act out verbs and verb sequences.
- Use Total Physical Response commands to build vocabulary comprehension.
- For long or unfamiliar word lists, introduce words by categories or select the words your students need most.
- Ask a series of questions to build comprehension and give students an opportunity to say the new words. Begin with *yes/no* questions: *Is #16 chalk?* Progress to *or* questions: *Is #16 chalk or a marker?* Finally, ask *Wh-* questions: *What can I use to write on this paper?*
- Focus on the words that students want to learn. Have them write 3–5 new words from each topic, along with meaning clues such as a drawing, translation, or sentence.

More vocabulary and **Grammar Point** sections provide additional presentation opportunities (see p. 5, School). For multilevel presentation ideas, see *OPD Lesson Plans*.

4. Check Comprehension

Make sure that students understand the target vocabulary. Here are two activities you can try:

- Say vocabulary words, and have students point to the correct items in their books. Walk around the room, checking if students are pointing to the correct pictures.
- Make true/false statements about the target vocabulary. Have students hold up two fingers for true, three for false.

5. Provide Guided and Communicative Practice

The exercise bands at the bottom of the topic pages provide a variety of guided and communicative practice opportunities and engage students' higher-level thinking.

6. Provide More Practice

OPD Second Edition offers a variety of components to facilitate vocabulary acquisition. Each of the print and electronic materials listed below offers suggestions and support for single and multilevel instruction.

OPD Lesson Plans Step-by-step multilevel lesson plans feature 3 CDs with multilevel listening, context-based pronunciation practice, and leveled reading practice. Includes multilevel teaching notes for *The OPD Reading Library*.

OPD Audio CDs or Audio Cassettes Each word in *OPD's* word list is recorded by topic.

Low-Beginning, High-Beginning, and Low-Intermediate Workbooks Guided practice for each page in *OPD* features linked visual contexts, realia, and listening practice.

Classic Classroom Activities A photocopiable resource of interactive multilevel activities, grammar practice, and communicative tasks.

The OPD Reading Library Readers include civics, academic content, and workplace themes.

Overhead Transparencies Vibrant transparencies help to focus students on the lesson.

OPD Presentation Software A multilevel interactive teaching tool using interactive whiteboard and LCD technology. Audio, animation, and video instructional support bring each dictionary topic to life.

The OPD CD-ROM An interactive learning tool featuring four-skill practice based on *OPD* topics.

Bilingual Editions *OPD* is available in numerous bilingual editions including Spanish, Chinese, Vietnamese, Arabic, Korean, and many more.

My hope is that OPD makes it easier for you to take your learners from comprehension to communication. Please share your thoughts with us as you make the book your own.

Jayme Adelson-Goldstein

Jayme Adelson-Goldstein

OPDteam.us@oup.com

Welcome to the OPD SECOND EDITION

The second edition of the *Oxford Picture Dictionary* expands on the best aspects of the 1998 edition with:

- New artwork presenting words within meaningful, real-life contexts
- An updated word list to meet the needs of today's English language learners
- 4,000 English words and phrases, including 285 verbs
- 40 new topics with 12 intro pages and 12 story pages
- Unparalleled support for vocabulary teaching

Subtopics present the words in easy-to-learn "chunks."

Color coding and icons make it easy to navigate through *OPD*.

New art and rich contexts improve vocabulary acquisition.

Revised practice activities help students from low-beginning through low-intermediate levels.

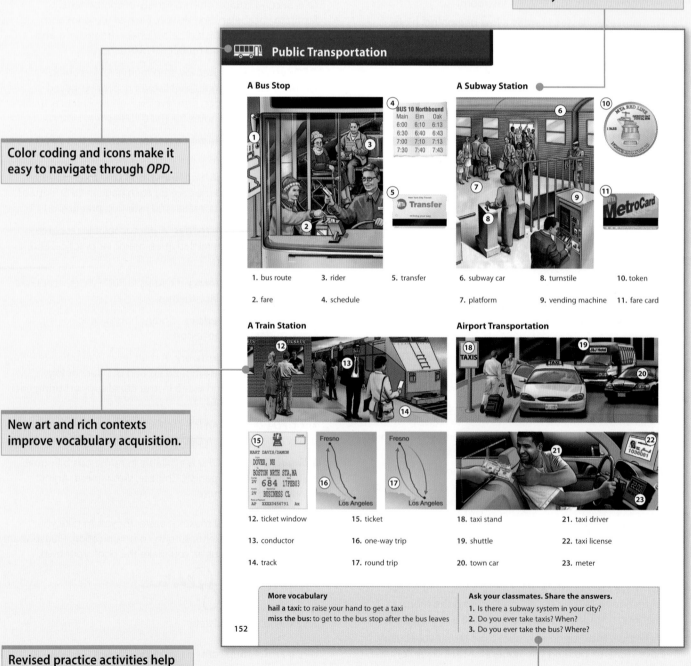

Public Transportation

A Bus Stop

BUS 10 Northbound
Main	Elm	Oak
6:00	6:10	6:13
6:30	6:40	6:43
7:00	7:10	7:13
7:30	7:40	7:43

1. bus route
2. fare
3. rider
4. schedule
5. transfer

A Subway Station

6. subway car
7. platform
8. turnstile
9. vending machine
10. token
11. fare card

A Train Station

12. ticket window
13. conductor
14. track
15. ticket
16. one-way trip
17. round trip

Airport Transportation

18. taxi stand
19. shuttle
20. town car
21. taxi driver
22. taxi license
23. meter

More vocabulary
hail a taxi: to raise your hand to get a taxi
miss the bus: to get to the bus stop after the bus leaves

Ask your classmates. Share the answers.
1. Is there a subway system in your city?
2. Do you ever take taxis? When?
3. Do you ever take the bus? Where?

152

x

NEW! Intro pages open each unit with key vocabulary related to the unit theme. Clear, engaging artwork promotes questions, conversations, and writing practice for all levels.

Each intro page teaches key vocabulary items within the unit theme.

Practice activities make it easy to manage multilevel classrooms.

Back from the Market

1. fish
2. meat
3. chicken
4. cheese
5. milk
6. butter
7. eggs
8. vegetables

9. fruit
10. rice
11. bread
12. pasta
13. grocery bag
14. shopping list
15. coupons

✓ milk
✓ bread
✓ lettuce
✓ grapes

Listen and point. Take turns.
A: *Point to the vegetables.*
B: *Point to the bread.*
A: *Point to the fruit.*

Pair Dictation
A: *Write vegetables.*
B: *Please spell vegetables for me.*
A: *V-e-g-e-t-a-b-l-e-s.*

Ways to talk about food.
Do we need eggs?
Do we have any pasta?
We have some vegetables, but we need fruit.

Role play. Talk about your shopping list.
A: *Do we need eggs?*
B: *No, we have some.*
A: *Do we have any...*

66   67

NEW! Story pages close each unit with a lively scene for reviewing vocabulary and teaching additional language. Meanwhile, rich visual contexts recycle words from the unit.

Pre-reading questions build students' previewing and predicting skills.

High-interest readings promote literacy skills.

Post-reading questions and role-play activities support critical thinking and encourage students to use the language they have learned.

A Family Reunion

LU FAMILY REUNION

I think large families are best.

Look at the picture. What do you see?

Answer the questions.
1. How many relatives are there at this reunion?
2. How many children are there? Which children are misbehaving?
3. What are people doing at this reunion?

Read the story.

A Family Reunion

Ben Lu has a lot of relatives and they're all at his house. Today is the Lu family reunion.

There is a lot of good food. There are also balloons and a banner. And this year there are four new babies!

People are having a good time at the reunion. Ben's grandfather and his aunt are talking about the baseball game. His cousins are laughing. His mother-in-law is giving her opinion. And many of the children are misbehaving.

Ben looks at his family and smiles. He loves his relatives, but he's glad the reunion is once a year.

Think about it.
1. Do you like to have large parties? Why or why not?
2. Imagine you see a little girl at a party. She's misbehaving. What do you do? What do you say?

1. banner
2. baseball game
3. opinion
4. balloons
5. glad
6. relatives

A. laugh
B. misbehave

44   45

The thematic word list previews words that students will encounter in the story.

A. **Say**, "Hello."
Dites, « Bonjour ».

B. **Ask**, "How are you?"
Demandez, « Comment allez-vous ? »

C. **Introduce** yourself.
Se **présenter**.

D. **Smile**.
Sourire.

E. **Hug**.
Embrasser.

F. **Wave**.
Faire un signe de la main.

Tell your partner what to do. Take turns.

1. *Say, "Hello."*   4. *Shake hands.*
2. *Bow.*   5. *Wave.*
3. *Smile.*   6. *Say, "Goodbye."*

Dictate to your partner. Take turns.

A: *Write smile.*
B: *Is it spelled s-m-i-l-e?*
A: *Yes, that's right.*

2

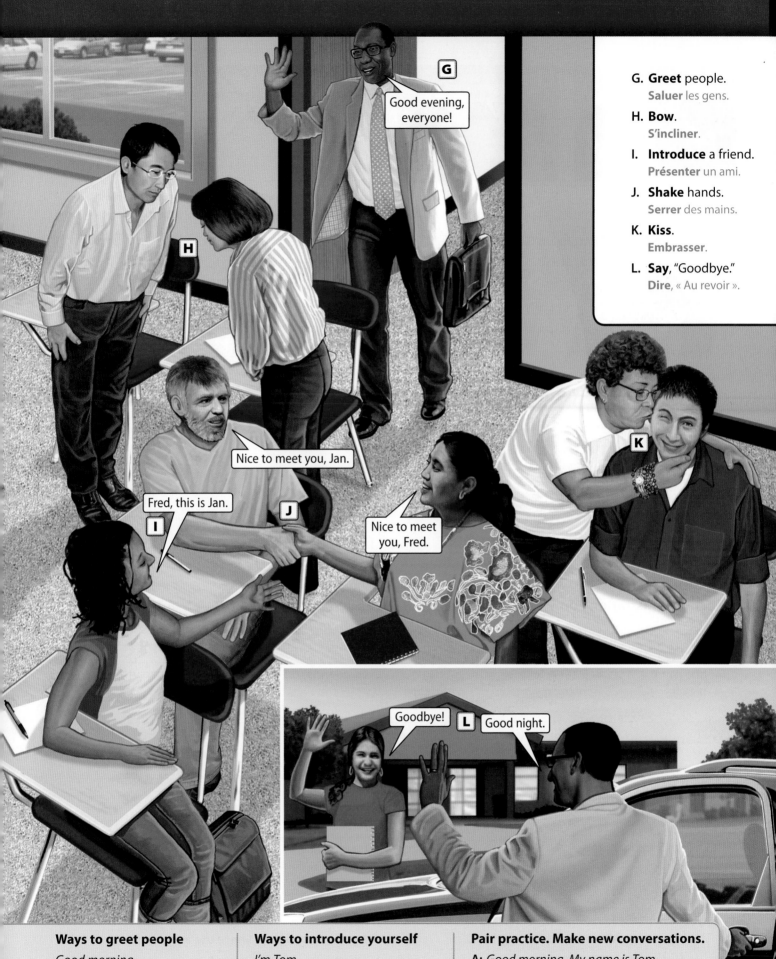

G. Greet people.
Saluer les gens.

H. Bow.
S'incliner.

I. Introduce a friend.
Présenter un ami.

J. Shake hands.
Serrer des mains.

K. Kiss.
Embrasser.

L. Say, "Goodbye."
Dire, « Au revoir ».

G Good evening, everyone!

I Fred, this is Jan.

J Nice to meet you, Jan.

Nice to meet you, Fred.

L Goodbye!

Good night.

Ways to greet people

Good morning.
Good afternoon.
Good evening.

Ways to introduce yourself

I'm Tom.
My name is Tom.

Pair practice. Make new conversations.

A: *Good morning. My name is Tom.*
B: *Nice to meet you, Tom. I'm Sara.*
A: *Nice to meet you, Sara.*

3

A. Say your name.
Dites votre nom.

B. Spell your name.
Épelez votre nom.

C. Print your name.
Écrivez votre nom en **majuscules**.

D. Sign your name.
Signez votre nom.

Filling Out a Form Remplir un formulaire

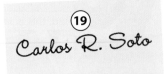

School Registration Form Formulaire d'inscription aux cours

1. name:
   nom :
   _____

2. first name   3. middle initial   4. last name   5. address   6. apartment number
   prénom   deuxième prénom   nom de famille   adresse   numéro d'appartement

7. city   8. state   9. ZIP code   10. area code   11. phone number
   ville   état   code ZIP / code postal indicatif régional   numéro de téléphone

12. cell phone number   13. date of birth (DOB)   14. place of birth
    numéro de téléphone cellulaire   date de naissance   lieu de naissance

15. Social Security number   16. sex: 17. male ☐   19. signature
    numéro de sécurité sociale   sexe :   homme   signature
                                          18. female ☐
                                              femme

Pair practice. Make new conversations.

A: *My first name is Carlos.*
B: *Please spell Carlos for me.*
A: *C-a-r-l-o-s*

Ask your classmates. Share the answers.

1. Do you like your first name?
2. Is your last name from your mother? father? husband?
3. What is your middle name?

Campus Campus

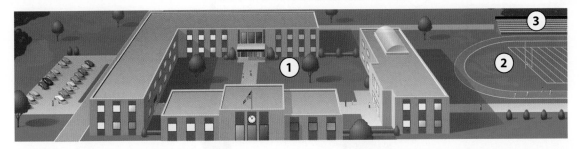

Administrators Administrateurs

Around Campus Sur le campus

1. quad
   la cour
2. field
   le terrain
3. bleachers
   les gradins
4. principal
   le directeur
5. assistant principal
   le directeur adjoint
6. counselor
   le conseiller
7. classroom
   la salle de classe
8. teacher
   le professeur
9. restrooms
   les toilettes
10. hallway
    le couloir
11. locker
    le casier
12. main office
    le bureau principal
13. clerk
    le préposé
14. cafeteria
    la cafétéria
15. computer lab
    la salle des ordinateurs
16. teacher's aide
    l'assistant du professeur
17. library
    la bibliothèque
18. auditorium
    l'auditorium
19. gym
    le gymnase
20. coach
    l'entraîneur
21. track
    la piste

More vocabulary

Students do not pay to go to a **public school**.
Students pay to go to a **private school**.
A church, mosque, or temple school is a **parochial school**.

Grammar Point: contractions of the verb *be*

He + is = He's   *He's a teacher.*
She + is = She's   *She's a counselor.*
They + are = They're   *They're students.*

1. chalkboard
   le tableau
2. screen
   l'écran

3. whiteboard
   le tableau blanc
4. teacher / instructor
   l'enseignant / l'instructeur

5. student
   l'étudiant
6. LCD projector
   le projecteur LCD

7. desk
   le pupitre
8. headphones
   les écouteurs

A. Raise your hand.
   Levez la main.

B. Talk to the teacher.
   Parlez au professeur.

C. Listen to a CD.
   Écoutez un CD.

D. Stand up.
   Levez-vous.

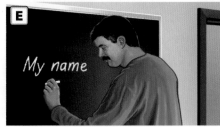

E. Write on the board.
   Écrivez au tableau.

F. Sit down. / Take a seat.
   Asseyez-vous. / Prenez place.

G. Open your book.
   Ouvrez votre livre.

H. Close your book.
   Fermez votre livre.

I. Pick up the pencil.
   Prenez le crayon.

J. Put down the pencil.
   Posez le crayon.

9. clock
l'horloge

10. bookcase
la bibliothèque

11. chair
la chaise

12. map
la carte (géographique)

13. alphabet
l'alphabet

14. bulletin board
le tableau d'affichage

15. computer
l'ordinateur

16. overhead projector
le rétroprojecteur

17. dry erase marker
le marqueur à essuyage à sec

18. chalk
la craie

19. eraser
la brosse à effacer

20. pencil
le crayon

21. (pencil) eraser
la gomme

22. pen
le stylo

23. pencil sharpener
le taille-crayon

24. marker
le marqueur

25. textbook
le livre

26. workbook
le cahier d'exercices

27. 3-ring binder / notebook
le classeur / cahier à 3 anneaux

28. notebook paper
les feuilles de cahier

29. spiral notebook
le cahier à spirale

30. dictionary
le dictionnaire

31. picture dictionary
le dictionnaire illustré

Look at the picture.
Describe the classroom.

A: There's a chalkboard.
B: There are fifteen students.

Ask your classmates. Share the answers.

1. Do you like to raise your hand in class?
2. Do you like to listen to CDs in class?
3. Do you ever talk to the teacher?

Learning New Words Apprendre des mots nouveaux

A. **Look up** the word.
Rechercher le mot.

B. **Read** the definition.
Lire la définition.

C. **Translate** the word.
Traduire le mot.

D. **Check** the pronunciation.
Vérifier la prononciation.

E. **Copy** the word.
Copier le mot.

F. **Draw** a picture.
Faire un dessin.

Working with Your Classmates Travailler avec vos camarades de classe

G. **Discuss** a problem.
Discuter d'un problème.

H. **Brainstorm** solutions / answers.
Trouver des solutions / réponses.

I. **Work** in a group.
Travailler en groupe.

J. **Help** a classmate.
Aider un camarade de classe.

Working with a Partner Travail avec un partenaire

K. **Ask** a question.
Poser une question.

L. **Answer** a question.
Répondre à une question.

M. **Share** a book.
Partager un livre.

N. **Dictate** a sentence.
Dicter une phrase.

Following Directions Suivre les instructions

O

Read a <u>book</u>.

O. Fill in the blank.
Remplir l'espace blanc.

P

5. How much is the book?
   a. $99.99
   b. $9.99
   c. $0.99

P. Choose the correct answer.
Choisir la réponse exacte.

Q

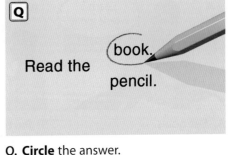

Read the (book.) pencil.

Q. Circle the answer.
Encercler la réponse.

R

pen
pencil
~~book~~
chalk
marker

R. Cross out the word.
Biffer le mot.

S

Underline the action.
1. <u>Open</u> the book.
2. <u>Close</u> the book.
3. <u>Give me</u> the book.

S. Underline the word.
Souligner le mot.

T

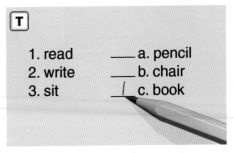

1. read   ___ a. pencil
2. write   ___ b. chair
3. sit   _1_ c. book

T. Match the items.
Faire correspondre les articles.

U

Check the box next to each action.

☑ stand   ☑ sit
☐ pen   ☑ write
☐ paper   ☐ book

U. Check the correct boxes.
Cocher les cases adéquates.

V

<u>book</u>

V. Label the picture.
Nommer l'illustration.

W

1. enp   <u>pen</u>
2. rappe   <u>paper</u>
3. okob   <u>book</u>

W. Unscramble the words.
Remettre les lettres dans l'ordre.

X

_4_ Close the book.
_1_ Pick up the book.
_2_ Open the book.
_3_ Read the book.

X. Put the sentences in order.
Mettre les phrases dans l'ordre.

Y

Y. Take out a piece of paper.
Prendre une feuille de papier.

Z

Z. Put away your books.
Rangez vos livres.

Ask your classmates. Share the answers.

1. Do you like to work in a group?
2. Do you ever share a book?
3. Do you like to answer questions?

Think about it. Discuss.

1. How can classmates help each other?
2. Why is it important to ask questions in class?
3. How can students check their pronunciation? Explain.

Ways to Succeed Façons de réussir

A. Set goals.
   Fixer des objectifs.

B. Participate in class.
   Participer en classe.

C. Take notes.
   Prendre des notes.

D. Study at home.
   Étudier à la maison.

E. Pass a test.
   Réussir un examen.

F. Ask for help.
   Demander de l'aide.

G. Make progress.
   Faire des progrès.

H. Get good grades.
   Obtenir de bonnes notes.

Taking a Test Passer un examen

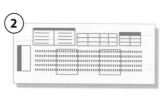

A	90%-100%	Outstanding
B	80%-89%	Very good
C	70%-79%	Satisfactory
D	60%-69%	Barely passing
F	0%-59%	Fail

1. test booklet
   le cahier d'examen

2. answer sheet
   la feuille de réponse

3. score
   le résultat

4. grades
   les notes

I. Clear off your desk.
   Nettoyer votre bureau.

J. Work on your own.
   Travailler seul.

K. Bubble in the answer.
   Griser la bonne réponse.

L. Check your work.
   Vérifier son travail.

M. Erase the mistake.
   Effacer l'erreur.

N. Correct the mistake.
   Corriger l'erreur.

O. Hand in your test.
   Rendre l'examen.

A Day at School

A. Enter the room.
Entrer dans la salle.

B. Turn on the lights.
Allumer les lumières.

C. Walk to class.
Marcher jusqu'à la salle de classe.

D. Run to class.
Courir jusqu'à la salle de classe.

E. Lift / Pick up the books.
Soulever / Ramasser les livres.

F. Carry the books.
Porter les livres.

G. Deliver the books.
Remettre les livres.

H. Take a break.
Faire une pause.

I. Eat.
Manger.

J. Drink.
Boire.

K. Buy a snack.
Acheter une collation.

L. Have a conversation.
Avoir une conversation.

M. Go back to class.
Retourner en classe.

N. Throw away trash.
Jeter des ordures.

O. Leave the room.
Sortir de la salle.

P. Turn off the lights.
Éteindre les lumières.

Grammar Point: present continuous

Use **be** + verb + **ing**
He is walking. They are entering.
Note: He is running. They are leaving.

Look at the pictures.
Describe what is happening.

A: *They are entering the room.*
B: *He is walking.*

11

A. **start** a conversation
   entamer une conversation

B. **make** small talk
   faire la conversation

C. **compliment** someone
   complimenter quelqu'un

D. **offer** something
   offrir quelque chose

E. **thank** someone
   remercier quelqu'un

F. **apologize**
   s'excuser

G. **accept** an apology
   accepter des excuses

H. **invite** someone
   inviter quelqu'un

I. **accept** an invitation
   accepter une invitation

J. **decline** an invitation
   refuser une invitation

K. **agree**
   être d'accord

L. **disagree**
   n'être pas d'accord

M. **explain** something
   expliquer quelque chose

N. **check** your understanding
   s'assurer de bien comprendre

More vocabulary

request: to ask for something

accept a compliment: to thank someone for a compliment

Pair practice. Follow the directions.

1. Start a conversation with your partner.
2. Make small talk with your partner.
3. Compliment each other.

Temperature Température

1. Fahrenheit
   Fahrenheit
2. Celsius
   Celsius
3. hot
   chaud
4. warm
   doux
5. cool
   frais
6. cold
   froid
7. freezing
   glacial
8. degrees
   degrés

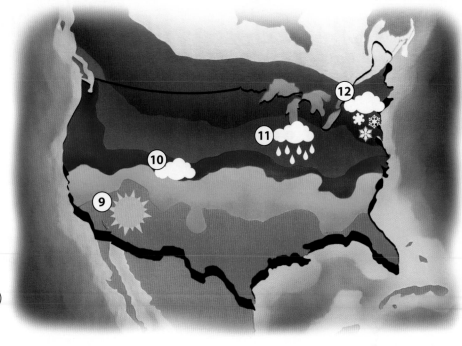

A Weather Map Une carte météorologique

9. sunny / clear
   ensoleillé / clair
10. cloudy
    nuageux
11. raining
    pluvieux
12. snowing
    neigeux

Weather Conditions Conditions météorologiques

13. heat wave
    vague de chaleur
14. smoggy
    obscurci par le brouillard
    de pollution
15. humid
    humide

16. thunderstorm
    orage
17. lightning
    foudre
18. windy
    venteux

19. dust storm
    tempête de poussière
20. foggy
    brumeux
21. hailstorm
    tempête de grêle

22. icy
    glacé
23. snowstorm / blizzard
    tempête de neige /
    blizzard

Ways to talk about the weather

It's <u>sunny</u> in <u>Dallas</u>.
What's the temperature?
It's <u>108</u>. They're having <u>a heat wave</u>.

Pair practice. Make new conversations.

A: What's the weather like in <u>Chicago</u>?
B: It's <u>raining</u> and it's <u>cold</u>. It's <u>30</u> degrees.

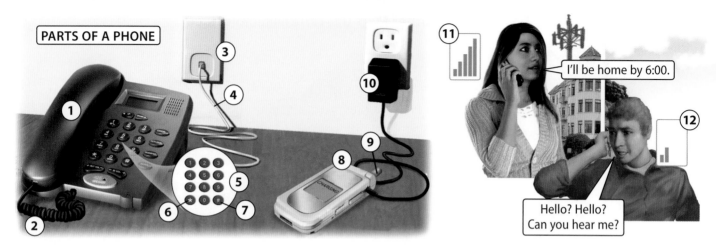

PARTS OF A PHONE

I'll be home by 6:00.

Hello? Hello? Can you hear me?

1. **receiver / handset**
   le combiné

2. **cord**
   le cordon

3. **phone jack**
   la prise téléphonique

4. **phone line**
   la ligne téléphonique

5. **key pad**
   le clavier

6. **star key**
   la touche étoile

7. **pound key**
   la touche dièse

8. **cellular phone**
   le téléphone cellulaire

9. **antenna**
   l'antenne

10. **charger**
    le chargeur

11. **strong signal**
    un signal puissant

12. **weak signal**
    un signal faible

Hi, Bob. It's Joe. Call me.

Hi Bob. Call me.

13. **headset**
    le casque

14. **wireless headset**
    le casque sans fil

15. **calling card**
    la carte d'appel

16. **access number**
    le numéro d'accès

17. **answering machine**
    le répondeur

18. **voice message**
    le message vocal

19. **text message**
    le message texte

Hi, Grandpa.

Hello, Jun.

Operator.

City and state, please.

For customer service, please press 2.

20. **Internet phone call**
    l'appel téléphonique par Internet

21. **operator**
    la téléphoniste

22. **directory assistance**
    l'assistance annuaire

23. **automated phone system**
    le système téléphonique automatisé

14

24. cordless phone
le téléphone sans fil

25. pay phone
le téléphone public

26. TDD*
ATS (Appareil de télécommunication pour malentendants)

27. smart phone
téléphone intelligent

Reading a Phone Bill   Lire une facture de téléphone

28. phone bill
la facture de téléphone

29. area code
l'indicatif régional

30. phone number
le numéro de téléphone

31. local call
l'appel local

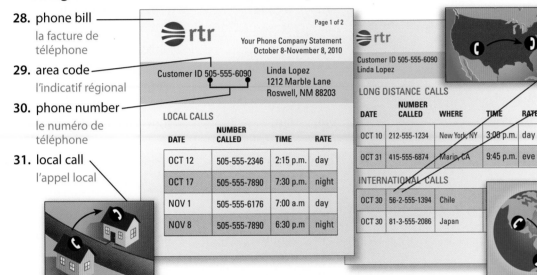

rtr

Page 1 of 2

Your Phone Company Statement
October 8-November 8, 2010

Customer ID 505-555-6090

Linda Lopez
1212 Marble Lane
Roswell, NM 88203

LOCAL CALLS

DATE	NUMBER CALLED	TIME	RATE
OCT 12	505-555-2346	2:15 p.m.	day
OCT 17	505-555-7890	7:30 p.m.	night
NOV 1	505-555-6176	7:00 a.m	day
NOV 8	505-555-7890	6:30 p.m	night

rtr

Customer ID 505-555-6090
Linda Lopez

LONG DISTANCE CALLS

DATE	NUMBER CALLED	WHERE	TIME	RATE
OCT 10	212-555-1234	New York, NY	3:00 p.m.	day
OCT 31	415-555-6874	Marin, CA	9:45 p.m.	eve

INTERNATIONAL CALLS

OCT 30	56-2-555-1394	Chile
OCT 30	81-3-555-2086	Japan

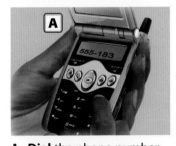

32. long distance call
l'appel interurbain

33. country code
le code du pays

34. city code
le code de la ville

35. international call
l'appel international

Making a Phone Call   Passer un appel téléphonique

A. Dial the phone number.
Composer le numéro de téléphone.

B. Press "send".
Appuyez sur « envoyer ».

C. Talk on the phone.
Parler au téléphone.

D. Hang up. / **Press** "end".
Raccrocher. / **Appuyer** sur « fin ».

Making an Emergency Call   Passer un appel d'urgence

E. Dial 911.
Composer le 911.

F. Give your name.
Donner votre nom.

This is Roy Chu.

G. State the emergency.
Expliquer l'urgence.

There's a fire on 5th and Oak.

H. Stay on the line.
Rester à l'écoute.

Please stay on the line.

*telecommunication device for the deaf

Cardinal Numbers Nombres cardinaux

0	zero / zéro	20	twenty / vingt
1	one / un	21	twenty-one / vingt et un
2	two / deux	22	twenty-two / vingt-deux
3	three / trois	23	twenty-three / vingt-trois
4	four / quatre	24	twenty-four / vingt-quatre
5	five / cinq	25	twenty-five / vingt-cinq
6	six / six	30	thirty / trente
7	seven / sept	40	forty / quarante
8	eight / huit	50	fifty / cinquante
9	nine / neuf	60	sixty / soixante
10	ten / dix	70	seventy / soixante-dix (septante)
11	eleven / onze	80	eighty / quatre-vingts (octante)
12	twelve / douze	90	ninety / quatre-vingt-dix (nonante)
13	thirteen / treize	100	one hundred / cent
14	fourteen / quatorze	101	one hundred one / cent un
15	fifteen / quinze	1,000	one thousand / mille
16	sixteen / seize	10,000	ten thousand / dix mille
17	seventeen / dix-sept	100,000	one hundred thousand / cent mille
18	eighteen / dix-huit	1,000,000	one million / un million
19	nineteen / dix-neuf	1,000,000,000	one billion / un milliard

Ordinal Numbers Nombres ordinaux

1st	first / premier (1e)	16th	sixteenth / seizième (16e)
2nd	second / deuxième (2e)	17th	seventeenth / dix-septième (17e)
3rd	third / troisième (3e)	18th	eighteenth / dix-huitième (18e)
4th	fourth / quatrième (4e)	19th	nineteenth / dix-neuvième (19e)
5th	fifth / cinquième (5e)	20th	twentieth / vingtième (20e)
6th	sixth / sixième (6e)	21st	twenty-first / vingt et unième (21e)
7th	seventh / septième (7e)	30th	thirtieth / trentième (30e)
8th	eighth / huitième (8e)	40th	fortieth / quarantième (40e)
9th	ninth / neuvième (9e)	50th	fiftieth / cinquantième (50e)
10th	tenth / dixième (10e)	60th	sixtieth / soixantième (60e)
11th	eleventh / onzième (11e)	70th	seventieth / soixante-dixième (70e)
12th	twelfth / douzième (12e)	80th	eightieth / quatre-vingtième (80e)
13th	thirteenth / treizième (13e)	90th	ninetieth / quatre-vingt dixième (90e)
14th	fourteenth / quatorzième (14e)	100th	one hundredth / centième (100e)
15th	fifteenth / quinzième (15e)	1,000th	one thousandth / millième (1 000e)

Roman Numerals Chiffres romains

I = 1	VII = 7	XXX = 30
II = 2	VIII = 8	XL = 40
III = 3	IX = 9	L = 50
IV = 4	X = 10	C = 100
V = 5	XV = 15	D = 500
VI = 6	XX = 20	M = 1,000

 **A. divide**
diviser
1 ÷ 4 = .25

 **B. calculate**
calculer
75% of 10 = 7.5

C. measure
mesurer
2 inches

 **D. convert**
convertir
1 mi. = 1.6 km
1 MILE TO LAKE

Fractions and Decimals Fractions et chiffres décimaux

1. one whole
$1 = 1.00$
un entier

2. one half
$1/2 = .5$
un demi

3. one third
$1/3 = .333$
un tiers

4. one fourth
$1/4 = .25$
un quart

5. one eighth
$1/8 = .125$
un huitième

Percents Pourcentages

6. calculator
la calculatrice

7. decimal point
le point décimal

8 100 percent — 100%
9 75 percent — 75%
10 50 percent — 50%
11 25 percent — 25%
12 10 percent — 10%

0% 10% 20% 30% 40% 50% 60% 70% 80% 90% 100%

8. 100 percent
100 pour cent

9. 75 percent
75 pour cent

10. 50 percent
50 pour cent

11. 25 percent
25 pour cent

12. 10 percent
10 pour cent

Measurement Mesure

13. ruler
la règle

14. centimeter [cm]
centimètre [cm]

15. inch [in.]
pouce [po]

Dimensions Dimensions

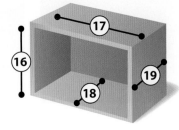

16. height
la hauteur

17. length
la longueur

18. depth
la profondeur

19. width
la largeur

Equivalencies

12 inches = 1 foot

3 feet = 1 yard

1,760 yards = 1 mile

1 inch = 2.54 centimeters

1 yard = .91 meters

1 mile = 1.6 kilometers

Telling Time Lire l'heure

1. hour
heure

2. minutes
minutes

3. seconds
secondes

4. a.m.
du matin

5. p.m.
de l'après-midi

6. 1:00
one o'clock
une heure

7. 1:05
one-oh-five
five after one
une heure cinq

8. 1:10
one-ten
ten after one
une heure dix

9. 1:15
one-fifteen
a quarter after one
une heure quinze
une heure et quart

10. 1:20
one-twenty
twenty after one
une heure vingt

11. 1:30
one-thirty
half past one
une heure trente
une heure et demie

12. 1:40
one-forty
twenty to two
une heure quarante
deux heures moins vingt

13. 1:45
one-forty-five
a quarter to two
une heure quarante-cinq
deux heures moins le quart

Times of Day Moments de la journée

14. sunrise
lever du soleil

15. morning
matin

16. noon
midi

17. afternoon
après-midi

18. sunset
coucher du soleil

19. evening
soir

20. night
nuit

21. midnight
minuit

Ways to talk about time

I wake up at 6:30 a.m.
I wake up at 6:30 in the morning.
I wake up at 6:30.

Pair practice. Make new conversations.

A: *What time do you wake up on weekdays?*
B: *At 6:30 a.m. How about you?*
A: *I wake up at 7:00.*

22. early
tôt

23. on time
à l'heure

24. late
tard

25. daylight saving time
heure d'été

26. standard time
heure normale

Time Zones Fuseaux horaires

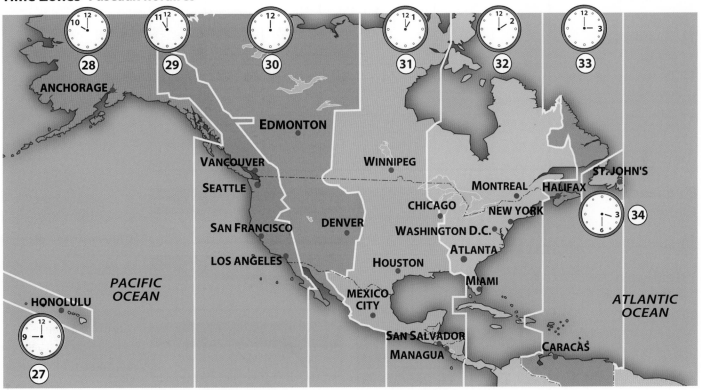

27. Hawaii-Aleutian time
heure d'Hawaï-des
Aléoutiennes

28. Alaska time
heure de l'Alaska

29. Pacific time
heure du Pacifique

30. Mountain time
heure des Rocheuses

31. Central time
heure du Centre

32. Eastern time
heure de l'Est

33. Atlantic time
heure de l'Atlantique

34. Newfoundland time
heure de Terre-Neuve

Ask your classmates. Share the answers.

1. When do you watch television? study? relax?
2. Do you like to stay up after midnight?
3. Do you like to wake up late on weekends?

Think about it. Discuss.

1. What is your favorite time of day? Why?
2. Do you think daylight saving time is a good idea?
Why or why not?

19

1. date
   date
2. day
   jour
3. month
   mois
4. year
   année

5. today
   aujourd'hui
6. tomorrow
   demain
7. yesterday
   hier

Days of the Week
Jours de la semaine

8. Sunday
   dimanche
9. Monday
   lundi
10. Tuesday
    mardi
11. Wednesday
    mercredi
12. Thursday
    jeudi
13. Friday
    vendredi
14. Saturday
    samedi

15. week
    semaine
16. weekdays
    jours de semaine
17. weekend
    fin de semaine

MAY

SUN	MON	TUE	WED	THU	FRI	SAT
1	2	3	4	5	6	7
8	9	10	11	12	13	14
15	16	17	18	19	20	21
22	23	24	25	26	27	28
29	30	31				

Frequency
Fréquence

18. last week
    la semaine dernière
19. this week
    cette semaine
20. next week
    la semaine prochaine

MAY

SUN	MON	TUE	WED	THU	FRI	SAT
X1	X2	X3	X4	X5	X6	X7
8	9	10	11	12	13	14
15	16	17	18	19	20	21
22	23	24	25	26	27	28

SUN	MON	TUE	WED	THU	FRI	SAT
✓	✓	✓	✓	✓	✓	✓

21. every day / daily
    chaque jour /
    quotidiennement

SUN	MON	TUE	WED	THU	FRI	SAT
	✓					

22. once a week
    une fois par semaine

SUN	MON	TUE	WED	THU	FRI	SAT
	✓		✓			

23. twice a week
    deux fois par semaine

SUN	MON	TUE	WED	THU	FRI	SAT
	✓	✓		✓		

24. three times a week
    trois fois par semaine

Ways to say the date

Today is __May 10th__. It's the __tenth__.
Yesterday was __May 9th__.
The party is on __May 21st__.

Pair practice. Make new conversations.

A: *The __test__ is on __Friday__, __June 14th__.*
B: *Did you say __Friday__, the __fourteenth__?*
A: *Yes, the __fourteenth__.*

25 JAN

SUN	MON	TUE	WED	THU	FRI	SAT
					1	2
3	4	5	6	7	8	9
10	11	12	13	14	15	16
17	18	19	20	21	22	23
24/31	25	26	27	28	29	30

26 FEB

SUN	MON	TUE	WED	THU	FRI	SAT
	1	2	3	4	5	6
7	8	9	10	11	12	13
14	15	16	17	18	19	20
21	22	23	24	25	26	27
28						

27 MAR

SUN	MON	TUE	WED	THU	FRI	SAT
	1	2	3	4	5	6
7	8	9	10	11	12	13
14	15	16	17	18	19	20
21	22	23	24	25	26	27
28	29	30	31			

28 APR

SUN	MON	TUE	WED	THU	FRI	SAT
				1	2	3
4	5	6	7	8	9	10
11	12	13	14	15	16	17
18	19	20	21	22	23	24
25	26	27	28	29	30	

29 MAY

SUN	MON	TUE	WED	THU	FRI	SAT
						1
2	3	4	5	6	7	8
9	10	11	12	13	14	15
16	17	18	19	20	21	22
23/30	24/31	25	26	27	28	29

30 JUN

SUN	MON	TUE	WED	THU	FRI	SAT
		1	2	3	4	5
6	7	8	9	10	11	12
13	14	15	16	17	18	19
20	21	22	23	24	25	26
27	28	29	30			

31 JUL

SUN	MON	TUE	WED	THU	FRI	SAT
				1	2	3
4	5	6	7	8	9	10
11	12	13	14	15	16	17
18	19	20	21	22	23	24
25	26	27	28	29	30	31

32 AUG

SUN	MON	TUE	WED	THU	FRI	SAT
1	2	3	4	5	6	7
8	9	10	11	12	13	14
15	16	17	18	19	20	21
22	23	24	25	26	27	28
29	30	31				

33 SEP

SUN	MON	TUE	WED	THU	FRI	SAT
			1	2	3	4
5	6	7	8	9	10	11
12	13	14	15	16	17	18
19	20	21	22	23	24	25
26	27	28	29	30		

34 OCT

SUN	MON	TUE	WED	THU	FRI	SAT
					1	2
3	4	5	6	7	8	9
10	11	12	13	14	15	16
17	18	19	20	21	22	23
24/31	25	26	27	28	29	30

35 NOV

SUN	MON	TUE	WED	THU	FRI	SAT
	1	2	3	4	5	6
7	8	9	10	11	12	13
14	15	16	17	18	19	20
21	22	23	24	25	26	27
28	29	30				

36 DEC

SUN	MON	TUE	WED	THU	FRI	SAT
		1	2	3	4
5	6	7	8	9	10	11
12	13	14	15	16	17	18
19	20	21	22	23	24	25
26	27	28	29	30	31	

Months of the Year
Mois de l'année

25. January
janvier

26. February
février

27. March
mars

28. April
avril

29. May
mai

30. June
juin

31. July
juillet

32. August
août

33. September
septembre

34. October
octobre

35. November
novembre

36. December
décembre

Seasons
Saisons

37. spring
printemps

38. summer
été

39. fall / autumn
automne

40. winter
hiver

Dictate to your partner. Take turns.

A: *Write <u>Monday</u>.*
B: *Is it spelled <u>M-o-n-d-a-y</u>?*
A: *Yes, that's right.*

Ask your classmates. Share the answers.

1. What is your favorite day of the week? Why?
2. What is your busiest day of the week? Why?
3. What is your favorite season of the year? Why?

1. birthday
anniversaire de naissance

2. wedding
mariage

3. anniversary
anniversaire

4. appointment
rendez-vous

5. parent-teacher conference
conseil de parents et professeurs

6. vacation
vacances

7. religious holiday
fête religieuse

8. legal holiday
jour férié

Legal Holidays Jours fériés

9. New Year's Day
Nouvel an

10. Martin Luther King Jr. Day
Fête de Martin Luther King Jr.

11. Presidents' Day
Fête des présidents

12. Memorial Day
Jour du souvenir

13. Fourth of July /
Independence Day
4 juillet / Fête de
l'indépendance nationale

14. Labor Day
Fête du travail

15. Columbus Day
Fête de Christophe Colomb

16. Veterans Day
Fête des anciens combattants

17. Thanksgiving
Action de grâce

18. Christmas
Noël

Pair practice. Make new conversations.

A: *When is your <u>birthday</u>?*
B: *It's on <u>January 31st</u>. How about you?*
A: *It's on <u>December 22nd</u>.*

Ask your classmates. Share the answers.

1. What are the legal holidays in your native country?
2. When is Labor Day in your native country?
3. When do you celebrate the New Year in your native country?

1. **little** hand
   petite main
2. **big** hand
   grosse main

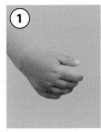 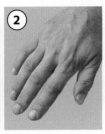

3. **fast** driver
   conducteur **rapide**
4. **slow** driver
   conducteur **lent**

5. **hard** chair
   chaise **dure**
6. **soft** chair
   chaise **moelleuse**

7. **thick** book
   livre **épais**
8. **thin** book
   livre **mince**

9. **full** glass
   verre **plein**
10. **empty** glass
    verre **vide**

11. **noisy** children /
    loud children
    enfants **bruyants** /
    enfants **tapageurs**
12. **quiet** children
    enfants **tranquilles**

 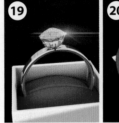

13. **heavy** box
    boîte **lourde**
14. **light** box
    boîte **légère**

15. **same** color
    même couleur
16. **different** colors
    couleurs **différentes**

17. **good** dog
    bon chien
18. **bad** dog
    vilain chien

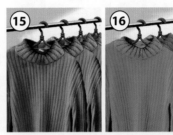 

19. **expensive** ring
    bague **coûteuse**
20. **cheap** ring
    bague **bon marché**

 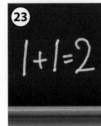

21. **beautiful** view
    vue **magnifique**
22. **ugly** view
    vue **laide**

23. **easy** problem
    problème **simple**
24. **difficult** problem /
    hard problem
    problème **difficile** /
    problème **compliqué**

Ask your classmates. Share the answers.

1. Are you a slow driver or a fast driver?
2. Do you prefer a hard bed or a soft bed?
3. Do you like loud parties or quiet parties?

Use the new words.

Look at page 150–151. Describe the things you see.

A: *The street* is *hard*.
B: *The truck* is *heavy*.

Basic Colors Couleurs de base

1. red
   rouge

2. yellow
   jaune

3. blue
   bleu

4. orange
   orange

5. green
   vert

6. purple
   mauve

7. pink
   rose

8. violet
   violet

9. turquoise
   turquoise

10. dark blue
    bleu foncé

11. light blue
    bleu pâle

12. bright blue
    bleu éclatant

Neutral Colors Couleurs neutres

13. black
    noir

14. white
    blanc

15. gray
    gris

16. cream / ivory
    crème / ivoire

17. brown
    brun

18. beige / tan
    beige / brun clair

Ask your classmates. Share the answers.

1. What colors are you wearing today?
2. What colors do you like?
3. Is there a color you don't like? What is it?

Use the new words. Look at pages 86–87.
Take turns naming the colors you see.

A: *His shirt is <u>blue</u>.*
B: *Her shoes are <u>white</u>.*

24

1. The yellow sweaters are **on the left**.
   Les pull-overs jaunes sont **sur la gauche**.

2. The purple sweaters are **in the middle**.
   Les pull-overs violets sont **au milieu**.

3. The brown sweaters are **on the right**.
   Les pull-overs marrons sont **sur la droite**.

4. The red sweaters are **above** the blue sweaters.
   Les pull-overs rouges sont **au-dessus** des pull-overs bleus.

5. The blue sweaters are **below** the red sweaters.
   Les pull-overs bleus sont **en desous** des pull-overs rouges.

6. The turquoise sweater is **in** the box.
   Le pull-over turquoise est **dans** la boîte.

7. The white sweater is **in front of** the black sweater.
   Le pull-over blanc est **devant** le pull-over noir.

8. The black sweater is **behind** the white sweater.
   Le pull-over noir est **derrière** le pull-over blanc.

9. The orange sweater is **on** the gray sweater.
   Le pull-over orange est **sur** le pull-over gris.

10. The violet sweater is **next to** the gray sweater.
    Le pull-over violet est **à côté du** pull-over gris.

11. The gray sweater is **under** the orange sweater.
    Le pull-over gris est **sous** le pull-over orange.

12. The green sweater is **between** the pink sweaters.
    Le pull-over vert est **entre** les pull-overs roses.

More vocabulary

near: in the same area
far from: not near

Role play. Make new conversations.

A: *Excuse me. Where are the <u>red</u> sweaters?*
B: *They're <u>on the left</u>, <u>above</u> the <u>blue</u> sweaters.*
A: *Thanks very much.*

Coins Pièces

1. $.01 = 1¢
   a penny / 1 cent
   1 cent

2. $.05 = 5¢
   a nickel / 5 cents
   5 cents

3. $.10 = 10¢
   a dime / 10 cents
   10 cents

4. $.25 = 25¢
   a quarter / 25 cents
   25 cents

5. $.50 = 50¢
   a half dollar
   50 cents

6. $1.00
   a dollar coin
   une pièce d'un dollar

Bills Billets

7. $1.00
   a dollar
   un dollar

8. $5.00
   five dollars
   cinq dollars

9. $10.00
   ten dollars
   dix dollars

10. $20.00
    twenty dollars
    vingt dollars

11. $50.00
    fifty dollars
    cinquante dollars

12. $100.00
    one hundred dollars
    cent dollars

A. **Get** change.
Obtenir de la monnaie.

B. **Borrow** money.
Emprunter de l'argent.

C. **Lend** money.
Prêter de l'argent.

D. **Pay back** the money.
Rembourser l'argent.

Pair practice. Make new conversations.

A: *Do you have change for a dollar?*
B: *Sure. How about two quarters and five dimes?*
A: *Perfect!*

Think about it. Discuss.

1. Is it a good idea to lend money to a friend? Why or why not?
2. Is it better to carry a dollar or four quarters? Why?
3. Do you prefer dollar coins or dollar bills? Why?

Ways to Pay Modes de paiement

A. pay cash
payer en espèces

B. use a credit card
utiliser une carte de crédit

C. use a debit card
utiliser une carte de débit

D. write a (personal) check
écrire un chèque personnel

E. use a gift card
utiliser une carte-cadeau

F. cash a traveler's check
encaisser un chèque de voyage

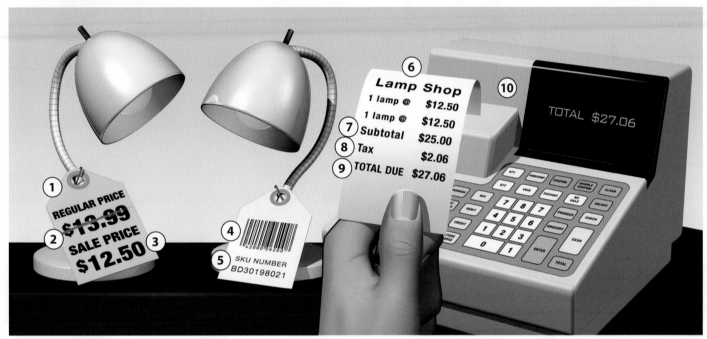

1. price tag
   étiquette

2. regular price
   prix courant

3. sale price
   prix réduit

4. bar code
   code à barres

5. SKU number
   numéro UGS

6. receipt
   reçu

7. price / cost
   prix / coût

8. sales tax
   taxe de vente

9. total
   total

10. cash register
    caisse

G. buy / pay for
acheter / payer

H. return
retourner

I. exchange
échanger

1. twins
   jumelles

2. sweater
   pull-over

3. matching
   identique

4. disappointed
   déçu

5. navy blue
   bleu marine

6. happy
   heureux (heureuse)

A. **shop**
   magasin

B. **keep**
   garder

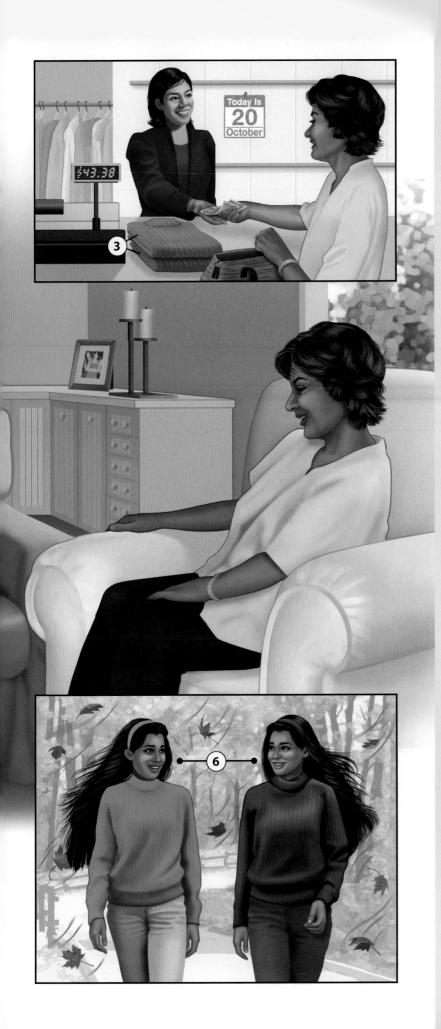

Look at the pictures.
What do you see?

Answer the questions.

1. Who is the woman shopping for?
2. Does she buy matching sweaters or different sweaters?
3. How does Anya feel about her green sweater? What does she do?
4. What does Manda do with her sweater?

 Read the story.

Same and Different

Mrs. Kumar likes to shop for her twins. Today she's looking at sweaters. There are many different colors on sale. Mrs. Kumar chooses two matching green sweaters.

The next day, Manda and Anya open their gifts. Manda likes the green sweater, but Anya is disappointed. Mrs. Kumar understands the problem. Anya wants to be different.

Manda keeps her sweater. But Anya goes to the store. She exchanges her green sweater for a navy blue sweater. It's an easy answer to Anya's problem. Now the twins can be warm, happy, and different.

Think about it.

1. Do you like to shop for other people? Why or why not?
2. Imagine you are Anya. Would you keep the sweater or exchange it? Why?

29

1. **man**
   homme

2. **woman**
   femme

3. **women**
   femmes

4. **men**
   hommes

5. **senior citizen**
   personne âgée

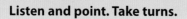

Listen and point. Take turns.

A: *Point to a woman.*
B: *Point to a senior citizen.*
A: *Point to an infant.*

Dictate to your partner. Take turns.

A: *Write woman.*
B: *Is that spelled w-o-m-a-n?*
A: *Yes, that's right, woman.*

30

6. infant
petit enfant

7. baby
bébé

8. toddler
enfant qui commence
à marcher

9. 6-year-old boy
garçon de 6 ans

10. 10-year-old girl
fille de 10 ans

11. teenager / teen
adolescent

Ways to talk about age

1 month – 3 months old = **infant**	13 – 19 years old = **teenager**
18 months – 3 years old = **toddler**	18+ years old = **adult**
3 years old – 12 years old = **child**	62+ years old = **senior citizen**

Pair practice. Make new conversations.

A: *How old is Sandra?*

B: *She's thirteen years old.*

A: *Wow, she's a teenager now!*

31

Age Âge

1. young
   jeune
2. middle-aged
   âge moyen
3. elderly
   âgé(e)

①　②　③

Height Taille

4. tall
   grand(e)
5. average height
   de taille moyenne
6. short
   petit(e)

④　⑤　⑥　⑦　⑧　⑨

Weight Poids

7. heavy / fat
   gros / gras
8. average weight
   de poids moyen
9. thin / slender
   mince / svelte

Disabilities Handicaps

10. physically challenged
    handicapé(e)
11. sight impaired / blind
    malvoyant(e) / aveugle
12. hearing impaired / deaf
    malentendant(e) / sourd(e)

⑩

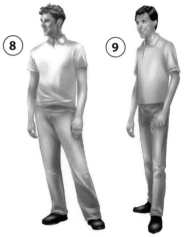
⑪

⑫

Prepositions of Motion p.153

Appearance Aspect physique

⑬　⑭

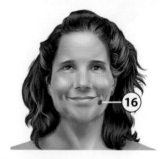
⑮

⑯

⑰　⑱

13. attractive
    attrayant(e)
14. cute
    mignon(ne)
15. pregnant
    enceinte
16. mole
    grain de beauté
17. pierced ear
    oreille percée
18. tattoo
    tatouage

Ways to describe people

He's a <u>heavy</u>, <u>young</u> man.
She's a <u>pregnant</u> woman with <u>a mole</u>.
He's <u>sight impaired</u>.

Use the new words. Look at pages 2–3.
Describe the people and point. Take turns.

A: *He's a <u>tall</u>, <u>thin</u>, <u>middle-aged</u> man.*
B: *She's a <u>short</u>, <u>average-weight</u> <u>young</u> woman.*

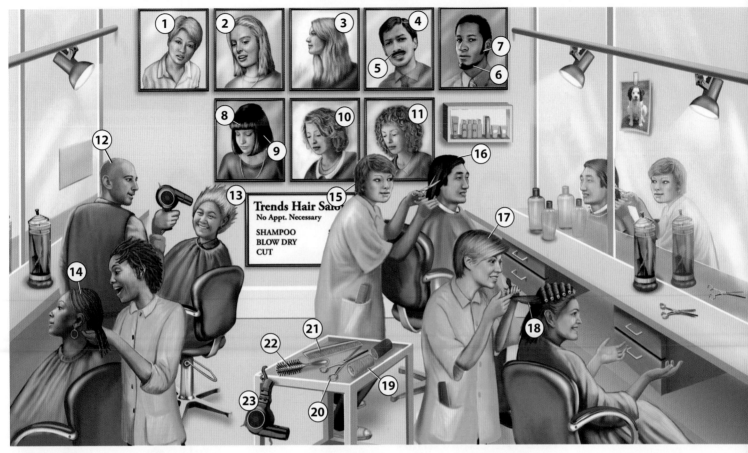

1. **short hair**
   cheveux courts

2. **shoulder-length hair**
   cheveux mi-longs

3. **long hair**
   cheveux longs

4. **part**
   raie

5. **mustache**
   moustache

6. **beard**
   barbe

7. **sideburns**
   favoris / pattes

8. **bangs**
   frange

9. **straight hair**
   cheveux raides

10. **wavy hair**
    cheveux ondulés

11. **curly hair**
    cheveux frisés

12. **bald**
    chauve

13. **gray hair**
    cheveux gris

14. **corn rows**
    tresses africaines

15. **red hair**
    cheveux roux

16. **black hair**
    cheveux noirs

17. **blond hair**
    cheveux blonds

18. **brown hair**
    cheveux bruns

19. **rollers**
    rouleaux

20. **scissors**
    ciseaux

21. **comb**
    peigne

22. **brush**
    brosse

23. **blow dryer**
    séchoir

Style Hair Coiffer les cheveux

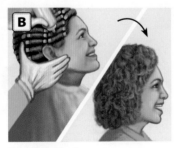

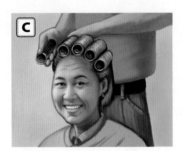

A. **cut** hair
couper les cheveux

B. **perm** hair
faire une permanente

C. **set** hair
faire une mise en pli
des cheveux

D. **color** hair / **dye** hair
colorer les cheveux /
teindre les cheveux

Ways to talk about hair

Describe hair in this order: length, style, and then color.
She has <u>long</u>, <u>straight</u>, <u>brown</u> hair.

Role play. Talk to a stylist.

A: *I need a new hairstyle.*
B: *How about <u>short</u> and <u>straight</u>?*
A: *Great. Do you think I should <u>dye</u> it?*

33

Families

Familles

1. **grandmother**
   grand-mère
2. **grandfather**
   grand-père
3. **mother**
   mère
4. **father**
   père
5. **sister**
   sœur
6. **brother**
   frère
7. **aunt**
   tante
8. **uncle**
   oncle
9. **cousin**
   cousin

Tim Lee's Family

GRANDPARENTS
Immediate Family

1 — Min
2 — Lu

PARENTS

3 — Rose
4 — Ken
7 — Lynn
8 — Dan

CHILDREN

Tim
5 — Lily
6 — Alex
9 — Emily

10. **mother-in-law**
    belle-mère
11. **father-in-law**
    beau-père
12. **wife**
    femme / épouse / conjointe
13. **husband**
    mari / époux / conjoint
14. **daughter**
    fille
15. **son**
    fils
16. **sister-in-law**
    belle-sœur
17. **brother-in-law**
    beau-frère
18. **niece**
    nièce
19. **nephew**
    neveu

Ana Garcia's Family

Extended Family

10 — Eva
11 — Sam

12 — Ana
13 — Tito
16 — Marta
17 — Carlos

14 — Sara
15 — Felix
18 — Alice
19 — Eddie

More vocabulary

Tim is Min and Lu's **grandson**.
Lily and Emily are Min and Lu's **granddaughters**.
Alex is Min's youngest **grandchild**.

Ana is Tito's **wife**.
Ana is Eva and Sam's **daughter-in-law**.
Carlos is Eva and Sam's **son-in-law**.

20. **married couple**
couple marié

21. **divorced couple**
couple divorcé

22. **single mother**
mère célibataire

23. **single father**
père célibataire

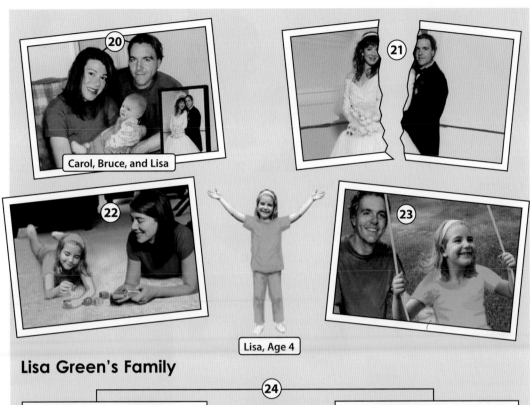

Carol, Bruce, and Lisa

Lisa, Age 4

Lisa Green's Family

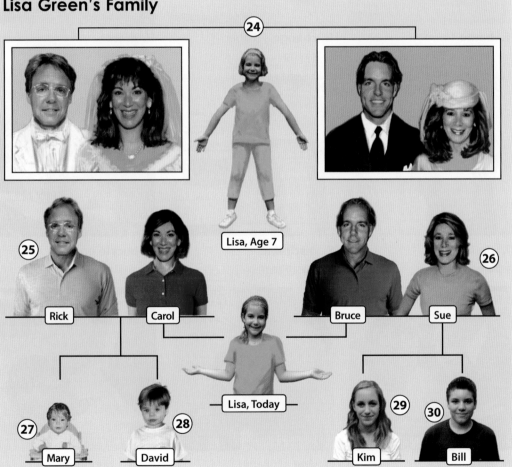

Lisa, Age 7

24. **remarried**
remarié(e)

25. **stepfather**
beau-père (adoptif)

26. **stepmother**
belle-mère (adoptive)

27. **half sister**
demi-sœur

28. **half brother**
demi-frère

29. **stepsister**
demi-sœur

30. **stepbrother**
demi-frère

Rick | Carol | Bruce | Sue

Lisa, Today

Mary | David | Kim | Bill

More vocabulary

Bruce is Carol's **former husband** or **ex-husband**.
Carol is Bruce's **former wife** or **ex-wife**.
Lisa is the **stepdaughter** of both Rick and Sue.

Look at the pictures.
Name the people.

A: Who is _Lisa's_ _half sister_?
B: _Mary_ is. Who is _Lisa's_ _stepsister_?

A. hold
porter

B. nurse
allaiter

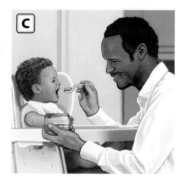

C. feed
nourrir

D. rock
bercer

E. undress
déshabiller

F. bathe
laver

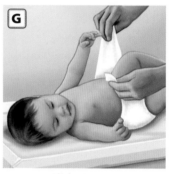

G. change a diaper
changer une couche

H. dress
habiller

I. comfort
réconforter

Good job!

J. praise
féliciter

No!

K. discipline
discipliner

L. buckle up
mettre la ceinture de sécurité

M. play with
jouer avec

N. read to
lire à

O. sing a lullaby
chanter une berceuse

P. kiss goodnight
embrasser avant de
mettre au lit

Look at the pictures.
Describe what is happening.

A: *She's <u>changing her baby's diaper</u>*.
B: *He's <u>kissing his son goodnight</u>*.

Ask your classmates. Share the answers.

1. Do you like to take care of children?
2. Do you prefer to read to children or play with them?
3. Can you sing a lullaby? Which one?

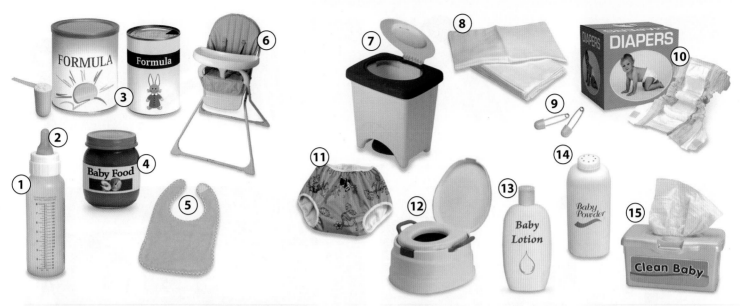

1. **bottle**
biberon

2. **nipple**
tétine

3. **formula**
formule

4. **baby food**
aliments pour bébés

5. **bib**
bavette

6. **high chair**
chaise haute

7. **diaper pail**
seau à couches

8. **cloth diaper**
couches lavables

9. **safety pins**
épingles de sûreté

10. **disposable diaper**
couches jetables

11. **training pants**
culottes de propreté

12. **potty seat**
pot

13. **baby lotion**
crème pour bébé

14. **baby powder**
poudre pour bébés

15. **wipes**
serviettes humides
pour bébés

16. **baby bag**
sac pour bébé

17. **baby carrier**
porte-bébé

18. **stroller**
poussette

19. **car safety seat**
siège de sécurité pour enfant

20. **carriage**
poussette

21. **rocking chair**
berceuse

22. **nursery rhymes**
comptines

23. **teddy bear**
ours en peluche

24. **pacifier**
sucette

25. **teething ring**
anneau de dentition

26. **rattle**
hochet

27. **night light**
veilleuse

Dictate to your partner. Take turns.

A: *Write pacifier.*
B: *Was that pacifier, p-a-c-i-f-i-e-r?*
A: *Yes, that's right.*

Think about it. Discuss.

1. How can parents discipline toddlers? teens?
2. What are some things you can say to praise a child?
3. Why are nursery rhymes important for young children?

37

A. wake up
se réveiller

B. get up
se lever

C. take a shower
prendre une douche

D. get dressed
s'habiller

E. eat breakfast
manger le petit déjeuner

F. make lunch
préparer le déjeuner

G. take the children to school /
drop off the kids
accompagner les enfants à l'école /
déposer les enfants

H. take the bus to school
prendre l'autobus pour aller à l'école

I. drive to work / **go** to work
aller travailler en voiture / aller travailler

J. go to class
aller en classe

K. work
travailler

L. go to the grocery store
aller à l'épicerie

M. pick up the kids
aller chercher les enfants

N. leave work
quitter le travail

Grammar Point: third person singular

For *he* and *she*, add **-s** or **-es** to the verb:

He wakes up.   *He watches TV.*

He gets up.   *She goes to the store.*

These verbs are different (irregular):

*Be: She **is** in school at 10:00 a.m.*

*Have: He **has** dinner at 6:30 p.m.*

38

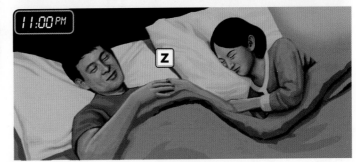

O. clean the house
 nettoyer la maison

P. exercise
 faire de l'exercice

Q. cook dinner / **make** dinner
 cuisiner le dîner / **préparer** le dîner

R. come home / **get** home
 revenir à la maison / se **rendre** à la maison

S. have dinner / **eat** dinner
 dîner

T. do homework
 faire ses devoirs

U. relax
 se détendre

V. read the paper
 lire le journal

W. check email
 vérifier son courriel

X. watch TV
 regarder la télévision

Y. go to bed
 aller se coucher

Z. go to sleep
 s'**endormir**

Pair practice. Make new conversations.

A: *When does he go to work?*
B: *He goes to work at 8:00 a.m. When does she go to class?*
A: *She goes to class at 10:00 a.m.*

Ask your classmates. Share the answers.

1. Who cooks dinner in your family?
2. Who goes to the grocery store?
3. Who goes to work?

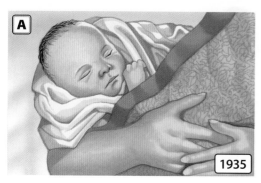

A. **be born**
naître

B. **start** school
commencer l'école

REGISTRO CIVIL
Acta de Nacimiento
MARTÍN PEREZ DE LÉON   B0983456
01-05-1935

Registro Civil
Acta de Nacimiento

1. birth certificate
acte de naissance

C. **immigrate**
émigrer / immigrer

D. **graduate**
obtenir un diplôme

PERMANENT RESIDENT CARD
PEREZ, MARTIN   A043398414

01-05-1935

2. Resident Alien card /
green card
carte verte

Los Angeles High School

Martin Perez

3. diploma
diplôme

E. **learn** to drive
apprendre à conduire

F. **get** a job
trouver un emploi

CALIFORNIA
DRIVER LICENSE
M06188
MARTIN PEREZ

4. driver's license
permis de conduire

G. **become** a citizen
obtenir sa citoyenneté

H. **fall in love**
tomber amoureux

SOCIAL SECURITY
987-65-4321
MARTIN PEREZ

5. Social Security card
carte de sécurité sociale

THE UNITED STATES OF AMERICA
CERTIFICATE OF   NATURALIZATION
MARTIN PEREZ DE LEON

6. Certificate of Naturalization
certificat de naturalisation

Grammar Point: past tense

start ⎫
learn ⎬ **+ed**
travel ⎭

immigrate   retire ⎫
graduate   die ⎬ **+d**
            ⎭

These verbs are different (irregular):

be – was   go – went   buy – bought
get – got   have – had
become – became   fall – fell

40

I. go to college
aller à l'université

1956

J. get engaged
se fiancer

1958

7. college degree
diplôme universitaire

City College
Martin Perez
Bachelor of Science

K. get married
se marier

1959

L. have a baby
avoir un bébé

1961

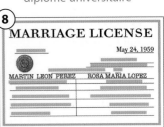

8. marriage license
certificat de publication des bans

MARRIAGE LICENSE
May 24, 1959
MARTIN LEON PEREZ   ROSA MARIA LOPEZ

M. buy a home
acheter une maison

FOR SALE
SOLD

1965

N. become a grandparent
devenir grand-parent

1986

9. deed
acte notarié

LAND DEED   6/7/1965
MARTIN LEON PEREZ
ROSA MARIA LOPEZ

GOODBYE MARTIN AND GOOD LUCK!

2000

O. retire
prendre sa retraite

2005

P. travel
voyager

10. passport
passeport

PASSPORT
United States of America

2006

Q. volunteer
faire du bénévolat

2008

R. die
mourir

11. death certificate
certificat de décès

CERTIFICATE OF DEATH
MARTIN LEON PEREZ
December 12th, 2008

More vocabulary

When a husband dies, his wife becomes a **widow**.
When a wife dies, her husband becomes a **widower**.

Ask your classmates. Share the answers.

1. When did you start school?
2. When did you get your first job?
3. Do you want to travel?

1. hot
   chaud

2. thirsty
   avoir soif

3. sleepy
   avoir sommeil

4. cold
   froid

5. hungry
   avoir faim

6. full / satisfied
   repu

7. disgusted
   être dégoûté(e)

8. calm
   (être) calme

9. uncomfortable
   être mal à l'aise

10. nervous
    nerveux (nerveuse)

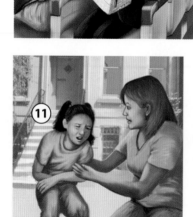

11. in pain
    avoir mal

12. sick
    être malade

13. worried
    être inquiet(e)

14. well
    être bien

15. relieved
    être soulagé(e)

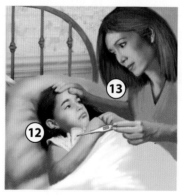

16. hurt
    être blessé(e) /
    peiné(e)

17. lonely
    seul(e)

18. in love
    être amoureux

Pair practice. Make new conversations.

A: *How are you doing?*
B: *I'm <u>hungry</u>. How about you?*
A: *I'm <u>hungry</u> and <u>thirsty</u>, too!*

Use the new words.
Look at pages 40–41. Describe what each person is feeling.

A: *Martin is <u>excited</u>.*
B: *Martin's mother is <u>proud</u>.*

19. sad
triste

20. homesick
mal du pays

21. proud
fier (fière)

22. excited
excité(e)

23. scared / afraid
avoir peur

24. embarrassed
embarrassé(e)

25. bored
blasé(e)

26. confused
confus(e)

27. frustrated
frustré(e)

In picture 26: $14\ (\tan 63°)$ $T = V_0 / g$ $79.00 - .40\ (79.00)$

In picture 27: $\sin^2 t + \cos^2 t + 1$ $\tan (\pi - t) = -\tan t$

28. upset
bouleversé(e)

29. angry
fâché(e)

30. surprised
surpris(e)

31. happy
heureux (heureuse)

32. tired
fatigué(e)

Ask your classmates. Share the answers.

1. Do you ever feel homesick?
2. What makes you feel frustrated?
3. Describe a time when you were very happy.

More vocabulary

exhausted: very tired
furious: very angry
humiliated: very embarrassed

overjoyed: very happy
starving: very hungry
terrified: very scared

1. banner
   bannière

2. baseball game
   match de base-ball

3. opinion
   opinion

4. balloons
   ballons

5. glad
   heureux / content

6. relatives
   parents

A. **laugh**
   rire

B. **misbehave**
   se conduire mal

Look at the picture. What do you see?

Answer the questions.

1. How many relatives are there at this reunion?

2. How many children are there? Which children are misbehaving?

3. What are people doing at this reunion?

 Read the story.

A Family Reunion

Ben Lu has a lot of <u>relatives</u> and they're all at his house. Today is the Lu family reunion.

There is a lot of good food. There are also <u>balloons</u> and a <u>banner</u>. And this year there are four new babies!

People are having a good time at the reunion. Ben's grandfather and his aunt are talking about the <u>baseball game</u>. His cousins <u>are laughing</u>. His mother-in-law is giving her <u>opinion</u>. And many of the children <u>are misbehaving</u>.

Ben looks at his family and smiles. He loves his relatives, but he's <u>glad</u> the reunion is once a year.

Think about it.

1. Do you like to have large parties? Why or why not?

2. Imagine you see a little girl at a party. She's misbehaving. What do you do? What do you say?

The Home La maison

1. **roof**
   toit
2. **bedroom**
   chambre
3. **door**
   porte
4. **bathroom**
   salle de bain
5. **kitchen**
   cuisine
6. **floor**
   plancher
7. **dining area**
   coin repas

Listen and point. Take turns.

A: *Point to the kitchen.*
B: *Point to the living room.*
A: *Point to the basement.*

Dictate to your partner. Take turns.

A: *Write kitchen.*
B: *Was that k-i-t-c-h-e-n?*
A: *Yes, that's right, kitchen.*

8. **attic**
grenier

9. **kids' bedroom**
chambre des enfants

10. **baby's room**
chambre du bébé

11. **window**
fenêtre

12. **living room**
salon

13. **basement**
sous-sol

14. **garage**
garage

Ways to give locations
I'm home.
I'm in the kitchen.
I'm on the roof.

Pair practice. Make new conversations.
A: *Where's the man?*
B: *He's in the attic. Where's the teenager?*
A: *She's in the laundry room.*

47

1. Internet listing
annonce sur Internet

2. classified ad
petite annonce

Abbreviations

apt = apartment

bdrm = bedroom

ba = bathroom

kit = kitchen

yd = yard

util = utilities

incl = included

mo = month

furn = furnished

unfurn = unfurnished

mgr = manager

eves = evenings

3. furnished apartment
appartement meublé

4. unfurnished apartment
appartement non meublé

Gas · Water · Electricity · Phone · Cable · DSL

5. utilities
services publics

Renting an Apartment · Location d'un appartement

A. Call the manager.
Appeler le gérant.

Are utilities included?

No, they aren't.

B. Ask about the features.
Se renseigner quant aux caractéristiques.

C. Submit an application.
Soumettre une demande.

D. Sign the rental agreement.
Signer un contrat de location.

E. Pay the first and last month's rent.
Payer le premier et le dernier mois de loyer.

F. Move in.
Emménager.

More vocabulary

lease: a monthly or yearly rental agreement
redecorate: to change the paint and furniture in a home
move out: to pack and leave a home

Ask your classmates. Share the answers.

1. How did you find your home?
2. Do you like to paint or arrange furniture?
3. Does gas or electricity cost more for you?

48

Buying a House Achat d'une maison

G. Meet with a realtor.
Rencontrer un agent immobilier.

H. Look at houses.
Visiter des maisons.

$$$$$$

I. Make an offer.
Faire une offre.

Congratulations!

J. Get a loan.
Obtenir un prêt.

K. Take ownership.
Prendre possession.

L. Make a mortgage payment.
Faire un versement hypothécaire.

Moving In Emménager

M. Pack.
Emballer.

N. Unpack.
Déballer.

We have a new address.

O. Put the utilities in your name.
Préciser son nom aux services publics.

P. Paint.
Peindre.

Q. Arrange the furniture.
Arranger les meubles.

Welcome!

R. Meet the neighbors.
Rencontrer les voisins.

Ways to ask about a home's features

Are utilities included?
Is the kitchen large and sunny?
Are the neighbors quiet?

Role play. Talk to an apartment manager.

A: *Hi. I'm calling about the apartment.*
B: *OK. It's unfurnished and rent is $800 a month.*
A: *Are utilities included?*

49

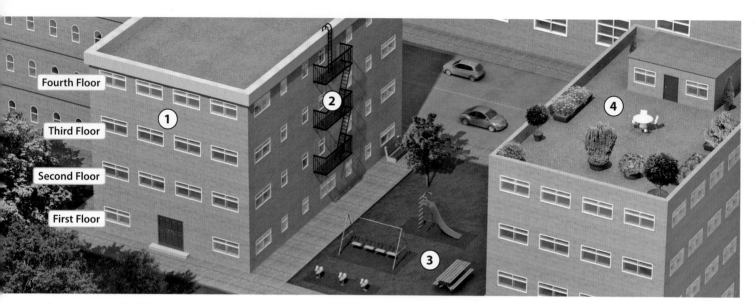

Fourth Floor
Third Floor
Second Floor
First Floor

1. apartment building
immeuble à appartements

2. fire escape
escalier de secours

3. playground
terrain de jeux

4. roof garden
jardin sur le toit

Entrance Entrée

Apartment Available
2BD + 2BA
555-4263

5. intercom / speaker
interphone / haut-parleur

6. tenant
locataire

7. vacancy sign
affiche de disponibilité

8. manager /
superintendent
gérant / concierge

Lobby Hall d'entrée

9. elevator
ascenseur

10. stairs / stairway
escaliers

11. mailboxes
boîtes aux lettres

Basement Sous-sol

SOAP SOFTENER

LAUNDRY ROOM

RECREATION ROOM

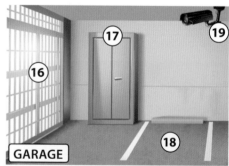

GARAGE

12. washer
lave-linge / laveuse

13. dryer
sèche-linge / sécheuse

14. big-screen TV
télé à grand écran

15. pool table
table de billard

16. security gate
barrière de sécurité

17. storage locker
casier de rangement

18. parking space
espace de stationnement

19. security camera
caméra de sécurité

Grammar Point: *there is / there are*

singular: there is   **plural:** there are
There is *a recreation room in the basement.*
There are *mailboxes in the lobby.*

Look at the pictures.
Describe the apartment building.

A: *There's <u>a pool table</u> in the recreation room.*
B: *There are <u>parking spaces</u> in the garage.*

APARTMENT COMPLEX

20. balcony
balcon

21. courtyard
cour

22. swimming pool
piscine

23. trash bin
bac à ordures

24. alley
ruelle

Hallway Couloir

25. emergency exit
sortie de secours

26. trash chute
vide-ordures

Rental Office Bureau de location

27. landlord
propriétaire

28. lease / rental agreement
bail / contrat de location

An Apartment Entryway Un vestibule d'appartement

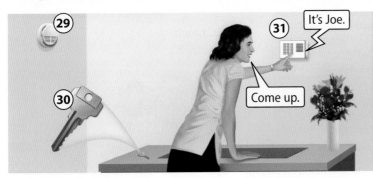

It's Joe.

Come up.

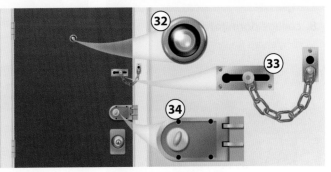

29. smoke detector
détecteur de fumée

30. key
clé

31. buzzer
sonnette

32. peephole
judas

33. door chain
chaîne de sûreté

34. dead-bolt lock
verrou

More vocabulary

upstairs: the floor(s) above you
downstairs: the floor(s) below you
fire exit: another name for emergency exit

Role play. Talk to a landlord.

A: Is there <u>a swimming pool</u> in this <u>complex</u>?
B: Yes, there is. It's near <u>the courtyard</u>.
A: Is there…?

51

1. the city / an urban area
la ville / une zone urbaine

2. the suburbs
la banlieue

3. a small town / a village
une petite ville / un village

4. the country / a rural area
la campagne / une zone rurale

5. condominium / condo
appartement en copropriété

6. townhouse
maison de ville

7. mobile home
maison mobile

8. college dormitory / dorm
résidences universitaires

9. farm
ferme

10. ranch
ranch

11. senior housing
maison de retraite

12. nursing home
maison de retraite

13. shelter
abri

More vocabulary

co-op: an apartment building owned by residents
duplex: a house divided into two homes
two-story house: a house with two floors

Think about it. Discuss.

1. What's good and bad about these places to live?
2. How are small towns different from cities?
3. How do shelters help people in need?

Une maison et un jardin

Front Yard and House Jardin de devant et maison

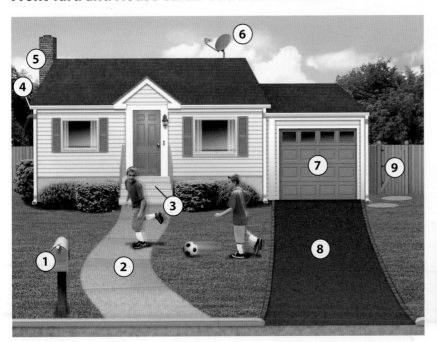

Front Porch Porche avant

1. **mailbox**
   boîte aux lettres

2. **front walk**
   trottoir

3. **steps**
   marches

4. **gutter**
   gouttière

5. **chimney**
   cheminée

6. **satellite dish**
   antenne parabolique

7. **garage door**
   porte de garage

8. **driveway**
   allée

9. **gate**
   portail

10. **storm door**
    double porte

11. **front door**
    porte d'entrée

12. **doorknob**
    poignée de porte

13. **porch light**
    lampe de porte

14. **doorbell**
    sonnette

15. **screen door**
    porte moustiquaire

Backyard Jardin à l'arrière

16. **patio**
    patio

17. **grill**
    gril

18. **sliding glass door**
    porte vitrée
    coulissante

19. **patio furniture**
    meubles de patio

20. **flower bed**
    plate-bande

21. **hose**
    boyau

22. **sprinkler**
    arroseur

23. **hammock**
    hamac

24. **garbage can**
    poubelle

25. **compost pile**
    tas de compost

26. **lawn**
    pelouse

27. **vegetable garden**
    jardin potager

A. **take** a nap
   faire une sieste

B. **garden**
   jardiner

Une cuisine

1. cabinet	**8. dishwasher**	**15. toaster oven**	**22. counter**
armoire	lave-vaisselle	grille-pain four	comptoir
2. shelf	**9. refrigerator**	**16. pot**	**23. drawer**
tablette	réfrigérateur	casserole	tiroir
3. paper towels	**10. freezer**	**17. teakettle**	**24. pan**
essuie-tout	congélateur	théière	poêlon
4. sink	**11. coffeemaker**	**18. stove**	**25. electric mixer**
évier	cafetière électrique	cuisinière	mélangeur électrique
5. dish rack	**12. blender**	**19. burner**	**26. food processor**
panier à vaisselle	mélangeur	brûleur	robot culinaire
6. toaster	**13. microwave**	**20. oven**	**27. cutting board**
grille-pain	micro-ondes	four	planche à découper
7. garbage disposal	**14. electric can opener**	**21. broiler**	**28. mixing bowl**
broyeur d'ordures	ouvre-boîte électrique	grilloir	saladier

Ways to talk about location using *on* and *in*

Use *on* for the counter, shelf, burner, stove, and cutting board. *It's **on** the counter.* Use *in* for the dishwasher, oven, sink, and drawer. *Put it **in** the sink.*

Pair practice. Make new conversations.

A: *Please move <u>the blender</u>.*
B: *Sure. Do you want it <u>in the cabinet</u>?*
A: *No, put it <u>on the counter</u>.*

1. dish / plate
   assiette

2. bowl
   bol

3. fork
   fourchette

4. knife
   couteau

5. spoon
   cuillère / cuiller

6. teacup
   tasse à thé

7. coffee mug
   grande tasse à café

8. dining room chair
   chaise de salle à manger

9. dining room table
   table de salle à manger

10. napkin
    serviette

11. placemat
    set de table

12. tablecloth
    nappe

13. salt and pepper shakers
    salière et poivrière

14. sugar bowl
    sucrier

15. creamer
    pot à crème

16. teapot
    théière

17. tray
    plateau

18. light fixture
    luminaire

19. fan
    ventilateur

20. platter
    plat

21. serving bowl
    saladier

22. hutch
    buffet

23. vase
    vase

24. buffet
    buffet

Ways to make requests at the table

May I have the sugar bowl?
Would you pass the creamer, please?
Could I have a coffee mug?

Role play. Request items at the table.

A: *What do you need?*
B: *Could I have a coffee mug?*
A: *Certainly. And would you...*

55

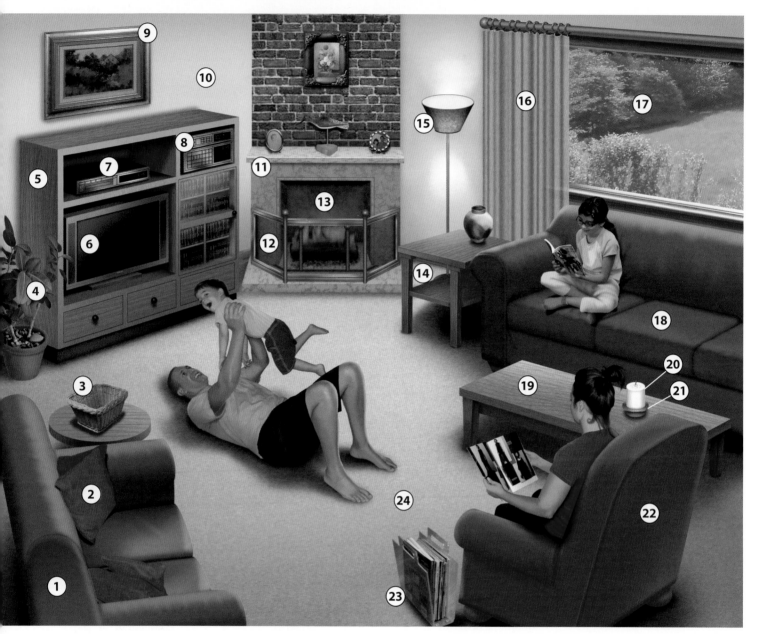

1. love seat causeuse	**7.** DVD player lecteur de DVD	**13.** fireplace foyer	**19.** coffee table table de salon / table basse
2. throw pillow coussin	**8.** stereo system chaîne stéréo	**14.** end table table d'extrémité	**20.** candle chandelle
3. basket panier	**9.** painting tableau	**15.** floor lamp lampe sur pied / lampadaire	**21.** candle holder bougeoir
4. houseplant plante d'intérieur	**10.** wall mur	**16.** drapes tentures	**22.** armchair / easy chair fauteuil
5. entertainment center centre de divertissement	**11.** mantle manteau	**17.** window fenêtre	**23.** magazine holder porte-journaux
6. TV (television) télé (téléviseur)	**12.** fire screen écran de cheminée	**18.** sofa / couch sofa / divan	**24.** carpet tapis / moquette

---

Use the new words.

Look at pages 44–45. Name the things in the room.

A: *There's a TV.*

B: *There's a carpet.*

More vocabulary

light bulb: the light inside a lamp

lampshade: the part of the lamp that covers the light bulb

sofa cushions: the pillows that are part of the sofa

1. hamper
   panier à linge

2. bathtub
   baignoire

3. soap dish
   porte savon

4. soap
   savon

5. rubber mat
   tapis de caoutchouc

6. washcloth
   gant de toilette

7. drain
   drain

8. faucet
   robinet

9. hot water
   eau chaude

10. cold water
    eau froide

11. grab bar
    barre d'appui

12. tile
    carrelage

13. showerhead
    pommeau de douche

14. shower curtain
    rideau de douche

15. towel rack
    porte-serviettes

16. bath towel
    serviette de bain

17. hand towel
    essuie-mains

18. mirror
    miroir

19. toilet paper
    papier hygiénique

20. toilet brush
    balayette

21. toilet
    cuvette

22. medicine cabinet
    armoire à pharmacie

23. toothbrush
    brosse à dents

24. toothbrush holder
    porte brosses à dents

25. sink
    lavabo

26. wastebasket
    corbeille à déchets

27. scale
    pèse-personne

28. bath mat
    tapis de bain

More vocabulary

stall shower: a shower without a bathtub
half bath: a bathroom with no shower or tub
linen closet: a closet for towels and sheets

Ask your classmates. Share the answers.

1. Is your toothbrush on the sink or in the medicine cabinet?
2. Do you have a bathtub or a shower?
3. Do you have a shower curtain or a shower door?

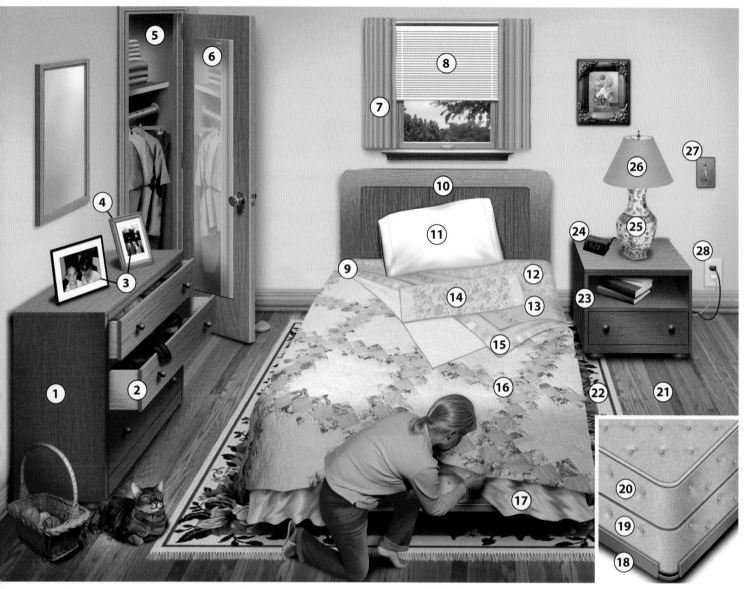

1. **dresser / bureau**
   commode-coiffeuse /
   commode

2. **drawer**
   tiroir

3. **photos**
   photos

4. **picture frame**
   cadre à photo

5. **closet**
   placard

6. **full-length mirror**
   miroir en pied

7. **curtains**
   rideaux

8. **mini-blinds**
   store (à lamelles)

9. **bed**
   lit

10. **headboard**
    tête de lit

11. **pillow**
    oreiller

12. **fitted sheet**
    drap-housse

13. **flat sheet**
    drap plat

14. **pillowcase**
    taie d'oreiller

15. **blanket**
    couverture

16. **quilt**
    courtepointe

17. **dust ruffle**
    volant de lit

18. **bed frame**
    cadre de lit

19. **box spring**
    sommier

20. **mattress**
    matelas

21. **wood floor**
    plancher en bois

22. **rug**
    carpette / tapis

23. **night table / nightstand**
    table de nuit

24. **alarm clock**
    réveil

25. **lamp**
    lampe

26. **lampshade**
    abat-jour

27. **light switch**
    interrupteur

28. **outlet**
    prise

Look at the pictures.
Describe the bedroom.

A: *There's a lamp on the nightstand.*
B: *There's a mirror in the closet.*

Ask your classmates. Share the answers.

1. Do you prefer a hard or a soft mattress?
2. Do you prefer mini-blinds or curtains?
3. How many pillows do you like on your bed?

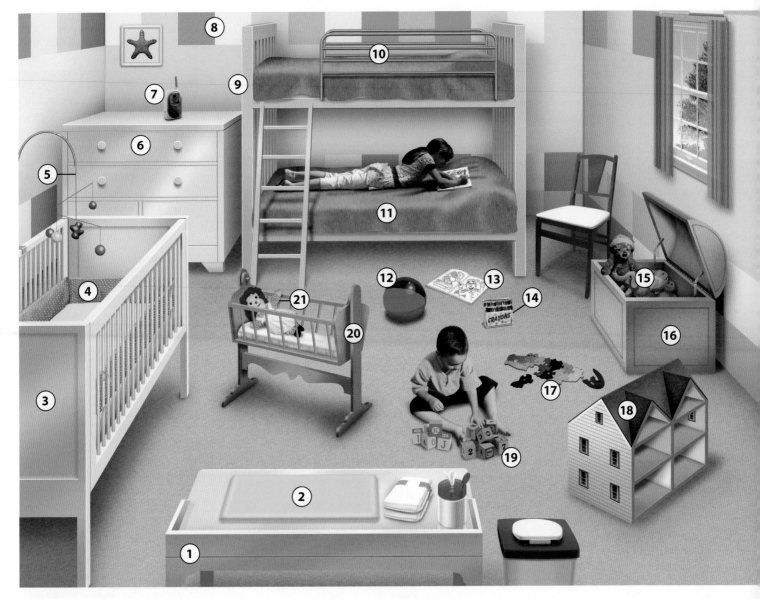

Furniture and Accessories Meubles et accessoires

1. changing table
   table à langer

2. changing pad
   matelas à langer

3. crib
   lit d'enfant

4. bumper pad
   bordure de protection

5. mobile
   mobile

6. chest of drawers
   commode

7. baby monitor
   moniteur de bébé

8. wallpaper
   papier peint

9. bunk beds
   lits superposés

10. safety rail
    rail de sécurité

11. bedspread
    couvre-lit

Toys and Games Jouets et jeux

12. ball
    balle / ballon

13. coloring book
    livre à colorier

14. crayons
    crayons

15. stuffed animals
    animaux en peluche

16. toy chest
    coffre à jouets

17. puzzle
    puzzle / casse-tête

18. dollhouse
    maison de poupées

19. blocks
    blocs

20. cradle
    berceau

21. doll
    poupée

Pair practice. Make conversations.

A: *Where's the changing pad?*
B: *It's on the changing table.*

Think about it. Discuss.

1. Which toys help children learn? How?
2. Which toys are good for older and younger children?
3. What safety features does this room need? Why?

A. **dust** the furniture
épousseter les meubles

B. **recycle** the newspapers
recycler les journaux

C. **clean** the oven
nettoyer le four

D. **mop** the floor
laver le plancher

E. **polish** the furniture
polir les meubles

F. **make** the bed
faire le lit

G. **put away** the toys
ranger les jouets

H. **vacuum** the carpet
passer l'aspirateur
sur le tapis

I. **wash** the windows
laver les vitres

J. **sweep** the floor
balayer le plancher

K. **scrub** the sink
récurrer l'évier

L. **empty** the trash
vider la poubelle

M. **wash** the dishes
laver la vaisselle

N. **dry** the dishes
essuyer la vaisselle

O. **wipe** the counter
essuyer le comptoir

P. **change** the sheets
changer les draps

Q. **take out** the garbage
sortir les ordures

Pair practice. Make new conversations.

A: *Let's clean this place. First, I'll <u>sweep the floor</u>.*
B: *I'll <u>mop the floor</u> when you finish.*

Ask your classmates. Share the answers.

1. Who does the housework in your home?
2. How often do you wash the windows?
3. When should kids start to do housework?

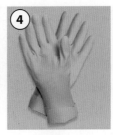
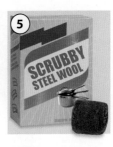

1. **feather duster**
   plumeau
2. **recycling bin**
   bac de recyclage
3. **oven cleaner**
   nettoyant à four
4. **rubber gloves**
   gants de caoutchouc
5. **steel-wool soap pads**
   tampons à récurer en laine d'acier
6. **sponge mop**
   balai-éponge
7. **bucket / pail**
   seau
8. **furniture polish**
   encaustique pour meubles

9. **rags**
   chiffons
10. **vacuum cleaner**
    aspirateur
11. **vacuum cleaner attachments**
    accessoires d'aspirateur
12. **vacuum cleaner bag**
    sacs d'aspirateur
13. **stepladder**
    escabeau
14. **glass cleaner**
    nettoyant à vitres
15. **squeegee**
    raclette
16. **broom**
    balai

17. **dustpan**
    ramasse-poussière
18. **cleanser**
    détergent
19. **sponge**
    éponge
20. **scrub brush**
    brosse à récurer
21. **dishwashing liquid**
    détergent à vaisselle
22. **dish towel**
    linge à vaisselle
23. **disinfectant wipes**
    serviettes désinfectantes
24. **trash bags**
    sacs à ordures

Ways to ask for something

Please hand me <u>the squeegee</u>.
Can you get me <u>the broom</u>?
I need <u>the sponge mop</u>.

Pair practice. Make new conversations.

A: *Please hand me <u>the sponge mop</u>.*
B: *Here you go. Do you need <u>the bucket</u>?*
A: *Yes, please. Can you get me <u>the rubber gloves</u>, too?*

61

1. The water heater is **not working**.
   Le chauffe-eau **ne fonctionne pas**.

2. The power is **out**.
   Il y a une **panne** de courant.

3. The roof is **leaking**.
   Le toit **coule**.

4. The tile is **cracked**.
   Le carreau est **fissuré**.

5. The window is **broken**.
   La vitre est **brisée**.

6. The lock is **broken**.
   La serrure est **cassée**.

7. The steps are **broken**.
   Les marches sont **abîmées**.

8. roofer
   couvreur

9. electrician
   électricien

10. repair person
    réparateur

11. locksmith
    serrurier

12. carpenter
    charpentier

13. fuse box
    boîte à fusibles

14. gas meter
    compteur à gaz

More vocabulary

fix: to repair something that is broken
pests: termites, fleas, rats, etc.
exterminate: to kill household pests

Pair practice. Make new conversations.

A: *The faucet is <u>leaking</u>.*
B: *Let's call <u>the plumber</u>. He can fix it.*

15. The furnace is **broken**.
L'appareil de chauffage est **cassé**.

16. The pipes are **frozen**.
Les tuyaux sont **gelés**.

17. The faucet is **dripping**.
Le robinet **coule**.

18. The sink is **overflowing**.
L'évier **déborde**.

19. The toilet is **stopped up**.
La cuvette est **bouchée**.

20. plumber
plombier

21. exterminator
exterminateur

22. termites
termites

23. ants
fourmis

24. bedbugs
punaises de lit

25. fleas
puces

26. cockroaches / roaches
cafards / blattes

27. rats
rats

28. mice*
souris

*****Note:** one mouse, two mice

Ways to ask about repairs

How much will this repair cost?
When can you begin?
How long will the repair take?

Role play. Talk to a repair person.

A: *Can you fix <u>the roof</u>?*
B: *Yes, but it will take <u>two weeks</u>.*
A: *How much will the repair cost?*

1. roommates colocataires	**3.** music musique	**5.** noise bruit	**7.** rules règles	**9.** invitation invitation
2. party fête	**4.** DJ DJ	**6.** irritated irrité	**8.** mess désordre	**A.** **dance** **danser**

Look at the pictures. What do you see?

Answer the questions.

1. What happened in apartment 2B? How many people were there?

2. How did the neighbor feel? Why?

3. What rules did they write at the tenant meeting?

4. What did the roommates do after the tenant meeting?

📖 Read the story.

The Tenant Meeting

Sally Lopez and Tina Green are <u>roommates</u>. They live in apartment 2B. One night they had a big <u>party</u> with <u>music</u> and a <u>DJ</u>. There was a <u>mess</u> in the hallway. Their neighbors were very unhappy. Mr. Clark in 2A was very <u>irritated</u>. He hates <u>noise</u>!

The next day there was a tenant meeting. Everyone wanted <u>rules</u> about parties and loud music. The girls were very embarrassed.

After the meeting, the girls cleaned the mess in the hallway. Then they gave each neighbor an <u>invitation</u> to a new party. Everyone had a good time at the rec room party. Now the tenants have two new rules and a new place to <u>dance</u>.

Think about it.

1. What are the most important rules in an apartment building? Why?

2. Imagine you are the neighbor in 2A. What do you say to Tina and Sally?

1. fish
   poisson
2. meat
   viande
3. chicken
   poulet
4. cheese
   fromage
5. milk
   lait
6. butter
   beurre
7. eggs
   oeufs
8. vegetables
   légumes

Listen and point. Take turns.

A: *Point to the vegetables.*
B: *Point to the bread.*
A: *Point to the fruit.*

Pair Dictation

A: *Write vegetables.*
B: *Please spell vegetables for me.*
A: *V-e-g-e-t-a-b-l-e-s.*

9. fruit
fruit

10. rice
riz

11. bread
pain

12. pasta
pâtes

13. grocery bag
sac à provisions

14. shopping list
liste des courses

15. coupons
coupons

Ways to talk about food.

Do we need eggs?
Do we have any pasta?
We have some vegetables, but we need fruit.

Role play. Talk about your shopping list.

A: *Do we need eggs?*
B: *No, we have some.*
A: *Do we have any...*

67

1. apples
   pommes

2. bananas
   bananes

3. grapes
   raisins

4. pears
   poires

5. oranges
   oranges

6. grapefruit
   pamplemousse

7. lemons
   citrons

8. limes
   limes

9. tangerines
   mandarines

10. peaches
    pêches

11. cherries
    cerises

12. apricots
    abricots

13. plums
    prunes

14. strawberries
    fraises

15. raspberries
    framboises

16. blueberries
    myrtilles

17. blackberries
    mûres

18. watermelons
    pastèques

19. melons
    melons

20. papayas
    papayes

21. mangoes
    mangues

22. kiwi
    kiwi

23. pineapples
    ananas

24. coconuts
    noix de coco

25. raisins
    raisins secs

26. prunes
    pruneaux

27. figs
    figues

28. dates
    dattes

29. a bunch of bananas
    un régime de bananes

30. **ripe** banana
    bananes **mûres**

31. **unripe** banana
    bananes **vertes**

32. **rotten** banana
    bananes **pourries**

Pair practice. Make new conversations.

A: *What's your favorite fruit?*
B: *I like __apples__. Do you?*
A: *I prefer __bananas__.*

Ask your classmates. Share the answers.

1. Which fruit do you put in a fruit salad?
2. What kinds of fruit are common in your native country?
3. What kinds of fruit are in your kitchen right now?

1. **lettuce**
   laitue

2. **cabbage**
   choux

3. **carrots**
   carottes

4. **radishes**
   radis

5. **beets**
   betteraves

6. **tomatoes**
   tomates

7. **bell peppers**
   poivrons

8. **string beans**
   haricots verts

9. **celery**
   céleri

10. **cucumbers**
    concombres

11. **spinach**
    épinards

12. **corn**
    maïs

13. **broccoli**
    brocoli

14. **cauliflower**
    choux-fleur

15. **bok choy**
    chou chinois

16. **turnips**
    navets

17. **potatoes**
    pommes de terre

18. **sweet potatoes**
    patates douces

19. **onions**
    oignons

20. **green onions / scallions**
    oignons verts / échalotes

21. **peas**
    pois

22. **artichokes**
    artichauts

23. **eggplants**
    aubergines

24. **squash**
    courges

25. **zucchini**
    courgettes

26. **asparagus**
    asperges

27. **mushrooms**
    champignons

28. **parsley**
    persil

29. **chili peppers**
    piments

30. **garlic**
    ail

31. a **bag of** lettuce
    un **sac de** laitue

32. a **head of** lettuce
    une **tête de** laitue

Pair practice. Make new conversations.

A: *Do you eat <u>broccoli</u>?*
B: *Yes. I like most vegetables, but not <u>peppers</u>.*
A: *Really? Well, I don't like <u>cauliflower</u>.*

Ask your classmates. Share the answers.

1. Which vegetables do you eat raw? cooked?
2. Which vegetables do you put in a green salad?
3. Which vegetables are in your refrigerator right now?

69

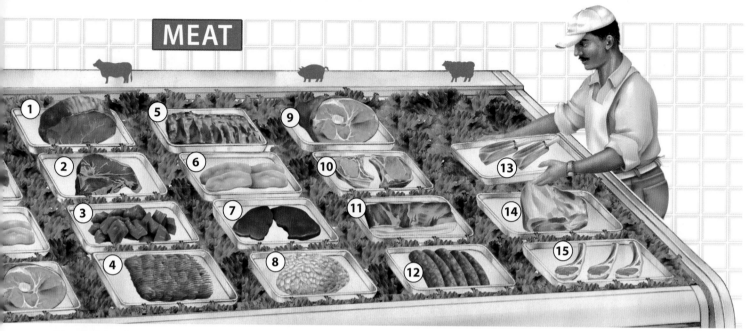

MEAT

Beef Bœuf

1. roast
   rôti
2. steak
   bifteck / steak
3. stewing beef
   bœuf à ragoût
4. ground beef
   boeuf haché

5. beef ribs
   côtes de bœuf
6. veal cutlets
   escalopes de veau
7. liver
   foie
8. tripe
   tripes

Pork Porc

9. ham
   jambon
10. pork chops
    côtelettes de porc
11. bacon
    lard / bacon
12. sausage
    saucisses

Lamb Agneau

13. lamb shanks
    jarrets d'agneau
14. leg of lamb
    gigot d'agneau
15. lamb chops
    côtelettes d'agneau

POULTRY

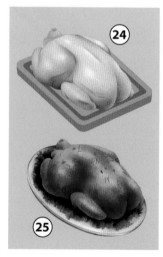

Poultry Volaille

16. chicken
    poulet
17. turkey
    dinde

18. duck
    canard
19. breasts
    poitrines

20. wings
    ailes
21. legs
    cuisses

22. thighs
    cuisses
23. drumsticks
    pilons

24. **raw** chicken
    poulet **cru**
25. **cooked** chicken
    poulet **cuit**

More vocabulary

vegetarian: a person who doesn't eat meat
boneless: meat and poultry without bones
skinless: poultry without skin

Ask your classmates. Share the answers.

1. What kind of meat do you eat most often?
2. What kind of meat do you use in soups?
3. What part of the chicken do you like the most?

Fish Poisson

1. trout
truite

2. catfish
poisson-chat

3. whole salmon
saumon entier

4. salmon steak
darne de saumon

5. swordfish
poisson-épée / espadon

6. halibut steak
pavé (steak) de flétan

7. tuna
thon

8. cod
morue

Shellfish Crustacés

9. crab
crabe

10. lobster
homard / langouste

11. shrimp
crevette

12. scallops
pétoncles

13. mussels
moules

14. oysters
huîtres

15. clams
palourdes

16. fresh fish
poisson **frais**

17. frozen fish
poisson **surgelé**

18. white bread
pain blanc / pain de froment

19. wheat bread
pain de blé

20. rye bread
pain de seigle

21. roast beef
rôti de bœuf / rosbif

22. corned beef
bœuf salé / bœuf en conserve

23. pastrami
pastrami

24. salami
salami

25. smoked turkey
dindon fumé

26. American cheese
cheddar américain

27. Swiss cheese
fromage gruyère

28. cheddar cheese
fromage cheddar

29. mozzarella cheese
mozzarella

Ways to order at the counter

I'd like some <u>roast beef</u>.
I'll have <u>a halibut steak</u> and some <u>shrimp</u>.
Could I get some <u>Swiss cheese</u>?

Pair practice. Make new conversations.

A: *What can I get for you?*
B: *<u>I'd like some roast beef</u>. How about a pound?*
A: *A pound of <u>roast beef</u> coming up!*

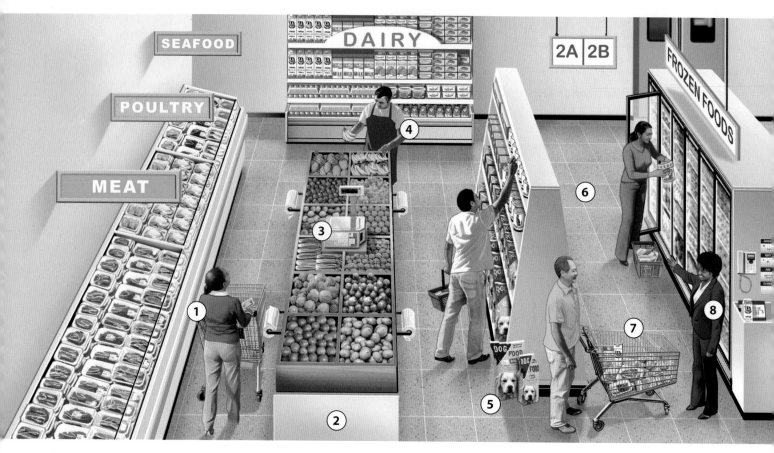

SEAFOOD

DAIRY

2A 2B

FROZEN FOODS

POULTRY

MEAT

1. **customer**
   client

2. **produce section**
   rayon des fruits et légumes

3. **scale**
   balance

4. **grocery clerk**
   commis épicier

5. **pet food**
   aliments pour animaux

6. **aisle**
   rayon

7. **cart**
   chariot

8. **manager**
   gérant

Canned Foods
Aliments en boîte

17. **beans**
    haricots

18. **soup**
    soupe

19. **tuna**
    thon

Dairy
Produits laitiers

20. **margarine**
    margarine

21. **sour cream**
    crème sûre / fermentée

22. **yogurt**
    yaourt / yogourt

Grocery Products
Emballages alimentaires

23. **aluminum foil**
    papier aluminium

24. **plastic wrap**
    film alimentaire

25. **plastic storage bags**
    sacs de stockage
    en plastique

Frozen Foods
Produits surgelés

26. **ice cream**
    crème glacée

27. **frozen vegetables**
    légumes surgelés

28. **frozen dinner**
    dîner surgelé

Ways to ask for information in a grocery store

Excuse me, where are the carrots?
Can you please tell me where to find the dog food?
Do you have any lamb chops today?

Pair practice. Make conversations.

A: *Can you please tell me where to find the dog food?*
B: *Sure. It's in aisle 1B. Do you need anything else?*
A: *Yes, where are the carrots?*

9. shopping basket
panier de provisions

10. self-checkout
caisse automatique

11. line
queue

12. checkstand
comptoir de caisse

13. cashier
caissier (caissière)

14. bagger
emballeur

15. cash register
caisse

16. bottle return
retour de bouteilles consignées

Baking Products
Produits de pâtisserie

29. flour
farine

30. sugar
sucre

31. oil
huile

Beverages
Boissons

32. apple juice
jus de pomme

33. coffee
café

34. soda / pop
boisson gazeuse

Snack Foods
En-cas

35. potato chips
chips

36. nuts
noix

37. candy bar
friandise

Baked Goods
Produits de boulangerie

38. cookies
biscuits

39. cake
gâteau

40. bagels
bagels

Ask your classmates. Share the answers.

1. What is your favorite grocery store?
2. Do you prefer to shop alone or with friends?
3. Which foods from your country are hard to find?

Think about it. Discuss.

1. Is it better to shop every day or once a week? Why?
2. Why do grocery stores put snacks near the checkstands?
3. What's good and what's bad about small grocery stores?

1. bottles
bouteilles

2. jars
bocaux

3. cans
boîtes de conserve

4. cartons
cartons

5. containers
contenants

6. boxes
boîtes

7. bags
sacs

8. packages
paquets

9. six-packs
pack de six

10. loaves
pains

11. rolls
petits pains

12. tubes
tubes

13. a bottle of water

14. a jar of jam

15. a can of beans

16. a carton of eggs

13. a bottle of water
une bouteille d'eau

14. a jar of jam
un bocal de confiture

15. a can of beans
une boîte de haricots

16. a carton of eggs
un carton d'œufs

17. a container of cottage cheese
un contenant de fromage cottage / blanc

18. a box of cereal
une boîte de céréales

19. a bag of flour
un sac de farine

20. a package of cookies
un paquet de biscuits

21. a six-pack of soda (pop)
un pack de six boissons gazeuses

22. a loaf of bread
un pain

23. a roll of paper towels
un rouleau d'essuie-tout

24. a tube of toothpaste
un tube de dentifrice

Grammar Point: count and non-count

Some foods can be counted: *an apple, two apples*.
Some foods can't be counted: *some rice, some water*.
For non-count foods, count containers: *two bags of rice*.

Pair practice. Make conversations.

A: *How many* <u>boxes of cereal</u> *do we need?*
B: *We need* <u>two boxes</u>.

Weights and Measurements

A. **Measure** the ingredients.
Mesurer les ingrédients.

B. **Weigh** the food.
Peser les aliments.

1 cup = 237 milliliters

C. **Convert** the measurements.
Convertir les mesures.

Liquid Measures Mesures de liquides

① 1 fl. oz.   ② 1 c.   ③ 1 pt.   ④ 1 qt.   ⑤ 1 gal.

Dry Measures Mesures de matières sèches

⑥ 1 tsp.   ⑦ 1 TBS.   ⑧ 1/4 c.   ⑨ 1/2 c.   ⑩ 1 c.

Weight Poids

1. a fluid ounce of milk
   une once liquide de lait

2. a cup of oil
   une tasse d'huile

3. a pint of frozen yogurt
   une pinte de yaourt glacé

4. a quart of milk
   un litre de lait

5. a gallon of water
   un galon d'eau

6. a teaspoon of salt
   une cuillerée à café de sel

7. a tablespoon of sugar
   une cuillerée à soupe de sucre

8. a quarter cup of brown sugar
   un quart de tasse de sucre brun

9. a half cup of raisins
   une demi-tasse de raisins secs

10. a cup of flour
    une tasse de farine

11. an ounce of cheese
    une once de fromage

12. a pound of roast beef
    une livre de rôti de bœuf / de rosbif

Equivalencies	
3 tsp. = 1 TBS.	2 c. = 1 pt.
2 TBS. = 1 fl. oz.	2 pt. = 1 qt.
8 fl. oz. = 1 c.	4 qt. = 1 gal.

Volume
1 fl. oz. = 30 ml
1 c. = 237 ml
1 pt. = .47 L
1 qt. = .95 L
1 gal. = 3.79 L

Weight
1 oz. = 28.35 grams (g)
1 lb. = 453.6 g
2.205 lbs. = 1 kilogram (kg)
1 lb. = 16 oz.

Food Safety Salubrité des aliments

A. **clean**
nettoyer

B. **separate**
séparer

C. **cook**
cuire

D. **chill**
faire refroidir

A — Clean counters! 20 SECONDS Wash your hands!

B — Use separate cutting boards for vegetables and meat!

C — Cook to the right temperature!

D — Refrigerate leftovers quickly!

Ways to Serve Meat and Poultry Façons de servir la viande et la volaille

1. fried chicken
poulet frit

2. barbecued / grilled ribs
côtes grillées

3. broiled steak
bifteck grillé

4. roasted turkey
dinde rôtie

5. boiled ham
jambon cuit

6. stir-fried beef
bœuf sauté

Ways to Serve Eggs Façons de servir les œufs

7. scrambled eggs
œufs brouillés

8. hardboiled eggs
œufs durs

9. poached eggs
œufs pochés

10. eggs sunny-side up
œufs sur le plat

11. eggs over easy
œufs tournés

12. omelet
omelette

Role play. Make new conversations.

A: *How do you like your eggs?*
B: *I like them <u>scrambled</u>. And you?*
A: *I like them <u>hardboiled</u>.*

Ask your classmates. Share the answers.

1. Do you use separate cutting boards?
2. What is your favorite way to serve meat? poultry?
3. What are healthy ways of preparing meat? poultry?

Cheesy Tofu Vegetable Casserole   Casserole de légumes et de tofu au fromage

A. Preheat the oven.
Faire préchauffer le four.

B. Grease a baking pan.
Graisser un plat à four.

C. Slice the tofu.
Découper le tofu **en tranches**.

D. Steam the broccoli.
Faire cuire le brocoli **à la vapeur**.

E. Saute the mushrooms.
Faire sauter les champignons.

F. Spoon sauce on top.
Verser la sauce à la cuiller.

G. Grate the cheese.
Râper le fromage.

H. Bake.
Cuire au four.

Easy Chicken Soup   Soupe de poulet facile à préparer

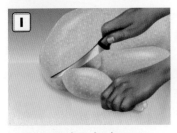

I. Cut up the chicken.
Couper le poulet.

J. Dice the celery.
Couper le céleri en cubes.

K. Peel the carrots.
Peler les carottes.

L. Chop the onions.
Hacher les oignons.

M. Boil the chicken.
Faire bouillir le poulet.

N. Add the vegetables.
Ajouter les légumes.

O. Stir.
Remuer.

P. Simmer.
Laisser mijoter.

Quick and Easy Cake   Gâteau facile et rapide

Q. Break 2 eggs into a microwave-safe bowl.
Casser 2 œufs dans un bol pour four micro-ondes.

R. Mix the ingredients.
Mélanger les ingrédients.

S. Beat the mixture.
Battre le mélange.

T. Microwave for 5 minutes.
Passer au micro-ondes pendant 5 minutes.

1. can opener
   ouvre-boîte

2. grater
   râpe

3. steamer
   cuit-vapeur

4. plastic storage container
   contenant de plastique

5. frying pan
   poêle à frire

6. pot
   casserole

7. ladle
   louche

8. double boiler
   bain-marie

9. wooden spoon
   cuiller en bois

10. casserole dish
    cocotte

11. garlic press
    presse-ail

12. carving knife
    couteau à découper

13. roasting pan
    rôtissoire / lèchefrite

14. roasting rack
    grille

15. vegetable peeler
    éplucheur / économe

16. paring knife
    couteau à éplucher

17. colander
    passoire

18. kitchen timer
    minuteur

19. spatula
    spatule

20. eggbeater
    batteur à œufs

21. whisk
    fouet

22. strainer
    tamis

23. tongs
    pinces

24. lid
    couvercle

25. saucepan
    casserole

26. cake pan
    moule à gâteau

27. cookie sheet
    tôle à biscuits

28. pie pan
    moule à tarte

29. pot holders
    poignées / maniques

30. rolling pin
    rouleau à pâtisserie

31. mixing bowl
    bol à mélanger

Pair practice. Make new conversations.

A: *Please hand me the whisk.*
B: *Here's the whisk. Do you need anything else?*
A: *Yes, pass me the casserole dish.*

Use the new words.

Look at page 77. Name the kitchen utensils you see.

A: *Here's a grater.*
B: *This is a mixing bowl.*

1. **hamburger**
   hamburger

2. **french fries**
   frites

3. **cheeseburger**
   cheeseburger / hamburger au fromage

4. **onion rings**
   rondelles d'oignon

5. **chicken sandwich**
   sandwich au poulet

6. **hot dog**
   hot-dog

7. **nachos**
   nachos

8. **taco**
   taco

9. **burrito**
   burrito

10. **pizza**
    pizza

11. **soda**
    boisson gazeuse

12. **iced tea**
    thé glacé

13. **ice-cream cone**
    cornet de glace

14. **milkshake**
    lait frappé

15. **donut**
    beignet

16. **muffin**
    muffin

17. **counterperson**
    préposé au comptoir

18. **straw**
    paille

19. **plastic utensils**
    couverts (ustensiles) en plastique

20. **sugar substitute**
    succédané de sucre

21. **ketchup**
    ketchup

22. **mustard**
    moutarde

23. **mayonnaise**
    mayonnaise

24. **salad bar**
    buffet de crudités

Grammar Point: yes/no questions (do)

Do you like hamburgers? Yes, I do.
Do you like nachos? No, I don't.

Think about it. Discuss.

1. Do you think that fast food is bad for people? Why or why not?
2. What fast foods do you have in your country?
3. Do you have a favorite fast food restaurant? Which one?

79

1. bacon
   lard / bacon

2. sausage
   saucisses

3. hash browns
   pommes de terre rissolées

4. toast
   toasts

5. English muffin
   muffin anglais

6. biscuits
   biscuits

7. pancakes
   crêpes

8. waffles
   gaufres

9. hot cereal
   céréales chaudes

10. grilled cheese sandwich
    sandwich au fromage grillé

11. pickle
    cornichon

12. club sandwich
    sandwich club

13. spinach salad
    salade d'épinards

14. chef's salad
    salade du chef

15. dinner salad
    salade

16. soup
    soupe

17. rolls
    petits pains

18. coleslaw
    salade de chou

19. potato salad
    salade de pommes de terre

20. pasta salad
    salade de pâtes

21. fruit salad
    salade de fruits

BREAKFAST SPECIAL
Served 6 a.m. to 11 a.m.

Two egg omelet with one side

HONEY

JELLY

SYRUP

LUNCH
Served 11 a.m. to 2 p.m.
All sandwiches come with soup or salad

CRACKERS

SIDE SALADS

SALAD DRESSINGS

Thousand Island   Ranch

Italian   Blue Cheese

Ways to order from a menu

I'd like a grilled cheese sandwich.
I'll have a bowl of tomato soup.
Could I get the chef's salad with ranch dressing?

Pair practice. Make conversations.

A: *I'd like a grilled cheese sandwich, please.*
B: *Anything else for you?*
A: *Yes, I'll have a bowl of tomato soup with that.*

A Coffee Shop Menu

DINNER

DESSERTS

BEVERAGES

22. **roast chicken**
    poulet rôti
23. **mashed potatoes**
    purée de pommes de terre
24. **steak**
    bifteck / steak
25. **baked potato**
    pomme de terre au four
26. **spaghetti**
    spaghetti
27. **meatballs**
    boulettes de viande
28. **garlic bread**
    pain à l'ail
29. **grilled fish**
    poisson grillé
30. **rice**
    riz
31. **meatloaf**
    pain de viande
32. **steamed vegetables**
    légumes cuits à la vapeur

33. **layer cake**
    gâteau à étages
34. **cheesecake**
    gâteau au fromage
35. **pie**
    tarte
36. **mixed berries**
    baies mélangées

37. **coffee**
    café
38. **decaf coffee**
    café déca
39. **tea**
    thé
40. **herbal tea**
    tisane
41. **cream**
    crème
42. **low-fat milk**
    lait écrémé

Ask your classmates. Share the answers.

1. Do you prefer vegetable soup or chicken soup?
2. Do you prefer tea or coffee?
3. Which desserts on the menu do you like?

Role play. Order a dinner from the menu.

A: *Are you ready to order?*
B: *I think so. I'll have <u>the roast chicken</u>.*
A: *Would you also like…?*

1. dining room
salle à manger

2. hostess
hôtesse

3. high chair
chaise haute

4. booth
box

5. to-go box
boîte à emporter

6. patron / diner
client / dîneur

7. menu
menu

8. server / waiter
serveur / garçon

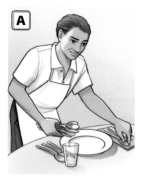    

A. set the table
mettre la table

B. seat the customer
faire asseoir le client

C. pour the water
verser l'eau

D. order from the menu
choisir dans le menu

E. take the order
prendre la commande

F. serve the meal
servir le repas

G. clear / bus the dishes
desservir la table

H. carry the tray
porter le plateau

I. pay the check
payer l'addition

J. leave a tip
laisser un pourboire

More Vocabulary

eat out: to go to a restaurant to eat
take out: to buy food at a restaurant and take it home to eat

Look at the pictures.
Describe what is happening.

A: She's <u>seating the customer</u>.
B: He's <u>taking the order</u>.

9. server / waitress
serveur / serveuse

10. dessert tray
plateau à desserts

11. bread basket
corbeille à pain

12. busser
aide-serveur

13. dish room
plonge

14. dishwasher
plongeur

15. kitchen
cuisine

16. chef
chef / cuisinier / cuisinière

 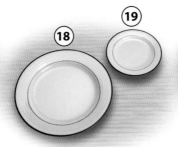 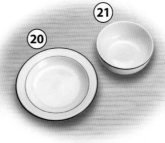 

17. place setting
couvert

18. dinner plate
grande assiette

19. bread-and-butter plate
assiette à pain et beurre

20. salad plate
assiette à salade

21. soup bowl
bol à soupe

22. water glass
verre à eau

23. wine glass
verre à vin

24. cup
tasse

25. saucer
soucoupe

26. napkin
serviette

27. salad fork
fourchette à salade

28. dinner fork
fourchette de table

29. steak knife
couteau à viande

30. knife
couteau

31. teaspoon
petite cuiller

32. soupspoon
cuiller à soupe

Pair practice. Make new conversations.

A: *Excuse me, this <u>spoon</u> is dirty.*
B: *I'm so sorry. I'll get you a clean <u>spoon</u> right away.*
A: *Thanks.*

Role play. Talk to a new busser.

A: *Do the <u>salad forks</u> go on <u>the left</u>?*
B: *Yes. They go <u>next to the dinner forks</u>.*
A: *What about the…?*

83

1. **live music**
   concert

2. **organic**
   biologique

3. **lemonade**
   limonade

4. **sour**
   aigre

5. **samples**
   échantillons

6. **avocados**
   avocats

7. **vendors**
   vendeurs

8. **sweets**
   sucreries

9. **herbs**
   fines herbes

A. **count**
   compter

HOT FOOD Cara's Bakery

CHIVES

DILL

PARSLEY

Look at the pictures. What do you see?

Answer the questions.

1. How many vendors are at the market today?

2. Which vegetables are organic?

3. What are the children eating?

4. What is the woman counting? Why?

📖 Read the story.

The Farmers' Market

On Saturdays, the Novaks go to the farmers' market. They like to visit the <u>vendors</u>. Alex Novak always goes to the hot food stand for lunch. His children love to eat the fruit <u>samples</u>. Alex's father usually buys some <u>sweets</u> and <u>lemonade</u>. The lemonade is very <u>sour</u>.

Nina Novak likes to buy <u>organic</u> <u>herbs</u> and vegetables. Today, she is buying <u>avocados</u>. The market worker <u>counts</u> eight avocados. She gives Nina one more for free.

There are other things to do at the market. The Novaks like to listen to the <u>live music</u>. Sometimes they meet friends there. The farmers' market is a great place for families on a Saturday afternoon.

Think about it.

1. What's good or bad about shopping at a farmers' market?

2. Imagine you are at the farmers' market. What will you buy?

BEST OF JAZZ CONCERT

1. shirt
   chemise
2. jeans
   jeans
3. dress
   robe
4. T-shirt
   T-shirt
5. baseball cap
   casquette de base-ball
6. socks
   chaussettes
7. athletic shoes
   chaussures athlétiques
A. **tie**
   lacer (ses souliers)

TICKETS

BEST OF JAZZ

Listen and point. Take turns.

A: *Point to the dress.*
B: *Point to the T-shirt.*
A: *Point to the baseball cap.*

Dictate to your partner. Take turns.

A: *Write dress.*
B: *Is that spelled d-r-e-s-s?*
A: *Yes. That's right.*

ONE NIGHT ONLY

DOORS OPEN AT 8:00

8. **blouse**
   chemisier
9. **handbag**
   sac à main
10. **skirt**
    jupe
11. **suit**
    costume
12. **slacks / pants**
    pantalons
13. **shoes**
    chaussures
14. **sweater**
    pull-over
B. **put on**
   mettre

Ways to compliment clothes

That's a pretty <u>dress</u>!
Those are great <u>shoes</u>!
I really like your <u>baseball cap</u>!

Role play. Compliment a friend.

A: *That's a pretty <u>dress</u>! <u>Green</u> is a great color on you.*
B: *Thanks! I really like your…*

87

Casual Clothes Vêtements décontractés

1. cap
   casquette

2. cardigan sweater
   cardigan

3. pullover sweater
   tricot / chandail

4. sports shirt
   chemise sport

5. maternity dress
   robe maternité / robe de grossesse

6. overalls
   salopette

7. knit top
   haut en tricot

8. capris
   pantalon capri / corsaire

9. sandals
   sandales

Work Clothes Vêtements de travail

10. uniform
    uniforme

11. business suit
    costume de ville

12. tie
    cravate

13. briefcase
    serviette

More vocabulary

three piece suit: matching jacket, vest, and slacks
outfit: clothes that look nice together
in fashion / in style: clothes that are popular now

Describe the people. Take turns.

A: *She's wearing a maternity dress.*
B: *He's wearing a uniform.*

Formal Clothes Vêtements de soirée

14. sports jacket / sports coat
veste / veston

15. vest
gilet

16. bow tie
noeud papillon

17. tuxedo
smoking

18. evening gown
robe du soir

19. clutch bag
pochette

20. cocktail dress
robe de cocktail

21. high heels
talon aiguille / talon haut

Exercise Wear Vêtements de sport

22. sweatshirt / hoodie
sweatshirt / sweatshirt à capuche

23. sweatpants
pantalon de survêtement

24. tank top
débardeur

25. shorts
short

Ask your classmates. Share the answers.

1. What's your favorite outfit?

2. Do you like to wear formal clothes? Why or why not?

3. Do you prefer to exercise in shorts or sweatpants?

Think about it. Discuss.

1. What jobs require formal clothes? Uniforms?

2. What's good and bad about wearing school uniforms?

3. What is your opinion of today's popular clothing?

1. hat
   chapeau
2. (over)coat
   pardessus
3. headband
   bandeau serre-tête
4. leather jacket
   veste de cuir

5. winter scarf
   écharpe d'hiver
6. gloves
   gants
7. headwrap
   écharpe entourant la tête
8. jacket
   veste

9. parka
   parka
10. mittens
    moufles / mitaines
11. ski hat
    bonnet de ski
12. leggings
    jambières

13. earmuffs
    protège-oreilles
14. down vest
    gilet en duvet
15. ski mask
    masque de ski
16. down jacket
    veste en duvet

17. umbrella
    parapluie
18. raincoat
    imperméable
19. poncho
    poncho

20. rain boots
    bottes de pluie
21. trench coat
    trench-coat / imperméable

22. swimming trunks
    maillot de bain
23. straw hat
    chapeau de paille
24. windbreaker
    coupe-vent

25. cover-up
    cache-maillot
26. swimsuit / bathing suit
    maillot de bain /
    costume de bain
27. sunglasses
    lunettes de soleil

Grammar Point: should

*It's raining. You **should** take an umbrella.*
*It's snowing. You **should** wear a scarf.*
*It's sunny. You **should** wear a straw hat.*

Pair practice. Make new conversations.

A: *It's snowing. You should wear a scarf.*
B: *Don't worry. I'm wearing my parka.*
A: *Good, and don't forget your mittens.*

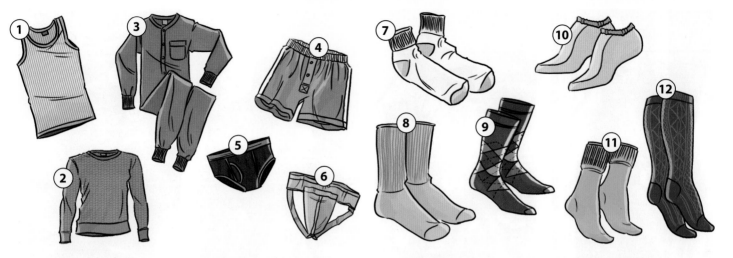

Unisex Underwear
Sous-vêtements unisexes

1. undershirt
   tricot / maillot de corps
2. thermal undershirt
   tricot de corps
3. long underwear
   caleçon-combinaison

Men's Underwear
Sous-vêtements pour hommes

4. boxer shorts
   caleçon boxeur
5. briefs
   caleçons
6. athletic supporter / jockstrap
   coquille

Unisex Socks
Chaussettes unisexes

7. ankle socks
   chaussettes jusqu'aux chevilles
8. crew socks
   chaussettes tube
9. dress socks
   chaussettes habillées

Women's Socks
Chaussettes pour femmes

10. low-cut socks
    chaussettes basses
11. anklets
    socquettes
12. knee highs
    mi-bas

Women's Underwear Sous-vêtements pour femmes

13. (bikini) panties
    slip
14. briefs / underpants
    petite culotte
15. body shaper / girdle
    gaine
16. garter belt
    porte-jarretelles
17. stockings
    bas
18. panty hose
    collants
19. tights
    collant
20. bra
    soutien-gorge
21. camisole
    camisole
22. full slip
    combinaison
23. half slip
    jupon

Sleepwear Vêtements de nuit

24. pajamas
    pyjama
25. nightgown
    robe de nuit
26. slippers
    pantoufles
27. blanket sleeper
    dormeuse molletonnée / pyjama-couverture / dors-bien ouverture
28. nightshirt
    chemise de nuit
29. robe
    robe de chambre

More vocabulary

lingerie: underwear or sleepwear for women
loungewear: very casual clothing for relaxing around the home

Ask your classmates. Share the answers.

1. What kind of socks are you wearing today?
2. What kind of sleepwear do you prefer?
3. Do you wear slippers at home?

91

Construction Worker

Road Worker

Automotive Painter

Food Processor

1. hard hat
   casque

2. work shirt
   chemise de travail

3. tool belt
   ceinture à outils

4. Hi-Visibility safety vest
   gilet de sécurité à haute visibilité

5. work pants
   pantalons de travail

6. steel toe boots
   bottes à embout d'acier

7. ventilation mask
   masque respiratoire

8. coveralls
   combinaison de travail

9. bump cap
   casque antichocs

10. safety glasses
    lunettes de sûreté

11. apron
    tablier

Manager

Salesperson

Farmworker

Ranch Hand

12. blazer
    blazer

13. tie
    cravate

14. polo shirt
    polo

15. name tag
    insigne d'identité

16. bandana
    bandana

17. work gloves
    gants de travail

18. cowboy hat
    chapeau de cowboy

19. jeans
    jeans

Pair practice. Make new conversations.

A: *What do <u>construction workers</u> wear to work?*
B: *They wear <u>hard hats</u> and <u>tool belts</u>.*
A: *What do <u>road workers</u> wear to work?*

Use the new words.

Look at pages 166–169. Name the workplace clothing you see.

A: *He's wearing <u>a hard hat</u>.*
B: *She's wearing <u>scrubs</u>.*

Security Guard

Emergency Worker

Counterperson

Chef

Line Cook

20. security shirt
chemise de sécurité

21. badge
badge

22. security pants
pantalons de sécurité

23. helmet
casque

24. jumpsuit
combinaison-pantalon

25. hairnet
filet à cheveux

26. smock
blouse

27. disposable gloves
gants jetables

28. chef's hat
toque de chef

29. chef's jacket
veste de chef

30. waist apron
tablier

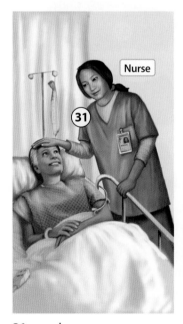

Nurse

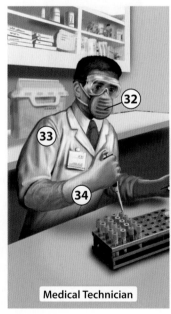

Medical Technician

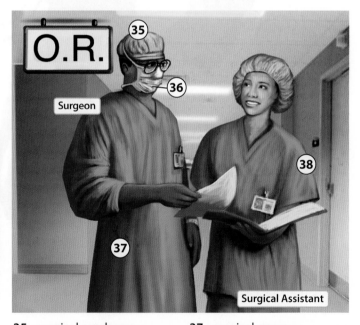

O.R.

Surgeon

Surgical Assistant

31. scrubs
tenue d'hôpital

32. face mask
masque facial

33. lab coat
blouse de laboratoire

34. latex gloves
gants de latex

35. surgical scrub cap
bonnet chirurgical

36. surgical mask
masque chirurgical

37. surgical gown
blouse de chirurgien(ne)

38. surgical scrubs
tenue chirurgicale

Ask your classmates. Share the answers.

1. Which of these outfits would you like to wear?
2. Which of these items are in your closet?
3. Do you wear safety clothing at work? What kinds?

Think about it. Discuss.

1. What other jobs require helmets? disposable gloves?
2. Is it better to have a uniform or wear your own clothes at work? Why?

93

A. purchase acheter	**1. suspenders** bretelles	**3. salesclerk** vendeur / commis	**5. display case** vitrine
B. wait in line faire la queue	**2. purses / handbags** sacs à main / sacoches	**4. customer** client	**6. belts** ceintures

13. wallet portefeuille	**17. shoulder bag** sac à bandoulière	**21. sole** semelle
14. change purse / coin purse porte-monnaie	**18. backpack** sac à dos	**22. heel** talon
15. cell phone holder porte-téléphone cellulaire	**19. tote bag** fourre-tout	**23. toe** bout / orteil
16. (wrist)watch montre-bracelet	**20. belt buckle** boucle de ceinture	**24. shoelaces** lacets de chaussures

More vocabulary

gift: something you give or receive from friends or family for a special occasion

present: a gift

Grammar Point: object pronouns

My **sister** loves jewelry. I'll buy **her** a necklace.
My **dad** likes belts. I'll buy **him** a belt buckle.
My **friends** love scarves. I'll buy **them** scarves.

7. shoe department	**9.** bracelets	**11.** hats	**C. try on** shoes
rayon des chaussures	bracelets	chapeaux	**essayer** des chaussures
8. jewelry department	**10.** necklaces	**12.** scarves	**D. assist** a customer
rayon de la bijouterie	colliers	écharpes	**aider** un client

25. high heels	**29.** oxfords	**33.** chain	**37.** clip-on earrings
talon aiguille / talon haut	souliers de ville /	chaîne	boucles d'oreilles
26. pumps	souliers lacés	**34.** beads	**38.** pin
escarpins	**30.** loafers	perles	épingle
27. flats	mocassins	**35.** locket	**39.** string of pearls
chaussures plates	**31.** hiking boots	médaillon	collier de perles
28. boots	bottes de randonnée	**36.** pierced earrings	**40.** ring
bottes	**32.** tennis shoes	boucles d'oreilles pour	bague
	chaussures de tennis	oreilles percées	

Ways to talk about accessories

I need a hat to wear with this scarf.
I'd like earrings to go with the necklace.
Do you have a belt that would go with my shoes?

Role play. Talk to a salesperson.

A: Do you have boots that would go with this skirt?
B: Let me see. How about these brown ones?
A: Perfect. I also need…

Sizes Tailles

1. **extra small**
   très petit

2. **small**
   petit

3. **medium**
   moyen

4. **large**
   grand

5. **extra large**
   très grand

6. **one-size-fits-all**
   taille unique

Styles Styles

Sweaters 50% off

7. **crewneck** sweater
   chandail / pull **à col rond**

8. **V-neck** sweater
   chandail / pull **à col en v**

9. **turtleneck** sweater
   chandail / pull **à col roulé**

10. **scoop neck** sweater
    chandail / pull **à col échancré**

11. **sleeveless** shirt
    chemise **sans manches**

12. **short-sleeved** shirt
    chemise **à manches courtes**

13. **3/4-sleeved** shirt
    chemise **à manches 3/4**

14. **long-sleeved** shirt
    chemise **à manches longues**

15. **mini**-skirt
    mini-jupe

16. **short** skirt
    jupe **courte**

17. **mid-length** / **calf-length** skirt
    jupe **mi-longue**

18. **long** skirt
    jupe **longue**

Patterns Motifs

19. solid
    uni (couleur)

20. striped
    rayé

21. polka-dotted
    à pois

22. plaid
    écossais

23. print
    imprimé

24. checked
    à carreaux

25. floral
    fleuri

26. paisley
    cachemire

Ask your classmates. Share the answers.

1. Do you prefer crewneck or V-neck sweaters?
2. Do you prefer checked or striped shirts?
3. Do you prefer short-sleeved or sleeveless shirts?

Role play. Talk to a salesperson.

A: *Excuse me. I'm looking for this V-neck sweater in large.*
B: *Here's a large. It's on sale for $19.99.*
A: *Wonderful! I'll take it. I'm also looking for…*

Comparing Clothing Comparaison de vêtements

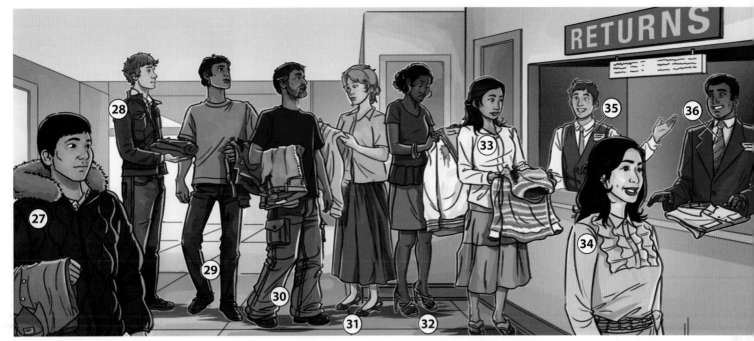

27. **heavy** jacket
    veste **épaisse**

28. **light** jacket
    veste **légère**

29. **tight** pants
    pantalons **serrés**

30. **loose / baggy** pants
    pantalons **larges**

31. **low** heels
    talons **plats**

32. **high** heels
    talons **aiguille /**
    talons **hauts**

33. **plain** blouse
    blouse **simple**

34. **fancy** blouse
    blouse **fantaisie**

35. **narrow** tie
    cravate **étroite**

36. **wide** tie
    cravate **large**

Clothing Problems Problèmes d'habillement

37. It's **too small**.
    C'est **trop petit**.

38. It's **too big**.
    C'est **trop grand**.

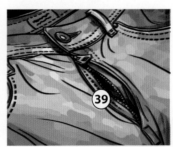

39. The zipper is **broken**.
    La fermeture éclair /
    à glissière est **cassée**.

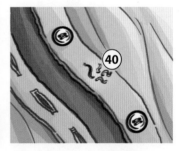

40. A button is **missing**.
    Un bouton **manque**.

41. It's **ripped / torn**.
    Il est **déchiré**.

42. It's **stained**.
    Il est **taché**.

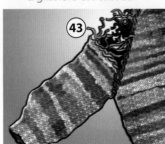

43. It's **unraveling**.
    Il est **effiloché**.

44. It's **too expensive**.
    Il est **trop cher**.

More vocabulary

refund: money you get back when you return an item to the store
complaint: a statement that something is not right
customer service: the place customers go with their complaints

Role play. Return an item to a salesperson.

A: *Welcome to Shopmart. How may I help you?*
B: *This sweater is new, but it's unraveling.*
A: *I'm sorry. Would you like a refund?*

97

Types of Material   Types de matériaux

1. cotton
coton

2. linen
lin

3. wool
laine

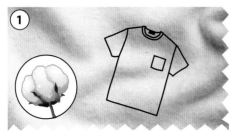

4. cashmere
cachemire

5. silk
soie

6. leather
cuir

A Garment Factory   Une usine de vêtements

Parts of a Sewing Machine
Pièces d'une machine à coudre

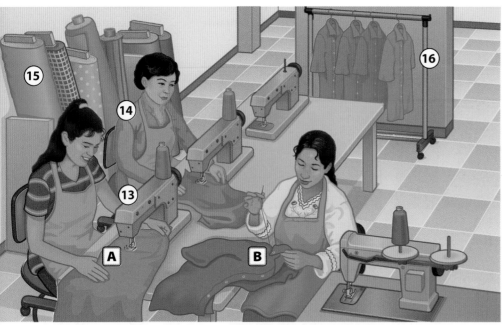

A. sew by machine	**14.** sewing machine operator
coudre à la machine	opératrice de machine à coudre
B. sew by hand	**15.** bolt of fabric
coudre à la main	coupe de tissu
13. sewing machine	**16.** rack
machine à coudre	présentoir

17. needle	**20.** feed dog / feed bar
aiguille	griffe d'entraînement
18. needle plate	**21.** bobbin
plaque à aiguille	canette
19. presser foot	
pied presseur	

More vocabulary

fashion designer: a person who makes original clothes
natural materials: cloth made from things that grow in nature
synthetic materials: cloth made by people, such as nylon

Use the new words.

Look at pages 86–87. Name the materials you see.

A: *That's denim.*
B: *That's leather.*

Types of Material Types de matériaux

7. denim
jean

8. suede
daim

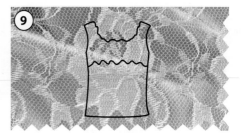

9. lace
dentelle

10. velvet
velours

11. corduroy
velours côtelé

12. nylon
nylon

A Fabric Store Un magasin de tissus

Closures Fermetures

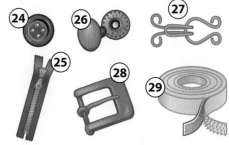

Trim Finition

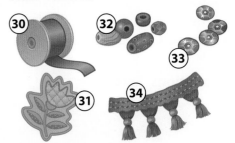

22. pattern motif	**25.** zipper fermeture éclair	**28.** buckle boucle
23. thread fil	**26.** snap pression	**29.** hook and loop fastener fermeture velcro
24. button bouton	**27.** hook and eye agrafe et œil	**30.** ribbon ruban

31. appliqué
application

32. beads
perles

33. sequins
sequins

34. fringe
frange

Ask your classmates. Share the answers.

1. Can you sew?
2. What's your favorite type of material?
3. How many types of material are you wearing today?

Think about it. Discuss.

1. Do most people make or buy clothes in your country?
2. Is it better to make or buy clothes? Why?
3. Which materials are best for formal clothes?

An Alterations Shop Un atelier de retouche

1. **dressmaker**
   couturière

2. **dressmaker's dummy**
   un mannequin de couturier

3. **tailor**
   tailleur

4. **collar**
   col

5. **waistband**
   ceinture montée

6. **sleeve**
   manche

7. **pocket**
   poche

8. **hem**
   ourlet

9. **cuff**
   revers

Sewing Supplies Fournitures de couture

10. **needle**
    aiguille

11. **thread**
    fil

12. **(straight) pin**
    épingle (droite)

13. **pin cushion**
    pelote à épingles

14. **safety pin**
    épingle de sûreté

15. **thimble**
    dé à coudre

16. **pair of scissors**
    (paire de) ciseaux

17. **tape measure**
    mètre-ruban

18. **seam ripper**
    découseur

Alterations Retouches

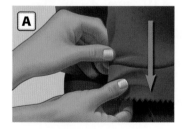   

A. **Lengthen** the pants.
Rallonger le pantaloon.

B. **Shorten** the pants.
Raccourcir le pantalon.

C. **Let out** the pants.
Allonger le pantalon.

D. **Take in** the pants.
Raccourcir le pantalon.

Pair practice. Make new conversations.

A: *Would you hand me <u>the thread</u>?*
B: *OK. What are you going to do?*
A: *I'm going to <u>take in</u> these <u>pants</u>.*

Ask your classmates. Share the answers.

1. Is there an alterations shop near your home?
2. Do you ever go to a tailor or a dressmaker?
3. What sewing supplies do you have at home?

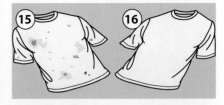

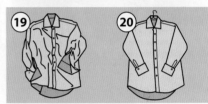

1. **laundry**
   lessive

2. **laundry basket**
   panier de lessive

3. **washer**
   lave-linge / laveuse

4. **dryer**
   sèche-linge / sécheuse

5. **dryer sheets**
   assouplisseur textile en feuilles / voiles sèche-linge

6. **fabric softener**
   produit assouplissant / adoucissant

7. **bleach**
   eau de javel

8. **laundry detergent**
   détergent à lessive

9. **clothesline**
   corde à linge

10. **clothespin**
    pince à linge

11. **hanger**
    cintre

12. **spray starch**
    amidon

13. **iron**
    fer à repasser

14. **ironing board**
    planche à repasser

15. **dirty** T-shirt
    T-shirt **sale**

16. **clean** T-shirt
    T-shirt **propre**

17. **wet** shirt
    chemise **mouillée**

18. **dry** shirt
    chemise **sèche**

19. **wrinkled** shirt
    chemise **froissée**

20. **ironed** shirt
    chemise **repassée**

A. Sort the laundry.
Trier la lessive.

B. Add the detergent.
Ajouter le détergent.

C. Load the washer.
Remplir le lave-linge / la laveuse.

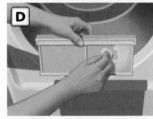

D. Clean the lint trap.
Nettoyer le filtre à charpie / filtre à air.

E. Unload the dryer.
Vider le sèche-linge / la sécheuse.

F. Fold the laundry.
Plier le linge.

G. Iron the clothes.
Repasser les vêtements.

H. Hang up the clothes.
Suspendre les vêtements.

 wash in cold water

 no bleach

line dry

dry clean only, do not wash

Pair practice. Make new Conversations.

A: *I have to <u>sort the laundry</u>. Can you help?*
B: *Sure. Here's <u>the laundry basket</u>.*
A: *Thanks a lot!*

A Garage Sale | Un vente-débarras

1. flyer	3. sticker	5. folding chair	7. VCR	B. **browse**
affiche	auto-collant	chaise pliante	magnétoscope	**regarder**
2. used clothing	4. folding card table	6. clock radio	A. **bargain**	
vêtements usagés	table pliante	radio-réveil	**marchander**	

Look at the pictures.
What do you see?

Answer the questions.

1. What kind of used clothing do you see?
2. What information is on the flyer?
3. Why are the stickers different colors?
4. How much is the clock radio? the VCR?

 Read the story.

A Garage Sale

Last Sunday, I had a garage sale. At 5:00 a.m., I put up <u>flyers</u> in my neighborhood. Next, I put price <u>stickers</u> on my <u>used clothing</u>, my <u>VCR</u>, and some other old things. At 7:00 a.m., I opened my <u>folding card table</u> and <u>folding chair</u>. Then I waited.

At 7:05 a.m., my first customer arrived. She asked, "How much is the sweatshirt?"

"Two dollars," I said.

She said, "It's stained. I can give you seventy-five cents." We <u>bargained</u> for a minute and she paid $1.00.

All day people came to <u>browse</u>, bargain, and buy. At 7:00 p.m., I had $85.00.

Now I know two things: Garage sales are hard work and nobody wants to buy an old <u>clock radio</u>!

Think about it.

1. Do you like to buy things at garage sales? Why or why not?
2. Imagine you want the VCR. How will you bargain for it?

103

1. **head**
   tête

2. **hair**
   cheveux

3. **neck**
   cou

4. **chest**
   poitrine

5. **back**
   dos

6. **nose**
   nez

7. **mouth**
   bouche

8. **foot**
   pied

Listen and Point. Take turns.

A: *Point to the chest.*
B: *Point to the neck.*
A: *Point to the mouth.*

Dictate to your partner. Take turns.

A: *Write hair.*
B: *Did you say hair?*
A: *That's right, h-a-i-r.*

9. leg
   jambe

10. toe
    orteil

11. eye
    œil

12. ear
    oreille

13. shoulder
    épaule

14. arm
    bras

15. hand
    main

16. finger
    doigt

Grammar Point: imperatives

Please touch your right foot.
Put your hands on your feet.
Don't put your hands on your shoulders.

Pair practice. Take turns giving commands.

A: *Raise* your *arms*.
B: *Touch* your *feet*.
A: *Put* your *hand* on your *shoulder*.

105

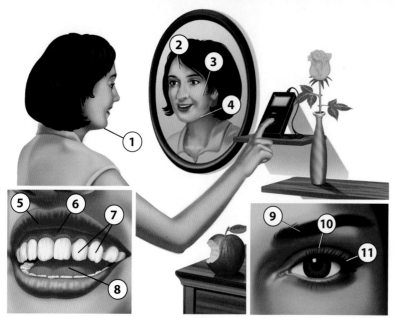
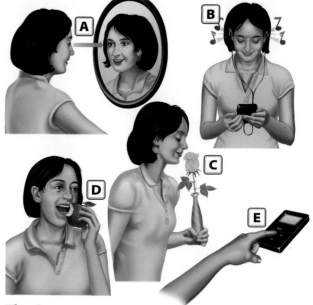
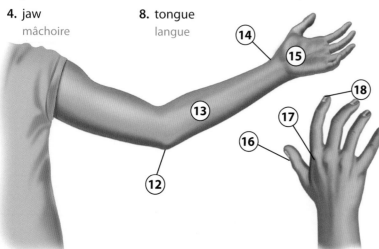
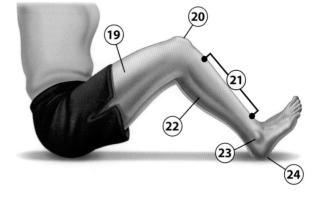

The Face
Le visage

1. chin
   menton
2. forehead
   front
3. cheek
   joue
4. jaw
   mâchoire

The Mouth
La bouche

5. lip
   lèvre
6. gums
   gencives
7. teeth
   dents
8. tongue
   langue

The Eye
L'œil

9. eyebrow
   sourcil
10. eyelid
    paupière
11. eyelashes
    cils

The Senses
Les sens

A. **see**
   voir
B. **hear**
   entendre
C. **smell**
   sentir

D. **taste**
   goûter
E. **touch**
   toucher

The Arm, Hand, and Fingers Le bras, la main, et les doigts

12. elbow
    coude
13. forearm
    avant-bras
14. wrist
    poignet

15. palm
    paume
16. thumb
    pouce

17. knuckle
    articulation
18. fingernail
    ongle

The Leg and Foot La jambe et le pied

19. thigh
    cuisse
20. knee
    genou
21. shin
    tibia

22. calf
    mollet
23. ankle
    cheville
24. heel
    talon

More vocabulary

torso: the part of the body from the shoulders to the pelvis
limbs: arms and legs
toenail: the nail on your toe

Pair practice. Make new conversations.

A: *Is your <u>arm</u> OK?*
B: *Yes, but now my <u>elbow</u> hurts.*
A: *I'm sorry to hear that.*

Inside and Outside the Body

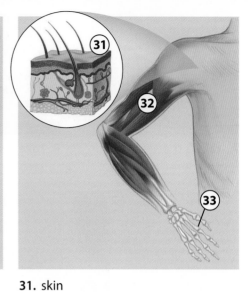

25. chest
poitrine

26. breast
sein

27. abdomen
abdomen

28. shoulder blade
omoplate

29. lower back
bas du dos

30. buttocks
fesses / postérieur

31. skin
peau

32. muscle
muscle

33. bone
os

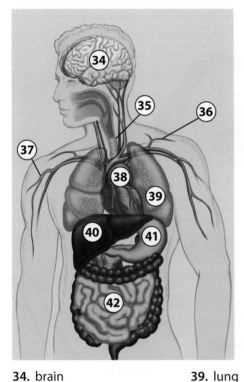

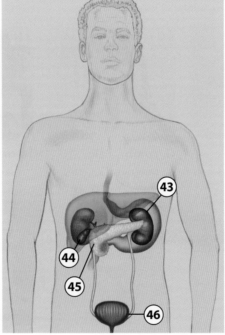

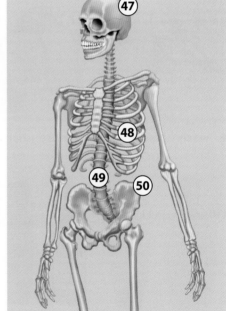

THE SKELETON

34. brain
cerveau

35. throat
gorge

36. artery
artère

37. vein
veine

38. heart
cœur

39. lung
poumon

40. liver
foie

41. stomach
estomac

42. intestines
intestins

43. kidney
rein

44. gallbladder
vésicule biliaire

45. pancreas
pancréas

46. bladder
vessie

47. skull
crâne

48. rib cage
cage thoracique

49. spinal column
colonne vertébrale

50. pelvis
bassin

A. take a shower
prendre une douche

B. take a bath / bathe
prendre un bain

C. use deodorant
mettre du déodorant

D. put on sunscreen
mettre de l'écran solaire

1. shower cap
bonnet de douche

2. shower gel
gel de douche

3. soap
savon

4. bath powder
poudre de bain

5. deodorant / antiperspirant
déodorant

6. perfume / cologne
parfum / eau de Cologne

7. sunscreen
écran solaire

8. sunblock
écran solaire

9. body lotion / moisturizer
crème pour le corps / crème hydratante

E. wash…hair
laver…les cheveux

F. rinse…hair
rincer…les cheveux

G. comb…hair
peigner…les cheveux

H. dry…hair
sécher…les cheveux

I. brush…hair
brosser…les cheveux

10. shampoo
shampooing

11. conditioner
après-shampooing

12. hair spray
fixatif capillaire

13. comb
peigne

14. brush
brosse

15. pick
fourchette à cheveux

16. hair gel
gel cheveux

17. curling iron
fer à friser

18. blow dryer
séchoir

19. hair clip
pince à cheveux

20. barrette
barrette

21. bobby pins
pinces à cheveux

More vocabulary

unscented: a product without perfume or scent
hypoallergenic: a product that is better for people
with allergies

Think about it. Discuss.

1. Which personal hygiene products should someone use
   before a job interview?
2. What is the right age to start wearing makeup? Why?

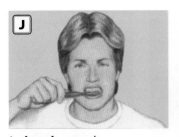 **J.** 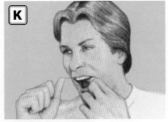 **K.**  **L.**   **M.**

J. brush…teeth
se brosser…les dents

K. floss…teeth
se passer la soie dentaire sur…les dents

L. gargle
se gargariser

M. shave
se raser

22. toothbrush
brosse à dents

23. toothpaste
pâte dentifrice

24. dental floss
soie dentaire

25. mouthwash
rince-bouche

26. electric shaver
rasoir électrique

27. razor
rasoir

28. razorblade
lame de rasoir

29. shaving cream
crème de rasage

30. aftershave
après-rasage (lotion)

 **N.**  **O.**  **P.**  **Q.**

N. cut…nails
se couper…les ongles

O. polish…nails
se mettre du vernis… à ongles

P. put on / apply
mettre / appliquer

Q. take off / remove
enlever / retirer

Makeup Maquillage

31. nail clipper
coupe-ongles

32. emery board
lime à ongles

33. nail polish
vernis à ongles

34. eyebrow pencil
crayon à sourcils

35. eye shadow
ombre à paupières

36. eyeliner
eye-liner

37. blush
fard à joue

38. lipstick
rouge à lèvres

39. mascara
rimmel / fard à cils

40. foundation
fond de teint

41. face powder
poudre pour le visage

42. makeup remover
démaquillant

 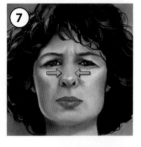 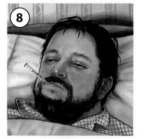  

    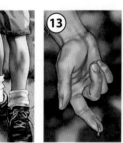

1. headache
   mal de tête

2. toothache
   mal de dents

3. earache
   mal d'oreille

4. stomachache
   mal d'estomac

5. backache
   mal de dos

6. sore throat
   mal de gorge

7. nasal congestion
   congestion nasale

8. fever / temperature
   fièvre / température

9. chills
   frissons

10. rash
    éruption cutanée

A. **cough**
   tousser

B. **sneeze**
   éternuer

C. **feel** dizzy
   se sentir étourdi

D. **feel** nauseous
   avoir la nausée

E. **throw up / vomit**
   rendre / vomir

  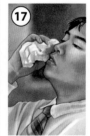

11. insect bite
    piqure d'insecte

12. bruise
    ecchymose

13. cut
    coupure

14. sunburn
    coup de soleil

15. blister
    ampoule

16. swollen finger
    doigt enflé

17. bloody nose
    saigner du nez

18. sprained ankle
    entorse

Look at the pictures.
Describe the symptoms and injuries.

A: *He has a backache.*
B: *She has a toothache.*

Think about it. Discuss.
1. What are some common cold symptoms?
2. What do you recommend for a stomachache?
3. What is the best way to stop a bloody nose?

Illnesses and Medical Conditions

Common Illnesses and Childhood Diseases Maladies communes et maladies de l'enfance

1. cold
rhume

2. flu
grippe

3. ear infection
infection de l'oreille

4. strep throat
angine streptococcique

5. measles
rougeole

6. chicken pox
varicelle

7. mumps
oreillons

8. allergies
allergies

Serious Medical Conditions and Diseases Affections et maladies graves

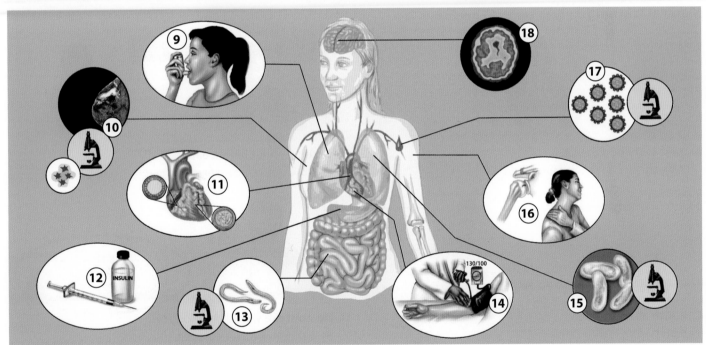

9. **asthma**
   asthme

10. **cancer**
    cancer

11. **heart disease**
    maladie cardiaque

12. **diabetes**
    diabète

13. **intestinal parasites**
    parasites intestinaux

14. **high blood pressure / hypertension**
    pression artérielle élevée / hypertension

15. **TB (tuberculosis)**
    TB (tuberculose)

16. **arthritis**
    arthrite

17. **HIV (human immunodeficiency virus)**
    VIH (virus de l'immunodéficience humaine)

18. **dementia**
    démence

More vocabulary

AIDS (acquired immune deficiency syndrome): a medical condition that results from contracting the HIV virus

Alzheimer's disease: a disease that causes dementia

coronary disease: heart disease

infectious disease: a disease that is spread through air or water

influenza: flu

DROP-OFF   PICK-UP

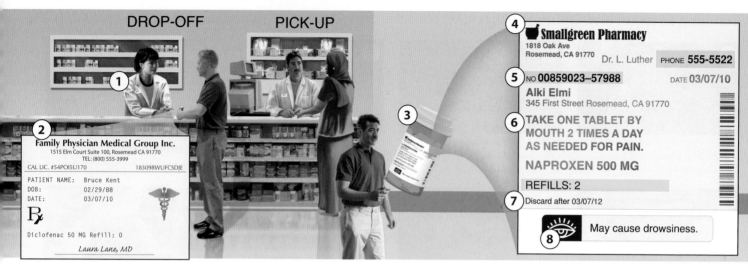

1. **pharmacist**
   pharmacien / pharmacienne

2. **prescription**
   prescription

3. **prescription medication**
   médicament d'ordonnance /
   médicament prescrit

4. **prescription label**
   étiquette de prescription /
   étiquette d'ordonnance

5. **prescription number**
   numéro d'ordonnance

6. **dosage**
   dose

7. **expiration date**
   date de péremption

8. **warning label**
   étiquette d'avertissement

Medical Warnings   Avertissements médicaux

A. **Take** with food or milk.
Prendre avec de la nourriture ou du lait.

B. **Take** one hour before eating.
Prendre une heure avant de manger.

C. **Finish** all medication.
Finir tous les médicaments.

D. **Do not take** with dairy products.
Ne pas prendre avec des produits laitiers.

E. **Do not drive or operate** heavy machinery.
Ne pas conduire ni manœuvrer des équipements lourds.

F. **Do not drink** alcohol.
Ne pas boire d'alcool.

More Vocabulary

prescribe medication: to write a prescription
fill prescriptions: to prepare medication for patients
pick up a prescription: to get prescription medication

Role play. Talk to the pharmacist.

A: *Hi. I need to pick up a prescription for Jones.*
B: *Here's your medication, Mr. Jones. Take these once a day with milk or food.*

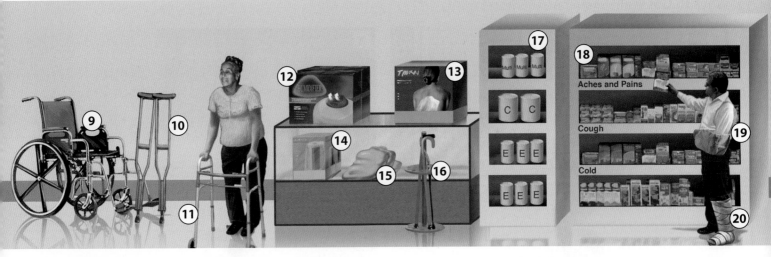

9. **wheelchair**
chaise roulante

10. **crutches**
béquilles

11. **walker**
ambulateur

12. **humidifier**
humidificateur

13. **heating pad**
coussin chauffant

14. **air purifier**
purificateur d'air

15. **hot water bottle**
bouillote

16. **cane**
canne

17. **vitamins**
vitamines

18. **over-the-counter medication**
médicament sans ordonnance

19. **sling**
écharpe

20. **cast**
plâtre

Types of Medication Types de médicaments

21. **pill**
pilule

22. **tablet**
comprimé

23. **capsule**
capsule

24. **ointment**
onguent

25. **cream**
crème

Over-the-Counter Medication Médicaments sans ordonnance

26. **pain reliever**
analgésique

27. **cold tablets**
comprimés contre le rhume

28. **antacid**
antiacide

29. **cough syrup**
sirop contre la toux

30. **throat lozenges**
pastilles pour la gorge

31. **eye drops**
gouttes pour les yeux

32. **nasal spray**
pulvérisation nasale

33. **inhaler**
inhalateur

Ways to talk about medication

Use *take* for pills, tablets, capsules, and cough syrup.
Use *apply* for ointments and creams.
Use *use* for drops, nasal sprays, and inhalers.

Ask your classmates. Share the answers.

1. What pharmacy do you go to?
2. Do you ever ask the pharmacist for advice?
3. Do you take any vitamins? Which ones?

Ways to Get Well Comment guérir

A. Seek medical attention.
   Aller chez le médecin.

B. Get bed rest.
   Rester au lit.

C. Drink fluids.
   Boire des liquides.

D. Take medicine.
   Prendre un médicament.

Ways to Stay Well Comment rester en bonne santé

E. Stay fit.
   Rester en forme.

F. Eat a healthy diet.
   Manger un régime équilibré.

G. Don't smoke.
   Ne pas fumer.

H. Have regular checkups.
   Faire des bilans de santé réguliers.

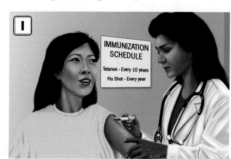

Ms. Jones, you must stop smoking!

I. Get immunized.
   Se faire vacciner.

IMMUNIZATION SCHEDULE
Tetanus – Every 10 years
Flu Shot – Every year

J. Follow medical advice.
   Suivre les conseils du médecin.

More vocabulary

injection: medicine in a syringe that is put into the body
immunization / vaccination: an injection that stops
serious diseases

Ask your classmates. Share the answers.

1. How do you stay fit?
2. What do you do when you're sick?
3. Which two foods are a part of your healthy diet?

Types of Health Problems Types de problèmes de santé

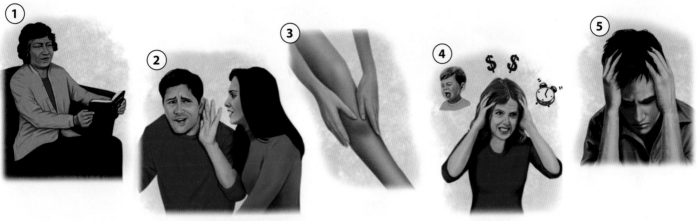

1. vision problems
problèmes de vue

2. hearing loss
perte de l'ouïe

3. pain
douleur

4. stress
stress

5. depression
dépression

Help with Health Problems Régler les problèmes de santé

6. optometrist
optométriste

8. contact lenses
verres de contact

9. audiologist
audiologiste

10. hearing aid
appareil auditif

7. glasses
lunettes

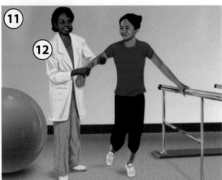
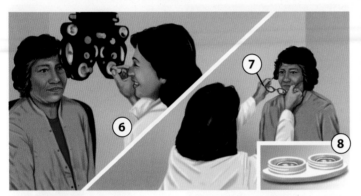

11. physical therapy
physiothérapie

13. talk therapy
thérapie verbale

15. support group
groupe de soutien

12. physical therapist
physiothérapeute

14. therapist
thérapeute

Ways to ask about health problems

Are you in pain?
Are you having vision problems?
Are you experiencing depression?

Pair practice. Make new conversations.

A: *Do you know a good optometrist?*
B: *Why? Are you having vision problems?*
A: *Yes, I might need glasses.*

115

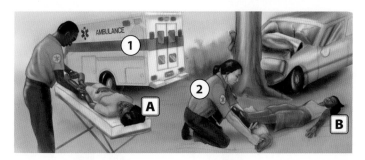

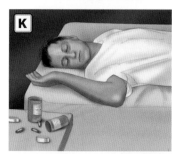
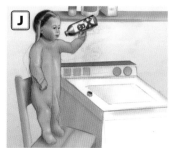

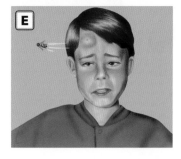

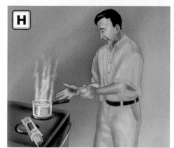

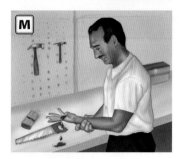

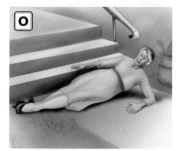
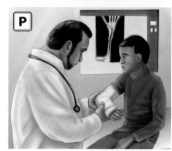

1. **ambulance**
   ambulance

2. **paramedic**
   ambulancier paramédical

A. **be** unconscious
   être inconscient

B. **be** in shock
   être en état de choc

C. **be** injured / **be** hurt
   être blessé

D. **have** a heart attack
   avoir une crise cardiaque

E. **have** an allergic reaction
   avoir une réaction allergique

F. **get** an electric shock
   subir un choc électrique

G. **get** frostbite
   avoir des gelures / engelures

H. **burn** (your)self
   se brûler

I. **drown**
   se noyer

J. **swallow** poison
   avaler du poison

K. **overdose** on drugs
   faire une overdose / **surdose** de drogues

L. **choke**
   s'étouffer

M. **bleed**
   saigner

N. **can't breathe**
   ne pas pouvoir respirer

O. **fall**
   tomber

P. **break** a bone
   se casser un os

Grammar Point: past tense

For past tense add –ed:
burned, drowned, swallowed,
overdosed, choked

These verbs are different (irregular):

be – was, were	bleed – bled	fall-fell
have – had	can't – couldn't	
get – got	break – broke	

First Aid

First Aid Premiers soins

1. first aid kit
trousse de premiers soins

2. first aid manual
manuel de premiers soins

3. medical emergency bracelet
bracelet d'urgence médicale

Inside the Kit Dans la trousse de premiers soins

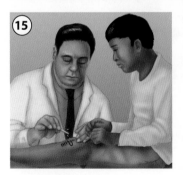

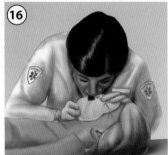

4. tweezers
pincettes

5. adhesive bandage
pansement adhésif

6. sterile pad
compresse stérile

7. sterile tape
sparadrap stérile

8. gauze
gaze

9. hydrogen peroxide
peroxyde d'hydrogène

10. antihistamine cream
crème antihistaminique

11. antibacterial ointment
onguent antibactérien

12. elastic bandage
bandage élastique

13. ice pack
poche de glace

14. splint
attelle

First Aid Procedures Premiers soins

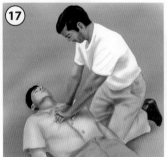

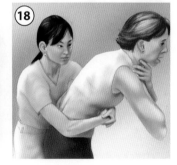

15. stitches
points de suture

16. rescue breathing
respiration artificielle

17. CPR (cardiopulmonary resuscitation)
RCR (réanimation cardio-respiratoire)

18. Heimlich maneuver
manœuvre de Heimlich

Pair practice. Make new conversations.

A: *What do we need in the first aid kit?*
B: *We need <u>tweezers</u> and <u>gauze</u>.*
A: *I think we need <u>sterile tape</u>, too.*

Think about it. Discuss.

1. What are the three most important first aid items? Why?
2. Which first aid procedures should everyone know? Why?
3. What are some good places to keep a first aid kit?

117

Medical Care
Soins médicaux

In the Waiting Room Dans la salle d'attente

HEALTH FIRST
Name: Andre Zolmar
Group Number: 98765
Membership Number: 60756789

Health Form
Name: *Andre Zolmar*
Date of birth: *July 8, 1973*
Current symptoms: *stomachache*

Health History:
Childhood Diseases:
☑ chicken pox
☑ diphtheria
☑ rubella
☑ measles
☐ mumps
☐ other

Description of symptoms:

1. appointment
rendez-vous

2. receptionist
réceptionniste

3. health insurance card
carte d'assurance maladie

4. health history form
fiche d'antécédents médicaux

In the Examining Room Dans la salle d'examen

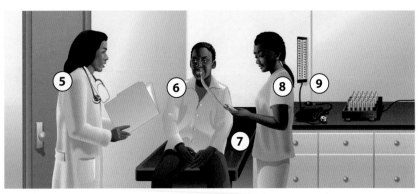

5. doctor
docteur

6. patient
patient(e)

7. examination table
table d'examen

8. nurse
infirmier / infirmière

9. blood pressure gauge
tensiomètre

10. stethoscope
stéthoscope

11. thermometer
thermomètre

12. syringe
seringue

Medical Procedures Procédures médicales

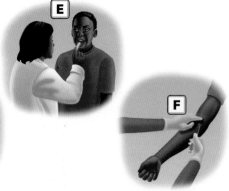

A. check…blood pressure
vérifier…la pression artérielle

B. take…temperature
prendre…la température

C. listen to…heart
écouter…le cœur

D. examine…eyes
examiner…les yeux

E. examine…throat
examiner…la gorge

F. draw…blood
prélever…du sang

Grammar Point: future tense with *will* + verb

To show a future action, use *will* + verb.
The subject pronoun contraction of *will* is -*'ll*.
*She **will draw** your blood.* = *She**'ll draw** your blood.*

Role play. Talk to a medical receptionist.

A: *Will the nurse <u>examine my eyes</u>?*
B: *No, but she'll <u>draw your blood</u>.*
A: *What will the doctor do?*

Dentistry Dentisterie

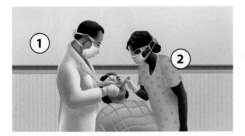 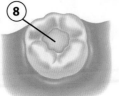 

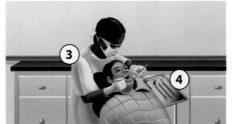 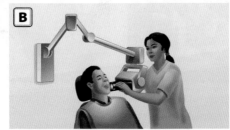 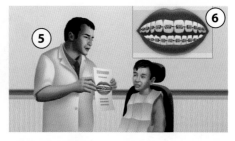

Orthodontics Orthodontie

1. dentist
dentiste

2. dental assistant
assistante dentaire

3. dental hygienist
hygiéniste dentaire

4. dental instruments
instruments dentaires

5. orthodontist
orthodontiste

6. braces
appareil orthodontique

Dental Problems Problèmes dentaires

7. cavity / decay
carie

8. filling
plombage

9. crown
couronne

10. dentures
dentier

11. gum disease
maladie des gencives

12. plaque
plaque dentaire

An Office Visit Une visite chez le dentiste

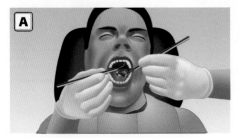 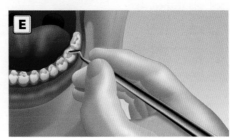 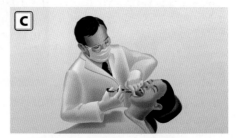

A. clean…teeth
nettoyer…les dents

B. take x-rays
prendre des radios

C. numb the mouth
endormir la bouche

 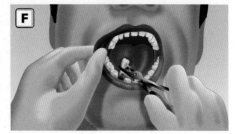

D. drill a tooth
percer une dent

E. fill a cavity
boucher une carie

F. pull a tooth
arracher une dent

Ask your classmates. Share the answers.

1. Do you know someone with braces? Who?
2. Do dentists make you nervous? Why or why not?
3. How often do you go to the dentist?

Role play. Talk to a dentist.

A: *I think I have a cavity.*
B: *Let me take a look.*
A: *Will I need a filling?*

Medical Specialists Spécialistes médicaux

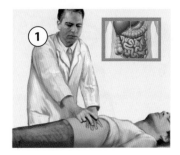

1. internist
interne

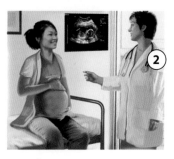

2. obstetrician
obstétricien(ne)

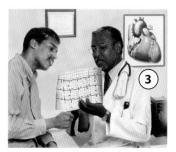

3. cardiologist
cardiologue

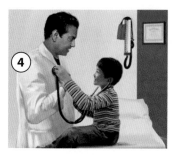

4. pediatrician
pédiatre

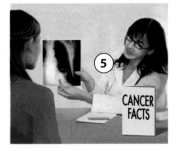

5. oncologist
oncologue

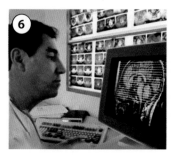

6. radiologist
radiologue

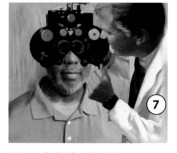

7. ophthalmologist
ophtalmologiste /
ophtalmologue / oculiste

8. psychiatrist
psychiatre

Nursing Staff Personnel soignant

9. surgical nurse
infirmier(ière) en chirurgie

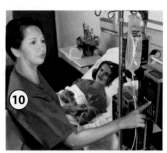

10. registered nurse (RN)
infirmier(ière) diplômé(e)

11. licensed practical nurse (LPN)
infirmier(ière) auxiliaire
diplômé(e)

12. certified nursing assistant (CNA)
infirmier(ière) auxiliaire
autorisé(e)

Hospital Staff Personnel de l'hôpital

13. administrator
administrateur

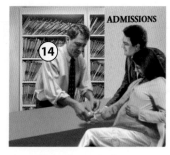

14. admissions clerk
responsable des admissions

15. dietician
diététicien

16. orderly
préposé(e) aux soins

More vocabulary

Gynecologists examine and treat women.
Nurse practitioners can give medical exams.
Nurse midwives deliver babies.

Chiropractors move the spine to improve health.
Orthopedists treat bone and joint problems.

A Hospital Room Une chambre d'hôpital

Lab Lab

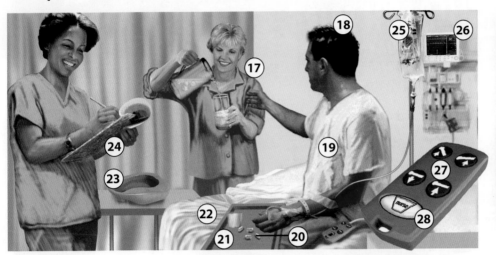

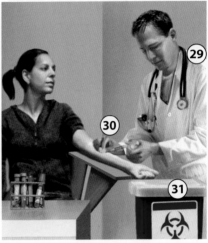

17. volunteer
bénévole

18. patient
patient(e)

19. hospital gown
chemise d'hôpital

20. medication
médicaments

21. bed table
table de chevet

22. hospital bed
lit d'hôpital

23. bed pan
bassin hygiénique

24. medical chart
fiche médicale

25. IV (intravenous drip)
I.V. (goutte-à-goutte
intraveineux)

26. vital signs monitor
moniteur de contrôle
des signes vitaux

27. bed control
commande de lit

28. call button
bouton d'appel

29. phlebotomist
phlébotomiste

30. blood work / blood test
analyse sanguine

31. medical waste disposal
dispositif d'évacuation des
déchets médicaux

Emergency Room Entrance
Entrée de la salle d'urgence

Operating Room
Salle d'opération

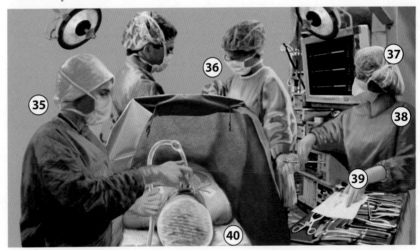

32. emergency medical technician (EMT)
technicien d'urgence médicale

33. stretcher / gurney
civière / brancard / civière roulante

34. ambulance
ambulance

35. anesthesiologist
anesthésiste

36. surgeon
chirurgien(ne)

37. surgical cap
bonnet de
chirurgien(ne)

38. surgical gown
blouse de
chirurgien(ne)

39. surgical gloves
gants de chirurgie

40. operating table
table d'opération

Dictate to your partner. Take turns.

A: *Write this sentence. She's a volunteer.*

B: *She's a what?*

A: *Volunteer. That's v-o-l-u-n-t-e-e-r.*

Role play. Ask about a doctor.

A: *I need to find a good surgeon.*

B: *Dr. Jones is a great surgeon. You should call him.*

A: *I will! Please give me his number.*

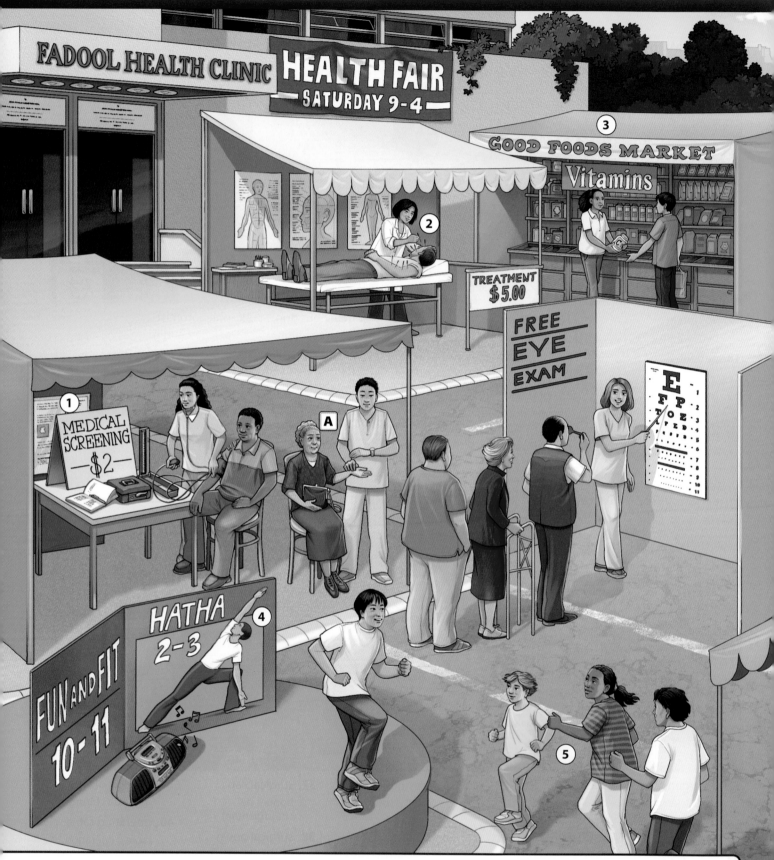

1. low-cost exam
   examen bon marché

2. acupuncture
   acupuncture

3. booth
   stand

4. yoga
   yoga

5. aerobic exercise
   aérobic

6. demonstration
   démonstration

7. sugar-free
   sans sucre

8. nutrition label
   étiquette de valeur
   nutritionnelle

A. **check**…pulse
   vérifier…le pouls

B. **give** a lecture
   faire une présentation

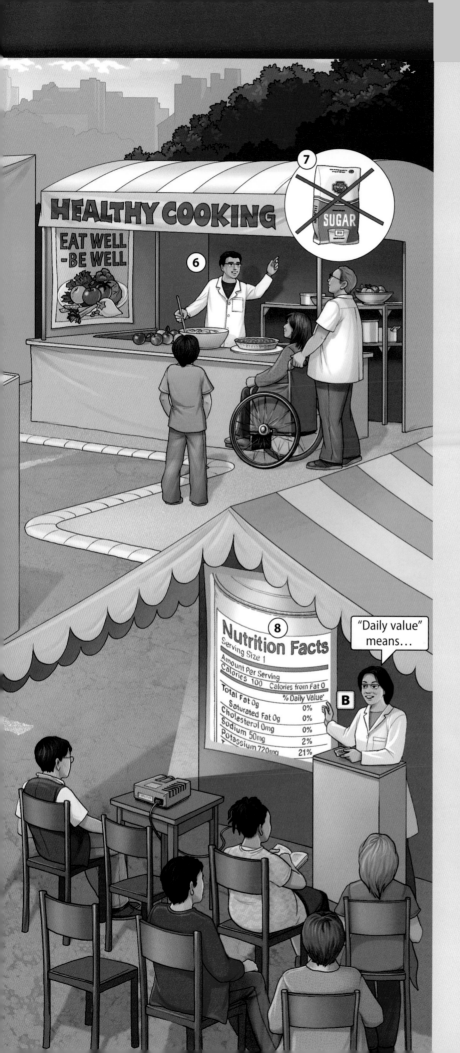

Answer the questions.

1. How many different booths are there at the health fair?

2. What kinds of exams and treatments can you get at the fair?

3. What kinds of lectures and demonstrations are there?

4. How much is an acupuncture treatment? a medical screening?

Read the story.

A Health Fair

Once a month the Fadool Health Clinic has a health fair. You can get a low-cost medical exam at one booth. The nurses check your blood pressure and check your pulse. At another booth you can get a free eye exam. And an acupuncture treatment is only $5.00.

You can learn a lot at the fair. This month a doctor is giving a lecture on nutrition labels. There is also a demonstration on sugar-free cooking. You can learn to do aerobic exercise and yoga, too.

Do you want to get healthy and stay healthy? Then come to the Fadool Clinic Health Fair!

Think about it.

1. Which booths at this fair look interesting to you? Why?

2. Do you read nutrition labels? Why or why not?

1. parking garage
   stationnement / parc
   de stationnement
2. office building
   immeuble de bureaux
3. hotel
   hôtel
4. Department of
   Motor Vehicles
   Préfecture (service
   des cartes grises)
5. bank
   banque
6. police station
   poste de police
7. bus station
   gare d'autobus
8. city hall
   hôtel de ville / mairie

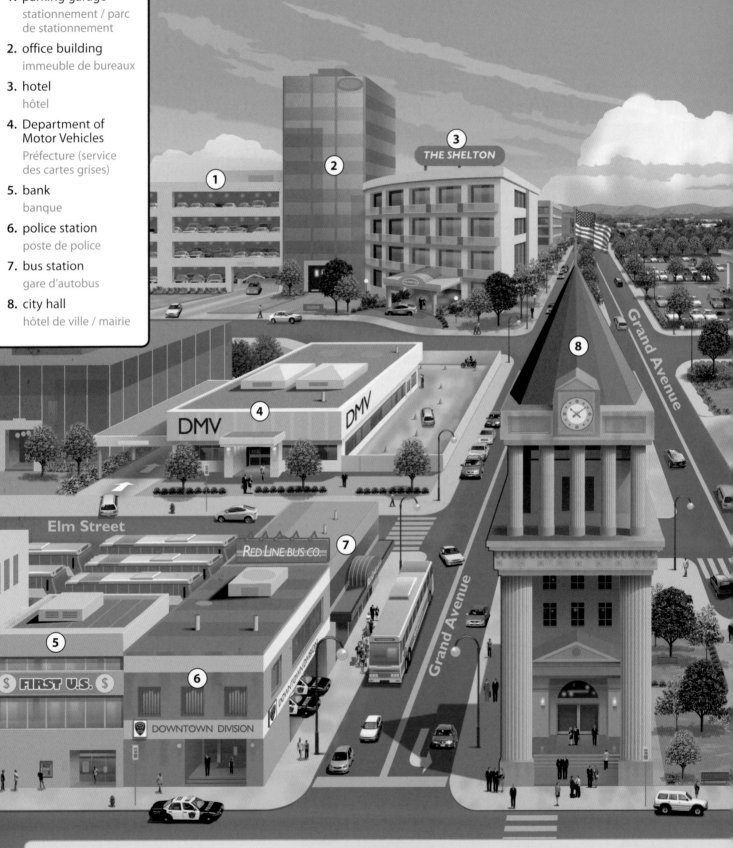

THE SHELTON

Grand Avenue

Elm Street

RED LINE BUS CO.

FIRST U.S.

DOWNTOWN DIVISION

Grand Avenue

Listen and point. Take turns.

A: *Point to the bank.*
B: *Point to the hotel.*
A: *Point to the restaurant.*

Dictate to your partner. Take turns.

A: *Write bank.*
B: *Is that spelled b-a-n-k?*
A: *Yes, that's right.*

9. **hospital**
   hôpital
10. **gas station**
    station service
11. **post office**
    poste
12. **fire station**
    caserne de pompiers
13. **courthouse**
    tribunal / palais de justice
14. **restaurant**
    restaurant
15. **library**
    bibliothèque

Grammar Point: *in* and *at* with locations

Use *in* when you are inside the building. *I am in (inside) the bank.* Use *at* to describe your general location. *I am at the bank.*

Pair practice. Make new conversations.

A: *I'm in the <u>bank</u>. Where are you?*
B: *I'm at the <u>bank</u>, too, but I'm outside.*
A: *OK. I'll meet you there.*

125

1. stadium
   stade

2. construction site
   chantier de construction

3. factory
   usine

4. car dealership
   concession d'automobiles

5. mosque
   mosquée

6. movie theater
   cinéma

7. shopping mall
   centre commercial

8. furniture store
   magasin de meubles

9. school
   école

10. gym
    centre de culture physique

11. coffee shop
    café-restaurant

12. motel
    motel

Ways to state your destination using *to* and *to the*

Use *to* for schools, churches, and synagogues.
*I'm going **to** <u>school</u>.*
Use *to the* for all other locations. *I have to go **to the** <u>bakery</u>.*

Pair practice. Make new conversations.

A: *Where are you going today?*
B: *I'm going to <u>school</u>. How about you?*
A: *I have to go to the <u>bakery</u>.*

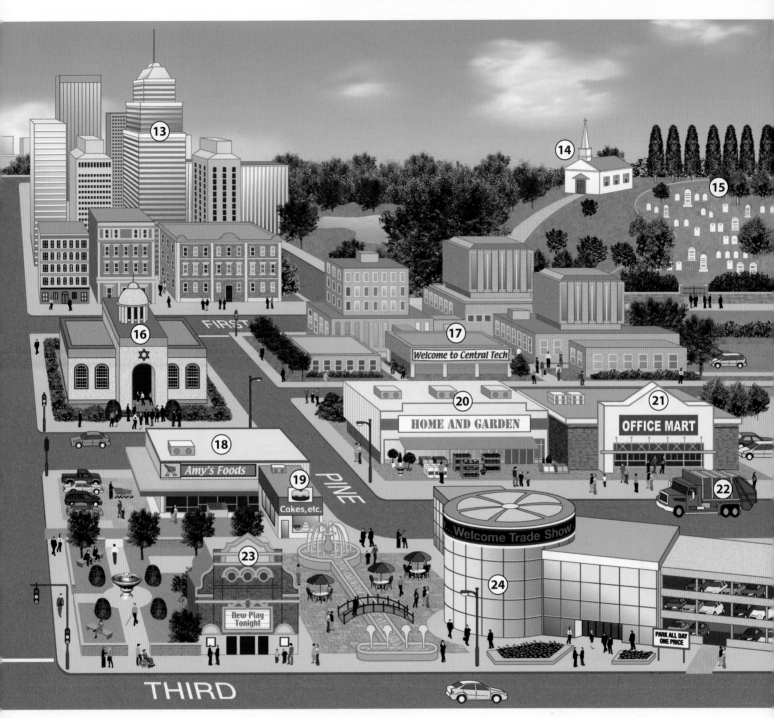

13. **skyscraper / high-rise**
gratte-ciel / tour

14. **church**
église

15. **cemetery**
cimetière

16. **synagogue**
synagogue

17. **community college**
centre universitaire de premier cycle

18. **supermarket**
supermarché

19. **bakery**
boulangerie

20. **home improvement store**
magasin d'amélioration de l'habitat

21. **office supply store**
magasin de fournitures de bureau

22. **garbage truck**
camion à ordures

23. **theater**
théâtre

24. **convention center**
palais des congrès

Ways to give locations

The mall is on 2nd Street.
The mall is on the corner of 2nd and Elm.
The mall is next to the movie theater.

Ask your classmates. Share the answers.

1. Where's your favorite coffee shop?
2. Where's your favorite supermarket?
3. Where's your favorite movie theater?

1. **laundromat**
   laverie

2. **dry cleaners**
   nettoyeur / teinturerie / pressing

3. **convenience store**
   dépanneur / commerce de proximité

4. **pharmacy**
   pharmacie

5. **parking space**
   espace de stationnement

6. **handicapped parking**
   stationnement pour personnes handicapées

7. **corner**
   coin

8. **traffic light**
   feu de signalisation / feu de circulation

9. **bus**
   autobus

10. **fast food restaurant**
    restaurant minute

11. **drive-thru window**
    service au volant / service à l'auto

12. **newsstand**
    kiosque à journaux

13. **mailbox**
    boîte aux lettres

14. **pedestrian**
    piéton

15. **crosswalk**
    passage pour piétons

A. **cross** the street
   traverser la rue

B. **wait for** the light
   attendre le changement de feu

C. **jaywalk**
   traverser en dehors des passages pour piétons

Pair practice. Make new conversations.

A: *I have a lot of errands to do today.*
B: *Me, too. First, I'm going to _the laundromat_.*
A: *I'll see you there after I stop at _the copy center_.*

Think about it. Discuss.

1. Which businesses are good to have in a neighborhood? Why?
2. Would you like to own a small business? If yes, what kind? If no, why not?

16. bus stop
arrêt d'autobus

17. donut shop
beignerie

18. copy center
centre de reprographie

19. barbershop
salon de coiffure pour hommes

20. video store
club vidéo

21. curb
bordure / bord de trottoir

22. bike
vélo / bicyclette

23. pay phone
téléphone public

24. sidewalk
trottoir

25. parking meter
parcomètre / parcmètre

26. street sign
plaque de rue

27. fire hydrant
bouche d'incendie

28. cart
chariot

29. street vendor
vendeur ambulant

30. childcare center
centre de garde d'enfants

D. ride a bike
faire du vélo

E. park the car
stationner / garer la voiture

F. walk a dog
promener un chien

More vocabulary

neighborhood: the area close to your home
do errands: to make a short trip from your home to buy or pick up things

Ask your classmates. Share the answers.

1. What errands do you do every week?
2. What stores do you go to in your neighborhood?
3. What things can you buy from a street vendor?

129

1. **music store**
   disquerie

2. **jewelry store**
   bijouterie

3. **nail salon**
   centre de manucure

4. **bookstore**
   librairie

5. **toy store**
   magasin de jouets

6. **pet store**
   animalerie

7. **card store**
   magasin de cartes

8. **florist**
   fleuriste

9. **optician**
   opticien

10. **shoe store**
    magasin de chaussures

11. **play area**
    zone de jeu

12. **guest services**
    services à la clientèle

More vocabulary

beauty shop: hair salon

men's store: men's clothing store

gift shop: a store that sells t-shirts, mugs, and other small gifts

Pair practice. Make new conversations.

A: *Where is the florist?*

B: *It's on the first floor, next to the optician.*

13. department store grand magasin	**17.** candy store confiserie	**21.** elevator ascenseur
14. travel agency agence de voyage	**18.** hair salon salon de coiffure	**22.** cell phone kiosk kiosque de téléphones cellulaires
15. food court aire de restauration	**19.** maternity store magasin de maternité	**23.** escalator escalier mécanique
16. ice cream shop glacier	**20.** electronics store magasin d'électronique	**24.** directory tableau d'information

Ways to talk about plans

Let's go to the <u>card store</u>.
I have to go to the <u>card store</u>.
I want to go to the <u>card store</u>.

Role play. Talk to a friend at the mall.

A: *Let's go to the <u>card store</u>. I need to buy <u>a card</u> for <u>Maggie's birthday</u>.*
B: *OK, but can we go to the <u>shoe store</u> next?*

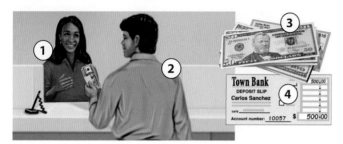

1. teller
   caissier (caissière)

2. customer
   client

3. deposit
   déposer

4. deposit slip
   bordereau de dépôt

5. security guard
   gardien de sécurité

6. vault
   chambre forte

7. safety deposit box
   coffre-fort

8. valuables
   objets de valeur

Opening an Account Ouvrir un compte

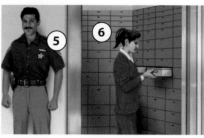

9. account manager
   gestionnaire de compte

10. passbook
    livret

11. savings account number
    numéro de compte d'épargne

12. check book
    carnet de chèques

13. check
    chèque

14. checking account number
    numéro de compte de chèque

15. ATM card
    carte de retrait

16. bank statement
    relevé de compte

17. balance
    solde

A. **Cash** a check.
   Encaisser un chèque.

B. **Make** a deposit.
   Faire un dépôt.

C. **Bank** online.
   Faire ses opérations bancaires en ligne.

The ATM (Automated Teller Machine) Le guichet automatique

D. **Insert** your ATM card.
   Introduire votre carte de retrait.

E. **Enter** your PIN.*
   Saisir le code PIN / le NIP.

F. **Withdraw** cash.
   Retirer de l'argent.

G. **Remove** your card.
   Retirer votre carte.

*PIN = personal identification number

A. get a library card
obtenir une carte de bibliothèque

B. look for a book
chercher un livre

C. check out a book
prendre un livre

D. return a book
rendre un livre

E. pay a late fine
payer une amende (de retard)

1. library clerk
bibliothécaire

2. circulation desk
comptoir de prêt

3. library patron
usager de la bibliothèque

4. periodicals
périodiques

5. magazine
magazine

6. newspaper
journal

7. headline
titre

8. atlas
atlas

9. reference librarian
bibliographe

10. self-checkout
caisse automatique

11. online catalog
catalogue en ligne

12. picture book
livre d'images

13. biography
biographie

14. title
titre

15. author
auteur

16. novel
roman

17. audiobook
livre audio

18. videocassette
cassette vidéo

19. DVD
DVD

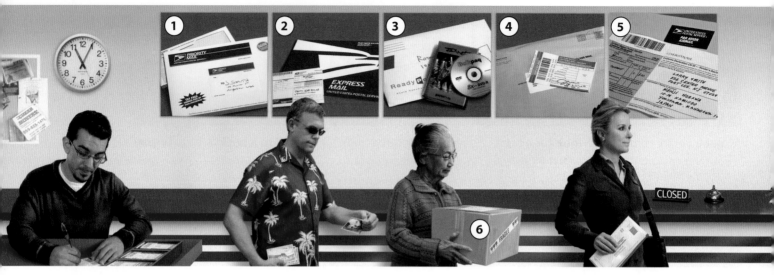

1. Priority Mail®
   courrier prioritaire
2. Express Mail®
   courrier express

3. media mail
   courrier média
4. Certified Mail™
   courrier recommandé

5. airmail
   courrier aérien
6. ground post / parcel post
   colis postal

13. letter
    lettre
14. envelope
    enveloppe

15. greeting card
    carte de vœux
16. post card
    carte postale

17. package
    emballage
18. book of stamps
    carnet de timbres

19. postal forms
    formulaires postaux
20. letter carrier
    facteur

21. return address
    adresse de retour

22. mailing address
    adresse postale

Sonya Enriquez
258 Quentin Avenue
Los Angeles, CA 90068-141

Cindy Lin
807 Glenn Drive
Charlotte, NC 28201

23. stamp
    timbre

24. postmark
    cachet de la poste

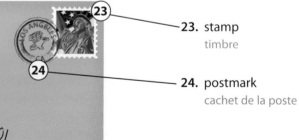

Ways to talk about sending mail

This letter has to get there tomorrow. (Express Mail®)
This letter has to arrive in two days. (Priority Mail®)
This letter can go in regular mail. (First Class)

Pair practice. Make new conversations.

A: *Hi. This letter has to get there tomorrow.*
B: *You can send it by Express Mail®.*
A: *OK. I need a book of stamps, too.*

7. postal clerk
postier(ère)

8. scale
pèse-lettre

9. post office box (PO box)
boîte postale

10. automated postal center (APC)
centre postal automatisé

11. stamp machine
distributeur de timbres

12. mailbox
boîte aux lettres

Sending a Card Envoyer une carte

A. Write a note in a card.
Écrire un mot sur une carte.

B. Address the envelope.
Adresser l'enveloppe.

C. Put on a stamp.
Coller un timbre.

D. Mail the card.
Poster la carte.

E. Deliver the card.
Livrer la carte.

F. Receive the card.
Recevoir la carte.

G. Read the card.
Lire la carte.

H. Write back.
Répondre.

More vocabulary

overnight / next day mail: Express Mail®
postage: the cost to send mail
junk mail: mail you don't want

Think about it. Discuss.

1. What kind of mail do you send overnight?
2. Do you want to be a letter carrier? Why or why not?
3. Do you get junk mail? What do you do with it?

135

1. **DMV handbook**
   code de la route

2. **testing area**
   zone de test

3. **DMV clerk**
   préposé du service
   des cartes grises

4. **photo**
   photo

5. **fingerprint**
   empreinte digitale

6. **vision exam**
   examen de la vue

7. **window**
   guichet

8. **proof of insurance**
   carte d'assurance

9. **driver's license**
   permis de conduire

10. **expiration date**
    date d'expiration

11. **driver's license number**
    numéro de permis de conduire

12. **license plate**
    plaque d'immatriculation

13. **registration sticker / tag**
    vignette

More vocabulary

expire: a license is no good, or **expires,** after the expiration date
renew a license: to apply to keep a license before it expires
vanity plate: a more expensive, personal license plate

Ask your classmates. Share the answers.

1. How far is the DMV from your home?
2. Do you have a driver's license? If yes, when does it expire? If not, do you want one?

Department of Motor Vehicles (DMV)

Getting Your First License Passer le premier permis de conduire

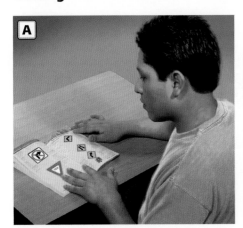

A. Study the handbook.
  Étudier le code de la route.

B. Take a driver education course.*
  Prendre des leçons de code de la route.

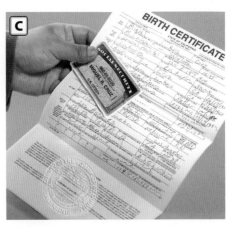

C. Show your identification.
  Montrer vos papiers d'identité.

D. Pay the application fee.
  Payer les frais de dossier.

E. Take a written test.
  Passer un examen écrit.

F. Get a learner's permit.
  Obtenir un permis d'apprentissage.

G. Take a driver's training course.*
  Prendre des leçons de conduite.

H. Pass a driving test.
  Réussir l'examen de conduite.

I. Get your license.
  Obtenir votre permis.

***Note:** This is not required for drivers 18 and older.

Ways to request more information

What do I do next?
What's the next step?
Where do I go from here?

Role play. Talk to a DMV clerk.

A: *I want to apply for a driver's license.*
B: *Did you study the handbook?*
A: *Yes, I did. What do I do next?*

Federal Government Gouvernement fédéral

Legislative Branch
Pouvoir législatif

1. U.S. Capitol
   Capitole
2. Congress
   Congrès
3. House of Representatives
   Chambre des représentants
4. congressperson
   député
5. Senate
   Sénat
6. senator
   sénateur / sénatrice

Executive Branch
Pouvoir exécutif

7. White House
   Maison Blanche
8. president
   président
9. vice president
   vice-président
10. Cabinet
    Ministère

Judicial Branch
Pouvoir judiciaire

11. Supreme Court
    Cour suprême
12. justices
    juges
13. chief justice
    président de la Court Suprême

The Military L'armée

14. Army
    Armée
15. Navy
    Marine
16. Air Force
    Force aérienne
17. Marines
    Fusilier marin
18. Coast Guard
    Garde-côte
19. National Guard
    Garde nationale

State Government Gouvernement de l'État

City Government Gouvernement de la ville

20. governor
gouverneur

21. lieutenant governor
lieutenant-gouverneur

22. state capital
capitale de l'État

23. Legislature
Pouvoir législatif

24. assemblyperson
député

25. state senator
sénateur d'État

26. mayor
maire

27. city council
conseil municipal

28. councilperson
conseiller municipal

An Election Une élection

A. run for office
se présenter aux élections

29. political campaign
campagne électorale

B. debate
débat

30. opponent
adversaire

C. get elected
être élu

31. election results
résultats des élections

D. serve
être en service

32. elected official
représentant élu

More vocabulary

term: the period of time an elected official serves
political party: a group of people with the same political goals

Think about it. Discuss.

1. Should everyone have to serve in the military? Why or why not?
2. Would you prefer to run for city council or mayor? Why?

139

Responsibilities Responsabilités

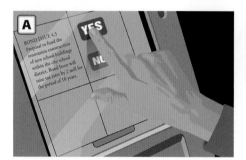

A. vote
voter

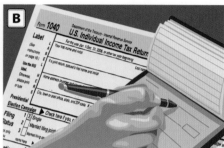

B. pay taxes
payer les impôts

C. obey the law
respecter les lois

D. register with Selective Service*
s'inscrire au Service sélectif

E. serve on a jury
siéger sur un jury

F. be informed
être informé

Citizenship Requirements Pour devenir citoyen(ne)

G. be 18 or older
avoir 18 ans ou plus

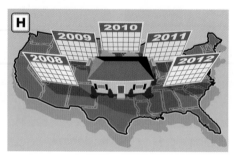

H. live in the U.S. for 5 years
vivre aux États-Unis pendant 5 ans

I. take a citizenship test
passer l'examen de citoyenneté

Rights Droits

1. peaceful assembly
rassemblement paisible

2. free speech
liberté d'expression

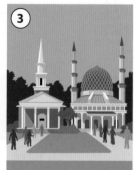

3. freedom of religion
liberté de religion

4. freedom of the press
liberté de la presse

5. fair trial
procès équitable

***Note:** All males 18 to 26 who live in the U.S. are required to register with Selective Service.

A. arrest a suspect
arrêter un suspect

1. police officer
   policier (policière)
2. handcuffs
   menottes

B. hire a lawyer / **hire** an attorney
engager un avocat

3. guard
   gardien
4. defense attorney
   avocat de la défense

C. appear in court
se présenter en cour

5. defendant
   accusé
6. judge
   juge

D. stand trial
passer en jugement

7. courtroom
   salle d'audience

8. jury
   jury
9. evidence
   preuves

10. prosecuting attorney
    procureur
11. witness
    témoin

12. court reporter
    greffier de la cour
13. bailiff
    huissier

E. convict the defendant
condamner l'accusé

14. verdict*
    verdict

F. sentence the defendant
prononcer une sentence

G. go to jail / **go** to prison
aller en prison

15. convict / prisoner
    condamné / prisonnier

H. be released
être relâché

*Note: There are two possible verdicts, "guilty" and "not guilty."

Look at the pictures.
Describe what happened.

A: The <u>police officer</u> <u>arrested a suspect</u>.
B: He put <u>handcuffs</u> on him.

Think about it. Discuss.

1. Would you want to serve on a jury? Why or why not?
2. Look at the crimes on page 142. What sentence would you give for each crime? Why?

1. **vandalism**
   vandalisme
2. **burglary**
   cambriolage

3. **assault**
   agression
4. **gang violence**
   violence des gangs

5. **drunk driving**
   conduite en état d'ivresse
6. **illegal drugs**
   drogues illégales

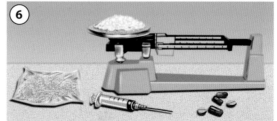

7. **arson**
   incendie criminel
8. **shoplifting**
   vol à l'étalage

9. **identity theft**
   vol d'identité
10. **victim**
    victime

11. **mugging**
    vol et agression
12. **murder**
    meurtre
13. **gun**
    pistolet

More vocabulary

steal: to take money or things from someone illegally
commit a crime: to do something illegal
criminal: someone who does something illegal

Think about it. Discuss.

1. Is there too much crime on TV or in the movies? Explain.
2. How can communities help stop crime?

A. **Walk** with a friend.
Marcher avec un ami.

B. **Stay** on well-lit streets.
Aller dans les rues bien éclairées.

C. **Conceal** your PIN number.
Dissimuler votre NIP.

D. **Protect** your purse or wallet.
Protéger votre sac ou votre porte-monnaie.

E. **Lock** your doors.
Verrouiller vos portes.

F. Don't **open** your door to strangers.
Ne pas ouvrir la porte à des étrangers.

G. Don't **drink** and **drive**.
Ne pas boire et conduire.

H. **Shop** on secure websites.
Acheter sur des sites Web sécurisés.

I. **Be** aware of your surroundings.
Être conscient de ce qui vous entoure.

J. **Report** suspicious packages.
Signaler les paquets suspects.

K. **Report** crimes to the police.
Signaler les crimes à la police.

L. **Join** a Neighborhood Watch.
Participer à un programme de surveillance de quartier.

More vocabulary

sober: not drunk
designated drivers: sober drivers who drive drunk people home safely

Ask your classmates. Share the answers.

1. Do you feel safe in your neighborhood?
2. Look at the pictures. Which of these things do you do?
3. What other things do you do to stay safe?

1. **lost child**
   enfant perdu

2. **car accident**
   accident d'automobile

3. **airplane crash**
   écrasement d'avion

4. **explosion**
   explosion

5. **earthquake**
   tremblement de terre

6. **mudslide**
   coulée de boue

7. **forest fire**
   incendie de forêt

8. **fire**
   incendie

9. **firefighter**
   pompier

10. **fire truck**
    camion de pompiers

Ways to report an emergency

First, give your name. *My name is <u>Tim Johnson</u>.*
Then, state the emergency and give the address.
There was <u>a car accident</u> at <u>219 Elm Street</u>.

Role play. Call 911.

A: *911 Emergency Operator.*

B: *My name is <u>Lisa Diaz</u>. There is <u>a fire</u> at <u>323 Oak Street</u>. Please hurry!*

Emergencies and Natural Disasters

11. drought
sécheresse

12. famine
famine

13. blizzard
blizzard

14. hurricane
ouragan

15. tornado
tornade

16. volcanic eruption
éruption volcanique

17. tidal wave / tsunami
raz-de-marée / tsunami

18. avalanche
avalanche

19. flood
inondation

20. search and rescue team
équipe de recherche et sauvetage

Ask your classmates. Share the answers.

1. Which natural disaster worries you the most?
2. Which natural disaster worries you the least?
3. Which disasters are common in your local area?

Think about it. Discuss.

1. What organizations can help you in an emergency?
2. What are some ways to prepare for natural disasters?
3. Where would you go in an emergency?

Before an Emergency Avant une urgence

A. Plan for an emergency.
Élaborer un plan d'urgence.

1. meeting place
lieu de rassemblement

2. out-of-state contact
contact en dehors de l'État

3. escape route
voie de sortie

4. gas shut-off valve
robinet de fermeture du gaz

5. evacuation route
itinéraire d'évacuation

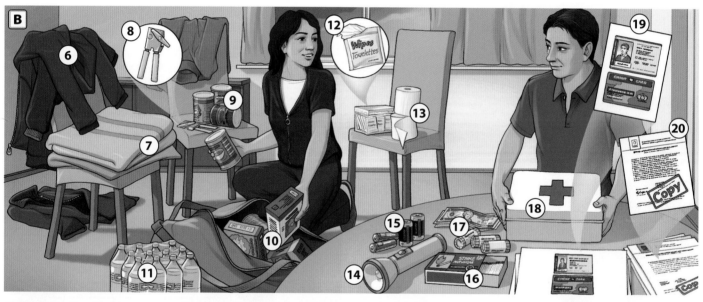

B. Make a disaster kit.
Préparer une trousse d'urgence en cas de catastrophe.

6. warm clothes
vêtements chauds

7. blankets
couvertures

8. can opener
ouvre-boîte

9. canned food
boîtes de conserve

10. packaged food
aliments emballés

11. bottled water
eau en bouteille

12. moist towelettes
serviettes humides

13. toilet paper
papier hygiénique

14. flashlight
lampe de poche

15. batteries
piles

16. matches
allumettes

17. cash and coins
espèces et pièces

18. first aid kit
trousse de premiers soins

19. copies of ID and credit cards
copies des papiers d'identité et des cartes de crédit

20. copies of important papers
copies des documents importants

Pair practice. Make new conversations.

A: *What do we need for our disaster kit?*
B: *We need blankets and matches.*
A: *I think we also need batteries.*

Ask your classmates. Share the answers.

1. Who would you call first after an emergency?
2. Do you have escape and evacuation routes planned?
3. Are you a calm person in case of an emergency?

During an Emergency   Durant une urgence

C. Watch the weather.
Consulter la météo.

D. Pay attention to warnings.
Faire attention aux avertissements.

E. Remain calm.
Rester calme.

F. Follow directions.
Suivre les instructions.

G. Help people with disabilities.
Aider les personnes handicapées.

H. Seek shelter.
Trouver un abri.

I. Stay away from windows.
Rester à l'écart des fenêtres.

J. Take cover.
Se mettre à l'abri.

K. Evacuate the area.
Évacuer la région.

After an Emergency   Après une urgence

L. Call out-of-state contacts.
Appeler vos contacts en dehors de l'État.

M. Clean up debris.
Nettoyer les débris.

N. Inspect utilities.
Vérifier l'eau, le gaz et l'électricité.

Ways to say you're OK	**Ways to say you need help**	**Role play. Prepare for an emergency.**
I'm fine.	*We need help.*	A: *They just issued <u>a hurricane</u> warning.*
We're OK here.	*Someone is hurt.*	B: *OK. We need to stay calm and follow directions.*
Everything's under control.	*I'm injured. Please get help.*	A: *What do we need to do first?*

1. graffiti
   graffiti

2. litter
   détritus

3. streetlight
   réverbère

4. hardware store
   quincaillerie

5. petition
   pétition

A. **give** a speech
   faire un discours

B. **applaud**
   applaudir

C. **change**
   changer

Look at the pictures.
What do you see?

Answer the questions.

1. What were the problems on Main Street?

2. What was the petition for?

3. Why did the city council applaud?

4. How did the people change the street?

📖 Read the story.

Community Cleanup

Marta Lopez has a donut shop on Main Street. One day she looked at her street and was very upset. She saw <u>graffiti</u> on her donut shop and the other stores. <u>Litter</u> was everywhere. All the <u>streetlights</u> were broken. Marta wanted to fix the lights and clean up the street.

Marta started a <u>petition</u> about the streetlights. Five hundred people signed it. Then she <u>gave a speech</u> to the city council. The council members voted to repair the streetlights. Everyone <u>applauded</u>. Marta was happy, but her work wasn't finished.

Next, Marta asked for volunteers to clean up Main Street. The <u>hardware store</u> manager gave the volunteers free paint. Marta gave them free donuts and coffee. The volunteers painted and cleaned. They <u>changed</u> Main Street. Now Main Street is beautiful and Marta is proud.

Think about it.

1. What are some problems in your community? How can people help?

2. Imagine you are Marta. What do you say in your speech to the city council?

1. car
   voiture
2. passenger
   passager
3. taxi
   taxi
4. motorcycle
   moto
5. street
   rue
6. truck
   camion
7. train
   train
8. (air)plane
   avion

Listen and point. Take turns.

A: *Point to the motorcycle*.
B: *Point to the truck*.
A: *Point to the train*.

Dictate to your partner. Take turns.

A: *Write motorcycle*.
B: *Could you repeat that for me?*
A: *Motorcycle. M-o-t-o-r-c-y-c-l-e*.

9. **helicopter**
   hélicoptère
10. **airport**
    aéroport
11. **subway station**
    station de métro
12. **subway**
    métro
13. **bus stop**
    arrêt d'autobus
14. **bus**
    autobus
15. **bicycle**
    bicyclette / vélo

SUBWAY

Mario's ITALIAN DELI

Ways to talk about using transportation

Use **take** for buses, trains, subways, taxis, planes, and helicopters. Use **drive** for cars and trucks. Use **ride** for bicycles and motorcycles.

Pair practice. Make new conversations.

A: *How do you get to school?*
B: *I take the bus. How about you?*
A: *I ride a bicycle to school.*

151

A Bus Stop Un arrêt d'autobus

BUS 10 Northbound

Main	Elm	Oak
6:00	6:10	6:13
6:30	6:40	6:43
7:00	7:10	7:13
7:30	7:40	7:43

New York City Transit
Transfer
◄ Going your way

1. bus route
   itinéraire d'autobus
2. fare
   tarif
3. rider
   passager
4. schedule
   horaire
5. transfer
   transfert

A Subway Station Une station de métro

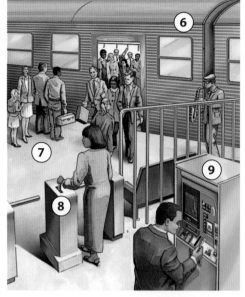

6. subway car
   rame de métro
7. platform
   quai
8. turnstile
   tourniquet
9. vending machine
   distributeur
   automatique
10. token
    jeton
11. fare card
    carte
    d'abonnement

A Train Station Une gare de chemin de fer

15.
HART DAVIS/DAMON
From
DOVER, NH
To
BOSTON NRTH STA,MA
Carrier   Train   Date
2V   684   17FEB03
Accom   Space/Car
2V   BUSINESS CL
Form of Payment
AP   XXXX0456791   Ax

Fresno → Los Angeles
Fresno → Los Angeles

12. ticket window
    guichet de vente des billets
13. conductor
    contrôleur
14. track
    voie ferrée
15. ticket
    billet
16. one-way trip
    aller simple
17. round trip
    aller-retour

Airport Transportation Moyens de transport à l'aéroport

TAXIS

J&J Hotel

18. taxi stand
    station de taxis
19. shuttle
    navette
20. town car
    voiture urbaine
21. taxi driver
    chauffeur de taxi
22. taxi license
    licence de taxi
23. meter
    compteur

More vocabulary

hail a taxi: to raise your hand to get a taxi
miss the bus: to get to the bus stop after the bus leaves

Ask your classmates. Share the answers.

1. Is there a subway system in your city?
2. Do you ever take taxis? When?
3. Do you ever take the bus? Where?

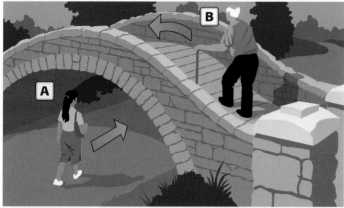

A. go under the bridge
passer sous le pont

B. go over the bridge
passer sur le pont

C. walk up the steps
monter les escaliers

D. walk down the steps
descendre les escaliers

E. get into the taxi
monter dans le taxi

F. get out of the taxi
descendre du taxi

G. run across the street
traverser la rue en courant

H. run around the corner
passer le coin en courant

I. get on the highway
s'engager sur l'autoroute

J. get off the highway
sortir de l'autoroute

K. drive through the tunnel
traverser le tunnel

Grammar Point: *into, out of, on, off*

Use *get into* for taxis and cars.
Use *get on* for buses, trains, planes, and highways.

Use *get out of* for taxis and cars.
Use *get off* for buses, trains, planes, and highways.

1. stop
stop / arrêt

2. do not enter / wrong way
ne pas s'engager / sens interdit

3. one way
voie à sens unique

4. speed limit
limite de vitesse

5. U-turn OK
demi-tour autorisé

6. no outlet / dead end
sans issue / cul-de-sac

7. right turn only
tourner à droite seulement

8. no left turn
défense de tourner à gauche

9. yield
ralentir

10. merge
converger

11. no parking
stationnement interdit

12. handicapped parking
stationnement pour
personnes handicapées

13. pedestrian crossing
passages pour piétons

14. railroad crossing
passage à niveau

15. school crossing
passage pour écoliers

16. road work
travaux routiers

17. U.S. route / highway marker
panneau d'autoroute

18. hospital
hôpital

Pair practice. Make new conversations.

A: *Watch out! The sign says <u>no left turn</u>.*
B: *Sorry, I was looking at the <u>stop</u> sign.*
A: *That's OK. Just be careful!*

Ask your classmates. Share the answers.

1. How many traffic signs are on your street?
2. What's the speed limit on your street?
3. What traffic signs are the same in your native country?

Directions Trajet

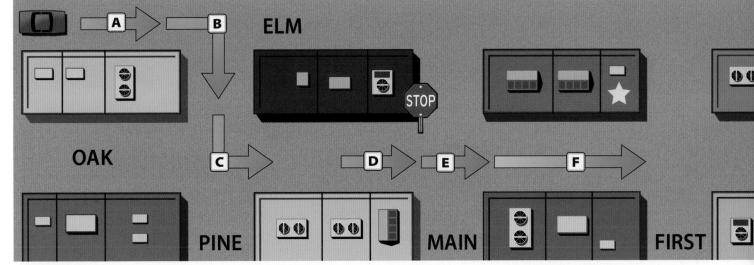

A. Go straight on Elm Street.
Aller tout droit sur Elm.

B. Turn right on Pine Street.
Tourner à droite sur Pine.

C. Turn left on Oak Street.
Tourner à gauche sur Oak.

D. Stop at the corner.
Arrêtez-vous au coin.

E. Go past Main Street.
Passer Main.

F. Go one block to First Street.
Continuer sur un pâté de maison sur First.

Maps Cartes

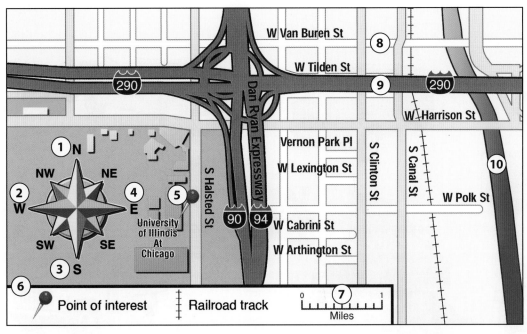

Point of interest — Railroad track — Miles

1. north
   nord

2. west
   ouest

3. south
   sud

4. east
   est

5. symbol
   symbole

6. key
   légende

7. scale
   échelle (des distances)

8. street
   rue

9. highway
   autoroute

10. river
    rivière

11. GPS (global positioning system)
    GPS (système mondial de localisation)

12. Internet map
    carte Internet

Role play. Ask for directions.

A: *I'm lost. I need to get to* <u>*Elm and Pine*</u>.
B: *Go* <u>*straight on Oak*</u> *and* <u>*make a right on Pine*</u>.
A: *Thanks so much.*

Ask your classmates. Share the answers.

1. How often do you use Internet maps? GPS? paper maps?
2. What was the last map you used? Why?

155

1. 4-door car / sedan
   voiture / berline 4 portes

2. 2-door car / coupe
   voiture / coupé 2 portes

3. hybrid
   voiture hybride

4. sports car
   voiture de sport

5. convertible
   décapotable

6. station wagon
   familiale / break

7. SUV (sport–utility vehicle)
   véhicule utilitaire sport

8. minivan
   mini-fourgonnette / monospace

9. camper
   camionnette de camping

10. RV (recreational vehicle)
    véhicule de camping

11. limousine / limo
    limousine

12. pickup truck
    camion léger

13. cargo van
    fourgonette

14. tow truck
    dépanneuse

15. tractor trailer / semi
    camion semi-remorque

16. cab
    cabine

17. trailer
    remorque

18. moving van
    camion de
    déménagement

19. dump truck
    camion à benne

20. tank truck
    camion citerne

21. school bus
    autobus d'écoliers

Pair practice. Make new conversations.

A: *I have a new car!*
B: *Did you get a hybrid?*
A: *Yes, but I really wanted a sports car.*

More vocabulary

make: the name of the company that makes the car
model: the style of the car

Buying and Maintaining a Car

Buying a Used Car Acheter une voiture d'occasion

'04 Compact. Only $3,000.

'05 Sedan. Must sell. Great deal!

A. Look at car ads.
Regarder les annonces de voitures.

How many miles does it have?

B. Ask the seller about the car.
Demander au vendeur des informations concernant la voiture.

It's in good condition.

C. Take the car to a mechanic.
Emmener la voiture chez le mécanicien.

It's $2,500.

I can give you $2,000.

D. Negotiate a price.
Négocier un prix.

E. Get the title from the seller.
Obtenir la carte grise du véhicule auprès du vendeur.

F. Register the car.
Immatriculer la voiture.

Taking Care of Your Car Entretenir votre voiture

G. Fill the tank with gas.
Remplir le réservoir d'essence.

H. Check the oil.
Vérifier l'huile.

I. Put in coolant.
Ajouter du liquide de refroidissement.

J. Go for a smog check.*
Passer le contrôle technique.

K. Replace the windshield wipers.
Remplacer les essuie-glaces.

L. Fill the tires with air.
Gonfler les pneus.

*smog check = emissions test

Ways to request service

Please check the oil.
Could you fill the tank?
Put in coolant, please.

Think about it. Discuss.

1. What's good and bad about a used car?
2. Do you like to negotiate car prices? Why?
3. Do you know any good mechanics? Why are they good?

At the Dealer
Chez le concessionnaire

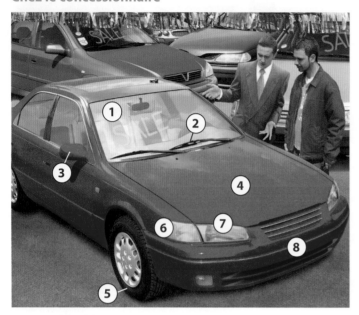

At the Mechanic
Chez le mécanicien

1. windshield
   pare-brise
2. windshield wipers
   essuie-glaces
3. sideview mirror
   rétroviseur extérieur
4. hood
   capot

5. tire
   pneu
6. turn signal
   clignotant
7. headlight
   phare
8. bumper
   pare-chocs

9. hubcap / wheel cover
   enjoliveur
10. gas tank
    réservoir d'essence
11. trunk
    coffre
12. license plate
    plaque d'immatriculation

13. tail light
    feu arrière
14. brake light
    feu de frein
15. tail pipe
    tuyau d'échappement
16. muffler
    silencieux

Under the Hood
Sous le capot

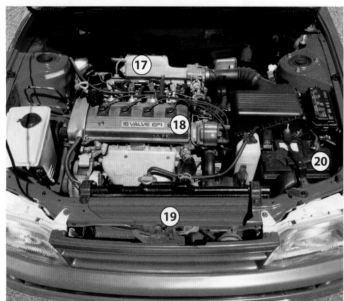

Inside the Trunk
Dans le coffre

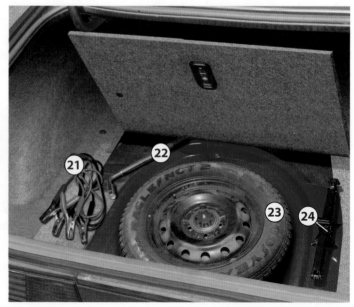

17. fuel injection system
    système d'injection
    de carburant
18. engine
    moteur

19. radiator
    radiateur
20. battery
    batterie

21. jumper cables
    câbles de démarrage
22. lug wrench
    démonte-roue

23. spare tire
    roue de secours
24. jack
    cric

The Dashboard and Instrument Panel
Le tableau de bord

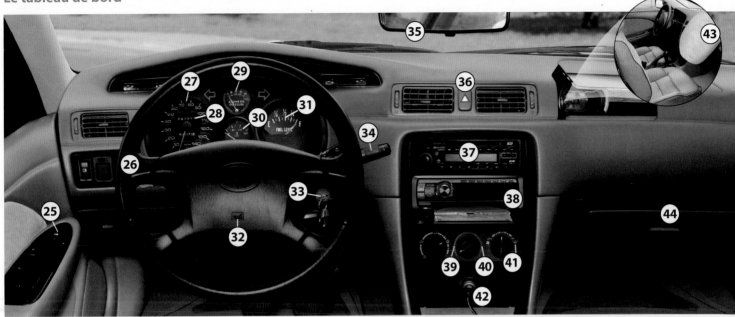

25. **door lock**
    verrouillage des portes

26. **steering wheel**
    volant

27. **speedometer**
    compteur de vitesse

28. **odometer**
    odomètre / compteur
    kilométrique

29. **oil gauge**
    jauge d'huile

30. **temperature gauge**
    indicateur de température du
    moteur

31. **gas gauge**
    jauge d'essence

32. **horn**
    klaxon

33. **ignition**
    allumage

34. **turn signal**
    clignotant

35. **rearview mirror**
    rétroviseur

36. **hazard lights**
    feux de détresse

37. **radio**
    radio

38. **CD player**
    lecteur de disques compacts

39. **air conditioner**
    climatiseur

40. **heater**
    appareil de chauffage

41. **defroster**
    dégivreur

42. **power outlet**
    prise d'alimentation

43. **air bag**
    coussin gonflable

44. **glove compartment**
    coffre à gant

An Automatic Transmission
Une transmission automatique

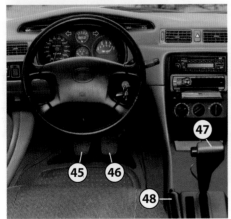

A Manual Transmission
Une transmission manuelle

Inside the Car
Intérieur de la voiture

45. **brake pedal**
    pédale de frein

46. **gas pedal /
    accelerator**
    pédale
    d'accélérateur

47. **gear shift**
    levier de vitesses

48. **hand brake**
    frein à main

49. **clutch**
    embrayage

50. **stick shift**
    levier de vitesses
    au plancher

51. **front seat**
    siège avant

52. **seat belt**
    ceinture de sécurité

53. **child safety seat**
    siège de sécurité
    pour enfant

54. **backseat**
    siège arrière

In the Airline Terminal
Dans le terminal de la compagnie aérienne

At the Security Checkpoint
Au passage de la sécurité

1. skycap
   porteur
2. check-in kiosk
   kiosque d'enregistrement
3. ticket agent
   préposé aux billets
4. screening area
   zone de fouilles
5. TSA* agent / security screener
   agent de l'AST / contrôleur de sécurité
6. bin
   bac

Taking a Flight   Prendre un avion

A. **Check in** electronically.
   S'enregistrer électroniquement.

B. **Check** your bags.
   Enregistrer vos bagages.

C. **Show** your boarding pass and ID.
   Montrer votre carte d'embarquement et votre pièce d'identité.

D. **Go through** security.
   Passer au contrôle de sécurité.

E. **Board** the plane.
   Monter à bord de l'avion.

F. **Find** your seat.
   Chercher le siège.

G. **Stow** your carry-on bag.
   Ranger les bagages à main.

H. **Fasten** your seat belt.
   Mettre la ceinture de sécurité.

I. **Turn off** your cell phone.
   Éteindre le téléphone cellulaire.

J. **Take off**. / **Leave**.
   Décoller. / **Partir**.

K. **Land**. / **Arrive**.
   Atterrir. / **Arriver**.

L. **Claim** your baggage.
   Récupérer vos bagages.

* Transportation Security Administration

At the Gate
À la porte d'embarquement

On the Airplane
Dans l'avion

At Customs
À la douane

7. arrival and departure monitors
écrans d'arrivée et de départ

8. gate
porte d'embarquement

9. boarding area
zone d'embarquement

10. cockpit
poste de pilotage

11. pilot
pilote

12. flight attendant
agent(e) de bord

13. overhead compartment
compartiment à bagages

14. emergency exit
sortie de secours

15. passenger
passager

16. declaration form
formulaire de déclaration

17. customs officer
agent des douanes

18. luggage / bag
bagage / sac

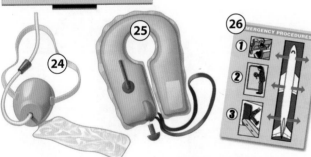

19. e-ticket
billet électronique

20. boarding pass
carte d'embarquement

21. tray table
tablette

22. turbulence
turbulence

23. baggage carousel
carroussel à bagages

24. oxygen mask
masque d'oxygène

25. life vest
gilet de sauvetage

26. emergency card
carte de mesures de sécurité

27. reclined seat
siège incliné

28. upright seat
siège droit

29. on-time
à l'heure

30. delayed flight
vol retardé

More vocabulary

departure time: the time the plane takes off
arrival time: the time the plane lands
direct flight: a trip with no stops

Pair practice. Make new conversations.

A: *Excuse me. Where do I* <u>check in</u>?
B: *At the* <u>check-in kiosk</u>.
A: *Thanks.*

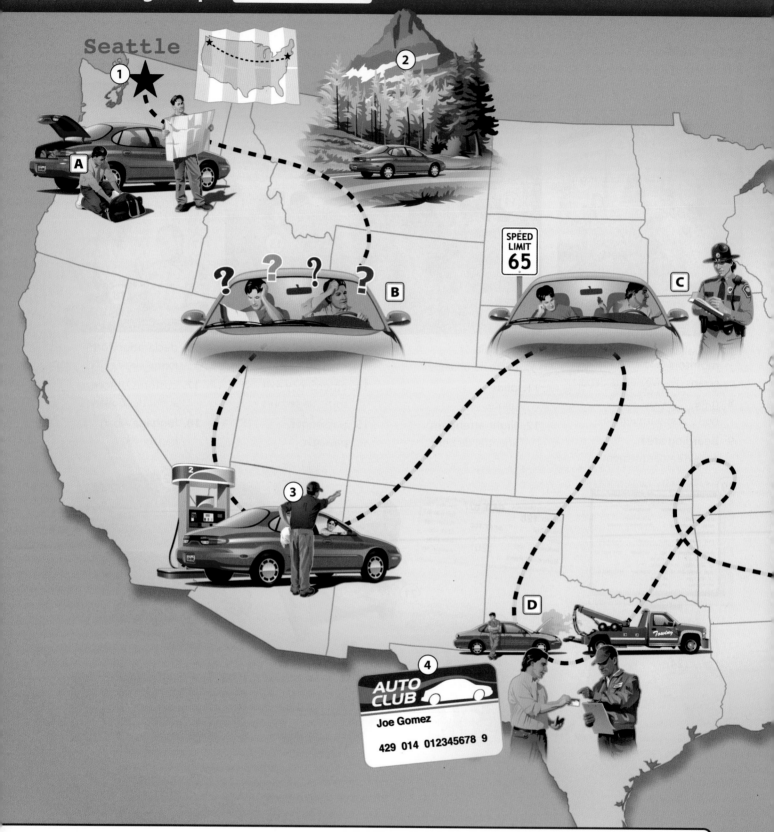

Seattle

SPEED LIMIT 65

AUTO CLUB
Joe Gomez
429 014 012345678 9

1. starting point
   point de départ

2. scenery
   paysage

3. gas station attendant
   pompiste

4. auto club card
   carte du club automobile

5. destination
   destination

A. **pack**
   préparer la voiture

B. **get** lost
   se perdre

C. **get** a speeding ticket
   recevoir une contravention

D. **break down**
   tomber en panne

E. **run out** of gas
   tomber en panne d'essence

F. **have** a flat tire
   avoir un pneu à plat / crevé

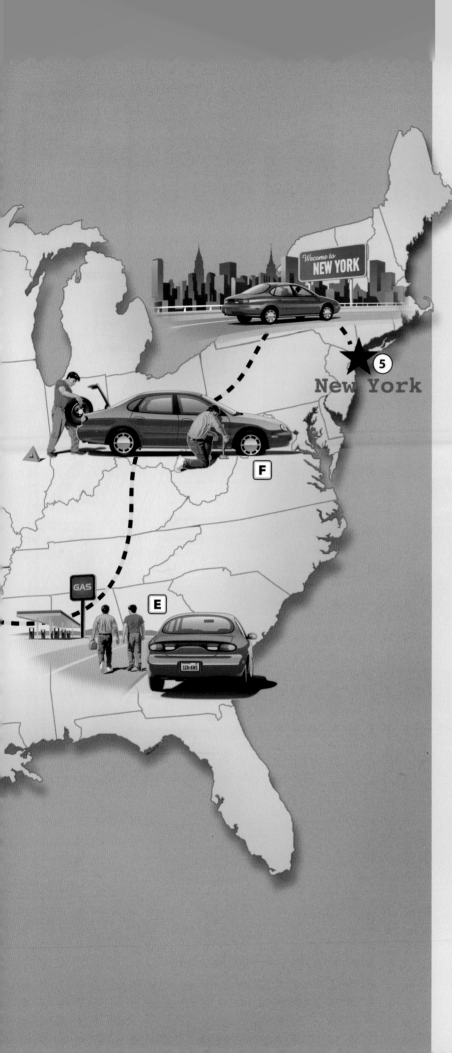

**Look at the pictures.
What do you see?**

Answer the questions.

1. What are the young men's starting point and destination?

2. What do they see on their trip?

3. What kinds of problems do they have?

 Read the story.

A Road Trip

On July 7th Joe and Rob <u>packed</u> their bags for a road trip. Their <u>starting point</u> was Seattle. Their <u>destination</u> was New York City.

The young men saw beautiful <u>scenery</u> on their trip. But there were also problems. They <u>got lost</u>. Then, a <u>gas station attendant</u> gave them bad directions. Next, they <u>got a speeding ticket</u>. Joe was very upset. After that, their car <u>broke down</u>. Joe called a tow truck and used his <u>auto club card</u>.

The end of their trip was difficult, too. They <u>ran out of gas</u> and then they had a <u>flat tire</u>.

After 7,000 miles of problems, Joe and Rob arrived in New York City. They were happy, but tired. Next time, they're going to take the train.

Think about it.

1. What is the best way to travel across the U.S.? by car? by plane? by train? Why?

2. Imagine your car breaks down on the road. Who can you call? What can you do?

1. entrance
   entrée
2. customer
   client
3. office
   bureau
4. employer /
   boss
   employeur / patron
5. receptionist
   réceptionniste
6. safety regulations
   réglementations
   de sécurité

IRINA'S COMPUTER SERVICE

OSHA
HAZARDS
SPILLS
CALL 911
SAFETY FIRST

COMPUTER NEWS

Irina Sarkov Owner

Listen and point. Take turns.

A: Point to <u>the front entrance</u>.
B: Point to <u>the receptionist</u>.
A: Point to <u>the time clock</u>.

Dictate to your partner. Take turns.

A: *Can you spell <u>employer</u>?*
B: *I'm not sure. Is it <u>e-m-p-l-o-y-e-r</u>?*
A: *Yes, that's right.*

7. **time clock**
pointeuse

8. **supervisor**
responsable

9. **employee**
employé

10. **payroll clerk**
employé(e) du service de la paye

11. **pay stub**
talon de chèque de paye

12. **wages**
salaires

13. **deductions**
déductions

14. **paycheck**
chèque de paie

Ways to talk about wages

I **earn** $250 a week.
He **makes** $7 an hour.
I'm **paid** $1,000 a month.

Role play. Talk to an employer.

A: *Is everything correct on your paycheck?*
B: *No, it isn't. I make $250 a week, not $200.*
A: *Let's talk to the payroll clerk. Where is she?*

165

1. accountant
comptable

2. actor
acteur (actrice)

3. administrative assistant
adjoint(e) administratif (ve)

4. appliance repair person
réparateur d'appareils électroménagers

5. architect
architecte

6. artist
artiste

7. assembler
monteur (monteuse)

8. auto mechanic
mécanicien (mécanicienne) auto

9. babysitter
gardienne d'enfant

10. baker
boulanger (boulangère)

11. business owner
propriétaire de magasin

12. businessperson
entrepreneur

13. butcher
boucher (bouchère)

14. carpenter
charpentier

15. cashier
caissier (caissière)

16. childcare worker
éducatrice (éducateur) en garderie

Ways to ask about someone's job

What's her job?
What does he do?
What kind of work do they do?

Pair practice. Make new conversations.

A: *What kind of work <u>does she</u> do?*
B: <u>*She's an accountant*</u>. *What <u>do they</u> do?*
A: <u>*They're actors*</u>.

17. commercial fisher
pêcheur commercial

18. computer software engineer
ingénieur en informatique

19. computer technician
technicien informatique

We have that shirt in red.

20. customer service representative
représentant du service à la clientèle

21. delivery person
livreur (livreuse)

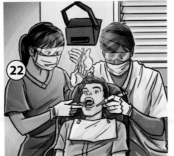

22. dental assistant
assistante dentaire

23. dockworker
docker

24. electronics repair person
réparateur de matériel électronique

25. engineer
ingénieur

26. firefighter
pompier

27. florist
fleuriste

28. gardener
jardinier (jardinière)

29. garment worker
confectionneur (confectionneuse) de vêtements

30. graphic designer
concepteur graphique

31. hairdresser / hair stylist
coiffeur / coiffeuse

32. home health care aide
aide aux soins à domicile

Ways to talk about jobs and occupations

*Sue's a <u>garment worker</u>. She works **in** a factory.*
*Tom's <u>an engineer</u>. He works **for** <u>a large company</u>.*
*Ann's a <u>dental assistant</u>. She works **with** <u>a dentist</u>.*

Role play. Talk about a friend's new job.

A: *Does your friend like <u>his</u> new job?*
B: *Yes, <u>he</u> does. <u>He's a graphic designer</u>.*
A: *Does <u>he</u> work <u>in an office</u>?*

33. homemaker
femme au foyer

34. housekeeper
femme de ménage

你好   He says, "Hi."

35. interpreter / translator
interprète / traducteur
(traductrice)

36. lawyer
avocat(e)

37. machine operator
opérateur (opératrice)
de machine

38. manicurist
manucure

39. medical records
technician
archiviste médicale

40. messenger / courier
coursier

41. model
mannequin

42. mover
déménageur

43. musician
musicien (musicienne)

44. nurse
infirmier / infirmière

45. occupational therapist
thérapeute occupationnel /
ergothérapeute

46. (house) painter
peintre en bâtiment

47. physician assistant
auxiliaire médical

48. police officer
policier (policière)

Grammar Point: past tense of be

I **was** a machine operator for 5 years.
She **was** a nurse for a year.
They **were** movers from 2003–2007.

Pair practice. Make new conversations.

A: What was your first job?
B: I was <u>a musician</u>. How about you?
A: I was <u>a messenger for a small company</u>.

49. postal worker
postier (postière)

50. printer
imprimeur

51. receptionist
réceptionniste

52. reporter
journaliste

53. retail clerk
vendeur au détail

54. sanitation worker
éboueur

55. security guard
gardien de sécurité

56. server
serveur (serveuse)

Here are some programs that will help you.

57. social worker
assistante sociale

58. soldier
soldat

59. stock clerk
commis aux stocks

Hello. I'm calling with a very special offer.

60. telemarketer
télé-vendeur (vendeuse)

61. truck driver
conducteur (conductrice)
de camions

62. veterinarian
vétérinaire

63. welder
soudeur (soudeuse)

Norma's Story

64. writer / author
écrivain / auteur

Ask your classmates. Share the answers.

1. Which of these jobs could you do now?

2. What is one job you don't want to have?

3. Which jobs do you want to have?

Think about it. Discuss.

1. Which jobs need special training?

2. What kind of person makes a good interpreter? A good nurse? A good reporter? Why?

A. assemble components
monter des éléments

B. assist medical patients
aider des malades

C. cook
cuisiner

D. do manual labor
faire des travaux manuels

E. drive a truck
conduire un camion

F. fly a plane
piloter un avion

G. make furniture
fabriquer des meubles

H. operate heavy machinery
conduire de la machinerie lourde

I. program computers
programmer des ordinateurs

J. repair appliances
réparer des appareils ménagers

K. sell cars
vendre des voitures

L. sew clothes
coudre des vêtements

M. solve math problems
résoudre des problèmes mathématiques

4% interest of 5K = x

ПРИВЕТ

N. speak another language
parler une langue étrangère

O. supervise people
encadrer des personnes

P. take care of children
prendre soin d'enfants

Q. teach
enseigner

R. type
taper

S. use a cash register
utiliser une caisse enregistreuse

T. wait on customers
servir des clients

Grammar Point: *can, can't*

*I am a chef. I **can** cook.*
*I'm not a pilot. I **can't** fly a plane.*
*I **can't** speak French, but I **can** speak Spanish.*

Role play. Talk to a job counselor.

A: *Tell me about your skills. Can you <u>type</u>?*
B: <u>*No, I can't*</u>, *but I <u>can use a cash register</u>.*
A: *OK. What other skills do you have?*

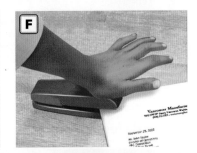

Office Skills
Compétences en
travail de bureau

A. **type** a letter
taper une lettre

B. **enter** data
saisir des données

C. **transcribe** notes
transcrire des notes

D. **make** copies
faire des photocopies

E. **collate** papers
classer des documents

F. **staple**
agrafer

G. **fax** a document
faxer un document

H. **scan** a document
scanner un document

I. **print** a document
imprimer un
document

J. **schedule** a meeting
planifier une réunion

K. **take** dictation
prendre des notes

L. **organize** materials
organiser des
documents

Telephone Skills
Service au téléphone

M. **greet** the caller
saluer l'appelant

N. **put** the caller on hold
mettre l'appelant
en attente

O. **transfer** the call
transférer l'appel

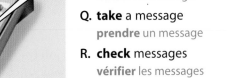

P. **leave** a message
laisser un message

Q. **take** a message
prendre un message

R. **check** messages
vérifier les messages

Career Path Développement de carrière

1. entry-level job
   poste de débutant

2. training
   formation

3. new job
   nouvel emploi

4. promotion
   promotion

Types of Job Training Types de formation professionnelle

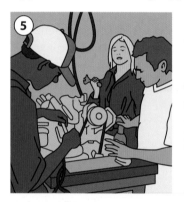

Enter the number here.

Medical Transcription 101
Log In
Password

5. vocational training
   formation professionnelle

6. internship
   stage

7. on-the-job training
   formation sur le tas

8. online course
   cours en ligne

Planning a Career Planifier une carrière

JOB BOARD

We offer training here.

Interests
Click on your interests. I like to work:
☑ Outside   ☐ With Children
☐ Inside   ☐ By Myself
☑ On a team

Skills
Click on your skills:
☐ Drive
☐ Speak Spanish
☑ Type

Work for Go-Mart

Why work for Go-Mart?

9. resource center
   centre de ressources professionnelles

10. career counselor
    conseiller professionnel

11. interest inventory
    inventaire d'intérêts

12. skill inventory
    inventaire des compétences

13. job fair
    forum de recrutement

14. recruiter
    recruteur

Ways to talk about job training

I'm looking into <u>an online course</u>.
I'm interested in <u>on-the-job training</u>.
I want to sign up for <u>an internship</u>.

Ask your classmates. Share the answers.

1. What kind of job training are you interested in?
2. Would your rather learn English in an online course or in a classroom?

A. talk to friends / **network**

parler à des amis / **entrer en contact**

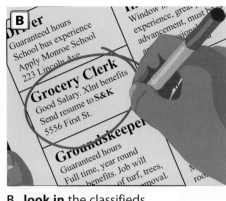

B. look in the classifieds

consulter les petites annonces

C. look for help wanted signs

chercher les panneaux offrant des emplois

D. check Internet job sites

vérifier les sites d'emploi sur Internet.

E. go to an employment agency

se rendre à une agence de recrutement

F. write a resume

écrire un curriculum vitae

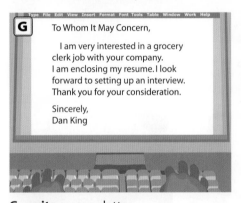

G. write a cover letter

écrire une lettre de présentation

H. send in your resume and cover letter

envoyer votre résumé et votre lettre de présentation

I. set up an interview

planifier une entrevue d'emploi

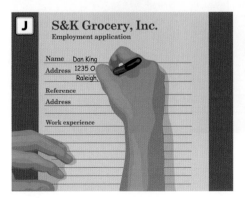

J. fill out an application

remplir une demande d'emploi

K. go on an interview

se présenter à une entrevue

L. get hired

être embauché

A. **Prepare** for the interview.
Se préparer pour une entrevue.

B. **Dress** appropriately.
S'habiller de manière adéquate.

C. **Be** neat.
Être soigné.

D. **Bring** your resume and ID.
Apporter votre curriculum vitae et votre pièce d'identité.

E. **Don't be** late.
Ne soyez pas en retard.

F. **Be** on time.
Soyez à l'heure.

G. **Turn off** your cell phone.
Éteindre le téléphone cellulaire.

H. **Greet** the interviewer.
Saluer l'intervieweur.

I. **Shake** hands.
Serrer la main.

Hello, I'm Elias Ortiz.

Hello, Mr. Ortiz. I'm Mrs. Perez.

J. **Make** eye contact.
Regarder dans les yeux.

K. **Listen** carefully.
Écouter attentivement.

L. **Talk** about your experience.
Parler de votre expérience.

Computer skills are important.

I have those skills.

I worked with computers on my last job.

M. **Ask** questions.
Poser des questions.

N. **Thank** the interviewer.
Remercier l'intervieweur.

O. **Write** a thank-you note.
Écrire un mot de remerciement.

Do you offer training?

Thank you for your time.

Dear Mrs. Perez, Thank you for the opportunity to meet with you.

More vocabulary

benefits: health insurance, vacation pay, or other things the employer can offer an employee
inquire about benefits: ask about benefits

Think about it. Discuss.

1. How can you prepare for an interview?
2. Why is it important to make eye contact?
3. What kinds of questions should you ask?

A Factory

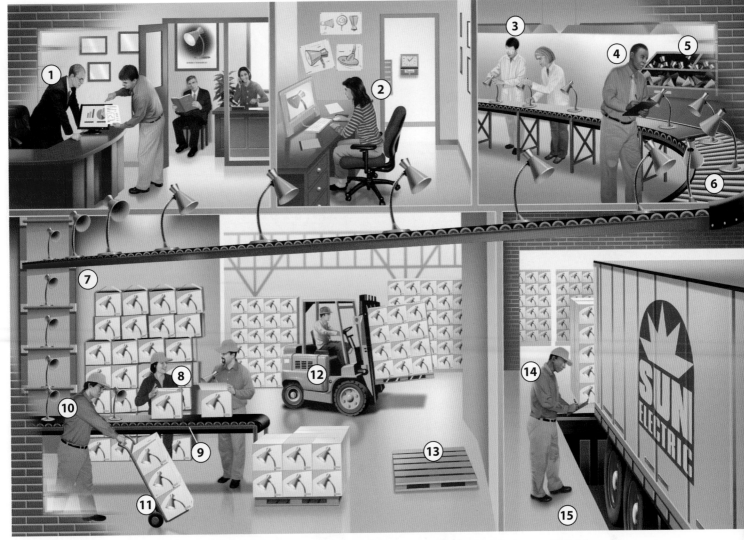

1. **factory owner**
   propriétaire de l'usine

2. **designer**
   concepteur

3. **factory worker**
   travailleur (travailleuse)

4. **line supervisor**
   agent de maîtrise

5. **parts**
   pièces

6. **assembly line**
   chaîne de montage

7. **warehouse**
   entrepôt

8. **packer**
   emballeur (emballeuse)

9. **conveyer belt**
   tapis roulant

10. **order puller**
    préposé aux commandes

11. **hand truck**
    chariot à main / diable

12. **forklift**
    chariot élévateur

13. **pallet**
    pallette

14. **shipping clerk**
    préposé à l'expédition

15. **loading dock**
    plate-forme de chargement

A. design
concevoir

B. manufacture
fabriquer

C. assemble
assembler

D. ship
expédier

1. gardening crew
   équipe de jardinage

2. leaf blower
   souffleuse à feuilles

3. wheelbarrow
   brouette

4. gardening crew leader
   chef de l'équipe de jardinage

5. landscape designer
   architecte paysagiste

6. lawn mower
   tondeuse à gazon

7. shovel
   pelle

8. rake
   râteau

9. pruning shears
   coupe-branches

10. trowel
    truelle

11. hedge clippers
    cisailles à haie

12. weed whacker / weed eater
    taille-bordures

A. **mow** the lawn
   tondre le gazon

B. **trim** the hedges
   tailler les bordures

C. **rake** the leaves
   ratisser (les feuilles)

D. **fertilize** / **feed** the plants
   fertiliser / **nourrir** les plantes

E. **plant** a tree
   planter un arbre

F. **water** the plants
   arroser (les plantes)

G. **weed** the flower beds
   désherber la plate-bande

H. **install** a sprinkler system
   installer un système d'arrosage

Use the new words.
Look at page 53. Name what you can do in the yard.

A: *I can mow the lawn.*
B: *I can weed the flower bed.*

Ask your classmates. Share the answers.

1. Do you know someone who does landscaping? Who?
2. Do you enjoy gardening? Why or why not?
3. Which gardening activity is the hardest to do? Why?

Crops Récoltes

1. rice
riz

2. wheat
blé

3. soybeans
soja

4. corn
maïs

5. alfalfa
luzerne

6. cotton
coton

7. field
champ

8. farmworker
ouvrier (ouvrière) agricole

9. tractor
tracteur

10. orchard
verger

11. barn
grange

12. farm equipment
matériel agricole

13. farmer / grower
fermier (fermière) /
producteur (productrice)

14. vegetable garden
jardin potager

15. livestock
bétail

16. vineyard
vignoble

17. corral
corral

18. hay
foin

19. fence
clôture

20. hired hand
ouvrier (ouvrière)
engagé(e)

21. cattle
bétail

22. rancher
cow-boy

A. **plant**
planter

B. **harvest**
récolter

C. **milk**
traire

D. **feed**
nourrir

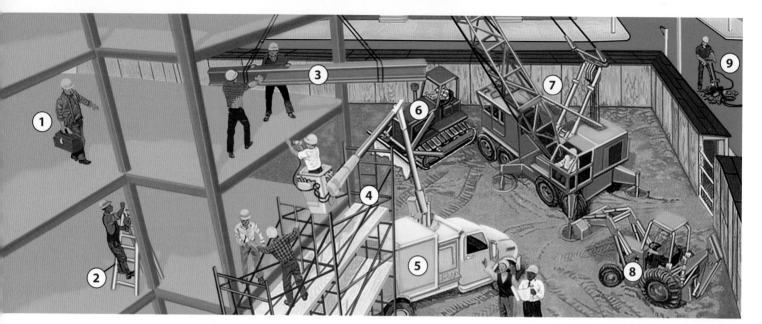

1. construction worker
ouvrier (ouvrière) du bâtiment

2. ladder
échelle

3. I beam/girder
poutre en I / poutrelle

4. scaffolding
échafaudage

5. cherry picker
engin élévateur à nacelle

6. bulldozer
bulldozer

7. crane
grue

8. backhoe
pelle rétrocaveuse

9. jackhammer / pneumatic drill
marteau pneumatique

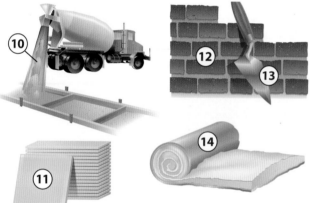
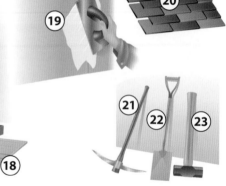

10. concrete
béton

11. tile
tuile

12. bricks
briques

13. trowel
truelle

14. insulation
isolation

15. stucco
stuc

16. window pane
vitre

17. wood / lumber
bois / bois de charpente

18. plywood
contreplaqué

19. drywall
placoplâtre

20. shingles
bardeaux

21. pickax
pioche

22. shovel
pelle

23. sledgehammer
masse

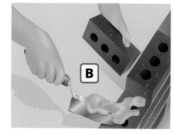

A. paint
peindre

B. lay bricks
poser des briques

C. install tile
carreler

D. hammer
frapper à coups de marteau

Safety Hazards and Hazardous Materials Risques d'accident et matériaux dangereux

1. **careless worker**
   ouvrier imprudent

2. **careful worker**
   ouvrier prudent

3. **poisonous fumes**
   vapeurs toxiques

4. **broken equipment**
   équipement endommagé

5. **frayed cord**
   cordage éraillé

6. **slippery floor**
   sol glissant

7. **radioactive materials**
   matériaux radioactifs

8. **flammable liquids**
   liquides inflammables

Safety Equipment Équipement de sécurité

9. **hard hat**
   casque

10. **safety glasses**
    lunettes de sûreté

11. **safety goggles**
    lunettes de sécurité

12. **safety visor**
    visière de sécurité

13. **respirator**
    masque respiratoire

14. **particle mask**
    masque à particules

15. **ear plugs**
    bouchons d'oreilles

16. **earmuffs**
    protège-oreilles

17. **work gloves**
    gants de travail

18. **back support belt**
    ceinture de soutien dorsal

19. **knee pads**
    genouillères

20. **safety boots**
    bottes de sécurité

21. **fire extinguisher**
    extincteur

22. **two-way radio**
    appareil radio émetteur récepteur

HAND TOOLS

HARDWARE

POWER TOOLS

1. hammer
marteau

2. mallet
maillet

3. ax
hache

4. handsaw
scie à main

5. hacksaw
scie à métaux

6. C-clamp
serre-joints en C

7. pliers
pinces

8. electric drill
perceuse électrique

9. circular saw
scie circulaire

10. jigsaw
scie sauteuse

11. power sander
ponceuse électrique

12. router
toupie

26. vise
étau

27. blade
lame

28. drill bit
foret

29. level
niveau

30. screwdriver
tournevis

31. Phillips screwdriver
tournevis Philips

32. machine screw
vis à métaux

33. wood screw
vis à bois

34. nail
clou

35. bolt
boulon

36. nut
écrou

37. washer
rondelle

38. toggle bolt
boulon de scellement

39. hook
crochet

40. eye hook
crochet à œillet

41. chain
chaîne

Use the new words.
Look at pages 62–63. Name the tools you see.

A: *There's a hammer*.
B: *There's a pipe wrench*.

Ask your classmates. Share the answers.

1. Are you good with tools?
2. Which tools do you have at home?
3. Where can you shop for building supplies?

13. wire
fil

14. extension cord
rallonge (électrique)

15. bungee cord
extenseur

16. yardstick
mètre

17. pipe
tuyau

18. fittings
raccords

19. 2 x 4 (two by four)
2 x 4 (deux par quatre)

20. particle board
aggloméré de bois

21. spray gun
pistolet à peinture

22. paintbrush
pinceau

23. paint roller
rouleau (à peinture)

24. wood stain
teinture pour bois

25. paint
peinture

42. wire stripper
pince à dénuder

43. electrical tape
chaterton / ruban isolant

44. work light
lampe de travail

45. tape measure
mètre-ruban

46. outlet cover
couvre-prise

47. pipe wrench
clé à tuyau

48. adjustable wrench
clé anglaise

49. duct tape
ruban adhésif en toile

50. plunger
débouchoir à ventouse

51. paint pan
bac à peinture

52. scraper
grattoir

53. masking tape
ruban à masquer

54. drop cloth
toile de peintre

55. chisel
burin

56. sandpaper
papier de verre

57. plane
rabot

Role play. Find an item in a building supply store.

A: *Where can I find <u>particle board</u>?*
B: *It's <u>on the back wall</u>, in the <u>lumber</u> section.*
A: *Great. And where <u>are the nails</u>?*

Think about it. Discuss.

1. Which tools are the most important to have? Why?
2. Which tools can be dangerous? Why?
3. Do you borrow tools from friends? Why or why not?

1. **supply cabinet**
   armoire de rangement des
   fournitures de bureau

2. **clerk**
   le préposé

3. **janitor**
   concierge

4. **conference room**
   salle de conférence

5. **executive**
   cadre

6. **presentation**
   présentation

7. **cubicle**
   poste de travail modulaire

8. **office manager**
   chef de bureau

9. **desk**
   bureau

10. **file clerk**
    préposé au classement

11. **file cabinet**
    meuble classeur

12. **computer technician**
    technicien informatique

13. **PBX**
    PBX

14. **receptionist**
    réceptionniste

15. **reception area**
    réception

16. **waiting area**
    salle d'attente

Ways to greet a receptionist

I'm here for a job interview.
I have a 9:00 a.m. appointment with Mr. Lee.
I'd like to leave a message for Mr. Lee.

Role play. Talk to a receptionist.

A: *Hello. How can I help you?*
B: *I'm here for a job interview with Mr. Lee.*
A: *OK. What is your name?*

Office Equipment Équipement de bureau

17. computer
ordinateur

18. inkjet printer
imprimante à jet d'encre

19. laser printer
imprimante laser

20. scanner
scanner

21. fax machine
télécopieur

22. paper cutter
massicot

23. photocopier
photocopieuse

24. paper shredder
déchiqueteuse

25. calculator
calculatrice

26. electric pencil sharpener
taille-crayons électrique

27. postal scale
pèse-lettre

Office Supplies Fournitures de bureau

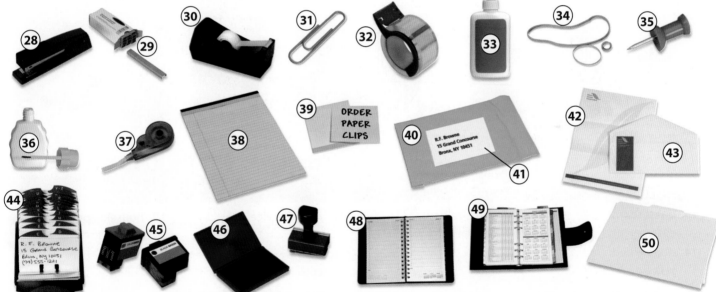

ORDER PAPER CLIPS

R.F. Browne
15 Grand Concourse
Bronx, NY 10451

R. F. Browne
15 Grand Concourse
Bronx, NY 10451
(718) 555-1221

28. stapler
agrafeuse

29. staples
agrafes

30. clear tape
ruban adhésif transparent

31. paper clip
trombone

32. packing tape
ruban d'emballage

33. glue
colle

34. rubber band
élastique

35. pushpin
clou à dessin

36. correction fluid
liquide correcteur

37. correction tape
ruban correcteur

38. legal pad
bloc format légal

39. sticky notes
notes autoadhésives

40. mailer
pochette matelassée

41. mailing label
étiquette d'expédition

42. letterhead / stationery
papier à en-tête

43. envelope
enveloppe

44. rotary card file
fichier rotatif

45. ink cartridge
cartouche d'encre

46. ink pad
tampon encreur

47. stamp
tampon

48. appointment book
carnet de rendez-vous

49. organizer
organiseur

50. file folder
chemise

1. doorman portier	**4.** concierge concierge	**7.** bellhop chasseur	**10.** guest client(e)
2. revolving door porte tambour	**5.** gift shop boutique de cadeaux	**8.** luggage cart chariot à bagages	**11.** desk clerk réceptionniste
3. parking attendant gardien de parking	**6.** bell captain chef chasseur	**9.** elevator ascenseur	**12.** front desk réception

13. guest room chambre	**15.** king-size bed très grand lit à deux places	**17.** room service service aux chambres	**19.** housekeeping cart chariot de ménage
14. double bed le lit à deux places	**16.** suite suite	**18.** hallway couloir	**20.** housekeeper femme de ménage

21. pool service nettoyage de la piscine	**23.** maintenance maintenance	**25.** meeting room salle de réunion
22. pool piscine	**24.** gym gymnase	**26.** ballroom salle de danse

A Restaurant Kitchen Une cuisine de restaurant

1. short-order cook
cuisinier-minute

2. dishwasher
plongeur

3. walk-in freezer
congélateur-chambre

4. food preparation worker
préposé à la préparation
alimentaire

5. storeroom
réserve

6. sous chef
sous chef

7. head chef / executive chef
chef de cuisine

Restaurant Dining Dîner au restaurant

8. server
serveur (serveuse)

9. diner
client / dineur

10. buffet
buffet

11. maitre d'
maître d'hôtel

12. headwaiter
maître d'hôtel

13. bus person
commis débarrasseur

14. banquet room
salle de banquet

15. runner
aide au service des tables

16. caterer
traiteur

More vocabulary

line cook: short-order cook
wait staff: servers, headwaiters, and runners

Ask your classmates. Share the answers.

1. Have you ever worked in a hotel? What did you do?
2. What is the hardest job in a hotel?
3. Would you prefer to stay at a hotel in the city or in the country?

185

1. dangerous
   dangereux
2. clinic
   clinique
3. budget
   budget
4. floor plan
   plan d'étage
5. contractor
   entrepreneur
6. electrical hazard
   danger électrique
7. wiring
   câblage
8. bricklayer
   maçon

A. **call in** sick
   se faire porter
   malade

Look at the picture. What do you see?

Answer the questions.

1. How many workers are there? How many are working?

2. Why did two workers call in sick?

3. What is dangerous at the construction site?

 Read the story.

A Bad Day at Work

Sam Lopez is the <u>contractor</u> for a new building. He makes the schedule and supervises the <u>budget</u>. He also solves problems. Today there are a lot of problems.

Two <u>bricklayers</u> <u>called in sick</u> this morning. Now Sam has only one bricklayer at work. One hour later, a construction worker fell. Now he has to go to the <u>clinic</u>. Sam always tells his workers to be careful. Construction work is <u>dangerous</u>. Sam's also worried because the new <u>wiring</u> is an <u>electrical hazard</u>.

Right now, the building owner is in Sam's office. Her new <u>floor plan</u> has 25 more offices. Sam has a headache. Maybe he needs to call in sick tomorrow.

Think about it.

1. What do you say when you can't come in to work? to school?

2. Imagine you are Sam. What do you tell the building owner? Why?

187

Schools and Subjects — Écoles et sujets

1. **preschool / nursery school**
   établissement préscolaire

2. **elementary school**
   école élémentaire / primaire

3. **middle school / junior high school**
   collège / école secondaire du 1er cycle

4. **high school**
   lycée / école secondaire du 2e cycle

5. **vocational school / technical school**
   école professionnelle / école de métiers

6. **community college**
   centre universitaire de 1er cycle

7. **college / university**
   collège / université

8. **adult school**
   centre d'éducation (de formation) des adultes / centre de formation continue (permanente)

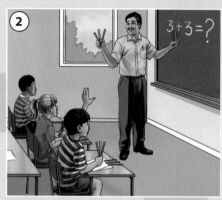

Listen and point. Take turns.

A: *Point to the preschool.*
B: *Point to the high school.*
A: *Point to the adult school.*

Dictate to your partner. Take turns.

A: *Write preschool.*
B: *Is that p-r-e-s-c-h-o-o-l?*
A: *Yes. That's right.*

188

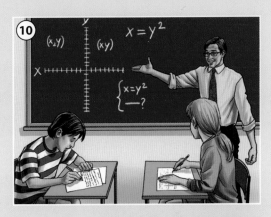

9. language arts
   arts du langage

10. math
    mathématiques

11. science
    science

12. history
    histoire

13. world languages
    langues du monde entier

14. ESL / ESOL
    anglais langue seconde

15. arts
    arts

16. music
    musique

17. physical education
    éducation physique

More vocabulary

core course: a subject students have to take. Math is a core course.

elective: a subject students choose to take. Art is an elective.

Pair practice. Make new conversations.

A: *I go to community college.*

B: *What subjects are you taking?*

A: *I'm taking history and science.*

189

English Composition　　　Composition anglaise

① factory

1. word
   mot

② I worked in a factory.

2. sentence
   phrase

③ Little by little, work and success came to me. My first job wasn't good. I worked in a small factory. Now, I help manage two factories.

3. paragraph
   paragraphe

④

4. essay
   rédaction

Parts of an Essay
Sections d'une rédaction

5. title
   titre
6. introduction
   introduction
7. body
   corps
8. conclusion
   conclusion
9. quotation
   citation
10. footnote
    note en bas
    de page

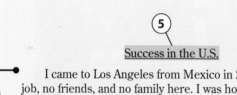

Carlos Lopez
Eng. Comp.
10/21/10

⑤ Success in the U.S.

⑥ I came to Los Angeles from Mexico in 2006. I had no job, no friends, and no family here. I was homesick and scared, but I did not go home. I took English classes (always at night) and I studied hard. I believed in my future success!

⑦ More than 400,000 new immigrants come to the U.S every year.[1] Most of us need to find work. During my first year here, my routine was the same: get up; look for work; go to class; go to bed. I had to take jobs with long hours and low pay. Often I had two or three jobs.

Little by little, work and success came to me. My first job wasn't good. I worked in a small factory. Now, I help manage two factories.

⑧ Hard work makes success possible. Henry David Thoreau said, **⑨** "Men are born to succeed, not fail." My story shows that he was right.

⑩ [1] U.S. Census

Punctuation
Ponctuation

11. period
    point
12. question mark
    point d'interrogation
13. exclamation mark
    point d'exclamation
14. comma
    virgule
15. quotation marks
    guillemets
16. apostrophe
    apostrophe
17. colon
    deux points
18. semicolon
    point virgule
19. parentheses
    parenthèses
20. hyphen
    trait d'union

Writing Rules　Règles d'écriture

A
Carlos
Mexico
Los Angeles

A. **Capitalize** names.
   Mettre des noms
   en majuscule.

B
Hard work makes success possible.

B. **Capitalize** the first letter in a sentence.
   Mettre la première lettre des phrases **en majuscule**.

C
I was homesick and scared, but I did not go home.

C. **Use** punctuation.
   Utiliser la ponctuation.

D
　I came to Los Angeles from Mexico in 2006. I had no job, no friends, and no family here. I was homesick and scared, but I did not go home. I took English classes (always at night) and I studied hard. I believed in my future success!

D. **Indent** the first sentence in a paragraph.
   Décaler la première phrase d'un paragraphe.

Ways to ask for suggestions on your compositions

What do you think of this <u>title</u>?
Is this <u>paragraph</u> OK? Is the <u>punctuation</u> correct?
Do you have any suggestions for the <u>conclusion</u>?

Pair practice. Make new conversations.

A: What do you think of this <u>title</u>?
B: *I think you need to <u>revise</u> it.*
A: *Thanks. Do you have any more suggestions?*

The Writing Process Le processus d'écriture

PREWRITING

E. Think about the assignment.
Penser au sujet.

F. Brainstorm ideas.
Trouver des idées.

G. Organize your ideas.
Organiser vos idées.

WRITING AND REVISING

H. Write a first draft.
Rédiger une version préliminaire.

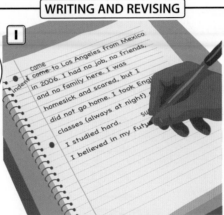

I. Edit. / Proofread.
Éditer. / Corriger.

J. Revise. / Rewrite.
Réviser. / Réécrire.

SHARING AND RESPONDING

K. Get feedback.
Recevoir des commentaires.

L. Write a final draft.
Rédiger une version finale.

M. Turn in your paper.
Rendre la rédaction.

Ask your classmates. Share the answers.

1. Do you like to write essays?
2. Which part of the writing process do you like best? least?

Think about it. Discuss.

1. In which jobs are writing skills important?
2. What tools can help you edit your writing?
3. What are some good subjects for essays?

191

Mathematics

Integers Nombres entiers

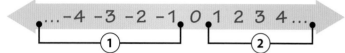

1. negative integers
entiers négatifs

2. positive integers
entiers positifs

Fractions Fractions

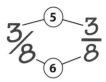

3. odd numbers
nombres impairs

4. even numbers
nombres pairs

5. numerator
numérateur

6. denominator
dénominateur

Math Operations Opérations mathématiques

A. add
ajouter

B. subtract
soustraire

C. multiply
multiplier

D. divide
diviser

7. sum
somme

8. difference
différence

9. product
produit

10. quotient
quotient

A Math Problem Un problème mathématique

11

Tom is 10 years older than Kim. Next year he will be twice as old as Kim. How old is Tom this year?

12 — x = Kim's age now
$x + 10$ = Tom's age now
$x + 1$ = Kim's age next year
$2(x + 1)$ = Tom's age next year

$x + 10 + 1 = 2(x + 1)$
$x + 11 = 2x + 2$ **13**
$11 - 2 = 2x - x$

$x = 9$, Kim is 9, Tom is 19 **14**

15

horizontal axis

vertical axis

11. word problem
problème de mot

12. variable
variable

13. equation
équation

14. solution
solution

15. graph
graphique

Types of Math Types de mathématiques

How much are they?

How many do I need?

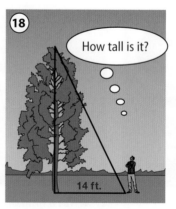
How tall is it?
14 ft.

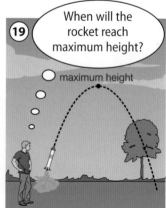
When will the rocket reach maximum height?
maximum height

x = the sale price
$x = 79.00 - .40(79.00)$
$x = \$47.40$

area of path = 24 square ft.
area of brick = 2 square ft.
24/2 = 12 bricks

$\tan 63° = $ height / 14 feet
height = 14 feet $(\tan 63°)$
height $\simeq 27.48$ feet

$s(t) = -\frac{1}{2}gt^2 + V_0 t + h$
$s'(t) = -gt + V_0 = 0$
$t = V_0 / g$

16. algebra
algèbre

17. geometry
géométrie

18. trigonometry
trigonométrie

19. calculus
calcul

192

Lines Lignes

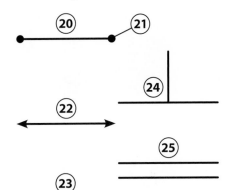

Angles Angles

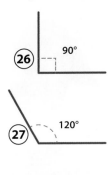

Shapes Formes

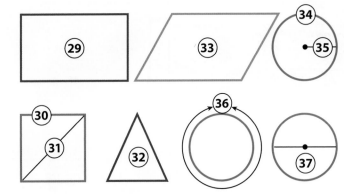

20. line segment
segment de ligne

21. endpoint
point d'extrémité

22. straight line
ligne droite

23. curved line
ligne courbée

24. perpendicular lines
lignes perpendiculaires

25. parallel lines
lignes parallèles

26. right angle / 90° angle
angle droit / angle à 90°

27. obtuse angle
angle obtus

28. acute angle
angle aigu

29. rectangle
rectangle

30. square
carré

31. diagonal
diagonale

32. triangle
triangle

33. parallelogram
parallélogramme

34. circle
cercle

35. radius
rayon

36. circumference
circonférence

37. diameter
diamètre

Geometric Solids
Solides géométriques

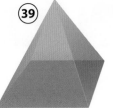

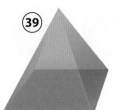

38. cube
cube

39. pyramid
pyramide

40. cone
cône

41. cylinder
cylindre

42. sphere
sphère

Measuring Area and Volume
Aire et volume

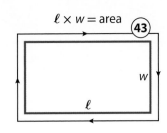

$\ell \times w =$ area

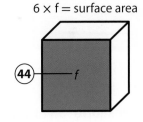

$6 \times f =$ surface area

43. perimeter
périmètre

44. face
face

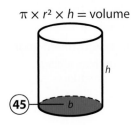

$\pi \times r^2 \times h =$ volume

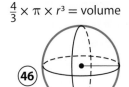

$\frac{4}{3} \times \pi \times r^3 =$ volume

$\pi \approx 3.14$

45. base
base

46. pi
pi

Ask your classmates. Share the answers.

1. Are you good at math?

2. Which types of math are easy for you?

3. Which types of math are difficult for you?

Think about it. Discuss.

1. What's the best way to learn mathematics?

2. How can you find the area of your classroom?

3. Which jobs use math? Which don't?

Biology Biologie

1. organisms
   organismes

2. biologist
   biologiste

3. slide
   lame

4. cell
   cellule

5. cell wall
   paroi cellulaire

6. cell membrane
   membrane cellulaire

7. nucleus
   noyau

8. chromosome
   chromosome

9. cytoplasm
   cytoplasme

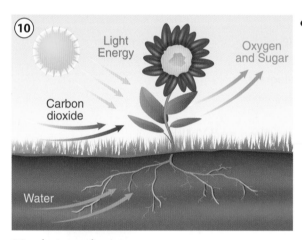

Light Energy

Oxygen and Sugar

Carbon dioxide

Water

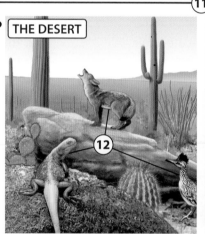

THE DESERT

THE OCEAN

10. photosynthesis
    photosynthèse

11. habitat
    habitat

12. vertebrates
    vertébrés

13. invertebrates
    invertébrés

A Microscope Un microscope

14. eyepiece
    oculaire

15. revolving nosepiece
    tourelle porte-objectif

16. objective
    objectif

17. stage
    platine

18. diaphragm
    diaphragme

19. light source
    source lumineuse

20. base
    socle

21. stage clips
    pinces de platine

22. fine adjustment knob
    bouton de réglage micrométrique

23. arm
    bras

24. coarse adjustment knob
    bouton de réglage macrométrique

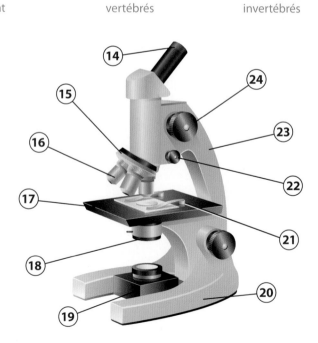

Chemistry Chimie

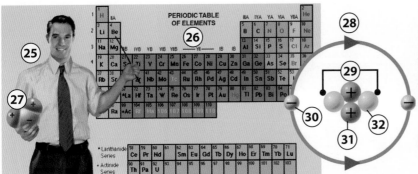

25. chemist
chimiste

26. periodic table
tableau périodique

27. molecule
molécule

28. atom
atome

29. nucleus
noyau

30. electron
électron

31. proton
proton

32. neutron
neutron

33. physicist
physicien

Physics Physique

34. formula
formule

35. prism
prisme

36. magnet
aimant

A Science Lab Un laboratoire scientifique

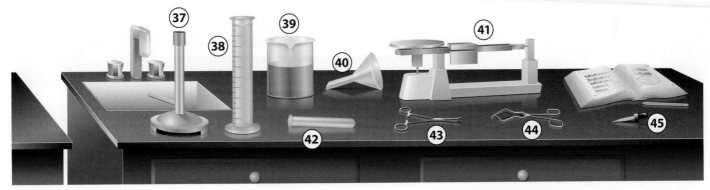

37. Bunsen burner
brûleur Bensen / bec Bensen

38. graduated cylinder
cylindre gradué / éprouvette graduée

39. beaker
bécher

40. funnel
entonnoir

41. balance / scale
balance

42. test tube
éprouvette

43. forceps
forceps

44. crucible tongs
pince à creusets

45. dropper
compte-gouttes

An Experiment Une expérience

A. State a hypothesis.
Faire une hypothèse.

B. Do an experiment.
Faire une expérience.

C. Observe.
Observer.

D. Record the results.
Consigner les résultats.

E. Draw a conclusion.
Tirer des conclusions.

195

Desktop Computer Ordinateur de bureau

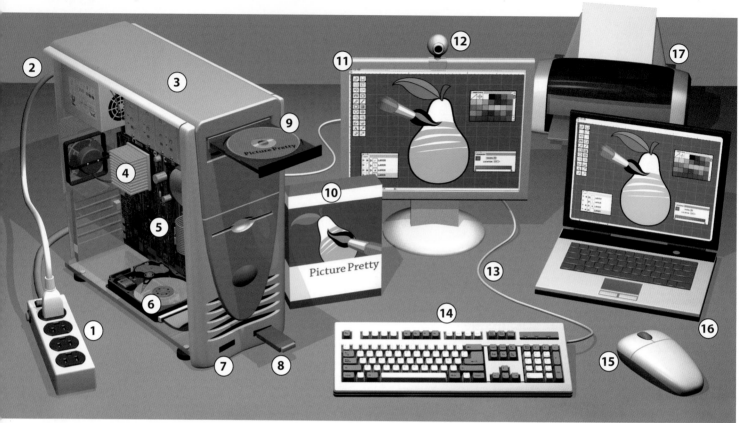

1. surge protector
   limiteur de surtension

2. power cord
   cordon d'alimentation

3. tower
   tour

4. microprocessor / CPU
   microprocesseur /
   unité centrale

5. motherboard
   carte mère

6. hard drive
   disque dur

7. USB port
   port USB

8. flash drive
   lecteur flash

9. DVD and CD-ROM drive
   lecteur de CD et DVD

10. software
    logiciel

11. monitor / screen
    moniteur / écran

12. webcam
    webcaméra

13. cable
    câble

14. keyboard
    clavier

15. mouse
    souris

16. laptop
    ordinateur portable

17. printer
    imprimante

Keyboarding Saisir au clavier

A

List the vocabulary:
1. towers |

A. **type**
   taper

B

List the vocabulary:
1. towers

B. **select**
   sélectionner

C

List the vocabulary:
1. tower |

C. **delete**
   supprimer

D

List the vocabulary:
1. tower

D. **go to** the next line
   aller à la ligne

Navigating a Webpage Naviguer sur une page Web

1. **menu bar**
   barre de menus

2. **back button**
   bouton Précédent

3. **forward button**
   bouton Suivant

4. **URL / website address**
   adresse URL / Web

5. **search box**
   boîte de recherche

6. **search engine**
   moteur de recherche

7. **tab**
   onglet

8. **drop-down menu**
   menu déroulant

9. **pop-up ad**
   fenêtre pub

10. **links**
    liens

11. **video player**
    lecteur de vidéo

12. **pointer**
    pointeur

13. **text box**
    boîte de texte

14. **cursor**
    curseur

15. **scroll bar**
    barre de défilement

Logging on and Sending Email Se connecter et envoyer un courriel

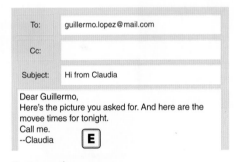

A. **type** your password
   taper votre mot de passe

B. **click** "sign in"
   cliquer sur « se connecter »

C. **address** the email
   adresser le courriel

D. **type** the subject
   taper l'objet

E. **type** the message
   taper le message

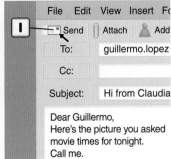

F. **check** your spelling
   vérifier l'orthographe

G. **attach** a picture
   joindre une photo

H. **attach** a file
   joindre un fichier

I. **send** the email
   envoyer un courriel

Colonial Period Période coloniale

1. **thirteen colonies**
   treize colonies

2. **colonists**
   colons

3. **Native Americans**
   Autochtones
   d'Amérique du Nord

4. **slave**
   esclave

5. **Declaration of Independence**
   Déclaration d'indépendance

6. **First Continental Congress**
   Premier congrès continental

7. **founders**
   fondateurs

8. **Revolutionary War**
   Guerre de
   l'Indépendance

9. **redcoat**
   Habit rouge

10. **minuteman**
    minuteman

11. **first president**
    premier
    président

12. **Constitution**
    constitution

13. **Bill of Rights**
    La Déclaration
    des droits

Western Expansion
1803 – 1893

Civil War
1861 – 1865

World War I
1914 – 1918

Jazz Age
1920 – 1929

World War II
1941 – 1945

Civil Rights Movement
1954 – 1972

Information Age
1959 – now

1800   1850   1900   1950   2000 →

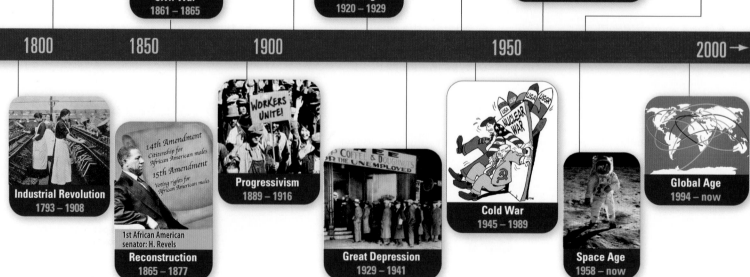

Industrial Revolution
1793 – 1908

1st African American
senator: H. Revels
Reconstruction
1865 – 1877

Progressivism
1889 – 1916

Great Depression
1929 – 1941

Cold War
1945 – 1989

Space Age
1958 – now

Global Age
1994 – now

Civilizations Civilisations

Pyramids | Parthenon
Times Square

Caesar
Qin Shi Huang

King Henry VIII
Queen Elizabeth I

Juarez

Mussolini | Churchill

1. **ancient**
   ancien

2. **modern**
   moderne

3. **emperor**
   empereur

4. **monarch**
   monarque

5. **president**
   président

6. **dictator**
   dictateur

7. **prime minister**
   premier ministre

Historical Terms Termes historiques

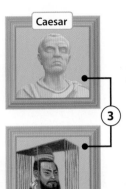
Vikings | Astronauts

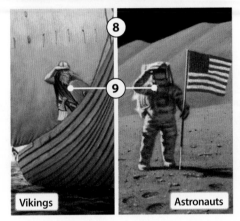

8. **exploration**
   exploration

9. **explorer**
   explorateur

10. **war**
    guerre

11. **army**
    armée

12. **immigration**
    immigration

13. **immigrant**
    immigrant

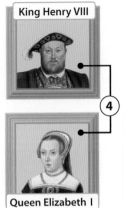
Mozart | Duke Ellington

Susan B. Anthony | César Chávez

Edison | Camarena

14. **composer**
    compositeur

15. **composition**
    composition

16. **political movement**
    mouvement politique

17. **activist**
    activiste

18. **inventor**
    inventeur

19. **invention**
    invention

Amérique du Nord et
Amérique centrale

ATLANTIC OCEAN

BERMUDA ISLANDS (UK)

BAHAMAS

Newfoundland and Labrador

Labrador Sea

GREENLAND

Baffin Bay

Devon Island

Ellesmere Island

Baffin Island

Prince Edward Island

⑥ Nova Scotia

New Brunswick

⑪

Vermont
New Hampshire
Massachusetts
Rhode Island
Connecticut

Maine

Delaware
Maryland
WASHINGTON, D.C.

New Jersey

⑤ Québec

New York

⑩ Pennsylvania

OTTAWA ★

West Virginia

Virginia

North Carolina

South Carolina

Georgia

Florida

Hudson Bay

④ Ontario

Michigan

Ohio

Kentucky

Tennessee

Alabama

Mississippi

Louisiana

Gulf of Mexico

Victoria Island

Banks Island

Nunavut

Manitoba

③ Saskatchewan

CANADA

Minnesota

Wisconsin

⑨

Illinois Indiana

Iowa

Missouri

Arkansas

Northwest Territories

①

Alberta

North Dakota

South Dakota

Nebraska

Kansas

Oklahoma

Texas

② British Columbia

Montana

⑧ Wyoming

Colorado

New Mexico

⑫

Coahuila

Nuevo León

Chihuahua

⑮

MÉXICO

Yukon

Idaho

Utah

Arizona

⑭

Sonora

Baja California Norte

Baja California Sur

Sinaloa

Gulf of California

Washington

Oregon

⑦

Nevada

California

UNITED STATES OF AMERICA

Alaska (US)

Beaufort Sea

ARCTIC OCEAN

Gulf of Alaska

Aleutian Islands

Bering Sea

Hawaii (US)

PACIFIC OCEAN

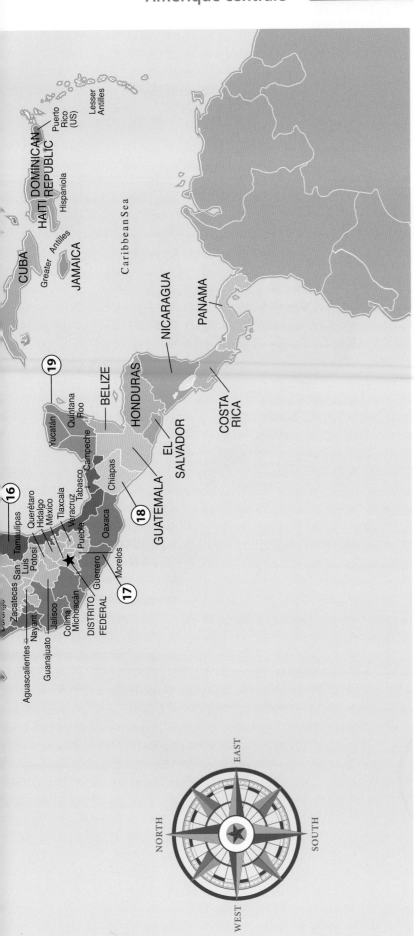

Puerto Rico (US)

Lesser Antilles

CUBA

HAITI DOMINICAN REPUBLIC

Hispaniola

Greater Antilles

JAMAICA

Caribbean Sea

NICARAGUA

PANAMA

BELIZE

Quintana Roo

Yucatán

Campeche

HONDURAS

Tabasco

Chiapas

EL SALVADOR

COSTA RICA

Veracruz

Puebla

Oaxaca

GUATEMALA

Tlaxcala

México

Hidalgo

Querétaro

San Luis Potosí

Tamaulipas

Zacatecas

Morelos

Guerrero

DISTRITO FEDERAL

Michoacán

Colima

Jalisco

Nayarit

Guanajuato

Aguascalientes

19 **16** **18** **17**

NORTH

EAST

SOUTH

WEST

Regions of Mexico
Régions du Mexique

14. **The Pacific Northwest**
    Le nord-ouest du Pacifique

15. **The Plateau of Mexico**
    Le plateau mexicain

16. **The Gulf Coastal Plain**
    La plaine côtière du Golfe

17. **The Southern Uplands**
    Les hautes terres du sud

18. **The Chiapas Highlands**
    Les hautes terres du Chiapas

19. **The Yucatan Peninsula**
    La péninsule du Yucatan

Regions of the United States
Régions des États-Unis

7. **The Pacific States / the West Coast**
   Les états du Pacifique / la côte ouest

8. **The Rocky Mountain States**
   Les états des Rocheuses

9. **The Midwest**
   Le Midwest

10. **The Mid-Atlantic States**
    Les états du centre du littoral de l'Atlantique

11. **New England**
    Nouvelle-Angleterre

12. **The Southwest**
    Le sud-ouest

13. **The Southeast / the South**
    Le sud-est / le sud

Regions of Canada
Régions du Canada

1. **Northern Canada**
   Nord du Canada

2. **British Columbia**
   Colombie Britannique

3. **The Prairie Provinces**
   Les provinces des Prairies

4. **Ontario**
   Ontario

5. **Québec**
   Québec

6. **The Maritime Provinces**
   Les provinces maritimes

Continents
Continents

1. **North America**
   Amérique du Nord
2. **South America**
   Amérique du Sud
3. **Europe**
   Europe
4. **Asia**
   Asie
5. **Africa**
   Afrique
6. **Australia**
   Australie
7. **Antarctica**
   Antarctique

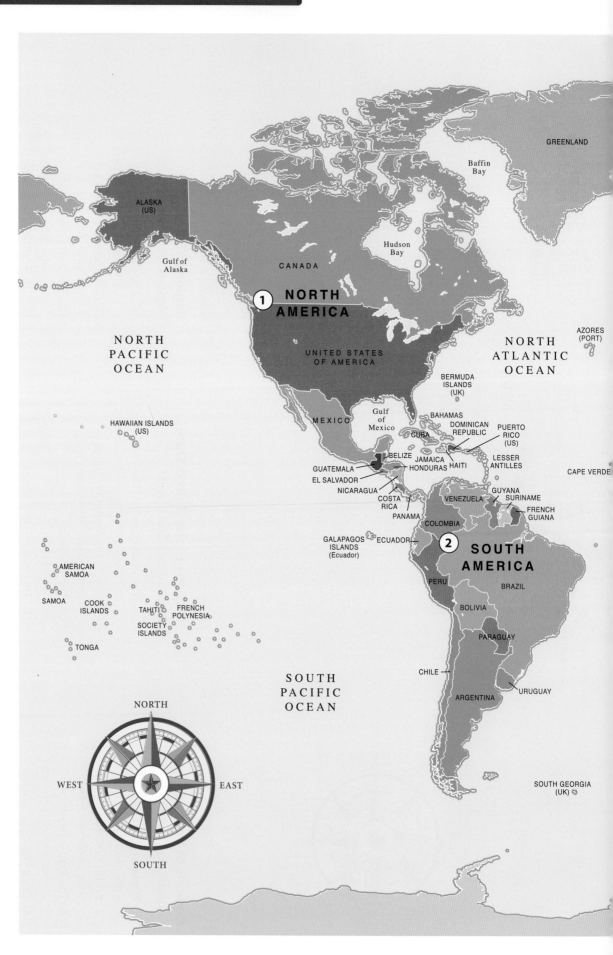

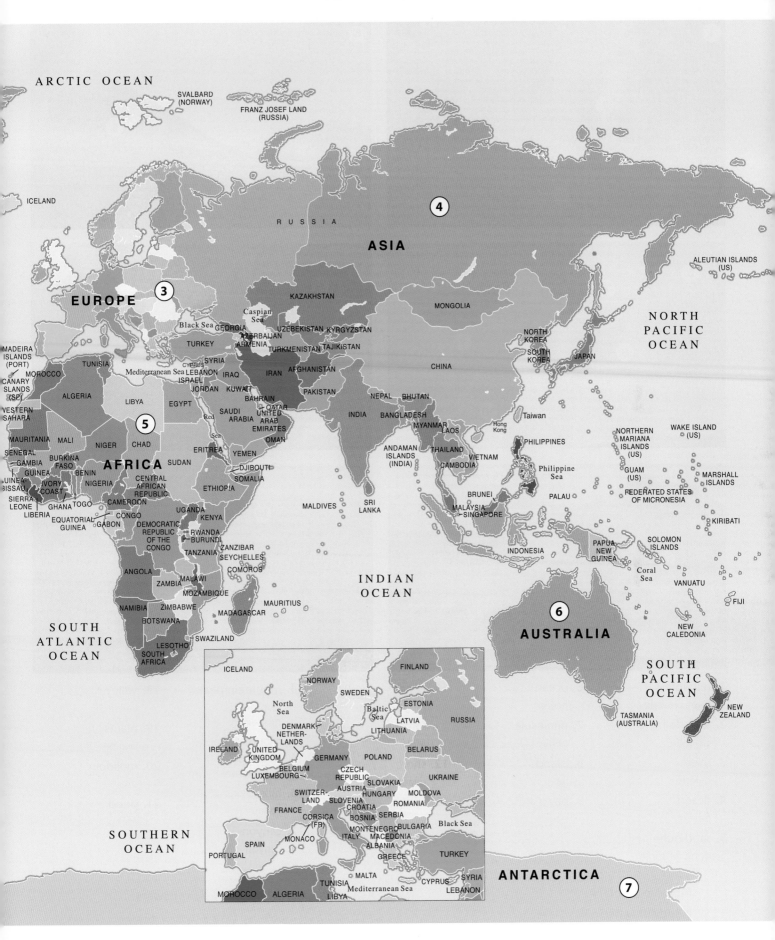

ARCTIC OCEAN

SVALBARD
(NORWAY)

FRANZ JOSEF LAND
(RUSSIA)

ICELAND

R U S S I A

4

ASIA

ALEUTIAN ISLANDS
(US)

KAZAKHSTAN

MONGOLIA

NORTH
PACIFIC
OCEAN

3

EUROPE

Caspian
Sea

Black Sea

GEORGIA

UZBEKISTAN KYRGYZSTAN

NORTH
KOREA

TURKEY

AZERBAIJAN
ARMENIA

TURKMENISTAN TAJIKISTAN

SOUTH
KOREA

JAPAN

MADEIRA
ISLANDS
(PORT)

SYRIA

CYPRUS

LEBANON
ISRAEL

IRAQ

AFGHANISTAN

CHINA

MOROCCO

TUNISIA

Mediterranean Sea

IRAN

CANARY
SLANDS
(SP)

ALGERIA

LIBYA

JORDAN KUWAIT

BAHRAIN

PAKISTAN

Taiwan

WESTERN
SAHARA

EGYPT

Red
Sea

SAUDI
ARABIA

QATAR
UNITED
ARAB
EMIRATES

NEPAL BHUTAN

INDIA BANGLADESH

Hong
Kong

NORTHERN
MARIANA
ISLANDS
(US)

WAKE ISLAND
(US)

5

MAURITANIA MALI

NIGER

CHAD

OMAN

MYANMAR

LAOS

GUAM
(US)

MARSHALL
ISLANDS

SENEGAL

BURKINA
FASO

BENIN

ERITREA

YEMEN

ANDAMAN
ISLANDS
(INDIA)

THAILAND

PHILIPPINES

GAMBIA

AFRICA

SUDAN

DJIBOUTI

VIETNAM

Philippine
Sea

FEDERATED STATES
OF MICRONESIA

UINEA
BISSAU

NIGERIA

CENTRAL
AFRICAN
REPUBLIC

SOMALIA

MALDIVES

SRI
LANKA

CAMBODIA

PALAU

KIRIBATI

SIERRA
LEONE

IVORY
COAST

GHANA TOGO

CAMEROON

ETHIOPIA

BRUNEI

LIBERIA

EQUATORIAL
GUINEA

GABON

CONGO

UGANDA

KENYA

MALAYSIA
SINGAPORE

DEMOCRATIC
REPUBLIC
OF THE
CONGO

RWANDA
BURUNDI

SOLOMON
ISLANDS

INDONESIA

PAPUA
NEW
GUINEA

TANZANIA

ZANZIBAR

SEYCHELLES

INDIAN
OCEAN

Coral
Sea

VANUATU

ANGOLA

ZAMBIA

MALAWI

COMOROS

FIJI

MOZAMBIQUE

NAMIBIA

ZIMBABWE

MAURITIUS

MADAGASCAR

6

SOUTH
ATLANTIC
OCEAN

BOTSWANA

SWAZILAND

LESOTHO
SOUTH
AFRICA

AUSTRALIA

NEW
CALEDONIA

SOUTH
PACIFIC
OCEAN

TASMANIA
(AUSTRALIA)

NEW
ZEALAND

ICELAND

FINLAND

NORWAY

SWEDEN

North
Sea

ESTONIA

Baltic
Sea

LATVIA

RUSSIA

IRELAND

UNITED
KINGDOM

DENMARK
NETHER-
LANDS

LITHUANIA

BELARUS

SOUTHERN
OCEAN

BELGIUM

GERMANY

POLAND

LUXEMBOURG

CZECH
REPUBLIC

SLOVAKIA

UKRAINE

SWITZER-
LAND

AUSTRIA

HUNGARY

MOLDOVA

FRANCE

SLOVENIA
CROATIA

ROMANIA

CORSICA
(FR)

BOSNIA

SERBIA

Black Sea

MONTENEGRO

BULGARIA

SPAIN

MONACO

ITALY

MACEDONIA

ALBANIA

PORTUGAL

GREECE

TURKEY

MALTA

ANTARCTICA

SYRIA

MOROCCO

ALGERIA

TUNISIA

Mediterranean Sea

CYPRUS

LEBANON

LIBYA

7

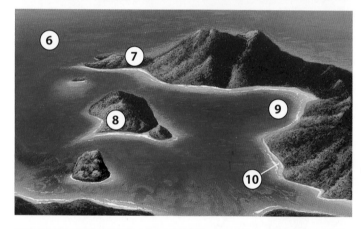

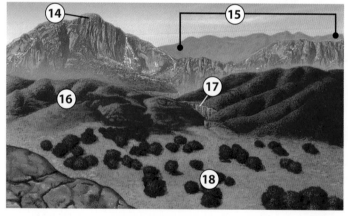

1. rain forest
   forêt pluviale

2. waterfall
   cascade

3. river
   rivière

4. desert
   désert

5. sand dune
   dune de sable

6. ocean
   océan

7. peninsula
   péninsule

8. island
   île

9. bay
   baie

10. beach
    plage

11. forest
    forêt

12. shore
    rivage

13. lake
    lac

14. mountain peak
    sommet de montagne

15. mountain range
    chaîne de montagnes

16. hills
    collines

17. canyon
    canyon

18. valley
    vallée

19. plains
    plaines

20. meadow
    pré

21. pond
    étang

More vocabulary

a body of water: a river, lake, or ocean

stream / creek: a very small river

Ask your classmates. Share the answers.

1. Would you rather live near a river or a lake?

2. Would you rather travel through a forest or a desert?

3. How often do you go to the beach or the shore?

204

The Solar System and the Planets Le système solaire et les planètes

Sun

Asteroid Belt

Orbit

1. Mercury Mercure	**3.** Earth Terre	**5.** Jupiter Jupiter	**7.** Uranus Uranus
2. Venus Vénus	**4.** Mars Mars	**6.** Saturn Saturne	**8.** Neptune Neptune

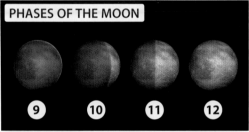

PHASES OF THE MOON

SPACE

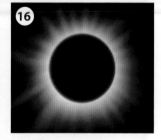

9. new moon nouvelle lune	**11.** quarter moon quart de lune	**13.** star étoile	**15.** galaxy galaxie
10. crescent moon croissant de lune	**12.** full moon pleine lune	**14.** constellation constellation	**16.** solar eclipse éclipse solaire

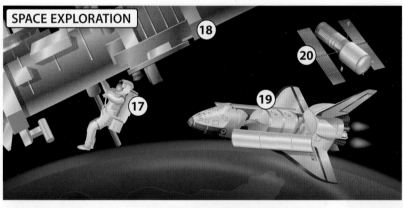

SPACE EXPLORATION

ASTRONOMY

17. astronaut astronaute	**19.** space shuttle navette spatiale	**21.** observatory observatoire	**23.** telescope télescope
18. space station station spatiale	**20.** satellite satellite	**22.** astronomer astronome	**24.** comet comète

More vocabulary

solar eclipse: when the moon is between the earth and the sun
Big Dipper: a famous part of the constellation Ursa Major
Sirius: the brightest star in the night sky

Ask your classmates. Share the answers.

1. How do you feel when you look at the night sky?
2. Can you name one or more constellations?
3. Do you want to travel in space?

205

MySpot.Edu | Help | SignOut

Home | Search | Invite | Mail |

All Adelia's photos

I loved Art History.

My last economics lesson

Marching Band is great!

The photographer was upset.

We look good!

I get my diploma.

Dad and his digital camera

1. **photographer**
   photographe

2. **funny photo**
   photo drôle

3. **serious photo**
   photo sérieuse

4. **guest speaker**
   conférencier
   (conférencière)
   invité(e)

5. **podium**
   podium

6. **ceremony**
   cérémonie

7. **cap**
   coiffe

8. **gown**
   toge

A. **take** a picture
   prendre une photo

B. **cry**
   pleurer

C. **celebrate**
   célébrer

206

Videos | Music | Classifieds |

People	Comments	
Sara	**June 29th 8:19 p.m.** Great pictures! What a day!	Delete
Zannie baby	**June 30th 10 a.m.** Love the funny photo.	Delete

I'm behind the mayor.

We're all very happy.

Look at the pictures. What do you see?

Answer the questions.

1. How many people are wearing caps and gowns?

2. How many people are being funny? How many are being serious?

3. Who is standing at the podium?

4. Why are the graduates throwing their caps in the air?

Read the story.

A Graduation

Look at these great photos on my web page! The first three are from my favorite classes, but the other pictures are from graduation day.

There are two pictures of my classmates in <u>caps</u> and <u>gowns</u>. In the first picture, we're laughing and the <u>photographer</u> is upset. In the second photo, we're serious. I like the <u>serious photo</u>, but I love the <u>funny photo</u>!

There's also a picture of our <u>guest speaker</u>, the mayor. She is standing at the <u>podium</u>. Next, you can see me at the graduation <u>ceremony</u>. My dad wanted to <u>take a picture</u> of me with my diploma. That's my mom next to him. She <u>cries</u> when she's happy.

After the ceremony, everyone was happy, but no one cried. We wanted to <u>celebrate</u> and we did!

Think about it.

1. What kinds of ceremonies are important for children? for teens? for adults?

2. Imagine you are the guest speaker at a graduation. What will you say to the graduates?

Nature Center

Centre d'initiation à la nature

1. trees
   arbres
2. soil
   terreau
3. path
   chemin
4. bird
   oiseau
5. plants
   plantes
6. rock
   pierre
7. flowers
   fleurs

OAK

WILLOW

ELM

PLANT SALE 50% OFF

$7.

Listen and point. Take turns.

A: *Point to the trees.*
B: *Point to a bird.*
A: *Point to the flowers.*

Dictate to your partner. Take turns.

A: *Write it's a tree.*
B: *Let me check that. I-t-'s -a- t-r-e-e?*
A: *Yes, that's right.*

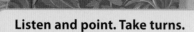

LOOK FOR ME!

ASH

GLASS PLASTIC ONLY

PLEASE DON'T FEED

OPEN DAILY 9-5

❀LILLO❀
Nature Center

8. sun
   soleil
9. sky
   ciel
10. mammals
    mammifères
11. insects
    insectes
12. nest
    nid
13. water
    eau
14. fish
    poisson

Ways to talk about nature

Look at the sky! Isn't it beautiful?
Did you see the fish / insects?
It's / They're so interesting.

Pair practice. Make new conversations.

A: *Do you know the name of that yellow flower?*
B: *I think it's a sunflower.*
A: *Oh, and what about that blue bird?*

PARTS OF A TREE

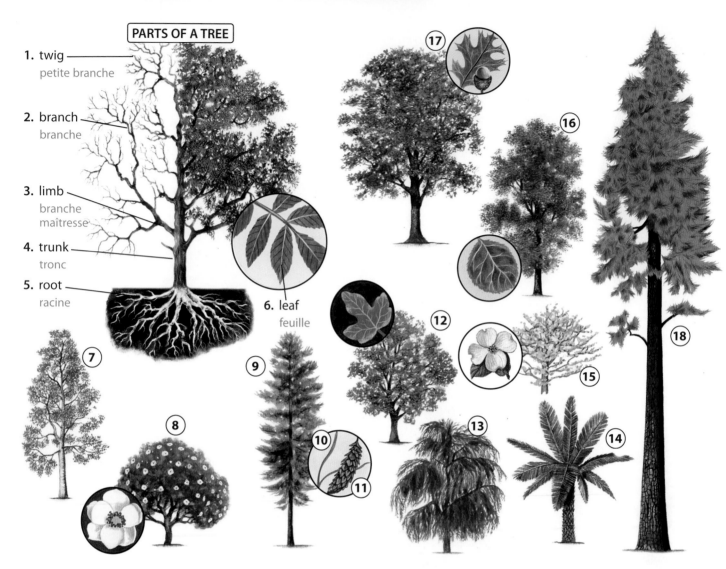

1. twig
petite branche

2. branch
branche

3. limb
branche maîtresse

4. trunk
tronc

5. root
racine

6. leaf
feuille

7. birch bouleau	**10.** needle aiguille	**13.** willow saule	**16.** elm orme
8. magnolia magnolia	**11.** pinecone cône de pin	**14.** palm palmier	**17.** oak chêne
9. pine pin	**12.** maple érable	**15.** dogwood cornouiller	**18.** redwood séquoia

Plants Plantes

19. holly
houx

20. berries
cerises

21. cactus
cactus

22. vine
vigne

23. poison sumac
sumac lustré

24. poison oak
sumac à feuille de chêne

25. poison ivy
sumac vénéneux /
herbe à puce

Parts of a Flower Parties d'une fleur

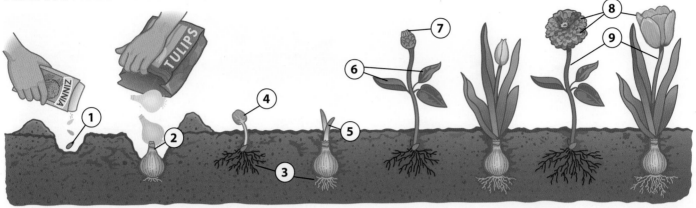

1. seed
   graine / semence

2. bulb
   bulbe

3. roots
   racines

4. seedling
   semis

5. shoot
   pousse

6. leaves
   feuilles

7. bud
   bourgeon

8. petals
   pétales

9. stems
   tiges

10. sunflower
    tournesol

11. tulip
    tulipe

12. hibiscus
    hibiscus

13. marigold
    souci

14. daisy
    marguerite

15. rose
    rose

16. iris
    iris

17. crocus
    crocus

18. gardenia
    gardénia

19. orchid
    orchidée

20. carnation
    œillet

21. chrysanthemum
    chrysanthème

22. jasmine
    jasmin

23. violet
    violette

24. poinsettia
    poinsettia

25. daffodil
    jonquille

26. lily
    lis

27. houseplant
    plante d'intérieur

28. bouquet
    bouquet

29. thorn
    épine

Sea Animals Animaux marins

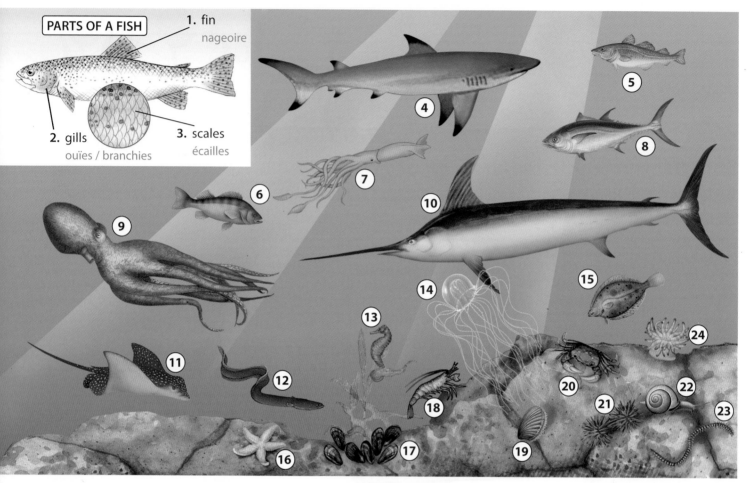

PARTS OF A FISH

1. fin
   nageoire
2. gills
   ouïes / branchies
3. scales
   écailles

4. shark
   requin

5. cod
   morue

6. bass
   perche (eau douce) /
   bar (eau salée)

7. squid
   calmar

8. tuna
   thon

9. octopus
   poulpe / pieuvre

10. swordfish
    poisson-épée /
    espadon

11. ray
    raie

12. eel
    anguille

13. seahorse
    hippocampe

14. jellyfish
    méduse

15. flounder
    flet / poisson plat

16. starfish
    étoile de mer

17. mussel
    moule

18. shrimp
    crevette

19. scallop
    pétoncle / coquille
    Saint-Jacques

20. crab
    crabe

21. sea urchin
    oursin

22. snail
    escargot

23. worm
    ver

24. sea anemone
    anémone de mer

Amphibians Amphibiens

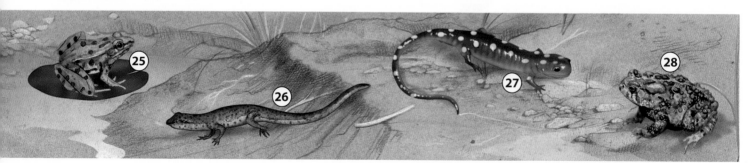

25. frog
    grenouille

26. newt
    triton

27. salamander
    salamandre

28. toad
    crapaud

Sea Mammals Mammifères marins

29. whale baleine	**31.** dolphin dauphin	**33.** sea lion otarie	**35.** sea otter loutre de mer
30. porpoise marsouin	**32.** walrus morse	**34.** seal phoque	

Reptiles Reptiles

36. alligator alligator	**38.** rattlesnake crotale / serpent à sonnettes	**40.** lizard lézard	**42.** tortoise tortue terrestre
37. crocodile crocodile	**39.** garter snake thamnophis	**41.** cobra cobra	**43.** turtle tortue

PARTS OF A BIRD

1. wing
aile

3. beak / bill
bec

4. feather
plume

2. claw
griffe / serre

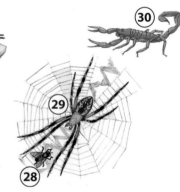

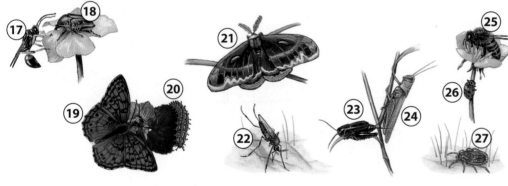

5. owl
hibou / chouette

6. blue jay
geai bleu

7. sparrow
moineau

8. woodpecker
pic

9. eagle
aigle

10. hummingbird
oiseau-mouche / colibri

11. penguin
pingouin

12. duck
canard

13. goose
oie

14. peacock
paon

15. pigeon
pigeon

16. robin
rouge-gorge / merle américain

Insects and Arachnids   Insectes et arachnides

17. wasp
guêpe

18. beetle
scarabée / coléoptère

19. butterfly
papillon

20. caterpillar
chenille

21. moth
papillon de nuit

22. mosquito
moustique

23. cricket
cricket / grillon

24. grasshopper
sauterelle

25. honeybee
abeille

26. ladybug
coccinelle

27. tick
tique

28. fly
mouche

29. spider
araignée

30. scorpion
scorpion

Domestic Animals and Rodents

Farm Animals Animaux de la ferme

1. cow
vache

2. pig
cochon

3. donkey
âne

4. horse
cheval

5. goat
chèvre

6. sheep
mouton

7. rooster
coq

8. hen
poule

Pets Animaux de compagnie

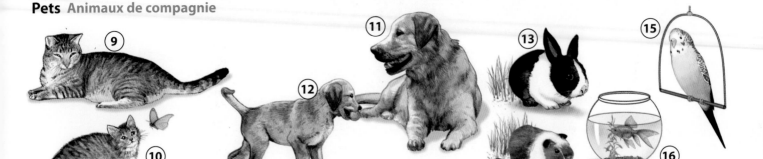

9. cat
chat

10. kitten
chaton

11. dog
chien

12. puppy
chiot

13. rabbit
lapin

14. guinea pig
cobaye

15. parakeet
perruche

16. goldfish
poisson rouge

Rodents Rongeurs

17. rat
rat

18. mouse
souris

19. gopher
gaufre / gauphre

20. chipmunk
tamia

21. squirrel
écureuil

22. prairie dog
chien de prairie

More vocabulary

domesticated: animals that work for and / or live with people

wild: animals that live away from people

Ask your classmates. Share the answers.

1. Have you worked with farm animals? Which ones?
2. Are you afraid of rodents? Which ones?
3. Do you have a pet? What kind?

215

1. **moose**
   élan / orignal

2. **mountain lion**
   couguar / puma

3. **coyote**
   coyote

4. **opossum**
   opossum

5. **wolf**
   loup

6. **buffalo / bison**
   bison

7. **bat**
   chauve-souris

8. **armadillo**
   tatou

9. **beaver**
   castor

10. **porcupine**
    porc-épic

11. **bear**
    ours

12. **skunk**
    mouffette

13. **raccoon**
    raton laveur

14. **deer**
    chevreuil

15. **fox**
    renard

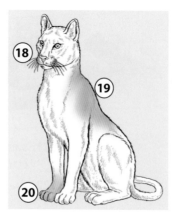

16. **antlers**
    ramure

17. **hooves**
    sabots

18. **whiskers**
    moustaches

19. **coat / fur**
    fourrure

20. **paw**
    patte

21. **horn**
    corne

22. **tail**
    queue

23. **quill**
    piquant

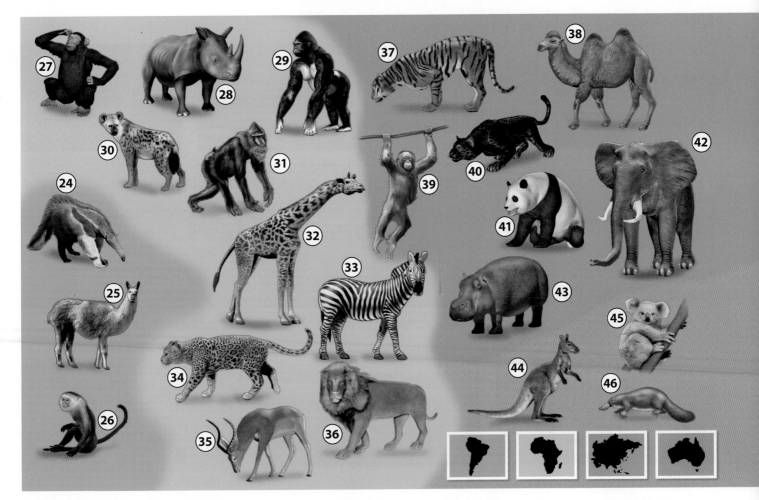

24. anteater tamanoir / fourmilier	**29.** gorilla gorille	**34.** leopard léopard	**39.** orangutan orang-outan	**44.** kangaroo kangourou
25. llama lama	**30.** hyena hyène	**35.** antelope antilope	**40.** panther panthère	**45.** koala koala
26. monkey singe	**31.** baboon babouin	**36.** lion lion	**41.** panda panda	**46.** platypus ornithorynque
27. chimpanzee chimpanzé	**32.** giraffe girafe	**37.** tiger tigre	**42.** elephant éléphant	
28. rhinoceros rhinocéros	**33.** zebra zèbre	**38.** camel chameau	**43.** hippopotamus hippopotame	

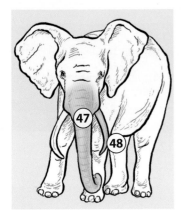

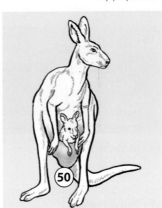

47. trunk <br> trompe

48. tusk <br> défense

49. mane <br> crinière

50. pouch <br> poche

51. hump <br> bosse

Energy Sources — Sources d'énergie

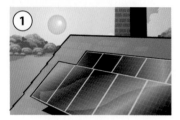

1. solar energy
énergie solaire

2. wind power
énergie éolienne

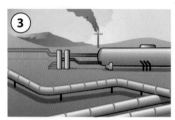

3. natural gas
gaz naturel

4. coal
charbon

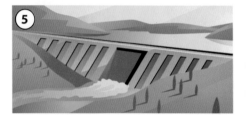

5. hydroelectric power
énergie hydroélectrique

6. oil / petroleum
pétrole

7. geothermal energy
énergie géothermique

8. nuclear energy
énergie nucléaire

9. biomass / bioenergy
biomasse / bioénergie

10. fusion
fusion

Pollution — Pollution

11. air pollution / smog
pollution de l'air

12. hazardous waste
déchets dangereux

13. acid rain
pluie acide

14. water pollution
pollution de l'eau

15. radiation
radioactivité

16. pesticide poisoning
pollution par les pesticides

17. oil spill
marée noire

Ask your classmates. Share the answers.

1. What types of things do you recycle?
2. What types of energy sources are in your area?
3. What types of pollution do you worry about?

Think about it. Discuss.

1. How can you save energy in the summer? winter?
2. What are some other ways that people can conserve energy or prevent pollution?

Ways to Conserve Energy and Resources   Méthodes de conservation d'énergie et des ressources

A. reduce trash
réduire la quantité de déchets

B. reuse shopping bags
réutiliser les sacs à provisions

C. recycle
recycler

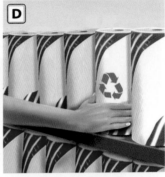

D. buy recycled products
acheter des produits recyclés

E. save water
conserver l'eau

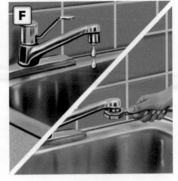

F. fix leaky faucets
réparer les robinets qui fuient

G. turn off lights
éteindre la lumière

H. use energy-efficient bulbs
utiliser des ampoules écoénergétiques

I. carpool
faire du covoiturage

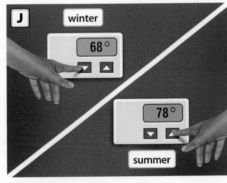

J. adjust the thermostat
régler le thermostat

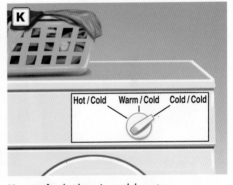

K. wash clothes in cold water
laver les vêtements dans de l'eau froide

L. don't litter
ne pas jeter des ordures

M. compost food scraps
composter les rebuts alimentaires

N. plant a tree
planter un arbre

219

Yosemite
NATIONAL PARK

Dry Tortugas
NATIONAL PARK

Half Dome ①

Fort Jefferson

②

④

③

⑤

1. landmarks
   points d'intérêt

2. park ranger
   conservateur de parc

3. wildlife
   faune et flore sauvage

4. ferry
   ferry

5. coral
   corail

6. cave
   grotte

7. caverns
   grottes / cavernes

A. **take** a tour
   faire un excursion

220

CARLSBAD CAVERNS
NATIONAL PARK

6

7

A

Look at the pictures. What do you see?

Answer the questions.

1. How many U.S. landmarks are in the pictures?

2. What kinds of wildlife do you see?

3. What can you do at Carlsbad Caverns?

Read the story.

U.S. National Parks

More than 200 million people visit U.S. National Parks every year. These parks protect the <u>wildlife</u> and <u>landmarks</u> of the United States. Each park is different, and each one is beautiful.

At Yosemite, in California, you can take a nature walk with a <u>park ranger</u>. You'll see waterfalls, redwoods, and deer there.

In south Florida, you can take a <u>ferry</u> to Dry Tortugas. It's great to snorkel around the park's <u>coral</u> islands.

There are 113 <u>caves</u> at Carlsbad <u>Caverns</u> in New Mexico. The deepest cave is 830 feet below the desert! You can <u>take a tour</u> of these beautiful caverns.

There are 391 national parks to see. Go online for information about a park near you.

Think about it.

1. Why are national parks important?

2. Imagine you are a park ranger at a national park. Give your classmates a tour of the landmarks and wildlife.

Places to Go

Endroits où aller

1. zoo
   jardin zoologique
2. movies
   films / cinéma
3. botanical garden
   jardin botanique
4. bowling alley
   bowling / quilles
5. rock concert
   concert de rock
6. swap meet / flea market
   marché aux puces
7. aquarium
   aquarium

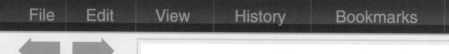

File   Edit   View   History   Bookmarks   Tools

Places to Go in Our City

T-SHIRTS $3 2 for $5

SUNGLASSES $10

ANTIQU

Listen and point. Take turns.

A: *Point to the zoo.*
B: *Point to the flea market.*
A: *Point to the rock concert.*

Dictate to your partner. Take turns.

A: *Write these words: zoo, movies, aquarium.*
B: *Zoo, movies, and what?*
A: *Aquarium.*

222

Search 🔍

8

9

10

11

12

13

14

BACH FESTIVAL

8. **play**
   pièce de théâtre

9. **art museum**
   musée d'art

10. **amusement park**
    parc d'attraction

11. **opera**
    opéra

12. **nightclub**
    boîte de nuit

13. **county fair**
    fête régionale /
    foire régionale

14. **classical concert**
    concert de musique
    classique

Ways to make plans using *Let's go*

Let's go to <u>the amusement park</u> tomorrow.
Let's go to <u>the opera</u> on Saturday.
Let's go to <u>the movies</u> tonight.

Pair practice. Make new conversations.

A: <u>*Let's go to the zoo this afternoon*</u>.
B: *OK. And let's go to <u>the movies tonight</u>.*
A: *That sounds like a good plan.*

223

1. **ball field**
   terrain de base-ball

2. **cyclist**
   cycliste

3. **bike path**
   piste cyclable

4. **jump rope**
   corde à sauter

5. **fountain**
   fontaine

6. **tennis court**
   court de tennis

7. **skateboard**
   skateboard (planche à roulettes)

8. **picnic table**
   table de pique-nique

9. **water fountain**
   fontaine

10. **bench**
    banc

11. **swings**
    balançoires

12. **tricycle**
    tricycle

13. **slide**
    glissade

14. **climbing apparatus**
    cage à poules

15. **sandbox**
    bac à sable

16. **seesaw**
    jeu de bascule

A. pull the wagon
tirer le wagonnet

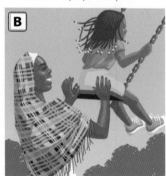

B. push the swing
pousser la balançoire

C. climb the bars
grimper aux barres

D. picnic / have a picnic
pique-niquer / faire un pique-nique

224

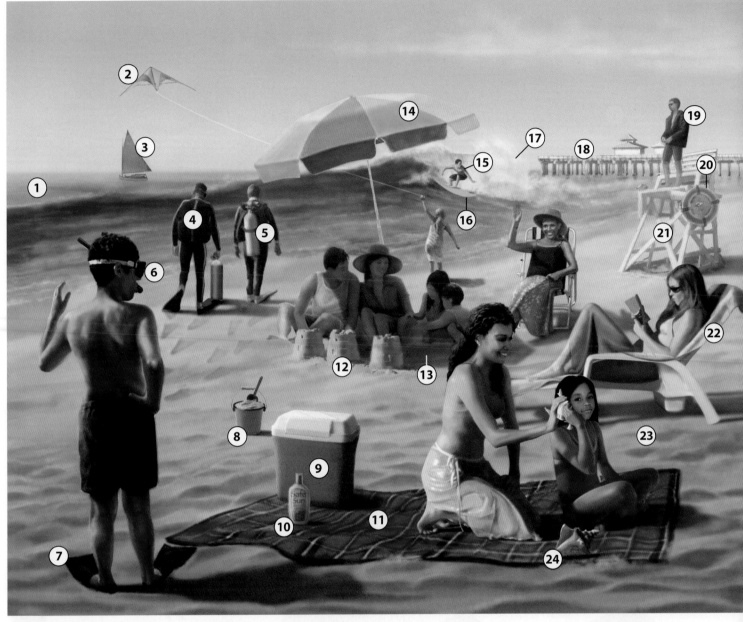

1. ocean / water océan / eau	**7.** fins palmes	**13.** shade ombre	**19.** lifeguard maître nageur
2. kite cerf-volant	**8.** pail / bucket seau	**14.** beach umbrella parasol de plage	**20.** lifesaving device matériel de sauvetage
3. sailboat voilier	**9.** cooler glacière	**15.** surfer surfeur	**21.** lifeguard station poste de secours
4. wet suit combinaison de plongée	**10.** sunscreen / sunblock écran solaire	**16.** surfboard planche de surf	**22.** beach chair chaise de plage
5. scuba tank bouteille de plongée	**11.** blanket couverture	**17.** wave vague	**23.** sand sable
6. diving mask masque de plongée	**12.** sand castle château de sable	**18.** pier jetée	**24.** seashell coquillage

More vocabulary

seaweed: a plant that grows in the ocean
tide: the level of the ocean. The tide goes in and out every 12 hours.

Ask your classmates. Share the answers.

1. Do you like to go to the beach?
2. Are there famous beaches in your native country?
3. Do you prefer to be on the sand or in the water?

225

1. boating
   canotage

2. rafting
   rafting

3. canoeing
   canoë / kayak

4. fishing
   pêche

5. camping
   camping

6. backpacking
   randonnées avec sac à dos

7. hiking
   randonnée

8. mountain biking
   faire du vélo tout terrain

9. horseback riding
   faire de l'équitation

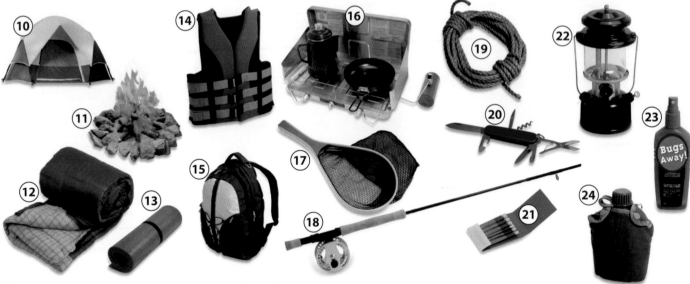

10. tent
    tente

11. campfire
    feu de camp

12. sleeping bag
    sac de couchage

13. foam pad
    matelas de mousse

14. life vest
    gilet de sauvetage

15. backpack
    sac à dos

16. camping stove
    réchaud de camping

17. fishing net
    épuisette

18. fishing pole
    canne à pêche

19. rope
    corde

20. multi-use knife
    couteau suisse

21. matches
    allumettes

22. lantern
    lanterne

23. insect repellent
    produit insectifuge

24. canteen
    bidon

Winter and Water Sports

1. downhill skiing
ski alpin

2. snowboarding
faire du surf des neiges

3. cross-country skiing
ski de randonnée

4. ice skating
patinage sur glace

5. figure skating
patinage artistique

6. sledding
faire de la luge

7. waterskiing
ski nautique

8. sailing
faire de la voile

9. surfing
faire du surf

10. windsurfing
faire de la planche à voile

11. snorkeling
plongée en apnée

12. scuba diving
plongée sous-marine

More vocabulary

speed skating: racing while ice skating
windsurfing: sailboarding

Ask your classmates. Share the Answers.

1. Which of these sports do you like?
2. Which of these sports would you like to learn?
3. Which of these sports is the most fun to watch?

227

1. archery
tir à l'arc

2. billiards / pool
billard

3. bowling
bowling / quilles

4. boxing
boxe

5. cycling / biking
cyclisme

6. badminton
badminton

7. fencing
escrime

8. golf
golf

9. gymnastics
gymnastique

10. inline skating
patinage avec patins
à roues alignées

11. martial arts
arts martiaux

12. racquetball
racquetball

13. skateboarding
faire du skateboard /
de la planche à
roulettes

14. table tennis
tennis de table /
ping-pong

15. tennis
tennis

16. weightlifting
haltérophilie

17. wrestling
lutte

18. track and field
athlétisme

19. horse racing
hippisme

Pair practice. Make new conversations.

A: *What sports do you like?*
B: *I like <u>bowling</u>. What do you like?*
A: *I like <u>gymnastics</u>.*

Think about it. Discuss.

1. Why do people like to watch sports?
2. Which sports can be dangerous?
3. Why do people do dangerous sports?

1. **score**
score

2. **coach**
entraîneur

3. **team**
équipe

4. **fan**
admirateur / fan

5. **player**
joueur

6. **official / referee**
officiel / arbitre

7. **basketball court**
terrain de basket

8. **basketball**
basket-ball

9. **baseball**
base-ball

10. **softball**
soft-ball

11. **football**
football américain

12. **soccer**
football

13. **ice hockey**
hockey sur glace

14. **volleyball**
volley-ball

15. **water polo**
water-polo

More Vocabulary

win: to have the best score
lose: the opposite of win
tie: to have the same score

captain: the team leader
umpire: the name of the referee in baseball
Little League: a baseball and softball program for children

A. **pitch**
décocher un lancer

B. **hit**
frapper

C. **throw**
envoyer

D. **catch**
attraper

E. **kick**
donner un coup de pied

F. **tackle**
bloquer

G. **pass**
passer

H. **shoot**
lancer au panier

I. **jump**
sauter

J. **dribble**
dribbler / faire rebondir le ballon

K. **dive**
plonger

L. **swim**
nager

M. **stretch**
s'étirer

N. **exercise / work out**
faire de l'exercice / s'entraîner

O. **bend**
se pencher

P. **serve**
servir

Q. **swing**
élan de golf

R. **start**
démarrer

S. **race**
courir

T. **finish**
finir

U. **skate**
patiner

V. **ski**
skier

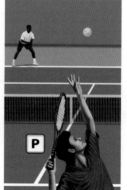

Use the new words.
Look on page 229. Name the actions you see.

A: *He's throwing.*
B: *She's jumping.*

Ways to talk about your sports skills

I can throw, but I can't catch.
I swim well, but I don't dive well.
I'm good at skating, but I'm terrible at skiing.

1. **golf club**
   club de golf

2. **tennis racket**
   raquette de tennis

3. **volleyball**
   balle de volley-ball

4. **basketball**
   balle de basket-ball

5. **bowling ball**
   boule de bowling

6. **bow**
   arc

7. **target**
   cible

8. **arrow**
   flèche

9. **ice skates**
   patins à glace

10. **inline skates**
    patins à roues alignées

11. **hockey stick**
    crosse de hockey

12. **soccer ball**
    ballon de football

13. **shin guards**
    protège-tibia

14. **baseball bat**
    batte de base-ball

15. **catcher's mask**
    masque d'attrapeur

16. **uniform**
    uniforme

17. **glove**
    gant

18. **baseball**
    balle de base-ball

19. **football helmet**
    casque de football américain

20. **shoulder pads**
    épaulières

21. **football**
    ballon de football américain

22. **weights**
    haltères

23. **snowboard**
    surf des neiges

24. **skis**
    skis

25. **ski poles**
    bâtons de ski

26. **ski boots**
    chaussures de ski

27. **flying disc***
    frisbee

* Note: one brand is
Frisbee®, of Wham-O, Inc.

Use the new words.

Look at pages 228–229. Name the sports equipment you see.

A: *Those are ice skates.*
B: *That's a football.*

Ask your classmates. Share the answers.

1. Do you own any sports equipment? What kind?
2. What do you want to buy at this store?
3. Where is the best place to buy sports equipment?

231

A. collect things
collectionner des objets

B. play games
jouer à des jeux

C. quilt
coudre une courtepointe

D. do crafts
faire de l'artisanat

1. figurine
   figurine

2. baseball cards
   cartes de base-ball

3. video game console
   console de jeu vidéo

4. video game control
   commande de jeu vidéo

5. board game
   jeu de société

6. dice
   dés

7. checkers
   jeu de dames

8. chess
   jeu d'échecs

9. model kit
   modèle réduit

10. acrylic paint
    peinture acrylique

11. glue stick
    tube de colle

12. construction paper
    papier de bricolage

13. doll making kit
    kit de confection de poupée

14. woodworking kit
    kit de menuisier

15. quilt block
    carré de courtepointe

16. rotary cutter
    coupeuse rotative

Grammar Point: *How often do you play cards?*

*I play **all the time**. (every day)*
*I play **sometimes**. (once a month)*
*I **never** play. (0 times)*

Pair practice. Make new conversations.

A: *How often do you do your hobbies?*
B: *I play games all the time. I love <u>chess</u>.*
A: *Really? I never play <u>chess</u>.*

232

E. paint
peindre

F. knit
tricoter

G. pretend
faire semblant

H. play cards
jouer aux cartes

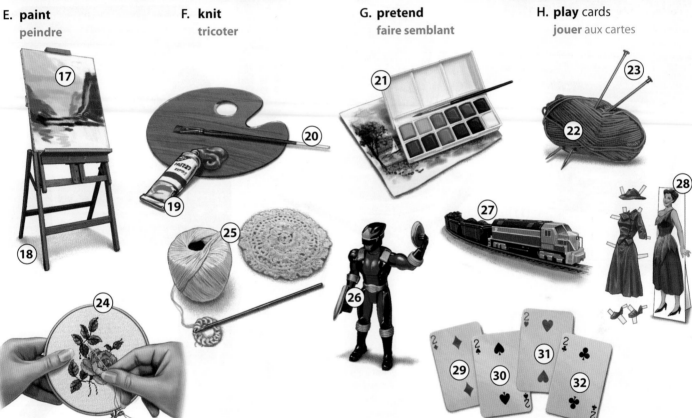

17. canvas
toile

18. easel
chevalet

19. oil paint
peinture à l'huile

20. paintbrush
pinceau

21. watercolor
aquarelle

22. yarn
fil

23. knitting needles
aiguilles à tricoter

24. embroidery
broderie

25. crocheting
faire du crochet

26. action figure
figurine

27. model trains
modèles réduits de train

28. paper dolls
poupées en papier

29. diamonds
carreaux

30. spades
pics

31. hearts
cœurs

32. clubs
trèfles

Ways to talk about hobbies and games

*This <u>board game</u> is **interesting**. It makes me think.*
*That <u>video game</u> is **boring**. Nothing happens.*
*I love to <u>play cards</u>. It's **fun** to play with my friends.*

Ask your classmates. Share the answers.

1. Do you collect anything? What?
2. Which games do you like to play?
3. What hobbies did you have as a child?

233

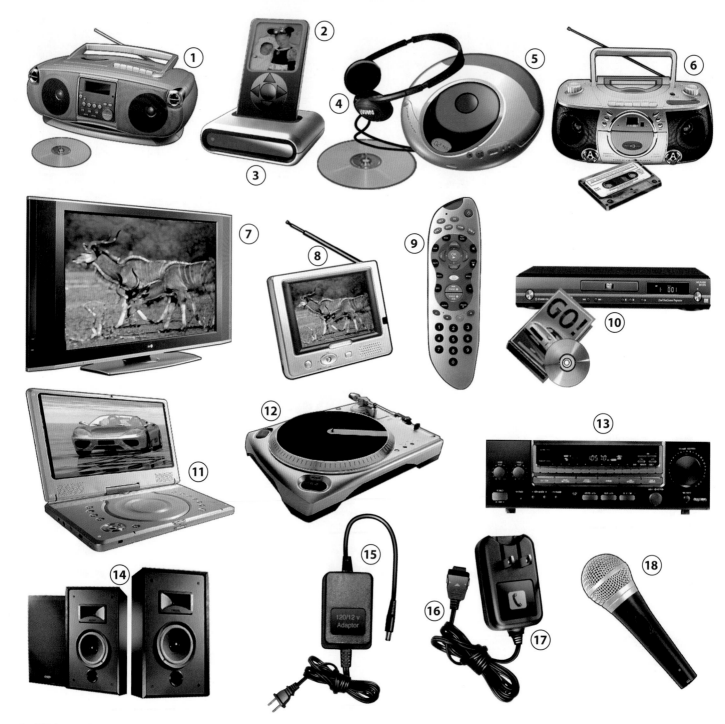

1. CD boombox
   radiocassette et lecteur de CD

2. MP3 player
   lecteur de MP3

3. dock
   station d'accueil

4. headphones
   écouteurs

5. personal CD player
   lecteur de CD personnel

6. portable cassette player
   magnétophone portable

7. flat screen TV / flat panel TV
   télévision à écran plat

8. portable TV
   téléviseur portable

9. universal remote
   télécommande universelle

10. DVD player
    lecteur de DVD

11. portable DVD player
    lecteur de DVD portable

12. turntable
    tourne-disque

13. tuner
    syntonisateur

14. speakers
    haut-parleurs

15. adapter
    adaptateur

16. plug
    fiche

17. charger
    chargeur

18. microphone
    micro

19. digital camera
    appareil photo numérique

20. memory card
    carte mémoire

21. film camera / 35 mm camera
    appareil-photo à pellicule /
    appareil-photo 35 mm

22. film
    pellicule

23. zoom lens
    zoom

24. camcorder
    caméscope

25. tripod
    trépied

26. battery pack
    bloc-piles

27. battery charger
    chargeur de piles

28. camera case
    étui à appareil-photo

29. LCD projector
    projecteur LCD

30. screen
    l'écran

31. photo album
    album de photos

32. digital photo album
    album de photos numériques

33. out of focus
    flou

34. overexposed
    surexposé

35. underexposed
    sous-exposé

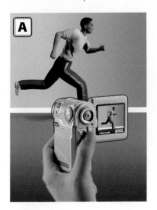 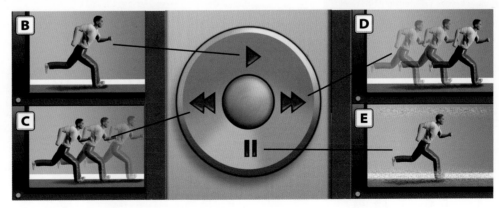

A. **record**
   enregistrer

B. **play**
   jouer

C. **rewind**
   rembobiner

D. **fast forward**
   avance rapide

E. **pause**
   pause

Types of TV Programs Types d'émissions télévisées

1. news program
informations

2. sitcom (situation comedy)
comédie de situation

3. cartoon
dessin animé

4. talk show
causerie

5. soap opera
feuilleton à l'eau de rose

6. reality show
télé réalité

7. nature program
programme sur la nature

8. game show
jeu-questionnaire

9. children's program
émission pour enfants

10. shopping program
émission sur le shopping / magasinage

11. sports program
émission sportive

12. drama
dramatique

Types of Movies   Types de film

13. comedy
comédie

14. tragedy
drame

15. western
western

16. romance
amour

17. horror story
horreur

18. science fiction story
science-fiction

19. action story / adventure story
action / aventure

20. mystery / suspense
mystère / suspens

Types of Music   Types de musique

21. classical
classique

22. blues
blues

23. rock
rock

24. jazz
jazz

25. pop
pop

26. hip hop
hip hop

27. country
country

28. R&B / soul
R&B / soul

29. folk
folk

30. gospel
gospel

31. reggae
reggae

32. world music
musiques du monde

A

A. play an instrument
jouer d'un instrument

B

B. sing a song
chanter une chanson

C

C. conduct an orchestra
conduire un orchestre

D

D. be in a rock band
jouer dans un groupe de rock

Woodwinds Bois

1. flute
   flûte
2. clarinet
   clarinette
3. oboe
   hautbois
4. bassoon
   basson
5. saxophone
   saxophone

Strings Instruments à corde

6. violin
   violon
7. cello
   violoncelle
8. bass
   basse
9. guitar
   guitare

Brass Cuivres (musique)

10. trombone
    trombone
11. trumpet /
    horn
    trompette
12. tuba
    tuba
13. French horn
    cor d'harmonie

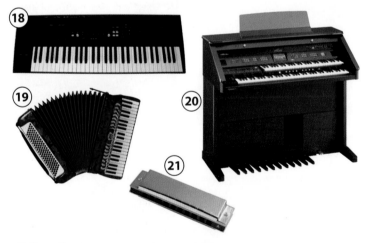

Percussion Percussion

14. piano
    piano
15. xylophone
    xylophone
16. drums
    batterie
17. tambourine
    tambourin

Other Instruments Autres instruments

18. electric keyboard
    clavier électrique
19. accordion
    accordéon
20. organ
    orgue
21. harmonica
    harmonica

1. **parade**
   défilé

2. **float**
   char

3. **confetti**
   confettis

4. **couple**
   couple

5. **card**
   carte

6. **heart**
   cœur

7. **fireworks**
   feu d'artifice

8. **flag**
   drapeau

9. **mask**
   masque

10. **jack-o'-lantern**
    feu follet

11. **costume**
    déguisement

12. **candy**
    bonbon

13. **feast**
    festin

14. **turkey**
    dindon

15. **ornament**
    ornement

16. **Christmas tree**
    arbre de Noël

17. **candy cane**
    canne en sucre

18. **string lights**
    lumières de Noël

*Thanksgiving is on the fourth Thursday in November.

HAPPY BIRTHDAY LOU and GANI

1. decorations décorations	**3.** present / gift présent / cadeau	**B. make** a wish **faire** un vœu	**D. hide** se cacher	**F. wrap** emballer
2. deck terrasse	**A. videotape** **cassette vidéo**	**C. blow out** **souffler**	**E. bring** **apporter**	

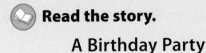
Happy Birthday!

Look at the picture.
What do you see?

Answer the questions.

1. What kinds of decorations do you see?
2. What are people doing at this birthday party?
3. What wish did the teenager make?
4. How many presents did people bring?

📖 Read the story.

A Birthday Party

Today is Lou and Gani Bombata's birthday barbecue. There are <u>decorations</u> around the backyard, and food and drinks on the <u>deck</u>. There are also <u>presents</u>. Everyone in the Bombata family likes to <u>bring</u> presents.

Right now, it's time for cake. Gani <u>is blowing out</u> the candles, and Lou <u>is making a wish</u>. Lou's mom wants to <u>videotape</u> everyone, but she can't find Lou's brother, Todd. Todd hates to sing, so he always <u>hides</u> for the birthday song.

Lou's sister, Amaka, has to <u>wrap</u> some <u>gifts</u>. She doesn't want Lou to see. Amaka isn't worried. She knows her family loves to sing. She can put her gifts on the present table before they finish the first song.

Think about it.

1. What wish do you think Gani made?
2. What kinds of presents do you give to relatives? What kinds of presents can you give to friends or co-workers?

Verb Guide

Verbs in English are either regular or irregular in the past tense and past participle forms.

Regular Verbs
The regular verbs below are marked 1, 2, 3, or 4 according to four different spelling patterns.
(See page 244 for the irregular verbs which do not follow any of these patterns.)

Spelling Patterns for the Past and the Past Participle	Example	
1. Add -ed to the end of the verb.	**ASK**	**ASKED**
2. Add -d to the end of the verb.	**LIVE**	**LIVED**
3. Double the final consonant and add -ed to the end of the verb.	**DROP**	**DROPPED**
4. Drop the final y and add -ied to the end of the verb.	**CRY**	**CRIED**

The Oxford Picture Dictionary List of Regular Verbs

accept (1)
add (1)
address (1)
adjust (1)
agree (2)
answer (1)
apologize (2)
appear (1)
applaud (1)
apply (4)
arrange (2)
arrest (1)
arrive (2)
ask (1)
assemble (2)
assist (1)
attach (1)
bake (2)
bank (1)
bargain (1)
bathe (2)
board (1)
boil (1)
borrow (1)
bow (1)
brainstorm (1)
breathe (2)
browse (2)
brush (1)
bubble (2)
buckle (2)
burn (1)
bus (1)
calculate (2)
call (1)
capitalize (2)
carpool (1)

carry (4)
cash (1)
celebrate (2)
change (2)
check (1)
chill (1)
choke (2)
chop (3)
circle (2)
claim (1)
clean (1)
clear (1)
click (1)
climb (1)
close (2)
collate (2)
collect (1)
color (1)
comb (1)
comfort (1)
commit (3)
compliment (1)
compost (1)
conceal (1)
conduct (1)
convert (1)
convict (1)
cook (1)
copy (4)
correct (1)
cough (1)
count (1)
cross (1)
cry (4)
dance (2)
debate (2)
decline (2)

delete (2)
deliver (1)
design (1)
dial (1)
dice (2)
dictate (2)
die (2)
disagree (2)
discipline (2)
discuss (1)
dive (2)
divide (2)
dress (1)
dribble (2)
drill (1)
drop (3)
drown (1)
dry (4)
dust (1)
dye (2)
edit (1)
empty (4)
enter (1)
erase (2)
evacuate (2)
examine (2)
exchange (2)
exercise (2)
expire (2)
explain (1)
exterminate (2)
fasten (1)
fast forward (1)
fax (1)
fertilize (2)
fill (1)
finish (1)

fix (1)
floss (1)
fold (1)
follow (1)
garden (1)
gargle (2)
graduate (2)
grate (2)
grease (2)
greet (1)
hail (1)
hammer (1)
hand (1)
harvest (1)
help (1)
hire (2)
hug (3)
immigrate (2)
indent (1)
inquire (2)
insert (1)
inspect (1)
install (1)
introduce (2)
invite (2)
iron (1)
jaywalk (1)
join (1)
jump (1)
kick (1)
kiss (1)
knit (3)
label (1)
land (1)
laugh (1)
learn (1)
lengthen (1)

lift (1)
listen (1)
litter (1)
live (2)
load (1)
lock (1)
look (1)
mail (1)
manufacture (2)
match (1)
measure (2)
microwave (2)
milk (1)
misbehave (2)
miss (1)
mix (1)
mop (3)
move (2)
mow (1)
multiply (4)
negotiate (2)
network (1)
numb (1)
nurse (2)
obey (1)
observe (2)
offer (1)
open (1)
operate (2)
order (1)
organize (2)
overdose (2)
pack (1)
paint (1)
park (1)
participate (2)
pass (1)
pause (2)
peel (1)
perm (1)
pick (1)

pitch (1)
plan (3)
plant (1)
play (1)
polish (1)
pour (1)
praise (2)
preheat (1)
prepare (2)
prescribe (2)
press (1)
pretend (1)
print (1)
program (3)
protect (1)
pull (1)
purchase (2)
push (1)
quilt (1)
race (2)
raise (2)
rake (2)
receive (2)
record (1)
recycle (2)
redecorate (2)
reduce (2)
register (1)
relax (1)
remain (1)
remove (2)
renew (1)
repair (1)
replace (2)
report (1)
request (1)
retire (2)
return (1)
reuse (2)
revise (2)
rinse (2)

rock (1)
sauté (1)
save (2)
scan (3)
schedule (2)
scrub (3)
seat (1)
select (1)
sentence (2)
separate (2)
serve (2)
share (2)
shave (2)
ship (3)
shop (3)
shorten (1)
sign (1)
simmer (1)
skate (2)
ski (1)
slice (2)
smell (1)
smile (2)
smoke (2)
sneeze (2)
solve (2)
sort (1)
spell (1)
spoon (1)
staple (2)
start (1)
state (2)
stay (1)
steam (1)
stir (3)
stop (3)
stow (1)
stretch (1)
study (4)
submit (3)
subtract (1)

supervise (2)
swallow (1)
tackle (2)
talk (1)
taste (2)
thank (1)
tie (2)
touch (1)
transcribe (2)
transfer (3)
translate (2)
travel (1)
trim (3)
try (4)
turn (1)
type (2)
underline (2)
undress (1)
unload (1)
unpack (1)
unscramble (2)
use (2)
vacuum (1)
videotape (2)
volunteer (1)
vomit (1)
vote (2)
wait (1)
walk (1)
wash (1)
watch (1)
water (1)
wave (2)
weed (1)
weigh (1)
wipe (2)
work (1)
wrap (3)

Irregular Verbs

These verbs have irregular endings in the past and/or the past participle.

The Oxford Picture Dictionary List of Irregular Verbs

simple	past	past participle	simple	past	past participle
be	was	been	make	made	made
beat	beat	beaten	meet	met	met
become	became	become	pay	paid	paid
bend	bent	bent	picnic	picnicked	picnicked
bleed	bled	bled	proofread	proofread	proofread
blow	blew	blown	put	put	put
break	broke	broken	read	read	read
bring	brought	brought	rewind	rewound	rewound
buy	bought	bought	rewrite	rewrote	rewritten
catch	caught	caught	ride	rode	ridden
choose	chose	chosen	run	ran	run
come	came	come	say	said	said
cut	cut	cut	see	saw	seen
do	did	done	seek	sought	sought
draw	drew	drawn	sell	sold	sold
drink	drank	drunk	send	sent	sent
drive	drove	driven	set	set	set
eat	ate	eaten	sew	sewed	sewn
fall	fell	fallen	shake	shook	shaken
feed	fed	fed	shoot	shot	shot
feel	felt	felt	show	showed	shown
find	found	found	sing	sang	sung
fly	flew	flown	sit	sat	sat
get	got	gotten	speak	spoke	spoken
give	gave	given	stand	stood	stood
go	went	gone	steal	stole	stolen
hang	hung	hung	sweep	swept	swept
have	had	had	swim	swam	swum
hear	heard	heard	swing	swung	swung
hide	hid	hidden	take	took	taken
hit	hit	hit	teach	taught	taught
hold	held	held	think	thought	thought
keep	kept	kept	throw	threw	thrown
lay	laid	laid	wake	woke	woken
leave	left	left	withdraw	withdrew	withdrawn
lend	lent	lent	write	wrote	written
let	let	let			

Index

Index Key

Font

Symbols

Numbers/Letters

Pronunciation Guide

The index includes a pronunciation guide for all the words and phrases illustrated in the book. This guide uses symbols commonly found in dictionaries for native speakers. These symbols, unlike those used in pronunciation systems such as the International Phonetic Alphabet, tend to use English spelling patterns and so should help you to become more aware of the connections between written English and spoken English.

Consonants

[b] as in back [băk]	[k] as in key [kē]	[sh] as in shoe [sho͞o]
[ch] as in cheek [chēk]	[l] as in leaf [lēf]	[t] as in tape [tāp]
[d] as in date [dāt]	[m] as in match [măch]	[th] as in three [thrē]
[dh] as in this [dhĭs]	[n] as in neck [něk]	[v] as in vine [vīn]
[f] as in face [fās]	[ng] as in ring [rĭng]	[w] as in wait [wāt]
[g] as in gas [găs]	[p] as in park [pärk]	[y] as in yams [yămz]
[h] as in half [hăf]	[r] as in rice [rīs]	[z] as in zoo [zo͞o]
[j] as in jam [jăm]	[s] as in sand [sănd]	[zh] as in measure [mĕzhər]

Vowels

[ā] as in bake [bāk]	[ī] as in line [līn]	[o͝o] as in cook [ko͝ok]
[ă] as in back [băk]	[ĭ] as in lip [lĭp]	[ow] as in cow [kow]
[ä] as in car [kär] or box [bäks]	[ï] as in near [nïr]	[oy] as in boy [boy]
[ē] as in beat [bēt]	[ō] as in cold [kōld]	[ŭ] as in cut [kŭt]
[ĕ] as in bed [bĕd]	[ö] as in short [shört] or claw [klö]	[ü] as in curb [kürb]
[ë] as in bear [bër]	[o͞o] as in cool [ko͞ol]	[ə] as in above [ə bŭv⁄]

All the pronunciation symbols used are alphabetical except for the schwa [ə]. The schwa is the most frequent vowel sound in English. If you use the schwa appropriately in unstressed syllables, your pronunciation will sound more natural.

Vowels before [r] are shown with the symbol [¨] to call attention to the special quality that vowels have before [r]. (Note that the symbols [ä] and [ö] are also used for vowels not followed by [r], as in *box* or *claw*.) You should listen carefully to native speakers to discover how these vowels actually sound.

Stress

This index follows the system for marking stress used in many dictionaries for native speakers.

1. Stress is not marked if a word consisting of a single syllable occurs by itself.
2. Where stress is marked, two levels are distinguished:
   a bold accent [⁄] is placed after each syllable with primary (or strong) stress, a light accent [⁄] is placed after each syllable with secondary (or weaker) stress. In phrases and other combinations of words, stress is indicated for each word as it would be pronounced within the whole phrase.

Syllable Boundaries

Syllable boundaries are indicated by a single space or by a stress mark.

Note: The pronunciations shown in this index are based on patterns of American English. There has been no attempt to represent all of the varieties of American English. Students should listen to native speakers to hear how the language actually sounds in a particular region.

Index

Abbreviations [ə brē/vē ā/shənz] **48**
abdomen [ăb/də mən] **107**–27
about [ə bowt/] **48**–B, **174**–L, **191**–E
above [ə bŭv/] **25**–4
accelerator [ĭk sĕl/ə rā/tər] **159**–46
accept [ĭk sĕpt/] **12**–G, **12**–I, **12** ✦
access number [ăk/sĕs/ nŭm/bər] **14**–16
Accessories [ĭk sĕs/ə rēz] **59, 94**–**95**
accident [ăk/sə dənt] **144**–2
accordion [ə kör/dē ən] **238**–19
account [ə kownt/] **132**–11, **132**–14
   account manager [ə kownt/ măn/ə jər] **132**–9
Account [ə kownt/] **132**
accountant [ə kown/tənt] **166**–1
ache [āk]
   backache [băk/āk/] **110**–5
   earache [ir/āk/] **110**–3
   headache [hĕd/āk/] **110**–1
   stomachache [stŭm/ək āk/] **110**–4
   toothache [tōōth/āk/] **110**–2
acid rain [ăs/əd rān/] **218**–13
across [ə krös] **153**–G
acrylic paint [ə krĭl/ĭk pānt] **232**–10
action [ăk/shən]
   action figure [ăk/shən fĭg/yər] **233**–26
   action story [ăk/shən stör/ē] **237**–19
activist [ăk/tə vĭst] **199**–17
actor [ăk/tər] **166**–2
acupuncture [ăk/yə pŭngk/chər] **122**–2
acute angle [ə kyōōt/ ăng/gəl] **193**–28
ad [ăd] **48**–2, **197**–9
adapter [ə dăp/tər] **234**–15
add [ăd] **77**–N, **101**–B, **192**–A
address [ə drĕs/, ă/drĕs] **4**–5
   mailing address [mā/lĭng ə drĕs/, –ā/drĕs] **134**–22
   return address [rĭ tŭrn/ ə drĕs/, –ā/drĕs] **134**–21
   website address [wĕb/sĭt ə drĕs/, –ā/drĕs] **197**–4
address [ə drĕs/] **135**–B, **197**–C
adhesive bandage [əd hē/sĭv băn/dĭj] **117**–5
adjust [ə jŭst/] **219**–J
   adjustable wrench [ə jŭs/tə bəl rĕnch/] **181**–48
   adjustment [ə jŭst/mənt] **194**–23, **194**–24
administrative assistant
   [əd mĭn/ə strā/tĭv ə sĭs/tənt] **166**–3
administrator [əd mĭn/ə strā/tər] **120**–13
Administrators [əd mĭn/ə strā/tərz] **5**
admissions clerk [əd mĭ/shənz klŭrk] **120**–14
ADULTS AND CHILDREN [ə dŭlts/ en chĭl/ drən] **30**–**31**
adult school [ə dŭlt/ skōōl/, ăd/ŭlt–] **188**–8
adventure story [əd vĕn/chər stör/ē] **237**–19
aerobic exercise [ə rō/bĭk ĕk/sər sĭz/] **122**–5
afraid [ə frād/] **43**–23
after [ăf/tər]
   afternoon [ăf/tər nōōn/] **18**–17
   aftershave [ăf/tər shāv/] **109**–30
   five after one [fĭv/ ăf/tər wŭn/] **18**–7
   quarter after one [kwör/tər ăf/tər wŭn/] **18**–9
   ten after one [tĕn/ ăf/tər wŭn/] **18**–8
   twenty after one [twĕn/tē ăf/tər wŭn/] **18**–10
After an Emergency [ăf/tər ən ĭ mür/jən sē] **147**
Age [āj] **32**
agency [ā/jən sē] **131**–14

agent [ā/jənt] **160**–3, **160**–5
agree [ə grē/] **12**–K
agreement [ə grē/mənt] **51**–28
aid [ād]
   first aid kit [fürst/ ād/ kĭt/] **117**–1, **146**–18
   first aid manual [fürst/ ād/ măn/yōō əl] **117**–2
   hearing aid [hĭr/ĭng ād/] **115**–10
aide [ād] **167**–32
AIDS (acquired immune deficiency syndrome) [ādz] /
   [ə kwi/rd ĭ myōōn/ də fĭ/shən sē sĭn/drōm] **111** ✦
air [ĕr]
   air bag [ĕr/ băg/] **159**–43
   air conditioner [ĕr/ kən dĭsh/ə nər] **159**–39
   Air Force [ĕr/ förs/] **138**–16
   airmail [ĕr/māl/] **134**–5
   airplane [ĕr/plān/] **150**–8
   airplane crash [ĕr/plān/ krăsh/] **144**–3
   air pollution [ĕr/ pə lōō/shən] **218**–11
   airport [ĕr/pört/] **151**–10
   air purifier [ĕr/ pyōōr/ə fĭ ər] **113**–14
Airline Terminal [ĕr/lĭn/ tür/mə nəl] **160**
Airplane [ĕr/plān/] **161**
AIRPORT [ĕr/pört/] **160**–**161**
Airport Transportation
   [ĕr/pört/ trăns/pər tā/shən] **152**
aisle [il] **72**–6
alarm clock [ə lärm/ kläk/] **58**–24
Alaska time [ə lăs/kə tĭm/] **19**–28
album [ăl/bəm] **235**–31, **235**–32
alfalfa [ăl făl/fə] **177**–5
algebra [al/jə brə] **192**–16
allergic reaction [ə lür/jĭk rē ăk/shən] **116**–E
allergies [ăl/ər jēz] **111**–8
alley [ăl/ē] **51**–24, **222**–4
alligator [ăl/ə gā/tər] **213**–36
alphabet [ăl/fə bĕt/] **7**–13
Alterations [öl/tə rā/shənz] **100**
ALTERATIONS [öl/tə rā/shənz] **100**
Alteration Shop [öl/tə rā/shən shăp/] **100**
aluminum foil [ə lōō/mə nəm foyl/] **72**–23
Alzheimer's disease [älts/hĭ mərz dĭ zēz/, älts–] **111** ✦
a.m. [ā/ĕm/] **18**–4
ambulance [ăm/byə ləns] **116**–1, **121**–34
AMERICA [ə mĕr/ə kə] **200**–**201**
American cheese [ə mĕr/ə kən chēz/] **71**–26
Americans [ə mĕr/ə kənz] **198**–3
Amphibians [ăm fĭb/ē ənz] **212**
AMPHIBIANS [ăm fĭb/ē ənz] **212**–**213**
amusement park [ə myōōz/mənt pärk/] **223**–10
ancient [ān/shənt] **199**–1
anemone [ə nĕ/mə nē] **212**–24
angle [ăng/gəl] **193**–26, **193**–27, **193**–28
Angles [ăng/gəlz] **193**
angry [ăng/grē] **43**–29
animals [ăn/ə məlz] **59**–15
Animals [ăn/ə məlz] **212, 215**
ANIMALS [ăn/ə məlz] **215**
ankle [ăng/kəl] **106**–23, **110**–18
   ankle socks [ăng/kəl säks/] **91**–7
anklets [ăngk/ləts] **91**–11
anniversary [ăn/ə vür/sə rē] **22**–3

answer [ăn/sər] **8**–L
answering machine [ăn/sə rĭng mə shēn/] **14**–17
answer sheet [ăn/sər shēt/] **10**–2
antacid [ănt ăs/əd] **113**–28
anteater [ănt/ē/tər] **217**–24
antelope [ăn/tə lōp/] **217**–35
antenna [ăn tĕ/nə] **14**–9
antibacterial ointment
   [ăn/tē băk tĭr/ē əl oynt/mənt] **117**–10
antihistamine cream [ăn/tĭ hĭs/tə mēn krēm/] **117**–11
antiperspirant [ăn/tē pürs/pə rənt] **108**–5
antlers [ănt/lərz] **216**–16
ants [ăntz] **63**–23
apartment [ə pärt/mənt] **48**–3, **48**–4
   apartment building [ə pärt/mənt bĭl/dĭng] **50**–1
   apartment number [ə pärt/mənt nŭm/bər] **4**–6
Apartment [ə pärt/mənt] **48**
Apartment Complex [ə pärt/mənt käm/plĕx] **51**
Apartment Entryway [ə pärt/mənt ĕn/trē wā/] **51**
APARTMENTS [ə pärt/məntz] **50**–**51**
APC (automated postal center) [ā/pē/sē/] /
   [ö/tə māt ĭd pōs/təl–sĕn/tər] **135**–10
apologize [ə päl/ə jĭz/] **12**–F
apostrophe [ə päs/trə fē] **190**–16
apparatus [ăp/ə rā/təs] **224**–14
appear [ə pĭr/] **141**–C
Appearance [ə pĭr/əns] **32**
applaud [ə plöd/] **148**–B
apples [ăp/əlz] **68**–1
   apple juice [ăp/əl jōōs/] **73**–32
appliance repair person
   [ə pli/əns rĭ pĕr/ pür/sən] **166**–4
appliqué [ăp/lə kā/] **99**–31
apply [ə pli/] **109**–P
appointment [ə poynt/mənt] **22**–4, **118**–1
   appointment book [ə poynt/mənt bōōk/] **183**–48
apricots [ăp/rə kăts/] **68**–12
April [ā/prəl] **21**–28
apron [ā/prən] **92**–11, **93**–30
aquarium [ə kwĕr/ē əm] **222**–7
Arachnids [ə răk/nĭdz/] **214**
ARACHNIDS [ə răk/nĭdz/] **214**
archery [är/chə rē] **228**–1
architect [är/kə tĕkt/] **166**–5
area [ĕr/ē ə]
   area code [ĕr/ē ə kōd/] **4**–10, **15**–29
   boarding area [bör/dĭng ĕr/ē ə] **161**–9
   dining area [dĭ/nĭng ĕr/ē ə] **46**–7
   play area [plā/ ĕr/ē ə] **130**–11
   reception area [rĭ sĕp/shən ĕr/ē ə] **182**–5
   rural area [rōōr/əl ĕr/ē ə] **52**–4
   screening area [skrē/nĭng ĕr/ē ə] **160**–4
   testing area [tĕs/tĭng ĕr/ē ə] **136**–2
   urban area [ür/bən ĕr/ē ə] **52**–1
AREA [ĕr/ē ə] **55**
Area and Volume [ĕr/ē ə ən văl/yəm, –yōōm] **193**
arm [ärm] **105**–14, **194**–15
   armchair [ärm/chĕr/] **56**–22
armadillo [är/mə dĭl/ō] **216**–8
Arm, Hand, and Fingers [ärm/ hănd/ ən fĭng/gərz] **106**
Army [är/mē] **138**–14, **199**–11
around [ə rownd/] **153**–H

Around Campus [ə rownd/ kăm/pəs] **5**
arrange [ə rănj/] **49**–Q
arrest [ə rĕst/] **141**–A
arrival [ə rī/vəl] **161**–7, **161** ✦
arrive [ə rīv/] **160**–K
arrow [ăr/ō] **231**–8
arson [är/sən] **142**–7
artery [är/tə rē] **107**–36
arthritis [är thrī/təs] **111**–16
artichokes [är/tə chōks/] **69**–22
artist [är/tĭst] **166**–6
arts [ärts] **189**–9, **189**–15, **228**–11
    art museum [ärt/ myōō zē/əm] **223**–9
ask [ăsk] **2**–B
    ask about [ăsk/ ə bowt/] **48**–B, **157**–B
    ask for [ăsk/ för/] **10**–F
    ask questions [ăsk/ kwĕs/chənz] **8**–K, **174**–M
asparagus [ə spĕr/ə gəs] **69**–26
assault [ə sölt/] **142**–3
assemble [ə sĕm/bəl] **170**–A, **175**–C
assembler [ə sĕm/blər] **166**–7
assembly [ə sĕm/blē] **140**–1
    assembly line [ə sĕm/blē līn/] **175**–6
    assemblyperson [ə sĕm/blē pür/sən] **139**–24
assist [ə sĭst/] **95**–D, **170**–B
assistance [ə sĭs/təns] **14**–22
assistant [ə sĭs/tənt]
    administrative assistant
        [əd mĭn/ ə strā/ tĭv ə sĭs/tənt] **166**–3
    assistant principal [ə sĭs/tənt prĭn/sə pəl] **5**–5
    certified nursing assistant (CNA) [sür/tə fīd/
        nür/sĭng ə sĭs/tənt] / [sē/ĕn/ā/] **120**–12
    dental assistant [dĕn/təl ə sĭs/tənt] **119**–2, **167**–22
    physician assistant [fə zĭ/shən ə sĭs/tənt] **168**–47
Assistant [ə sĭs/tənt] **93**
asthma [ăz/mə] **111**–9
astronaut [ăs/trə nöt/] **205**–17
astronomer [ə strä/nə mər] **205**–22
Astronomy [ə strä/nə mē] **205**
At Customs [ăt/ kŭs/təmz] **161**
athletic [ăth lĕt/ĭk]
    athletic shoes [ăth lĕt/ĭk shōōz/] **86**–7
    athletic supporter [ăth lĕt/ĭk sə pör/tər] **91**–6
Atlantic time [ət lăn/tĭk tīm/] **19**–33
atlas [ăt/ləs] **133**–8
ATM (Automated Teller Machine) [ā/tē/ĕm/] /
    [ö/tə māt ĭd tĕ/lər mə shēn/] **132**
ATM card [ā/tē/ĕm/ kärd/] **132**–15
atom [ăt/əm] **195**–28
attach [ə tăch/] **197**–G, **197**–H
attachments [ə tăch/mənts] **61**–11
attack [ə tăk/] **116**–D
attendant [ə tĕn/dənt] **161**–12, **162**–3, **184**–3
At the Dealer [ăt/ dhə dē/lər] **158**
At the Gate [ăt/ dhə gāt/] **161**
At the Mechanic [ăt/ dhə mə kăn/ĭk] **158**
At the Security Checkpoint
    [ăt/ dhə sə kyōō/ rə tē/ chĕk/ poynt/] **160**
attic [ăt/ĭk] **47**–7
attorney [ə tür/nē] **141**–4, **141**–10
attractive [ə trăk/tĭv] **32**–13
audiobook [ö/dē ō bōōk/] **133**–17

audiologist [ö dē ä/lə jĭst] **115**–9
auditorium [ö/də tör/ē əm] **5**–18
August [ö/gəst] **21**–32
aunt [ănt] **34**–7
author [ö/thər] **133**–15, **169**–64
auto [ö/tō]
    auto club card [ö/tō klŭb/ kärd/] **162**–4
    auto mechanic [ö/tō mə kăn/ĭk] **166**–8
automated [ö/tə māt ĭd]
    automated phone system
        [ö/tə māt ĭd fōn/ sĭs/təm] **14**–23
    automated postal center (APC)
        [ö/tə māt ĭd pōs/təl sĕn/tər] / [ā/pē/sē/] **135**–10
Automated Teller Machine
    [ö/tə māt ĭd tĕl/ər mə shēn/] **132**
Automatic Transmission
    [ö tə māt/ĭk trănz mĭ/shən] **159**
Automotive Painter [ö tə mōt/ĭv pān/tər] **92**
autumn [ö/təm] **21**–39
avalanche [ăv/ə lănch/] **145**–18
average [ăv/rĭj]
    average height [ăv/rĭj hīt/] **32**–5
    average weight [ăv/rĭj wāt/] **32**–8
avocados [ä/və kä/dōz, ăv/ə–] **84**–6
ax [ăks] **180**–3
baboon [bă bōōn/] **217**–31
baby [bā/bē] **31**–7
    baby bag [bā/bē băg/] **37**–16
    baby carrier [bā/bē kă/rē/ər] **37**–17
    baby food [bā/bē fōōd/] **37**–4
    baby lotion [bā/bē lō/shən] **37**–13
    baby monitor [bā/bē măn/ə tər] **59**–7
    baby powder [bā/bē pow/dər] **37**–14
    babysitter [bā/bē sĭt/ər] **166**–9
    baby's room [bā/bēz/ rōōm/] **47**–10
back [băk] **104**–5
    backache [băk/āk/] **110**–5
    back button [băk/ bŭt/n] **197**–2
    backhoe [băk/hō/] **178**–8
    backpack [băk/păk/] **94**–18, **226**–15
    backpacking [băk/păk/ĭng] **226**–6
    backseat [băk/sēt/] **159**–54
    back support belt [băk/ sə pört/ bĕlt/] **179**–18
    go back [gō/ băk/] **11**–M
    horseback riding [hörs/băk/ rī/dĭng] **226**–9
    lower back [lō/ər băk/] **107**–29
    pay back [pā/ băk/] **26**–D
Backyard [băk/yärd/] **53**
BACK FROM THE MARKET
    [băk/ frəm dhə mär/kət] **66**–67
bacon [bā/kən] **70**–11, **80**–1
bad [băd] **23**–18
BAD DAY AT WORK [băd/ dā/ ăt würk/] **186**–187
badge [băj] **93**–21
badminton [băd/mĭn tən] **228**–6
bag [băg] **69**–31, **74**–7, **74**–19, **161**–18
    air bag [ĕr/ băg/] **159**–43
    baby bag [bā/bē băg/] **37**–16
    clutch bag [klŭch/ băg/] **89**–19
    grocery bag [grōs/rē băg/] **67**–13
    handbag [hănd/ băg/] **87**–9, **94**–2
    plastic storage bags [plăs/tĭk stör/ĭj băgz/] **72**–25

    shoulder bag [shōl/dər băg/] **94**–17
    sleeping bag [slē/pĭng băg/] **226**–12
    totebag [tōt/ băg/] **94**–19
    trash bags [trăsh/ băgz/] **61**–24
    vacuum cleaner bag
        [văk/yōōm klē/nər băg/] **61**–12
bagels [bā/gəlz] **73**–40
baggage [băg/ĭj]
    baggage carousel [băg/ĭj kăr/ə sĕl/] **161**–23
bagger [băg/ər] **73**–14
baggy [băg/ē] **97**–30
bailiff [bā/lĭf] **141**–13
bake [bāk] **77**–H
Baked Goods [bākt/ gŏŏdz/] **73**
baked potato [bākt/ pə tā/tō] **81**–25
baker [bā/kər] **166**–10
bakery [bā/kə rē] **127**–19
Baking Products [bā/kĭng präd/ŭkts] **73**
balance [băl/əns] **132**–17, **195**–41
balcony [băl/kə nē] **51**–20
bald [böld] **33**–12
ball [böl] **59**–12, **231**–5, **231**–12
    ball field [böl/ fēld/] **224**–1
    ballroom [böl/rōōm/] **184**–26
    baseball [bās/böl/] **231**–18, **231**–14
    basketball [băs/kət böl/] **229**–8, **231**–4
    basketball court [băs/kət böl/ kört/] **229**–7
    football [fŏŏt/böl/] **229**–11, **231**–21
    meatballs [mēt/bölz/] **81**–27
    racquetball [răk/ət böl/] **228**–12
    softball [söft/böl/] **229**–10
    volleyball [väl/ē böl/] **229**–14, **231**–3
balloons [bə lōōnz/] **44**–4
bananas [bə năn/əz] **68**–2
band [bănd] **183**–34
    headband [hĕd/bănd/] **90**–3
    waistband [wāst/bănd/] **100**–5
bandage [băn/dĭj] **117**–5, **117**–12
bandana [băn dă/nə] **92**–16
bangs [băngz] **33**–8
bank [băngk] **124**–5
    bank statement [băngk/ stāt/mənt] **132**–16
bank online [băngk/ än līn/] **132**–C
BANK [băngk] **132**
banner [băn/ər] **44**–1
banquet room [băng/kwət rōōm/] **185**–14
bar [bär]
    bar code [bär/ kōd/] **27**–4
    candy bar [kăn/dē bär/] **73**–37
    grab bar [grăb/ bär/] **57**–9
    menu bar [mĕn/yōō bär/] **197**–1
    salad bar [săl/əd bär/] **79**–24
    scroll bar [skröl/ bär/] **197**–15
barbecued ribs [bär/bĭ kyōō/d rĭbz/] **76**–2
barbershop [bär/bər shäp/] **129**–19
bargain [bär/gən] **102**–A
barn [bärn] **177**–11
barrette [bə rĕt/] **108**–20
base [bās] **193**–45, **194**–20
baseball [bās/böl/] **229**–9, **231**–18
    baseball bat [bās/böl/ băt/] **231**–14
    baseball cap [bās/böl/ kăp/] **86**–5

Index

baseball cards [bās/bȯl/ kärds/] **232**–2
baseball game [bās/bȯl/ gām/] **44**–2
basement [bās/mənt] **47**–13
Basement [bās/mənt] **50**
Basic Colors [bā/sĭk kŭ/lərz] **24**
BASIC TRANSPORTATION
   [bā/sĭk trănz/pər tā/shən] **150**–151
basket [băs/kət] **56**–3
   basketball [băs/kət bȯl/] **229**–8, **231**–4
   basketball court [băs/kət bȯl kört/] **229**–7
   bread basket [brĕd/ băs/kət] **83**–11
   laundry basket [lȯn/drē băs/kət] **101**–2
   shopping basket [shäp/ĭng băs/kət] **73**–9
   wastebasket [wāst/băs/kət] **57**–26
bass [băs] **212**–6, [bās] **238**–8
bassoon [bə sōōn/] **238**–4
bat [băt] **216**–7, **231**–14
bath [băth]
   bath mat [băth/ măt/] **57**–28
   bath powder [băth/ pow/dər] **108**–4
   bathroom [băth/rōōm/] **46**–4
   bath towel [băth/ tow/əl] **57**–13
   bathtub [băth/tŭb/] **57**–2
   half bath [hăf/ băth/] **57** ✦
bathe [bādh] **36**–F, **108**–B
bathing suit [bā/dhĭng sōōt/] **90**–26
BATHROOM [băth/rōōm/] **57**
battery / batteries [băt/ə rē] / [băt/ə rēz]
   146–15, **158**–20
   battery charger [băt/ə rē chär/jər] **235**–27
   battery pack [băt/ə rē păk/] **235**–26
bay [bā] **204**–9
be [bē]
   be aware [bē ə wër/] **143**–I
   be born [bē börn/] **40**–A
   be 18 or older [bē ā/tēn/ ör ōld/ər] **140**–G
   be hurt [bē hürt/] **116**–C
   be in a rock band [bē ĭn ə räk/ bănd/] **238**–D
   be informed [bē ĭn förmd/] **140**–F
   be injured [bē ĭn/jərd] **116**–C
   be in shock [bē ĭn shäk/] **116**–B
   be neat [bē nēt/] **174**–C
   be on time [bē ön tīm/] **174**–F
   be released [bē rĭ lēst/] **141**–H
   be unconscious [bē ŭn kän/shəs] **116**–A
   don't be late [dōnt/ bē lāt/] **174**–D
beach [bēch] **204**–10
   beach chair [bēch/ chër/] **225**–22
   beach umbrella [bēch/ ŭm brĕl/ə] **225**–14
BEACH [bēch] **225**
beads [bēdz] **95**–34, **99**–32
beak [bēk] **214**–3
beaker [bē/kər] **195**–39
beam [bēm] **178**–3
beans [bēnz] **69**–8, **72**–17
   soybeans [soy/bēnz/] **177**–3
bear [bër] **37**–23, **216**–11
beard [bërd] **33**–6
beat [bēt] **77**–S
beater [bē/tər]
   eggbeater [ĕg/bē/tər] **78**–20
beautiful [byōō/tə fəl] **23**–21

beauty shop [byōō/tē shäp/] **130** ✦
beaver [bē/vər] **216**–9
become [bē kŭm/] **40**–G, **41**–N
bed [bĕd] **58**–9
   bedbugs [bĕd/bŭgz/] **63**–24
   bed control [bĕd/ kən trōl/] **121**–27
   bed frame [bĕd/ frām/] **58**–18
   bed pan [bĕd/ păn/] **121**–23
   bedroom [bĕd/rōōm/] **46**–2
   bedspread [bĕd/sprĕd/] **59**–11
   bed table [bĕd/ tā/bəl] **121**–21
   bunk beds [bŭnk/ bĕdz/] **59**–9
   double bed [dŭb/əl bĕd/] **184**–14
   flower bed [flow/ər bĕd/] **53**–20
   hospital bed [häs/pĭ tl bĕd/] **121**–22
   kids' bedroom [kĭdz/ bĕd/rōōm/] **47**–9
   king-size bed [kĭng/sīz/ bĕd/] **184**–15
BEDROOM [bĕd/rōōm/] **58, 59**
bee [bē]
   honeybee [hŭn/ē bē/] **214**–25
beef [bēf]
   beef ribs [bēf/ rĭbz/] **70**–5
   corned beef [körnd/ bēf/] **71**–22
   ground beef [grownd/ bēf/] **70**–4
   roast beef [rōst/ bēf/] **71**–21
   stewing beef [stōō/ĭng bēf/] **70**–3
   stir-fried beef [stür/frīd/ bēf/] **76**–6
Beef [bēf] **70**
beetle [bēt/l] **214**–18
beets [bēts] **69**–5
Before an Emergency [bĭ för/ ən ĭ mür/ jən sē] **146**
behind [bĭ hīnd/] **25**–8
beige [bāzh] **24**–18
bell [bĕl]
   bell captain [bĕl/ kăp/tən] **184**–6
   bellhop [bĕl/häp/] **184**–7
   bell peppers [bĕl/ pĕp/ərz] **69**–7
   doorbell [dör/bĕl/] **53**–14
below [bĭ lō/] **25**–5
belts [bĕlts] **94**–6
   back support belt [băk/ sə pört/ bĕlt/] **179**–18
   belt buckle [bĕlt/ bŭk/əl] **94**–20
   conveyor belt [kən vā/ər bĕlt/] **175**–9
   garter belt [gär/tər bĕlt/] **91**–16
   seat belt [sēt/ bĕlt/] **159**–52
   tool belt [tōōl/ bĕlt/] **92**–3
bench [bĕnch] **224**–10
bend [bĕnd] **230**–O
benefits [bĕn/ə fĭts] **174** ✦
berries [bĕr/ēz] **210**–20
   blackberries [blăk/bĕr/ēz] **68**–17
   blueberries [blōō/bĕr/ēz] **68**–16
   mixed berries [mĭkst/ bĕr/ēz] **81**–36
   raspberries [răz/bĕr/ēz] **68**–15
   strawberries [strö/bĕr/ēz] **68**–14
between [bĭ twēn/] **25**–12
Beverages [bĕv/rə jəz] **73, 81**
bib [bĭb] **37**–5
bicycle / bike [bī/sĭ kəl] / [bīk] **129**–22, **151**–15
big [bĭg] **23**–2, **97**–38
   Big Dipper [bĭg/ dĭ/pər] **205** ✦
   big-screen TV [bĭg/skrēn/ tē/vē/] **50**–15

bike / bicycle [bīk] / [bī/sĭ kəl] **129**–22, **151**–15
   bike path [bīk/ păth/] **224**–3
biking [bī/kĭng] **226**–8, **228**–5
bikini panties [bə kē/nē păn/tēz] **91**–13
bill [bĭl] **214**–3
Bill [bĭl] **15**
billiards [bĭl/yərdz] **228**–2
Bill of Rights [bĭl/ əv rīts/] **198**–10
Bills [bĭlz] **26**
bin [bĭn] **51**–23, **61**–2, **160**–6
bioenergy [bī/ō ĕn/ər jē] **218**–9
biography [bī ä/grə fē] **133**–15
biologist [bī ä/lə jĭst] **194**–2
Biology [bī ä/lə jē] **194**
biomass [bī/ō măs/] **218**–9
birch [bürch] **210**–7
bird [bürd] **208**–4
Bird [bürd] **214**
BIRDS, INSECTS, AND ARACHNIDS
   [bürdz/ ĭn/sĕkts ən ə răk/nĭdz] **214**
birth [bürth]
   birth certificate [bürth/ sər tĭf/ə kət] **40**–1
   birthday [bürth/dā/] **22**–1
BIRTHDAY PARTY [bürth/dā/ pär/tē] **240**–241
biscuits [bĭs/kəts] **80**–6
bison [bī/sən] **216**–6
bit [bĭt] **180**–28
bite [bīt] **110**–11
black [blăk] **24**–13
   blackberries [blăk/bĕr/ēz] **68**–17
   black hair [blăk/ hër/] **33**–16
bladder [blăd/ər] **107**–46
blade [blād] **107**–28, **109**–28, **180**–27
blankets [blăng/kəts] **58**–15, **146**–7, **225**–11
   blanket sleeper [blăng/kət slē/pər] **91**–27
blazer [blā/zər] **92**–12
bleach [blēch] **101**–7
bleachers [blē/chərz] **5**–3
bleed [blēd] **116**–M
blender [blĕn/dər] **54**–12
blind [blīnd] **32**–11
blister [blĭs/tər] **110**–15
blizzard [blĭz/ərd] **13**–23, **145**–13
blocks [blăks] **59**–19
   quilt block [kwĭlt/ blăk/] **232**–15
   sunblock [sŭn/blăk/] **108**–8, **225**–10
blond hair [bländ/ hër/] **33**–17
blood [blŭd] **111**–14
   blood pressure gauge [blŭd/ prĕsh/ər gāj/] **118**–9
   blood test [blŭd/ tĕst/] **121**–30
   blood work [blŭd/ würk/] **121**–30
   bloody nose [blŭd/ē nōz/] **110**–17
blouse [blows] **87**–8
blow dryer [blō/ drī/ər] **33**–23, **108**–18
blower [blō/ər] **176**–2
blow out [blō/ owt/] **240**–C
blue [blōō] **24**–3
   blueberries [blōō/bĕr/ēz] **68**–16
   blue jay [blōō/ jā/] **214**–6
   bright blue [brīt/ blōō/] **24**–12
   dark blue [därk/ blōō/] **24**–10
   light blue [līt/ blōō/] **24**–11
   navy blue [nā/vē blōō/] **28**–5

blues [blooz] **237**–22
blush [blŭsh] **109**–37
board [börd]
    board game [börd/ gām/] **232**–5
    bulletin board [bŏŏl/ə tn börd/] **7**–14
    chalkboard [chök/börd/] **6**–1
    cutting board [kŭt/ĭng börd/] **54**–27
    emery board [ĕm/ə rē börd/, ĕm/rē–] **109**–32
    headboard [hĕd/börd/] **58**–10
    ironing board [ī/ər nĭng börd/] **101**–14
    motherboard [mŭdh/ər börd/] **196**–5
    particle board [pär/tə kəl börd/] **181**–20
    skateboard [skāt/börd/] **224**–7
    snowboard [snō/börd/] **231**–23
    surfboard [sürf/börd/] **225**–16
    whiteboard [wīt/börd/] **6**–3
board [börd] **160**–E
boarding [bör/dĭng]
    boarding area [bör/dĭng ër/ē ə] **161**–9
    boarding pass [bör/dĭng păs/] **161**–20
    sailboarding [sāl/bör/dĭng] **227** ✦
    skateboarding [skāt/bör/dĭng] **228**–13
    snowboarding [snō/bör/dĭng] **227**–2
boat [bōt]
    sailboat [sāl/bōt/] **225**–3
boating [bō/tĭng] **226**–1
bobbin [bä/bĭn] **98**–21
bobby pins [bäb/ē pĭnz/] **108**–21
body [bäd/ē] **190**–7
    body lotion [bäd/ē lō/shən] **108**–9
    body of water [bäd/ē əv wö/tər] **204** ✦
    body shaper [bäd/ē/ shā/pər] **91**–15
BODY [bäd/ē] **104**–105, **106**–107
boil [boyl] **77**–M
boiled ham [boyld/ hăm/] **76**–5
boiler [boy/lər] **78**–8
bok choy [bäk/ choy/] **69**–15
bolt [bōlt] **51**–34, **180**–35, **180**–38
    bolt of fabric [bōlt/ əv făb/rĭk] **98**–15
bone [bōn] **107**–33, **116**–P
    boneless [bōn/ləs] **70** ✦
book [bŏŏk]
    appointment book [ə poynt/mənt bŏŏk/] **183**–48
    audiobook [ö/dē ō bŏŏk/] **133**–17
    bookkeeper [bŏŏk/ kē/pər] **175**–2
    book of stamps [bŏŏk/ əv stămps/] **134**–18
    bookcase [bŏŏk/ kās/] **7**–10
    bookstore [bŏŏk/ stör/] **130**–4
    check book [chĕk/ bŏŏk/] **132**–12
    coloring book [kŭl/ə rĭng bŏŏk/] **59**–13
    DMV handbook [dē/ĕm/vē/ hănd/bŏŏk/] **136**–1
    notebook [nōt/bŏŏk/] **7**–27
    passbook [păs/bŏŏk/] **132**–10
    picture book [pĭk/chər bŏŏk/] **133**–12
    spiral notebook [spī/rəl nōt/bŏŏk/] **7**–29
    test booklet [tĕst/ bŏŏk/lət] **10**–1
    textbook [tĕkst/bŏŏk/, tĕks/–] **7**–25
    workbook [würk/bŏŏk/] **7**–26
boombox [bōōm/bäks/] **234**–1
booth [bōōth] **82**–4, **122**–3

boots [bōōts] **95**–28
    hiking boots [hī/kĭng bōōts/] **95**–31
    rain boots [răn/ bōōts/] **90**–20
    safety boots [sāf/tē bōōts/] **179**–20
    ski boots [skē/ bōōts/] **231**–26
    steel toe boots [stēl/ tō/ bōōts/] **92**–6
bored [börd] **43**–25
borrow [bär/ō, bör/ō] **26**–B
boss [bäs] **164**–4
botanical garden [bə tăn/ĭ kəl gär/dn] **222**–3
bottle [bät/l] **37**–1, **74**–1, **74**–13
    bottle return [bät/l rĭ türn/] **73**–16
    hot water bottle [hät/ wö/tər bät/l] **113**–15
bottled water [bät/ld wö/tər] **146**–11
bouquet [bō kā/, bōō–] **211**–28
bow [bō] **231**–6
    bow tie [bō/ tī/] **89**–16
bow [bow] **3**–H
bowl [bōl] **55**–2
    mixing bowl [mĭks/ĭng bōl/] **54**–28, **78**–31
    serving bowl [sürv/ĭng bōl/] **55**–21
    soup bowl [sōōp/ bōl/] **83**–21
    sugar bowl [shŏŏg/ər bōl/] **55**–14
bowling [bō/lĭng] **228**–3
    bowling alley [bō/lĭng ăl/ē] **222**–4
    bowling ball [bō/lĭng bōl/] **231**–5
box / boxes [bäks/, bäks/ĭz] **74**–6, **74**–18
    box spring [bäks/ sprĭng/] **58**–19
    CD boombox [sē/dē/ bōōm/bäks/] **234**–1
    fuse box [fyōōz/ bäks/] **62**–13
    mailboxes [māl/băk/səz] **50**–11, **128**–13
    post office box (PO box)
        [pōst/ ö/fəs bäks/] / [pē/ō bäks/] **135**–9
    safety deposit box [sāf/tē dĭ päz/ət bäks/] **132**–7
    sandbox [sănd/bäks/] **224**–15
    search box [sürch/ bäks/] **197**–5
    text box [tĕkst/ bäks/] **197**–13
    to-go box [tə gō/ bäks/] **82**–5
boxer shorts [bäk/sər shörts/] **91**–4
boxing [bäks/ĭng] **228**–4
boy [boy] **31**–9
bra [brä] **91**–20
bracelets [brās/ləts] **95**–9, **117**–3
braces [brā/səz] **119**–6
brain [brān] **107**–34
brainstorm [brān/störm/] **8**–H, **191**–F
brake [brāk] **159**–48
    brake light [brāk/ līt/] **158**–14
    brake pedal [brāk/ pĕd/l] **159**–45
branch [brănch] **210**–2
Branch [brănch] **138**
Brass [brăs] **238**
bread [brĕd] **67**–11
    bread-and-butter plate [brĕd/ n bŭt/ər plāt/] **83**–19
    bread basket [brĕd/ băs/kət] **83**–11
    garlic bread [gär/lĭk brĕd/] **81**–28
    rye bread [rī/ brĕd/] **71**–20
    wheat bread [wēt/ brĕd/] **71**–19
    white bread [wīt/ brĕd/] **71**–18
break [brāk] **77**–Q, **116**–P
    break down [brāk/ down/] **162**–D

Breakfast Special [brĕk/fəst spĕ/shəl] **80**
breasts [brĕsts] **70**–19, **107**–26
breathe [brēdh] **116**–N
breathing [brē/dhĭng] **117**–16
bricklayer [brĭk/lā/ər] **186**–8
bricks [brĭks] **178**–12, **178**–B
briefcase [brēf/kās/] **88**–13
briefs [brēfs] **91**–5, **91**–14
bright blue [brīt/ blōō/] **24**–12
bring [brĭng] **174**–D, **240**–E
broccoli [bräk/ə lē] **69**–13
broiled steak [broyld/ stāk/] **76**–3
broiler [broy/lər] **54**–21
broken [brō/kən] **62**–5, **62**–6, **62**–7, **63**–15, **97**–39
    broken equipment [brō/kən ĭ kwĭp/mənt] **179**–4
broom [brōōm] **61**–16
brother [brŭdh/ər] **34**–6, **35**–28
    brother-in-law [brŭdh/ər ĭn lö/] **34**–17
    stepbrother [stĕp/brŭdh/ər] **35**–30
brown [brown] **24**–17
    brown hair [brown/ hër/] **33**–18
    hash browns [hăsh/ brownz/] **80**–3
browse [browz] **102**–B
bruise [brōōz] **110**–12
brush [brŭsh] **33**–22, **108**–14
    paintbrush [pānt/brŭsh/] **181**–22, **233**–20
    scrub brush [skrŭb/ brŭsh/] **61**–20
    toilet brush [toy/lət brŭsh/] **57**–18
    toothbrush [tōōth/brŭsh/] **109**–22
brush [brŭsh] **108**–I, **109**–J
bubble in [bŭ/bəl ĭn/] **10**–K
bucket [bŭk/ət] **61**–7, **225**–8
buckle [bŭk/əl] **94**–20, **99**–28
buckle up [bŭk/əl ŭp/] **36**–L
bud [bŭd] **211**–7
budget [bŭ jĭt/] **186**–3
buffalo [bŭf/ə lō] **216**–6
buffet [bə fā/] **55**–24, **185**–10
bugs [bŭgz]
    bedbugs [bĕd/bŭgz/] **63**–24
building [bĭl/dĭng] **50**–1, **124**–2
BUILDING SUPPLIES [bĭl/dĭng sə plīz/] **180**–181
bulb [bŭlb] **56** ✦, **211**–2
bulldozer [bŏŏl/dō/zər] **178**–6
bulletin board [bŏŏl/ə tn börd/] **7**–14
bump cap [bŭmp/ kăp/] **92**–9
bumper [bŭm/pər] **158**–8
    bumper pad [bŭm/pər păd/] **59**–4
bunch [bŭnch] **68**–29
bunk beds [bŭngk/ bĕdz/] **59**–9
Bunsen burner [bŭn/sən bür/nər] **195**–37
bureau [byōōr/ō] **58**–1
burger [bür/gər]
    cheeseburger [chēz/bür/gər] **79**–3
    hamburger [hăm/bür/gər] **79**–1
burglary [bür/glə rē] **142**–2
burn [bürn]
    sunburn [sŭn/bürn/] **110**–14
burn [bürn] **116**–H
burner [bür/nər] **54**–19, **195**–37
burrito [bə rē/tō] **79**–9

bus [bŭs] **128–9, 151–14**
   bus person [bŭs/ pür/sən] **185–13**
   bus route [bŭs/ rōōt/, –rowt/] **152–1**
   bus station [bŭs/ stā/shən] **124–7**
   bus stop [bŭs/ stäp/] **129–16, 151–13**
   miss the bus [mĭs/ dhə bŭs/] **152 ✦**
bus [bŭs] **82–G**
business [bĭz/nəs]
   business owner [bĭz/nəs ō/nər] **166–11**
   businessperson [bĭz/nəs pür/sən] **166–12**
   business suit [bĭz/nəs sōōt/] **88–11**
busser [bŭ/sər] **83–12**
Bus Stop [bŭs/ stäp/] **152**
butcher [bŏŏch/ər] **166–13**
butter [bŭt/ər] **66–6, 83–19**
butterfly [bŭt/ər flī/] **214–19**
buttocks [bŭt/əks] **107–30**
button [bŭt/n] **99–24**
   back button [băk/ bŭt/n] **197–2**
   call button [köl/ bŭt/n] **121–28**
   forward button [för/wərd bŭt/n] **197–3**
buy [bī] **27–G**
   buy a home [bī/ ə hōm/] **41–M**
   buy a snack [bī/ ə snăk/] **11–K**
   buy recycled products
     [bī/ rē sī/kəld präd/ŭkts] **219–D**
Buying a House [bī/ĭng ə hows/] **49**
BUYING AND MAINTAINING A CAR
   [bī/ĭng ən măn tā/nĭng ə kär/] **157**
Buying a Used Car [bī/ĭng ə yōōzd/ kär/] **157**
buzzer [bŭz/ər] **51–31**
cab [kăb] **156–16**
cabbage [kăb/ĭj] **69–2**
Cabinet [kăb/ə nət] **138–10**
cabinet [kăb/ə nət] **54–1**
   file cabinet [fīl/ kăb/ə nət] **182–11**
   medicine cabinet [mĕd/ə sən kăb/ə nət] **57–20**
   supply cabinet [sə plī/ kăb/ə nət] **182–1**
cables [kā/bəlz] **158–21, 196–13**
cactus [kăk/təs] **210–21**
cafeteria [kăf/ə tïr/ē ə] **5–14**
cage [kāj] **107–48**
cake [kāk] **73–39, 81–33**
   cake pan [kāk/ păn/] **78–26**
   cheesecake [chēz/kāk/] **81–34**
   pancakes [păn/kāks/] **80–7**
Cake [kāk] **77**
calculate [kăl/kyə lāt/] **17–B**
calculator [kăl/kyə lā/tər] **17–6, 183–25**
calculus [kăl/kyə ləs] **192–19**
CALENDAR [kăl/ən dər] **20–21**
CALENDAR EVENTS [kăl/ən dər ĭ vĕnts/] **22**
calf [kăf] **106–22**
   calf-length [kăf/ lĕnth/] **96–17**
call [köl]
   call button [köl/ bŭt/n] **121–28**
   international call [ĭn/tər năsh/ə nəl köl/] **15–35**
   Internet phone call [ĭn/tər nĕt/ fōn/ köl/] **14–20**
   local call [lō/kəl köl/] **15–31**
   long distance call [löng/ dĭs/təns köl/] **15–32**
call [köl] **48–A, 147–L**
   call in [köl/ ĭn/] **186–A**

calling card [kö/lĭng kärd/] **14–15**
calm [köm] **42–8**
camcorder [kăm/kör dər] **235–24**
camel [kăm/əl] **217–38**
camera [kăm/rə]
   camera case [kăm/rə kās/] **235–28**
   digital camera [dĭ/jə təl kăm/rə] **235–19**
   film camera [fĭlm/ kăm/rə] **235–21**
   security camera [sĭ kyōōr/ə tē kăm/rə] **50–19**
   35 mm camera
     [thür/tē fïv/ mïl/ə mē/tər kăm/rə] **235–21**
camisole [kăm/ə sōl/] **91–21**
campaign [kăm pān/] **139–29**
camper [kăm/pər] **156–9**
campfire [kămp/fïr/] **226–11**
camping [kăm/pĭng] **226–5**
   camping stove [kăm/pĭng stōv/] **226–16**
Campus [kăm/pəs] **5**
can [kăn] **74–3, 74–15**
   can opener [kăn/ ō/pə nər] **78–1, 146–8**
   electric can opener [ĭ lĕk/trĭk/ kăn/ ō/pə nər] **54–14**
   garbage can [gär/bĭj kăn/] **53–24**
cancer [kăn/sər] **111–10**
candle [kăn/dl] **56–20**
   candle holder [kăn/dl hōl/dər] **56–21**
candy [kăn/dē] **239–12**
   candy bar [kăn/dē bär/] **73–37**
   candy cane [kăn/dē kān/] **239–17**
   candy store [kăn/dē stör/] **131–17**
cane [kăn] **113–16, 239–17**
canned food [kănd/ fōōd/] **146–9**
Canned Foods [kănd/ fōōdz/] **72**
canoeing [kə nōō/ĭng] **226–3**
can't breathe [kănt/ brēdh/] **116–N**
canteen [kăn tēn/] **226–24**
canvas [kăn/vəs] **233–17**
canyon [kăn/yən] **204–17**
cap [kăp] **88–1, 206–7**
   baseball cap [bās/böl/ kăp/] **86–5**
   bump cap [bŭmp/ kăp/] **92–9**
   shower cap [show/ər kăp/] **108–1**
   surgical cap [sür/jĭ kəl kăp/] **121–37**
   surgical scrub cap [sür/jĭ kəl skrŭb/ kăp/] **93–35**
capital [kă/pət əl] **139–22**
capitalize [kă/pət əl īz/] **190–A, 190–B**
Capitol [kă/pət əl] **138–1**
capris [kə prēz/] **88–8**
capsule [kăp/səl] **113–23**
car [kär] **150–1**
   car accident [kär/ ăk/sə dənt] **144–2**
   car dealership [kär/ dē/lər shĭp/] **126–4**
   car safety seat [kär/ săf/tē sēt/] **37–19**
   4-door car [för/dör/ kär/] **156–1**
   sports car [spörts/kär/] **156–4**
   subway car [sŭb/wā/ kär/] **152–6**
   town car [town/ kär/] **152–20**
   2-door car [tōō/dör/ kär/] **156–2**
Car [kär] **157, 159**
CAR [kär] **156, 157, 158–159**
card [kärd] **239–5**
   ATM card [ā/tē/ĕm/ kärd/] **132–15**
   auto club card [ö tō/ klŭb/ kärd/] **162–4**

baseball cards [bās/böl/ kärdz/] **232–2**
card store [kärd/ stör/] **130–7**
copies of ID and credit cards
   [kä/pēz əv ī/dē/ ən krĕd/ət/ kärdz/] **146–19**
emergency card [ĭ mür/jən sē/ kärd/] **161–23**
fare card [fër/ kärd/] **152–11**
folding card table [fōl/dĭng/ kärd/ tā/bəl] **102–4**
green card [grēn/ kärd/] **40–2**
greeting card [grē/tĭng kärd/] **134–15**
health insurance card
   [hĕlth/ ĭn shŏŏr/əns kärd/] **118–3**
memory card [mĕm/ə rē kärd/] **235–20**
post card [pōst/ kärd/] **134–16**
Resident Alien card [rĕz/ə dənt ā/lē ən kärd/] **40–2**
rotary card file [rō/tə rē kärd/ fïl/] **183–44**
Social Security card
   [sō/shəl sĭ kyŏŏr/ə tē kärd/] **40–5**
Card [kärd] **135**
cardigan sweater [kär/də gən swĕt/ər] **88–2**
Cardinal Numbers [kärd/nəl nŭm/bərz] **16**
cardiologist [kär/dē äl/ə jīst] **120–3**
cardiopulmonary resuscitation (CPR)
   [kär/dē ō pŏŏl mə nër/ē rĭ sŭs/ə tā/shən /
   [sē/pē/är/] **117–17**
care [kër] **167–32**
careful worker [kër/fəl wür/kər] **179–2**
careless worker [kër/ləs wür/kər] **179–1**
childcare worker [chïld/kër wür/kər] **166–16**
CARE [kër] **114–115, 118, 119**
Care of Your Car [kër/ əv yər kär/] **157**
career counselor [kə rër/ kown/slər] **172–10**
Career Path [kə rër/ păth/] **172**
CAREER PLANNING [kə rër/ plăn/ïng] **172**
cargo van [kär/gō văn/] **156–13**
carnation [kär nā/shən] **211–20**
carousel [kär/ə sĕl/] **161–23**
carpenter [kär/pən tər] **62–12, 166–14**
carpet [kär/pət] **56–24**
carpool [kär/pōōl/] **219–I**
carriage [kär/ĭj] **37–20**
carrier [kär/ē ər] **37–17, 134–20**
carrots [kär/əts] **69–3**
carry [kär/ē] **11–F, 82–H**
CARS AND TRUCKS [kärz/ ən trŭks/] **156**
cart [kärt] **72–7, 129–28**
   housekeeping cart [hows/kē/pĭng kärt/] **184–19**
   luggage cart [lŭg/ĭj/ kärt/] **184–8**
carton [kär/tn] **74–4, 74–16**
cartoon [kär/tōōn] **236–3**
cartridge [kär/trĭj] **183–45**
carving knife [kär/vĭng nïf/] **78–12**
case [kās] **94–5, 235–28**
cash [kăsh]
   cash and coins [kăsh/ ən koynz/] **146–17**
   cash register [kăsh/ rĕj/ə stər] **27–10, 73–15**
cash [kăsh] **27–F, 132–A**
cashier [kă shïr/] **73–13, 166–15**
cashmere [kăzh/mïr/] **98–4**
Casserole [kăs/ə röl] **77**
casserole dish [kăs/ə röl dĭsh/] **78–10**
cassette [kə sĕt/] **234–6**
   videocassette [vĭ/dē ō kə sĕt/] **133–18**

cast [kăst] **113**–20
castle [kă/səl] **225**–12
Casual Clothes [kăzh/ōō əl klōz/] **88**
CASUAL, WORK, AND FORMAL CLOTHES
[kăzh/ōō əl würk/ ən för/məl klōz/] **88**–**89**
cat [kăt] **215**–9
catfish [kăt/fĭsh/] **71**–2
catalog [kăt ə /lög] **133**–11
catch [kăch] **230**–D
catcher's mask [kăch/ərz măsk/] **231**–15
caterer [kā/tər ər] **185**–16
caterpillar [kăt/ə pĭl/ər, kăt/ər–] **214**–20
cattle [kăt/l] **177**–21
cauliflower [kö/lĭ flow/ər, kä/–] **69**–14
cave [kāv] **220**–6
caverns [că/vərnz] **220**–7
cavity [kăv/ə tē] **119**–7
C-clamp [sē/klămp/] **180**–6
CD [sē/dē/] **196**–9, **234**–5
CD boombox [sē/dē/ bōōm/băks/] **234**–1
CD player [sē/dē/ plā/ər] **159**–38
celebrate [sĕl/ə brāt] **206**–C
celery [sĕl/ə rē] **69**–9
cell [sĕl] **194**–4
cell membrane [sĕl/ mĕm/brān] **194**–6
cell phone holder [sĕl/ fōn/ hōl/dər] **94**–15
cell phone kiosk [sĕl/ fōn/ kē/ösk] **131**–22
cell phone number [sĕl/ fōn/ nŭm/bər] **4**–12
cell wall [sĕl/ wäl/] **194**–5
cello [chĕl/ō] **238**–7
cellular phone [sĕl/yə lər fōn/] **14**–8
Celsius [sĕl/sē əs] **13**–2
cemetery [sĕ/mə tĕr/ē] **127**–15
cent [sĕnt] **26**–1, **26**–2, **26**–3, **26**–4
center [sĕn/tər]
automated postal center (APC)
[ö/tə māt ĭd pōs/təl sĕn/tər] / [ā/pē/sē/] **135**–10
childcare center [chĭld/kĕr/ sĕn/tər] **129**–30
convention center [kən vĕn/shən sĕn/tər] **127**–24
copy center [käp/ē sĕn/tər] **129**–18
entertainment center
[ĕn/tər tān/mənt sĕn/tər] **56**–5
resource center [rē/sörs sĕn/tər] **172**–9
CENTER [sĕn/tər] **208**–**209**
centimeter [cm] [sĕn/tə mē/tər] **17**–14
CENTRAL AMERICA [sĕn/trəl ə mĕr/ə kə] **200**–**201**
Central time [sĕn/trəl tīm/] **19**–31
cereal [sĭr/ē əl] **80**–9
ceremony [sĕr/ə mō/nē] **206**–6
certificate [sər tĭf/ə kət] **40**–1, **41**–11
Certificate of Naturalization
[sər tĭf/ə kət əv năch/rə lə zā/shən] **40**–6
certified [sür/tə fīd/]
Certified Mail® [sür/tə fīd/ māl/] **134**–4
certified nursing assistant (CNA)
[sür/tə fīd/ nür/sĭng ə sĭs/tənt] / [sē/ĕn/ā/]
120–12
chain [chān] **51**–33, **95**–33, **180**–41
chair [chĕr] **7**–11
armchair [ärm/chĕr/] **56**–22
beach chair [bēch/ chĕr/] **225**–22
dining room chair [dī/nĭng rōōm/chĕr/] **55**–8

easy chair [ē/zē/ chĕr/] **56**–22
folding chair [fōld/ĭng chĕr/] **102**–5
high chair [hī/ chĕr/] **37**–6, **82**–3
rocking chair [räk/ĭng chĕr/] **37**–21
wheelchair [wēl/chĕr/] **113**–9
chalk [chök] **7**–18
chalkboard [chök/börd/] **6**–1
challenged [chăl/əngd] **32**–10
change [chānj] **36**–G, **60**–P, **148**–C
change purse [chānj/ pürs/] **94**–14
changing [chān/jĭng]
changing pad [chān/jĭng păd/] **59**–2
changing table [chān/jĭng tā/bəl] **59**–1
charger [chär/jər] **14**–10, **234**–17, **235**–27
chart [chärt] **121**–24
cheap [chēp] **23**–20
check [chĕk] **132**–13
check book [chĕk/ bŏŏk/] **132**–12
check-in kiosk [chĕk/ĭn kē/ösk] **160**–2
checkstand [chĕk/stănd/] **73**–12
paycheck [pā/chĕk/] **165**–14
check [chĕk]
check blood pressure [chĕk/ blŭd/ prĕsh/ər] **118**–A
check email [chĕk/ ē/ māl/] **39**–W
check in [chĕk/ ĭn/] **160**–A
check Internet job sites
[chĕk/ ĭn/tər nĕt/ jäb/ sīts/] **173**–D
check messages [chĕk/ mĕs/ə jĭz] **171**–R
check out [chĕk/ owt/] **133**–C
check the correct boxes
[chĕk/ dhə kə rĕkt/ bäk/səz] **9**–U
check the oil [chĕk/ dhə oyl/] **157**–H
check the pronunciation
[chĕk/ dhe prə nən sē ā/ shən] **8**–D
check your bags [chĕk/ yər băgz/] **160**–B
check pulse [chĕk/ pŭls/] **122**–A
check your spelling [chĕk/ yər spĕl/ĭng] **197**–F
check your understanding
[chĕk/ yər ŭn/dər stănd/ĭng] **12**–N
check your work [chĕk/ yər würk/] **10**–L
checked [chĕkt] **96**–24
checkers [chĕk/ərz] **232**–7
checking account number
[chĕk/ĭng ə kownt/ nŭm/bər] **132**–14
checkout [chĕk/owt/] **133**–10
Checkpoint [chĕk/poynt/] **160**
cheddar cheese [chĕd/ər chēz/] **71**–28
cheek [chēk] **106**–3
cheese [chēz] **66**–4
American cheese [ə mĕr/ə kən chēz/] **71**–26
cheddar cheese [chĕd/ər chēz/] **71**–28
cheeseburger [chēz/bür/gər] **79**–3
cheesecake [chēz/kāk/] **81**–34
grilled cheese sandwich
[grĭld/ chēz/ săn/wĭch, –sănd/–] **80**–10
Swiss cheese [swĭs/ chēz/] **71**–27
Cheesy Tofu Vegetable Casserole
[chē/zē tō/fōō vĕj/tə bəl kăs/ə rōl] **77**
chef [shĕf] **83**–16
chef's hat [shĕfs/ hăt/] **93**–28
chef's jacket [shĕfs/ jăk/ət] **93**–29
chef's salad [shĕfs/ săl/ əd] **80**–14

executive chef [ĭg zĕk/yə tĭv shĕf/] **185**–7
head chef [hĕd/ shĕf/] **185**–7
sous chef [sōō/ shĕf/] **185**–6
Chef [shĕf] **93**
chemist [kĕm/ĭst] **195**–25
Chemistry [kĕm/ə strē] **195**
cherries [chĕr/ēz] **68**–11
cherry picker [chĕr/ē pĭk/ər] **178**–5
chess [chĕs] **232**–8
chest [chĕst] **59**–16, **104**–4, **107**–25
chest of drawers [chĕst/ əv drörz/] **59**–6
chicken [chĭk/ən] **66**–3, **70**–16
chicken pox [chĭk/ən päks/] **111**–6
chicken sandwich [chĭk/ən săn/wĭch, –sănd–] **79**–5
fried chicken [frīd/ chĭk/ən] **76**–1
roast chicken [rōst/ chĭk/ən] **81**–22
Chicken [chĭk/ən] **77**
chief justice [chēf/ jŭs/təs] **138**–13
CHILDCARE AND PARENTING
[chīld/kĕr ən pĕr/ən tĭng] **36**–**37**
child / children [chīld] / [chĭl/ drən]
childcare center [chīld/kĕr sĕn/tər] **129**–30
childcare worker [chīld/kĕr wür/kər] **166**–16
children's program [chĭl/drənz prō/grăm] **236**–9
child safety seat [chīld/ sāf/tē sēt/] **159**–53
grandchild [grăn/chīld/, grănd/–] **34** ✦
lost child [löst/ chīld/] **144**–1
Childhood Diseases [chīld/hŏŏd dĭ zē/zəz] **111**
chili peppers [chĭl/ē pĕp/ərz] **69**–29
chill [chĭl] **76**–D
chills [chĭlz] **110**–9
chimney [chĭm/nē] **53**–5
chimpanzee [chĭm/păn zē/] **217**–27
chin [chĭn] **106**–1
chipmunk [chĭp/mŭngk] **215**–20
chips [chĭps] **73**–35
chiropractors [kī/rō prăk/tərz] **120**
chisel [chĭz/əl] **181**–55
choke [chōk] **116**–L
choose [chōōz] **9**–P
chop [chäp] **77**–L
chops [chäps] **70**–10, **70**–15
Christmas [krĭs/məs] **22**–18
Christmas tree [krĭs/məs trē/] **239**–16
chromosome [krō/mə zōm/] **194**–8
chrysanthemum [krī săn/thə məm] **211**–21
church [chürch] **127**–14
chute [shōōt] **51**–26
circle [sür/ kəl] **193**–34
circle [sür/ kəl] **9**–Q
circular saw [sür/kyə lər sö/] **180**–9
circulation desk [sür/kyə lā/shən dĕsk/] **133**–2
circumference [sər küm/frəns] **193**–36
citizen [sĭt/ə zən] **30**–5
Citizenship Requirements
[sĭt/ə zən shĭp/ rĭ kwīr/mənts] **140**
city [sĭt/ē] **4**–7, **52**–1
city code [sĭt/ē kōd/] **15**–34
city council [sĭt/ē kown/səl] **139**–27
city hall [sĭt/ē häl/] **124**–8
City Government [sĭt/ē gŭ/vərn mənt] **139**
CITY STREETS [sĭt/ē strēts/] **126**–**127**

CIVIC RIGHTS AND RESPONSIBILITIES
[sī/vĭk rīts n rĭ spän/sə bĭl/ə tēz] **140**
Civilizations [sĭ/və lə zā/shenz] **199**
claim [klām] **160**–L
clamp [klămp] **180**–6
clams [klămz] **71**–15
clarinet [klăr/ə nĕt/] **238**–2
classical [kla/sĭ kəl] **237**–21
   classical concert [kla/sĭ kəl kän/sərt] **223**–14
classified ad [klăs/e fīd] **48**–2
Classmates [klăs/māts/] **8**
classroom [klăs/rōōm/] **5**–7
CLASSROOM [klăs/rōōm/] **6**–7
claw [klö] **214**–2
clean [klēn] **101**–16
clean [klēn] **76**–A
   clean teeth [klēn/ tēth/] **119**–A
   clean the house [klēn/ dhə hows/] **39**–O
   clean the lint trap [klēn/ dhə lĭnt/ trăp/] **101**–D
   clean the oven [klēn/ dhə ŭv/ən] **60**–C
   clean up [klēn/ ŭp/] **147**–M
cleaner [klēn/ər]
   dry cleaners [drī/ klēn/ərz] **128**–2
   glass cleaner [glăs/ klēn/ər] **61**–14
   oven cleaner [ŭv/ən klēn/ər] **61**–3
   vacuum cleaner [văk/yōōm klēn/ər] **61**–10
   vacuum cleaner attachments
      [văk/yōōm klēn/ər ə tăch/mənts] **61**–11
   vacuum cleaner bag [văk/yəm klēn/ər băg/] **61**–12
CLEANING SUPPLIES [klē/nĭng sə plīz/] **61**
cleanser [klēn/zər] **61**–18
CLEANUP [klēn/ŭp/] **148**–149
clear [klĭr] **13**–9
   clear tape [klĭr/tāp/] **183**–30
clear [klĭr] **82**–G
   clear off [klĭr/ äf/] **10**–I
clerk [klürk] **5**–13, **182**–2
   admissions clerk [əd mĭsh/ənz klürk/] **120**–14
   desk clerk [dĕsk/ klürk/] **184**–11
   DMV clerk [dē/ĕm/vē/ klürk/] **136**–3
   file clerk [fīl/ klürk/] **182**–10
   grocery clerk [grōs/rē klürk/, grōsh/–, grō/sə–] **72**–4
   library clerk [lī/brĕr ē klürk/] **133**–1
   payroll clerk [pā/rōl/ klürk/] **165**–10
   postal clerk [pō/stəl klürk/] **135**–7
   retail clerk [rē/tāl/ klürk/] **169**–53
   salesclerk [sālz/klürk/] **94**–3
   shipping clerk [shĭp/ĭng klürk/] **175**–16
   stock clerk [stäk/ klürk/] **169**–59
click [klĭk] **197**–B
climb [klĭm] **224**–C
climbing apparatus [klĭm/ĭng ă/pə ră/təs] **224**–14
clinic [klĭn/ĭk] **186**–2
clip-on earrings [klĭp/än ĭr/ĭngz, –ön–] **95**–37
clipper [klĭp/ər] **109**–31, **176**–11
clips [klĭps] **108**–19, **183**–31, **194**–24
clock [kläk] **7**–9, **58**–24, **165**–7
   clock radio [kläk/ rā/dē ō] **102**–6
close [klōz] **6**–H
closet [kläz/ət] **57** ✦, **58**–5
Closures [klō/zhərz] **99**

cloth [klöth] **181**–54
   cloth diaper [klöth/ dī/pərz] **37**–8
   tablecloth [tā/bəl klöth/] **55**–12
   washcloth [wäsh/klöth/] **57**–4
clothes [klōz] **146**–6
   clothesline [klōz/līn/] **101**–9
   clothespin [klōz/pĭn/] **101**–10
CLOTHES [klōz] **86**–87, **88**–89, **96**–97, **98**–99
clothing [klō/dhĭng] **102**–2
CLOTHING [klō/dhĭng] **90**, **92**–93
Clothing Problems [klō/dhĭng präb/ləmz] **97**
cloudy [klow/dē] **13**–10
club [klŭb] **162**–4, **223**–12, **231**–1
   club sandwich [klŭb săn/wĭch/, –sănd–] **80**–12
clubs [klŭbz] **233**–32
clutch [klŭch] **159**–49
   clutch bag [klŭch/ băg/] **89**–19
CNA (certified nursing assistant) [sē/ĕn/ā/] /
   [sür/tə tə fīd/ nür/sĭng ə sĭs/tənt] **120**–12
coach [kōch] **5**–20, **229**–2
coal [kōl] **218**–4
coarse adjustment knob
   [körs/ ə jüst/mənt näb/] **194**–22
Coast Guard [kōst/ gärd/] **138**–18
coat [kōt] **90**–2, **216**–19
   lab coat [lăb/ kōt/] **93**–33
   raincoat [rān/ kōt/] **90**–18
   sports coat [spörts/ kōt/] **89**–14
   trench coat [trĕnch/ kōt/] **90**–21
cobra [kō/brə] **213**–41
cockpit [käk/pĭt/] **161**–10
cockroaches [käk/rō/chəz] **63**–26
cocktail dress [käk/tāl/ drĕs/] **89**–20
coconuts [kō/kə nŭts/] **68**–24
cod [käd] **71**–8, **212**–5
code [kōd]
   area code [ĕr/ē ə kōd/] **15**–29
   bar code [bär/ kōd/] **27**–4
   city code [sĭt/ē kōd/] **15**–34
   country code [kŭn/trē kōd/] **15**–33
coffee [kö/fē] **73**–33, **81**–37, **81**–38
   coffeemaker [kö/fē mā/kər] **54**–11
   coffee mug [kö/fē mŭg/] **55**–7
   coffee shop [kö/fē shäp/] **126**–11
   coffee table [kö/fē tā/bəl] **56**–19
COFFEE SHOP MENU [kö/fē shäp/ mĕn/yōō] **80**–81
coins [koynz] **146**–17
   coin purse [koyn/ pürs/] **94**–14
Coins [koynz] **26**
colander [käl/ən dər] **78**–17
cold [kōld] **13**–6, **42**–4, **111**–1
   cold tablets [kōld tăb/ləts] **113**–27
   cold water [kōld wö/tər] **57**–7
coleslaw [kōl/slö/] **80**–18
collar [käl/ər] **100**–4
collate [kō/lāt/, kə lāt/] **171**–E
collect [kə lĕkt/] **232**–A
college [käl/ĭj] **127**–17, **188**–6, **188**–7
   college degree [käl/ĭj də grē/] **41**–7
   college dormitory [käl/ĭj dör/mə tör/ē] **52**–8
cologne [kə lōn/] **108**–6
colon [kō/lən] **190**–17

Colonial Period [kə lō/nē əl pĭr/ē əd] **198**
colonies [kä/lə nēz] **198**–1
colonists [kä/lə nĭsts] **198**–2
color [kŭl/ər]
   watercolor [wö/tər kŭl/ər] **233**–21
color [kŭl/ər] **33**–D
coloring book [kŭl/ə rĭng bŏŏk/] **59**–13
Colors [kŭl/ərs] **24**
COLORS [kŭl/ərs] **24**
Columbus Day [kə lŭm/bəs dā/] **22**–15
column [käl/ŭm] **107**–49
comb [kōm] **33**–21, **108**–13
comb [kōm] **108**–G
come [kŭm] **39**–R
comedy [käm/ə dē] **236**–2, **237**–13
comet [käm/ət] **205**–24
comfort [kŭm/fərt] **36**–I
comma [käm/ə] **190**–14
commercial fisher [kə mür/shəl fĭsh/ər] **167**–17
commit a crime [kə mĭt/ ə krīm/] **142** ✦
Common Illnesses and Childhood Diseases
   [käm/ən ĭl/nə səz ən chīld/hŏŏd-dĭ zē/zəz] **111**
COMMUNITY CLEANUP
   [kə myōō/nə tē klēn/ŭp] **148**–149
community college
   [kə myōō/nə tē käl/ĭj] **127**–17, **188**–6
Comparing Clothing [kəm pĕr/ĭng klō/dhĭng] **97**
compartment [kəm pärt/mənt] **159**–44, **161**–13
complaint [kəm plānt/] **97** ✦
Complex [käm/plĕks/] **51**
compliment [käm/plə mĕnt/] **12** ✦
compliment [käm/plə mĕnt/] **12**–C
composer [kəm pō/zər] **199**–15
composition [käm/pə zĭsh/ən] **199**–14
compost [käm/pōst/] **219**–M
compost pile [käm/pōst pīl/] **53**–25
computer [kəm pyōō/tər] **7**–15, **183**–17
   computer lab [kəm pyōō/tər lăb/] **5**–15
   computer software engineer
      [kəm pyōō/tər söft/wĕr/ ĕn/jə nĭr/] **167**–18
   computer technician [kəm pyōō/tər tĕk nĭsh/ən]
      167–19, **182**–12
Computer [kəm pyōō/tər] **196**
COMPUTERS [kəm pyōō/tərz] **196**
conceal [kən sēl/] **143**–C
concert [kän/sərt] **222**–5, **223**–14
concierge [kän/sē ĕrzh/, kōn/–] **184**–4
conclusion [kən klōō/zhən] **190**–8
concrete [käng/krēt, kän krēt/] **178**–10
conditioner [kən dĭsh/ə nər] **108**–11, **159**–39
Conditions [kən dĭsh/ənz] **13**, **111**
CONDITIONS [kən dĭsh/ənz] **111**
condominium [kän/də mĭn/ē əm] **52**–5
conduct [kən dŭkt/] **238**–C
conductor [kən dŭk/tər] **152**–13
cone [kōn] **79**–13, **193**–40
   pinecone [pīn/kōn] **210**–11
conference room [kän/frəns rōōm/] **182**–4
confetti [kən fĕt/ē] **239**–3
confused [kən fyōōzd/] **43**–26
congestion [kən jĕs/chən] **110**–7
Congress [käng/grəs] **138**–2, **198**–6

congressperson [kän/grəs pür/sən] **138**–4
CONSERVATION [kän/sər vā/shən] **218–219**
Conserve Energy and Resources
[kən sürv/ ĕn/ər jē ən rē/sörs/əz] **219**
console [kän/söl] **232**–3
constellation [kän/stə lā/shən] **205**–14
Constitution [kän/stə tōō/shən] **198**–19
construction [kən strŭk/shən]
construction paper [kən strŭk/shən pā/pər] **232**–12
construction site [kən strŭk/shən sīt/] **126**–2
construction worker
[kən strŭk/shən wür/kər] **178**–1
CONSTRUCTION [kən strŭk/shən] **178**
Construction Worker [kən strŭk/shən wür/kər] **92**
contact [kän/tăkt] **146**–2
contact lenses [kän/tăkt lĕn/zəz] **115**–8
container [kən tā/nər] **74**–5, **74**–17, **78**–4
CONTAINERS AND PACKAGING
[kən tā/nərz ən păk/ĭ jĭng] **74**
continental [kän/tə nĕnt/əl] **198**–6
contractor [kän/trăk tər] **186**–5
control [kən tröl/] **121**–27, **232**–4
convenience store [kən vēn/yəns stör/] **128**–3
convention center [kən vĕn/shən sĕn/tər] **127**–24
convert [kən vürt/] **17**–D, **75**–C
convertible [kən vür/tə bəl] **156**–5
conveyor belt [kən vā/ər bĕlt/] **175**–16
convict [kän/vĭkt/] **141**–15
convict [kən vĭkt/] **141**–E
cook [kŏŏk] **185**–1, **185** ✦
cook [kŏŏk] **39**–Q, **76**–C, **170**–C
cooked [kŏŏkt] **70**–25
cookies [kŏŏk/ēz] **73**–38
cookie sheet [kŏŏk/ē shēt/] **78**–27
cool [kōōl] **13**–5
cooler [kōō/lər] **225**–19
co-op [kō/äp/] **52** ✦
copier [kä/pē ər]
photocopier [fō/tō kä/pē ər] **183**–23
copies / copy [kä/pēz] / [kä/pē]
copies of ID and credit cards
[käp/ēz əv ī/dē ən krĕd/ət kärdz/] **146**–19
copies of important papers
[käp/ēz əv ĭm pört/ənt pā/pərz] **146**–20
copy center [käp/ē sĕn/tər] **129**–18
copy [käp/ē] **8**–E
coral [kör/əl] **220**–5
cord [körd] **14**–2
bungee cord [bŭn/jē körd/] **181**–15
cordless phone [körd/ləs fōn/] **15**–24
extension cord [ĭk stĕn/shən körd/] **181**–14
frayed cord [frād/ körd/] **179**–5
power cord [pow/ər körd/] **196**–2
corduroy [kör/də roy/] **99**–11
core course [kör/ körs/] **189** ✦
corn [körn] **69**–12, **177**–4
corn rows [körn/ rōz/] **33**–14
corned beef [körnd/ bēf/] **71**–22
corner [kör/nər] **128**–7
coronary disease [kör/ə nĕ/rē dĭ zēz/] **111** ✦
corral [kə răl/] **177**–17
correct [kə rĕkt/] **10**–N

correction [kə rĕk/shən]
correction fluid [kə rĕk/shən flōō/əd] **183**–36
correction tape [kə rĕk/shən tāp/] **183**–37
cost [köst] **27**–7, **122**–1
costume [käs/tōōm] **239**–11
cotton [kät/n] **98**–1, **177**–6
couch [kowch] **56**–18
cough [köf] **110**–A
cough syrup [köf/ sĭr/əp, –sür/–] **113**–29
council [kown/səl] **139**–27
councilperson [kown/səl pür/sən] **139**–28
counselor [kown/slər] **5**–6, **172**–10
count [kownt] **84**–A
counter [kown/tər] **54**–22, **113**–18
counterperson [kown/tər pür/sən] **79**–17
Counterperson [kown/tər pür/sən] **93**
country [kŭn/trē] **52**–4, **227**–3, **237**–27
country code [kŭn/trē kōd/] **15**–33
county fair [kown/tē fĕr/] **223**–13
coupe [kōōp] **156**–2
couple [kŭ/pəl] **35**–20, **35**–21, **239**–4
coupons [kōō/pönz/] **67**–15
courier [kür/ē ər, kŏōr/–] **168**–40
course [körs] **172**–8, **189** ✦
court [kört]
basketball court [băs/kət böl/ kört/] **229**–7
courthouse [kört/hows/] **125**–13
courtroom [kört/rōōm/] **141**–7
court reporter [kört/ rĭ pör/tər] **141**–12
courtyard [kört/yärd/] **51**–21
food court [fōōd/ kört/] **131**–15
Supreme Court [sə prēm/ kört/] **138**–11
tennis court [tĕ/nəs kört/] **224**–6
cousin [kŭz/ən] **34**–9
cover [kŭv/ər] **158**–9, **181**–46
coveralls [kŭv/ər ölz/] **92**–8
cover-up [kŭv/ər ŭp/] **90**–25
cow [kow] **215**–1
cowboy hat [kow/boy/ hăt/] **92**–18
coyote [kī ō/tē, kī/ōt/] **216**–3
CPR (cardiopulmonary resuscitation) [sē/ pē/är/] /
[kär/dē ō pŏōl/mə nĕr/ē-rē sŭs/ə tā/shən] **117**–17
CPU [sē/ pē/yōō/] **196**–4
crab [krăb] **71**–9, **212**–20
cracked [krăkt] **62**–4
cradle [krād/l] **59**–20
crane [krān] **178**–7
crash [krăsh] **144**–3
crayons [krā/änz] **59**–14
cream [krēm] **24**–16, **81**–41, **113**–25
antihistamine cream
[ăn/tĭ hĭs/tə mēn krēm/] **117**–11
ice-cream [īs/ krēm/] **72**–26
ice-cream cone [īs/ krēm kōn/] **79**–13
ice cream shop [īs/ krēm shäp/] **131**–16
shaving cream [shā/vĭng krēm/] **109**–29
sour cream [sow/ər krēm/] **72**–21
creamer [krē/mər] **55**–15
credit [krĕd/ət] **146**–19
creek [krēk, krĭk] **204** ✦
crescent moon [krĕs/ənt mōōn/] **205**–10

crew [krōō] **176**–1, **176**–4
crewneck [krōō/nĕk] **96**–7
crew socks [krōō/säks/] **91**–8
crib [krĭb] **59**–3
cricket [krĭk/ət] **214**–23
crime [krīm] **142** ✦
CRIME [krīm] **142**
criminal [krīm/ə nəl] **142** ✦
crocheting [krō shā/ĭng] **233**–25
crocodile [krăk/ə dīl/] **213**–37
crocus [krō/kəs] **211**–17
Crops [kräps] **177**
cross [krös]
cross-country skiing [krös/kŭn/trē skē/ĭng] **227**–3
crosswalk [krös/wök/] **128**–15
cross [krös] **128**–A
cross out [krös/ owt/] **9**–R
crossing [krö/sĭng] **154**–13, **154**–14, **154**–15
crown [krown] **119**–9
crucible tongs [krōō/sə bəl tängz/, –töngz/] **195**–44
crutches [krŭch/əz] **113**–10
cry [krī] **206**–B
cube [kyōōb] **193**–38
cubicle [kyōōb/ə kəl] **182**–7
cucumbers [kyōō/kŭm bərz] **69**–10
cuff [kŭf] **100**–9
cup [kŭp] **75**–2, **75**–10, **83**–24
1/2 cup [hăf/ kŭp/] **75**–9
1/4 cup [kwör/tər kŭp/] **75**–8
teacup [tē/kŭp/] **55**–6
curb [kürb] **129**–21
curling iron [kür/lĭng ī/ərn] **108**–17
curly hair [kür/lē hĕr/] **33**–11
cursor [kür/sər] **197**–14
curtains [kür/tnz] **57**–12, **58**–7
curved line [kürvd/ līn/] **193**–23
cushion [kŏŏ/shən] **56** ✦, **100**–13
customer [kŭs/tə mər] **72**–1, **94**–4, **132**–2, **164**–2
customer service [kŭs/tə mər sür/vəs] **97** ✦
customer service representative
[kŭs/tə mər-sür/vəs rĕ/prə zĕn/tə tĭv] **167**–20
Customs [kŭs/təmz] **161**
customs officer [kŭs/təmz ö/fə sər] **161**–17
cut [kŭt] **91**–10, **110**–13
cut [kŭt] **33**–A, **109**–N
cut up [kŭt/ ŭp/] **77**–I
cute [kyōōt] **32**–14
cutlets [kŭt/ləts] **70**–6
cutter [kut/ər] **183**–22, **232**–16
cutting board [kŭt/ĭng börd/] **54**–27
cycling [sī/klĭng] **228**–5
cyclist [sī/klĭst] **224**–2
cylinder [sĭl/ən dər] **193**–41, **195**–38
cytoplasm [sī/tə plăzm] **194**–9
daffodil [dăf/ə dĭl/] **211**–25
daily [dā/lē] **20**–21
DAILY ROUTINES [dā/lē rōō tēnz/] **38–39**
Dairy [dĕr/ē] **72**
daisy [dā/zē] **211**–14
dance [dăns] **64**–A
dangerous [dān/jər əs] **186**–1
dark blue [därk/ blōō/] **24**–10

Index

Dashboard and Instrument Panel
[dăsh/börd/ ən ĭn/strə mənt păn/əl] **159**
dates [dāts] **20**–1, **68**–28
   date of birth [dāt əv bürth/] **4**–13
   expiration date
     [ĕk/spə rā/shən dāt/] **112**–7, **136**–10
daughter [dö/tər] **34**–14
   daughter-in-law [dö/tər ĭn lö/] **34** ✦
   granddaughters [grăn/dö/tərz] **34** ✦
   stepdaughter [stĕp/dö/tər] **35** ✦
day [dā] **20**–2
   birthday [bürth/dā/] **22**–1
   Columbus Day [kə lŭm/bəs dā] **22**–15
   daylight saving time [dā/līt/ sā/vĭng tīm/] **19**–25
   every day [ĕv/rē dā/] **20**–21
   Independence Day [ĭn/də pĕn/dəns dā/] **22**–13
   Labor Day [lā/bər dā/] **22**–14
   Martin Luther King Jr. Day
     [mär/tən lōō/thər kĭng/ jōōn/yər-dā/] **22**–10
   Memorial Day [mə mör/ē əl dā/] **22**–12
   New Year's Day [nōō/ yïrz/ dā/] **22**–9
   Presidents' Day [prĕz/ə dənts dā/] **22**–11
   Veterans Day [vĕt/ər ənz dā/] **22**–16
Day [dā] **18**
DAY AT SCHOOL [dā/ ăt skōōl/] **11**
DAY AT WORK [dā/ ăt würk/] **186**–187
Days of the Week [dāz/ əv dhə wēk/] **20**
dead [dĕd]
   dead-bolt lock [dĕd/bōlt/ läk/] **51**–34
   dead end [dĕd/ ĕnd/] **154**–6
deaf [dĕf] **32**–12
Dealer [dē/lər] **158**
dealership [dē/lər shĭp/] **126**–4
death certificate [dĕth/ sər tĭf/ə kət] **41**–11
debate [də bāt/] **139**–B
decaf coffee [dē/kăf/ kö/fē] **81**–38
decay [də kā/] **119**–7
December [dĭ sĕm/bər] **21**–36
decimal point [dĕ/sə məl poynt/] **17**–7
Decimals [dĕ/sə məlz] **17**
deck [dĕk] **240**–2
declaration [dĕk/lə rā/shən]
   declaration form [dĕk/lə rā/shən förm/] **161**–16
   Declaration of Independence
     [dĕk/lə rā/shən əv ĭn/də pĕn/dəns] **198**–5
decline [də klīn/] **12**–J
decorations [dĕk/ə rā/shənz] **240**–1
deductions [də dŭk/shənz] **165**–13
deed [dĕd] **41**–9
deer [dïr] **216**–14
defendant [dĭ fĕn/dənt] **141**–5
defense attorney [dĭ fĕns/ ə tür/nē] **141**–4
defroster [də fräs/tər] **159**–41
degrees [də grēz/] **13**–8, **193**–26
delayed flight [də lād/ flīt/] **161**–30
delete [də lēt/] **196**–C
DELI [dĕl/ē] **71**
deliver [də lĭv/ər] **11**–G, **135**–E
delivery person [də lĭv/ə rē pür/sən] **167**–21
dementia [də mĕn/shə] **111**–18
demonstration [dĕ/mən strā/shən] **122**–6
denim [dĕ/nəm] **99**–7

denominator [də nömə nā/tər] **192**–6
dental [dĕn/təl]
   dental assistant [dĕn/təl ə sĭs/tənt] **119**–2, **167**–22
   dental floss [dĕn/təl flös/, –fläs/] **109**–24
   dental hygienist [dĕn/təl hī jē/nĭst, –jē/nĭst] **119**–3
   dental instruments [dĕn/təl ĭn/strə mənts] **119**–4
DENTAL CARE [dĕn/təl kër/] **119**
Dental Problems [dĕn/təl präb/ləmz] **119**
dentist [dĕn/tĭst] **119**–1
Dentistry [dĕn/təs trē/] **119**
dentures [dĕn/chərz] **119**–10
deodorant [dē ō/dər ənt] **108**–5
department [dĭ pärt/mənt] **95**–7, **95**–8
   Department of Motor Vehicles
     [dĭ pärt/mənt əv mō/tər vē/ĭ kəlz] **124**–4
   department store [dĭ pärt/mənt stör/] **131**–13
DEPARTMENT OF MOTOR VEHICLES (DMV)
   [dĭ pärt/mənt əv mō/tər vē/ĭ kəlz] / [dē/ĕm/vē/]
   136–137
departure [dĭ pär/chər] **161**–5, **161**–7
deposit [dĭ päz/ət] **132**–3, **132**–7
   deposit slip [dĭ päz/ət slĭp/] **132**–4
depression [də prĕ/shən] **115**–5
depth [dĕpth] **17**–18
DESCRIBING CLOTHES [dĭ skrī/bĭng klōz/] **96**–97
DESCRIBING HAIR [dĭ skrī/bĭng hër/] **33**
DESCRIBING PEOPLE [dĭ skrī/bĭng pē/pəl] **32**
DESCRIBING THINGS [dĭ skrī/bĭng thĭngz/] **23**
desert [dĕz/ərt] **204**–4
design [dĭ zīn/] **175**–A
designated drivers [dĕz/ĭg nā/təd drī/vərz] **143** ✦
designer [dĭ zī/nər] **98** ✦, **167**–30, **175**–2, **176**–5
desk [dĕsk] **6**–7, **182**–9
   circulation desk [sür/kyə lā/shən dĕsk/] **133**–2
   desk clerk [dĕsk klürk/] **184**–11
   front desk [frŭnt/ dĕsk/] **184**–12
Desktop Computer [dĕsk/täp/ kəm pyōō/tər] **196**
Desserts [dĭ zürts] **81**
dessert tray [dĭ zürt/ trā/] **83**–10
destination [dĕs/tə nā/shən] **161** ✦
detector [dĭ tĕk/tər] **51**–29
detergent [dĭ tür/jənt] **101**–8
device [də vīs/] **225**–20
diabetes [dī/ə bē/tēz, –təs] **111**–12
diagonal [dī ăg/ə nəl, –ăg/nəl] **193**–31
dial [dī/əl] **15**–A, **15**–E
diameter [dī ăm/ə tər] **193**–37
diamonds [dī/məndz] **233**–29
diaper [dī/pər] **37**–8, **37**–10
   diaper pail [dī/pər pāl/] **37**–7
diaphragm [dī/ə frăm/] **194**–19
dice [dīs] **232**–6
dice [dīs] **77**–J
dictate [dĭk/tāt/] **8**–N
dictator [dĭk/tā/tər] **199**–6
dictionary [dĭk/shə nër/ē] **7**–30, **7**–31
die [dī] **41**–R
dietician [dī/ə tĭsh/ən] **120**–15
difference [dĭf/rəns] **192**–8
different [dĭf/rənt, dī/fə rənt] **23**–16
DIFFERENT [dĭf/rənt, dī/fə rənt] **28**–29

DIFFERENT PLACES TO LIVE
   [dĭ/frənt plā/səz tə lĭv/, dī/fə rənt] **52**
difficult [dĭf/ĭ kült/] **23**–24
digital [dĭ/jə təl]
   digital camera [dĭ/jə təl kăm/rə] **235**–19
   digital photo album [dĭ/jə təl fō/tō ăl/bəm] **235**–32
dime [dīm] **26**–3
Dimensions [də mĕn/shənz] **17**
diner [dī/nər] **82**–6, **185**–9
dining [dī/nĭng]
   dining area [dī/nĭng ër/ē ə] **46**–7
   dining room [dī/nĭng rōōm/] **82**–1
   dining room chair [dī/nĭng rōōm/ chër/] **55**–8
   dining room table [dī/nĭng rōōm/tā/bəl] **55**–9
Dining [dī/nĭng] **185**
DINING AREA [dī/nĭng ër/ē ə] **55**
dinner [dĭn/ər] **72**–28
   dinner fork [dĭn/ər förk/] **83**–28
   dinner plate [dĭn/ər plāt/] **83**–18
   dinner salad [dĭn/ər săl/əd] **80**–15
Dinner [dĭn/ər] **81**
diploma [də plō/mə] **40**–3
direct flight [də rĕkt/ flīt/, dī–] **161** ✦
Directions [də rĕk/shənz] **9, 155**
DIRECTIONS AND MAPS
   [də rĕk/shənz ən măps/, dī–] **155**
directory [də rĕk/tə rē, dī–] **131**–24
   directory assistance
     [də rĕk/tə rē ə sĭs/təns, dī–] **14**–22
dirty [dür/tē] **101**–15
Disabilities [dĭs/sə bĭl/ə tēz] **32**
disagree [dĭs/sə grē/] **12**–L
disappointed [dĭ/sə poyn/təd] **28**–4
DISASTERS [dĭ/zăs tərz] **144**–145
disc [dĭsk] **231**–27
discipline [dĭs/ə plən] **36**–K
discuss [dĭ skŭs/] **8**–G
disease [dĭ zēz/] **111**–11, **111** ✦, **119**–11
Diseases [dĭ zē/zəz] **111**
disgusted [dĭ skŭs/təd] **42**–7
dish [dĭsh] **55**–1
   casserole dish [kăs/ə rōl dĭsh/] **78**–10
   dish rack [dĭsh/ răk/] **54**–5
   dish room [dĭsh/ rōōm/] **83**–13
   dish towel [dĭsh/ tow/əl] **61**–22
   dishwasher [dĭsh/wä/shər, –wö/–]
     54–8, **83**–14, **185**–2
   dishwashing liquid [dĭsh/wä/shĭng lĭk/wəd] **61**–21
   satellite dish [să/tə līt dĭsh/] **53**–6
   soap dish [sōp/ dĭsh/] **57**–25
disinfectant wipes [dĭs/ən fĕk/tənt wīps/] **61**–23
display case [dĭ splā/ kās/] **94**–5
disposable [dĭ spō/zə bəl]
   disposable diaper [dĭ spō/zə bəl dī/pər] **37**–10
   disposable gloves [dĭ spō/zə bəl glŭvz/] **93**–27
disposal [dĭ spō/zəl] **54**–7, **121**–31
dive [dīv] **230**–K
divide [də vīd/] **17**–A, **192**–D
diving [dī/vĭng] **227**–12
   diving mask [dī/vĭng măsk/] **225**–6
divorced couple [də vörst/ kŭ/pəl] **35**–21
DJ [dē/jā/] **64**–4

DMV [dē/ĕm/vē/]
DMV clerk [dē/ĕm/vē/ klŭrk/] **136**–3
DMV handbook [dē/ĕm/vē/ hănd/bŏŏk/] **136**–1
do [dōō] **39**–T
do an experiment [dōō ən ĭk spĕr/ə mənt] **195**–B
do crafts [dōō krăfts/] **232**–D
do errands [dōō ĕr/əndz] **128** ✦
do manual labor [dōō măn/yōō əl lā/bər] **170**–D
do not drink [dōō nät drĭnk/] **112**–F
do not enter [dōō nät/ ĕn/tər] **154**–2
do not operate [dōō nät/ äp/ə rāt/] **112**–E
do not take [dōō nät/ tāk/] **112**–F
don't be late [dōnt/ bē/ lāt/] **174**–E
don't litter [dōnt/ lĭ/tər] **219**–L
don't smoke [dōnt/smōk/] **114**–G
dock [däk] **175**–15, **234**–3
dockworker [däk/wür/kər] **167**–23
doctor [däk/tər] **118**–5
DOCUMENTS [dä/kyə mənts] **40**–**41**
dog [dög] **79**–6, **215**–11, **215**–22
dogwood [dög/wŏŏd/] **210**–15
DOING THE LAUNDRY [dō/ĭng dhə lön/drē] **101**
doll [däl] **59**–21, **233**–28
dollhouse [däl/hows/] **59**–16
doll making kit [däl/ mā/kĭng kĭt/] **232**–13
dollar [däl/ər] **26**–7
dollar coin [däl/ər koyn/] **26**–6
fifty dollars [fĭf/tē däl/ərz] **26**–11
five dollars [fiv/ däl/ərz] **26**–8
half dollar [hăf/ däl/ər] **26**–5
one hundred dollars
[wŭn/ hŭn/drəd däl/ərz] **26**–12
ten dollars [tĕn/ däl/ərz] **26**–9
twenty dollars [twĕn/tē däl/ərz] **26**–10
dolphin [däl/fən, döl/–] **213**–31
domesticated [də mĕs/tə kā/təd] **215** ✦
DOMESTIC ANIMALS AND RODENTS
[də mĕs/tĭk ăn/ə məlz ən rōd/nts] **215**
donkey [däng/kē, dŭng/–, döng/–] **215**–3
donut [dō/nŭt] **79**–15
donut shop [dō/nŭt shäp/] **129**–17
door [dör] **46**–3
doorbell [dör/bĕl/] **53**–14
door chain [dör/ chān/] **51**–33
doorknob [dör/näb/] **53**–12
door lock [dör/ läk/] **159**–25
doorman [dör/măn/] **184**–1
4-door car [för/dör kär/] **156**–1
front door [frŭnt/ dör/] **53**–11
garage door [gə räj/ dör/] **53**–7
revolving door [rĭ väl/vĭng dör/] **184**–2
screen door [skrēn/ dör/] **53**–15
sliding glass door [sli/dĭng glăs/dör/] **53**–18
storm door [störm/ dör/] **53**–10
2-door car [tōō/dör kär/] **156**–2
dorm / dormitory [dörm/] / [dör/mə tör/ē] **52**–8
dosage [dō/sĭj] **112**–6
double [dŭb/əl]
double bed [dŭb/əl bĕd/] **184**–14
double boiler [dŭb/əl boy/lər] **78**–8

down [down]
break down [brāk/ down/] **162**–D
downhill skiing [down/hĭl/ skē/ĭng] **227**–1
down jacket [down jăk/ət] **90**–16
down vest [down vĕst/] **90**–14
drop-down menu [drăp/ down/ mĕn/yōō/] **197**–8
put down [pŏŏt/ down/] **6**–J
sit down [sĭt down/] **6**–F
walk down [wäk down/] **153**–D
downstairs [down/stērz/] **51** ✦
DOWNTOWN [down/town/] **124**–**125**
drain [drān] **57**–5
drama [drä/mə] **236**–12
drapes [drāps] **56**–16
draw [drö] **8**–F, **118**–F, **195**–E
drawer [drör] **54**–23, **58**–2, **59**–6
dress [drĕs] **86**–3, **88**–5, **89**–20
dressmaker [drĕs/mā/kər] **100**–1
dressmaker's dummy [drĕs/mā/kərz dŭ/mē] **100**–2
dress socks [drĕs/ säks/] **91**–9
dress [drĕs] **36**–H, **174**–B
dressed [drĕst] **38**–D
dresser [drĕs/ər] **58**–1
Dressings [drĕs/ĭngz] **80**
dribble [drĭb/əl] **230**–J
drill [drĭl] **178**–9, **180**–8
drill bit [drĭl bĭt] **180**–28
drill [drĭl] **119**–D
drink [drĭnk] **11**–J
do not drink alcohol
[dōō/ nät/ drĭnk/ ăl/kə höl/] **112**–F
don't drink and drive [dōnt/ drĭnk ən drĭv/] **143**–G
drink fluids [drĭnk flōō/ədz] **114**–C
drip [drĭp] **121**–25
dripping [drĭp/ĭng] **63**–17
drive [drĭv] **196**–6, **196**–8, **196**–9
drive-thru window [drĭv/thrōō/ wĭn/dō] **128**–11
driveway [drĭv/wā/] **53**–8
drive [drĭv]
don't drink and drive [dōnt/drĭnk ən drĭv/] **143**–G
drive a truck [drĭv ə trŭk] **170**–E
drive through [drĭv/ thrōō] **153**–K
drive to work [drĭv/ tə würk/] **38**–I
driver [drī/vər] **152**–21, **169**–61
designated drivers [dĕz/ĭg nā/təd drī/vərz] **143** ✦
driver's license [drī/vərz li/səns] **40**–4, **136**–9
driver's license number
[drī/vərz li/səns nŭm/bər] **136**–11
Phillips screwdriver [fĭl/ĭps skrōō/drī/vər] **180**–31
screwdriver [skrōō/drī/vər] **180**–30
driving [drī/vĭng] **142**–5
drop [drăp]
drop cloth [drăp/ klöth/] **181**–54
drop-down menu [drăp/ down/ mĕn/yōō/] **197**–8
drop off [drăp/ öf/] **38**–G
dropper [drăp/ər] **195**–45
drops [drăps] **113**–31
drought [drowt] **145**–11
drown [drown] **116**–I
drugs [drŭgz] **116**–K, **142**–6
drums [drŭmz] **238**–16
drumsticks [drŭm/stĭks/] **70**–23
drunk driving [drŭngk/ drī/vĭng] **142**–5

dry [drī] **101**–18
dry cleaners [drī/ klē/nərz] **128**–2
dry erase marker [drī/ ĭ răs/ mär/kər] **7**–17
drywall [drī/wöl/] **178**–19
dry [drī] **60**–N, **108**–H
dryer [drī/ər] **50**–13, **101**–4
blow dryer [blō/ drī/ər] **33**–23, **108**–18
dryer sheets [drī/ər shēts/] **101**–5
Dry Measures [drī/ mĕzh/ərz] **75**
duck [dŭk] **70**–18, **214**–12
duct tape [dŭkt/ tāp/] **181**–49
dummy [dŭ/mē] **100**–2
dump truck [dŭmp/ trŭk/] **156**–19
dune [dōōn] **204**–5
duplex [dōō/plĕks/] **52** ✦
During an Emergency [dōō/rĭng ən ĭ mür/jən sē] **147**
dust [dŭst]
dustpan [dŭst/păn/] **61**–17
dust ruffle [dŭst/ rŭf/əl] **58**–17
dust storm [dŭst/ störm/] **13**–19
dust [dŭst] **60**–A
duster [dŭs/tər] **61**–1
DVD [dē/vē/dē/] **133**–19, **234**–11
DVD and CD-ROM drive
[dē/vē/dē/ ən sē/dē/räm/ drīv/] **196**–9
DVD player [dē/vē/dē/ plā/ ər] **56**–7, **234**–10
dye [dī] **33**–D
eagle [ē/gəl] **214**–9
ear [ïr] **32**–17, **105**–11
earache [ïr/āk/] **110**–3
ear infection [ïr/ ĭn fĕk/shən] **111**–3
earmuffs [ïr/mŭfs/] **90**–13, **179**–16
ear plugs [ïr/ plŭgz/] **179**–15
pierced earrings [pïrst/ ïr/ĭngz] **95**–36
early [ür/lē] **19**–22
Earth [ürth] **205**–3
earthquake [ürth/kwāk/] **144**–5
easel [ē/zəl] **233**–18
east [ēst] **155**–4
Eastern time [ē/stərn tīm/] **19**–32
easy [ē/zē] **23**–23, **76**–11
easy chair [ē/zē chër/] **56**–22
Easy Chicken Soup [ē/zē chĭk/ən sōōp/] **77**
eat [ēt] **11**–1
eat a healthy diet [ēt ə hĕl/thē dī/ət] **114**–F
eat breakfast [ēt brĕk/fəst] **38**–E
eat dinner [ēt dĭn/ər] **39**–S
eat out [ēt/ owt/] **82** ✦
eater [ē/tər] **176**–12
eclipse [ĭ klĭps/] **205**–16, **205** ✦
edit [ĕd/ət] **191**–I
education [ĕ jyōō/ kā/shən] **189**–17
eel [ēl] **212**–12
eggs [ĕgz] **66**–7
eggbeater [ĕg/bē/tər] **78**–20
eggs over easy [ĕgz ō/vər ē/zē] **76**–11
eggs sunny-side up [ĕgz sŭn/ē sīd/ ŭp/] **76**–10
hardboiled eggs [härd/ boyld/ ĕgz/] **76**–8
poached eggs [pōcht/ ĕgz/] **76**–9
scrambled eggs [skrăm/bəld ĕgz/] **76**–7
Eggs [ĕgz] **76**

Index

eight [āt] **16**

eighteen [ā/tēn/] **16**

eighteenth [ā/tēnth/] **16**

eighth [ātth, āth] **16**

eightieth [ā/tē/əth] **16**

eighty [ā/tē] **16**

elastic bandage [ĭ lăs/tĭk băn/dĭj] **117**–12

elbow [ĕl/bō] **106**–12

elderly [ĕl/dər lē] **32**–3

elected [ĭ lĕk/təd] **139**–C

elected official [ĭ lĕk/təd ə fĭ/shəl] **139**–32

Election [ĭ lĕk/shən] **139**

election results [ĭ lĕk/shən rĭ zŭltz/] **139**–31

elective [ĭ lĕk/tĭv] **189** ✦

electric [ĭ lĕk/trĭk] **116**–F

electric can opener [ĭ lĕk/trĭk kăn/ ō/pə nər] **54**–14

electric drill [ĭ lĕk/trĭk drĭl/] **180**–8

electric keyboard [ĭ lĕk/trĭk kē/börd] **238**–18

electric mixer [ĭ lĕk/trĭk mĭk/sər] **54**–25

electric pencil sharpener
[ĭ lĕk/trĭk pĕn/səl shär/pə nər] **183**–26

electric shaver [ĭ lĕk/trĭk shā/vər] **109**–26

electrical [ĭ lĕk/trĭ kəl]

electrical hazard [ĭ lĕk/trĭ kəl hăz/ərd] **186**–6

electrical tape [ĭ lĕk/trĭ kəl tāp/] **181**–43

electrician [ĭ lĕk trĭsh/ən] **62**–9

electron [ĭ lĕk/trän] **195**–30

electronics [ĭ lĕk trän/ĭks]

electronics repair person
[ĭ lĕk trän/ĭks rĭ pĕr/ pür/sən] **167**–24

electronics store [ĭ lĕk trän/ĭks stör/] **131**–20

ELECTRONICS AND PHOTOGRAPHY
[ĭ lĕk trän/ĭks ən fə täg/rə fē] **234**–235

elementary school [ĕl/ə mĕn/trē skool/] **188**–2

elephant [ĕl/ə fənt] **217**–42

elevator [ĕl/ə vā/tər] **50**–9, **131**–21, **184**–9

eleven [ĭ lĕv/ən] **16**

eleventh [ĭ lĕv/ənth] **16**

elm [ĕlm] **210**–16

Email [ē/māl/] **197**

embarrassed [ĭm băr/əst] **43**–24

embroidery [ĭm broy/də rē] **233**–24

EMERGENCIES [ĭ mür/jən sēz] **116**

EMERGENCIES AND NATURAL DISASTERS
[ĭ mür/jən sēz ən năch/rəl dĭ zăs/tərz,–năch/ə rəl–]
144–145

emergency [ĭ mür/jən sē] **117**–3

emergency card [ĭ mür/jən sē kärd/] **161**–26

emergency exit
[ĭ mür/jən sē ĕg/zăt,–ĕk/sət] **51**–25, **161**–14

emergency medical technician (EMT) [ĭ mür/jən sē
mĕd/ĭ kəl tĕk nĭsh/ən] / [ē/ĕm/tē/] **121**–32

Emergency [ĭ mür/jən sē] **146**–147

Emergency Call [ĭ mür/jən sē köl] **15**

EMERGENCY PROCEDURES
[ĭ mür/jən sē prə sē/jərz] **146**–147

Emergency Room Entrance
[ĭ mür/jən sē room/ ĕn/trəns] **121**

Emergency Worker [ĭ mür/jən sē wür/kər] **93**

emery board [ĕm/ə rē börd/, ĕm/rē-] **109**–32

emperor [ĕm/pər ər] **199**–3

employee [ĕm ploy/ē] **165**–9

employer [ĕm ploy/ər] **164**–4

empty [ĕmp/tē] **23**–10

empty [ĕmp/tē] **60**–L

EMT (emergency medical technician) [ē/ĕm/tē/] /
[ĭ mür/jən sē mĕd/ĭ kəl tĕk nĭsh/ən] **121**–32

end [ĕnd] **154**–6

endpoint [ĕnd/poynt/] **193**–21

end table [ĕnd/ tā/bəl] **56**–14

energy [ĕn/ər jē] **218**–1, **218**–7, **218**–8

bioenergy [bī/ō ĕn/ər jē] **218**–9

ENERGY AND CONSERVATION
[ĕn/ər jē ən kän/sər vā/shən] **218**–219

Energy and Resources [ĕn/ər jē ən rē/sör/səz] **219**

Energy Sources [ĕn/ər jē sör/səz] **218**

engine [ĕn/jən] **158**–18, **197**–6

engineer [ĕn/jə nïr/] **167**–18, **167**–25

ENGLISH COMPOSITION
[ĭng/glĭsh käm/pə zĭsh/ən] **190**–191

English muffin [ĭng/glĭsh mŭf/ən] **80**–5

enter [ĕn/tər]

do not **enter** [doo/ nät/ ĕn/tər] **154**–2

enter data [ĕn/tər dā/tə] **171**–B

enter the room [ĕn/tər dhe room/] **11**–A

enter your PIN [ĕn/tər yər pĭn/] **132**–E

ENTERTAINMENT [ĕn/tər tān/mənt] **236**–237

entertainment center [ĕn/tər tān/mənt sĕn/tər] **56**–5

entrance [ĕn/trəns] **164**–1

Entrance [ĕn/trəns] **50**, **121**

entry-level job [ĕn/trē lĕv/əl jäb/] **172**–1

Entryway [ĕn/trē wā/] **51**

envelope [ĕn/və lōp/] **134**–14, **183**–43

equation [ĭ kwā/zhən] **192**–13

equipment [ĭ kwĭp/mənt] **177**–12, **179**–4

Equipment [ĭ kwĭp/mənt] **179**, **183**

EQUIPMENT [ĭ kwĭp/mənt] **231**

Equivalencies [ĭ kwĭ/və lən sēz/] **17**, **75**

erase [ĭ rās/] **10**–M

eraser [ĭ rā/sər] **7**–19, **7**–21

errands [ĕr/əndz] **128** ✦

eruption [ĭ rŭp/shən] **145**–16

escalator [ĕs/kə lā/tər] **131**–23

escape [ĭs kāp/] **50**–2

escape route [ĭs kāp/ root/, rowt/] **146**–3

ESL [ē/ĕs/ĕl/] **189**–14

ESOL [ē/ĕs/ō/ĕl/] **189**–14

essay [ĕs/ā] **190**–4

Essay [ĕs/ā] **190**

e-ticket [ē/tĭ kət] **161**–19

evacuate [ĭ văk/yoo/ āt] **147**–K

evacuation route [ĭ văk/yoo/ā shən root/, rowt/] **146**–5

evening [ĕv/nĭng] **18**–19

evening gown [ĕv/nĭng gown/] **89**–18

even numbers [ē/vən nŭm/bərz] **192**–4

EVENTS [ĭ vĕnts/] **22**, **40**–41

every day [ĕv/rē dā/] **20**–21

EVERYDAY CLOTHES [ĕv/rē dā/ klōz] **86**–87

EVERDAY CONVERSATION
[ĕv/rē dā/ kän/vər sā/shən] **12**

evidence [ĕv/ĭ dəns/] **141**–9

exam [ĭg zăm/] **122**–1, **136**–6

examination table [ĭg zăm/ə nā/shən tā/bəl] **118**–7

examine [ĭg zăm/ən] **118**–D, **118**–E

Examining Room [ĭg zăm/ə nĭng room/] **118**

exchange [ĭks chănj/] **27**–I

excited [ĭk sī/təd] **43**–22

exclamation mark [ĕk/sklə mā/shən märk/] **190**–13

executive [ĭg zĕk/yə tĭv] **182**–5

executive chef [ĭg zĕk/yə tĭv shĕf/] **185**–7

Executive Branch [ĭg zĕk/yə tĭv brănch/] **138**

exercise [ĕk/sər sīz/] **122**–4

exercise [ĕk/sər sīz/] **39**–P, **230**–N

Exercise Wear [ĕk/sər sīz/wër] **89**

exhausted [ĭg zö/stəd] **43** ✦

ex-husband [ĕks/ hŭz/bənd] **35** ✦

exit [ĕg/zət, ĕk/sət] **51**–25, **51** ✦, **161**–14

expensive [ĭk spĕn/sĭv] **23**–19, **97**–44

Experiment [ĭk spër/ə mənt] **195**

expiration date [ĕk/spə rā/shən dāt/] **112**–7, **136**–10

expire [ĕk/spīr/] **136** ✦

explain [ĭk splān/] **12**–M

exploration [ĕk/splə rā/shən] **199**–8

explorer [ĭk splör/ər] **199**–9

explosion [ĭk splō/zhən] **144**–4

exposed [ĭk spōzd/]

overexposed [ō/vər ĭk spōzd/] **235**–34

underexposed [ŭn/dər ĭk spōzd/] **235**–35

Express Mail® [ĭk sprĕs/ māl/] **134**–2

Extended Family [ĭk stĕn/dəd făm/lē, făm/ə lē] **34**

extension cord [ĭk stĕn/shən körd/] **181**–14

exterminate [ĭk stür/mə nāt/] **62** ✦

exterminator [ĭk stür/mə nā/tər] **63**–21

extinguisher [ĭk stĭn/gwə shər] **179**–21

extra [ĕk/strə]

extra large [ĕk/strə lärj/] **96**–5

extra small [ĕk/strə smöl/] **96**–1

ex-wife [ĕks/ wīf/] **35** ✦

eye [ī] **99**–27, **105**–11

eyebrow [ī/brow/] **106**–9

eyebrow pencil [ī/brow/ pĕn/səl] **109**–34

eye drops [ī/dräps/] **113**–31

eye hook [ī/hook/] **180**–40

eyelashes [ī/lăsh/əz] **106**–11

eyelid [ī/lĭd/] **106**–10

eyeliner [ī/lī/nər] **109**–36

eyepiece [ī/pēs/] **194**–14

eye shadow [ī/shă/dō] **109**–35

Eye [ī] **106**

fabric [făb/rĭk] **98**–15

fabric softener [făb/rĭk sö/fə nər] **101**–6

Fabric Store [făb/rĭk stör/] **99**

face [fās] **193**–44

face mask [fās măsk/] **93**–32

face powder [fās/ pow/dər] **109**–41

Face [fās] **106**

factory [făk/tə rē, –trē] **126**–3

factory owner [făk/tə rē ō/nər] **175**–1

factory worker [făk/tə rē wür/kər] **175**–3

Factory [făk/tə rē] **98**

FACTORY [făk/tə rē] **175**

Fahrenheit [făr/ən hīt/] **13**–1

fair [fër] **172**–13, **223**–13

fair trial [fër/ trī/əl] **140**–5

FAIR [fër] **122**–123

fall [föl] **21**–39

fall [föl] **40**–H, **116**–O
FAMILIES [făm/lēz, făm/ə lēz] **34**–**35**
Family [făm/lē, făm/ə lē] **34**
FAMILY REUNION
    [făm/lē rē yōōn/yən, făm/ə lē] **44**–**45**
famine [fă/mĭn] **145**–12
fan [făn] **55**–19, **229**–4
fancy [făn/sē] **97**–34
far from [fär/ frŭm/, –frəm/] **25** ✦
fare [fër] **152**–2
    fare card [fër kärd/] **152**–11
farm [färm] **52**–9
    farm equipment [färm ĭ kwĭp/mənt] **177**–12
    farmworker [färm/ wür/kər] **177**–8
Farm Animals [färm/ ăn/ə məlz] **215**
farmer [fär/mər] **177**–13
FARMERS' MARKET [fär/mərz mär/kət] **84**–**85**
FARMING AND RANCHING
    [fär/mĭng ən răn/chĭng] **177**
Farmworker [färm/ wür/kər] **92**
fashion [făsh/ən] **88** ✦
    fashion designer [făsh/ən dĭ zī/nər] **98** ✦
fast [făst] **23**–3
    fast food restaurant [făst/ fōōd/ rĕs/tə rənt, –ränt]
        128–10
fasten [făs/ən] **160**–H
fastener [făs/nər] **99**–29
FAST FOOD RESTAURANT
    [făst/ fōōd/ rĕs/tə rənt, –ränt] **79**
fast forward [făst/ för/wərd] **235**–D
fat [făt] **32**–7
father [fä/dhər] **34**–4, **35**–23
    father-in-law [fä/dhər ĭn lö/] **34**–11
    grandfather [grăn/fä/dhər, grănd/–] **34**–2
    stepfather [stĕp/fädhər] **35**–25
faucet [fö/sət] **57**–6
fax [făks] **171**–G
fax machine [făks/ mə shēn/] **183**–21
feast [fēst] **239**–13
feather [fĕdh/ər] **214**–4
    feather duster [fĕdh/ər dŭs/tər] **61**–1
February [fĕb/yōō ër/ē, fĕb/rōō–] **21**–26
Federal Government
    [fĕ/də rəl gŭ/vərn mənt, fĕ/drəl] **138**
feed [fēd] **36**–C, **176**–D, **177**–D
feed dog / feed bar [fēd/dög/ / fēd/ bär/] **98**–20
feel [fēl] **110**–C, **110**–D
FEELINGS [fē/lĭngz] **42**–**43**
female [fē/māl/] **4**–18
fence [fĕns] **177**–19
fencing [fĕn/sĭng] **228**–7
ferry [fĕr/ē] **220**–4
fertilize [fürt/ əl īz/] **176**–D
fever [fē/vər] **110**–8
fiction [fĭk/shən] **237**–18
field [fēld] **5**–2, **177**–7
    ball field [böl/ fēld/] **224**–1
    track and field [trăk/ ən fēld/] **228**–18
fifteen [fĭf/tēn/] **16**
fifteenth [fĭf/tēnth/] **16**
fifth [fĭfth] **16**
fiftieth [fĭf/tē əth] **16**

fifty [fĭf/tē] **16**
    fifty dollars [fĭf/tē däl/ərz] **26**–11
    50 percent [fĭf/tē pər sĕnt/] **17**–10
fighter [fī/tər]
    firefighter [fīr/fī/tər] **144**–9, **167**–26
figs [fĭgz] **68**–27
figure [fĭg/yər] **233**–26
    figure skating [fĭg/yər skā/tĭng] **227**–5
figurine [fĭg/yə rēn/] **232**–1
file [fīl] **183**–44
    file cabinet [fīl kăb/ə nət] **182**–11
    file clerk [fīl klürk/] **182**–10
    file folder [fīl fōl/dər] **183**–50
fill [fĭl]
    fill a cavity [fĭl/ ə kăv/ə tē] **119**–E
    fill prescriptions [fĭl/ prĭ skrĭp/shənz] **112** ✦
    fill in [fĭl/ ĭn] **9**–O
    fill out [fĭl/ owt/] **173**–J
    fill the tank [fĭl/ dhe tănk/] **157**–G
    fill the tires [fĭl/ dhe tīrz/] **157**–L
filling [fĭl/ĭng] **119**–8
Filling Out a Form [fĭl/ĭng owt ə förm/] **4**
film [fĭlm] **235**–22
    film camera [fĭlm kăm/rə] **235**–21
find [fīnd] **160**–F
FINDING A HOME [fīn/dĭng ə hōm/] **48**–**49**
fine adjustment knob [fīn/ ə jŭst/mənt näb/] **194**–23
fingers [fĭng/gərz] **105**–16, **110**–16
    fingernail [fĭng/gər nāl/] **106**–18
    fingerprint [fĭng/gər prĭnt/] **136**–5
Fingers [fĭng/gərz] **106**
finish [fĭn/ĭsh] **112**–C, **230**–T
fins [fĭnz] **212**–1, **225**–7
fire [fīr] **144**–7, **144**–8
    campfire [kămp/fīr/] **226**–11
    fire escape [fīr ĭ skāp/] **50**–2
    fire exit [fīr/ ĕg/zət, –ĕk/sət] **51** ✦
    fire extinguisher [fīr ĭk stĭng/gwĭ shər] **179**–21
    firefighter [fīr/fī/tər] **144**–9, **167**–26
    fire hydrant [fīr hī/drənt] **129**–27
    fireplace [fīr/plās/] **56**–13
    fire screen [fīr skrēn/] **56**–12
    fire station [fīr stā/shən] **125**–12
    fire truck [fīr trŭk/] **144**–10
    fireworks [fīr/würks/] **239**–7
first [fürst] **16**
    first aid kit [fürst/ ād/ kĭt/] **117**–1, **146**–18
    first aid manual [fürst/ ād/ măn/yōō əl] **117**–2
    First Continental Congress
        [fürst/ kän/tə nĕnt/ əl kăng/grəs] **198**–6
    first name [fürst/ nām/] **4**–2
    first president [fürst/ prĕz/ə dənt] **198**–11
First Aid [fürst/ ād/] **117**
FIRST AID [fürst/ ād/] **117**
First Aid Procedures [fürst/ ād/ prə sē/ jərz] **117**
First Floor [fürst/ flör/] **50**
First License [fürst/ lī/səns] **137**
fish [fĭsh] **66**–1, **81**–29, **209**–14
    catfish [kăt/fĭsh/] **71**–2
    goldfish [gōld/fĭsh/] **215**–16
    jellyfish [jĕ/lē fĭsh/] **212**–14
    starfish [stär/fĭsh/] **212**–16
    swordfish [sörd/fĭsh/] **71**–5

Fish [fĭsh] **71, 212**
fisher [fĭsh/ər] **167**–17
fishing [fĭsh/ĭng] **226**–4
    fishing net [fĭsh/ĭng nĕt/] **226**–17
    fishing pole [fĭsh/ĭng pōl/] **226**–18
fitted sheet [fĭt/əd shēt/] **58**–12
fittings [fĭt/ĭngz] **181**–18
five [fīv] **16**
    five after one [fīv ăf/tər wŭn/] **18**–7
    five dollars [fīv däl/ərz] **26**–8
fix [fĭks] **62** ✦, **219**–F
fixture [fĭks/chər] **55**–18
flag [flăg] **239**–8
flammable liquids [flăm/ə bəl lĭk/wədz] **179**–8
flashlight [flăsh/līt/] **146**–14
flat [flăt]
    flat panel TV [flăt/ păn/əl tē/vē/] **234**–7
    flat screen TV [flăt/ skrēn/ tē/vē/] **234**–7
    flat sheet [flăt/ shēt] **58**–13
    have a flat tire [hăv/ ə flăt/ tīr/] **162**–F
flats [flăts] **95**–27
fleas [flēz] **63**–25
    flea market [flē/ mär/kət] **222**–6
flight [flīt] **161**–30, **161** ✦
    flight attendant [flīt/ ə tĕn/dənt] **161**–12
Flight [flīt] **160**
float [flōt/] **239**–2
flood [flŭd] **145**–19
floor [flör] **46**–6, **58**–21, **179**–6
    floor lamp [flör lămp/] **56**–15
    floor plan [flör plăn/] **186**–4
Floor [flör] **50**
floral [flör/əl] **96**–25
florist [flör/ĭst] **130**–8, **167**–27
floss [flös, fläs] **109**–24
floss [flös, fläs] **109**–K
flounder [flown/dər] **212**–15
flour [flow/ər] **73**–29
Flower [flow/ər] **211**
flowers [flow/ərz] **208**–7
    flower bed [flow/ər bĕd/] **53**–20
FLOWERS [flow/ərz] **211**
flu [flōō] **111**–2
fluid [flōō/əd] **183**–36
    fluid ounce [flōō/əd owns/] **75**–1
flute [flōōt] **238**–1
fly [flī] **214**–28
fly [flī] **170**–F
flyer [flī/ər] **102**–1
flying disc [flī/ĭng dĭsk/] **231**–27
foam pad [fōm/ păd/] **226**–13
focus [fō/kəs] **235**–33
foggy [fö/gē, fäg/ē] **13**–20
foil [foyl] **72**–23
fold [fōld] **101**–F
folder [fōl/dər] **183**–50
folding [fōl/dĭng]
    folding card table [fōl/dĭng kärd/ tā/bəl] **102**–4
    folding chair [fōl/dĭng chër/] **102**–5
folk [fōk] **237**–29
follow [fäl/ō] **114**–J, **147**–F
Following Directions [fäl/ō də rek/shənz, –dī–] **9**

Index

food [fo͞od]
  baby food [bā/bē fo͞od/] **37**–4
  canned food [kănd/ fo͞od/] **146**–9
  fast food restaurant [făst/ fo͞od/ rĕs/tə ränt] **128**–10
  food court [fo͞od/kört] **131**–15
  food preparation worker
      [fo͞od/ prĕ/pə rā/shən wür/kər] **185**–4
  food processor [fo͞od/ prä/sĕ sər] **54**–26
  packaged food [păk/ĭjd fo͞od/] **146**–10
  pet food [pĕt/ fo͞od/] **72**–5
FOOD [fo͞od] **79**
FOOD PREPARATION AND SAFETY
    [fo͞od/ prĕ/pə rā/shən ən săf/tē] **76**–77
Food Processor [fo͞od/ prä/sĕ sər] **92**
Foods [fo͞odz] **72, 73**
Food Safety [fo͞od/ săf/tē] **76**
FOOD SERVICE [fo͞od/sür/vəs] **185**
foot [fo͝ot] **104**–8
  football [fo͝ot/böl/] **229**–11, **231**–21
  football helmet [fo͝ot/böl/ hĕl/mət] **231**–19
  footnote [fo͝ot/nōt/] **190**–10
Foot [fo͝ot] **106**
for [för] **128**–B, **173**–C
forceps [för/səps, –sĕps] **195**–43
forearm [för/ärm/] **106**–13
forehead [för/əd/, –hĕd/, fär/–] **106**–2
forest [för/əst, fär/–] **204**–1, **204**–11
  forest fire [för/əst fir/] **144**–7
fork [förk] **55**–3, **83**–27, **83**–28
  forklift [förk/lĭft/] **175**–12
Form [förm] **4**
Formal Clothes [förm/əl klōz/] **89**
former husband [för/mər hŭz/bənd] **35** ✦
former wife [för/mər wif/] **35** ✦
forms [förmz] **118**–4, **134**–19, **161**–16
formula [för/myə lə] **37**–3, **195**–34
fortieth [för/tē əth] **16**
forty [för/tē] **16**
forward [för/wərd] **235**–D
  forward button [för/wərd bŭt/n] **197**–3
foundation [fown dā/shən] **109**–40
founders [fown/dərz] **198**–7
fountain [fown/tn] **224**–5, **224**–9
four [för] **16**
  4-door car [för/dör kär/] **156**–1
  2 x 4 (two by four) [to͞o/ bī för/] **181**–19
fourteen [för/tēn] **16**
fourteenth [för/tēnth] **16**
fourth [förth] **16**
Fourth Floor [förth flör/] **50**
Fourth of July [förth əv jo͞o lī/] **22**–13
fox [fäks] **216**–15
Fractions [frăk/shənz] **192**
Fractions and Decimals [frăk/shənz ən dĕ/sə məlz] **17**
frame [frām] **58**–4, **58**–18
frayed cord [frād/ körd/] **179**–5
free [frē] **122**–7
  free speech [frē/ spēch/] **140**–2
freedom [frē/dəm]
  freedom of religion [frē/dəm əv rĭ lĭ/jən] **140**–3
  freedom of the press [frē/dəm əv dhə prĕs/] **140**–4
freezer [frē/zər] **54**–10, **185**–3

freezing [frē/zĭng] **13**–7
French [frĕnch]
  french fries [frĕnch/ friz/] **79**–2
  French horn [frĕnch/ hörn/] **238**–13
Frequency [frē/kwən sē/] **20**
fresh [frĕsh] **71**–16
Friday [fri/dā, –dē] **20**–13
fried [frid] **76**–6
  fried chicken [frid/ chĭk/ən] **76**–1
fringe [frĭnj] **99**–34
frog [frög, fräg] **212**–25
front [frŭnt] **25**–7
  front desk [frŭnt/ dĕsk/] **184**–12
  front door [frŭnt/ dör/] **53**–11
  front seat [frŭnt/ sĕt/] **159**–51
  front walk [frŭnt/ wök/] **53**–2
Front Porch [frŭnt/ pörch/] **53**
Font Yard and House [frŭnt/ yärd/ en hows/] **53**
frostbite [fräst/bit/] **116**–G
frozen [frō/zən] **63**–16, **71**–17
  frozen dinner [frō/zən dĭn/ər] **72**–28
  frozen vegetables [frō/zən vĕj/tə bəlz] **72**–27
Frozen Foods [frō/zən fo͞odz/] **72**
fruit [fro͞ot] **67**–9
  fruit salad [fro͞ot săl/əd] **80**–21
FRUIT [fro͞ot] **68**
frustrated [frŭs/trā/təd] **43**–27
frying pan [fri/ĭng păn/] **78**–5
fuel injection system
    [fyo͞o/əl ĭn jĕk/shən sĭs/təm] **158**–17
full [fo͝ol] **23**–9, **42**–6
  full-length mirror [fo͝ol/lĕnth/ mĭr/ər] **58**–6
  full moon [fo͝ol/ mo͞on/] **205**–12
  full slip [fo͝ol/ slĭp/] **91**–22
fumes [fyo͞omz] **179**–3
funnel [fŭn/əl] **195**–40
funny photo [fŭn/ē fō/tō] **206**–2
fur [für] **216**–19
furious [fyo͝or/ē əs] **43** ✦
furnished apartment [für/nĭsht ə pärt/mənt] **48**–3
furniture [für/nĭ chər] **53**–19
  furniture polish [für/nĭ chər päl/ĭsh] **61**–8
  furniture store [für/nĭ chər stör/] **126**–8
Furniture and Accessories
    [für/nĭ chər ən ĭk sĕs/ə rēz] **59**
fuse box [fyo͞oz/ băks/] **62**–13
fusion [fyo͞o/zhən] **218**–10
galaxy [găl/ək sē] **205**–15
gallbladder [göl/blăd/ər] **107**–44
gallon [găl/ən] **75**–5
game [gām]
  baseball game [bās/böl gām/] **44**–2
  board game [börd/ gām/] **232**–5
  game show [gām/ shō/] **236**–8
  video game console [vĭd/ē ō gām/ kän/sōl] **232**–3
  video game control [vĭd/ē ō gām kən tröl/] **232**–4
Games [gāmz] **59**
GAMES [gāmz] **232**–233
gang violence [găng/ vi/ə ləns] **142**–4
garage [gə räzh/, –räj/] **47**–14, **124**–1
  garage door [gə räzh/ dör/] **53**–7
Garage [gə räzh/, –räj/] **50**

GARAGE SALE [gə räzh/ sāl/] **102**–103
garbage [gär/bĭj]
  garbage can [gär/bĭj kăn/] **53**–24
  garbage disposal [gär/bĭj dĭ spō/zəl] **54**–7
  garbage truck [gär/bĭj trŭk/] **127**–22
garden [gär/dn]
  botanical garden [bə tăn/ə kəl gär/dn] **222**–3
  roof garden [ro͞of/gär/dn] **50**–4
  vegetable garden [vĕj/tə bəl gär/dn] **53**–27, **177**–14
garden [gär/dn] **53**–B
gardener [gär/dn er, gärd/nər] **167**–28
gardenia [gär dēn/yə] **211**–18
gardening [gärd/nĭng]
  gardening crew [gärd/nĭng kro͞o/] **176**–1
  gardening crew leader
      [gärd/nĭng kro͞o lĕd/ər] **176**–4
GARDENING [gärd/nĭng] **176**
gargle [gär/gəl] **109**–L
garlic [gär/lĭk] **69**–30
  garlic bread [gär/lĭk brĕd/] **81**–28
  garlic press [gär/lĭk prĕs/] **78**–11
Garment Factory [gär/mənt făk/tə rē, făk/trē] **98**
garment worker [gär/mənt wür/kər] **167**–29
garter [gär/tər]
  garter belt [gär/tər bĕlt/] **91**–16
  garter snake [gär/tər snāk/] **213**–39
gas [găs] **218**–3
  gas gauge [găs/gāj/] **159**–31
  gas meter [găs mē/tər] **62**–14
  gas pedal [găs pĕd/l] **159**–46
  gas shut-off valve [găs/ shŭt/öf vălv/] **146**–4
  gas station [găs stā/shən] **125**–10
  gas station attendant
      [găs stā/shən ə tĕn/dənt] **162**–3
  gas tank [găs tăngk/] **158**–10
gate [gāt] **50**–16, **53**–9, **161**–8
Gate [gāt] **161**
gauge [gāj]
  blood pressure gauge [blŭd/ prĕsh/ər gāj/] **118**–9
  gas gauge [găs/gāj/] **159**–31
  oil gauge [oyl/gāj/] **159**–29
  temperature gauge [tĕm/prə chər gāj/] **159**–30
gauze [göz] **117**–8
gear shift [gir/ shĭft/] **159**–47
gel [jĕl] **108**–2, **108**–16
GEOGRAPHY AND HABITATS
    [jē äg/rə fē ən hă/bə tăts/] **204**
Geometric Solids [jē/ə mĕ/trĭk säl/ədz] **193**
geometry [jē äm/ə trē] **192**–17
geothermal energy [jē/ō thür/məl ĕn/ər jē] **218**–7
get [gĕt]
  get a job [gĕt/ ə jäb/] **40**–F
  get a learner's permit
      [gĕt/ ə lürn/ərz pür/mĭt] **137**–F
  get a library card [gĕt/ ə li/brĕr ē kärd/] **133**–A
  get a loan [gĕt/ ə lōn/] **49**–J
  get an electric shock [gĕt/ ən ĭ lĕk/trĭk shäk/] **116**–F
  get a speeding ticket [gĕt/ ə spē/dĭng tĭk/ət] **162**–C
  get bed rest [gĕt/ bĕd/ rĕst/] **114**–B
  get change [gĕt/ chānj/] **26**–A
  get dressed [gĕt/ drĕst/] **38**–D
  get elected [gĕt/ ĭ lĕk/təd] **139**–C

get engaged [gĕt/ ĭn gājd/] **41**–J

get feedback [gĕt/ fēd/băk/] **191**–K

get frostbite [gĕt/ frŏst/bīt/] **116**–G

get good grades [gĕt/ gŏŏd/ grādz/] **10**–H

get hired [gĕt/ hīrd/] **173**–L

get home [gĕt/ hōm/] **39**–R

get immunized [gĕt/ ĭm/yə nīzd] **114**–I

get into [gĕt/ ĭn/tōō] **153**–E

get lost [gĕt/ löst/] **162**–B

get married [gĕt/ măr/ēd] **41**–K

get off [gĕt/ öf/] **153**–J

get on [gĕt/ än/, ön/] **153**–I

get out of [gĕt/ owt/ əv] **153**–F

get the title [gĕt/ dhə tīt/l] **157**–E

get up [gĕt/ ŭp/] **38**–B

get your license [gĕt/ yər lī/səns] **137**–I

Getting Your First License
[gĕt/ĭng yər fürst/ lī/səns] **137**

Get Well [gĕt/ wĕl/] **114**

gift [gĭft] **94 ✦, 240**–3

gift shop [gĭft/ shäp/] **130 ✦, 184**–5

gills [gĭlz] **212**–2

giraffe [jə răf/] **217**–32

girder [gür/dər] **178**–3

girdle [gür/dl] **91**–15

girl [gürl] **31**–10

give [gĭv] **15**–F, **122**–B, **148**–A,

glad [glăd] **44**–5

glass [glăs] **53**–18, **83**–22, **83**–23

    glass cleaner [glăs klē/nər] **61**–14

glasses [glăs/əz] **92**–10, **115**–7, **179**–10

    sunglasses [sŭn/glăs/əz] **90**–27

global positioning system (GPS) [glō/bəl
pə zĭ/shə nĭng sĭs/təm] / [jē/pē/ĕs/] **155**–11

gloves [glŭvz] **90**–6, **231**–17

    disposable gloves [dĭ spō/ zə bəl glŭvz/] **93**–27

    glove compartment [glŭv/ kəm pärt/mənt] **159**–44

    latex gloves [lā/tĕks glŭvz/] **93**–34

    rubber gloves [rŭb/ər glŭvz/] **61**–4

    surgical gloves [sür/jĭ kəl glŭvz/] **121**–39

    work gloves [würk/ glŭvz/] **92**–17, **179**–17

glue [glōō] **183**–33

    glue stick [glōō/ stĭk] **232**–11

go [gō]

    go back [gō/ băk/] **11**–M

    go for [gō/ fər] **157**–J

    go on [gō/ än] **173**–K

    go over [gō/ ō/vər] **153**–B

    go past [gō/ păst/] **155**–E

    go straight [gō/ strāt/] **155**–A

    go through [gō/ throō/] **160**–D

    go to an employment agency
        [gō/ tə ən ĭm ploy/mənt ā/jən sē] **173**–E

    go to bed [gō/ tə bĕd/] **39**–Y

    go to college [gō/ tə käl/ĭj] **41**–I

    go to jail [gō/ tə jāl/] **141**–G

    go to prison [gō/ tə prĭz/ən] **141**–G

    go to school [gō/ tə skōōl] **38**–J

    go to sleep [gō/ tə slēp/] **39**–Z

    go to the grocery store
        [gō/ tə dhə grōs/rē stör/, grōsh/rē] **38**–L

    go to the next line [gō/ tə dhə nĕkst/ līn] **196**–D

    go to work [gō/ tə würk/] **38**–I

    go under [gō/ ŭn/dər] **153**–A

    to-go box [tə gō/ bäks/] **82**–5

GO [gō] **222–223**

goat [gōt] **215**–5

goggles [gäg/əlz] **179**–11

goldfish [gōld/fĭsh/] **215**–16

golf [gälf, gölf] **228**–8

    golf club [gälf/ klŭb/] **231**–1

good [gŏŏd] **23**–17

Goods [gŏŏdz] **73**

goose [gōōs] **214**–13

gopher [gō/fər] **215**–19

gorilla [gə rĭl/ə] **217**–29

gospel [gäs/pəl] **237**–30

Government [gŭ/ vərn mənt] **138–139**

GOVERNMENT AND MILITARY SERVICE
[gŭ/ vərn mənt ən mĭ/ lə tër ē sür/vəs]**138–139**

governor [gŭ/ vər nər] **139**–20, **139**–21

gown [gown] **206**–8

    evening gown [ēv/nĭng gown/] **89**–18

    hospital gown [häs/pĭ tl gown/] **121**–19

    nightgown [nīt/gown/] **91**–25

    surgical gown [sür/jə kəl gown/] **93**–37, **121**–38

GPS (global positioning system) [jē/pē/ĕs/] /
[glō/bəl pə zĭ/shə nĭng sĭs/təm] **155**–11

grab bar [grăb/ bär/] **57**–9

grades [grādz] **10**–4

graduate [grăj/ōō āt/] **40**–D

graduated cylinder [grăj/ōō ā/təd sĭl/ən dər] **195**–38

GRADUATION [grăj/ōō ā/shən] **206–207**

graffiti [grə fēt/tē] **148**–1

grandchild [grăn/chīld/, grănd/–] **34 ✦**

granddaughters [grăn/dö/tərz] **34 ✦**

grandfather [grăn/fä/dhər, grănd/–] **34**–2

grandmother [grăn/mŭdh/ər, grănd/–] **34**–1

Grandparents [grăn/për/ənts, grănd/–] **34**

grandson [grăn/sŭn/, grănd/–] **34 ✦**

grapefruit [grāp/frōōt/] **68**–6

grapes [grăps] **68**–3

graph [grăf] **192**–15

graphic designer [grăf/ĭk dĭ zī/nər] **167**–30

grasshopper [grăs/häp/ər] **214**–24

grate [grāt] **77**–G

grater [grā/tər] **78**–2

gray [grā] **24**–15

    gray hair [grā hër/] **33**–13

grease [grēs] **77**–B

green [grēn] **24**–5

    green card [grēn/ kärd/] **40**–2

    green onions [grēn/ ŭn/yənz] **69**–20

greet [grēt] **3**–G, **171**–M, **174**–H

GREETING [grē/tĭng] **2–3**

greeting card [grē/tĭng kärd/] **134**–15

grill [grĭl] **53**–17

grilled [grĭld/]

    grilled cheese sandwich
        [grĭld/ chēz/ săn/wĭch, –sănd/–] **80**–10

grilled fish [grĭld/ fĭsh/] **81**–29

grilled ribs [grĭld/ rĭbz/] **76**–2

grocery [grōs/rē, grōsh/rē]

    grocery bag [grōs/rē băg/] **67**–13

    grocery clerk [grōs/rē klürk/] **72**–4

Grocery Products [grōs/rē präd/ŭkts] **72**

GROCERY STORE [grōs/ rē stör/] **72–73**

ground [grownd]

    ground beef [grownd/ bēf/] **70**–4

    ground post [grownd/ pōst/] **134**–6

    playground [plā/grownd/] **50**–3

group [grōōp] **115**–15

grower [grō/ər] **177**–13

guard [gärd] **141**–3

    Coast Guard [kōst/ gärd/] **138**–18

    lifeguard [līf/gärd] **225**–19

    lifeguard station [līf/gärd stā/shən] **225**–21

    National Guard [nă/shə nəl gärd/] **138**–19

    security guard [sĭ kyōōr/ə tē gärd/] **132**–5, **169**–55

    shin guards [shĭn/ gärdz/] **231**–13

guest [gĕst] **184**–10

    guest room [gĕst/ rōōm] **184**–13

    guest services [gĕst/ sür/vəs əs] **130**–12

    guest speaker [gĕst/ spē/kər] **206**–4

guinea pig [gĭn/ē pĭg/] **215**–14

guitar [gĭ tär/] **238**–9

gums [gŭmz] **106**–6

    gum disease [gŭm/ dĭ zēz/] **119**–11

gun [gŭn] **142**–13, **181**–21

gurney [gür/nē] **121**–33

gutter [gŭt/ər] **53**–4

gym [jĭm] **5**–19, **126**–10, **184**–24

gymnastics [jĭm năs/tĭks] **228**–9

gynecologists [gī/nə käl/ə jĭsts] **120 ✦**

habitat [hă/bə tăt/] **194**–12

HABITATS [hă/bə tăts/] **204**

hacksaw [hăk/sö/] **180**–5

hail a taxi [hāl/ ə tăx/ē/] **152 ✦**

hailstorm [hāl/störm/] **13**–21

hair [hër] **104**–2

    black hair [blăk/ hër/] **33**–16

    blond hair [bländ/ hër/] **33**–17

    brown hair [brown/ hër/] **33**–18

    curly hair [kür/lē hër/] **33**–11

    gray hair [grā/ hër] **33**–13

    hair clip [hër klĭp/] **108**–19

    hairdresser [hër/drĕs/ər] **167**–31

    hair gel [hër jĕl/] **108**–16

    hairnet [hër nĕt/] **93**–25

    hair salon [hër sə län/] **131**–18

    hair spray [hër sprā/] **108**–12

    hair stylist [hër stī/lĭst] **167**–31

    long hair [löng/ hër/] **33**–3

    red hair [rĕd/ hër/] **33**–15

    short hair [shört/hër/] **33**–1

    shoulder-length hair [shōl/dər lĕnth/ hër/] **33**–2

    straight hair [strāt/ hër/] **33**–9

    wavy hair [wā/vē hër/] **33**–10

HAIR [hër] **33**

Index

half [hăf]
half bath [hăf/ băth/] **57** ✦
half brother [hăf/ brŭdh/ər] **35**–28
1/2 cup [hăf/ kŭp/] **75**–9
half dollar [hăf/ däl/ər] **26**–5
half past one [hăf/ păst/ wŭn/] **18**–11
half sister [hăf/ sĭs/tər] **35**–27
half slip [hăf/ slĭp/] **91**–23
halibut steak [hăl/ə bət stāk/] **71**–6
hall [höl] **124**–8
hallway [höl/wā/] **5**–10, **184**–18
Hallway [höl/wā/] **51**
ham [hăm] **70**–9, **76**–5
hamburger [hăm/bŭr/gər] **79**–1
hammer [hăm/ər] **180**–1
jackhammer [jăk/hăm/ər] **178**–9
sledgehammer [slĕj/ hăm/ər] **178**–23
hammer [hăm/ər] **178**–D
hammock [hăm/ək] **53**–23
hamper [hăm/pər] **57**–1
hand [hănd] **105**–15, **177**–20
DMV handbook [dē/ĕm/vē/ hănd/boōk] **136**–1
handbag [hănd/băg/] **87**–9, **94**–2
handbrake [hănd/ brāk/] **59**–48
handcuffs [hănd/kŭfs/] **141**–2
handsaw [hănd/sö/] **180**–4
handset [hănd/sĕt] **14**–1
hand towel [hănd tow/əl] **57**–15
hand truck [hănd trŭk/] **175**–11
Hand [hănd] **106**
handicapped parking [hăn/dē kăpt pär/kĭng]
128–6, **154**–12
hand in [hănd/ ĭn/] **10**–O
hanger [hăng/gər] **101**–11
hang up [hăng/ ŭp/] **15**–D, **101**–H
happy [hăp/ē] **28**–6, **43**–31
hard [härd] **23**–5, **23**–24
hardboiled eggs [härd/boyld/ ĕgz/] **76**–8
hard drive [härd/ drīv/] **196**–6
hard hat [härd/ hăt/] **92**–1, **179**–9
hardware store [härd/wër/stör/] **148**–4
harmonica [här mä/ nĭ kə] **238**–21
harvest [här/vəst] **177**–B
hash browns [hăsh/ brownz/] **80**–3
hats [hăts] **90**–1, **95**–11
chef's hat [shĕfs/ hăt/] **93**–28
cowboy hat [kow/boy/ hăt/] **92**–18
hard hat [härd/ hăt/] **92**–1, **179**–9
ski hat [skē/ hăt/] **90**–11
straw hat [strö/ hăt/] **90**–23
have [hăv]
have a baby [hăv/ ə bā/bē] **41**–L
have a conversation [hăv/ ə kän/vər sā/shən] **11**–L
have a heart attack [hăv/ ə härt/ ə tăk/] **116**–D
have an allergic reaction
[hăv/ ən ə lür/jĭk rē ăk/shən] **116**–E
have a picnic [hăv/ ə pĭk/nĭk] **224**–D
have dinner [hăv/ dĭn/ər] **39**–S
have regular checkups
[hăv/ rĕg/yə lər chĕk/ups] **114**–H
Hawaii-Aleutian time [hə wī/ē ə loō/shən tim/] **19**–27

hay [hā] **177**–18
hazard [hăz/ərd] **186**–6
hazard lights [hăz/ərd līts/] **159**–36
Hazardous Materials [hăz/ər dəs mə tïr/ē əlz] **179**
hazardous waste [hăz/ər dəs wäst/] **218**–12
Hazards [hăz/ərdz] **179**
head [hĕd] **69**–32, **104**–1
headache [hĕd/āk/] **110**–1
headband [hĕd/bănd/] **90**–3
headboard [hĕd/börd/] **58**–10
head chef [hĕd/ shĕf/] **185**–7
headlight [hĕd/līt/] **158**–7
headline [hĕd/līn] **133**–7
headphones [hĕd/fōnz/] **6**–8, **234**–4
headset [hĕd/sĕt] **14**–13
headwaiter [hĕd/wā/tər] **185**–12
headwrap [hĕd/răp/] **90**–7
letterhead [lĕt/ər hĕd] **183**–42
overhead compartment
[ō/vər hĕd/ kəm pärt/mənt] **161**–13
overhead projector [ō/vər hĕd/prə jĕk/tər] **7**–16
wireless headset [wïr/ləs hĕd/sĕt] **14**–14
health [hĕlth] **167**–32
health history form [hĕlth/ hĭs/tə rē förm/] **118**–4
health insurance card
[hĕlth/ ĭn shoōr/əns kärd/] **118**–3
HEALTH [hĕlth] **114**–115
HEALTH FAIR [hĕlth/ fër/] **122**–123
Health Problems [hĕlth/ präb/ləmz] **115**
hear [hïr] **106**–B
hearing [hïr/ĭng]
hearing aid [hïr/ĭng ād/] **115**–10
hearing impaired [hïr/ĭng ĭm përd/] **32**–12
hearing loss [hïr/ĭng lös/] **115**–2
heart [härt] **107**–38, **116**–D, **239**–6
heart disease [härt/ dĭ zēz/] **111**–11
hearts [härts] **233**–31
heater [hē/tər] **159**–40
heating pad [hē/tĭng păd/] **113**–13
heat wave [hēt/ wāv/] **13**–13
heavy [hĕv/ē] **23**–13, **32**–7, **97**–27
hedge clippers [hĕj/ klĭp/ərz] **176**–11
heel [hēl] **94**–22, **106**–24
high heels [hī/ hēlz/] **89**–21, **95**–25
height [hīt] **17**–16, **32**–5
Height [hīt] **32**
Heimlich maneuver [hīm/lĭk mə noō/vər] **117**–18
helicopter [hĕl/ə käp/tər] **151**–9
helmet [hĕl/mət] **93**–23, **231**–19
help [hĕlp] **8**–J, **147**–G
Help with Health Problems
[hĕlp/ wĭth/ hĕlth/ präb/ləmz] **115**
hem [hĕm] **100**–8
hen [hĕn] **215**–8
herbal tea [ür/bəl tē/, hür/bəl–] **81**–40
herbs [ürbz, hürbz] **84**–9
hibiscus [hī bĭs/kəs, hĭ–] **211**–12
high [hī] **91**–12, **97**–32, **188**–3
high blood pressure [hī/ blŭd/ prĕsh/ər] **111**–14
high chair [hī/ chër/] **37**–6, **82**–3
high heels [hī/ hēlz/] **89**–21, **95**–25

high-rise [hī/ rīz/] **127**–13
high school [hī/ skoōl] **188**–4
highway [hī/wā] **155**–9
highway marker [hī/wā mär/kər] **154**–17
hiking [hī/kĭng] **226**–7
hiking boots [hī/kĭng boōts/] **95**–31
hills [hĭlz] **204**–16
downhill skiing [down/hĭl/ skē/ĭng] **227**–1
hip hop [hĭp/häp] **237**–26
hippopotamus [hĭp/ə pät/ə məs] **217**–43
hire [hīr] **141**–B
hired hand [hīrd/ hănd/] **177**–20
Historical Terms [hĭs/tör/ə kəl türmz/] **199**
history [hĭs/tə rē] **118**–4, **189**–12
HISTORY [hĭs/tə rē] **198**–199
hit [hĭt] **230**–B
HIV (human immunodeficiency virus)
[āch/ī/vē/] / [hyoō/mən ĭm/yə nō
dĭ fĭsh/ən sē vī/rəs] **111**–17
Hi-Visibility safety vest [hī/vĭ/zə bĭl/ə tē vĕst/] **92**–4
HOBBIES AND GAMES [häb/ēz ən gämz/] **232**–233
hockey [häk/ē] **229**–13
hockey stick [häk/ē stĭk/] **231**–11
hold [hōld] **36**–A
holder [hōl/dər]
candle holder [kăn/dl hōl/dər] **56**–21
cell phone holder [sĕl/ fōn/ hōld/ər] **94**–15
magazine holder [măg/ə zēn/ hōld/ər] **56**–23
pot holders [pät/ hōl/dərz] **78**–29
toothbrush holder [toōth/brŭsh/ hōld/ər] **57**–22
holiday [hăl/ə dā/] **22**–7, **22**–8
Holidays [hăl/ə dāz/] **22**
HOLIDAYS [hăl/ə dāz/] **239**
holly [hăl/ē] **210**–19
home [hōm] **52**–7, **52**–12
home health care aide [hōm/ hĕlth/ kër ād] **167**–32
home improvement store
[hōm/ ĭm proōv/mənt stör/] **127**–20
homemaker [hōm/mā/kər] **168**–33
homesick [hōm/sĭk/] **43**–20
HOME [hōm] **46**–47, **48**–49
honeybee [hŭn/ē bē/] **214**–25
hood [hoōd] **158**–4
Hood [hoōd] **158**
hoof / hooves [hoōf] / [hoōvz] **216**–17
hook [hoōk] **180**–39, **180**–40
hook and eye [hoōk/ ən ī/] **99**–27
hook and loop fastener
[hoōk/ ən loōp/ fä/sən ər] **99**–29
horn [hörn] **159**–32, **216**–21, **238**–11
French horn [frĕnch/ hörn] **238**–13
horror story [hör/ər stör/ē, här/–] **237**–17
horse [hörs] **215**–4
horseback riding [hörs/băk rī/dĭng] **226**–9
horse racing [hörs/ rā/sĭng] **228**–19
seahorse [sē/hörs/] **212**–13
hose [hōz] **53**–21, **91**–18
hospital [häs/pĭ tl] **125**–9, **154**–18
hospital bed [häs/pĭ tl bĕd/] **121**–22
hospital gown [häs/pĭ tl gown/] **121**–19
HOSPITAL [häs/pĭ tl] **120**–121
Hospital Room [häs/pĭ tl roōm/] **121**

Hospital Staff [häs/pĭ tl stäf/] **120**
hostess [hō/stəs] **82**–2
hot [hät] **13**–3, **42**–1
  hot cereal [hät sïr/ē əl] **80**–9
  hot dog [hät/ dög/] **79**–6
  hot water [hät/ wö/tər] **57**–8
  hot water bottle [hät/ wö/tər bät/l] **113**–15
hotel [hō tĕl/] **124**–3
A HOTEL [hō tĕl/] **184**
hour [ow/ər] **18**–1
house [hows]
  courthouse [kört/hows/] **125**–13
  dollhouse [däl/hows/] **59**–18
  housekeeper [hows/kē/pər] **168**–34, **184**–20
  housekeeping cart [hows/kē/pĭng kärt/] **184**–19
  House of Representatives
    [hows/ əv rĕp/rĭ zĕn/tə tĭvz] **138**–3
  house painter [hows/ pān/tər] **168**–46
  houseplant [hows/plănt/] **56**–4, **211**–27
  townhouse [town/hows/] **52**–6
  two-story house [tōō/stör/ē hows/] **52** ✦
  warehouse [wër/hows/] **175**–7
  White House [wït/ hows/] **138**–7
House [hows] **49, 53**
A HOUSE AND YARD [hows/ən yärd/] **53**
HOUSEHOLD PROBLEMS AND REPAIRS
  [hows/hōld/ präb/ləmz ən rĭ përz/] **62**–**63**
HOUSEWORK [hows/würk/] **60**
housing [how/zĭng] **52**–11
hubcap [hŭb/kăp/] **158**–9
hug [hŭg] **2**–E
human immunodeficiency virus (HIV)
  [hyōō/mən ĭm/yə nō dĭ fĭsh/ən sē vī/rəs] /
  [āch/ī/vē/] **111**–17
humid [hyōō/məd] **13**–15
humidifier [hyōō mĭd/ə fī/ər] **113**–11
humiliated [hyōō mĭl/ē ā/təd] **43** ✦
hummingbird [hŭm/ĭng bürd/] **214**–10
hump [hŭmp] **217**–51
hungry [hŭng/grē] **42**–5
hurricane [hür/ə kān/] **145**–14
hurt [hürt] **42**–16, **116**–C
husband [hŭz/bənd] **34**–13
  ex-husband [ĕks/ hŭz/bənd] **35** ✦
  former husband [för/mər hŭz/bənd] **35** ✦
hutch [hŭch] **55**–22
hybrid [hy/brĭd] **156**–3
hydrant [hī/drənt] **129**–27
hydroelectric power [hī/drō ĭ lĕk/trĭk pow/ər] **218**–5
hydrogen peroxide [hī/drə jən pə räk/sīd] **117**–9
hyena [hī ē/nə] **217**–30
HYGIENE [hy/jēn] **108**–**109**
hygienist [hī jē/nĭst, –jĕn/ĭst] **119**–3
hypertension [hī/pər tĕn/shən] **111**–14
hyphen [hy/fən] **190**–20
hypoallergenic [hī/pō ăl/ər jĕn/ĭk] **108** ✦
I beam [ī/ bēm/] **178**–3
ice [īs]
  ice cream [īs/ krēm/] **72**–26
  ice-cream cone [īs/ krēm/ kōn] **79**–13
  ice cream shop [īs/ krēm/ shäp/] **131**–16
  ice hockey [īs/ häk/ē] **229**–13

ice pack [īs/ păk/] **117**–13
ice skates [īs/ skāts/] **231**–9
ice skating [īs/ skā/tĭng] **227**–4
iced tea [īst/ tē/] **79**–12
icy [ī/sē] **13**–22
ID [ī/dē/] **146**–19
identity theft [ī dĕn/tə tē thĕft/] **142**–9
ignition [ĭg nĭsh/ən] **159**–33
illegal drugs [ĭ lē/gəl drŭgz/] **142**–6
Illnesses and Childhood Diseases
  [ĭl/nə səz ən chïld/hōŏd dĭ zēz/ əz] **111**
ILLNESSES AND MEDICAL CONDITIONS
  [ĭl/nə səz ən mĕd/ĭ kəl kən dĭsh/ənz] **111**
Immediate Family
  [ĭ mē/ dē ət făm/lē, –fā/məlē] **34**
immigrant [ĭm/ə grənt] **199**–19
immigrate [ĭm/ə grāt/] **40**–C
immigration [ĭm/ə grā/shən] **199**–18
immunization [ĭm/yə nə zā/shən] **114** ✦
immunodeficiency [ĭm/yə nō dĭ fĭsh/ən sē] **111**–17
impaired [ĭm përd/] **32**–11, **32**–12
important [ĭm pört/ənt] **146**–19
improvement [ĭm prōōv/mənt] **127**–20
in [ĭn] **25**–6
  be in shock [bē/ ĭn shäk/] **116**–B
  bubble in [bŭb/l ĭn/] **10**–K
  call in [käl/ ĭn/] **186**–A
  check in [chĕk/ ĭn/] **160**–A
  check-in kiosk [chĕk/ĭn kē/äsk/] **160**–2
  fall in love [fäl/ ĭn lŭv/] **40**–H
  fill in [fĭl/ ĭn/] **9**–O
  hand in [hănd/ĭn/] **10**–O
  in fashion [ĭn făsh/ən] **88** ✦
  in front of [ĭn frŭnt/ əv] **24**–7
  in love [ĭn lŭv/] **42**–18
  in pain [ĭn pān/] **42**–11
  in style [ĭn stīl/] **88** ✦
  in the middle [ĭn dhə mĭd/l] **24**–2
  look in [lōŏk/ ĭn] **173**–B
  move in [mōōv/ ĭn/] **48**–F
  send in [sĕnd/ ĭn/] **173**–H
  take in [tāk/ ĭn/] **100**–D
  turn in [türn/ ĭn/] **191**–M
  walk-in freezer [wäk/ĭn frē/zər] **185**–3
inch [ĭnch] **17**–15
indent [ĭn dĕnt/] **190**–D
independence [ĭn/də pĕn/dəns]
  Declaration of Independence
    [dĕk/lə rā/shən əv ĭn/də pĕn/dəns] **198**–5
  Independence Day [ĭn/də pĕn/dəns dā/] **22**–13
INDIVIDUAL SPORTS [ĭn/də vĭj/ōō əl spörts/] **228**
infant [ĭn/fənt] **31**–6
infection [ĭn fĕk/shən] **111**–3
infectious disease [ĭn fĕk/shəs dĭ zēz/] **111** ✦
influenza [ĭn/flōō ĕn/zə] **111** ✦
INFORMATION [ĭn/fər mā/shən] **4**
inhaler [ĭn hā/lər] **113**–33
injection [ĭn jək/shən] **114** ✦, **158**–17
injured [ĭn/ jərd] **116**–C
INJURIES [ĭn/jə rēz] **110**

ink [ĭnk]
  ink cartridge [ĭnk/ kär/trĭj] **183**–45
  inkjet printer [ĭnk/jĕt prĭn/tər] **183**–18
  ink pad [ĭnk/ păd/] **183**–46
inline [ĭn/līn/]
  inline skates [ĭn/līn/ skāts/] **231**–10
  inline skating [ĭn/līn/ skā/tĭng] **228**–10
inquire about benefits
  [ĭn kwïr/ ə bowt/bĕn/ə fĭts] **174** ✦
insects [ĭn/sĕkts] **209**–11
  insect bite [ĭn/sĕkt bīt/] **110**–11
  insect repellent [ĭn/sĕkt rĭ pĕl/ənt] **226**–23
Insects [ĭn/sĕkts] **214**
INSECTS [ĭn/sĕkts] **214**
insert [ĭn sürt/] **132**–D
INSIDE AND OUTSIDE THE BODY
  [ĭn/sīd/ ən owt/sīd/ dhə băd/ē] **106**–**107**
Inside the Car [ĭn/sīd/ dhə kär/] **159**
Inside the Kit [ĭn/sīd/ dhə kĭt/] **117**
Inside the Trunk [ĭn/sīd/ dhə trŭnk/] **158**
inspect [ĭn spĕkt/] **147**–N
install [ĭn stäl/] **176**–H, **178**–C
instructor [ĭn strŭk/tər] **6**–4
Instrument Panel [ĭn/strə mənt păn/əl] **159**
instruments [ĭn/strə mənts] **119**–4, **238**
insulation [ĭn/sə lā/shən] **178**–14
insurance [ĭn shōŏr/əns] **118**–3, **136**–8
integers [ĭn/tə jərz] **192**–1, **192**–2
Integers [ĭn/tə jərz] **192**
intercom [ĭn/tər käm/] **50**–5
interest inventory [ĭn/trəst ĭn/vən tör/ ē] **172**–11
international call [ĭn/tər năsh/ə nəl köl/] **15**–35
Internet [ĭn/tər nĕt/]
  Internet listing [ĭn/tər nĕt/ lĭst/ĭng] **48**–1
  Internet map [ĭn/tər nĕt/ măp/] **155**–12
  Internet phone call [ĭn/tər nĕt/ fōn/ käl] **14**–20
INTERNET [ĭn/tər nĕt/] **197**
internist [ĭn/tür/nĭst] **120**–1
internship [ĭn/türn shĭp/] **172**–6
interpreter [ĭn tür/prə tər] **168**–35
INTERSECTION [ĭn/tər sĕk/shən] **128**–**129**
INTERVIEW SKILLS [ĭn/tər vyōō/ skĭlz/] **174**
intestinal parasites [ĭn tĕs/tə nəl păr/ə sīts/] **111**–13
intestines [ĭn tĕs/tənz] **107**–42
In the Airline Terminal [ĭn dhə ër/līn tür/mə nəl] **160**
In the Examining Room
  [ĭn dhə ĭg zăm/ə nĭng rōōm/] **118**
In the Waiting Room [ĭn dhə wā/tĭng rōōm/] **118**
into [ĭn/tōō, –tə] **153**–E
intravenous drip (IV)
  [ĭn/trə vē/nəs drĭp/] / [ī/vē/] **121**–25
introduce [ĭn/trə dōōs/] **2**–C, **3**–I
introduction [ĭn/trə dŭk/shən] **190**–6
invention [ĭn vĕn/shən] **199**–12
inventor [ĭn vĕn/tər] **199**–13
inventory [ĭn/vən tör/ ē] **172**–11, **172**–12
invertebrates [ĭn vür/ tə brəts/] **194**–13
invitation [ĭn və tā/shən] **12**–I, **12**–J, **64**–9
invite [ĭn vīt/] **12**–H
iris [ī/rəs] **211**–16
iron [ī/ərn] **101**–13, **108**–17
iron [ī/ərn] **101**–G

ironed [ī/ərnd] **101**–20
ironing board [ī/ər nĭng börd/] **101**–14
irritated [ĭr/ə tā/təd] **64**–6
island [ī/lənd] **204**–8
IV (intravenous drip)
    [ī/vē/] / [ĭn/trə vē/nəs drĭp/] **121**–25
ivory [ī/vər ē] **24**–16
ivy [ī/vē] **210**–25
jack [jăk] **158**–24
jacket [jăk/ət] **90**–8
    chef's jacket [shĕfs/ jăk/ət] **93**–29
    down jacket [down/ jăk/ət] **90**–16
    leather jacket [lĕdh/ər jăk/ət] **90**–4
    sports jacket [spörts/ jăk/ət] **89**–14
jackhammer [jăk/ hăm/ər] **178**–9
jack-o'-lantern [jăk/ə lăn/tərn] **239**–10
janitor [jăn/ĭ tər] **182**–3
January [jăn/yōō ër/ē] **21**–25
jar [jär] **74**–2, **74**–14
jasmine [jăz/mən] **211**–22
jaw [jö] **106**–4
jay [jā] **214**–6
jaywalk [jā/wäk] **128**–C
jazz [jăz] **237**–24
jeans [jēnz] **86**–2, **92**–19
jellyfish [jĕl/ē fĭsh] **212**–14
jewelry [jōō/əl rē]
    jewelry department [jōō/əl rē dĭ pärt/mənt] **95**–8
    jewelry store [jōō/əl rē stör/] **130**–2
jigsaw [jĭg/sö/] **180**–10
job [jäb] **172**–1, **172**–3, **172**–7
    job fair [jäb/ fër] **172**–13
JOB SAFETY [jäb/ săf/tē] **179**
JOBS AND OCCUPATIONS
    [jäbz/ ən äk/yə pā/shənz] **166**–**169**
JOB SEARCH [jäb/ sürch/] **173**
JOB SKILLS [jäb/ skĭlz/] **170**
Job Training [jäb/ trān/ĭng] **172**
jockstrap [jäk/străp/] **91**–6
join [joyn] **143**–L
judge [jŭj] **141**–6
Judicial Branch [jōō dĭ/shəl brănch/] **138**
juice [jōōs] **73**–32
July [jōō lī/] **21**–31
jump [jŭmp] **230**–I
jumper cables [jŭm/pər kā/bəlz] **158**–21
jump rope [jŭmp/ rōp/] **224**–4
jumpsuit [jŭmp/sōōt/] **93**–24
June [jōōn] **21**–30
junior high school [jōōn/yər hī/ skōōl] **188**–3
junk mail [jŭnk/ māl/] **135** ✦
Jupiter [jōō/pə tər] **205**–5
jury [jür/ē] **141**–8
justices [jŭs/tə səz] **138**–12, **138**–13
kangaroo [kăng/gə rōō/] **217**–44
keep [kēp] **28**–B
ketchup [kĕch/əp, kăch/–] **79**–21
kettle [kĕt/l] **54**–21
key [kē] **51**–30, **155**–9
    key pad [kē/ păd/] **14**–5
    pound key [pownd/ kē/] **14**–7
    star key [stär/ kē/] **14**–6

keyboard [kē/börd/] **196**–14, **238**–18
Keyboarding [kē/börd/ĭng] **196**
kick [kĭk] **230**–E
kidney [kĭd/nē] **107**–43
kids' bedroom [kĭdz/ bĕd/rōōm/] **47**–9
KIDS' BEDROOM [kĭdz/ bĕd/rōōm/] **59**
king-size bed [kĭng/sīz/ bĕd/] **184**–15
kiosk [kē/äsk/] **131**–22, **160**–2
kiss [kĭs] **3**–K, **36**–P
kit [kĭt]
    doll making kit [däl/ mā/kĭng kĭt/] **232**–13
    first aid kit [fürst/ ād/ kĭt/] **117**–1, **146**–18
    model kit [mäd/l kĭt/] **232**–9
    woodworking kit [wōōd/wür/kĭng kĭt/] **232**–14
Kit [kĭt] **117**
kitchen [kĭch/ən] **46**–5, **83**–15
    kitchen timer [kĭch/ən tī/mər] **78**–18
A KITCHEN [ə kĭch/ən] **54**
Kitchen [kĭch/ən] **185**
KITCHEN UTENSILS [kĭch/ən yōō tĕn/səlz] **78**
kite [kīt] **225**–2
kitten [kĭt/n] **215**–10
kiwi [kē/wē] **68**–22
knee [nē] **106**–20
    knee highs [nē/hīz/] **91**–12
    knee pads [nē/ pădz/] **179**–19
knife [nīf] **55**–4, **83**–30
    carving knife [kär/vĭng nīf/] **78**–12
    multi-use knife [mŭl/tē yōōs/nīf/, mŭl/tī–] **226**–20
    paring knife [për/ĭng nīf/] **78**–16
    steak knife [stāk/ nīf/] **83**–29
knit [nĭt] **233**–F
knitting needles [nĭt/ĭng nēd/lz] **233**–23
knit top [nĭt/ täp/] **88**–7
knob [näb] **194**–22, **194**–23
    doorknob [dör/näb/] **53**–12
knuckle [nŭk/l] **106**–17
koala [kō ä/lə] **217**–45
lab [lăb] **5**–15
    lab coat [lăb/ kōt/] **93**–33
Lab [lăb] **195**
label [lā/bəl]
    mailing label [mā/lĭng lā/bəl] **183**–41
    nutrition label [nōō trĭ/shən lā/bəl] **122**–8
    prescription label [prĭ skrĭp/shən lā/bəl] **112**–4
    warning label [wär/nĭng lā/bəl] **112**–8
label [lā/bəl] **9**–V
Labor Day [lā/bər dā/] **22**–14
lace [lās] **99**–9
    shoelaces [shōō/lā səz] **94**–24
ladder [lăd/ər] **178**–2
ladle [lā/dl] **78**–7
ladybug [lā/dē bŭg/] **214**–26
lake [lāk] **204**–13
lamb [lăm] **70**–14
    lamb chops [lăm/ chäps/] **70**–15
    lamb shanks [lăm/ shăngks/] **70**–13
Lamb [lăm] **70**
lamp [lămp] **56**–15, **58**–25
    lampshade [lămp/shād/] **56** ✦, **58**–26
land [lănd] **160**–K
landlord [lănd/lörd/] **51**–27

landmarks [lănd/märks/] **220**–1
landscape designer [lănd/skāp/ dĭ zī/nər] **176**–5
LANDSCAPING AND GARDENING
    [lănd/skā/pĭng ən gärd/nĭng] **176**
languages [lăng/gwĭ jəz] **189**–13
    language arts [lăng/gwĭj ärts/] **189**–9
lantern [lăn/tərn] **226**–22, **239**–10
laptop [lăp/täp/] **196**–16
large [lärj] **96**–4, **96**–5
laser printer [lā/zər prĭn/tər] **183**–19
lashes [lăsh/əz]
    eyelashes [ī/lăsh/əz] **106**–11
last [lăst]
    last name [lăst/ nām/] **4**–4
    last week [lăst/wēk/] **20**–18
late [lāt] **19**–24
latex gloves [lā/tĕks glŭvz/] **93**–34
laugh [lăf] **44**–A
laundromat [lön/drə mät/] **128**–1
laundry [lön/drē] **101**–1
    laundry basket [lön/drē băs/kət] **101**–2
    laundry detergent [lön/drē dĭ tür/jənt] **101**–8
LAUNDRY [lön/drē] **101**
Laundry Room [lön/drē rōōm/] **50**
lawn [lön] **53**–26
    lawn mower [lön/ mō/ər] **176**–6
lawyer [lö/yər] **168**–36
lay [lā] **178**–B
layer cake [lā/ər kāk] **81**–33
LCD projector [ĕl/sē/dē/ prə jĕk/tər] **6**–6, **235**–29
leader [lē/dər] **176**–4
leaf / leaves [lēf] / [lēvz] **210**–6, **211**–6
    leaf blower [lēf/ blō/ər] **176**–2
leaking [lē/kĭng] **62**–3
learn [lürn] **40**–E
Learning New Words [lür/nĭng nōō/ würdz/] **8**
lease [lēs] **48** ✦, **51**–28
leather [lĕdh/ər] **98**–6
    leather jacket [lĕdh/ər jăk/ət] **90**–4
leave [lēv] **11**–O, **38**–N, **82**–J, **160**–J, **171**–P
leaves / leaf [lēvz] / [lēf] **210**–6, **211**–6
    leaf blower [lēf/ blō/ər] **176**–2
lecture [lĕk/chər] **122**–9
left [lĕft] **25**–1, **154**–8, **155**–C
legal [lē/gəl]
    legal holiday [lē/gəl hăl/ə dā/] **22**–8
    legal pad [lē/gəl păd/] **183**–38
Legal Holidays [lē/gəl hăl/ə dāz/] **22**
LEGAL SYSTEM [lē/gəl sĭs/təm] **141**
Leg and Foot [lĕg/ ən fōōt/] **106**
leggings [lĕg/ĭngz] **90**–12
Legislature [lĕ/jəs lā/chər] **139**–23
legs [lĕgz] **70**–21, **105**–9
    leg of lamb [lĕg/ əv lăm/] **70**–14
lemonade [lĕm/ə nād/] **84**–2
lemons [lĕm/ənz] **68**–7
lend [lĕnd] **26**–C
length [lĕngkth] **17**–17, **96**–17
lengthen [lĕngk/thən] **100**–A
lens / lenses [lĕnz] / [lĕnz/əz] **115**–8, **235**–23
leopard [lĕp/ərd] **217**–34
let out [lĕt/ owt/] **100**–C

letter [lĕt/ər] **134**–13
    letter carrier [lĕt/ər kăr/ē ər] **134**–20
    letterhead [lĕt/ər hĕd/] **183**–42
lettuce [lĕt/əs] **69**–1
level [lĕv/əl] **172**–1, **180**–29
librarian [lī brër/ē ən] **133**–9
library [lī/brër ē] **5**–17, **125**–15
    library clerk [lī/brër ē klürk/] **133**–1
    library patron [lī/brër ē pā/trən] **133**–3
LIBRARY [lī/brër ē] **133**
license [lī/səns]
    driver's license [drī/vərz lī/səns] **40**–4, **136**–9
    driver's license number
      [drī/vərz lī/səns nŭm/bər] **136**–11
    license plate [lī/səns plāt/] **136**–12, **158**–12
    marriage license [măr/ĭj lī/səns] **41**–8
    renew a license [rĭ nōō/ ə lī/səns, –nyōō/–] **136** ✦
    taxi license [tăk/sē lī/səns] **152**–22
License [lī/səns] **137**
licensed practical nurse (LPN)
    [lī/sənst prăk/tə kəl nürs/] / [ĕl/pē/ĕn/] **120**–11
lid [lĭd] **78**–24
lieutenant governor [lōō tĕ/nənt gŭ/ vər nər] **139**–21
life [līf]
    lifeguard [līf/gärd/] **225**–19
    lifeguard station [līf/gärd/ stā/shən] **225**–21
    lifesaving device [līf/sā/vĭng dĭ vīs/] **225**–20
    life vest [līf/ vĕst/] **161**–25, **226**–14
    wildlife [wīld/ līf/] **220**–3
LIFE [līf] **212**–**213**
LIFE EVENTS AND DOCUMENTS
    [līf/ ĭ vĕnts/ ən dä/kyə mənts] **40**–**41**
lift [lĭft] **11**–E
light [līt] **23**–14, **97**–28
    brake light [brāk/ līt/] **158**–14
    daylight saving time [dā/līt/ sā/vĭng tīm/] **19**–25
    flashlight [flăsh/līt/] **146**–14
    hazard lights [hăz/ərd līts/] **159**–36
    headlight [hĕd/ līt/] **158**–7
    light blue [līt/ blōō/] **24**–11
    light bulb [līt/ bŭlb/] **56** ✦
    light fixture [līt/ fĭks/chər] **55**–18
    light source [līt/ sörs/] **194**–21
    light switch [līt/ swĭch/] **58**–27
    night light [nīt/ līt/] **37**–27
    porch light [pörch/ līt/] **53**–13
    streetlight [strēt/līt/] **148**–3
    string lights [strĭng/ lītz/] **239**–18
    tail light [tāl/ līt/] **158**–13
    traffic light [trăf/ĭk līt/] **128**–8
    work light [würk/ līt/] **181**–44
lightning [līt/nĭng] **13**–17
lily [lĭl/ē] **211**–26
limbs [lĭmz] **106** ✦, **210**–3
limes [līmz] **68**–8
limit [lĭ/mət] **154**–4
limo / limousine [lĭ/mō] / [lĭ/mə zēn] **156**–11
line [līn] **73**–11
    assembly line [ə sĕm/blē līn] **175**–6
    clothesline [klōz/līn/] **101**–9
    curved line [kürvd/ līn/] **193**–23
    headline [hĕd/līn/] **133**–7

line cook [līn/ kŏŏk/] **93**, **185** ✦
line segment [līn/ sĕg/mənt] **193**–20
line supervisor [līn/ sōō/pər vī zər] **175**–4
    parallel lines [pă/rə lĕl līnz/] **193**–25
    perpendicular lines
      [pür/pən dĭk/yə lər līnz/] **193**–24
    straight line [strāt/ līn/] **193**–22
linen [lĭn/ən] **98**–2
    linen closet [lĭn/ən kläz/ət] **57** ✦
liner [lī/nər]
    eyeliner [ī/lī/nər] **109**–36
Lines [līnz] **193**
lingerie [län/zhə rā/, –jə–] **91** ✦
links [lĭnkz] **197**–10
lion [lī/ən] **213**–33, **216**–2, **217**–36
lip [lĭp] **106**–5
    lipstick [lĭp/stĭk/] **109**–38
Liquid Measures [lĭk/wəd mĕzh/ərz] **75**
liquids [lĭk/wədz] **61**–21, **179**–8
list [lĭst] **67**–14
listen [lĭs/ən] **6**–C, **118**–C, **174**–K
listing [lĭst/ĭng] **48**–1
litter [lĭt/ər] **148**–2
litter [lĭt/ər] **219**–L
little [lĭt/l] **23**–1
Little League [lĭt/l lēg/] **229** ✦
live [lĭv] **140**–H
LIVE [lĭv] **52**
live music [lĭv/ myōō/zĭk] **84**–1
liver [lĭv/ər] **70**–7, **107**–40
livestock [līv/stäk/] **177**–15
living room [lĭv/ĭng rōōm/] **47**–12
LIVING ROOM [lĭv/ĭng rōōm/] **56**
lizard [lĭz/ərd] **213**–40
llama [lä/mə] **217**–25
load [lōd] **101**–C
loading dock [lō/dĭng däk/] **175**–15
loaf [lōf] **74**–10, **74**–22
    meatloaf [mēt/lōf/] **81**–31
loafers [lō/fərz] **95**–30
Lobby [läb/ē] **50**
lobster [läb/stər] **71**–10
local call [lō/kəl köl/] **15**–31
lock [läk] **51**–34, **159**–25
    locksmith [läk/smĭth/] **62**–11
lock [läk] **143**–E
locker [lä/kər] **5**–11, **50**–17
locket [läk/ət] **95**–35
Logging on and Sending Email
    [lög/ĭng än/ ən sĕnd/ĭng ē/māl, –ön–] **197**
lonely [lōn/lē] **42**–17
long [löng] **96**–18
    long distance call [löng/dĭs/təns köl/] **15**–32
    long hair [löng/ hër/] **33**–3
    long-sleeved [löng/slēvd/] **96**–14
    long underwear [löng/ ŭn/dər wër/] **91**–3
look [lŏŏk]
    look at [lŏŏk/ ăt/, –ət] **49**–H, **157**–A
    look for [lŏŏk/ för/] / [lŏŏk/ fər] **133**–B, **173**–C
    look in [lŏŏk/ ĭn] **173**–B
    look up [lŏŏk/ ŭp] **8**–A
loop [lōōp] **99**–29

loose [lōōs] **97**–30
lose [lōōz] **229** ✦
loss [lös] **115**–2
lost child [löst/ chīld/] **144**–1
lotion [lō/shən] **37**–13, **108**–9
loud [lowd] **23**–11
loungewear [lownj/wër/] **91** ✦
love [lŭv] **40**–H, **42**–18
    love seat [lŭv/ sēt/] **56**–1
low [lō] **97**–31
    low-cost exam [lō/köst ĭg zăm/] **122**–1
    low-cut socks [lō/kŭt/ säks/] **91**–10
    low-fat milk [lō/făt/ mĭlk/] **81**–42
lower back [lō/ər băk/] **107**–29
lozenges [läz/ən jəz] **113**–30
LPN (licensed practical nurse) [ĕl/pē/ĕn/] /
    [lī/sənst prăk/tə kəl nürs/] **120**–11
luggage [lŭg/ĭj] **161**–18
    luggage cart [lŭg/ĭj kärt/] **184**–8
lug wrench [lŭg/ rĕnch/] **158**–22
lumber [lŭm/bər] **178**–17
Lunch [lŭnch] **80**
lung [lŭng] **107**–39
machine [mə shēn/]
    answering machine [ăn/sər ĭng mə shēn/] **14**–17
    ATM (Automated Teller Machine) [ā/tē/ĕm/] /
      [ö/tə māt ĭd tĕ/lər mə shēn/] **132**
    fax machine [făks/ mə shēn/] **183**–21
    machine operator [mə shēn/ äp/ə rā tər] **168**–37
    machine screw [mə shēn/ skrōō/] **180**–32
    sewing machine [sō/ĭng mə shēn/] **98**–13
    sewing machine operator
      [sō/ĭng mə shēn/ äp/ə rā/tər] **98**–14
    stamp machine [stămp/ mə shēn/] **135**–11
    vending machine [vĕnd/ĭng mə shēn/] **152**–9
Machine [mə shēn/] **98**, **132**
magazine [măg/ə zēn, măg/ə zēn/] **133**–5
    magazine holder [măg/ə zēn/ hōl/dər] **56**–23
magnet [măg/nət] **195**–36
magnolia [măg nōl/yə] **210**–8
mail
    airmail [ër/māl/] **134**–5
    Certified Mail® [sür/tə fīd māl/] **134**–4
    Express Mail® [ĭk sprĕs/ māl/] **134**–2
    junk mail [jŭnk/ māl/] **135** ✦
    mailboxes [māl/bäk/səz] **50**–11, **53**–1, **128**–13,
      135–12
    media mail [mē/dē ə māl/] **134**–3
    overnight / next day mail
      [ō/vər nīt/ / nĕkst/ dā/ māl/] **135** ✦
    Priority Mail® [prī/ör ə tē māl/] **134**–1
mail [māl/] **135**–D
mailer [mā/lər] **183**–40
mailing [mā/lĭng]
    mailing address [mā/lĭng ə drĕs/, ă/drĕs] **134**–22
    mailing label [mā/lĭng lā/bəl] **183**–41
main office [mān/ ö/fəs] **5**–12
MAINTAINING A CAR [mān/tā nĭng ə kär/] **157**
maintenance [mān/tn əns] **184**–23
maitre d' [mā/trə dē/] **185**–11
make [māk] **156** ✦

make [māk]
    make a deposit [māk/ ə dĭ päz/ət] **132**–B
    make a disaster kit [māk/ ə dĭz/ăs tər kĭt/] **146**–B
    make a mortgage payment
        [māk/ ə mör/gəj pā/mənt] **49**–L
    make an offer [māk/ ən ö/fər] **49**–I
    make a wish [māk/ ə wĭsh/] **240**–B
    make copies [māk/ käp/ēz] **171**–D
    make dinner [māk/ dĭn/ər] **39**–Q
    make eye contact [māk/ ī/ kän/täkt] **174**–J
    make furniture [māk/ für/nĭ chər] **170**–G
    make lunch [māk/ lŭnch/] **38**–F
    make progress [māk/ prä/grəs] **10**–G
    make small talk [māk/ smöl/tök] **12**–B
    make the bed [māk/dhə bĕd/] **60**–F
maker [mā/kər]
    dressmaker [drĕs/mā/kər] **100**–1
    dressmaker's dummy [drĕs/mā/kərz dŭ/mē] **100**–2
    homemaker [hōm/mā/kər] **168**–33
Makeup [māk/ŭp] **109**
makeup remover [māk/ŭp rĭ mōōv/ər] **109**–42
making [mā/kĭng] **232**–13
MAKING ALTERATIONS [māk/ĭng öl/tə rā/shənz] **100**
MAKING CLOTHES [māk/ĭng klōz/] **98–99**
Making an Emergency Call
    [mā/kĭng ən ĭ mür/jən sē köl/] **15**
Making a Phone Call [mā/kĭng ə fōn/ köl/] **15**
male [māl] **4**–17
mall [möl] **126**–7
MALL [möl] **130–131**
mallet [măl/ət] **180**–2
mammals [măm/əlz] **209**–10
Mammals [măm/əlz] **213**
MAMMALS [măm/əlz] **216–217**
manager [măn/ĭ jər] **50**–8, **72**–8
    account manager [ə kownt/ măn/ĭ jər] **132**–9
    office manager [ö/fəs măn/ĭ jər] **182**–8
Manager [măn/ĭ jər] **92**
mane [mān] **217**–49
maneuver [mə nōō/vər] **117**–18
mangoes [măng/gōz] **68**–21
manicurist [mă/nə kyōō/rĭst] **168**–38
man / men [măn] / [mĕn] **30**–1, **30**–4
    doorman [dör/măn/] **184**–1
mantle [măn/təl] **56**–11
manual [măn/yōō əl] **117**–2
Manual Transmission [măn/yōō əl trănz mĭsh/ən] **159**
manufacture [măn/yə făk/chər] **175**–B
map [măp] **7**–12, **155**–12
Map [măp] **13**
maple [mā/pəl] **210**–12
Maps [măps] **155**
MAPS [măps]**155**
March [märch] **21**–27
margarine [mär/jər ən] **72**–20
marigold [mär/ə göld] **211**–13
MARINE LIFE, AMPHIBIANS, AND REPTILES
    [mə rēn/ lĭf/ ăm fĭb/ē ənz ən rĕp/tĭlz] **212–213**
Marines [mə rēnz/] **138**–17
mark [märk] **190**–12, **190**–13, **190**–15
    postmark [pōst/märk/] **134**–24

markers [mär/kərz] **7**–17, **7–24**, **154**–17
market [mär/kət] **222**–6
    supermarket [sōō/pər mar/kət] **127**–18
MARKET [mär/kət] **66–67**
marriage license [măr/ĭj lĭ/səns] **41**–8
married couple [măr/ēd kŭ/pəl] **35**–20
Mars [märz] **205**–4
martial arts [mär/shəl ärts/] **228**–11
Martin Luther King Jr. Day
    [mär/tən lōō/thər-kĭng/ jōōn/yər dā/] **22**–10
mascara [mă skăr/ə] **109**–39
mashed potatoes [măsht/ pə tā/tōz] **81**–23
mask [măsk] **239**–9
    catcher's mask [kăch/ərz măsk/] **231**–15
    diving mask [dī/vĭng măsk/] **225**–6
    face mask [fās/ măsk/] **93**–32
    oxygen mask [äk/sĭ jən măsk/] **161**–24
    particle mask [pär/tĭ kəl măsk/] **179**–14
    ski mask [skē/ măsk/] **90**–15
    surgical mask [sür/jĭ kəl măsk/] **93**–36
    ventilation mask [vĕnt/əl ā/shən măsk/] **92**–7
masking tape [măs/kĭng tāp/] **181**–53
mat [măt] **57**–3, **57**–28
    placemat [plās/măt] **55**–11
match [măch] **9**–T
matches [măch/əz] **146**–16, **226**–21
matching [mă/chĭng] **28**–3
Material [mə tïr/ē əl] **98**
materials [mə tïr/ē əlz] **98** ✦, **179**–7
Materials [mə tïr/ē əlz] **179**
maternity [mə tür/nə tē]
    maternity dress [mə tür/nə tē drĕs/] **88**–5
    maternity store [mə tür/nə tē stör/] **131**–19
math [măth] **189**–10
MATHEMATICS [măth/ə măt/ĭks] **192–193**
Math Operations [măth/ äp/ə rā/shənz] **192**
Math Problem [măth/ präb/ləmz] **192**
mattress [mă/trəs] **58**–20
May [mā] **21**–29
mayonnaise [mā/ə nāz/, mā/ə nāz/] **79**–23
mayor [mā/ər] **139**–26
meadow [mĕd/ō] **204**–20
measles [mē/zəlz] **111**–5
measure [mĕzh/ər] **100**–17, **181**–45
measure [mĕzh/ər] **17**–C
Measurement [mĕzh/ər mənt] **17**
MEASUREMENTS [mĕzh/ər mənts] **17, 75**
Measures [mĕzh/ərz] **75**
Measuring Area and Volume
    [mē/zhər ĭng ër/ē ə ən văl/yəm, -yōōm] **193**
meat [mēt] **66**–2
    meatballs [mēt/bölz] **81**–27
    meatloaf [mēt/löf/] **81**–31
Meat [mēt] **70, 76**
MEAT AND POULTRY [mēt/ n pōl/trē] **70**
mechanic [mə kăn/ĭk] **166**–8
Mechanic [mə kăn/ĭk] **158**
media mail [mē/dē ə māl/] **134**–3
medical [mĕd/ĭ kəl] **121**–32
    medical chart [mĕd/ĭ kəl chärt/] **121**–24
    medical emergency bracelet
        [mĕd/ĭ kəl ĭ mür/jən sē brās/lət] **117**–3

medical records technician
    [mĕd/ĭ kəl rĕkərdz tĕk nĭsh/ən] **168**–39
medical waste disposal
    [mĕd/ĭ kəl wāst/ dĭ spō/zəl] **121**–31
MEDICAL CARE [mĕd/ĭ kəl kër/] **118**
MEDICAL CONDITIONS [mĕd/ĭ kəl kən dĭsh/ənz] **111**
MEDICAL EMERGENCIES [mĕd/ĭ kəl ĭ mür/jən sēz] **116**
Medical Procedures [mĕd/ĭ kəl prə se/jərz] **118**
Medical Specialists [mĕd/ĭ kəl spē/shə lĭsts] **120**
Medical Technician [mĕd/ĭ kəl tĕk nĭsh/ən] **93**
Medical Warnings [mĕd/ĭ kəl wör/nĭngz] **112**
medication [mĕd/ə kā/shən] **112**–3, **112** ✦,
    113–18, **121**–20
Medication [mĕd/ə kā/shən] **113**
medicine cabinet [mĕd/ə sən kăb/ə nət] **57**–20
medium [mē/dē əm] **96**–3
meet [mēt] **222**–6
meet [mēt] **49**–G, **49**–R
meeting [mē/tĭng]
    meeting place [mē/tĭng plās/] **146**–1
    meeting room [mē/tĭng rōōm/] **184**–25
MEETING AND GREETING [mē/tĭng ən grē/tĭng] **2–3**
melons [mĕl/ənz] **68**–19
    watermelons [wö/tər mĕl/ənz] **68**–18
membrane [mĕm/brān] **194**–6
Memorial Day [mə mör/ē əl dā/] **22**–12
memory card [mĕm/ə rē kärd/] **235**–20
men / man [mĕn] / [măn] **30**–1, **30**–4
    doorman [dör/măn/] **184**–1
    men's store [mĕnz/ stör/] **130** ✦
Men's Underwear [mĕnz/ un/dər wër/] **91**
menu [mĕn/yōō] **82**–7, **197**–8
    menu bar [mĕn/yōō bär/] **197**–1
MENU [mĕn/yōō] **80–81**
Mercury [mür/kyə rē] **205**–1
merge [mürj] **154**–10
mess [mĕs] **64**–8
message [mĕs/ĭj] **14**–18, **14**–19
messenger [mĕs/ən jər] **168**–40
meter [mē/tər] **62**–14, **129**–25, **152**–23
mice / mouse [mīs] / [mows] **63**–28, **196**–15, **215**–18
microphone [mī/krə fōn/] **234**–18
microprocessor [mī/krō prä/sĕ sər] **196**–4
Microscope [mī/krə skōp/] **194**
microwave [mī/krə wāv/] **77**–T
microwave oven [mī/krə wāv/ ŭv/ən] **54**–13
middle [mĭd/l] **25**–2
    middle-aged [mĭd/l ājd/] **32**–2
    middle initial [mĭd/l ĭ nĭsh/əl] **4**–3
    middle school [mĭd/l skōōl/] **188**–3
mid-length [mĭd/lĕnth] **96**–17
midnight [mĭd/nīt/] **18**–21
Military [mĭ/lə tër ē] **138**
MILITARY SERVICE [mĭ/lə tër ē sür/vəs] **138–139**
milk [mĭlk] **66**–5, **81**–42
    milkshake [mĭlk shāk/] **79**–14
milk [mĭlk] **177**–C
mini [mĭn/ē] **96**–15
    mini-blinds [mĭn/ē blīndz/] **58**–8
    minivan [mĭn/ē văn/] **156**–8
minister [mĭ/nə stər] **199**–7

minutes [mĭn/əts] **18**–2
mirror [mĭr/ər] **57**–16
   full-length mirror [fŏŏl/lĕnth mĭr/ər] **58**–6
   rearview mirror [rĭr/vyōō/ mĭr/ər] **159**–35
   sideview mirror [sīd/vyōō/ mĭr/ər] **158**–3
misbehave [mĭs/bĭ hāv/] **44**–B
miss the bus [mĭs dhə bŭs/] **152** ✦
missing [mĭs/ĭng] **97**–40
mittens [mĭt/nz] **90**–10
mix [mĭks] **77**–R
mixed berries [mĭkst/ bĕr/ēz] **81**–36
mixer [mĭk/sər] **54**–25
mixing bowl [mĭk/sĭng bōl/] **54**–28, **78**–31
mobile [mō/bēl] **59**–5
   mobile home [mō/bəl hōm/] **52**–7
model [mäd/l] **156** ✦, **168**–41
   model kit [mäd/l kĭt/] **232**–9
   model trains [mäd/l trānz/] **233**–27
modern [mä/dərn] **199**–2
moist towelettes [moyst/ tow/əl ĕts] **146**–12
moisturizer [moys/chə rī/zər] **108**–9
mole [mōl] **32**–16
molecule [mäl/ĭ kyōōl/] **195**–27
monarch [mä/nərk, mä/närk/] **199**–4
Monday [mŭn/dā, –dē] **20**–9
MONEY [mŭn/ē] **26**
monitor [män/ə tər] **196**–11
   arrival and departure monitors
      [ə rī/vəl ən dĭ pär/chər män/ə tərz] **161**–7
   baby monitor [bā/bē män/ə tər] **59**–7
   vital signs monitor [vī/təl sīnz män/ə tər] **121**–26
monkey [mŭng/kē] **217**–26
month [mŭnth] **20**–3
Months of the Year [mŭnths/ əv dhə yïr/] **21**
moon [mōōn]
   crescent moon [krĕs/ənt mōōn/] **205**–10
   full moon [fŏŏl/ mōōn/] **205**–12
   new moon [nōō/ mōōn/] **205**–9
   quarter moon [kwör/tər mōōn/] **205**–11
Moon [mōōn] **205**
moose [mōōs] **216**–1
mop [mäp] **61**–6
mop [mäp] **60**–D
morning [mör/nĭng] **18**–15
mosque [mäsk] **126**–5
mosquito [mə skē/tō] **214**–22
motel [mō tĕl/] **126**–12
moth [möth] **214**–21
mother [mŭdh/ər] **34**–3, **35**–22
   grandmother [grän/mŭdh/ər, gränd/–] **34**–1
   motherboard [mŭdh/ər börd/] **196**–5
   mother-in-law [mŭdh/ər ĭn lö/] **34**–10
   stepmother [stĕp/mŭdh/ər] **35**–26
MOTION [mō/shən] **153**
motor [mō/tər] **124**–4
motorcycle [mō/tər sī/kəl] **150**–4
mountain [mown/tn]
   mountain biking [mown/tn bī/kĭng] **226**–8
   mountain lion [mown/tn lī/ən] **216**–2
   mountain peak [mown/tn pēk/] **204**–14
   mountain range [mown/tn rānj/] **204**–15
   Mountain time [mown/tn tīm/] **19**–30

mouse / mice [mows] / [mīs] **63**–28, **196**–15, **215**–18
mouth [mowth] **104**–7
   mouthwash [mowth/wäsh/, –wösh/] **109**–25
Mouth [mowth] **106**
move in [mōōv/ ĭn/] **48**–F
move out [mōōv/ owt/] **48** ✦
movement [mōōv/mənt] **199**–16
mover [mōō/vər] **168**–42
movies [mōō/vēz] **222**–2
   movie theater [mōō/vē thē/ə tər] **126**–6
Movies [mōō/vēz] **237**
Moving In [mōō/vĭng ĭn] **49**
moving van [mōō/vĭng văn/] **156**–18
mow [mō] **176**–A
mower [mō/ər] **176**–6
mozzarella cheese [möts/ə rĕ lə chēz/] **71**–29
MP3 player [ĕm/pē/thrē/ plā/ər] **234**–2
mudslide [mŭd/slīd/] **144**–6
muffin [mŭf/ən] **79**–16, **80**–5
muffler [mŭf/lər] **158**–16
muffs [mŭfs] **179**–16
mug [mŭg] **55**–7
mugging [mŭg/ĭng] **142**–11
multiply [mŭl/tə plī] **192**–C
multi-use knife [mŭl/tē yōōs/ nīf/, mŭl/tī–] **226**–20
mumps [mŭmps] **111**–7
murder [mür/dər] **142**–12
muscle [mŭs/əl] **107**–32
mushrooms [mŭsh/rōōmz/] **69**–27
music [myōō/zĭk] **64**–3, **189**–15
   live music [līv/ myōō/zĭk] **84**–1
   music store [myōō/zĭk stör/] **130**–1
   world music [würld/ myōō/zĭk] **237**–32
Music [myōō/zĭk] **237**
MUSIC [myōō/zĭk] **238**
musician [myōō zĭsh/ən] **168**–43
mussels [mŭs/əlz] **71**–13, **212**–17
mustache [mŭs/tăsh] **33**–5
mustard [mŭs/tərd] **79**–22
mystery [mĭs/tə rē] **237**–20
nachos [nä/chōz] **79**–7
nail [nāl] **180**–34
   fingernail [fĭng/gər nāl/] **106**–18
   nail clipper [nāl klĭp/ər] **109**–31
   nail polish [nāl päl/ĭsh] **109**–33
   nail salon [nāl sə län/] **130**–3
   toenail [tō/nāl/] **106** ✦
name [nām] **4**–1, **4**–2, **4**–4
   name tag [nām/ tăg/] **92**–15
napkin [năp/kĭn] **55**–10, **83**–26
narrow [năr/ō] **97**–35
nasal [nā/zəl]
   nasal congestion [nā/zəl kən jĕs/chən] **110**–7
   nasal spray [nā/zəl sprā/] **113**–32
National Guard [nă/shə nəl gärd/] **138**–19
NATIONAL PARKS [nă/shə nəl pärks/] **220**–221
Native Americans [nā/tĭv ə mĕr/ə kənz] **198**–3
natural [năch/rəl, năch/ər əl/]
   natural gas [năch/rəl găs/] **218**–3
   natural materials [năch/rəl mə tïr/ē əlz] **98** ✦
NATURE CENTER [nā/chər sĕn/tər] **208**–209
nature program [nā/chər prō/grăm] **236**–7

Navigating a Webpage [nă/və gā/tĭng ə wĕb/pāj] **197**
Navy [nā/vē] **138**–15
navy blue [nā/vē blōō/] **28**–5
near [nïr] **25** ✦
neck [nĕk] **96**–8, **96**–10, **104**–3
   crewneck [krōō/nĕk] **96**–7
   necklaces [nĕk/lə sĕz] **95**–10
   turtleneck [tür/tl nĕk/] **96**–9
needle [nēd/l] **98**–17, **100**–10, **210**–10, **233**–23
   needle plate [nēd/l plāt/] **98**–18
negative integers [nĕ/gə tĭv ĭn/tə jərz] **192**–1
negotiate [nĭ gō/shē āt/] **157**–D
neighborhood [nā/bər hŏŏd/] **128** ✦
nephew [nĕf/yōō] **34**–19
Neptune [nĕp/tōōn] **205**–8
nervous [nür/vəs] **42**–10
nest [nĕst] **209**–12
net [nĕt] **226**–17
   hairnet [hĕr/nĕt/] **93**–25
network [nĕt/würk/] **173**–A
Neutral Colors [nōō/trəl kŭl/ərz] **24**
neutron [nōō/trän] **195**–32
new [nōō]
   new job [nōō/ jäb/] **172**–3
   new moon [nōō/ mōōn/] **205**–9
   New Year's Day [nōō/ yïrz/ dā/] **22**–9
Newfoundland time [nōō/fən lənd tīm/, –fənd–] **19**–34
news [nōōz]
   newspaper [nōōz/pā/pər] **133**–6
   news program [nōōz prō/grăm] **236**–1
   newsstand [nōōz/stănd/] **128**–12
newt [nōōt] **212**–26
New Words [nōō/ würdz/] **8**
next [nĕkst]
   next day mail [nĕkst/ dā/ māl/] **135** ✦
   next to [nĕkst/ tōō, –tə] **24**–9
   next week [nĕkst/ wēk/] **20**–20
nickel [nĭk/əl] **26**–2
niece [nēs] **34**–18
night [nīt] **18**–20
   nightclub [nīt/klŭb/] **223**–12
   nightgown [nīt/gown/] **91**–25
   night light [nīt/līt/] **37**–27
   nightshirt [nīt/shürt/] **91**–28
   nightstand [nīt/stănd/] **58**–23
   night table [nīt/ tā/bəl] **58**–23
nine [nīn] **16**
nineteen [nīn/tēn/] **16**
nineteenth [nīn/tēnth/] **16**
ninetieth [nīn/tē əth] **16**
ninety [nīn/tē] **16**
   90° angle [nīn/tē də grē/ ăng/gəl] **193**–26
ninth [nīnth] **16**
nipple [nĭp/əl] **37**–2
no [nō]
   no left turn [nō/ lĕft/ türn] **154**–8
   no outlet [nō/ owt/lĕt, –lət] **154**–6
   no parking [nō/ pär/kĭng] **154**–11
noise [noyz] **64**–5
noisy [noy/zē] **23**–11
noon [nōōn] **18**–16
   afternoon [ăf/tər nōōn/] **18**–17

north [nörth] **155**–1

NORTH AMERICA AND CENTRAL AMERICA
[nörth/ ə měr/ə kə ən sěn/trəl ə měr/ə kə] **200–201**

nose [nōz] **104**–6, **110**–17

revolving nosepiece [rə väl/ving nōz/pēs] **194**–17

not [nät]

can't breathe [kănt/ brēdh/] **116**–N

do not drink [dōō/ nät/ drĭnk] **112**–F

do not enter [dōō/ nät/ ĕn/tər] **154**–2

do not operate [dōō/ nät/ äp/ər ät/] **112**–E

do not take [dōō nät/ tāk/] **112**–D

don't be late [dōnt/ bē/ lāt/] **174**–E

don't litter [dōnt/ lĭt/ər] **219**–L

don't smoke [dōnt/ smōk/] **114**–G

not working [nät/ wür/kĭng] **62**–1

note [nōt] **183**–39

footnote [fŏŏt/nōt/] **190**–10

notebook [nōt/bŏŏk/] **7**–27

notebook paper [nōt/bŏŏk/ pāp/ər] **7**–28

spiral notebook [spī/rəl nōt/bŏŏk/] **7**–29

novel [nä/vəl] **133**–16

November [nō věm/bər] **21**–35

nuclear energy [nōō/klē ər ĕn/ər jē] **218**–8

nucleus [nōō/klē əs] **194**–7, **195**–29

numb [nŭm] **119**–C

number [nŭm/bər]

access number [ăk/sĕs/ nŭm/bər] **14**–16

apartment number [ə pärt/mənt nŭm/bər] **4**–6

cell phone number [sĕl/ fōn/ nŭm/bər] **4**–12

checking account number
[chĕk/ĭng ə kownt/ nŭm/bər] **132**–14

driver's license number
[drī/vərz lī/səns nŭm/bər] **136**–11

even numbers [ĕv/ən nŭm/bərz] **192**–4

odd numbers [öd/ nŭm/bərz] **192**–3

phone number [fōn/ nŭm/bər] **4**–11, **15**–30

prescription number
[prĭ skrĭp/shən nŭm/bər] **112**–5

savings account number
[sā/vĭngz ə kownt/ nŭm/bər] **132**–11

SKU number [ĕs/kā/yōō/ nŭm/bər] **27**–5

Social Security number
[sō/shəl sĭ kyŏŏr/ə tē nŭm/bər] **4**–15

Numbers [nŭm/bərz] **16**

NUMBERS [nŭm/bərz] **16**

Numerals [nōō/mər əlz] **16**

numerator [nōō/mər ā/ tər] **192**–5

nurse [nürs] **118**–8, **168**–44

licensed practical nurse (LPN) [lī/sənst
prăk/tə kəl nürs/] / [ĕl/pē/ĕn/] **120**–11

nurse midwives [nürs/ mĭd/wīvz/] **120** ✦

nurse practitioners [nürs/ prăk tĭ/shən ərz] **120** ✦

registered nurse (RN) [rĕj/ə stərd nürs/] / [är/ĕn/]
120–10

surgical nurse [sür/jĭ kəl nürs/] **120**–9

nurse [nürs] **36**–B

Nurse [nürs] **93**

nursery [nür/sə rē]

nursery rhymes [nür/sə rē rīmz/] **37**–22

nursery school [nür/sə rē skōōl/] **188**–1

nursing [nür/sĭng] **120**–12

nursing home [nür/sĭng hōm/] **52**–12

Nursing Staff [nür/sĭng stăf/] **120**

nutrition label [nōō trĭ/shən lā/bəl] **122**–8

nuts [nŭts] **73**–36, **180**–36

nylon [nī/län] **99**–12

oak [ōk] **210**–17, **210**–24

obey [ō bā/] **140**–C

objective [əb jĕk/tĭv] **194**–18

oboe [ō/bō] **238**–3

observatory [əb zür/və tör/ē] **205**–21

observe [əb zürv/] **195**–C

obstetrician [äb/stə trĭsh/ən] **120**–2

obtuse angle [äb/tōōs ăng/gəl] **193**–27

occupational therapist
[äk/yə pā/shən əl thĕr/ə pĭst] **168**–45

OCCUPATIONS [äk/yə pā/shənz] **166–169**

ocean [ō/shən] **204**–6, **225**–1

o'clock [ə kläk/] **18**–6

October [äk tō/bər] **21**–34

octopus [äk/tə pəs] **212**–9

odd numbers [öd/ nŭm/bərz] **192**–3

odometer [ō däm/ə tər] **159**–28

off [öf]

clear off [klĭr/ öf/] **10**–I

drop off [dräp/ öf/] **38**–G

gas shut-off valve [găs/ shŭt/öf vălv/] **146**–4

get off [gĕt/ öf/] **153**–J

take off [tāk/ öf/] **109**–Q

turn off [türn/ öf/] **11**–P, **160**–I, **174**–G, **219**–G

offer [ö/fər] **12**–D

office [ö/fəs] **164**–3

main office [mān/ ö/fəs] **5**–12

office building [ö/fəs bĭld/ĭng] **124**–2

office manager [ö/fəs măn/ĭ jər] **182**–8

office supply store [ö/fəs sə plī/ stör/] **127**–21

post office [pōst/ ö/fəs] **125**–11

post office box (PO box) [pōst/ ö/fəs bäks/] /
[pē/ō bäks/] **135**–9

run for office [rŭn/ fər ö/fəs] **139**–A

Office [ö/fəs] **51**

OFFICE [ö/fəs] **134–135**, **182–183**

Office Equipment [ö/fəs ĭ kwĭp/mənt] **183**

officer [ö/fə sər] **161**–17, **168**–48

Office Skills [ö/fəs skĭlz/] **171**

OFFICE SKILLS [ö/fəs skĭlz/] **171**

Office Supplies [ö/fəs sə plīz/] **183**

Office Visit [ö/fəs vĭ/zət] **119**

official [ə fĭsh/əl] **139**–32, **229**–6

oil [oyl] **73**–31, **218**–6

oil gauge [oyl/ gāj/] **159**–29

oil paint [oyl/ pānt/] **233**–19

oil spill [oyl/ spĭl/] **218**–17

ointment [oynt/mənt] **113**–24, **117**–10

OK [ō kā/] **154**–5

old [ōld] **31**–9, **31**–10

omelet [äm/lət, ä/mə lət] **76**–12

on [än, ön] **25**–11

get on [gĕt/ än, –ön] **153**–I

go on [gō/ än, –ön] **173**–K

on-the-job training [än dhə jäb/ trā/nĭng, –ön]
172–7

on the left [än dhə lĕft/, –ön] **25**–1

on the right [än dhə rīt/, –ön] **25**–3

on time [än tīm/, –ön] **19**–23, **16**–29

overdose on drugs [ō/vər dōs/ än drŭgz/] **116**–K

put on [pŏŏt/ än/, –ön/] **87**–B, **108**–D, **109**–P

try on [trī/ än/, –ön/] **95**–C

turn on [türn/ än/, –ön/] **11**–B

once a week [wŭns/ə wēk/] **20**–22

oncologist [ön/kö lə jĭst/] **120**–5

one [wŭn] **16**

five after one [fīv/ ăf/ tər wŭn/] **18**–7

one billion [wŭn/ bĭl/yən] **16**

one eighth [wŭn/ ätth/, –āth/] **17**–5

one-fifteen [wŭn/fĭf/tēn/] **18**–9

one-forty [wŭn/för/tē] **18**–12

one-forty-five [wŭn/för/tē fīv/] **18**–13

one fourth [wŭn/ förth/] **17**–4

one half [wŭn/ hăf/] **17**–2

one hundred [wŭn/ hŭn/drəd] **16**

one hundred dollars
[wŭn/ hŭn/drəd däl/ərz] **26**–12

one hundred one [wŭn/ hŭn/drəd wŭn/] **16**

100 percent [wŭn/ hŭn/drəd pər sĕnt/] **17**–8

one hundredth [wŭn/ hŭn/drəth] **16**

one hundred thousand
[wŭn/ hŭn/drəd thow/zənd] **16**

one million [wŭn/ mĭl/yən] **16**

one o'clock [wŭn/ ə kläk/] **18**–6

one-oh-five [wŭn/ō fīv/] **18**–7

one-size-fits-all [wŭn/sīz fĭts/äl] **96**–6

one-ten [wŭn/tĕn/] **18**–8

one third [wŭn/ thürd/] **17**–3

one-thirty [wŭn/thür/tē] **18**–11

one thousand [wŭn/ thow/zənd] **16**

one thousandth [wŭn/ thow/zənth] **16**

one-twenty [wŭn/twĕn/tē] **18**–10

one way [wŭn/ wā/] **154**–3

one-way trip [wŭn/wā/ trĭp/] **152**–16

one whole [wŭn/hōl/] **17**–1

quarter after one [kwör/tər ăf/tər wŭn/] **18**–9

ten after one [tĕn/ ăf/tər wŭn/] **18**–8

twenty after one [twĕn/tē ăf/tər wŭn/] **18**–10

onions [ŭn/yənz] **69**–19, **69**–20

onion rings [ŭn/yən rĭngz/] **79**–4

online [än/līn/, ön–]

online catalog [än/līn/ kä/tə lög, ön–] **133**–11

online course [än/lĭn/ körs/, ön–] **172**–8

only [ōn/lē] **154**–7

On the Airplane [än/ dhe ĕr/plān/] **161**

open [ō/pən] **6**–G, **143**–F

opener [ō/pən ər] **54**–8, **78**–1, **146**–8

Opening an Account [ō/pə nĭng ən ə kownt/] **132**

opera [äp/rə] **223**–11, **236**–5

operate [äp/ə rāt/] **112**–E, **170**–H

Operating Room [äp/ə rā/tĭng rōōm/] **121**

operating table [äp/ə rā/tĭng tā/bəl] **121**–40

Operations [äp/ə rā/shənz] **192**

operator [äp/ə rā/tər] **14**–21, **98**–14, **168**–37

ophthalmologist
[äf/thəl mäl/ə jĭst, –thə mäl/–, äp/–] **120**–7

opinion [ə pĭn/yən] **44**–3

opossum [ə päs/əm, päs/əm] **216**–4

opponent [ə pō/nənt] **139**–30

optician [äp tĭsh/ən] **130**–9

optometrist [äp täm/ə trĭst] **115**–6
orange [ör/ənj, är/–] **24**–4
oranges [ör/ən jəz, är/–] **68**–5
orangutan [ə răng/ə tăng/, –tăn/] **217**–39
orchard [ör/chərd] **177**–10
orchid [ör/kĭd] **211**–19
order [ör/dər] **185**–1
    order puller [ör/dər pŏŏl/ər] **175**–10
order [ör/dər] **82**–D
orderly [ör/dər lē] **120**–16
Ordinal Numbers [ör/dn əl nŭm/bərz] **16**
organ [ör/gən] **238**–20
organic [ör gă/nĭk] **84**–2
organisms [ör/gə nĭzmz] **194**–1
organize [ör/gə nīz/] **171**–L, **191**–G
organizer [ör/gə nī/zər] **183**–49
ornament [ör/nə mənt] **239**–15
Orthodontics [ör/thə dän/tĭks] **119**
orthodontist [ör/thə dän/tĭst] **119**–5
orthopedists [ör/thə pē/dĭsts] **120** ✦
Other Instruments [ŭdh/ər ĭn/strə mənts] **238**
otter [ät/ər] **213**–35
ounce [owns] **75**–1, **75**–11
out [owt] **62**–2
    blow out [blō/ owt/] **240**–C
    check out [chĕk/ owt/] **133**–C
    cross out [krös/ owt/] **9**–R
    eat out [ēt/ owt/] **82** ✦
    fill out [fĭl/ owt/] **173**–J
    get out of [gĕt/ owt/ əv] **153**–F
    let out [lĕt/ owt/] **100**–C
    move out [mōōv/ owt/] **48** ✦
    outfit [owt/fĭt] **88** ✦
    out of focus [owt/ əv fō/kəs] **235**–33
    out-of-state contact [owt/əv stāt/ kän/täkt] **146**–2
    run out of gas [rŭn/ owt/ əv gäs/] **162**–E
    take out [tāk/ owt/] **9**–Y, **60**–Q, **82** ✦
    work out [würk/ owt/] **230**–N
OUTDOOR RECREATION [owt/dör rĕk/rē ā/shən] **226**
outlet [owt/lĕt, –lət] **58**–28, **154**–6, **159**–42
    outlet cover [owt/lĕt kŭv/ər] **181**–46
OUTSIDE THE BODY [owt/sīd/ dhe bä/dē] **106**–**107**
oven [ŭv/ən] **54**–15, **54**–20
    oven cleaner [ŭv/ən klē/nər] **61**–3
over [ō/vər] **76**–11, **153**–B
    overalls [ō/vər ölz/] **88**–6
    overcoat [ō/vər kōt/] **90**–2
    overexposed [ō/vər ĭk spōzd/] **235**–34
    overflowing [ō/vər flō/ĭng] **63**–17
    overhead compartment
        [ō/vər hĕd/ kəm pärt/mənt] **161**–13
    overhead projector [ō/vər hĕd/ prə jĕk/tər] **7**–16
    overjoyed [ō/vər joyd/] **43** ✦
    overnight mail [ō/vər nīt/ māl/] **135** ✦
    over-the-counter medication
        [ō/vər dhə -kown/tər mĕd/ə kā/shən] **113**–18
overdose [ō/vər dōs, ō/vər dōs/] **116**–K
Over-the-Counter Medication
    [ō/vər dhə kown/tər mĕd/ə kā/shən] **113**
owl [owl] **214**–5
owner [ō/nər] **166**–11, **175**–1
oxfords [äks/fərdz] **95**–29

oxygen mask [äk/sĭ jən mäsk/] **161**–24
oysters [oy/stərz] **71**–14
Pacific time [pə sĭf/ĭk tīm/] **19**–29
pacifier [păs/ə fī/ər] **37**–24
pack [päk] **74**–9, **117**–13, **235**–26
    backpack [băk/päk/] **94**–18, **226**–15
pack [päk] **49**–M, **162**–A
package [păk/ĭj] **74**–8, **74**–20, **134**–17
packaged food [păk/ĭjd fōōd/] **146**–10
PACKAGING [păk/ə jĭng] **74**
packer [păk/ər] **175**–18
packing tape [păk/ĭng tāp/] **183**–32
pad [păd]
    bumper pad [bŭm/pər păd/] **59**–4
    changing pad [chānj/ĭng păd/] **59**–2
    foam pad [fōm/ păd/] **226**–13
    heating pad [hē/tĭng păd/] **113**–13
    ink pad [ĭnk/ păd/] **183**–46
    knee pads [nē/ pădz/] **179**–19
    legal pad [lē/gəl păd/] **183**–38
    shoulder pads [shōl/dər pădz/] **231**–20
    steel-wool soap pads [stēl/wŏŏl/sōp/ pădz/] **61**–5
    sterile pad [stĕr/əl păd/] **117**–6
pail [pāl] **37**–7, **61**–7, **225**–8
pain [pān] **42**–11, **115**–3
    pain reliever [pān rĭ lē/vər] **113**–26
paint [pānt] **181**–25, **232**–10, **233**–19
    paintbrush [pānt/brŭsh/] **181**–22, **233**–20
    paint pan [pānt/ păn/] **181**–51
    paint roller [pānt/ rō/lər] **181**–23
paint [pānt] **49**–P, **178**–A, **233**–E
painter [pān/tər] **168**–46
Painter [pān/tər] **92**
painting [pān/tĭng] **56**–9
pair of scissors [pĕr/ əv sĭz/ərz] **100**–16
paisley [pāz/lē] **96**–26
pajamas [pə jä/məz, –jä/–] **91**–24
pallet [pă/lət] **175**–13
palm [päm] **106**–15, **210**–14
pan [păn] **54**–24
    bed pan [bĕd/ păn/] **121**–28
    cake pan [kāk/ păn/] **78**–26
    dustpan [dŭst/ păn/] **61**–17
    frying pan [frī/ĭng păn/] **78**–5
    paint pan [pānt/ păn/] **181**–51
    pancakes [păn/kāks/] **80**–7
    pie pan [pī/ păn/] **78**–28
    roasting pan [rō/stĭng păn/] **78**–13
    saucepan [sös/păn/] **78**–25
pancreas [păng/krē əs] **107**–45
panda [păn/də] **217**–41
pane [pān] **178**–16
panel [păn/əl] **234**–7
Panel [păn/əl] **159**
panther [păn/thər] **217**–40
panties [păn/tēz] **91**–13
pants [pănts] **87**–12
    security pants [sĭ kyŏŏr/ə tē pănts/] **93**–22
    training pants [trā/nĭng pănts/] **37**–11
    work pants [würk/ pănts/] **92**–5
panty hose [păn/tē hōz/] **91**–18
papayas [pə pī/əz] **68**–20

paper [pā/pər]
    construction paper [kən strŭk/shən pā/pər] **232**–12
    copies of important papers
        [kä/pēz əv ĭm pört/ənt pā/pərz] **146**–20
    newspaper [nōōz/pā/pər] **133**–6
    notebook paper [nōt/bŏŏk/ pā/pər] **7**–28
    paper clip [pā/pər klĭp/] **183**–31
    paper cutter [pā/pər kŭt/ər] **183**–22
    paper dolls [pā/pər dälz/] **233**–28
    paper shredder [pā/pər shrĕd/ər] **183**–24
    paper towels [pā/pər tow/əlz] **54**–3
    sandpaper [sănd/ pā/pər] **181**–56
    toilet paper [toy/lət pā/pər] **57**–17, **146**–13
    wallpaper [wäl/ pā/pər] **59**–8
parade [pə rād/] **239**–1
paragraph [păr/ə grăf/] **190**–3
parakeet [păr/ə kēt/] **215**–15
parallel lines [păr/ə lĕl/ līnz/] **193**–25
parallelogram [păr/ə lĕl/ə grăm/] **193**–33
paramedic [păr/ə mĕ/dĭk] **116**–2
parasites [păr/ə sīts/] **111**–13
parcel post [păr/səl pōst/] **134**–6
parentheses [pə rĕn/thə sēz/] **190**–19
PARENTING [păr/ən tĭng, pĕr/–] **36**–**37**
Parents [păr/ənts, pĕr/–] **34**
parent-teacher conference
    [păr/ənt tē/chər kän/frəns, pĕr/–] **22**–5
paring knife [pĕr/ĭng nīf/] **78**–16
park [pärk] **223**–10
    park ranger [pärk/ rāng/jər] **220**–2
park [pärk] **129**–E
parka [pär/kə] **90**–9
PARK AND PLAYGROUND [pärk/ ən plā/grownd/] **224**
parking [pär/kĭng] **128**–6, **154**–11, **154**–12
    parking attendant [pär/kĭng ə tĕn/dənt] **184**–3
    parking garage [pär/kĭng gə räzh/, –räj/] **124**–1
    parking meter [pär/kĭng mē/tər] **129**–25
    parking space [pär/kĭng spās/] **50**–18, **128**–5
PARKS [pärks] **220**–**221**
parochial school [pə rō/kē əl skōōl/] **5** ✦
parsley [pär/slē] **69**–28
part [pärt] **33**–4
participate [pär tĭ/sə pāt/] **10**–B
particle [pär/tĭ kəl]
    particle board [pär/tĭ kəl börd/] **181**–20
    particle mask [pär/tĭ kəl măsk/] **179**–14
Partner [pärt/nər] **8**
parts [pärts] **175**–5
Parts of a Bird [pärts/ əv ə bürd/] **214**
PARTS OF A CAR [pärts/ əv ə kär/] **158**–**159**
Parts of a Fish [pärts/ əv ə fĭsh/] **212**
Parts of a Flower [pärts/ əv ə flow/ər] **211**
Parts of an Essay [pärts/ əv ən ĕs/ā] **190**
Parts of a Phone [pärts/ əv ə fōn/] **14**
Parts of a Sewing Machine
    [pärts/ əv ə sō/ĭng mə shēn] **98**
Parts of a Tree [pärts/ əv ə trē/] **210**
party [pär/tē] **64**–2
pass [păs] **161**–20
    passbook [păs/bŏŏk/] **132**–10
    passport [păs/pört/] **41**–10
pass [păs] **10**–E, **137**–H, **230**–G

Index

passenger [păs/ən jər] **150**–2, **161**–15

past [păst] **155**–E

pasta [päs/tə] **67**–12

    pasta salad [päs/tə săl/əd] **80**–20

paste [pāst]

    toothpaste [tōōth/pāst/] **109**–23

pastrami [pə strä/mē] **71**–23

path [păth] **208**–3, **224**–3

Path [păth] **172**

patient [pā/shənt] **118**–6, **121**–18

patio [păt/ē ō] **53**–16

    patio furniture [păt/ē ō fűr/nĭ chər] **53**–19

patron [pā/trən] **82**–6, **133**–3

pattern [păt/ərn] **99**–22

PATTERNS [păt/ərnz] **96**

pause [pöz] **235**–E

paw [pö] **216**–20

pay [pā]

    paycheck [pā/chĕk/] **165**–14

    payroll clerk [pā/rōl klürk/] **165**–10

    pay stub [pā/ stŭb/] **165**–11

pay [pā]

    pay a late fine [pā/ ə lāt/ fīn/] **133**–E

    pay attention [pā/ ə tĕn/shən] **147**–D

    pay back [pā/ băk/] **26**–D

    pay cash [pā/ kăsh/] **27**–A

    pay for [pā/ för/, –fər/] **27**–G

    pay phone [pā/ fōn] **15**–25, **129**–23

    pay taxes [pā/ tăks/əz] **140**–B

    pay the application fee

        [pā/ dhe ăp/lə kā/shən fē/] **137**–D

    pay the check [pā/ dhe chĕk/] **82**–I

    pay the rent [pā/ dhe rĕnt/] **48**–E

Pay [pā] **27**

PBX [pē/ bē/ ĕks/] **182**–13

peaceful assembly [pēs/fəl ə sĕm/blē] **140**–1

peaches [pē/chəz] **68**–10

peacock [pē/käk/] **214**–14

peak [pēk] **204**–14

pearls [pürlz] **95**–39

pears [përz] **68**–4

peas [pēz] **69**–21

pedal [pĕd/əl] **159**–45, **159**–46

pedestrian [pə dĕs/trē ən] **128**–14

    pedestrian crossing [pə dĕs/trē ən krö/sĭng] **154**–13

pediatrician [pē/dē ə trĭsh/ən] **120**–4

peel [pēl] **77**–K

peeler [pē/lər] **78**–15

peephole [pēp/hōl/] **51**–32

pelvis [pĕl/vəs] **107**–50

pen [pĕn] **7**–22

pencil [pĕn/səl] **7**–20, **109**–34

    pencil eraser [pĕn/səl ĭ rā/sər] **7**–21

    pencil sharpener [pĕn/səl shär/pə nər] **7**–23, **183**–26

penguin [pĕng/wĭn] **214**–11

peninsula [pə nĭn/sə lə] **204**–7

penny [pĕn/ē] **26**–1

PEOPLE [pē/pəl] **32**

pepper [pĕp/ər] **55**–13, **69**–7, **69**–29

percent [pər sĕnt/]

    50 percent [fĭf/tē pər sĕnt/] **17**–10

    100 percent [wŭn/ hŭn/drəd pər sĕnt/] **17**–8

    75 percent [sĕv/ən tē fīv/ pər sĕnt/] **17**–9

    10 percent [tĕn/ pər sĕnt/] **17**–12

    25 percent [twĕn/tē fīv/ pər sĕnt/] **17**–11

Percents [pər sĕnts/] **17**

Percussion [pər kŭsh/ən] **238**

perfume [pür/fyōōm/, pər fyōōm/] **108**–6

perimeter [pə rĭ/mə tər] **193**–43

period [pïr/ē əd] **190**–11

Period [pïr/ē əd] **198**

periodicals [pïr/ē äd/ĭ kəlz] **133**–4

periodic table [pïr/ē äd/ĭk tā/bəl] **195**–26

perm [pürm] **33**–B

peroxide [pə räk/ sïd] **117**–9

perpendicular lines [pür/pən dĭk/yə lər līnz/] **193**–24

person [pür/sən]

    appliance repair person

        [ə plī/əns rĭ për/ pür/sən] **166**–4

    assemblyperson [ə sĕm/blē pür/sən] **139**–24

    businessperson [bĭz/nəs pür/sən] **166**–12

    bus person [bŭs/ pür/sən] **185**–13

    congressperson [kän/grəs pür/sən] **138**–4

    councilperson [kown/səl pür/sən] **139**–28

    counterperson [kown/tər pür/sən] **79**–17

    delivery person [də lĭv/ə rē pür/sən] **167**–21

    electronics repair person

        [ĭ lĕk trän/ĭks rĭ për/ pür/sən] **167**–24

    repair person [rĭ për/ pür/sən] **62**–10

personal CD player [pür/sə nəl sē/dē/ plā/ər] **234**–5

PERSONAL HYGIENE [pür/sə nəl hī/jēn] **108**–**109**

PERSONAL INFORMATION

    [pür/sə nəl ĭn/fər mā/shən] **4**

pesticide poisoning [pĕs/tə sïd/ poy/zə nĭng] **218**–16

pests [pĕsts] **62** ✦

pet [pĕt]

    pet food [pĕt fōōd/] **72**–5

    pet store [pĕt stör/] **130**–6

petals [pĕt/lz] **211**–8

petition [pə tĭ/shən] **148**–5

petroleum [pə trō/lē əm] **218**–6

Pets [pĕts] **215**

pharmacist [fär/mə sïst] **112**–1

pharmacy [fär/mə sē] **128**–4

PHARMACY [fär/mə sē] **112**–**113**

Phase of the Moon [fāz/ əf dhə mōōn/] **205**

Phillips screwdriver [fĭl/ĭps skrōō/drī/vər] **180**–31

phlebotomist [flĭ bä/tə mĭst] **121**–29

phone [fōn]

    automated phone system

        [ö/tə māt ĭd fōn/ sĭs/təm] **14**–23

    cell phone holder [sĕl/ fōn/ hōl/dər] **94**–15

    cell phone kiosk [sĕl/ fōn/ kē/ösk] **131**–22

    cell phone number [sĕl/ fōn/ nŭm/bər] **4**–12

    cellular phone [sĕl/yə lər fōn/] **14**–8

    cordless phone [körd/ləs fōn/] **15**–24

    headphones [hĕd/ fōnz/] **6**–8, **234**–4

    Internet phone call [ĭn/tər nĕt/ fōn/ käl/] **14**–20

    microphone [mī/krə fōn/] **234**–18

    pay phone [pā/ fōn/] **15**–25, **129**–23

    phone bill [fōn/ bĭl/] **15**–28

    phone jack [fōn/ jäk/] **14**–3

    phone line [fōn/ lĭn/] **14**–4

    phone number [fōn/ nŭm/bər] **4**–11, **15**–30

    smart phone [smärt/ fōn/] **15**–27

Phone [fōn] **14**

Phone Bill [fōn/ bĭl/] **15**

Phone Call [fōn/ köl/] **15**

photo [fō/tō] **58**–3, **136**–4

    digital photo album [dĭ/jə təl fō/tō ăl/bəm] **235**–32

    funny photo [fŭn/ē fō/tō] **206**–2

    photo album [fō/tō ăl/bəm] **235**–31

    photocopier [fō/tə käp/ē ər] **183**–23

    serious photo [sïr/ē əs fō/tō] **206**–3

photographer [fə täg/rə fər] **206**–1

PHOTOGRAPHY [fə täg/rə fē] **234**–**235**

photosynthesis [fō/tō sĭn/thə səs] **194**–10

physical [fĭz/ĭ kəl]

    physical education [fĭz/ĭ kəl ĕ jə kā/shən] **189**–17

    physical therapist [fĭz/ĭ kəl thër/ə pïst] **115**–12

    physical therapy [fĭz/ĭ kəl thër/ə pē] **115**–11

physically challenged [fĭz/ĭ klē chăl/ənjd] **32**–10

physician assistant [fĭz/ĭ shən ə sĭs/tənt] **168**–47

physicist [fĭz/ĭ sïst] **195**–33

Physics [fĭz/ĭks] **195**

pi (π) [pī] **193**–46

piano [pē ăn/ō] **238**–14

pick [pĭk] **108**–15

pickax [pĭk/äks/] **178**–21

picker [pĭ/kər] **178**–5

pickle [pĭk/l] **80**–11

pick up [pĭk/ ŭp/] **6**–I, **11**–E, **38**–M, **112** ✦

pickup truck [pĭk/ŭp trŭk/] **156**–12

picnic [pĭk/nĭk] **224**–D

picnic table [pĭk/nĭk tā/bəl] **224**–8

picture [pĭk/chər]

    picture book [pĭk/chər bōōk/] **133**–12

    picture dictionary [pĭk/chər dĭk/shə nër ē] **7**–31

    picture frame [pĭk/chər frām/] **58**–4

pie [pī] **81**–35

    pie pan [pī/ păn/] **78**–28

pier [pïr] **225**–18

pierced [pïrst]

    pierced ear [pïrst/ ïr/] **32**–17

    pierced earrings [pïrst/ ïr/ĭngz] **95**–36

pig [pĭg] **215**–2, **215**–14

pigeon [pĭj/ən] **214**–15

pile [pïl] **53**–25

pill [pĭl] **113**–21

pillow [pĭl/ō] **56**–2, **58**–11

    pillowcase [pĭl/ō kās/] **58**–14

pilot [pī/lət] **161**–11

pin [pĭn] **95**–38

    bobby pins [bäb/ē pĭnz/] **108**–21

    clothespin [klōz/ pĭn/] **101**–10

    pin cushion [pĭn/ kōōsh/ən] **100**–13

    pushpin [pōōsh/pĭn/] **183**–35

    rolling pin [rō/lĭng pĭn/] **78**–30

    safety pin [săf/tē pĭn/] **37**–9, **100**–14

    straight pin [strāt pĭn/] **100**–12

pine [pĭn] **210**–9

    pinecone [pĭn/kōn/] **210**–11

pineapples [pī/năp/əlz] **68**–23

pink [pĭnk] **24**–7

pint [pïnt] **75**–3

pipe [pïp] **158**–15, **181**–17

    pipe wrench [pïp rĕnch/] **181**–47

pitch [pĭch] **230**–A
pizza [pēt′sə] **79**–10
place [plās] **146**–1
  fireplace [fīr′plās′] **56**–13
  placemat [plās′ măt′] **55**–11
  place of birth [plās′ əv bürth′] **4**–14
  place setting [plās′ sĕt′ĭng] **83**–17
PLACES TO GO [plā′səz tə gō′] **222**–223
PLACES TO LIVE [plā′səz tə lĭv′] **52**
plaid [plăd] **96**–22
plain [plān] **97**–33
plains [plānz] **204**–19
plan [plăn] **186**–4
plan [plăn] **146**–A
plane [plān] **144**–3, **150**–8, **181**–57
Planets [plăn′əts] **205**
Planning a Career [plă′nĭng ə kə rēr′] **172**
plant [plănt] **176**–E, **177**–A, **219**–N
plants [plănts] **208**–5
  houseplant [hows′plănt′] **56**–4, **211**–27
Plants [plănts] **210**
PLANTS [plănts] **210**
plaque [plăk] **119**–12
plastic [plăs′tĭk]
  plastic storage bags [plăs′tĭk stör′ĭj băgz′] **72**–25
  plastic storage container
    [plăs′tĭk stör′ĭj kən tā′nər] **78**–4
  plastic utensils [plăs′tĭk yōō tĕn′ səlz] **79**–19
  plastic wrap [plăs′tĭk răp′] **72**–24
plate [plāt] **55**–1
  bread-and-butter plate [brĕd′n bŭt′ər plāt′] **83**–19
  dinner plate [dĭn′ər plāt′] **83**–18
  license plate [lī′səns plāt′] **136**–12, **158**–12
  salad plate [săl′əd plāt′] **83**–20
  vanity plate [vă′nə tē plāt′]**136** ✦
platform [plăt′förm′] **152**–7
platter [plăt′ər] **55**–20
platypus [plăt′ĭ pəs, –pŏŏs′] **217**–46
play [plā] **223**–8
  play area [plā′ ĕr′ē ə] **130**–11
  playground [plā′grownd′] **50**–3
play [plā] **235**–B
  play an instrument [plā′ ən ĭn′strə mənt] **238**–A
  play cards [plā′ kärdz′] **233**–H
  play games [plā′ gāmz′] **232**–B
  play with [plā′ wĭth′] **36**–M
player [plā′ər] **229**–5
  CD player [sē′dē plā′ər] **159**–38
  DVD player [dē′vē′dē′ plā′ər] **56**–7, **234**–10
  MP3 player [ĕm′pē′thrē′ plā′ər] **234**–2
  personal CD player [pür′sə nəl sē′dē plā′ər] **234**–5
  portable cassette player
    [pör′tə bəl kə sĕt′ plā′ər] **234**–6
  portable DVD player
    [pör′tə bəl dē′vē′dē′ plā′ər] **234**–11
  video player [vĭd′ē ō plā′ər] **197**–11
PLAYGROUND [plā′grownd′] **224**
pliers [plī′ərz] **180**–7
plugs [plŭgz] **179**–15, **234**–16
plumber [plŭm′ər] **63**–20
plums [plŭmz] **68**–13
plunger [plŭn′jər] **181**–50

plywood [plī′wŏŏd′] **178**–18
p.m. [pē′ĕm′] **18**–5
pneumatic drill [nŏŏ măt′ĭk drĭl′] **178**–9
poached eggs [pōcht′ ĕgz′] **76**–9
PO box (post office box) [pē′ō bäks′] /
    [pōst′ ö′fəs bäks′] **135**–9
pocket [päk′ət] **100**–7
podium [pō′dē əm] **206**–5
poinsettia [poyn sĕt′ē ə, –sĕt′ə] **211**–24
point [poynt] **17**–7,
    endpoint [ĕnd′poynt′] **193**–21
pointer [poyn′tər] **197**–12
poison [poy′zən] **116**–J
  poison ivy [poy′zən ī′vē] **210**–25
  poison oak [poy′zən ōk′] **210**–24
  poison sumac [poy′zən sōō′măk, –shōō′–] **210**–23
poisoning [poy′zən ĭng] **218**–16
poisonous fumes [poy′zən əs fyōōmz′] **179**–3
poles [pōlz] **226**–18, **231**–25
police [pə lēs′]
  police officer [pə lēs′ ö′fə sər] **141**–1, **168**–48
  police station [pə lēs′ stā′shən] **124**–6
polish [päl′ĭsh] **61**–8, **109**–33
polish [päl′ĭsh] **60**–E, **109**–O
political [pə lĭ′tĭ kəl]
  political campaign [pə lĭ′tĭ kəl kăm păn′] **139**–29
  political movement [pə lĭ′tĭ kəl mōōv′mənt] **199**–16
  political party [pə lĭ′tĭ kəl pär′tē] **139** ✦
polka-dotted [pō′kə dät′əd] **96**–21
pollution [pə lōō′shən] **218**–11, **218**–14
Pollution [pə lōō′shən] **218**
polo [pō′lō] **229**–15
  polo shirt [pō′lō shĭrt′] **92**–14
poncho [pän′chō] **90**–19
pond [pänd] **204**–21
pool [pōōl] **51**–22, **184**–22, **228**–2
  pool service [pōōl′ sür′vəs] **184**–21
  pool table [pōōl′ tā′bəl] **50**–14
pop [päp] **73**–34, **237**–25
  pop-up ad [päp′ŭp′] **197**–9
porch light [pörch′ lĭt′] **53**–13
porcupine [pör′kyə pīn′] **216**–10
Pork [pörk] **70**
pork chops [pörk′ chäps′] **70**–10
porpoise [pör′pəs] **213**–30
port [pört] **196**–7
  airport [ĕr′pört′] **151**–10
portable [pör′tə bəl]
  portable cassette player
    [pör′tə bəl kə sĕt′ plā′ər] **234**–6
  portable DVD player
    [pör′tə bəl dē′vē′dē′ plā′ər] **234**–11
  portable TV [pör′tə bəl tē′ vē′] **234**–8
positive integers [pö′zə tĭv ĭn′tə jərz] **192**–2
post [pōst] **134**–6
  post card [pōst′kärd′] **134**–16
  postmark [pōst′märk] **134**–24
  post office [pōst′ ö′fəs] **125**–11
  post office box (PO box) [pōst′ ö′fəs bäks′] /
    [pē′ō bäks′] **135**–9
postage [pō′stĭj] **135** ✦

postal [pō′stəl] **135**–10
  postal clerk [pō′stəl klürk′] **135**–7
  postal forms [pō′stəl förmz′] **134**–19
  postal scale [pō′stəl skāl′] **183**–27
  postal worker [pō′stəl wür′kər] **169**–49
POST OFFICE [pōst′ ö′fəs] **134**–135
pot [pät] **54**–16, **78**–6
  pot holders [pät hōl′dərz] **78**–29
  teapot [tē′pät′] **55**–16
potatoes [pə tā′tōz] **69**–17
  baked potato [bākt′ pə tā′tō] **81**–25
  mashed potatoes [măsht′ pə tā′tōz] **81**–23
  potato chips [pə tā′tō chĭps′] **73**–35
  potato salad [pə tā′tō săl′əd] **80**–19
  sweet potatoes [swĕt′ pə tā′tōz] **69**–18
potty seat [pät′ē sēt′] **37**–12
pouch [powch] **217**–50
Poultry [pōl′trē] **70, 76**
POULTRY [pōl′trē] **70**
pound [pownd] **75**–12
  pound key [pownd′ kē′] **14**–7
pour [pör] **82**–C
powder [pow′dər] **37**–14, **108**–4, **109**–41
power [pow′ər] **218**–2, **218**–5
  power cord [pow′ər körd′] **196**–2
  power outlet [pow′ər owt′lĕt] **159**–42
  power sander [pow′ər săn′dər] **180**–11
pox [pöks] **111**–6
practical [prăk′tə kəl] **120**–11
prairie dog [prĕr′ē dög′] **215**–22
praise [prāz] **36**–J
pregnant [prĕg′nənt] **32**–15
preheat [prē′hēt′] **77**–A
preparation [prĕ′pə rā′shən] **185**–4
PREPARATION [prĕ′pə rā′shən] **76**–77
prepare [prĭ′pĕr′] **174**–A
PREPOSITIONS [prĕp′ə zĭsh′ənz] **25**
PREPOSITIONS OF MOTION
    [prĕp′ə zĭsh′ənz əv mō′shən] **153**
preschool [prē′skōōl′] **188**–1
prescribe medication [prĭ skrĭb′mĕd′ə kā′shən] **112** ✦
prescription [prĭ skrĭp′shən] **112**–2
  pick up a prescription
    [pĭk′ ŭp′ə prĭ skrĭp′shən] **112** ✦
  prescription label [prĭ skrĭp′shən lā′bəl] **112**–4
  prescription medication
    [prĭ skrĭp′shən mĕd′ə kā′shən] **112**–3
  prescription number [prĭ skrĭp′shən nŭm′bər]
    112–5
present [prĕz′ənt] **94** ✦, **240**–3
presentation [prĕ′zən tā′shən] **182**–6
president [prĕz′ə dənt] **138**–8, **199**–5
  first president [fürst′ prĕz′ə dənt] **198**–11
  Presidents′ Day [prĕz′ə dənts dā′] **22**–11
  vice president [vīs′ prĕz′ə dənt] **138**–9
press [prĕs] **78**–11, **140**–4
press [prĕs] **15**–B, **15**–D
presser foot [prĕs′ər fŏŏt′] **98**–19
pressure [prĕsh′ər] **111**–14, **118**–9
pretend [prĭ tĕnd′] **233**–G
Prewriting [prē′rī′tĭng] **191**

Index

price [prīs] **27**–2, **27**–3, **27**–7
  price tag [prīs tăg/] **27**–1
prime minister [prīm/ mĭn/ə stər] **199**–7
principal [prĭn/sə pəl] **5**–4
print [prĭnt] **96**–23
  fingerprint [fĭng/gər prĭnt/] **136**–5
print [prĭnt] **4**–C, **171**–I
printer [prĭn/tər] **169**–50, **196**–17
  inkjet printer [ĭnk/jĕt prĭn/tər] **183**–18
  laser printer [lā/zər prĭn/tər] **183**–19
Priority Mail® [prī ör/ə tē māl/, –är/–] **134**–1
prism [prĭz/əm] **195**–35
prisoner [prĭz/nər] **141**–15
private school [prī/vət skool/] **5** ✦
Problem [präb/ləm] **192**
problems [präb/ləmz] **115**–1, **192**–11
Problems [präb/ləmz] **115**, **119**
PROBLEMS [präb/ləmz] **62**–**63**
Procedures [prə sē/jərz] **117**, **118**
PROCEDURES [prə sē/jərz] **146**–**147**
Process [prä/sĕs] **191**
processor [prä/sĕ sər] **54**–26
Processor [prä/sĕ sər] **92**
produce section [prō/doos sĕk/shən] **72**–2
product [präd/ŭkt] **192**–9
Products [präd/ŭkts] **72**, **73**
program [prō/grăm]
  children's program [chĭl/drənz prō/grăm] **236**–9
  nature program [nā/chər prō/grăm] **236**–7
  news program [nooz/ prō/grăm] **236**–1
  shopping program [shäp/ĭng prō/grăm] **236**–10
  sports program [spörtz/ prō/grăm] **236**–11
program [prō/grăm] **170**–I
Programs [prō/grămz] **236**
projector [prə jĕk/tər] **6**–6, **7**–16, **235**–29
promotion [prə mō/shən] **172**–4
proof of insurance [proof/ əv/ĭn shoor/əns] **136**–8
proofread [proof/rĕd/] **191**–I
prosecuting attorney
  [präs/ĭ kyoo/tĭng ə tür/nē] **141**–10
protect [prə tĕkt/] **143**–D
protector [prə tĕk/tər] **196**–1
proton [prō/tön] **195**–31
proud [prowd] **43**–21
prunes [proonz] **68**–26
pruning shears [proo/nĭng shĭrz/] **176**–11
psychiatrist [sī kī/ə trĭst, sə–] **120**–8
PUBLIC SAFETY [pŭb/lĭk sāf/tē] **143**
public school [pŭb/lĭk skool/] **5** ✦
PUBLIC TRANSPORTATION
  [pŭb/lĭk trăns/pər tā/shən] **152**
pull [pool] **119**–F, **224**–A
puller [pool/ər] **175**–10
pullover sweater [pool/ō/vər swĕt/ər] **88**–3
pulse [pŭls] **122**–A
pumps [pŭmps] **95**–26
Punctuation [pŭngk/choo ā/shən] **190**
puppy [pŭp/ē] **215**–12
purchase [pür/chəs] **94**–A
purifier [pyoo/rə fī/ ər] **113**–13
purple [pür/pəl] **24**–6
purses [pür/səz] **94**–2, **94**–14

push [poosh] **224**–B
pushpin [poosh/pĭn/] **183**–35
put [poot] **9**–X
put away
  [poot/ə wā/] **9**–Z, **60**–G
  put down [poot/ down/] **6**–J
  put in coolant [poot/ ĭn koo/lənt] **157**–I
  put on [poot/ än/, –ön/] **87**–B, **108**–D, **109**–P, **135**–C
  put on hold [poot/ än hōld/, –ön] **171**–N
  put the utilities in your name
    [poot/ dhe yoo tĭl/ə tēz ĭn yər nām/] **49**–O
puzzle [pŭz/əl] **59**–17
pyramid [pĭr/ə mĭd] **193**–39
quad [kwäd] **5**–1
quart [kwört] **75**–4
quarter [kwör/tər] **26**–4
  quarter after one [kwör/tər ăf/tər wŭn/] **18**–9
  1/4 cup [kwör/tər kŭp/] **75**–8
  quarter moon [kwör/tər moon/] **205**–11
  quarter to two [kwör/tər tə too/] **18**–13
  3/4 sleeved [thrē/ kwör/tər slēvd/] **96**–13
question mark [kwĕs/chən märk/] **190**–12
Quick and Easy Cake [kwĭk/ ən ē/zē kāk/] **77**
quiet [kwī/ət] **23**–12
quill [kwĭl] **216**–23
quilt [kwĭlt] **58**–16
  quilt block [kwĭlt/ bläk/] **232**–15
quilt [kwĭlt] **232**–C
quotation [kwō tā/shən] **190**–9
  quotation marks [kwō tā/shən märks/] **190**–15
quotient [kwō /shənt] **192**–10
rabbit [răb/ət] **215**–13
raccoon [ră koon/] **216**–13
race [rās] **230**–S
racing [rā/sĭng] **228**–19
rack [răk] **98**–16
  dish rack [dĭsh/ răk/] **54**–5
  roasting rack [rō/stĭng räk/] **78**–14
  towel rack [tow/əl räk/] **57**–13
racket [răk/ət] **231**–2
racquetball [răk/ət böl/] **228**–12
radiation [rā/dē ā/shən] **218**–15
radiator [rā/dē ā/tər] **158**–19
radio [rā/dē ō] **102**–6, **159**–37, **179**–22
radioactive materials
  [rā/dē ō ăk/tĭv mə tïr/ē əlz] **179**–7
radiologist [rā/dē äl/ə jĭst] **120**–6
radishes [răd/ĭ shəz] **69**–4
radius [rā/dē əs] **193**–35
rafting [răf/tĭng] **226**–2
rags [răgz] **61**–9
rail [rāl] **59**–10
railroad crossing [rāl/rōd krö/sĭng] **154**–14
rain [rān] **218**–13
  rain boots [rān/ boots/] **90**–20
  raincoat [rān/kōt/] **90**–18
  rain forest [rān/ för/əst, fär/–] **204**–1
raining [rā/nĭng] **13**–11
raise [rāz] **6**–A
raisins [rā/zənz] **68**–25
rake [rāk] **176**–8
rake [rāk] **176**–C

ranch [rănch] **52**–10
rancher [răn/chər] **177**–22
Ranch Hand [rănch hănd/] **92**
RANCHING [răn/chĭng] **177**
R&B [är/n bē/] **237**–28
range [rānj] **204**–15
ranger [rān/jər] **220**–2
rash [răsh] **110**–10
raspberries [răz/bĕr/ēz] **68**–15
rats [răts] **63**–27, **215**–17
rattle [răt/l] **37**–26
  rattlesnake [răt/l snāk/] **213**–38
raw [rö] **70**–24
ray [rā] **212**–11
razor [rā/zər] **109**–27
  razorblade [rā/zər blād/] **109**–28
reaction [rē/ăk shən] **116**–E
read [rēd]
  proofread [proof/rĕd/] **191**–I
  read the card [rēd/ dhe kärd/] **135**–G
  read the definition [rēd/ dhe dĕ/fə nĭ/shən] **8**–B
  read the paper [rēd/ dhe pā/pər] **39**–V
  read to [rēd/ too] **36**–N
Reading a Phone Bill [rē/dĭng ə fōn/ bĭl/] **15**
reality show [rē ă lə tē shō/] **236**–6
rearview mirror [rĭr/vyoo/ mĭr/ər] **159**–35
receipt [rĭ sēt/] **27**–6
receive [rĭ sēv/] **135**–F
receiver [rĭ sē/vər] **14**–1
reception area [rĭ sĕp/shən ĕr/ē ə] **182**–15
receptionist [rĭ sĕp/shə nĭst] **118**–2, **164**–5,
  169–51, **182**–14
reclined seat [rĭ klīnd/ sēt/] **161**–27
record [rĭ körd/] **195**–D, **235**–A
records [rĕk/ərdz] **168**–39
RECREATION [rĕk/rē ā/shən] **226**
recreational vehicle (RV)
  [rĕk/rē ā/shən əl vē/ə kəl] / [är/vē/] **156**–10
Recreation Room [rĕk/rē ā/shən room/] **50**
recruiter [rə kroo/tər] **172**–14
rectangle [rĕk/tăng/gəl] **193**–29
recycle [rē sī/kəl] **60**–B, **219**–C
recycling bin [rē sī/klĭng bĭn/] **61**–2
red [rĕd] **24**–1
  red hair [rĕd/ hër/] **33**–15
  redwood [rĕd/wood/] **210**–18
redecorate [rē dĕk/ə rāt/] **48** ✦
reduce [rĭ doos/] **219**–A
referee [rĕf/ə rē/] **229**–6
reference librarian [rĕf/rəns lī brër/ē ən] **133**–9
refrigerator [rĭ frĭj/ə rā/tər] **54**–9
refund [rē/fŭnd] **97** ✦
reggae [rĕ gā/] **237**–31
register [rĕj/ə stər] **73**–15
register [rĕj/ə stər] **140**–D, **157**–F
registered nurse (RN)
  [rĕj/ə stərd nürs/] / [är/ĕn/] **120**–10
registration [rĕj/ə strā/shən]
  registration sticker
    [rĕj/ə strā/shən stĭk/ər] **136**–13
  registration tag [rĕj/ə strā/shən tăg/] **136**–13
regular price [rĕg/yə lər prĭs/] **27**–2

regulations [rĕ gyə lā/shənz] **164**–6
relatives [rĕ lə tĭvz] **44**–6
relax [rĭ lăks/] **39**–U
relieved [rĭ lēvd/] **42**–15
reliever [rĭ lēv/ər] **113**–26
religious holiday [rĭ lĭj/əs häl/ə dā/] **22**–7
remain [rē/mān] **147**–E
remarried [rē mǎr/ēd] **35**–24
remote [rĭ mōt/] **234**–9
remove [rĭ mōōv/] **109**–Q, **132**–G
remover [rĭ mōō/vər] **109**–42
renew a license [rĭ nōō/ ə lī/səns, –nyōō/–] **136** ✦
rental agreement [rĕn/təl ə grē/mənt] **51**–28
Rental Office [rĕn/təl ö/fəs] **51**
Renting an Apartment [rĕn/tĭng ən ə pärt/mənt] **48**
repair [rĭ për/] **166**–4, **167**–24
    repair person [rĭ për/ pür/sən] **62**–10
repair [rĭ për/] **170**–J
REPAIRS [rĭ përz/] **62**–63
repellent [rĭ pĕl/ənt] **226**–23
replace [rĭ plās/] **157**–K
report [rĭ pört/] **143**–J, **143**–K
reporter [rĭ pör/tər] **169**–52
representative [rĕ/prĭ zĕn/tə tĭv] **138**–3, **167**–20
Reptiles [rĕp/tĭlz] **213**
REPTILES [rĕp/tĭlz] **212**–213
request [rĭ kwĕst/] **12** ✦
Requirements [rĭ kwīr/mənts] **140**
rescue [rĕs/kyōō] **145**–20
    rescue breathing [rĕs/kyōō brē/dhĭng] **117**–16
Resident Alien card [rĕz/ə dənt ā/lē ən kärd/] **40**–2
resource center [rē/sörs sĕn/tər] **172**–9
Resources [rē/sörs/səz, rĭ sör/səz] **219**
respirator [rĕs/pə rā/tər] **179**–13
Responding [rĭ spän/dĭng] **191**
Responsibilities [rĭ spän/sə bĭl/ə tēz] **140**
RESPONSIBILITIES [rĭ spän/sə bĭl/ə tēz] **140**
restaurant [rĕs/tə rənt, –ränt/] **125**–14, **128**–10
RESTAURANT [rĕs/tə rənt, –ränt/] **79, 82**–83
Restaurant Dining [rĕs/tə rənt dī/nĭng, –ränt/] **185**
Restaurant Kitchen [rĕs/tə rənt kĭ/chən, –ränt/] **185**
restrooms [rĕst/ rōōmz/] **5**–10
results [rĭ zŭltz/] **139**–31
resuscitation [rĭ sə sə tā/shən] **117**–17
retail clerk [rē/tāl/ klürk/] **169**–53
retire [rĭ tīr/] **41**–O
return [rĭtürn/] **73**–16
    return address [rĭ türn/ ə drĕs/, –ă/drĕs] **134**–21
return [rĭ türn/] **27**–H, **133**–D
REUNION [rē yōōn/yən] **44**–45
reuse [rē yōōz/] **219**–B
revise [rĭ vīz/] **191**–J
Revising [rĭ vī/zĭng] **191**
Revolutionary War [rĕ/və lōō/shə nër ē wör/] **198**–8
revolving [rĭ väl/vĭng]
    revolving door [rĭ väl/vĭng dör/] **184**–2
    revolving nosepiece [rĭ väl/vĭng nōz/pēs/] **194**–17
rewind [rē wīnd/] **235**–C
rewrite [rē rīt/] **191**–J
rhinoceros [rī näs/ər əs] **217**–28
ribbon [rĭ/bən] **99**–30

ribs [rĭbz] **70**–5, **76**–2
    rib cage [rĭb/ kāj/] **107**–48
rice [rīs] **67**–10, **81**–30, **177**–1
ride [rīd] **129**–D
rider [rī/dər] **152**–3
riding [rī/dĭng] **226**–9
right [rīt] **25**–3, **155**–B, **198**–10
    right angle [rīt/ ăng/gəl] **193**–26
    right turn only [rīt/ türn/ ōn/lē] **154**–7
Rights [rīts] **140**
RIGHTS AND RESPONSIBILITIES
    [rīts/ ən rĭ spän/sə bĭl/ə tēz] **140**
ring [rĭng] **37**–25, **79**–4, **95**–40
    clip-on earrings [klĭp/än ïr/ĭngz, –ön–] **95**–37
    pierced earrings [pïrst/ ïr/ĭngz] **95**–36
rinse [rĭns] **108**–F
ripe [rīp] **68**–30
ripped [rĭpt] **97**–41
ripper [rĭ/pər] **100**–18
rise [rīz] **127**–13
    sunrise [sŭn/rīz/] **18**–14
river [rĭv/ər] **155**–10, **204**–3
RN (registered nurse) [är/ĕn/] / [rĕj/ə stərd nürs/]
    120–10
road work [rōd/ würk/] **154**–16
Road Worker [rōd/ wür/kər] **92**
roast [rōst] **70**–1
    roast beef [rōst bēf/] **71**–21
    roast chicken [rōst chĭk/ən] **81**–22
    roasted turkey [rō/stəd tür/kē] **76**–4
    roasting pan [rō/stĭng păn/] **78**–13
    roasting rack [rō/stĭng răk/] **78**–14
robe [rōb] **91**–29
robin [räb/ən] **214**–16
rock [räk] **36**–D
rock concert [räk/ kän/sərt] **222**–5
rocking chair [räk/ĭng chër/] **37**–21
rocks [räks] **208**–6, **237**–23
Rodents [rōd/nts] **215**
RODENTS [rōd/nts] **215**
rollers [rō/lərz] **33**–19, **181**–23
rolling pin [rō/lĭng pĭn/] **78**–30
rolls [rōlz] **74**–11, **74**–23, **80**–17
romance [rō mǎns/, rō/mǎns] **237**–16
Roman Numerals [rō/mən nōō/mər əlz] **16**
roof [rōōf] **46**–1
roof garden [rōōf/ gär/dn] **50**–4
roofer [rōō/fər] **62**–8
room [rōōm]
    baby's room [bā/bēz rōōm/] **47**–10
    ballroom [böl/ rōōm/] **184**–26
    banquet room [băn/kwət rōōm/] **185**–14
    bathroom [băth/rōōm/] **46**–4
    bedroom [bĕd/rōōm/] **46**–2
    conference room [kän/frəns rōōm/] **182**–4
    dining room [dī/nĭng rōōm/] **82**–1
    dining room chair [dī/nĭng rōōm/ chër/] **55**–8
    dining room table [dī/nĭng rōōm/ tā/bəl] **55**–9
    dish room [dĭsh/ rōōm/] **83**–13
    guest room [gĕst/ rōōm/] **184**–13
    kids' bedroom [kĭdz/ bĕd/rōōm/] **47**–9

living room [lĭv/ĭng rōōm/] **47**–12
meeting room [mē/tĭng rōōm/] **184**–25
roommates [rōōm/māts/] **64**–1
room service [rōōm/ sür/vəs] **184**–17
storeroom [stör/rōōm/] **185**–5
Room [rōōm] **50, 118, 121**
ROOM [rōōm] **56**
rooster [rōō/stər] **215**–7
roots [rōōts] **210**–5, **211**–3
rope [rōp] **224**–4, **226**–19
rose [rōz] **211**–15
rotary [rō/tə rē]
    rotary card file [rō/tə rē kärd/ fīl/] **183**–44
    rotary cutter [rō/tə rē kŭt/ər] **232**–16
rotten [rät/n] **68**–32
round trip [rownd/ trĭp/] **152**–17
route [rōōt] / [rowt]
    bus route [bŭs/ rōōt, –rowt] **152**–1
    escape route [ĕs/kāp rōōt, –rowt] **146**–3
    evacuation route
        [ĭ văk/yōō/ā shən rōōt, –rowt] **146**–5
    U.S. route [yōō/ĕs/ rōōt, –rowt] **154**–17
router [row/tər] **180**–12
ROUTINES [rōō tēnz/] **38**–39
rubber [rŭb/ər]
    rubber band [rŭb/ər bănd/] **183**–34
    rubber gloves [rŭb/ər glŭvz/] **61**–4
    rubber mat [rŭb/ər măt/] **57**–3
ruffle [rŭ/fəl] **58**–17
rug [rŭg] **58**–22
ruler [rōō/lər] **17**–13
rules [rōōlz] **64**–8
Rules [rōōlz] **190**
run [rŭn] **11**–D
    run across [rŭn/ə krös/] **153**–G
    run around [rŭn/ə rownd/] **153**–H
    run for office [rŭn/ fər ö/fəs] **139**–A
    run out [rŭn/owt/] **162**–E
runner [rŭ/nər] **185**–15
rural area [rŏŏr/əl ër/ē ə] **52**–4
RV (recreational vehicle)
    [är/vē/] / [rĕk/rē ā/shən əl vē/ə kəl] **156**–10
rye bread [rī/ brĕd/] **71**–20
sad [săd] **43**–19
safety [sāf/tē] **37**–19, **92**–4, **159**–53
    safety boots [sāf/tē bōōts/] **179**–20
    safety deposit box [sāf/tē dĭ päz/ət bäks/] **132**–7
    safety glasses [sāf/tē glăs/əz] **92**–10, **179**–10
    safety goggles [sāf/tē găg/əlz] **179**–11
    safety pin [sāf/tē pĭn/] **37**–9, **100**–14
    safety rail [sāf/tē rāl/] **59**–10
    safety regulations [sāf/tē rĕ/gyə lā/shənz] **164**–6
    safety visor [sāf/tē vī/zər] **179**–12
Safety [sāf/tē] **76**
SAFETY [sāf/tē] **76**–77, **143, 179**
Safety Equipment [sāf/tē ĭ kwĭp/mənt] **179**
Safety Hazards and Hazardous Materials
    [sāf/tē hăz/ərdz ən hăz/ər dəs-mə tïr/ē əlz] **179**
sailboat [sāl/bōt/] **225**–3
sailing [sā/lĭng] **227**–8

271

Index

salad [săl/əd]

   chef's salad [shĕfs/ săl/əd] **80**–14

   dinner salad [dĭn/ər săl/əd] **80**–15

   fruit salad [frōōt/ săl/əd] **80**–21

   pasta salad [päs/tə săl/əd] **80**–20

   potato salad [pə tā/tō săl/əd] **80**–19

   salad bar [săl/əd bär/] **79**–24

   salad fork [săl/əd förk/] **83**–27

   salad plate [săl/əd plāt/] **83**–20

   spinach salad [spĭ/nĭch săl/əd] **80**–13

Salad Dressings [săl/əd drĕ/sĭngz] **80**

Salads [săl/ədz] **80**

salamander [săl/ə măn/dər] **212**–27

salami [sə lä/mē] **71**–24

SALE [sāl] **102**–**103**

sales [sālz]

   sale price [sāl/ prīs/] **27**–3

   salesclerk [sālz/klürk/] **94**–3

   sales tax [sālz/ tăks/] **27**–8

Salesperson [sālz/pür/sən] **92**

salmon [săm/ən] **71**–3

   salmon steak [săm/ən stāk/] **71**–4

salon [sə lön/] **130**–3, **131**–18

salt and pepper shakers

   [sölt/ n pĕp/ər shā/kərz] **55**–13

same [sām] **23**–15

SAME AND DIFFERENT

   [sām/ ən dĭ/frənt, –dĭ fə rənt] **28**–**29**

samples [săm/pəlz] **84**–5

sand [sănd] **225**–23

   sandbox [sănd/bäks/] **224**–15

   sand castle [sănd kăs/əl] **225**–12

   sand dune [sănd dōōn/] **204**–5

   sandpaper [sănd/pā/pər] **181**–56

sandals [săn/dlz] **88**–9

sander [săn/dər] **180**–11

sandwich [săn/wĭch, –sănd/–] **79**–5, **80**–10, **80**–12

sanitation worker [săn/ə tā/shən wür/kər] **169**–54

satellite [săt/əl īt/] **205**–20

   satellite dish [săt/əl līt/ dĭsh/] **53**–6

satisfied [săt/ĭs fīd/] **42**–6

Saturday [săt/ər dā/, –dē] **20**–14

Saturn [săt/ərn] **205**–6

saucepan [sös/păn/] **78**–25

saucer [sö/sər] **83**–25

sausage [sö/sĭj] **70**–12, **80**–2

sauté [sö tā/, sō –] **77**–E

save [sāv] **219**–E

saving [sā/vĭng] **19**–25, **225**–20

savings account number

   [sā/vĭngz ə kownt/ nŭm/bər] **132**–11

saw [sö] **180**–9

   hacksaw [hăk/sö/] **180**–5

   jigsaw [jĭg/sö/] **180**–10

saxophone [săk/sə fōn/] **238**–5

say [sā] **2**–A, **3**–L, **4**–A

scaffolding [skăf/əl dĭng] **178**–4

scales [skālz] **57**–27, **72**–3, **135**–8, **155**–7, **195**–41, **212**–3

   postal scale [pō/stəl skāl/] **183**–27

scallions [skăl/yənz] **69**–20

scallops [skăl/əps, skäl/–] **71**–12, **212**–19

scan [skăn] **171**–H

scanner [skăn/ər] **183**–20

scared [skĕrd] **43**–23

scarf / scarves [skärf/ / skärvz] **95**–12

   winter scarf [wĭn/tər skärf/] **90**–5

scenery [sē/ nə rē] / [sēn/rē] **162**–3

schedule [skĕj/ōōl, –ōō əl] **152**–4

schedule [skĕj/ōōl, –ōō əl] **171**–J

school [skōōl] **126**–9

   adult school [[ə dŭlt/–, ăd/ŭlt skōōl/] **188**–8

   elementary school [ĕl/ə mĕn/trē skōōl/] **188**–2

   high school [hī/ skōōl/] **188**–4

   junior high school [jōōn/yər hī/ skōōl/] **188**–3

   middle school [mĭd/l skōōl/] **188**–3

   nursery school [nür/sə rē skōōl/] **188**–1

   parochial school [pə rō/kē əl skōōl/] **5** ✦

   preschool [prē/skōōl] **188**–1

   private school [prī/vət skōōl/] **5** ✦

   public school [pŭb/lĭk skōōl/] **5** ✦

   school bus [skōōl/ bŭs/] **156**–21

   school crossing [skōōl/ krö/sĭng] **154**–15

   technical school [tĕk/nĭ kəl skōōl/] **188**–5

   vocational school [vō kā/shə nəl skōōl/] **188**–5

SCHOOL [skōōl] **5, 10, 11**

School Registration Form

   [skōōl/ rĕj/ə strā/shən förm/] **4**

SCHOOLS AND SUBJECTS

   [sklōōz ən sŭb/jĭkts] **188**–**189**

science [sī/əns] **189**–11

SCIENCE [sī/əns] **194**–**195**

Science Lab [sī/əns lăb/] **195**

scissors [sĭz/ərz] **33**–20, **100**–16

scoop neck [skōōp/ nĕk/] **96**–10

score [skör] **10**–3, **229**–1

scorpion [skör/pē ən] **214**–30

scrambled eggs [skrăm/bəld ĕgz/] **76**–7

scraper [skrā/pər] **181**–52

screen [skrēn] **6**–2, **196**–11, **235**–30

   big-screen TV [bĭg/skrēn/ tē/ vē/] **50**–15

   fire screen [fīr/ skrēn/] **56**–12

   flat screen TV [flăt/ skrēn/ tē/vē/] **234**–7

   screen door [skrēn/ dör/] **53**–15

   sunscreen [sŭn/skrēn/] **108**–7, **225**–10

screener [skrēn/ər] **160**–5

screening area [skrē/nĭng ĕr/ē ə] **160**–4

screw [skrōō] **180**–32, **180**–33

   Phillips screwdriver [fĭl/ĭps skrōō/drī/vər] **180**–31

   screwdriver [skrōō/drī/vər] **180**–30

scroll bar [skröl/bär/] **197**–15

scrub [skrŭb] **60**–K

scrubs [skrŭbz] **93**–31

   scrub brush [skrŭb/ brŭsh/] **61**–20

   surgical scrub cap [sür/jĭ kəl skrŭb/ kăp/] **93**–35

   surgical scrubs [sür/jĭ kəl skrŭbz/] **93**–38

scuba [skōō/bə]

   scuba diving [skōō/bə dī/vĭng] **227**–12

   scuba tank [skōō/bə tăngk/] **225**–5

sea [sē]

   sea anemone [sē/ ə nĕm/ə nē] **212**–24

   seahorse [sē/ hörs/] **212**–13

   sea lion [sē/ lī/ən] **213**–33

   sea otter [sē/ ät/ər] **213**–35

seashell [sē/shĕl/] **225**–24

sea urchin [sē/ ür/chən] **212**–21

seaweed [sē/ wēd/] **225** ✦

Sea Animals [sē/ ăn/ə məlz] **212**

SEAFOOD AND DELI [sē/fōōd/ ən dĕ/lī] **71**

seal [sēl] **213**–34

Sea Mammals [sē/ măm/əlz] **213**

seam ripper [sēm/ rĭp/ər] **100**–18

search [sürch]

   search and rescue team

     [sürch/ ən rĕs/kyōō tēm/] **145**–20

   search box [sürch/ bäks/] **197**–5

   search engine [sürch/ ĕn/jən] **197**–6

SEARCH [sürch] **173**

SEASONAL CLOTHING [sē/zə nəl klö/dhĭng] **90**

Seasons [sē/zənz] **21**

seat [sēt]

   backseat [băk/ sēt/] **159**–54

   car safety seat [kär/ sāf/tē sēt/] **37**–19

   child safety seat [chīld/ sāf/tē sēt/] **159**–53

   front seat [frŭnt/ sēt/] **159**–51

   love seat [lŭv/ sēt/] **56**–1

   potty seat [pät/ē sēt/] **37**–12

   reclined seat [rĭ klīnd/ sēt/] **161**–27

   seat belt [sēt/ bĕlt/] **159**–52

   upright seat [ŭp/rīt/ sēt/] **161**–28

seat [sēt] **82**–B

second [sĕk/ənd] **16**

Second Floor [sĕk/ənd flör/] **50**

seconds [sĕk/əndz] **18**–3

section [sĕk/shən] **72**–2

security [sĭ kyŏŏr/ə tē]

   security camera [sĭ kyŏŏr/ə tē kăm/rə] **50**–19

   security gate [sĭ kyŏŏr/ə tē gāt/] **50**–16

   security guard [sĭ kyŏŏr/ə tē gärd/] **132**–5, **169**–55

   security pants [sĭ kyŏŏr/ə tē pănts/] **93**–22

   security screener [sĭ kyŏŏr/ə tē skrē/nər] **160**–5

   security shirt [sĭ kyŏŏr/ə tē shürt/] **93**–20

Security Checkpoint [sĭ kyŏŏr/ə tē chĕk/poynt/] **160**

Security Guard [sĭ kyŏŏr/ə tē gärd/] **93**

sedan [sə dăn/] **156**–1

see [sē] **106**–A

seed [sēd] **211**–1

   seedling [sēd/lĭng] **211**–4

seek [sēk] **114**–A, **147**–H

seesaw [sē/sö/] **224**–16

select [sə lĕkt/] **196**–B

self-checkout [sĕlf/ chĕk/owt/] **73**–10, **133**–10

sell [sĕl] **170**–K

semi [sĕm/ī] **156**–15

semicolon [sĕm/ē kō/lən] **190**–18

Senate [sĕn/ət] **138**–5

senator [sĕn/ə tər] **138**–6

   state senator [stāt/ sĕn/ə tər] **139**–25

send [sĕnd] **197**–I

   send in [sĕnd/ ĭn] **173**–H

Sending a Card [sĕn/dĭng ə kärd/] **135**

Sending Email [sĕn/dĭng ē/māl/] **197**

senior [sēn/yər]

   senior citizen [sēn/yər sĭt/ə zən] **30**–5

   senior housing [sēn/yər howz/ĭng] **52**–11

Senses [sĕn/səz] **106**

sentence [sĕn/tns] **190**–2
sentence [sĕn/tns] **141**–E
separate [sĕ/pə rāt/] **76**–B
September [sĕp tĕm/bər] **21**–33
sequins [sē/kwĭnz] **99**–33
Serious Medical Conditions
[sïr/ē əs mĕd/ĭ kəl kən dĭsh/ənz] **111**
serious photo [sïr/ē əs fō/tō] **206**–3
serve [sürv] **139**–D, **230**–P
serve on a jury [sürv/ ăn ə jŏŏr/ē, –ōn–] **140**–E
serve the meal [sürv/ dhə mēl/] **82**–F
Serve [sürv] **76**
server [sür/vər] **82**–8, **83**–9, **169**–56, **185**–8
service [sür/vəs]
customer service [kŭs/tə mər sür/vəs] **97** ✦
customer service representative
[kŭs/tə mər-sür/vəs rĕ/prə zĕn/tə tĭv] **167**–20
guest services [gĕst/ sür/vəs əz] **130**–12
pool service [pōōl/ sür/vəs] **184**–21
room service [rōōm/ sür/vəs] **184**–17
SERVICE [sür/vəs] **138**–**139**, **185**
serving bowl [sür/vĭng bōl/] **55**–21
set [sĕt] **10**–A, **33**–C, **82**–A
set up [sĕt/ ŭp/] **173**–I
sunset [sŭn/sĕt/] **18**–18
setting [sĕ/tĭng] **83**–17
seven [sĕv/ən] **16**
seventeen [sĕv/ən tēn/] **16**
seventeenth [sĕv/ən tēnth/] **16**
seventh [sĕv/ənth] **16**
seventieth [sĕv/ən tē əth] **16**
seventy [sĕv/ən tē] **16**
75 percent [sĕv/ən tē fīv/ pər sĕnt/] **17**–9
sew [sō] **98**–A, **98**–B, **170**–L
sewing [sō/ĭng]
sewing machine [sō/ĭng mə shēn/] **98**–13
sewing machine operator
[sō/ĭng mə shēn/ äp/ə rā/ tər] **98**–14
Sewing Machine [sō/ĭng mə shēn/] **98**
Sewing Supplies [sō/ĭng sə plīz/] **100**
sex [sĕks] **4**–16
shade [shād] **225**–13
lampshade [lămp/shād/] **56** ✦, **58**–26
shadow [shă/dō/] **109**–35
shake [shāk]
milkshake [mĭlk/shāk/] **79**–14
shake [shāk] **3**–J, **174**–I
shakers [shā/kərz] **55**–13
shampoo [shăm pōō/] **108**–10
shanks [shănks] **70**–13
shaper [shā/pər] **91**–15
Shapes [shāps] **193**
share [shĕr] **8**–M
Sharing and Responding
[shĕr/ĭng ən rĭ spän/dĭng] **191**
shark [shärk] **212**–4
sharpener [shär/pən ər] **183**–26
shave [shāv]
aftershave [ăf/tər shāv/] **109**–30
shave [shāv] **109**–M
shaver [shā/vər] **109**–26
shaving cream [shā/vĭng krēm/] **109**–29

shears [shïrz] **176**–9
sheep [shēp] **215**–6
sheet [shēt]
cookie sheet [kŏŏk/ē shēt/] **78**–27
dryer sheets [drī/ər shēts/] **101**–5
fitted sheet [fĭt/əd shēt/] **58**–12
flat sheet [flăt/ shēt/] **58**–13
shelf [shĕlf] **54**–2
shell [shĕl]
seashell [sē/shĕl/] **225**–24
Shellfish [shĕl/fĭsh/] **71**
shelter [shĕl/tər] **52**–13
shield [shēld]
windshield [wĭnd/shēld/] **158**–1
windshield wipers [wĭnd/shēld wī/pərz] **158**–2
shift [shĭft] **159**–49, **159**–50
shin [shĭn] **106**–21
shin guards [shĭn/ gärdz/] **231**–13
shingles [shĭng/gəlz] **178**–20
ship [shĭp] **175**–D
shipping clerk [shĭp/ĭng klürk/] **175**–14
shirt [shürt] **86**–1
nightshirt [nīt/shürt/] **91**–28
polo shirt [pō/lō shürt/] **92**–14
security shirt [sĭ kyŏŏr/ə tē shürt/] **93**–20
sports shirt [spörts/ shürt/] **88**–4
T-shirt [tē/shürt/] **86**–4
work shirt [würk/ shürt/] **92**–2
shock [shäk] **116**–B, **116**–F
shoes [shōōz] **86**–7, **87**–13, **95**–32
shoe department [shōō/ dĭ pärt/mənt] **95**–7
shoelaces [shōō/lās əz] **94**–24
shoe store [shōō/ stör/] **130**–10
SHOES AND ACCESSORIES
[shōōz/ ən ĭk sĕs/ə rēz] **94**–**95**
shoot [shōōt] **211**–5
shoot [shōōt] **230**–H
shop [shäp]
barbershop [bär/bər shäp/] **129**–19
beauty shop [byōō/tē shäp/] **130** ✦
coffee shop [kö/fē shäp/] **126**–11
donut shop [dō/nŭt shäp/] **129**–17
gift shop [gĭft/ shäp/] **130** ✦, **184**–5
ice cream shop [īs/ krēm shäp] **131**–16
shop [shäp] **28**–A, **143**–H
Shop [shäp] **100**
SHOP [shäp] **80**–**81**
shoplifting [shäp/lĭf/tĭng] **142**–8
shopping [shäp/ĭng]
shopping basket [shäp/ĭng băs/kət] **73**–9
shopping list [shäp/ĭng lĭst/] **67**–14
shopping mall [shäp/ĭng mäl/] **126**–7
shopping program [shäp/ĭng mäl/] **236**–10
SHOPPING [shäp/ĭng] **27**
shore [shör] **204**–12
short [shört] **32**–6, **96**–16
short hair [shört/ hër/] **33**–1
short-order cook [shört/ör/dər kŏŏk/] **185**–1
short-sleeved [shört/slēvd/] **96**–12
shorten [shört/ən] **100**–B
shorts [shörts] **89**–25, **91**–4

shoulder [shōl/dər] **105**–13
shoulder bag [shōl/dər băg/] **94**–17
shoulder blade [shōl/dər blād/] **107**–28
shoulder-length hair [shōl/dər lĕngkth/ hër/] **33**–2
shoulder pads [shōl/dər pădz/] **231**–20
shovel [shŭv/əl] **176**–7, **178**–22
show [shō] **236**–4, **236**–6, **236**–8
show [shō] **137**–C, **160**–C
shower [show/ər]
shower cap [show/ər kăp/] **108**–1
shower curtain [show/ər kür/tn] **57**–12
shower gel [show/ər jĕl/] **108**–2
showerhead [show/ər hĕd/] **57**–11
stall shower [stöl/ show/ər/] **57** ✦
shredder [shrĕ/dər] **183**–24
shrimp [shrĭmp] **71**–11, **212**–18
shut [shŭt] **146**–4
shuttle [shŭt/l] **152**–19, **205**–19
sick [sĭk] **42**–12
homesick [hōm/sĭk/] **43**–20
side [sīd] **76**–10
sideburns [sīd/bürnz/] **33**–7
sideview mirror [sīd/vyōō/ mïr/ər] **158**–3
Side Salads [sīd/ săl/ədz] **80**
sidewalk [sīd/wök/] **129**–24
sight impaired [sīt/ ĭm përd/] **32**–11
sign [sīn] **4**–D
street sign [strēt/ sīn/] **129**–26
vacancy sign [vā/kən sē sīn/] **50**–7
vital signs monitor [vīt/l sīnz/ män/ə tər] **121**–26
sign [sīn] **48**–D
signal [sĭg/nəl]
strong signal [ströng/ sĭg/nəl] **14**–11
turn signal [türn/ sĭg/nəl] **158**–6, **159**–34
weak signal [wēk/ sĭg/nəl] **14**–12
signature [sĭg/nə chər] **4**–19
SIGNS [sīnz] **154**
silk [sĭlk] **98**–5
simmer [sĭm/ər] **77**–P
sing [sĭng] **36**–O, **238**–B
single [sĭng/gəl]
single father [sĭng/gəl fä/dhər] **35**–23
single mother [sĭng/gəl mŭdh/ər] **35**–22
sink [sĭnk] **54**–4, **57**–23
Sirius [sïr/ē əs] **205** ✦
sister [sĭs/tər] **34**–5, **35**–27
sister-in-law [sĭs/tər ĭn lö/] **34**–16
stepsister [stĕp/sĭs/tər] **35**–29
sitcom (situation comedy)
[sĭt/käm/] / [sĭch/ōō ā/shən käm/ə dē] **236**–2
sit down [sĭt/ down/] **6**–F
site [sīt] **126**–2
sitter [sĭt/ər] **166**–9
situation comedy (sitcom)
[sĭch/ōō ā/shən-käm/ə dē] / [sĭt/käm/] **236**–2
six [sĭks] **16**
six-pack [sĭks/păk/] **74**–9, **74**–21
6-year-old boy [sĭks/yïr öld/boy/] **31**–9
sixteen [sĭks/tēn/] **16**
sixteenth [sĭks/tēnth/] **16**
sixth [sĭksth] **16**
sixtieth [sĭks/tē əth] **16**

Index

sixty [sĭks/tē] **16**
Sizes [sī/zəz] **96**
skate [skāt] **230**–U
skates [skāts] **231**–9, **231**–10
    skateboard [skāt/bördʹ] **224**–7
    skateboarding [skāt/bör/dĭng] **228**–13
skating [skā/tĭng] **227**–4, **227**–5, **227** ✦, **228**–10
ski [skē] **230**–V
skiing [skē/ĭng] **227**–1, **227**–3
    waterskiing [wö/tər skē/ĭng] **227**–7
skill inventory [skĭl/ ĭn/vən tör/ē] **172**–12
Skills [skĭlz] **171**
SKILLS [skĭlz] **170, 171, 174**
skin [skĭn] **107**–31
    skinless [skĭn/ləs] **70** ✦
skirt [skürt] **87**–10
skis [skēz] **231**–24
    ski boots [skē/ bööts] **231**–26
    ski hat [skē/ hăt/] **90**–11
    ski mask [skē/ măsk/] **90**–15
    ski poles [skē/ pōlz/] **231**–25
skull [skŭl] **107**–47
skunk [skŭngk] **216**–12
SKU number [ĕs/kā/yoo/ nŭm/bər, skyoo/] **27**–5
sky [skī] **209**–9
    skycap [skē/kăp/] **160**–1
    skyscraper [skī/skrā/pər] **127**–13
slacks [slăks] **87**–12
slaves [slāvz] **198**–4
sledding [slĕd/ĭng] **227**–6
sledgehammer [slĕj/hăm/ər] **178**–23
sleeper [slē/pər] **91**–27
sleeping bag [slē/pĭng băg/] **226**–12
Sleepwear [slēp/wër] **91**
SLEEPWEAR [slēp/wër] **91**
sleepy [slē/pē] **42**–3
sleeve [slēv] **100**–6
    long-sleeved [löng/slēvd/] **96**–14
    short-sleeved [shört/slēvd/] **96**–12
    sleeveless [slēv/ləs] **96**–11
    3/4 sleeved [thrē/kwör/tər slēvd/] **96**–13
slender [slĕn/dər] **32**–9
slice [slīs] **77**–C
slide [slīd] **194**–3, **224**–13
    mudslide [mŭd/slīd/] **144**–6
sliding glass door [slī/dĭng glăs/ dör/] **53**–18
sling [slĭng] **113**–19
slip [slĭp] **91**–22, **91**–23, **132**–4
slippers [slĭp/ərz] **91**–26
slippery floor [slĭ/pər ē flör/] **179**–6
slow [slō] **23**–4
small [smöl] **96**–1, **96**–2, **97**–37
    small town [smöl/ town/] **52**–3
smart phone [smärt/ fōn/] **15**–27
smell [smĕl] **106**–C
smile [smīl] **2**–D
smock [smök] **93**–26
smog [smäg, smög] **218**–11
smoggy [smä/gē, smö/–] **13**–14
smoke [smōk] **114**–G
smoke detector [smōk/ dĭ tĕk/tər] **51**–29
smoked turkey [smōkt/ tür/kē] **71**–25

Snack Foods [snăk/ foodz/] **73**
snail [snāl] **212**–22
snake [snāk] **213**–39
    rattlesnake [ră/təl snāk] **213**–38
snap [snăp] **99**–26
sneeze [snēz] **110**–B
snorkeling [snör/kə lĭng] **227**–11
snow [snō]
    snowboard [snō/börd/] **231**–23
    snowboarding [snō/bör/dĭng] **227**–2
    snowstorm [snō/störm/] **13**–23
snowing [snō/ĭng] **13**–12
soap [sōp] **57**–24, **61**–5, **108**–3
    soap dish [sōp/ dĭsh/] **57**–25
    soap opera [sōp/ äp/rə] **236**–5
sober [sō/ bər] **143** ✦
soccer [säk/ər] **229**–12
    soccer ball [säk/ər böl/] **231**–12
social [sō/shəl]
    Social Security card
      [sō/shəl sĭ kyoor/ə tē kärd/] **40**–5
    Social Security number
      [sō/shəl sĭ kyoor/ə tē nŭm/bər] **4**–15
    social worker [sō/shəl wür/kər] **169**–57
socks [säks] **86**–6
    ankle socks [ang/kəl säks/] **91**–7
    crew socks [kroo/ säks/] **91**–8
    dress socks [drĕs/ säks/] **91**–9
    low-cut socks [lō/kŭt säks/] **91**–10
Socks [säks] **91**
soda [sō/də] **73**–34, **79**–11
sofa [sō/fə] **56**–18
    sofa cushions [sō/fə koo/shənz] **56** ✦
soft [söft] **23**–6
    softball [söft/böl/] **229**–10
softener [sö/fən ər] **101**–6
software [söft/wër/] **167**–18, **196**–10
soil [soyl] **208**–2
solar [sō/lər]
    solar eclipse [sō/lər ĭ klĭps/] **205**–16, **205** ✦
    solar energy [sō/lər ĕn/ər jē] **218**–1
Solar System and the Planets
    [sō/lər sĭs/təm ən dhə plăn/əts] **205**
soldier [sōl/jər] **169**–58
sole [sōl] **94**–21
solid [säl/əd] **96**–19
Solids [säl/ədz] **193**
solution [sə loo/ shən] **192**–14
solve [sölv] **170**–M
son [sŭn] **34**–15
    grandson [grăn/sŭn/, gränd/–] **34** ✦
    son-in-law [sŭn/ĭn lö/] **34** ✦
sore throat [sör/ thrōt/] **110**–6
sort [sört] **101**–A
soul [sōl] **237**–28
soup [soop] **72**–18, **80**–16
    soup bowl [soop/ böl/] **83**–21
    soupspoon [soop/spoon/] **83**–32
Soup [soop] **77**
sour [sow/ər] **84**–4
    sour cream [sow/ər krēm/] **72**–21
Sources [sör/səz] **218**

sous chef [soo/ shĕf/] **185**–6
south [sowth] **155**–3
soybeans [soy/bēnz/] **177**–3
space [spās] **50**–18, **128**–5
    space shuttle [spās/ shŭt/əl] **205**–19
    space station [spās/ stā/shən] **205**–18
Space [spās] **205**
Space Exploration [spās/ ĕk/splə rā/shən] **205**
spades [spādz] **233**–30
spaghetti [spə gĕt/ē] **81**–26
spare tire [spër/ tīr/] **158**–23
sparrow [spăr/ō] **214**–7
spatula [spăch/ə lə] **78**–19
speak [spēk] **170**–N
speakers [spē/kərz] **50**–5, **206**–4, **234**–14
Special [spĕ/shəl] **80**
Specialists [spĕsh/ə lĭsts/] **120**
speech [spēch] **140**–2
speed limit [spēd/ lĭm/ət] **154**–4
speedometer [spī däm/ə tər] **159**–27
speed skating [spēd/skā/tĭng] **227** ✦
spell [spĕl] **4**–B
sphere [sfĭr] **193**–42
spider [spī/dər] **214**–29
spill [spĭl] **218**–17
spinach [spĭn/ĭch] **69**–11
    spinach salad [spĭn/ĭch săl/əd] **80**–13
spinal column [spī/nəl käl/əm] **107**–49
spiral notebook [spi/rəl nōt/book/] **7**–29
splint [splĭnt] **117**–14
sponge [spŭnj] **61**–19
    sponge mop [spŭnj/ mäp/] **61**–6
spoon [spoon] **55**–5, **78**–9
    soupspoon [soop/spoon/] **83**–32
    tablespoon [tā/bəl spoon/] **75**–7
    teaspoon [tē/spoon/] **75**–6, **83**–31
spoon [spoon] **77**–F
sports [spörts]
    sports car [spörts/ kär/] **156**–4
    sports coat [spörts/ kōt/] **89**–14
    sports jacket [spörts/ jăk/ət] **89**–14
    sports program [spörts/ prō/grăm] **236**–11
    sports shirt [spörts/ shürt/] **88**–4
    sport-utility vehicle (SUV) [spört/
      yoo tĭl/ə tē vē/ĭ kəl] / [ĕs/yoo/vē/] **156**–7
SPORTS [spörts] **228, 229, 230, 231**
SPORTS EQUIPMENT [spörts/ ĭ kwĭp/mənt] **231**
SPORTS VERBS [spörts/ vürbz/] **230**
sprained ankle [sprānd/ ăng/kəl] **110**–18
spray [sprā] **108**–12, **113**–32
    spray gun [sprā/ gŭn/] **181**–21
    spray starch [sprā/ stärch/] **101**–12
spread [sprĕd]
    bedspread [bĕd/sprĕd] **59**–11
spring [sprĭng] **21**–37, **58**–19
sprinkler [sprĭng/klər] **53**–22
square [skwër] **193**–30
squash [skwäsh, skwösh] **69**–24
squeegee [skwē/jē] **61**–15
squid [skwĭd] **212**–7
squirrel [skwür/əl] **215**–21
stadium [stā/dē əm] **126**–1

274

staff [stăf] **185** ✦
Staff [stăf] **120**
stage [stāj] **194**–16
    stage clips [stāj/ klĭps/] **194**–24
stain [stān] **181**–24
stained [stānd] **97**–42
stairs [stërz] **50**–10
stairway [stër/wā/] **50**–10
stall shower [stöl/ show/ər] **57** ✦
stamps [stămps] **134**–18, **134**–23, **183**–47
    stamp machine [stămp/ mə shēn/] **135**–11
stand [stănd] **152**–18
    checkstand [chĕk/stănd/] **73**–12
    newsstand [nōōz/stănd/] **128**–12
    nightstand [nīt/stănd/] **58**–23
stand [stănd] **141**–D
    stand up [stănd/ ŭp/] **6**–D
standard time [stăn/dərd tīm/] **19**–26
staple [stā/pəl] **171**–F
stapler [stā/plər] **183**–28
staples [stā/pəlz] **183**–29
star [stär] **205**–13
    starfish [stär/fĭsh/] **212**–16
    star key [stär/ kē/] **14**–6
starch [stärch] **101**–12
start [stärt] **12**–A, **40**–B, **230**–R
starting point [stär/tĭng poynt/] **162**–1
starving [stär/vĭng] **43** ✦
state [stāt] **4**–8, **146**–2
    state capital [stāt kă/pət əl] **139**–22
    state senator [stāt sĕn/ə tər] **139**–25
state [stāt] **15**–G, **195**–A
State Government [stāt gŭ/ vərn mənt] **139**
statement [stāt/mənt] **132**–16
station [stā/shən]
    bus station [bŭs/ stā/shən] **124**–7
    fire station [fīr/ stā/shən] **125**–12
    gas station [găs/ stā/shən] **125**–10
    gas station attendant
        [găs/ stā/shən ə tĕn/dənt] **162**–3
    lifeguard station [līf/gärd/ stā/shən] **225**–21
    police station [pə lēs/ stā/shən] **124**–6
    space station [spās/ stā/shən] **205**–18
    station wagon [stā/shən wăg/ən] **156**–6
    subway station [sŭb/wā/ stā/shən] **151**–11
Station [stā/shən] **152**
stationery [stā/shə nër/ ē] **183**–42
stay [stā]
    stay away [stā ə wā/] **147**–I
    stay fit [stā fĭt/] **114**–E
    stay on the line [stā ön dhə līn/] **15**–H
    stay on well-lit streets [stā ön wĕl lĭt/ strēts/] **143**–B
Stay Well [stā wĕl/] **114**
steak [stāk] **70**–2, **81**–24
    broiled steak [broyld/ stāk/] **76**–3
    halibut steak [hăl/ə bŭt stāk/] **71**–6
    salmon steak [săm/ən stāk/] **71**–4
    steak knife [stāk/ nīf/] **83**–29
steal [stēl] **142** ✦
steam [stēm] **77**–D
steamed vegetables [stēmd/ vĕj/tə bəlz] **81**–32
steamer [stē/mər] **78**–3

steel [stēl]
    steel toe boots [stēl/ tō/ bōōts/] **92**–6
    steel-wool soap pads [stēl/wōōl/ sōp/ pădz/] **61**–5
steering wheel [stïr/ĭng wēl/] **159**–26
stems [stĕmz] **211**–9
step [stĕp]
    stepbrother [stĕp/brŭdh/ər] **35**–30
    stepdaughter [stĕp/dö/tər] **35** ✦
    stepfather [stĕp/fä/dhər] **35**–25
    stepladder [stĕp/lăd/ər] **61**–13
    stepmother [stĕp/mŭdh/ər] **35**–26
    steps [stĕps] **53**–3
    stepsister [stĕp/sĭs/tər] **35**–29
stereo system [stĕr/ē ō sĭs/təm] **56**–8
sterile [stĕr/əl]
    sterile pad [stĕr/əl păd/] **117**–6
    sterile tape [stĕr/əl tāp/] **117**–7
stethoscope [stĕth/ə skōp/] **118**–10
stewing beef [stōō/ĭng bēf/] **70**–3
stick [stĭk] **231**–11, **232**–11
    drumsticks [drŭm/stĭks/] **70**–23
    lipstick [lĭp/stĭk/] **109**–38
    stick shift [stĭk/ shĭft/] **159**–50
    yardstick [yärd/stĭk/] **181**–16
sticker [stĭk/ər] **102**–3, **136**–13
sticky notes [stĭk/ē nōts/] **183**–39
stir [stür] **77**–O
    stir-fried beef [stür/frīd/ bēf/] **76**–6
stitches [stĭch/əz] **117**–15
stock clerk [stäk/ klürk/] **169**–59
stockings [stäk/ĭngz] **91**–17
stomach [stŭm/ək] **107**–41
    stomachache [stŭm/ək āk/] **110**–4
stop [stäp] **129**–16, **151**–13, **154**–1
    stopover [stäp/ō/vər] **161** ✦
stop [stäp] **155**–D
Stop [stäp] **152**
stopped up [stäpt/ ŭp/] **63**–19
storage [stör/ĭj] **72**–25, **78**–4
    storage locker [stör/ĭj läk/ər] **50**–17
store [stör]
    bookstore [bŏŏk/stör/] **130**–4
    candy store [kăn/dē stör/] **131**–17
    card store [kärd/stör/] **130**–7
    convenience store [kən vēn/yəns stör/] **128**–3
    department store [dĭ pärt/mənt stör/] **131**–13
    electronics store [ē lĕk trän/ĭks stör/] **131**–20
    furniture store [für/nĭ chər stör/] **126**–8
    hardware store [härd/wër/ stör/] **148**–4
    home improvement store
        [hōm/ ĭm prōōv/mənt stör/] **127**–20
    jewelry store [jōō/əl rē stör/] **130**–2
    maternity store [mə tür/nə tē stör/] **131**–19
    men's store [mĕnz/ stör/] **130** ✦
    music store [myōō/zĭk stör/] **130**–1
    office supply store [ö/fəs sə plī/ stör/] **127**–21
    pet store [pĕt/ stör/] **130**–6
    shoe store [shōō/ stör/] **130**–10
    toy store [toy/ stör/] **130**–5
    video store [vĭd/ē ō stör/] **129**–20
Store [stör] **99**
STORE [stör] **72**–73

storeroom [stör/rōōm/] **185**–3
storm [störm] **13**–19
    hailstorm [hāl/störm/] **13**–21
    snowstorm [snō/störm/] **13**–23
    storm door [störm/ dör/] **53**–10
    thunderstorm [thŭn/dər störm/] **13**–16
story [stör/ē]
    action story [ăk/shən stör/ē] **237**–19
    adventure story [ăd vĕn/chər stör/ē] **237**–19
    horror story [hör/ər stör/ē, här/–] **237**–17
    science fiction story [sī/əns fĭk/shən stör/ē] **237**–18
    two-story house [tōō/stör/ē hows/] **52** ✦
stove [stōv] **54**–18, **226**–16
stow [stō] **160**–G
straight [strāt] **155**–A
    straight hair [strāt/ hër/] **33**–9
    straight line [strāt/ līn/] **193**–22
    straight pin [strāt/ pĭn/] **100**–12
strainer [strā/nər] **78**–22
straw [strö] **79**–18
    strawberries [strö/bĕr/ēz] **68**–14
    straw hat [strö/ hăt/] **90**–23
stream [strēm] **204** ✦
street [strēt] **150**–5, **155**–8
    streetlight [strēt/līt/] **148**–3
    street sign [strēt/ sīn/] **129**–26
    street vender [strēt/ vĕn/dər] **129**–29
STREETS [strēts] **126**–127
strep throat [strĕp/ thrōt/] **111**–4
stress [strĕs] **115**–4
stretch [strĕch] **230**–M
stretcher [strĕch/ər] **121**–33
string [strĭng]
    string beans [strĭng/ bēnz/] **69**–8
    string lights [strĭng/ līts/] **239**–18
    string of pearls [strĭng/ əv pürlz/] **95**–39
Strings [strĭngz] **238**
striped [strīpt] **96**–20
stripper [strĭ/pər] **181**–42
stroller [strō/lər] **37**–18
strong signal [sträng/ sĭg/nəl] **14**–11
stub [stŭb] **165**–11
stucco [stŭk/ō] **178**–15
student [stōōd/nt] **6**–5
study [stŭ/dē] **10**–D, **137**–A
STUDYING [stŭ/dē ĭng] **8**–9
stuffed animals [stŭft/ ăn/ə məlz] **59**–15
style [stīl/] **88** ✦
Styles [stīlz] **96**
STYLES [stīlz] **96**
stylist [stī/lĭst] **167**–31
SUBJECTS [sŭb/jĭkts/] **188**–189
submit [səb mĭt/] **48**–C
substitute [sŭb/stə tōōt/] **79**–20
subtract [səb trăkt/] **192**–B
suburbs [sŭb/ürbz] **52**–2
subway [sŭb/wā/] **151**–12
    subway car [sŭb/wā/ kär/] **152**–6
    subway station [sŭb/wā/ stā/shən] **151**–11
Subway Station [sŭb/wā/ stā/shən] **152**
Succeed [sək sēd/] **10**
SUCCEEDING IN SCHOOL [sək sē/dĭng ən skōōl/] **10**

suede [swād] **99**–8
sugar [shŏŏg/ər] **73**–30
　sugar bowl [shŏŏg/ər bōl/] **55**–14
　sugar-free [shŏŏg/ər frē/] **122**–7
　sugar substitute [shŏŏg/ər sŭb/stə tōōt/] **79**–20
suit [sōōt] **87**–11
　bathing suit [bā/dhǐng sōōt/] **90**–26
　business suit [bǐz/nəs sōōt/] **88**–11
　jumpsuit [jŭmp/sōōt/] **93**–24
　three piece suit [thrē/ pēs/ sōōt/] **88** ✦
　wet suit [wĕt/ sōōt/] **225**–4
suite [swēt] **184**–16
sum [sŭm] **192**–7
sumac [sōō/măk] **210**–23
summer [sŭm/ər] **21**–38
sun [sŭn] **209**–8
　sunblock [sŭn/blăk/] **108**–8, **225**–0
　sunburn [sŭn/bŭrn] **110**–14
　sunflower [sŭn/flow/ər] **211**–10
　sunglasses [sŭn/glăs/əz] **90**–27
　sunrise [sŭn/ rīz] **18**–14
　sunscreen [sŭn/skrēn/] **108**–7, **225**–10
　sunset [sŭn/ sĕt] **18**–19
Sunday [sŭn/dā, –dē] **20**–8
sunny [sŭn/ē] **13**–9, **76**–10
superintendent [sōō/prǐn tĕn/dənt, sōō/pər ǐn–] **50**–8
supermarket [sōō/pər/ mär/kət] **127**–18
supervise [sōō/pər vīz/] **170**–O
supervisor [sōō/pər vī/zər] **165**–8, **175**–4
Supplies [sə plīz] **100, 183**
SUPPLIES [sə plīz] **61, 180–181**
supply [sə plī/] **127**–21
　supply cabinet [sə plī/ kăb/ə nət] **182**–1
support [sə pört/] **179**–18
　support group [sə pört/ grōōp/] **115**–15
supporter [sə pör/tər] **91**–6
Supreme Court [sə prēm/ kört/] **138**–11
surfboard [sürf/börd/] **225**–16
surfer [sür/fər] **225**–15
surfing [sür/fǐng] **227**–9, **227**–10, **227** ✦
surgeon [sür/jən] **121**–36
Surgeon [sür/jən] **93**
surge protector [sürj/ prə tĕk/tər] **196**–1
surgical [sür/jǐ kəl]
　surgical cap [sür/jǐ kəl kăp/] **121**–37
　surgical gloves [sür/jǐ kəl glŭvz/] **121**–39
　surgical gown [sür/jǐ kəl gown/] **93**–37, **121**–38
　surgical mask [sür/jǐ kəl măsk/] **93**–36
　surgical nurse [sür/jǐ kəl nürs/] **120**–9
　surgical scrub cap [sür/jǐ kəl skrŭb/ kăp/] **93**–35
　surgical scrubs [sür/jǐ kəl skrŭbz/] **93**–38
Surgical Assistant [sür/jǐ kəl ə sǐs/tənt] **93**
surprised [sər prīzd/, sə–] **43**–30
suspenders [sə spĕn/dərz] **94**–1
suspense [sŭs/pĕns] **237**–20
SUV (sport-utility vehicle) [ĕs/yōō/vē/] /
　[spört/ yōō tǐl/ə tē vē/ǐ kəl] **156**–7
swallow [swäl/ō] **116**–J
swap meet [swäp/ mēt/] **222**–6
sweat [swĕt]
　sweatpants [swĕt/pănts/] **89**–23
　sweatshirt [swĕt/shürt/] **89**–22

sweater [swĕt/ər] **28**–2, **87**–14
　cardigan sweater [kär/də gən swĕt/ər] **88**–2
　pullover sweater [pŏŏl/ō/vər swĕt/ər] **88**–3
sweep [swēp] **60**–J
sweet potatoes [swēt pə tā/tōz] **69**–18
sweets [swēts] **84**–9
swim [swǐm] **230**–L
　swimsuit [swǐm/sōōt/] **90**–26
swimming [swǐm/ǐng]
　swimming pool [swǐm/ǐng pōōl/] **51**–22
　swimming trunks [swǐm/ǐng trŭngks/] **90**–22
swing [swǐng] **230**–Q
swings [swǐngz] **224**–11
Swiss cheese [swǐs/ chēz/] **71**–27
switch [swǐch] **58**–27
swollen finger [swŏ/lən fǐng/gər] **110**–16
swordfish [sörd/fǐsh] **71**–5, **212**–10
symbol [sǐm/bəl] **155**–8
SYMPTOMS AND INJURIES
　[sǐmp/təmz ə ǐn/jə rēz] **110**
synagogue [sǐn/ə gäg/] **127**–16
synthetic materials [sǐn thĕ/tǐk mə tǐr/ē əlz] **98** ✦
syringe [sə rǐnj/] **118**–12
syrup [sǐr/əp, sür/–] **113**–29
system [sǐs/təm]
　fuel injection system
　　[fyōō/əl ǐn jĕk/shən sǐs/təm] **158**–17
　stereo system [stĕr/ē ō sǐs/təm] **56**–8
SYSTEM [sǐs/təm] **141**
tab [tăb] **197**–7
table [tā/bəl]
　bed table [bĕd/ tā/bəl] **121**–21
　changing table [chān/jǐng tā/bəl] **59**–1
　coffee table [kö/fē tā/bəl] **56**–19
　dining room table [dī/nǐng rōōm/ tā/bəl] **55**–9
　end table [ĕnd/ tā/bəl] **56**–14
　examination table [ǐg zăm/ə nā/shən tā/bəl] **118**–7
　folding card table [fōl/dǐng kärd/ tā/bəl] **102**–4
　night table [nǐt/ tā/bəl] **58**–23
　operating table [äp/ə rā/tǐng tā/bəl] **121**–40
　periodic table [pǐr/ē äd/ǐk tā/bəl] **195**–26
　picnic table [pǐk/nǐk tā/bəl] **224**–8
　pool table [pōōl/ tā/bəl] **50**–15
　tablecloth [tā/bəl klöth/] **55**–12
　tablespoon [tā/bəl spōōn/] **75**–7
　table tennis [tā/bəl tĕn/əs] **228**–14
　tray table [trā/ tā/bəl] **161**–21
　turntable [türn/tā/bəl] **234**–12
tablet [tăb/lət] **113**–22, **113**–27
tackle [tăk/əl] **230**–F
taco [tä/kō] **79**–8
tags [tăgz] **92**–15, **136**–13
tail [tāl] **216**–22
tail light [tāl/ līt/] **158**–13
tail pipe [tāl/ pīp/] **158**–15
tailor [tā/lər] **100**–3
take [tāk]
　do not take with dairy products
　　[dōō nät/ tāk/ wǐth dĕr/ē prăd/ŭkts] **112**–A
　take a bath [tāk/ ə băth/] **108**–B
　take a break [tāk/ ə brāk/] **11**–H
　take a citizenship test
　　[tāk/ ə sǐt/ə zən shǐp tĕst/] **140**–I

take a driver education course
　[tāk/ ə drī/vərz ĕj/ə kā/shən körs/] **137**–B
take a driver's training course
　[tāk/ ə drī/vərz trā/nǐng körs/] **137**–G
take a message [tāk/ ə mĕs/ǐj] **171**–Q
take a nap [tāk/ ə năp/] **53**–A
take a picture [tāk/ ə pǐk/chər] **206**–B
take a seat [tāk/ ə sēt/] **6**–F
take a shower [tāk/ ə show/ər] **38**–C, **108**–A
take a tour [tāk/ ə tōōr/] **220**–A
take a written test [tāk/ ə rǐt/ən tĕst] **137**–E
take care of children [tāk/ kĕr/ əv chǐl/drən] **170**–P
take cover [tāk/ kŭv/ər] **147**–J
take dictation [tāk/ dǐk/tā shən] **171**–K
take in [tāk/ ǐn] **100**–D
take medicine [tāk/ mĕd/ə sən] **114**–D
take notes [tāk/ nōts/] **10**–C
take off [tāk/ öf/] **109**–Q, **160**–J
take one hour before eating
　[tāk/ wŭn/ ow/ər bǐ för/ ē/tǐng] **112**–B
take out [tāk/ owt/] **9**–Y, **60**–Q, **82** ✦
take ownership [tāk/ ō/nər shǐp/] **49**–K
take temperature [tāk/ tĕm/prə chər] **118**–B
take the bus to school
　[tāk/ dhə bŭs/ tə skōōl/] **38**–H
take the car to a mechanic
　[tāk/ dhə kär/ tə dhə mə kăn/ǐk] **157**–C
take the children to school
　[tāk/ dhə chǐl/drən tə skōōl/] **38**–G
take the order [tāk/ dhē ör/dər] **82**–E
take with food [tāk/ wǐth fōōd/] **112**–A
take x-rays [tāk/ ĕks/rāz/] **119**–B
Taking a Flight [tā/kǐng ə flīt/] **160**
Taking a Test [tā/kǐng ə tĕst/] **10**
TAKING A TRIP [tā/kǐng ə trǐp/] **162–163**
Taking Care of Your Car [tā/kǐng kĕr/ əv yər kär/] **157**
TAKING CARE OF YOUR HEALTH
　[tā/kǐng kĕr əv yər hĕlth/] **114–115**
talk [tök]
　talk show [tök/ shō/] **236**–4
　talk therapy [tök/ thĕr/ ə pē] **115**–13
talk [tök]
　talk about [tök ə bowt/] **174**–L
　talk on the phone [tök/ ön dhə fōn/] **15**–C
　talk to friends [tök/ tə frĕndz/] **173**–A
　talk to the teacher [tök/ tə dhə tē/chər] **6**–B
tall [töl] **32**–4
tambourine [tăm/bə rēn/] **238**–17
tan [tăn] **24**–18
tangerines [tăn/jə rēnz/] **68**–9
tank [tăngk] **158**–10, **225**–5
　tank top [tăngk/ täp/] **89**–24
　tank truck [tăngk/ trŭk/] **156**–20
tape [tāp]
　clear tape [klĕr/ tāp/] **183**–30
　correction tape [kə rĕk/shən tāp/] **183**–37
　duct tape [dŭkt/ tāp/] **181**–49
　electrical tape [ǐ lĕk/trǐ kəl tāp/] **181**–43
　masking tape [măs/kǐng tāp/] **181**–53
　packing tape [păk/ǐng tāp/] **183**–32
　sterile tape [stĕr/ əl tāp/] **117**–7
　tape measure [tāp mĕzh/ər] **100**–17, **181**–45

target [tär**/**gət] **231**–7
taste [tāst] **106**–D
tattoo [tă tōō**/**] **32**–18
tax / taxes [tăks] / [tăks**/**əz] **27**–8
taxi [tăk**/**sē] **150**–3
    hail a taxi [hāl**/** ə tăk**/**sē] **152** ✦
    taxi driver [tăk**/**sē drī**/**vər] **152**–21
    taxi license [tăk**/**sē lī**/**səns] **152**–22
    taxi stand [tăk**/**sē stănd**/**] **152**–18
TB (tuberculosis) [tē**/**bē**/**] / [tōō bür**/**kyə lō**/**səs] **111**–15
TDD [tē**/**dē**/**dē**/**] **15**–26
tea [tē] **79**–12, **81**–39, **81**–40
    teacup [tē**/**kŭp] **55**–6
    tea kettle [tē**/** kĕt**/**l] **54**–21
    teapot [tē**/**pät] **55**–16
    teaspoon [tē**/**spōōn] **75**–6, **83**–31
teach [tēch] **170**–Q
teacher [tē**/**chər] **5**–8, **6**–4, **22**–5
    teacher's aide [tē**/**chərz ād**/**] **5**–16
team [tēm] **145**–20, **229**–3
TEAM SPORTS [tēm**/** spörts**/**] **229**
technical school [tĕk**/**nĭ kəl skōōl**/**] **188**–5
technician [tĕk nĭsh**/**ən]
    computer technician
        [kəm pyōō**/**tər tĕk nĭsh**/**ən] **167**–19, **182**–12
    emergency medical technician (EMT)
        [ĭ mür**/**jən sē mĕd**/**ĭ kəl tĕk nish**/**ən] / [ē**/**ĕm**/**tē]
        121–32
    medical records technician
        [mĕd**/**ĭ kəl rĕk**/**ərdz tĕk nish**/**ən] **168**–39
Technician [tĕk nĭsh**/**ən] **93**
teddy bear [tĕd**/**ē bër**/**] **37**–23
teen / teenager [tēn] / [tē**/**nā**/**jər] **31**–11
teething ring [tē**/**dhĭng rĭng**/**] **37**–25
teeth / tooth [tēth] / [tōōth] **106**–7
    toothache [tōōth**/**āk**/**] **110**–2
    toothbrush [tōōth**/**brŭsh**/**] **57**–21, **109**–22
    toothbrush holder [tōōth**/**brŭsh**/** hōl**/**dər] **57**–22
    toothpaste [tōōth**/**pāst**/**] **109**–23
telemarketer [tĕl**/**ə mär**/**kə tər] **169**–60
TELEPHONE [tĕl**/**ə fōn**/**] **14**–15
Telephone Skills [tĕl**/**ə fōn**/** skĭlz**/**] **171**
telescope [tĕl**/**ə skōp**/**] **205**–23
television / TV [tĕl**/**ə vĭzh**/**ən] / [tē**/**vē**/**] **56**–6
    big-screen TV [bĭg**/**skrēn**/** tē**/**vē**/**] **50**–14
    flat panel TV [flăt**/** păn**/**əl tē**/**vē**/**] **234**–7
    flat screen TV [flăt**/** skrēn**/** tē**/**vē**/**] **234**–7
    portable TV [pör**/**tə bəl tē**/**vē**/**] **234**–8
teller [tĕl**/**ər] **132**–1
Teller [tĕl**/**ər] **132**
Telling Time [tĕ**/**lĭng tīm**/**] **18**
temperature [tĕm**/**prə chər] **110**–8
    temperature gauge [tĕm**/**prə chər gāj**/**] **159**–30
Temperature [tĕm**/**prə chər] **13**
ten [tĕn] **16**
    ten after one [tĕn**/** ăf**/**tər wŭn**/**] **18**–8
    ten dollars [tĕn**/** däl**/**ərz] **26**–9
    10 percent [tĕn**/** pər sĕnt**/**] **17**–12
    ten thousand [tĕn**/** thow**/**zənd] **16**
    10-year-old girl [tĕn**/**yïr ōld**/** gürl**/**] **31**–10
tenant [tĕn**/**ənt] **50**–6
TENANT MEETING [tĕn**/**ənt mē**/**tĭng] **64**–65

tennis [tĕn**/**əs] **228**–15
    table tennis [tā**/**bəl tĕn**/**əs] **228**–14
    tennis court [tĕn**/**əs kört**/**] **224**–6
    tennis racket [tĕn**/**əs răk**/**ət] **231**–2
    tennis shoes [tĕn**/**əs shōōz**/**] **95**–32
tent [tĕnt] **226**–10
tenth [tĕnth] **16**
Terminal [tür**/**mə nəl] **160**
termites [tür**/**mīts] **63**–22
term [türm] **139** ✦
Terms [türmz] **199**
terrified [tĕr**/**ə fīd**/**] **43** ✦
test [tĕst] **121**–30
    test booklet [tĕst**/** bŏŏk**/**lət] **10**–1
    testing area [tĕs**/**tĭng ër**/**ē ə] **136**–2
    test tube [tĕst**/** tōōb**/**] **195**–42
Test [tĕst] **10**
text [tĕkst]
    textbook [tĕkst**/**bŏŏk**/**, tĕks**/**-] **7**–25
    text box [tĕkst**/** bäks**/**, tĕks**/**-] **197**–13
    text message [tĕkst**/** mĕs**/**ĭj, tĕks**/**-] **14**–19
thank [thăngk] **12**–E, **174**–N
Thanksgiving [thăngks gĭv**/**ĭng] **22**–17
theater [thē**/**ə tər] **126**–6, **127**–23
theft [thĕft] **142**–9
therapist [thĕr**/** ə pĭst] **115**–12, **115**–14, **168**–45
therapy [thĕr**/** ə pē] **115**–11, **115**–13
thermal undershirt [thür**/**məl ŭn**/**dər shürt**/**] **91**–2
thermometer [thər măm**/**ə tər] **118**–11
thick [thĭk] **23**–7
thighs [thīz] **70**–22, **106**–19
thimble [thĭm**/**bəl] **100**–15
thin [thĭn] **23**–8, **32**–9
THINGS [thĭngz] **23**
think [thĭnk] **191**–E
third [thürd] **16**
Third Floor [thürd**/** flör**/**] **50**
thirsty [thür**/**stē] **42**–2
thirteen [thür**/**tēn**/**] **16**
    thirteen colonies [thür**/**tēn**/** kä**/**lə nēz] **198**–1
thirteenth [thür**/**tēnth**/**] **16**
thirtieth [thür**/**tē əth] **16**
thirty [thür**/**tē] **16**
    35 mm camera
        [thür**/**tē fïv**/** mĭl**/**ə mē**/**tər kăm**/**rə] **235**–21
this week [dhĭs**/** wēk**/**] **20**–19
thorn [thörn] **211**–29
thread [thrĕd] **99**–23, **100**–11
three [thrē] **16**
    three piece suit [thrē**/**pēs**/** sōōt**/**] **88** ✦
    3-ring binder [thrē**/** rĭng**/** bīn**/**dər] **7**–27
    3/4 sleeved [thrē**/**kwör**/**tər slēv**/**] **96**–13
    three times a week [thrē**/** tīmz**/** ə wēk**/**] **20**–24
throat [thrōt] **107**–35, **110**–6, **111**–4
    throat lozenges [thrōt**/** läz**/**ən jəz] **113**–30
through [thrōō] **153**–K
throw [thrō] **230**–C
    throw away [thrō**/** ə wā**/**] **11**–N
    throw up [thrō**/** ŭp**/**] **110**–E
throw pillow [thrō**/** pĭl**/**ō] **56**–2
thumb [thŭm] **106**–16
thunderstorm [thŭn**/**dər störm**/**] **13**–16

Thursday [thürz**/**dā, –dē] **20**–12
tick [tĭk] **214**–27
ticket [tĭk**/**ət] **152**–15, **161**–19
    ticket agent [tĭk**/**ət ā**/**jənt] **160**–3
    ticket window [tĭk**/**ət wĭn**/**dō**/**] **152**–12
tidal wave [tīd**/**l wāv**/**] **145**–17
tide [tīd] **225** ✦
tie [tī] **88**–12, **89**–16, **92**–13, **229** ✦
tie [tī] **86**–A
tiger [tī**/**gər] **217**–37
tight [tīt] **97**–29
tights [tīts] **91**–19
tile [tīl] **57**–10, **178**–11, **178**–D
time [tīm]
    Alaska time [ə lăs**/**kə tīm**/**] **19**–28
    arrival time [ə rī**/**vəl tīm**/**] **161** ✦
    Atlantic time [ət lăn**/**tĭk tīm**/**] **19**–33
    Central time [sĕn**/**trəl tīm**/**] **19**–31
    daylight saving time [dā**/**līt**/** sā**/**vĭng tīm**/**] **19**–25
    departure time [dĭ pär**/**chər tīm**/**]**161** ✦
    Eastern time [ē**/**stərn tīm**/**] **19**–32
    Hawaii-Aleutian time
        [hə wī**/**ē ə lōō**/**shən tīm**/**] **19**–27
    Mountain time [mown**/**tn tīm**/**] **19**–30
    Newfoundland time
        [nōō**/**fən lənd tīm**/**, –fənd–] **19**–34
    on time [än**/** tīm**/**, ön**/** tīm**/**] **19**–23, **161**–29
    Pacific time [pə sĭf**/**ĭk tīm**/**] **19**–29
    standard time [stăn**/**dərd tīm**/**] **19**–26
    three times a week [thrē tīmz**/** ə wēk**/**] **20**–24
    time clock [tīm**/** kläk**/**] **165**–7
Time [tīm] **18**
TIME [tīm] **18**–19
timer [tī**/**mər] **78**–18
Times of Day [tīmz**/** əv dā**/**] **18**
Time Zones [tīm**/** zōnz**/**] **19**
tire [tīr] **158**–5, **158**–23, **162**–F
tired [tīrd] **43**–32
title [tīt**/**l] **133**–14, **190**–5
toad [tōd] **212**–28
toast [tōst] **80**–4
toaster [tō**/**stər] **54**–6
    toaster oven [tō**/**stər ŭv**/**ən] **54**–15
today [tə dā**/**] **20**–5
toddler [täd**/**lər] **31**–8
toe [tō] **92**–6, **94**–23, **105**–10
    toenail [tō**/**nāl**/**] **106** ✦
Tofu [tō**/**fōō] **77**
toggle bolt [täg**/**əl bōlt**/**] **180**–38
to-go box [tə gō**/** bäks**/**] **82**–5
toilet [toy**/**lət] **57**–19
    toilet brush [toy**/**lət brŭsh**/**] **57**–18
    toilet paper [toy**/**lət pā**/**pər] **57**–17, **146**–13
token [tō**/**kən] **152**–10
tomatoes [tə mā**/**tōz] **69**–6
tomorrow [tə mär**/**ō, –mör**/**ō] **20**–6
tongs [tängz, töngz] **78**–23, **195**–44
tongue [tŭng] **106**–8
too [tōō]
    too big [tōō**/** bĭg**/**] **97**–38
    too expensive [tōō**/** ĭk spĕn**/**sĭv] **97**–44
    too small [tōō**/** smöl**/**] **97**–37

Index

tool belt [tōōl/ bĕlt/] **92**–3
TOOLS AND BUILDING SUPPLIES
[tōōlz/ ən bĭl/dĭng sə plīz/] **180**–**181**
tooth / teeth [tōōth] / [tĕth] **106**–7
toothache [tōōth/āk/] **110**–2
toothbrush [tōōth/brŭsh/] **57**–21, **109**–22
toothbrush holder [tōōth/brŭsh/ hōl/dər] **57**–22
toothpaste [tōōth/pāst/] **109**–23
top [täp] **88**–7, **89**–24
torn [törn] **97**–41
tornado [tör nā/dō] **145**–15
torso [tör/sō/] **106** ✦
tortoise [tör/təs] **213**–42
total [tōt/l] **27**–9
totebag [tōt/ băg/] **94**–19
touch [tŭch] **106**–E
towel [tow/əl]
bath towel [băth/ tow/əl] **57**–14
dish towel [dĭsh/ tow/əl] **61**–22
hand towel [hănd/ tow/əl] **57**–15
paper towels [pā/pər tow/əlz] **54**–3
towel rack [tow/əl răk/] **57**–13
towelettes [tow/əl ĕts] **146**–12
tower [tow/ər] **196**–3
town [town] **52**–3
town car [town/ kär/] **152**–20
townhouse [town/hows/] **52**–6
tow truck [tō/ trŭk/] **156**–14
toy [toy]
toy chest [toy/ chĕst/] **59**–16
toy store [toy/ stör/] **130**–5
Toys and Games [toyz/ ən gāmz/] **59**
track [trăk] **5**–21, **152**–14
track and field [trăk/ ən fēld/] **228**–18
tractor [trăk/tər] **177**–9
tractor trailer [trăk/tər trā/lər] **156**–15
traffic light [trăf/ĭk līt/] **128**–8
TRAFFIC SIGNS [trăf/ĭk sīnz/] **154**
tragedy [trăj/ə dē] **237**–14
trailer [trā/lər] **156**–15, **156**–17
train [trān] **150**–7, **233**–27
training [trā/nĭng] **172**–2, **172**–5, **172**–7
training pants [trā/nĭng pănts/] **37**–11
Training [trā/nĭng] **172**
Train Station [trān/ stā/shən] **152**
transcribe [trăn skrīb/] **171**–C
transfer [trăns für/, trăns/fər] **152**–5
transfer [trăns für/, trăns/fər] **171**–O
translate [trănz/lāt] **8**–C
translator [trănz/lā/tər, trăns/–] **168**–35
Transmission [trănz mĭsh/ən, trăns–] **159**
Transportation [trăns/pər tā/shən] **152**
TRANSPORTATION [trăns/pər tā/shən] **150**–**151**, **152**
trash [trăsh]
trash bags [trăsh/ băgz/] **61**–24
trash bin [trăsh/ bĭn/] **51**–23
trash chute [trăsh/ shōōt/] **51**–26
travel [trăv/əl] **41**–P
travel agency [trăv/əl ā/jən sē] **131**–14
tray [trā] **55**–17, **83**–10
tray table [trā tā/bəl] **161**–21
Tree [trē] **210**

trees [trēz] **208**–1, **239**–16
TREES AND PLANTS [trēz/ ən plănts/] **210**
trench coat [trĕnch/ kōt/] **90**–21
trial [trī/əl] **140**–5
triangle [trī/ăng/gəl] **193**–32
tricycle [trī/sĭ kəl] **224**–12
trigonometry [trĭg/ə näm/ə trē] **192**–18
trim [trĭm] **176**–B
trip [trĭp] **152**–16, **152**–17
tripe [trīp] **70**–8
tripod [trī/päd] **235**–25
trombone [träm bōn/] **238**–10
trout [trowt] **71**–1
trowel [trow/əl] **176**–10, **178**–13
truck [trŭk] **150**–5
dump truck [dŭmp/trŭk/] **156**–19
fire truck [fīr/ trŭk/] **144**–10
garbage truck [gär/bĭj trŭk/] **127**–22
hand truck [hănd/ trŭk/] **175**–11
pickup truck [pĭk/ŭp trŭk/] **156**–12
tank truck [tăngk/ trŭk/] **156**–20
tow truck [tō/ trŭk/] **156**–14
truck driver [trŭk/ drī/vər] **169**–61
TRUCKS [trŭks] **156**
trumpet [trŭm/pət] **238**–11
Trunk [trŭngk] **158**
trunks [trŭngks] **158**–11, **210**–4, **217**–47
swimming trunks [swĭm/ĭng trŭngks/] **90**–22
try on [trī/ŏn] **95**–C
TSA agent [tē/ĕs/ā/ ā/jənt] **160**–5
T-shirt [tē/shürt/] **86**–4
tsunami [sōō nä/ mē/, tsōō–] **145**–17
tub [tŭb]
bathtub [băth/tŭb/] **57**–2
tuba [tōō/bə] **238**–12
tube [tōōb] **74**–12, **74**–24, **195**–42
tuberculosis (TB)
[tōō bür/kyə lō/səs] / [tē/bē/] **111**–15
Tuesday [tōōz/dā, –dē] **20**–10
tulip [tōō/ləp] **211**–11
tuna [tōō/nə] **71**–7, **72**–19, **212**–8
tuner [tōō/nər] **234**–13
turbulence [tür/byə ləns] **161**–22
turkey [tür/kē] **70**–17, **239**–14
roasted turkey [rōs/təd tür/kē] **76**–4
smoked turkey [smōkt/ tür/kē] **71**–25
turn [türn] **154**–5, **154**–7, **154**–8
turn signal [türn/ sĭg/nəl] **158**–6, **159**–34
turnstile [türn/stīl/] **152**–8
turntable [türn/tā/bəl] **234**–12
turn [türn]
turn in [türn/ ĭn/] **191**–M
turn left [türn/ lĕft/] **155**–C
turn off [türn/ öf/] **11**–P, **160**–I, **174**–G, **219**–G
turn on [türn/ ön/, –än/] **11**–B
turn right [türn/ rīt/] **155**–B
turnips [tür/nəps] **69**–16
turquoise [tür/koyz, –kwoyz] **24**–9
turtle [tür/tl] **213**–43
turtleneck [tür/tl nĕk/] **96**–9
tusk [tŭsk] **217**–48
tuxedo [tŭk sē/dō] **89**–17

TV Programs [tē/vē/ prō/grămz] **236**
TV / television [tē/vē/] / [tĕl/ə vĭzh/ən] **56**–6
big-screen TV [bĭg/skrēn/ tē/vē/] **50**–14
flat panel TV [flăt/ păn/əl tē/vē/] **234**–7
flat screen TV [flăt/ skrēn/ tē/ vē/] **234**–7
portable TV [por/tə bəl tē/vē/] **234**–8
tweezers [twē/zərz] **117**–4
twelfth [twĕlfth] **16**
twelve [twĕlv] **16**
twentieth [twĕn/tē ĕth] **16**
twenty [twĕn/tē] **16**
twenty after one [twĕn/tē ăf/tər wŭn/] **18**–10
twenty dollars [twĕn/tē däl/ərz] **26**–10
twenty-first [twĕn/tē fürst/] **16**
twenty-five [twĕn/tē fīv/] **16**
25 percent [twĕn/fīv/ pər sĕnt/] **17**–11
twenty-four [twĕn/tē för/] **16**
twenty-one [twĕn/tē wŭn/] **16**
twenty-three [twĕn/tē thrē/] **16**
twenty to two [twĕn/tē tə tōō/] **18**–12
twenty-two [twĕn/tē tōō/] **16**
twice a week [twīs/ ə wēk/] **20**–23
twig [twĭg] **210**–1
twins [twĭnz] **28**–1
two [tōō] **16**
2-door car [tōō/dör kär/] **156**–2
two-story house [tōō/stör/ē hows/] **52** ✦
two-way radio [tōō/wā rā/dē ō] **179**–22
2 x 4 (two by four) [tōō/ bī/ för/] **181**–19
type [tīp] **170**–R, **196**–A
type a letter [tīp/ə lĕt/ər] **171**–A
type the message [tīp/ dhə mĕs/ĭj] **197**–E
type the subject [tīp/ dhə sŭb/jĭkt] **197**–D
type your password [tīp/ yər păs/würd/] **197**–A
Types of Health Problems
[tīps/ əv hĕlth/ präb/ləmz] **115**
Types of Job Training [tīps/ əv jäb/ trā/nĭng] **172**
Types of Material [tīps/ əv mə tïr/ē əl] **99**
Types of Math [tīps/ əv măth/] **192**
Types of Medication [tīps/ əv mĕd/ə kā/shən] **113**
Types of Movies [tīps/ əv mōō/vēz] **237**
Types of Music [tīps/ əv myōō/zĭk] **237**
Types of TV Programs [tīps/ əv tē/vē/ prō/grămz] **236**
ugly [ŭg/lē] **23**–22
umbrella [ŭm brĕl/ə] **90**–17, **225**–14
umpire [ŭm/pīr] **229** ✦
uncle [ŭng/kəl] **34**–8
uncomfortable [ŭn kŭmf/tə bəl, –tər–] **42**–9
unconscious [ŭn/kän/shəs] **116**–A
under [ŭn/dər] **25**–10, **153**–A
long underwear [löng/ ŭn/dər wër/] **91**–3
thermal undershirt [thür/məl ŭn/dər shürt/] **91**–2
underexposed [ŭn/dər ĭk spōzd/] **235**–35
underpants [ŭn/dər pănts/] **91**–14
undershirt [ŭn/dər shürt/] **91**–1
underline [ŭn/dər līn/] **9**–S
Under the Hood [ŭn/dər dhə hōōd/] **158**
Underwear [ŭn/dər wër/] **91**
UNDERWEAR AND SLEEPWEAR
[ŭn/dər wër/ ən slēp/wër/] **91**
undress [ən drĕs/] **36**–E

278

unfurnished apartment
   [ŭn/fûr nĭsht ə pärt/ mənt] **48**–4
uniform [yōō/nə förm/] **88**–10, **231**–16
Unisex Socks [yōō/nə sĕks/ säks/] **91**
Unisex Underwear [yōō/nə sĕks/ ŭn/dər wër] **91**
universal remote [yōō/nə vûr/səl rĭ mōt/] **234**–9
UNIVERSE [yōō/nə vûrs/] **205**
university [yōō/nə vûr/sə tē] **188**–7
unload [ŭn lōd/] **101**–E
unpack [ŭn păk/] **49**–N
unraveling [ŭn răv/əl ĭng] **97**–43
unripe [ŭn rip/] **68**–31
unscented [ŭn sĕn/təd] **108** ✦
unscramble [ŭn skrăm/bəl] **9**–W
up [ŭp]
   buckle up [bŭk/əl ŭp/] **36**–L
   clean up [klēn/ ŭp/] **147**–M
   cut up [kŭt/ ŭp/] **77**–I
   eggs sunny-side up [ĕgz/ sŭn/ē sid/ ŭp/] **76**–10
   get up [gĕt/ ŭp/] **38**–B
   hang up [hăng/ ŭp/] **15**–D, **101**–H
   look up [lŏŏk/ ŭp/] **8**–A
   pick up [pĭk/ ŭp/] **6**–I, **11**–E, **38**–M
   pop-up ad [päp/ ŭp ăd/] **197**–9
   set up [sĕt/ ŭp/] **173**–I
   stand up [stănd/ ŭp/] **6**–D
   stopped up [stäpt/ ŭp/] **63**–19
   throw up [thrō/ ŭp/] **110**–E
   wake up [wāk/ ŭp/] **38**–A
   walk up [wök/ ŭp/] **153**–C
upright seat [ŭp/rit/ sēt/] **161**–28
upset [ŭp sĕt/] **43**–28
upstairs [ŭp/stërz/] **51** ✦
Uranus [yŏŏr/ə nəs, yŏŏ rā/nəs] **205**–7
urban area [ûr/bən ër/ē ə] **52**–1
urchin [ûr/chən] **212**–21
URL [yōō/ärl/ĕl/] **197**–4
U.S. [yōō/ĕs/]
   U.S. Capitol [yōō/ĕs/ kă/pət əl] **138**–1
   U.S. route [yōō/ĕs/ rōōt/, –rowt/] **154**–17
USB port [yōō/ĕs/ bē/ pört/] **196**–7
use [yōōz]
   use a cash register [yōōz/ə kăsh/ rĕj/ə stər] **170**–S
   use a credit card [yōōz/ə krĕ/dət kärd/] **27**–B
   use a debit card [yōōz/ə dĕ/bət kärd/] **27**–C
   use a gift card [yōōz/ ə gĭft/ kärd/] **27**–E
   use deodorant [yōōz/dē ō/dər ənt] **108**–C
   use energy-efficient bulbs
      [yōōz/ ĕn/ər jē ĭ fĭ/shənt bŭlbz] **219**–H
   use punctuation [yōōz/ pŭngk/chōō ā/shən] **190**–C
Used Car [yōōzd/ kär/] **157**
used clothing [yōōzd/ klō/dhĭng] **102**–2
U.S. HISTORY [yōō/ĕs/ hĭs/tə rē] **198**
U.S. NATIONAL PARKS
   [yōō/ĕs năsh/ə nəl pärks/] **220**–**221**
utensils [yōō tĕn/səlz] **79**–19
utility / utilities [yōō tĭl/ə tē] / [yōō tĭl/ə tēz]
   48–5, **156**–7
U-turn [yōō/tûrn/] **154**–5
vacancy sign [vă/kən sē sin/] **50**–7
vacation [vā kā/shən] **22**–6
vaccination [văk/sə nā/shən] **114** ✦

vacuum [văk/yōōm]
   vacuum cleaner [văk/yōōm klē/nər] **61**–10
   vacuum cleaner attachments
      [văk/yōōm klē/nər ə tăch/mənts] **61**–11
   vacuum cleaner bag
      [văk/yōōm klē/nər băg/] **61**–12
   vacuum [văk/yōōm] **60**–H
valley [văl/ē] **204**–17
valuables [văl/yə bəlz, –yə wə–] **132**–8
valve [vălv/] **146**–4
van [văn] **156**–13, **156**–18
vandalism [văn/də lĭz/əm] **142**–1
vanity plate [vă/nə tē plăt/] **136** ✦
variable [vër/ē ə bəl] **192**–12
vase [vās, văz, väz] **55**–23
vault [völt] **132**–6
VCR [vē/sē/är/] **102**–7
veal cutlets [vēl/ kŭt/ləts] **70**–6
Vegetable [vĕj/tə bəl] **77**
vegetables [vĕj/tə bəlz] **66**–8, **72**–27, **81**–32
   vegetable garden [vĕj/tə bəl gär/dn] **53**–27, **177**–14
   vegetable peeler [vĕj/tə bəl pē/lər] **78**–15
VEGETABLES [vĕj/tə bəlz] **69**
vegetarian [vĕj/ə tër/ē ən] **70** ✦
vehicles [vē/ĭ kəlz] **124**–4, **156**–7, **156**–10
vein [vān] **107**–37
velvet [vĕl/vət] **99**–10
vending machine [vĕn/dĭng mə shēn/] **152**–9
vendors [vĕn/dərz] **84**–7, **129**–29
ventilation mask [vĕnt/əl ā/shən măsk/] **92**–7
Venus [vē/nəs] **205**–2
verdict [vûr/dĭkt] **141**–14
vertebrates [vûr/ tə brəts] **194**–13
vest [vĕst] **89**–15
   down vest [down/ vĕst] **90**–14
   Hi-Visibility safety vest
      [hi/vĭz/ə bĭl/ə tē săf/tē vĕst] **92**–6
   life vest [lif/ vĕst/] **161**–25, **226**–14
Veterans Day [vĕt/ər ənz dā/] **22**–16
veterinarian [vĕt/ər ə nër/ē ən] **169**–62
vice president [vis/ prĕz/ə dənt] **138**–9
victim [vĭk/təm] **142**–10
video [vĭd/ē ō]
   videocassette [vĭd/ē ō kə sĕt/] **133**–18
   video game console [vĭd/ē ō găm/ kän/sōl/] **232**–3
   video game control [vĭd/ē ō găm/ kän trōl/] **232**–4
   video player [vĭd/ē ō plā ər] **197**–11
   video store [vĭd/ē ō stör/] **129**–20
   videotape [vĭd/ē ō tāp/] **240**–A
view [vyōō]
   rearview mirror [rïr/vyōō/ mïr/ər] **159**–35
   sideview mirror [sid/vyōō/ mïr/ər] **158**–3
village [vĭ/lĭj] **52**–3
vine [vin] **210**–22
vineyard [vĭn/yərd] **177**–16
violence [vi/ləns, vi/ə–] **142**–4
violet [vi/ə lət, vi/lət] **24**–8, **211**–23
violin [vi/ə lĭn/] **238**–6
virus [vi/rəs] **111**–17
vise [vis] **180**–26
vision [vĭ/zhən]
   vision exam [vĭ/zhən ĭg zăm/] **136**–6
   vision problems [vĭ/zhən präb/ləmz] **115**–1

Visit [vĭ/zət] **119**
visor [vi/zər] **179**–12
vital signs monitor [vit/l sinz/ män/ə tər] **121**–26
vitamins [vi/tə mənz] **113**–17
v-neck [vē/nĕk/] **96**–8
vocational [vō kā/shə nəl]
   vocational school [vō kā/shə nəl skōōl/] **188**–5
   vocational training [vō kā/shə nəl trā/nĭng] **172**–5
voice message [voys mĕs/ïj] **14**–18
volcanic eruption [väl kăn/ïk ĭ rŭp/shən] **145**–16
volleyball [väl/ē böl/] **229**–14, **231**–3
Volume [väl/yəm, –yōōm] **75**, **193**
volunteer [väl/ən tïr/] **121**–17
volunteer [väl/ən tïr/] **41**–Q
vomit [văm/ət] **110**–E
vote [vōt] **140**–A
waffles [wä/fəlz, wö/–] **80**–8
wages [wā/jïz] **165**–12
wagon [wă/gən] **156**–6
waist [wāst]
   waist apron [wāst/ ā/prən] **93**–30
   waistband [wāst/bănd/] **100**–5
wait [wāt] **94**–B, **128**–B, **170**–T
waiter [wā/tər] **82**–8
   headwaiter [hĕd/wā/tər] **185**–12
waiting area [wā/tĭng ër/ē ə] **182**–16
Waiting Room [wā/tĭng rōōm/] **118**
waitress [wā/trəs] **83**–9
wait staff [wāt/ stäf/] **185** ✦
wake up [wāk/ ŭp/] **38**–A
walk [wök] **53**–2
   crosswalk [krös/wök/] **128**–15
   walk-in freezer [wök/ĭn frē/zər] **185**–3
walk [wök]
   walk a dog [wök ə dög/] **129**–F
   walk down [wök/ down/] **153**–D
   walk to class [wök/ tə kläs/] **11**–C
   walk up [wök/ ŭp/] **153**–C
   walk with a friend [wök/ wïth ə frĕnd/] **143**–A
walker [wö/kər] **113**–11
wall [wöl] **56**–10, **194**–5
   drywall [dri/wöl/] **178**–19
   wallpaper [wöl/pā/pər] **59**–8
wallet [wä/lət, wö/–] **94**–13
walrus [wöl/rəs] **213**–32
war [wör] **199**–10
   Revolutionary War [rĕ/və lōō/shə nër/ē wör/] **198**–8
warehouse [wër/hows/] **175**–7
warm [wörm] **13**–4
   warm clothes [wörm/ klöz/] **146**–6
warning label [wör/nĭng lā/bəl] **112**–8
Warnings [wör/nĭngz] **112**
wash [wäsh, wösh]
   mouthwash [mowth/wäsh/, –wösh/–] **109**–25
   washcloth [wäsh/klöth/, wösh/–] **57**–4
wash [wäsh, wösh]
   wash clothes [wäsh/ klöz/, wösh/–] **219**–K
   wash hair [wäsh/ här/, wösh/–] **108**–E
   wash the dishes [wäsh/ dhə dĭsh/əz, wösh/–] **60**–M
   wash the windows
      [wäsh/ dhə wĭn/dōz, wösh/–] **60**–I
washer [wä/shər, wö/–] **50**–12, **101**–3, **180**–37
   dishwasher [dĭsh/wäsh/ər, –wö/–] **54**–8, **185**–2

Index

washing [wä′shǐng, wö′–] **61**–21

wasp [wäsp, wösp] **214**–17

waste [wāst] **121**–31, **218**–12

   wastebasket [wāst′bās′kət] **57**–26

watch [wäch, wöch] **94**–16

watch [wäch, wöch] **39**–X, **147**–C

water [wö′tər] **209**–3, **225**–1

   body of water [bäd′ē əv wö′tər] **204** ✦

   bottled water [bät′ld wö′tər] **146**–11

   cold water [kōld′ wö′tər] **57**–7

   hot water [hät′ wö′tər] **57**–8

   hot water bottle [hät′ wö′tər böt′l] **113**–15

   watercolor [wö′tər kŭl′ər] **233**–21

   waterfall [wä′tər föl′] **204**–2

   water fountain [wö′tər fown′tn] **224**–9

   water glass [wö′tər gläs′] **83**–22

   watermelons [wö′tər mĕl′ənz] **68**–18

   water pollution [wö′tər pə lōō′shən] **218**–14

   water polo [wö′tər pō′lō] **229**–15

   waterskiing [wö′tər skē′ĭng] **227**–7

water [wö′tər] **176**–F

WATER SPORTS [wö′tər spörts′] **227**

wave [wāv] **145**–17, **225**–17

wave [wāv] **2**–F

wavy hair [wā′vē hër′] **33**–10

way [wā]

   hallway [häl′wā′] **184**–18

   one way [wŭn′ wā′] **154**–3

   one-way trip [wŭn′wā′ trĭp′] **152**–16

   two-way radio [tōō′wā′ rā′dē ō] **179**–22

   wrong way [röng′ wā′] **154**–2

Ways to Conserve Energy and Resources

   [wāz′ tə kən sürv′ ĕn′ər jē n rē′sör′səz,
   –rĭ sör′səz] **219**

Ways to Get Well [wāz′ tə gĕt′ wĕl′] **114**

Ways to Pay [wāz′ tə pā′] **27**

Ways to Serve Eggs [wāz′ tə sürv′ ĕgz′] **76**

Ways to Serve Meat and Poultry

   [wāz′ tə sürv′ mēt′ n pōl′trē′] **76**

Ways to Stay Well [wāz′ tə stā′ wĕl′] **114**

Ways to Succeed [wāz′tə sək sēd′] **10**

weak signal [wēk′ sĭg′nəl] **14**–12

WEATHER [wĕdh′ər] **13**

Weather Conditions [wĕdh′ər kən dĭsh′ənz] **13**

Weather Map [wĕdh′ər măp′] **13**

webcam [wĕb′kăm′] **196**–12

Webpage [wĕb′pāg′] **197**

website address [wĕb′sīt ə drĕs′] **197**–4

wedding [wĕ′dĭng] **22**–2

Wednesday [wĕnz′dā, –dē] **20**–11

weed [wēd]

   seaweed [sē′ wēd′] **225** ✦

   weed eater [wēd′ ē′tər] **176**–12

   weed whacker [wēd′ wăk′ər] **176**–12

weed [wēd] **176**–G

week [wēk] **20**–15

   last week [lăst′ wēk′] **20**–18

   next week [nĕkst′ wēk′] **20**–20

   once a week [wŭns′ ə wēk′] **20**–22

   this week [dhĭs′ wēk′] **20**–19

   three times a week [thrē′ tīmz′ ə wēk′] **20**–24

   twice a week [twīs′ ə wēk′] **20**–23

weekdays [wēk′dāz′] **20**–16

weekend [wēk′ĕnd′] **20**–17

Week [wēk] **20**

weigh [wā] **75**–B

weight [wāt] **32**–8

Weight [wāt] **32, 75**

weightlifting [wāt′lĭf′tĭng] **228**–16

weights [wāts] **231**–22

WEIGHTS AND MEASUREMENTS

   [wāts′ ən mĕzh′ər mənts] **75**

welder [wĕl′dər] **169**–63

well [wĕl] **42**–14

Well [wĕl] **114**

west [wĕst] **155**–2

western [wĕs′tərn] **237**–15

wet [wĕt] **101**–17

   wet suit [wĕt′ sōōt′] **225**–4

whacker [wăk′ər] **176**–12

whale [wāl] **213**–29

wheat [wēt] **177**–2

   wheat bread [wēt′ brĕd′] **71**–19

wheel [wēl] **159**–26

   wheelbarrow [wēl′băr′ō] **176**–3

   wheelchair [wēl′chër′] **113**–9

   wheel cover [wēl′ kŭv′ər] **158**–9

whisk [wĭsk] **78**–21

whiskers [wĭs′kərz] **216**–18

white [wīt] **24**–14

   whiteboard [wīt′börd′] **6**–3

   white bread [wīt′ brĕd′] **71**–18

   White House [wīt′ hows′] **138**–7

whole salmon [hōl′ săm′ən] **71**–3

wide [wīd] **97**–36

widow [wĭd′ō] **41** ✦

widower [wĭd′ō ər] **41** ✦

width [wĭdth, wĭtth] **17**–19

wife [wīf] **34**–12

   ex-wife [ĕks′ wīf′] **35** ✦

   former wife [för′mər wīf′] **35** ✦

wild [wīld] **215** ✦

wildlife [wīld′līf′] **220**–3

willow [wĭl′ō] **210**–13

win [wĭn] **229** ✦

wind [wĭnd]

   windbreaker [wĭnd′brā′kər] **90**–24

   wind power [wĭnd′ pow′ər] **218**–2

   windshield [wĭnd′ shēld′] **158**–1

   windshield wipers [wĭnd′shēld′wī′pərz] **158**–2

   windsurfing [wĭnd′sür′fĭng] **227**–10, **227** ✦

window [wĭn′dō] **47**–11, **56**–17, **136**–7

   drive-thru window [drīv′throō′ wĭn′dō] **128**–11

   ticket window [tĭk′ət wĭn′dō] **152**–12

   window pane [wĭn′dō pān′] **178**–16

windy [wĭn′dē] **13**–18

wine glass [wīn′ gläs′] **83**–23

wing [wĭng] **70**–20, **214**–1

winter [wĭn′tər] **21**–40

   winter scarf [wĭn′tər skärf′] **90**–5

WINTER AND WATER SPORTS

   [wĭn′tər ən wö′tər spörts′] **227**

wipe [wīp] **60**–O

wipers [wī′pərz] **158**–2

wipes [wīps] **37**–15, **61**–23

wire [wīr] **181**–13

   wire stripper [wīr′ strĭp′ər] **181**–42

wireless headset [wīr′ləs hĕd′sĕt] **14**–14

wiring [wīr′ĭng] **186**–7

withdraw [wĭdh drö′, wĭth–] **132**–F

witness [wĭt′nəs] **141**–11

wolf [wŏolf] **216**–5

woman [wŏom′ən] **30**–2

women [wĭ′mən] **30**–3

Women's Socks [wĭ′mənz säks′] **91**

Women's Underwear [wĭ′mənz ŭn′dər wër′] **91**

wood [wŏod] **178**–18

   plywood [plī′wŏod] **178**–17

   redwood [rĕd′wŏod] **210**–18

   wood floor [wŏod′ flör′] **58**–21

   woodpecker [wŏod′pĕk′ər] **214**–8

   wood screw [wŏod′ skrōo′] **180**–33

   wood stain [wŏod′ stān′] **181**–24

   woodworking kit [wŏod′wür′kĭng kĭt′] **232**–14

wooden spoon [wŏod′n spōōn′] **78**–9

Woodwinds [wŏod′wĭndz′] **238**

wool [wŏol] **61**–5, **98**–3

word [würd] **190**–1

   word problem [würd′ prä′bləm] **192**–11

Words [würdz] **8**

work [würk′] **121**–30, **154**–16

   workbook [würk′bŏok′] **7**–26

   work gloves [würk′ glŭvz′] **92**–17, **179**–17

   work light [würk′ līt′] **181**–44

   work pants [würk′ pănts′] **92**–5

   work shirt [würk′ shürt′] **92**–2

work [würk] **8**–I, **10**–J, **38**–K

WORK [würk] **186**–187

Work Clothes [würk′ klōz′] **88**

worker [wür′kər]

   careful worker [kër′fəl wür′kər] **179**–2

   careless worker [kër′ləs wür′kər] **179**–1

   childcare worker [chĭld′kër wür′kər] **166**–16

   construction worker

     [kən strŭk′shən wür′kər] **178**–1

   dockworker [däk′wür′kər] **167**–23

   factory worker [făk′tə rē wür′kər, –trē] **175**–3

   farmworker [färm′wür′kər] **177**–8

   food preparation worker

     [fōōd′ prĕp ə rā′shən wür′kər] **185**–4

   garment worker [gär′mənt wür′kər] **167**–29

   postal worker [pō′stəl wür′kər] **169**–49

   sanitation worker [săn′ə tā′shən wür′kər] **169**–54

   social worker [sō′shəl wür′kər] **169**–57

Worker [wür′kər] **92, 93**

working [wür′kĭng]

   not working [nät′ wür′kĭng] **62**–1

   woodworking kit [wŏod′wür′kĭng kĭt′] **232**–14

Working with a Partner [wür′kĭng wĭth ə pärt′nər] **8**

Working with Your Classmates

   [wür′kĭng wĭth yər kläs′māts′] **8**

work out [würk′ owt′] **230**–N

WORKPLACE [würk′ plās′] **164**–165

WORKPLACE CLOTHING

   [würk′ plās′ klō′dhĭng] **92**–93

world [würld]
    world languages [würld/ lăng/gwĭ jəz] **189**–13
    world music [würld/ myōō/zĭk] **237**–32
WORLD MAP [würld/măp/] **202**–**203**
WORLD HISTORY [würld hĭs/tə rē] **199**
worm [würm] **212**–23
worried [wür/ēd] **42**–13
wrap [răp] **72**–24
wrap [răp] **240**–F
wrench [rĕnch] **158**–22, **181**–47, **181**–48
wrestling [rĕs/lĭng] **228**–17
wrinkled [rĭng/kəld] **101**–19
wrist [rĭst] **106**–14
    wristwatch [rĭst/wäch/, –wŏch/] **94**–16
write [rīt]
    write a check [rīt/ ə chĕk/] **27**–D
    write a cover letter [rīt/ ə kŭv/ər lĕt/ər] **173**–G
    write a final draft [rīt/ ə fī/nəl drăft/] **191**–L
    write a first draft [rīt/ ə fürst/ drăft/] **191**–H
    write a note [rīt/ ə nōt/] **135**–A
    write a resume [rīt/ ə rĕ/zə mā/] **173**–F
    write a thank-you note
        [rīt/ ə thăngk/ yōō nōt/] **174**–O
    write back [rīt/ băk/] **135**–H
    write on the board [rīt/ ŏn dhə börd/] **6**–E
writer [rī/tər] **169**–64
Writing and Revising [rī/tĭng ən rĭ vī/ zĭng] **191**
Writing Process [rī/tĭng prä/sĕs] **191**
Writing Rules [rī/tĭng rōōlz] **190**
wrong way [rŏng/ wā/] **154**–2
xylophone [zī/lə fōn/] **238**–15
yard [yärd]
    courtyard [kört/ yärd/] **51**–21
    yardstick [yärd/stĭk/] **181**–16
YARD [yärd] **53**
yarn [yärn] **233**–22
year [yĭr] **20**–4, **31**–9, **31**–10
Year [yĭr] **21**
yellow [yĕl/ō] **24**–2
yesterday [yĕs/tər dā/, –dē] **20**–7
yield [yēld] **154**–9
yoga [yō/gə] **122**–4
yogurt [yō/gərt] **72**–22
young [yŭng] **32**–1
Your First License [yər fürst/ lī/səns] **137**
YOUR HEALTH [yər hĕlth/] **114**–**115**
zebra [zē/brə] **217**–33
zero [zĭr/ō] **16**
ZIP code [zĭp/ kōd/] **4**–9
zipper [zĭp/ər] **99**–25
Zones [zōnz] **19**
zoo [zōō] **222**–1
zoom lens [zōōm/ lĕnz/] **235**–23
zucchini [zōō kē/nē] **69**–25

Geographical Index

Continents

Africa [ăf′rĭ kə] **202–5**

Antarctica [ănt ärk′tĭ kə, –är′tĭ–] **202–7**

Asia [ā′zhə] **202–4**

Australia [ö strāl′yə] **202–6**

Europe [yŏŏr′əp] **202–3**

North America [nôrth′ ə mĕr′ə kə] **200–201, 202–1**

South America [sowth′ ə mĕr′ə kə] **202–2**

Countries and other locations

Afghanistan [ăf găn′ə stăn′] **203**

Albania [ăl bā′nē ə] **203**

Aleutian Islands [ə lōō′shən ī′ləndz] **200, 203**

Algeria [ăl jïr′ē ə] **203**

American Samoa [ə mĕr′ə kən sə mō′ə] **202**

Andaman Islands [ăn′də mən ī′ləndz] **203**

Angola [ăng gō′lə] **203**

Argentina [är′jən tē′nə] **202**

Armenia [är mē′nē ə] **203**

Austria [ö′strē ə] **203**

Azerbaijan [ăz′ər bī jän′] **203**

Azores [ā′zörz] **202**

Baffin Island [băf′ən ī′lənd] **200**

Bahamas [bə hä′məz] **200, 202**

Bahrain [bä rān′] **203**

Bangladesh [băng′glə dĕsh′, băng′–] **203**

Banks Island [băngks′ ī′lənd] **200**

Belarus [bĕ′lə rōōs′, byĕl′ə–] **203**

Belgium [bĕl′jəm] **203**

Belize [bə lēz′] **201, 202**

Benin [bə nĭn′, –nēn′] **203**

Bermuda Islands [bər myōō′də ī′ ləndz] **200, 202**

Bhutan [bōō tän′] **203**

Bolivia [bə lĭv′ē ə] **202**

Bosnia [băz′nē ə] **203**

Botswana [bät swä′nə] **203**

Brazil [brə zĭl′] **202**

Brunei [brōō nī′] **203**

Bulgaria [bŭl gĕr′ē ə] **203**

Burkina Faso [bər kē′nə fä′sō] **203**

Burma [bür′mə] **203**

Burundi [bōŏ rōōn′dē] **203**

Cambodia [kăm bō′dē ə] **203**

Cameroon [kăm′ə rōōn′] **203**

Canada [kăn′ə də] **200, 202**

Canary Islands [kə nĕr′ē ī′ ləndz] **203**

Cape Verde [kāp′ vürd′] **202**

Central African Republic
[sĕn′trəl ăf′rĭ kən rĭ pŭb′lĭk] **203**

Chad [chăd] **203**

Chile [chĭl′ē] **202**

China [chī′nə] **203**

Colombia [kə lŭm′bē ə] **202**

Comoros [kăm′ə rōz] **203**

Congo [kăng′gō] **203**

Cook Islands [kŏŏk′ ī′ləndz] **202**

Corsica [kôr′sĭ kə] **203**

Costa Rica [kôs′tə rē′kə, käs′–] **201, 202**

Croatia [krō ā′shə] **203**

Cuba [kyōō′bə] **201, 202**

Cyprus [sī′prəs] **203**

Czech Republic [chĕk′ rĭ pŭb′lĭk] **203**

Democratic Republic of the Congo
[dĕm′ə krăt′ĭk rĭ pŭb′lĭk əv dhə käng′gō] **203**

Denmark [dĕn′märk] **203**

Devon Island [dĕv′ən ī′lənd] **200**

Djibouti [jĭ bōō′tē] **203**

Dominican Republic [də mĭn′ĭ kən rĭ pŭb′lĭk] **201, 202**

Ecuador [ĕk′wə dör′] **202**

Egypt [ē′jĭpt] **203**

Ellesmere Island [ĕl′əs mïr′ ī′lənd] **200**

El Salvador [ĕl săl′və dör′] **201, 202**

Equatorial Guinea [ē′kwə tör′ē əl gĭn′ē, ĕk′wə–] **203**

Eritrea [ĕr′ə trē′ə] **203**

Estonia [ĕ stō′nē ə] **203**

Ethiopia [ē′thē ō′pē ə] **203**

Federated States of Micronesia
[fĕ′də rā′təd stāts′ əv mī′krə nē′zhə] **203**

Fiji [fē′jē] **203**

Finland [fĭn′lənd] **203**

France [frăns] **203**

Franz Josef Land [fränz′ yō′səf länd′] **203**

French Guiana [frĕnch′ gē än′ə, –ä′nə] **202**

French Polynesia [frĕnch′ păl′ə nē′zhə] **202**

Gabon [gă bōn′] **203**

Galápagos Islands [gə lä′pə gōs ī′ləndz] **202**

Gambia [găm′bē ə] **203**

Georgia [jör′jə] **203**

Germany [jür′mə nē] **203**

Ghana [gä′nə] **203**

Greater Antilles [grā′tər ăn tĭl′ēz] **201**

Greece [grēs] **203**

Greenland [grēn′lənd, –lănd′] **200, 202**

Guam [gwäm] **203**

Guatemala [gwä′tə mä′lə] **201, 202**

Guinea [gĭn′ē] **203**

Guinea-Bissau [gĭn′ē bĭ sow′] **203**

Guyana [gī än′ə] **202**

Haiti [hā′tē] **201, 202**

Hawaiian Islands [hə wī′ən ī′ləndz] **200, 202**

Hispaniola [hĭs′pən yō′lə] **201**

Honduras [hän dōŏr′əs] **201, 202**

Hong Kong [häng′ käng′] **203**

Hungary [hŭng′gə rē] **203**

Iceland [īs′lənd] **203**

India [ĭn′dē ə] **203**

Indonesia [ĭn′də nē′zhə] **203**

Iran [ĭ rän′, ĭ răn′] **203**

Iraq [ĭ räk′, ĭ răk′] **203**

Ireland [īr′lənd] **203**

Israel [ĭz′rē əl, –rā–] **203**

Italy [ĭt′l ē] **203**

Ivory Coast [īv′rē kōst′] **203**

Jamaica [jə mā′kə] **201, 202**

Japan [jə păn′] **203**

Jordan [jör′dn] **203**

Kazakhstan [kä′zäk stän′] **203**

Kenya [kĕn′yə, kēn′–] **203**

Kiribati [kïr′ə bäs′] **203**

Kuwait [kōō wāt′] **203**

Kyrgyzstan [kïr′gĭ stän′, –stän′] **203**

Laos [lows, lä′ōs] **203**

Latvia [lăt′vē ə] **203**

Lebanon [lĕb′ə nən, –nän′] **203**

Lesotho [lə sō′tō, –sōō′tōō] **203**

Lesser Antilles [lĕ′sər ăn tĭl′ēz] **201, 202**

Liberia [lī bïr′ē ə] **203**

Libya [lĭb′ē ə] **203**

Lithuania [lĭth′ōō ā′nē ə] **203**

Luxembourg [lŭk′səm bürg′] **203**

Macedonia [măs′ə dō′nē ə] **203**

Madagascar [măd′ə găs′kər] **203**

Madeira Islands [mə dïr′ə ī′ləndz] **203**

Malawi [mə lä′wē] **203**

Malaysia [mə lā′zhə] **203**

Maldives [möl′dēvz, măl′–] **203**

Mali [mä′lē] **203**

Malta [möl′tə] **203**

Marshall Islands [mär′shəl ī′ləndz] **203**

Mauritania [mör′ə tā′nē ə] **203**

Mauritius [mö rĭsh′əs] **203**

Mexico [mĕk′sĭ kō′] **200, 201, 202**

Moldova [möl dō′və, măl–] **203**

Monaco [măn′ə kō′] **203**

Mongolia [mäng gō′lē ə] **203**

Montenegro [măn′tə nē′grō, –nĕ′–] **203**

Morocco [mə räk′ō] **203**

Mozambique [mō′zəm bēk′] **203**

Namibia [nə mĭb′ē ə] **203**

Nepal [nə pöl′, –päl′] **203**

Netherlands [nĕdh′ər ləndz] **203**

New Caledonia [nōō′ kăl′ə dō′nē ə] **203**

New Zealand [nōō′ zē′lənd] **203**

Nicaragua [nĭk′ə rä′gwə] **201, 202**

Niger [nī′jər, nē zhĕr′] **203**

Nigeria [nī jïr′ē ə] **203**

Northern Mariana Islands
[nördh′ərn mär′rē ä′nə ī′ləndz] **203**

North Korea [nôrth′ kə rē′ə] **203**

Norway [nör′wā] **203**

Oman [ō män′] **203**

Pakistan [păk′ə stăn′] **203**

Palau [pə low′] **203**

Panama [păn′ə mä′] **201, 202**

Papua New Guinea [păp′yōō ə nōō′ gĭn′ē] **203**

Paraguay [păr′ə gwī′, –gwä′] **202**

Peru [pə rōō′] **202**

Philippines [fĭl′ə pēnz′, fĭl′ə pēnz′] **203**

Poland [pō′lənd] **203**

Portugal [pör′chə gəl] **203**

Puerto Rico [pwĕr′tə rē′kō, pör′tə–] **201, 202**

Qatar [kä′tär, kə tär′] **203**

Romania [rō mā′nē ə, rōō–] **203**

Russia [rŭsh′ə] **203**

Rwanda [rōō än′də] **203**

Samoa [sə mō′ə] **202**

Saudi Arabia [sow′dē ə rā′bē ə, sö′dē–] **203**

Senegal [sĕn′ə göl′, –gäl′] **203**

Serbia [sür′bē ə] **203**

Seychelles [sā shĕlz′, –shĕl′] **203**

Sierra Leone [sē ĕr′ə lē ōn′, –lē ō′nē] **203**

Singapore [sĭng′ə pör′] **203**

Slovakia [slō vä′kē ə] **203**

Slovenia [slō vē′nē ə] **203**

Society Islands [sə sī′ə tē ī′ləndz] **202**

Solomon Islands [säl′ə mən ī′ləndz] **203**

Somalia [sə mä/lē ə] **203**
South Africa [sowth/ ăf/rĭ kə] **203**
South Georgia [sowth/ jör/jə] **202**
South Korea [sowth/ kə rē/ə] **203**
Spain [spān] **203**
Sri Lanka [srē/ läng/kə, shrē/–] **203**
Sudan [sōō dăn/] **203**
Suriname [sŏŏr/ə nä/mə] **202**
Svalbard [sväl/bärd] **203**
Swaziland [swä/zē länd/] **203**
Sweden [swēd/n] **203**
Switzerland [swĭt/sər lənd] **203**
Syria [sĭr/ē ə] **203**
Tahiti [tə hē/tē] **202**
Taiwan [tī/wän/] **203**
Tajikistan [tä jĭk/ə stän/, –stän/] **203**
Tanzania [tăn/zə nē/ə] **203**
Tasmania [tăz mā/nē ə] **203**
Thailand [tī/lănd/, –lənd] **203**
Togo [tō/gō] **203**
Tonga [täng/gə] **202**
Tunisia [tōō nē/zhə] **203**
Turkey [tür/kē] **203**
Turkmenistan [türk mĕn/ə stän/, –stän/] **203**
Uganda [yōō găn/də] **203**
Ukraine [yōō/krān, yōō krān/] **203**
United Arab Emirates [yōō nī/təd är/əb ĕm/ər əts] **203**
United Kingdom [yōō nī/təd kĭng/dəm] **203**
United States of America
    [yōō nī/təd stāts/ əv ə mĕr/ə kə] **200, 202**
Uruguay [yŏŏr/ə gwī/, –gwā/] **202**
Uzbekistan [ŏŏz bĕk/ə stän/, –stän/] **203**
Vanuatu [vä/nōō ä/tōō] **203**
Venezuela [vĕn/ə zwā/lə] **202**
Victoria Island [vĭk/tör ē ə ī/lənd] **200**
Vietnam [vē/ĕt näm/, –näm/] **203**
Wake Island [wāk/ ī/lənd] **203**
Western Sahara [wĕs/tərn sə hăr/ə] **203**
Yemen [yĕm/ən] **203**
Zambia [zăm/bē ə] **203**
Zanzibar [zăn/zə bär] **203**
Zimbabwe [zĭm bäb/wā] **203**

Bodies of water
Arctic Ocean [ärk/tĭk ō/shən] **200, 203**
Atlantic Ocean [ət lăn/ tĭk ō/shən] **200, 202–203**
Baffin Bay [băf/ən bā/] **200, 202**
Baltic Sea [böl/tĭk sē/] **203**
Beaufort Sea [bō/fərt sē/] **200**
Bering Sea [bër/ĭng sē/, bĭr/–] **200**
Black Sea [blăk/ sē/] **203**
Caribbean Sea [kăr/ə bē/ən sē/, kə rĭb/ē ən–] **201**
Caspian Sea [kăs/pē ən sē/] **203**
Coral Sea [kör/əl sē/] **203**
Gulf of Alaska [gŭlf/ əv ə lăs/kə] **200, 202**
Gulf of California [gŭlf/ əv kăl/ə förn/yə] **200**
Gulf of Mexico [gŭlf/ əv mĕk/sĭ kō/] **200, 202**
Hudson Bay [hŭd/sən bā/] **200, 202**
Indian Ocean [ĭn/dē ən ō/shən] **203**
Labrador Sea [lăb/rə dör/ sē/] **200**
Mediterranean Sea [mĕd/ə tə rā/nē ən sē/] **203**

North Atlantic Ocean [nörth/ ət lăn/tĭk ō/shən] **202**
North Pacific Ocean [nörth/ pə sĭf/ĭk ō/shən] **202, 203**
North Sea [nörth/ sē/] **203**
Pacific Ocean [pə sĭf/ĭk ō/shən] **200, 202, 203**
Philippine Sea [fĭl/ə pēn/ sē/] **203**
Red Sea [rĕd/ sē/] **203**
South Atlantic Ocean [sowth/ ət lăn/tĭk ō/shən] **203**
Southern Ocean [sŭdh/ərn ō/shən] **203**
South Pacific Ocean [sowth/ pə sĭf/ĭk ō/shən] **202, 203**

The United States of America
Capital: Washington, D.C. (District of Columbia)
    [wä/shĭng tən dē/sē/, wö/–] **200**

Regions of the United States
Mid–Atlantic States [mĭd/ət lăn/tĭk stāts/] **201–10**
Midwest [mĭd/wĕst/] **201–9**
New England [nōō/ ĭng/glənd] **201–11**
Pacific States [pə sĭf/ĭk stāts/] **201–7**
Rocky Mountain States [räk/ē mown/tn stāts/] **201–8**
South [sowth] **201–13**
Southeast [sowth/ēst/] **201–13**
Southwest [sowth/wĕst/] **201–12**
West Coast [wĕst/ kōst/] **201–7**

States of the United States
Alabama [ăl/ə băm/ə] **200**
Alaska [ə lăs/kə] **200, 202**
Arizona [ăr/ə zō/nə] **200**
Arkansas [är/kən sö/] **200**
California [kăl/ə förn/yə] **200**
Colorado [kăl/ə răd/ō, –ra/dō] **200**
Connecticut [kə nĕt/ĭ kət] **200**
Delaware [dĕl/ə wër/] **200**
Florida [flör/ə də, flär/–] **200**
Georgia [jör/jə] **200**
Hawaii [hə wī/ē] **200**
Idaho [ī/də hō/] **200**
Illinois [ĭl/ə noy/] **200**
Indiana [ĭn/dē ăn/ə] **200**
Iowa [ī/ə wə] **200**
Kansas [kăn/zəs] **200**
Kentucky [kən tŭk/ē] **200**
Louisiana [lōō ē/zē ăn/ə] **200**
Maine [mān] **200**
Maryland [mĕr/ə lənd] **200**
Massachusetts [măs/ə chōō/səts] **200**
Michigan [mĭsh/ĭ gən] **200**
Minnesota [mĭn/ə sō/tə] **200**
Mississippi [mĭs/ə sĭp/ē] **200**
Missouri [mə zŏŏr/ē, –zŏŏr/ə] **200**
Montana [män tăn/ə] **200**
Nebraska [nə brăs/kə] **200**
Nevada [nə văd/ə, –vä/də] **200**
New Hampshire [nōō/ hămp/shər] **200**
New Jersey [nōō/ jür/zē] **200**
New Mexico [nōō/ mĕk/sĭ kō/] **200**
New York [nōō/ york/] **200**
North Carolina [nörth/ kăr/ə lī/nə] **200**
North Dakota [nörth/ də kō/tə] **200**
Ohio [ō hī/ō] **200**
Oklahoma [ō/klə hō/mə] **200**
Oregon [ör/ĭ gən, –găn/, är/–] **200**

Pennsylvania [pĕn/səl vān/yə] **200**
Rhode Island [rōd/ ī/lənd] **200**
South Carolina [sowth/ kăr/ə lī/nə] **200**
South Dakota [sowth/ də kō/tə] **200**
Tennessee [tĕn/ə sē/] **200**
Texas [tĕk/səs] **200**
Utah [yōō/tö, –tä] **200**
Vermont [vər mänt/] **200**
Virginia [vər jĭn/yə] **200**
Washington [wä/shĭng tən, wö/–] **200**
West Virginia [wĕst/ vər jĭn/yə] **200**
Wisconsin [wĭs kän/sən] **200**
Wyoming [wī ō/mĭng] **200**

Canada
Capital: Ottawa [ät/ə wə] **201**

Regions of Canada
British Columbia [brĭt/ĭsh kə lŭm/bē ə] **201–2**
Maritime Provinces [mĕr/ə tīm präv/ən səz] **201–6**
Northern Canada [nör/dhərn kăn/ə də] **201–1**
Ontario [än tër/ē ō/] **201–4**
Prairie Provinces [prër/ē präv/ən səz] **201–3**
Québec [kwĭ bĕk/] **201–5**

Provinces of Canada
Alberta [ăl bür/tə] **200**
British Columbia [brĭt/ĭsh kə lŭm/bē ə] **200**
Manitoba [măn/ə tō/bə] **200**
New Brunswick [nōō/ brŭnz/wĭk] **200**
Newfoundland and Labrador
    [nōō/fən lənd ən lă/brə dör/] **200**
Northwest Territories [nörth/wĕst/ tër/ə tör/ēz] **200**
Nova Scotia [nō/və skō/shə] **200**
Nunavut [nōō/nə vōōt/] **200**
Ontario [än tër/ē ō/] **200**
Prince Edward Island [prĭns/ ĕd/wərd ī/lənd] **200**
Québec [kwĭ bĕk/] **200**
Saskatchewan [sə skăch/ə wən, –wän/] **200**
Yukon [yōō/kän] **200**

Mexico
Capital: Mexico (City) [mĕk/sĭ kō/ (sĭt/ē)] **201**

Regions of Mexico
Chiapas Highlands [chē ä/pəs hī/ləndz] **201–18**
Gulf Coastal Plain [gŭlf/ kō/stəl plān/] **201–16**
Pacific Northwest [pə sĭf/ĭk nörth/wĕst] **201–14**
Plateau of Mexico [plă tō/ əv mĕk/sĭ kō/] **201–15**
Southern Uplands [sŭdh/ərn ŭp/ləndz] **201–17**
Yucatan Peninsula
    [yōō/kə tän/ pə nĭn/sə lə, yōō/kə tän/–] **201–19**

States of Mexico
Aguascalientes [ä/gwəs kăl yĕn/tās] **201**
Baja California Norte [bä/hä kăl/ə förn/yə nör/tā] **200**
Baja California Sur [bä/hä kăl/ə förn/yə sŏŏr/] **200**
Campeche [käm pā/chā, käm pē/chē] **201**
Chiapas [chē ä/pəs] **200**
Chihuahua [chĭ wä/wä, –wə] **200**
Coahuila [kō/ə wē/lə] **200**
Colima Michoacán [kə lē/mə mē/chō ə kän/] **201**
Distrito Federal [dĭ strē/tō fĕd/ə räl/] **201**
Durango [dŏŏ răng/gō, –räng/–] **201**

283

Geographical Index

1 cent **26**–1
10 cents **26**–3
10 pour cent **17**–12
100 pour cent **17**–8
2 x 4 (deux par quatre) **181**–19
25 cents **26**–4
25 pour cent **17**–11
4 juillet **22**–13
5 cents **26**–2
50 cents **26**–5
50 pour cent **17**–10
75 pour cent **17**–9
abat-jour **58**–26
abdomen **107**–27
abeille **214**–252
abri **52**–13
abricots **68**–12
accepter des excuses **12**–G
accepter une invitation **12**–I
accessoires d'aspirateur **61**–11
ACCESSOIRES DE NETTOYAGE **61**
accident d'automobile **144**–2
accompagner les enfants à l'école **38**–G
accordéon **238**–19
accusé **141**–5
achat d'une maison **49**
acheter **27**–G, **94**–A
acheter des produits recyclés **219**–D
ACHETER ET ENTRETENIR UNE
    VOITURE **157**
acheter sur des sites Web
    sécurisés **143**–H
acheter une collation **11**–K
acheter une maison **41**–M
acheter une voiture d'occasion **157**
acte de naissance **40**–1
acte notarié **41**–9
acteur (actrice) **166**–2
action **237**–19
Action de grâce **22**–17
activiste **199**–17
ACTIVITÉS DE PLEIN AIR **226**
ACTIVITÉS QUOTIDIENNES **38**–39
acupuncture **122**–2
adaptateur **234**–15
adjoint(e) administratif (ve) **166**–3
administrateur **120**–13
administrateurs **5**
admirateur **229**–4
adolescent **31**–11
adresse **4**–5
adresse de retour **134**–21
adresse postale **134**–22
adresse URL **197**–4
adresse Web **197**–4
adresser l'enveloppe **135**–B
adresser le courriel **197**–C
ADULTES ET ENFANTS **30**–31

adversaire **139**–30
aérobic **122**–5
aéroport **151**–10
AÉROPORT **160**–161
affections et maladies graves **111**
affiche **102**–1
affiche de disponibilité **50**–7
Afrique **202**–5
âge **32**–3
âge moyen **32**–2
agence de voyage **131**–14
agent de l'AST **160**–5
agent de maîtrise **175**–4
agent des douanes **161**–17
agent(e) de bord **161**–12
aggloméré de bois **181**–20
agneau **70**
agrafe et œil **99**–27
agrafer **171**–F
agrafes **183**–29
agrafeuse **183**–28
agression **142**–3
aide au service des tables **185**–15
aide aux soins à domicile **167**–32
aider des malades **170**–B
aider les personnes handicapées **147**–G
aider un camarade de classe **8**–J
aider un client **95**–D
aide-serveur **83**–12
aigle **214**–9
aigre **84**–4
aiguille **98**–17, **100**–10, **210**–10
aiguilles à tricoter **233**–23
ail **69**–30
aile **214**–1
ailes **70**–20
aimant **195**–36
aire de restauration **131**–15
aire et volume **193**
ajouter **192**–A
ajouter du liquide de
    refroidissement **157**–I
ajouter le détergent **101**–B
ajouter les légumes **77**–N
album de photos **235**–31
album de photos numériques **235**–32
algèbre **192**–16
aliments emballés **146**–10
aliments en boîte **72**
aliments pour animaux **72**–5
aliments pour bébés **37**–4
allaiter **36**–B
allée **53**–8
aller à l'épicerie **38**–L
aller à l'université **41**–I
aller à la ligne **196**–D
aller chercher les enfants **38**–M
aller chez le médecin **114**–A

aller dans les rues bien éclairées **143**–B
aller en classe **38**–J
aller en prison **141**–G
aller se coucher **39**–Y
aller simple **152**–16
aller tout droit sur Elm **155**–A
aller travailler en voiture **38**–I
aller travailler **38**–I
allergies **111**–8
aller-retour **152**–17
alligator **213**–36
allonger le pantalon **100**–C
allumage **159**–33
allumer les lumières **11**–B
allumettes **146**–16, **226**–21
alphabet **7**–13
ambulance **116**–1, **121**–34
ambulancier paramédical **116**–2
ambulateur **113**–11
AMÉNAGEMENT DU PAYSAGE ET
    JARDINAGE **176**
Amérique du Nord **202**–1
AMÉRIQUE DU NORD ET AMÉRIQUE
    CENTRALE **200**–201
Amérique du Sud **202**–2
amidon **101**–12
amour **237**–16
amphibiens **212**
ampoule **110**–15
analgésique **113**–26
analyse sanguine **121**–30
ananas **68**–23
ancien **199**–1
âne **215**–3
anémone de mer **212**–24
anesthésiste **121**–35
angine streptococcique **111**–4
angle à 90° **193**–26
angle aigu **193**–28
angle droit **193**–26
angle obtus **193**–27
angles **193**
anguille **212**–12
animalerie **130**–6
animaux de compagnie **215**
animaux de la ferme **215**
ANIMAUX DOMESTIQUES ET
    RONGEURS **215**
animaux en peluche **59**–15
animaux marins **212**
anneau de dentition **37**–25
année **20**–4
anniversaire **22**–3
anniversaire de naissance **22**–1
annonce sur Internet **48**–1
antenne **14**–9

antenne parabolique **53**–6
antiacide **113**–28
antilope **217**–35
août **21**–32
apostrophe **190**–16
appareil auditif **115**–10
appareil de chauffage **159**–40
appareil de chauffage est cassé **63**–15
appareil orthodontique **119**–6
appareil photo numérique **235**–19
appareil radio émetteur
    récepteur **179**–22
appareil-photo 35 mm **235**–21
appareil-photo à pellicule **235**–21
appartement en copropriété **52**–5
appartement meublé **48**–3
appartement non meublé **48**–4
APPARTEMENTS **50**–51
appel international **15**–35
appel interurbain **15**–32
appel local **15**–31
appel téléphonique par Internet **14**–20
appeler le gérant **48**–A
appeler vos contacts en dehors
    de l'État **147**–L
applaudir **148**–B
application **99**–31
appliquer **109**–P
apporter **240**–E
apporter votre curriculum vitae et
    votre pièce d'identité **174**–D
apprendre à conduire **40**–E
apprendre des mots nouveaux **8**
appuyer sur « fin » **15**–D
appuyez sur « envoyer » **15**–B
après une urgence **147**
après-midi **18**–17
après-rasage (lotion) **109**–30
après-shampooing **108**–11
aquarelle **233**–21
aquarium **222**–7
araignée **214**–29
arbitre **229**–6
arbre de Noël **239**–16
arbres **208**–1
ARBRES ET PLANTES **210**
arc **231**–6
architecte **166**–5
architecte paysagiste **176**–5
archiviste médicale **168**–39
ARGENT **26**
armée **138**–14, **199**–11
armoire **54**–1
armoire à pharmacie **57**–22
armoire de rangement des fournitures
    de bureau **182**–1
arracher une dent **119**–F
arranger les meubles **49**–Q

arrêt **154**–1
arrêt d'autobus **129**–16, **151**–13, **152**
arrêter un suspect **141**–A
arrêtez-vous au coin **155**–D
arriver **160**–K
arroser (les plantes) **176**–F
arroseur **53**–22
artère **107**–36
arthrite **111**–16
artichauts **69**–22
ARTICLES DE SPORT **231**
articulation **106**–17
artiste **166**–6
arts **189**–15
arts du langage **189**–9
arts martiaux **228**–11
ascenseur **50**–9, **131**–21, **184**–9
Asie **202**–4
aspect physique **32**
asperges **69**–26
aspirateur **61**–10
assembler **175**–C
asseyez-vous **6**–F
assiette **55**–1
assiette à pain et beurre **83**–19
assiette à salade **83**–20
assistance annuaire **14**–22
assistant du professeur **5**–16
assistante dentaire **119**–2, **167**–22
assistante sociale **169**–57
assouplisseur textile en feuilles **101**–5
asthme **111**–9
astronaute **205**–17
astronome **205**–22
atelier de retouche **100**
athlétisme **228**–18
atlas **133**–8
atome **195**–28
ATS (appareil de télécommunication
     pour malentendants) **15**–26
attelle **117**–14
attendre le changement de feu **128**–B
atterrir **160**–K
attraper **230**–D
attrayant(e) **32**–13
aubergines **69**–23
audiologiste **115**–9
auditorium **5**–18
aujourd'hui **20**–5
Australie **202**–6
auteur **133**–15, **169**–64
autobus **128**–9, **151**–14
autobus d'écoliers **156**–21
autochtones d'Amérique du
     Nord **198**–3
auto-collant **102**–3
automne **21**–39
autoroute **155**–9

autres instruments **238**
auxiliaire médical **168**–47
avalanche **145**–18
avaler du poison **116**–J
avance rapide **235**–D
avant une urgence **146**
avant-bras **106**–13
aventure **237**–19
avertissements médicaux **112**
aveugle **32**–11
avion **150**–8
avocat de la défense **141**–4
avocat(e) **168**–36
avocats **84**–6
avoir 18 ans ou plus **140**–G
avoir des gelures **116**–G
avoir faim **42**–5
avoir la nausée **110**–D
avoir mal **42**–11
avoir peur **43**–23
avoir soif **42**–2
avoir sommeil **42**–3
avoir un bébé **41**–L
avoir une conversation **11**–L
avoir une crise cardiaque **116**–D
avoir une réaction allergique **116**–E
avoir un pneu à plat **162**–F
avoir un pneu crevé **162**–F
avril **21**–28
babouin **217**–31
bac **160**–6
bac à ordures **51**–23
bac à peinture **181**–51
bac à sable **224**–15
bac de recyclage **61**–2
bacon **70**–11, **80**–1
badge **93**–21
badminton **228**–6
bagage **161**–18
bagels **73**–40
bague **95**–40
bague bon marché **23**–20
bague coûteuse **23**–19
baie **204**–9
baies mélangées **81**–36
baignoire **57**–2
bail **51**–28
bain-marie **78**–8
balai **61**–16
balai-éponge **61**–6
balance **72**–3, **195**–41
balançoires **224**–11
balayer le plancher **60**–J
balayette **57**–20
balcon **51**–20
baleine **213**–29
balle **59**–12
balle de base-ball **231**–18

balle de basket-ball **231**–4
balle de volley-ball **231**–3
ballon **59**–12
ballon de football **231**–12
ballon de football américain **231**–21
ballons **44**–4
bananes **68**–2
bananes mûres **68**–30
bananes pourries **68**–32
bananes vertes **68**–31
banc **224**–10
bandage élastique **117**–12
bandana **92**–16
bandeau serre-tête **90**–3
banlieue **52**–2
bannière **44**–1
banque **124**–5
BANQUE **132**
bar (eau salée) **212**–6
barbe **33**–6
bardeaux **178**–20
barre d'appui **57**–11
barre de défilement **197**–15
barre de menus **197**–1
barrette **108**–20
barrière de sécurité **50**–16
bas **91**–17
bas du dos **107**–29
base **193**–45
base-ball **229**–9
basket-ball **229**–8
basse **238**–8
bassin **107**–50
bassin hygiénique **121**–23
basson **238**–4
bâtons de ski **231**–25
batte de base-ball **231**–14
batterie **158**–20, **238**–16
batteur à œufs **78**–20
battre le mélange **77**–S
bavette **37**–5
beau-frère **34**–17
beau-père **34**–11
beau-père (adoptif) **35**–25
bébé **31**–7
bec **214**–3
bec Bensen **195**–37
bécher **195**–39
beige **24**–18
beignerie **129**–17
beignet **79**–15
belle-mère **34**–10
belle-mère (adoptive) **35**–26
belle-sœur **34**–16
bénévole **121**–17
béquilles **113**–10
berceau **59**–20
bercer **36**–D

berceuse **37**–21
berline 4 portes **156**–1
bétail **177**–15, **177**–21
béton **178**–10
betteraves **69**–5
beurre **66**–6
biberon **37**–1
bibliographe **133**–9
bibliothécaire **133**–1
BIBLIOTHÈQUE **133**
bibliothèque **5**–17, **7**–10, **125**–15
bicyclette **129**–22, **151**–15
bidon **226**–24
biffer le mot **9**–R
bifteck **70**–2, **81**–24
bifteck grillé **76**–3
bijouterie **130**–2
billard **228**–2
billet **152**–15
billet électronique **161**–19
billets **26**
bioénergie **218**–9
biographie **133**–13
biologie **194**
biologique **84**–2
biologiste **194**–2
biomasse **218**–9
biscuits **73**–38, **80**–6
bison **216**–6
blanc **24**–14
blasé(e) **43**–25
blattes **63**–26
blazer **92**–12
blé **177**–2
bleu **24**–3
bleu éclatant **24**–12
bleu foncé **24**–10
bleu marine **28**–5
bleu pâle **24**–11
blizzard **13**–23, **145**–13
bloc format légal **183**–38
bloc-piles **235**–26
blocs **59**–19
bloquer **230**–F
blouse **93**–26
blouse de
     chirurgien(ne) **93**–37, **121**–38
blouse de laboratoire **93**–33
blouse fantaisie **97**–34
blouse simple **97**–33
blues **237**–22
bocal de confiture **74**–14
bocaux **74**–2
bœuf **70**
bœuf à ragoût **70**–3
bœuf en conserve **71**–22
boeuf haché **70**–4
bœuf salé **71**–22

bœuf sauté **76**–6
boire **11**–J
boire des liquides **114**–C
bois **178**–17, **238**
bois de charpente **178**–17
boisson gazeuse **73**–34, **79**–11
boissons **73**
boîte à emporter **82**–5
boîte à fusibles **62**–13
boîte aux lettres **53**–1, **128**–13, **135**–12
boîte de céréales **74**–18
boîte de haricots **74**–15
boîte de nuit **223**–12
boîte de recherche **197**–5
boîte de texte **197**–13
boîte légère **23**–14
boîte lourde **23**–13
boîte postale **135**–9
boîtes **74**–6
boîtes aux lettres **50**–11
boîtes de conserve **74**–3, **146**–9
bol **55**–2
bol à mélanger **78**–31
bol à soupe **83**–21
bon chien **23**–17
bonbon **239**–12
bonnet chirurgical **93**–35
bonnet de chirurgien(ne) **121**–37
bonnet de douche **108**–1
bonnet de ski **90**–11
bord de trottoir **129**–21
bordereau de dépôt **132**–4
bordure **129**–21
bordure de protection **59**–4
bosse **217**–51
bottes **95**–28
bottes à embout d'acier **92**–6
bottes de pluie **90**–20
bottes de randonnée **95**–31
bottes de sécurité **179**–20
bouche **104**–7, **106**
bouche d'incendie **129**–27
boucher (bouchère) **166**–13
boucher une carie **119**–E
bouchons d'oreilles **179**–15
boucle **99**–28
boucle de ceinture **94**–20
boucles d'oreilles **95**–37
boucles d'oreilles pour oreilles
    percées **95**–363
bougeoir **56**–21
bouillote **113**–15
boulanger (boulangère) **166**–10
boulangerie **127**–19
boule de bowling **231**–5
boule de quilles **231**–5
bouleau **210**–7
boulettes de viande **81**–27

bouleversé(e) **43**–28
boulon **180**–35
boulon de scellement **180**–38
bouquet **211**–28
bourgeon **211**–7
bout **94**–23
bouteille d'eau **74**–13
bouteille de plongée **225**–5
bouteilles **74**–1
boutique de cadeaux **184**–5
bouton **99**–24
bouton d'appel **121**–28
bouton de réglage
    macrométrique **194**–24
bouton de réglage
    micrométrique **194**–22
bouton manque **97**–40
bouton Précédent **197**–2
bouton Suivant **197**–3
bowling **222**–4, **228**–3
box **82**–4
boxe **228**–4
boyau **53**–21
bracelet d'urgence médicale **117**–3
bracelets **95**–9
brancard **121**–33
branche **210**–2
branche maîtresse **210**–3
branchies **212**–2
bras **105**–14, **194**–23
bras, la main et les doigts **106**
break **156**–7
bretelles **94**–1
briques **178**–12
brocoli **69**–13
broderie **233**–24
brosse **33**–22, **108**–14
brosse à dents **57**–23, **109**–22
brosse à effacer **7**–19
brosse à récurer **61**–20
brosser…les cheveux **108**–I
brouette **176**–3
broyeur d'ordures **54**–7
bruit **64**–5
brûleur **54**–19
brûleur Bensen **195**–37
brumeux **13**–20
brun **24**–17
brun clair **24**–18
budget **186**–3
buffet **55**–22, **55**–24, **185**–10
buffet de crudités **79**–24
bulbe **211**–2
bulldozer **178**–6
BUREAU **182**–183
bureau **164**–3, **182**–9
bureau de location **51**
bureau principal **5**–12

burin **181**–55
burrito **79**–9
c'est trop grand **97**–38
c'est trop petit **97**–37
cabine **156**–16
câblage **186**–7
câble **196**–13
câbles de démarrage **158**–21
cache-maillot **90**–25
cachemire **96**–26, **98**–4
cachet de la poste **134**–24
cactus **210**–21
cadeau **240**–3
cadre **182**–5
cadre à photo **58**–4
cadre de lit **58**–18
cafards **63**–26
café **73**–33, **81**–37
café déca **81**–38
café-restaurant **126**–11
cafétéria **5**–14
cafetière électrique **54**–11
cage à poules **224**–14
cage thoracique **107**–48
cahier à 3 anneaux **7**–27
cahier à spirale **7**–29
cahier d'examen **10**–1
cahier d'exercices **7**–26
caisse **27**–10, **73**–15
caisse automatique **73**–10, **133**–10
caissier (caissière) **73**–13,
    132–1, **166**–15
calcul **192**–19
calculatrice **17**–6, **183**–5
calculer **17**–B
caleçon boxeur **91**–4
caleçon-combinaison **91**–3
caleçons **91**–5
CALENDRIER **20**–21
CALENDRIER D'ÉVÈNEMENTS **22**
calmar **212**–7
cambriolage **142**–2
caméra de sécurité **50**–19
caméscope **235**–24
camion **150**–6
camion à benne **156**–19
camion à ordures **127**–22
camion citerne **156**–20
camion de déménagement **156**–18
camion de pompiers **144**–10
camion léger **156**–12
camion semi-remorque **156**–15
camionnette de camping **156**–9
camisole **91**–21
campagne **52**–4
campagne électorale **139**–29
camping **226**–5
campus **5**

canard **70**–18, **214**–12
cancer **111**–10
canette **98**–21
canne **113**–16
canne à pêche **226**–18
canne en sucre **239**–17
canoë **226**–3
canotage **226**–1
canyon **204**–17
capitale de l'État **139**–22
Capitole **138**–1
capot **158**–4
capsule **113**–23
cardigan **88**–2
cardiologue **120**–3
carie **119**–7
carnet de chèques **132**–12
carnet de rendez-vous **183**–48
carnet de timbres **134**–18
carottes **69**–3
carpette **58**–22
carré **193**–30
carré de courtepointe **232**–15
carreau est fissuré **62**–4
carreaux **96**–24, **233**–29
carrelage **57**–12
carreler **178**–C
carrousel à bagages **161**–23
carte **239**–5
carte (géographique) **7**–12
carte d'abonnement **152**–11
carte d'appel **14**–15
carte d'assurance **136**–8
carte d'assurance maladie **118**–3
carte d'embarquement **161**–20
carte de mesures de sécurité **161**–26
carte de retrait **132**–15
carte de sécurité sociale **40**–5
carte de vœux **134**–15
carte du club automobile **162**–4
CARTE DU MONDE **202**–203
carte Internet **155**–12
carte mémoire **235**–20
carte mère **196**–5
carte météorologique **13**
carte postale **134**–16
carte verte **40**–2
cartes **155**
cartes de base-ball **232**–2
carton d'œufs **74**–16
cartons **74**–4
cartouche d'encre **183**–45
cascade **204**–2
caserne de pompiers **125**–12
casier **5**–11
casier de rangement **50**–17
casque **14**–13, **92**–1, **93**–23, **179**–9
casque antichocs **92**–9

casque de football américain **231**–19
casque sans fil **14**–14
casquette de base-ball **86**–5
casser 2 œufs dans un bol pour
    four micro-ondes **77**–Q
casserole **54**–16, **78**–6, **78**–25
casserole de légumes et de tofu au
    fromage **77**
casse-tête **59**–17
cassette vidéo **133**–18, **240**–A
castor **216**–9
catalogue en ligne **133**–11
causerie **236**–4
causeuse **56**–1
cavernes **220**–7
ceinture à outils **92**–3
ceinture de sécurité **159**–52
ceinture de soutien dorsal **179**–18
ceinture montée **100**–5
ceintures **94**–6
célébrer **206**–C
céleri **69**–9
cellule **194**–4
celsius **13**–2
cent **16**
cent dollars **26**–12
cent mille **16**
cent un **16**
centième **16**
centimètre [cm] **17**–14
centre commercial **126**–7
CENTRE COMMERCIAL **130**–131
centre d'éducation (de formation)
    des adultes **188**–8
CENTRE D'INITIATION À LA
    NATURE **208**–209
centre de culture physique **126**–10
centre de divertissement **56**–5
centre de formation continue
    (permanente) **188**–8
centre de garde d'enfants **129**–30
centre de manucure **130**–3
centre de reprographie **129**–18
centre de ressources
    professionnelles **172**–9
centre postal automatisé **135**–10
centre universitaire de premier
    cycle **127**–17
centre universitaire de 1er cycle **188**–6
CENTRE-VILLE **124**–125
cercle **193**–34
céréales chaudes **80**–9
cérémonie **206**–6
cerf-volant **225**–2
cerises **68**–11, **210**–20
certificat de décès **41**–11
certificat de naturalisation **40**–6
certificat de publication des bans **41**–8

cerveau **107**–34
cette semaine **20**–19
chaîne **95**–33, **180**–41
chaîne de montage **175**–6
chaîne de montagnes **204**–15
chaîne de sûreté **51**–33
chaîne stéréo **56**–8
chaise **7**–11
chaise de plage **225**–22
chaise de salle à manger **55**–8
chaise dure **23**–5
chaise haute **37**–6, **82**–3
chaise moelleuse **23**–6
chaise pliante **102**–5
chaise roulante **113**–9
chambre **46**–2, **184**–13
CHAMBRE À COUCHER **58**
chambre d'hôpital **121**
chambre des enfants **47**–9
CHAMBRE DES ENFANTS **59**
Chambre des représentants **138**–3
chambre du bébé **47**–10
chambre forte **132**–6
chameau **217**–38
champ **177**–7
champignons **69**–27
chandail **88**–3
chandail à col échancré **96**–10
chandail à col en v **96**–8
chandail à col rond **96**–7
chandail à col roulé **96**–9
chandelle **56**–20
changer **148**–C
changer les draps **60**–P
changer une couche **36**–G
chanter une berceuse **36**–O
chanter une chanson **238**–B
chantier de construction **126**–2
chapeau **90**–1
chapeau de cowboy **92**–18
chapeau de paille **90**–23
chapeaux **95**–11
chaque jour **20**–21
char **239**–2
charbon **218**–4
CHARCUTERIE ET FRUITS DE MER **71**
chargeur **14**–10, **234**–17
chargeur de piles **235**–27
chariot **72**–7, **129**–28
chariot à bagages **184**–8
chariot à main **175**–11
chariot de ménage **184**–19
chariot élévateur **175**–12
charpentier **66**–14, **162**–12
chasseur **184**–7
chat **215**–9
château de sable **225**–12
chaterton **181**–43

chaton **215**–10
chaud **13**–3, **42**–1
chauffe-eau ne fonctionne pas **62**–1
chauffeur de taxi **152**–21
chaussettes **86**–6
chaussettes basses **91**–10
chaussettes habillées **91**–9
chaussettes jusqu'aux chevilles **91**–7
chaussettes pour femmes **91**
chaussettes tube **91**–8
chaussettes unisexes **91**
chaussures **87**–13
chaussures athlétiques **86**–7
chaussures de ski **231**–26
chaussures de tennis **95**–32
CHAUSSURES ET ACCESSOIRES **94**–95
chaussures plates **95**–27
chauve **33**–12
chauve-souris **216**–7
cheddar américain **71**–26
cheeseburger **79**–3
chef **83**–16
chef chasseur **184**–6
chef de bureau **182**–8
chef de cuisine **185**–7
chef de l'équipe de jardinage **176**–4
chemin **208**–3
cheminée **53**–5
chemise **86**–1, **183**–50
chemise à manches 3/4 **96**–13
chemise à manches courtes **96**–12
chemise à manches longues **96**–14
chemise d'hôpital **121**–19
chemise de nuit **91**–28
chemise de sécurité **93**–20
chemise de travail **92**–2
chemise froissée **101**–19
chemise mouillée **101**–17
chemise repassée **101**–20
chemise sans manches **96**–11
chemise sèche **101**–18
chemise sport **88**–4
chemisier **87**–8
chêne **210**–17
chenille **214**–20
chèque **132**–13
chèque de paie **165**–14
chercher le siège **160**–F
chercher les panneaux offrant
    des emplois **173**–C
chercher un livre **133**–B
cheval **215**–4
chevalet **233**–18
cheveux **104**–2
cheveux blonds **33**–17
cheveux bruns **33**–18
cheveux courts **33**–1
cheveux frisés **33**–11

cheveux gris **33**–13
cheveux longs **33**–3
cheveux mi-longs **33**–2
cheveux noirs **33**–16
cheveux ondulés **33**–10
cheveux raides **33**–9
cheveux roux **33**–15
cheville **106**–23
chèvre **215**–5
chevreuil **216**–14
chez le concessionnaire **158**
chez le mécanicien **158**
chien **215**–11
chien de prairie **215**–22
chiffons **61**–9
chiffres romains **16**
chimie **195**
chimiste **195**–25
chimpanzé **217**–27
chiot **215**–12
chips **73**–35
chirurgien(ne) **121**–36
choisir dans le menu **82**–D
choisir la réponse exacte **9**–P
chou chinois **69**–15
chouette **214**–5
choux **69**–2
choux-fleur **69**–14
chromosome **194**–8
chrysanthème **211**–21
cible **231**–7
ciel **209**–9
cils **106**–11
cimetière **127**–15
cinéma **126**–6, **222**–2
cinq **16**
cinq dollars **26**–8
cinquante **16**
cinquante dollars **26**–11
cinquantième **16**
cinquième **16**
cintre **101**–11
circonférence **193**–36
cisailles à haie **176**–11
ciseaux **33**–20
citation **190**–9
citrons **68**–7
civière **121**–33
civière roulante **121**–33
civilisations **199**
clair **13**–9
clarinette **238**–2
classer des documents **171**–E
classeur **7**–27
classique **237**–21
clavier **14**–5, **196**–14
clavier électrique **238**–18
clé **51**–30

clé à tuyau **181**–47
clé anglaise **181**–48
client **72**–1, **82**–6, **94**–4, **132**–2, **164**–2, **184**–10, **185**–9
clignotant **158**–6, **159**–34
CLIMAT **13**
climatiseur **159**–39
clinique **186**–2
cliquer sur « se connecter » **197**–B
clôture **177**–19
clou **180**–34
clou à dessin **183**–35
club de golf **231**–1
club vidéo **129**–20
cobaye **215**–4
cobra **213**–41
coccinelle **214**–26
cocher les cases adéquates **9**–U
cochon **215**–2
cocotte **78**–10
code à barres **27**–4
code de la route **136**–1
code de la ville **15**–34
code du pays **15**–33
code postal **4**–9
code ZIP **4**–9
cœur **107**–38, **239**–6
cœurs **233**–31
coffre **158**–11
coffre à gant **159**–44
coffre à jouets **59**–16
coffre-fort **132**–7
coiffe **88**–1, **206**–7
coiffer les cheveux **33**
coiffeur **167**–31
coiffeuse **167**–31
coin **128**–7
coin repas **46**–7
col **100**–4
coléoptère **214**–18
colibri **214**–10
colis postal **134**–6
collant **91**–19
collants **91**–18
colle **183**–33
collectionner des objets **232**–A
collège **188**–3, **188**–7
coller un timbre **135**–C
collier de perles **95**–39
colliers **95**–10
collines **204**–16
colocataires **64**–1
Colombie Britannique **201**–2
colonne vertébrale **107**–49
colons **198**–2
colorer les cheveux **33**–D
combinaison **91**–22
combinaison de plongée **225**–4

combinaison de travail **92**–8
combinaison-pantalon **93**–24
combiné **14**–1
comédie **237**–13
comédie de situation **236**–2
comète **205**–24
commande de jeu vidéo **232**–4
commande de lit **121**–27
commencer l'école **40**–B
comment guérir **114**
comment rester en bonne santé **114**
commerce de proximité **128**–3
commis **94**–3
commis aux stocks **169**–59
commis débarrasseur **185**–13
commis épicier **72**–4
commode **58**–1, **59**–6
commode-coiffeuse **58**–1
comparaison de vêtements **97**
compartiment à bagages **161**–13
COMPÉTENCES EN MATIÈRE D'ENTREVUE **174**
COMPÉTENCES EN TRAVAIL DE BUREAU **171**
COMPÉTENCES PROFESSIONNELLES **170**
complimenter quelqu'un **12**–C
composer le 911 **15**–E
composer le numéro de téléphone **15**–A
compositeur **199**–14
composition **199**–15
COMPOSITION ANGLAISE **190**–**191**
composter les rebuts alimentaires **219**–M
compresse stérile **117**–6
comprimé **113**–22
comprimés contre le rhume **113**–27
comptable **166**–1
compte-gouttes **195**–45
compter **84**–A
compteur **152**–23
compteur à gaz **62**–14
compteur de vitesse **159**–27
compteur kilométrique **159**–28
comptines **37**–22
comptoir **54**–22
comptoir de caisse **73**–12
comptoir de prêt **133**–2
concepteur **175**–2
concepteur graphique **167**–30
concert **84**–1
concert de musique classique **223**–14
concert de rock **222**–5
concession d'automobiles **126**–4
concevoir **175**–A
concierge **50**–8, **182**–3, **184**–4
conclusion **190**–8

concombres **69**–10
condamné **141**–15
condamner l'accusé **141**–E
conditions météorologiques **13**
conducteur (conductrice) de camions **169**–61
conducteur lent **23**–4
conducteur rapide **23**–3
conduire de la machinerie lourde **170**–H
conduire un camion **170**–E
conduire un orchestre **238**–C
conduite en état d'ivresse **142**–5
cône **193**–40
cône de pin **210**–11
confectionneur (confectionneuse) de vêtements **167**–29
conférencier (conférencière) invité(e) **206**–4
confettis **239**–3
confiserie **131**–17
confus(e) **43**–26
congélateur **54**–10
congélateur-chambre **185**–3
congestion nasale **110**–7
Congrès **138**–2
conjoint **34**–13
conjointe **34**–12
conseil de parents et professeurs **22**–5
conseil municipal **139**–27
conseiller **5**–6
conseiller municipal **139**–28
conseiller professionnel **172**–10
conservateur de parc **220**–2
conserver l'eau **219**–E
consigner les résultats **195**–D
console de jeu vidéo **232**–3
constellation **205**–14
constitution **198**–12
CONSTRUCTION **178**
consulter la météo **147**–C
consulter les petites annonces **173**–B
contact en dehors de l'État **146**–2
contenant de fromage blanc **74**–17
contenant de fromage cottage **74**–17
contenant de plastique **78**–4
contenants **74**–5
content **44**–5
continents **202**
continuer sur un pâté de maison sur First **155**–F
contrat de location **51**–28
contreplaqué **178**–18
contrôleur **152**–13
contrôleur de sécurité **160**–5
converger **154**–10
CONVERSATION COURANTE **12**
convertir **17**–D

convertir les mesures **75**–C
copier le mot **8**–E
copies des documents importants **146**–20
copies des papiers d'identité et des cartes de crédit **146**–19
coq **215**–7
coquillage **225**–24
coquille **91**–6
coquille Saint-Jacques **212**–19
cor d'harmonie **238**–13
corail **220**–5
corbeille à déchets **57**–26
corbeille à pain **83**–11
cordage éraillé **179**–5
corde **226**–19
corde à linge **101**–9
corde à sauter **224**–4
cordon **14**–2
cordon d'alimentation **196**–2
corne **216**–21
cornet de glace **79**–13
cornichon **80**–11
cornouiller **210**–15
CORPS **104**–**105**
corps **190**–7
corral **177**–17
corriger **191**–I
corriger l'erreur **10**–N
costume **87**–11
costume de bain **90**–26
costume de ville **88**–11
côte ouest **201**–7
côtelettes d'agneau **70**–15
côtelettes de porc **70**–10
côtes de bœuf **70**–5
côtes grillées **76**–2
coton **98**–1, **177**–6
cou **104**–3
coucher du soleil **18**–18
couches jetables **37**–10
couches lavables **37**–8
coude **106**–12
coudre à la machine **98**–A
coudre à la main **98**–B
coudre des vêtements **170**–L
coudre une courtepointe **232**–C
couguar **216**–2
coulée de boue **144**–6
COULEURS **24**
couleurs de base **24**
couleurs différentes **23**–16
couleurs neutres **24**
couloir **5**–10, **51**, **184**–18
country **237**–27
coup de soleil **110**–14
coupé 2 portes **156**–2
coupe de tissu **98**–15

coupe-branches **176**–9
coupe-ongles **109**–31
couper le céleri en cubes **77**–J
couper le poulet **77**–I
couper les cheveux **33**–A
coupeuse rotative **232**–16
coupe-vent **90**–24
couple **239**–4
couple divorcé **35**–21
couple marié **35**–20
coupons **67**–15
coupure **110**–13
cour **5**–1, **51**–21
Cour suprême **138**–11
courges **69**–24
courgettes **69**–25
courir **230**–S
courir jusqu'à la salle de classe **11**–D
couronne **119**–9
courrier aérien **134**–5
courrier express **134**–2
courrier média **134**–3
courrier prioritaire **134**–1
courrier recommandé **134**–4
cours en ligne **172**–8
coursier **168**–40
court de tennis **224**–6
courtepointe **58**–16
cousin **34**–9
coussin **56**–2
coussin chauffant **113**–13
coussin gonflable **159**–43
coût **27**–7
couteau **55**–4, **83**–30
couteau à découper **78**–12
couteau à éplucher **78**–16
couteau à viande **83**–29
couteau suisse **226**–20
couturière **100**–1
couvercle **78**–24
couvert **83**–17
couverts (ustensiles) en
    plastique **79**–19
couverture **58**–15, **225**–11
couvertures **146**–7
couvre-lit **59**–11
couvre-prise **181**–46
couvreur **62**–8
cow-boy **177**–22
coyote **216**–3
crabe **71**–9, **212**–20
craie **7**–18
crâne **107**–47
crapaud **212**–28
cravate **88**–12, **92**–13
cravate étroite **97**–35
cravate large **97**–36
crayon **7**–20

crayon à sourcils **109**–34
crayons **59**–14
crème **24**–16, **81**–41, **113**–25
crème antihistaminique **117**–10
crème de rasage **109**–29
crème fermentée **72**–21
crème glacée **72**–26
crème hydratante **108**–9
crème pour bébé **37**–13
crème pour le corps **108**–9
crème sure **72**–21
crêpes **80**–7
crevette **71**–11, **212**–18
cric **158**–24
cricket **214**–23
CRIMINALITÉ **142**
crinière **217**–49
crochet **180**–39
crochet à œillet **180**–40
crocodile **213**–37
crocus **211**–17
croissant de lune **205**–10
crosse de hockey **231**–11
crotale **213**–38
crustacés **71**
cube **193**–38
cuiller **55**–5
cuiller à soupe **83**–32
cuiller en bois **78**–9
cuillère **55**–5
cuillerée à café de sel **75**–6
cuillerée à soupe de sucre **75**–7
cuir **98**–6
cuire **76**–C
cuire au four **77**–H
cuisine **46**–5, **83**–15
CUISINE **54**
cuisine de restaurant **185**
cuisiner **170**–C
cuisiner le dîner **39**–Q
cuisinier **83**–16
cuisinière **54**–18, **83**–16
cuisinier-minute **185**–1
cuisse **106**–19
cuisses **70**–21, **70**–22
cuit-vapeur **78**–3
cuivres (musique) **238**
cul-de-sac **154**–6
culottes de propreté **37**–11
curseur **197**–14
cuvette **57**–21
cuvette est bouchée **63**–19
cyclisme **228**–5
cycliste **224**–2
cylindre **193**–41
cylindre gradué **195**–38
cytoplasme **194**–9
daim **99**–8

danger électrique **186**–6
dangereux **186**–1
dans l'avion **161**
dans la salle d'attente **118**
dans la salle d'examen **118**
dans la trousse de premiers soins **117**
dans le coffre **158**
dans le terminal de la compagnie
    aérienne **160**
danser **64**–A
darne de saumon **71**–4
date **20**–1
date d'expiration **136**–10
date de naissance **4**–13
date de péremption **112**–7
dattes **68**–28
dauphin **213**–31
dé à coudre **100**–15
de l'après-midi **18**–5
de poids moyen **32**–8
de taille moyenne **32**–5
déballer **49**–N
débardeur **89**–24
débat **139**–B
débouchoir à ventouse **181**–50
décaler la première phrase d'un
    paragraphe **190**–D
décapotable **156**–5
décembre **21**–36
déchets dangereux **218**–12
déchiqueteuse **183**–24
Déclaration d'indépendance **198**–5
Déclaration des droits **198**–13
décocher un lancer **230**–A
décoller **160**–J
décorations **240**–1
découper le tofu en tranches **77**–C
découseur **100**–18
déçu **28**–4
déductions **165**–13
défense **217**–48
défense de tourner à gauche **154**–8
défilé **239**–1
dégivreur **159**–41
degrés **13**–8
déguisement **239**–11
DÉLINQUANCE **142**
demain **20**–6
demander au vendeur des informations
    concernant la voiture **157**–B
demander de l'aide **10**–F
demandez, « comment allez-vous » **2**–B
démaquillant **109**–42
démarrer **230**–R
déménageur **168**–42
démence **111**–18
demi **17**–2
demi-frère **35**–28, **35**–30

demi-sœur **35**–27, **35**–29
demi-tasse de raisins secs **75**–9
demi-tour autorisé **154**–5
démonstration **122**–6
démonte-roue **158**–22
dénominateur **192**–6
dentelle **99**–9
dentier **119**–10
dentiste **119**–1
dentisterie **119**
dents **106**–7
déodorant **108**–5
dépanneur **128**–3
dépanneuse **156**–14
déposer **132**–3
déposer les enfants **38**–G
dépression **115**–5
député **138**–4, **139**–24
dés **232**–6
descendre du taxi **153**–F
descendre les escaliers **153**–D
DESCRIPTION DE CHOSES **23**
DESCRIPTION DE PERSONNES **32**
DESCRIPTION DE VÊTEMENTS **96**–97
DESCRIPTION DES CHEVEUX **33**
désert **204**–4
déshabiller **36**–E
désherber la plate-bande **176**–G
désordre **64**–8
desservir la table **82**–G
dessin animé **236**–3
destination **162**–5
détecteur de fumée **51**–29
détergent **61**–18
détergent à lessive **101**–8
détergent à vaisselle **61**–21
détritus **148**–2
deux **16**
deux fois par semaine **20**–23
deux heures moins le quart **18**–13
deux heures moins vingt **18**–12
deux points **190**–17
deuxième **16**
deuxième prénom **4**–3
développement de carrière **172**
devenir grand-parent **41**–N
diabète **111**–12
diable **175**–11
diagonale **193**–31
diamètre **193**–37
diaphragme **194**–18
dictateur **199**–6
dicter une phrase **8**–N
dictionnaire **7**–30
dictionnaire illustré **7**–31
diététicien **120**–15
différence **192**–8
dimanche **20**–8

dimensions **17**
dinde **70**–17
dinde rôtie **76**–4
dindon **239**–14
dindon fumé **71**–25
dîner **39**–S
dîner au restaurant **185**
dîner surgelé **72**–28
dineur **82**–6, **185**–9
diplôme **40**–3
diplôme universitaire **41**–7
dire, « au revoir » **3**–L
directeur **5**–4
directeur adjoint **5**–5
DIRECTIONS ET CARTES **155**
discipliner **36**–K
discuter d'un problème **8**–G
dispositif d'évacuation des déchets
    médicaux **121**–31
disque dur **196**–6
disquerie **130**–1
dissimuler votre NIP **143**–C
distributeur automatique **152**–9
distributeur de timbres **135**–11
dites votre nom **4**–A
dites, « bonjour » **2**–A
divan **56**–18
DIVERTISSEMENTS **236**–237
diviser **17**–A, **192**–D
dix **16**
dix dollars **26**–9
dix mille **16**
dix-huit **16**
dix-huitième **16**
dixième **16**
dix-neuf **16**
dix-neuvième **16**
dix-sept **16**
dix-septième **16**
DJ **64**–4
docker **167**–23
docteur **118**–5
doigt **105**–16
doigt enflé **110**–16
donner un coup de pied **230**–E
donner votre nom **15**–F
dormeuse molletonnée **91**–27
dors-bien ouverture **91**–27
dos **104**–5
dose **112**–6
douane **161**
double porte **53**–10
douleur **115**–3
doux **13**–4
douze **16**
douzième **16**
drain **57**–7
dramatique **236**–12

drame **237**–14
drap plat **58**–13
drapeau **239**–8
drap-housse **58**–12
dribbler **230**–J
drogues illégales **142**–6
droits **140**
DROITS ET RESPONSABILITÉS
    CIVIQUES **140**
du matin **18**–4
dune de sable **204**–5
durant une urgence **147**
DVD **133**–19
eau **209**–13, **225**–1
eau chaude **57**–9
eau de Cologne **108**–6
eau de javel **101**–7
eau en bouteille **146**–11
eau froide **57**–10
ébeuer **169**–54
écailles **212**–3
ecchymose **110**–12
échafaudage **178**–4
échalotes **69**–20
échanger **27**–I
échantillons **84**–5
écharpe **113**–19
écharpe d'hiver **90**–5
écharpe entourant la tête **90**–7
écharpes **95**–12
échelle **178**–2
échelle (des distances) **155**–7
éclipse solaire **205**–16
école **126**–9
ÉCOLE **5**
école de métiers **188**–5
école élémentaire **188**–2
école primaire **188**–2
école professionnelle **188**–5
école secondaire du 1er cycle **188**–3
école secondaire du 2e cycle **188**–4
ÉCOLES ET SUJETS **188**–189
économe **78**–15
écossais **96**–22
écouter attentivement **174**–K
écouter…le cœur **118**–C
écouteurs **6**–8, **234**–4
écoutez un CD **6**–C
écran **6**–2, **196**–11, **235**–30
écran de cheminée **56**–12
écran solaire **108**–7, **108**–8, **225**–10
écrans d'arrivée et de départ **161**–7
écrasement d'avion **144**–3
écrire un chèque personnel **27**–D
écrire un curriculum vitae **173**–F
écrire un mot de remerciement **174**–O
écrire un mot sur une carte **135**–A
écrire une lettre de présentation **173**–G

écrivain **169**–64
écrivez au tableau **6**–E
écrivez votre nom en majuscules **4**
écrou **180**–36
écureuil **215**–21
éditer **191**–I
éducation physique **189**–17
éducatrice (éducateur) en
    garderie **166**–16
effacer l'erreur **10**–M
église **127**–14
élaborer un plan d'urgence **146**–A
élan **216**–1
élan de golf **230**–Q
élastique **183**–34
élection **139**
électricien **62**–9
électron **195**–30
ÉLECTRONIQUE ET
    PHOTOGRAPHIE **234**–235
éléphant **217**–42
emballage **134**–17
emballages alimentaires **72**
emballer **49**–M, **240**–F
emballeur **73**–14
emballeur (emballeuse) **175**–8
embarrassé(e) **43**–24
embrasser **2**–E, **3**–K
embrasser avant de mettre au lit **36**–P
embrayage **159**–49
émigrer **40**–C
émission pour enfants **236**–9
émission sportive **236**–11
émission sur le magasinage **236**–10
émission sur le shopping **236**–10
emménager **48**–F, **49**
emmener la voiture chez le
    mécanicien **157**–C
empereur **199**–3
EMPLOIS ET PROFESSIONS **166**–169
employé **165**–9
employé(e) du service de
    la paye **165**–10
employeur **164**–4
empreinte digitale **136**–5
emprunter de l'argent **26**–B
encadrer des personnes **170**–O
encaisser un chèque **132**–A
encaisser un chèque de voyage **27**–F
en-cas **73**
encaustique pour meubles **61**–8
enceinte **32**–15
encercler la réponse **9**–Q
endormir la bouche **119**–C
ENDROITS OÙ ALLER **222**–223
énergie éolienne **218**–2
ÉNERGIE ET CONSERVATION **218**–219
énergie géothermique **218**–7

énergie hydroélectrique **218**–5
énergie nucléaire **218**–8
énergie solaire **218**–1
enfant perdu **144**–1
enfant qui commence à marcher **31**–8
enfants bruyants **23**–11
enfants tapageurs **23**–11
enfants tranquilles **23**–12
engager un avocat **141**–B
engelures **116**–G
engin élévateur à nacelle **178**–5
enjoliveur **158**–9
enlever **109**–Q
enregistrer **235**–A
enregistrer vos bagages **160**–B
enseignant **6**–4
enseigner **170**–Q
ensoleillé **13**–9
entamer une conversation **12**–A
entendre **106**–B
entier **17**–1
entiers négatifs **192**–1
entiers positifs **192**–2
entonnoir **195**–40
entorse **110**–18
entraîneur **5**–20, **229**–2
entrée **50**, **164**–1
entrée de la salle d'urgence **121**
entrepôt **175**–7
entrepreneur **166**–12, **186**–5
entrer dans la salle **11**–A
entrer en contact **173**–A
entretenir votre voiture **157**
enveloppe **134**–14, **183**–43
envoyer **230**–C
envoyer un courriel **197**–I
envoyer une carte **135**
envoyer votre résumé et votre lettre
    de présentation **173**–H
épaule **105**–13
épaulières **231**–20
épelez votre nom **4**–B
ÉPICERIE **72**–73
épinards **69**–11
épine **211**–29
épingle **95**–38
épingle (droite) **100**–12
épingle de sûreté **100**–14
épingles de sûreté **37**–9
éplucheur **78**–15
éponge **61**–19
épouse **34**–12
épousseter les meubles **60**–A
époux **34**–13
éprouvette **195**–42
éprouvette graduée **195**–38
épuisette **226**–17
équation **192**–13

équipe **229**–3
équipe de jardinage **176**–1
équipe de recherche et
 sauvetage **145**–20
équipement de bureau **183**
équipement de sécurité **179**
équipement endommagé **179**–4
érable **210**–12
ergothérapeute **168**–45
éruption cutanée **110**–10
éruption volcanique **145**–16
escabeau **61**–13
escalier de secours **50**–2
escalier mécanique **131**–23
escaliers **50**–10
escalopes de veau **70**–6
escargot **212**–22
escarpins **95**–26
esclave **198**–4
escrime **228**–7
espace de stationnement **50**–18, **128**–5
espadon **71**–5, **212**–10
espèces et pièces **146**–17
essayer des chaussures **95**–C
essuie-glaces **158**–2
essuie-mains **57**–17
essuie-tout **54**–3
essuyer la vaisselle **60**–N
essuyer le comptoir **60**–O
est **155**–4
estomac **107**–41
établissement préscolaire **188**–1
étang **204**–21
état **4**–8
états des Rocheuses **201**–8
états du centre du littoral de
 l'Atlantique **201**–10
états du Pacifique **201**–7
étau **180**–26
été **21**–38
éteindre la lumière **219**–G
éteindre le téléphone
 cellulaire **160**–I, **174**–G
éteindre les lumières **11**–P
éternuer **110**–B
étiquette **27**–1
étiquette d'avertissement **112**–8
étiquette d'expédition **183**–41
étiquette d'ordonnance **112**–4
étiquette de prescription **112**–4
étiquette de valeur
 nutritionnelle **122**–8
étoile **205**–13
étoile de mer **212**–16
être amoureux **42**–18
être bien **42**–14
être blessé **42**–16, **116**–C
être calme **42**–8

Être conscient de ce qui vous
 entoure **143**–I
être d'accord **12**–K
être dégoûté(e) **42**–7
être élu **139**–C
être embauché **173**–L
être en état de choc **116**–B
être en service **139**–D
être inconscient **116**–A
être informé **140**–F
être inquiet(e) **42**–13
être mal à l'aise **42**–9
être malade **42**–12
être peiné(e) **42**–16
être relâché **141**–H
Être soigné **174**–C
être soulagé(e) **42**–15
ÉTUDE **8**–9
étudiant **6**–5
étudier à la maison **10**–D
étudier le code de la route **137**–A
étui à appareil-photo **235**–28
Europe **202**–3
évacuer la région **147**–K
ÉVÈNEMENTS DE LA VIE ET DOCUMENTS
 OFFICIELS **40**–41
évier **54**–4
évier déborde **63**–18
examen bon marché **122**–1
examen de la vue **136**–6
examiner...la gorge **118**–E
examiner...les yeux **118**–D
excité(e) **43**–22
expédier **175**–D
expérience **195**
expliquer l'urgence **15**–G
expliquer quelque chose **12**–M
explorateur **199**–9
exploration **199**–8
explosion **144**–4
EXPRESSIONS INDIQUANT LE
 MOUVEMENT **153**
extenseur **181**–15
exterminateur **63**–21
extincteur **179**–21
eye-liner **109**–36
fabriquer **175**–B
fabriquer des meubles **170**–G
FABRIQUER DES VÊTEMENTS **98**–99
face **193**–44
fâché(e) **43**–29
façons de réussir **10**
façons de servir la viande et la
 volaille **76**
façons de servir les œufs **76**
facteur **134**–20
facture de téléphone **15**–28
fahrenheit **13**–1

faire asseoir le client **82**–B
faire attention aux
 avertissements **147**–D
faire bouillir le poulet **77**–M
faire correspondre les articles **9**–T
faire cuire le brocoli à la vapeur **77**–D
faire de l'artisanat **232**–D
faire de l'équitation **226**–9
faire de l'exercice **39**–P, **230**–N
faire de la luge **227**–6
faire de la planche à roulettes **228**–13
faire de la planche à voile **227**–10
faire de la voile **227**–8
faire des bilans de santé
 réguliers **114**–H
FAIRE DES COURSES **27**
faire des photocopies **171**–D
faire des progrès **10**–G
FAIRE DES RETOUCHES **100**
faire des travaux manuels **170**–D
faire du bénévolat **41**–Q
faire du covoiturage **219**–I
faire du crochet **233**–25
faire du skateboard **228**–13
faire du surf **227**–9
faire du surf des neiges **227**–2
faire du vélo **129**–D
faire du vélo tout terrain **226**–8
faire la conversation **12**–B
FAIRE LA LESSIVE **101**
faire la queue **94**–B
faire le lit **60**–F
faire préchauffer le four **77**–A
faire rebondir le ballon **230**–J
faire refroidir **76**–D
faire sauter les champignons **77**–E
faire semblant **233**–G
faire ses devoirs **39**–T
faire ses opérations bancaires en
 ligne **132**–C
faire un dépôt **132**–B
faire un dessin **8**–F
faire un discours **148**–A
faire un excursion **220**–A
faire un pique-nique **224**–D
faire un signe de la main **2**–F
faire un versement hypothécaire **49**–L
faire un vœu **240**–B
faire une expérience **195**–B
faire une hypothèse **195**–A
faire une mise en pli des cheveux **33**–C
faire une offre **49**–I
faire une overdose **116**–K
faire une pause **11**–H
faire une permanente **33**–B
faire une présentation **122**–B
faire une sieste **53**–A
familiale **156**–6

FAMILLES **34**–35
famine **145**–12
fan **229**–4
fard à cils **109**–39
fard à joue **109**–37
farine **73**–29
fatigué(e) **43**–32
faune et flore sauvage **220**–3
FAUNE MARINE, AMPHIBIENS ET
 REPTILES **212**–213
fauteuil **56**–22
favoris **33**–7
faxer un document **171**–G
féliciter **36**–J
femme **4**–18, **30**–2, **34**–12
femme au foyer **168**–33
femme de ménage **168**–34, **184**–20
femmes **30**–3
fenêtre **47**–11, **56**–17
fenêtre pub **197**–9
fer à friser **108**–17
fer à repasser **101**–13
ferme **52**–9
ferme et au ranch **177**
fermeture éclair **99**–25
fermeture éclair à glissière
 est cassée **97**–39
fermeture éclair est cassée **97**–39
fermeture velcro **99**–29
fermetures **99**
fermez votre livre **6**–H
fermier (fermière) **177**–13
ferry **220**–4
fertiliser **176**–D
fesses **107**–30
festin **239**–13
fête **64**–2,
FÊTE D'ANNIVERSAIRE **240**–241
fête de Christophe Colomb **22**–15
fête de l'indépendance nationale **22**–13
fête de Martin Luther King Jr **22**–10
fête des anciens combattants **22**–16
fête des présidents **22**–11
fête du travail **22**–14
fête régionale **223**–13
fête religieuse **22**–7
feu arrière **158**–13
feu d'artifice **239**–7
feu de camp **226**–11
feu de circulation **128**–8
feu de frein **158**–14
feu de signalisation **128**–8
feu follet **239**–10
feuille **210**–6
feuille de réponse **10**–2
feuilles **211**–6
feuilles de cahier **7**–28
feuilleton à l'eau de rose **236**–5

feux de détresse **159**–36
février **21**–26
fiche **234**–16
fiche d'antécédents médicaux **118**–4
fiche médicale **121**–24
fichier rotatif **183**–44
fier (fière) **43**–21
fièvre **110**–8
figues **68**–27
figurine **232**–1, **233**–26
fil **99**–23, **100**–11, **181**–13, **233**–22
filet à cheveux **93**–25
fille **34**–14
fille de 10 ans **31**–10
film alimentaire **72**–24
films **222**–2
fils **34**–15
fin de semaine **20**–17
fines herbes **84**–9
finir **230**–T
finir tous les médicaments **112**–C
finition **99**
fixatif capillaire **108**–12
fixer des objectifs **10**–A
flèche **231**–8
flet **212**–15
fleuri **96**–25
fleuriste **130**–8, **167**–27
fleurs **208**–7
FLEURS **211**
flou **235**–33
flûte **238**–1
foie **70**–7, **107**–40
foin **177**–18
foire régionale **223**–13
FOIRE SUR LA SANTÉ **122**–**123**
folk **237**–29
fond de teint **109**–40
fondateurs **198**–7
fontaine **224**–5, **224**–9
football **229**–12
football américain **229**–11
force aérienne **138**–16
forceps **195**–43
foret **180**–28, **204**–11
forêt pluviale **204**–1
formation **172**–2
formation professionnelle **172**–5
formation sur le tas **172**–7
formes **193**
formulaire d'inscription aux cours **4**
formulaire de déclaration **161**–16
formulaires postaux **134**–19
formule **37**–3, **195**–34
forum de recrutement **172**–13
foudre **13**–17
fouet **78**–21
four **54**–20

fourchette **55**–3
fourchette à cheveux **108**–15
fourchette à salade **83**–27
fourchette de table **83**–28
fourgonette **156**–13
fourmilier **217**–24
fourmis **63**–23
fournitures de bureau **183**
fournitures de couture **100**
fourre-tout **94**–19
fourrure **216**–19
foyer **56**–13
fractions **192**
fractions et chiffres décimaux **17**
frais **13**–5
fraises **68**–14
framboises **68**–15
frange **33**–8, **99**–34
frapper **230**–B
frapper à coups de marteau **178**–D
frein à main **159**–48
fréquence **20**
frère **34**–6
friandise **73**–37
frisbee **231**–27
frissons **110**–9
frites **79**–2
froid **13**–6, **42**–4
fromage **66**–4
fromage cheddar **71**–28
fromage gruyère **71**–27
front **106**–2
fruit **67**–9
FRUITS **68**
frustré(e) **43**–27
fuseaux horaires **19**
Fusilier marin **138**–17
fusion **218**–10
gaine **91**–15
galaxie **205**–15
galon d'eau **75**–5
gant **231**–17
gant de toilette **57**–6
gants **90**–6
gants de caoutchouc **61**–4
gants de chirurgie **121**–39
gants de latex **93**–34
gants de travail **92**–17, **179**–17
gants jetables **93**–27
garage **47**–14
garçon **82**–8
garçon de 6 ans **31**–9
GARDE ET ÉDUCATION
    DES ENFANTS **36**–**37**
Garde nationale **138**–19
Garde-côte **138**–18
gardénia **211**–18
garder **28**–B

gardien **141**–3
gardien de parking **184**–3
gardien de sécurité **132**–5, **169**–55
gardienne d'enfant **166**–9
gare d'autobus **124**–7
gare de chemin de fer **152**
garer la voiture **129**–E
gâteau **73**–39
gâteau à étages **81**–33
gâteau au fromage **81**–34
gâteau facile et rapide **77**
gaufre **215**–19
gaufres **80**–8
gauphre **215**–19
gaz naturel **218**–3
gaze **117**–8
geai bleu **214**–6
gel cheveux **108**–16
gel de douche **108**–2
gencives **106**–6
genou **106**–20
genouillères **179**–19
GÉOGRAPHIE ET HABITATS **204**
géométrie **192**–17
gérant **50**–8, **72**–8
gestionnaire de compte **132**–9
gigot d'agneau **70**–14
gilet **89**–15
gilet de sauvetage **161**–25, **226**–14
gilet de sécurité à haute visibilité **92**–4
gilet en duvet **90**–14
girafe **217**–32
glacé **13**–22
glacial **13**–7
glacier **131**–16
glacière **225**–9
glissade **224**–13
golf **228**–8
gomme **7**–21
gonfler les pneus **157**–L
gorge **107**–35
gorille **217**–29
gospel **237**–30
goûter **106**–D
gouttes pour les yeux **113**–31
gouttière **53**–4
gouvernement de la ville **139**
gouvernement de l'État **139**
gouvernement fédéral **138**
gouverneur **139**–20
GPS (système mondial de
    localisation) **155**–11
gradins **5**–3
graffiti **148**–1
grain de beauté **32**–16
graine **211**–1
graisser un plat à four **77**–B
grand **96**–4

grand magasin **131**–13
grand(e) **32**–4
grande assiette **83**–18
grande tasse à café **55**–7
grand-mère **34**–1
grand-père **34**–2
grange **177**–11
graphique **192**–15
gras **32**–7
gratte-ciel **127**–13
grattoir **181**–52
greffier de la cour **141**–12
grenier **47**–8
grenouille **212**–25
griffe **214**–2
griffe d'entraînement **98**–20
gril **53**–17
grille **78**–14
grille-pain **54**–6
grille-pain four **54**–15
grilloir **54**–21
grillon **214**–23
grimper aux barres **224**–C
grippe **111**–2
gris **24**–15
griser la bonne réponse **10**–K
gros **32**–7
grosse main **23**–2
grotte **220**–6
grottes **220**–7
groupe de soutien **115**–15
grue **178**–7
guêpe **214**–17
guerre **199**–10
guerre de l'Indépendance **198**–8
guichet **136**–7
guichet automatique **132**
guichet de vente des billets **152**–12
guillemets **190**–15
guitare **238**–9
gymnase **5**–19, **184**–24
gymnastique **228**–9
habiller **36**–H
habit rouge **198**–9
habitat **194**–11
HABITATIONS **52**
hache **180**–3
hacher les oignons **77**–L
hall d'entrée **50**
haltères **231**–22
haltérophilie **228**–16
hamac **53**–23
hamburger **79**–1
hamburger au fromage **79**–3
handicapé(e) **32**–10
handicaps **32**
haricots **72**–17
haricots verts **69**–8

harmonica **238**–21
haut en tricot **88**–7
hautbois **238**–3
hautes terres du Chiapas **201**–18
hautes terres du sud **201**–17
hauteur **17**–16
haut-parleur **50**–5
haut-parleurs **234**–14
hélicoptère **151**–9
herbe à puce **210**–25
HEURE **18–19**
heure **18**–1, **19**–23, **161**–29
heure d'été **19**–25
heure d'Hawaï-des Aléoutiennes **19**–27
heure de l'Alaska **19**–28
heure de l'Atlantique **19**–33
heure de l'Est **19**–32
heure de Terre-Neuve **19**–34
heure des Rocheuses **19**–30
heure du Centre **19**–31
heure du Pacifique **19**–29
heure normale **19**–26
heureux (heureuse) **28**–6, **43**–31, **44**–5
hibiscus **211**–12
hibou **214**–5
hier **20**–7
hip hop **237**–26
hippisme **228**–19
hippocampe **212**–13
hippopotame **217**–43
histoire **189**–12
HISTOIRE DES ÉTATS-UNIS **198**
HISTOIRE DU MONDE **199**
hiver **21**–40
hochet **37**–26
hockey sur glace **229**–13
homard **71**–10
homme **4**–17, **30**–1
hommes **30**–4
HÔPITAL **120–121**
hôpital **125**–9, **154**–18
horaire **152**–4
horloge **7**–9
horreur **237**–17
hot-dog **79**–6
hôtel **124**–3
HÔTEL **184**
hôtel de ville **124**–8
hôtesse **82**–2
houx **210**–19
huile **73**–31
huissier **141**–13
huit **16**
huitième **16**, **17**–5
huîtres **71**–14
humide **13**–15
humidificateur **113**–12

hyène **217**–30
HYGIÈNE PERSONNELLE **108–109**
hygiéniste dentaire **119**–3
hypertension **111**–14
I.V. (goutte-à-goutte intraveineux) **121**–25
identique **28**–3
il est déchiré **97**–41
il est effiloché **97**–43
il est taché **97**–42
il est trop cher **97**–44
il y a une panne de courant **62**–2
île **204**–8
immatriculer la voiture **157**–F
immeuble à appartements **50**–1
immeuble de bureaux **124**–2
immigrant **199**–13
immigration **199**–12
immigrer **40**–C
imperméable **90**–18, **90**–21
imprimante **196**–17
imprimante à jet d'encre **183**–18
imprimante laser **183**–19
imprimé **96**–23
imprimer un document **171**–I
imprimeur **169**–50
incendie **144**–8
incendie criminel **142**–7
incendie de forêt **144**–7
indicateur de température du moteur **159**–30
indicatif régional **4**–10, **15**–29
infection de l'oreille **111**–3
infirmier **118**–8, **168**–44
infirmier(ière) auxiliaire autorisé(e) **120**–12
infirmier(ière) auxiliaire diplômé(e) **120**–11
infirmier(ière) diplômé(e) **120**–10
infirmier(ière) en chirurgie **120**–9
infirmière **118**–8, **168**–44
informations **236**–1
ingénieur **167**–25
ingénieur en informatique **167**–18
inhalateur **113**–33
inondation **145**–19
insectes **209**–11
insectes et arachnides **214**
insigne d'identité **92**–15
installer un système d'arrosage **176**–H
instructeur **6**–4
instruments à corde **238**
instruments dentaires **119**–4
intérieur de la voiture **159**
INTÉRIEUR ET À L'EXTÉRIEUR DU CORPS **106–107**
interne **120**–1

hyène **217**–30
INTERNET **197**
interphone **50**–5
interprète **168**–35
interrupteur **58**–27
INTERSECTION **128–129**
intestins **107**–42
introduction **190**–6
introduire votre carte de retrait **132**–D
inventaire d'intérêts **172**–11
inventaire des compétences **172**–12
inventeur **199**–18
invention **199**–19
invertébrés **194**–13
invitation **64**–9
inviter quelqu'un **12**–H
iris **211**–16
irrité **64**–6
isolation **178**–14
itinéraire d'autobus **152**–1
itinéraire d'évacuation **146**–5
ivoire **24**–16
jambe **105**–9
jambe et le pied **106**
jambières **90**–12
jambon **70**–9
jambon cuit **76**–5
janvier **21**–25
jardiner **53**–B
jardin à l'arrière **53**
jardin botanique **222**–3
jardin de devant et maison **53**
jardin potager **53**–27, **177**–14
jardin sur le toit **50**–4
jardin zoologique **222**–1
jardinier (jardinière) **167**–28
jarrets d'agneau **70**–13
jasmin **211**–22
jauge d'essence **159**–31
jauge d'huile **159**–29
jaune **24**–2
jazz **237**–24
jean **99**–7
jeans **86**–2, **92**–19
jetée **225**–18
jeter des ordures **11**–N
jeton **152**–10
jeu d'échecs **232**–8
jeu de bascule **224**–16
jeu de dames **232**–7
jeu de société **232**–5
jeudi **20**–12
jeune **32**–1
jeu-questionnaire **236**–8
joindre un fichier **197**–H
joindre une photo **197**–G
jonquille **211**–25
joue **106**–3

jouer **235**–B
jouer à des jeux **232**–B
jouer aux cartes **233**–H
jouer avec **36**–M
jouer d'un instrument **238**–A
jouer dans un groupe de rock **238**–D
jouets et jeux **59**
joueur **229**–5
jour **20**–2
jour du souvenir **22**–12
jour férié **22**–8
journal **133**–6
journaliste **169**–52
JOURNÉE À L'ÉCOLE **11**
jours de la semaine **20**
jours de semaine **20**–16
Jours fériés **22**
JOURS FÉRIÉS **239**
judas **51**–32
juge **141**–6
juges **138**–12
juillet **21**–31
juin **21**–30
jumelles **28**–1
jupe **87**–10
jupe courte **96**–16
jupe longue **96**–18
jupe mi-longue **96**–17
Jupiter **205**–5
jupon **91**–23
jury **141**–8
jus de pomme **73**–32
kangourou **217**–44
kayak **226**–3
ketchup **79**–21
kiosque à journaux **128**–12
kiosque d'enregistrement **160**–2
kiosque de téléphones cellulaires **131**–22
kit de confection de poupée **232**–13
kit de menuisier **232**–4
kiwi **68**–22
klaxon **159**–32
koala **217**–45
lab **121**
laboratoire scientifique **195**
lac **204**–13
lacer (ses souliers) **86**–A
lacets de chaussures **94**–24
laine **98**–3
laisser mijoter **77**–P
laisser un message **171**–P
laisser un pourboire **82**–J
lait **66**–5
lait écrémé **81**–42
lait frappé **79**–14
laitue **69**–1

lama **217**–25
lame **180**–27, **194**–3
lame de rasoir **109**–28
lampadaire **56**–15
lampe **58**–25
lampe de poche **146**–14
lampe de porte **53**–13
lampe de travail **181**–44
lampe sur pied **56**–15
lancer au panier **230**–H
langouste **71**–10
langue **106**–8
langues du monde entier **189**–13
lanterne **226**–22
lapin **215**–13
lard **70**–11, **80**–1
largeur **17**–19
lavabo **57**–25
lave-linge **50**–12, **101**–3
laver **36**–F
laver la vaisselle **60**–M
laver le plancher **60**–D
laver les vêtements dans de l'eau
      froide **219**–K
laver les vitres **60**–I
laver…les cheveux **108**–E
laverie **128**–1
laveuse **50**–12, **101**–3
lave-vaisselle **54**–8
lèchefrite **78**–13
lecteur de CD et DVD **196**–9
lecteur de CD personnel **234**–5
lecteur de disques compacts **159**–38
lecteur de DVD **56**–7, **234**–10
lecteur de DVD portable **234**–11
lecteur de MP3 **234**–2
lecteur de vidéo **197**–11
lecteur flash **196**–8
légende **155**–6
légumes **66**–8
LÉGUMES **69**
légumes cuits à la vapeur **81**–32
légumes surgelés **72**–27
léopard **217**–34
lessive **101**–1
lettre **134**–13
lever du soleil **18**–14
levez la main **6**
levez-vous **6**–D
levier de vitesses **159**–47
levier de vitesses au plancher **159**–50
lèvre **106**–5
lézard **213**–40
liberté d'expression **140**–2
liberté de la presse **140**–4
liberté de religion **140**–3
librairie **130**–4

licence de taxi **152**–22
liens **197**–10
lieu de naissance **4**–14
lieu de rassemblement **146**–1
LIEU DE TRAVAIL **164**–165
lieutenant-gouverneur **139**–21
ligne courbée **193**–23
ligne droite **193**–22
ligne téléphonique **14**–4
lignes **193**
lignes parallèles **193**–25
lignes perpendiculaires **193**–24
lime à ongles **109**–32
limes **68**–8
limite de vitesse **154**–4
limiteur de surtension **196**–1
limonade **84**–3
limousine **156**–11
lin **98**–2
linge à vaisselle **61**–22
lion **217**–36
liquide correcteur **183**–36
liquides inflammables **179**–8
lire à **36**–N
lire l'heure **18**
lire la carte **135**–G
lire la définition **8**–B
lire le journal **39**–V
lire une facture de téléphone **15**
lis **211**–26
liste des courses **67**–14
lit **58**–9
lit à deux places **184**–14
lit d'enfant **59**–3
lit d'hôpital **121**–22
litre de lait **75**–4
lits superposés **59**–9
livre **7**–25
livre à colorier **59**–13
livre audio **133**–17
livre d'images **133**–12
livre de rosbif **75**–12
livre de rôti de bœuf **75**–12
livre épais **23**–7
livre mince **23**–8
livrer la carte **135**–E
livret **132**–10
livreur (livreuse) **167**–21
locataire **50**–6
location d'un appartement **48**
logiciel **196**–10
longueur **17**–17
louche **78**–7
loup **216**–5
loutre de mer **213**–35
lumières de Noël **239**–18
luminaire **55**–18

lundi **20**–9
lunettes **115**–7
lunettes de sécurité **179**–11
lunettes de soleil **90**–27
lunettes de sûreté **92**–10, **179**–10
lutte **228**–17
luzerne **177**–5
lycée **188**–4
machine à coudre **98**–13
mâchoire **106**–4
maçon **186**–8
magasin **28**–A
magasin d'amélioration de
      l'habitat **127**–20
magasin d'électronique **131**–20
magasin de cartes **130**–7
magasin de chaussures **130**–10
magasin de fournitures de
      bureau **127**–21
magasin de jouets **130**–5
magasin de maternité **131**–19
magasin de meubles **126**–8
magasin de tissus **99**
magazine **133**–5
magnétophone portable **234**–6
magnétoscope **102**–7
magnolia **210**–8
mai **21**–29
maillet **180**–2
maillot de bain **90**–22, **90**–26
maillot de corps **91**–1
main **105**–15
maintenance **184**–23
maire **139**–26
mairie **124**–8
maïs **69**–12, **177**–4
MAISON **46**–47
Maison Blanche **138**–7
maison de poupées **59**–18
maison de retraite **52**–11, **52**–12
maison de ville **52**–6
MAISON ET UN JARDIN **53**
maison mobile **52**–7
maître d'hôtel **185**–11, **185**–12
maître nageur **225**–19
mal d'estomac **110**–4
mal d'oreille **110**–3
mal de dents **110**–2
mal de dos **110**–5
mal de gorge **110**–6
mal de tête **110**–1
mal du pays **43**–20
maladie cardiaque **111**–11
maladie des gencives **119**–11
maladies communes et maladies
      de l'enfance **111**

MALADIES ET AFFECTIONS
      MÉDICALES **111**
malentendant(e) **32**–12
malvoyant(e) **32**–11
mammifères **209**–10
MAMMIFÈRES **216**–217
mammifères marins **213**
manche **100**–6
mandarines **68**–9
manger **11**–I
manger le petit déjeuner **38**–E
manger un régime équilibré **114**–F
mangues **68**–21
maniques **78**–29
mannequin **168**–41
mannequin de couturier **100**–2
manœuvre de Heimlich **117**–18
manteau **56**–11
manucure **168**–38
manuel de premiers soins **117**–2
maquillage **109**
marchander **102**–A
marché aux puces **222**–6
MARCHÉ DES PRODUCTEURS **84**–85
marcher avec un ami **143**–A
marcher jusqu'à la salle de classe **11**–C
marches **53**–3
marches sont abîmées **62**–7
mardi **20**–10
marée noire **218**–17
margarine **72**–20
marguerite **211**–14
mari **34**–13
mariage **22**–2
Marine **138**–15
marqueur **7**–24
marqueur à essuyage à sec **7**–17
Mars **205**–4
mars **21**–27
marsouin **213**–30
marteau **180**–1
marteau pneumatique **178**–9
masque **239**–9
masque à particules **179**–14
masque chirurgical **93**–36
masque d'attrapeur **231**–15
masque d'oxygène **161**–24
masque de plongée **225**–6
masque de ski **90**–15
masque facial **93**–32
masque respiratoire **92**–7, **179**–13
masse **178**–23
massicot **183**–22
match de base-ball **44**–2
matelas **58**–20
matelas à langer **59**–2
matelas de mousse **226**–13

matériaux radioactifs **179**–7
matériel agricole **177**–12
matériel de sauvetage **225**–20
mathématiques **189**–10
MATHÉMATIQUES **192–193**
matin **18**–15
MAUVAISE JOURNÉE AU
    TRAVAIL **186–187**
mauve **24**–6
mayonnaise **79**–23
mécanicien (mécanicienne) auto **166**–8
médaillon **95**–35
médicament d'ordonnance **112**–3
médicament prescrit **112**–3
médicament sans ordonnance **113**–18
médicaments **121**–20
médicaments sans ordonnance **113**
méduse **212**–14
mélanger les ingrédients **77**–R
mélangeur **54**–12
mélangeur électrique **54**–25
melons **68**–19
membrane cellulaire **194**–6
même couleur **23**–15
menottes **141**–2
menton **106**–1
menu **82**–7
MENU DE CAFÉTÉRIA **80–81**
menu déroulant **197**–8
mercredi **20**–11
Mercure **205**–1
mère **34**–3
mère célibataire **35**–22
merle américain **214**–16
message texte **14**–19
message vocal **14**–18
mesure **17**
mesurer **17**–C
mesurer les ingrédients **75**–A
MESURES **17**
mesures de liquides **75**
mesures de matières sèches **75**
méthodes de conservation d'énergie
    et des ressources **219**
mètre **181**–16
métro **151**–12
mètre-ruban **100**–17, **181**–45
mettre **87**–B, **109**–P
mettre de l'écran solaire **108**–D
mettre des noms en majuscule **190**–A
mettre du déodorant **108**–C
mettre l'appelant en attente **171**–N
mettre la ceinture de sécurité **160**–H
mettre la ceinture de sécurité **36**–L
mettre la première lettre des phrases
    en majuscule **190**–B
mettre la table **82**–A

mettre les phrases dans l'ordre **9**–X
meuble classeur **182**–11
meubles de patio **53**–19
meubles et accessoires **59**
meurtre **142**–12
mi-bas **91**–12
micro **234**–18
micro-ondes **54**–13
microprocesseur **196**–4
microscope **194**
midi **18**–16
midwest **201**–9
mignon(ne) **32**–14
mille **16**
millième **16**
mince **32**–9
mini-fourgonnette **156**–8
mini-jupe **96**–15
Ministère **138**–10
minuit **18**–21
minuteman **198**–10
minutes **18**–2
minuteur **78**–18
miroir **57**–18
miroir en pied **58**–6
mitaines **90**–10
mobile **59**–5
mocassins **95**–30
modèle réduit **232**–9
modèles réduits de train **233**–27
moderne **199**–2
modes de paiement **27**
moineau **214**–7
mois **20**–3
mois de l'année **21**
molécule **195**–27
mollet **106**–22
moments de la journée **18**
monarque **199**–4
moniteur **196**–11
moniteur de bébé **59**–7
moniteur de contrôle des signes
    vitaux **121**–26
monospace **156**–8
monter à bord de l'avion **160**–E
monter dans le taxi **153**–E
monter des éléments **170**–A
monter les escaliers **153**–C
monteur (monteuse) **166**–7
montre-bracelet **94**–16
montrer vos papiers d'identité **137**–C
montrer votre carte d'embarquement et
    votre pièce d'identité **160**–C
moquette **56**–24
morse **213**–32
morue **71**–8, **212**–5
mosquée **126**–5

mot **190**–1
motel **126**–12
moteur **158**–18
moteur de recherche **197**–6
motif **99**–22
motifs **96**
moto **150**–4
mouche **214**–28
mouffette **216**–12
moufles **90**–10
moule **212**–17
moule à gâteau **78**–26
moule à tarte **78**–28
moules **71**–13
mourir **41**–R
moustache **33**–5
moustaches **216**–18
moustique **214**–22
moutarde **79**–22
mouton **215**–6
mouvement politique **199**–16
moyen **96**–3
MOYENS DE TRANSPORT **150–151**
moyens de transport à l'aéroport **152**
mozzarella **71**–29
muffin **79**–16
muffin anglais **80**–5
multiplier **192**–C
mur **56**–10
mûres **68**–17
muscle **107**–32
musée d'art **223**–9
musicien (musicienne) **168**–43
musique **189**–16
MUSIQUE **238**
musique **64**–3
musiques du monde **237**–32
myrtilles **68**–16
mystère **237**–20
n'être pas d'accord **12**–L
nachos **79**–7
nageoire **212**–1
nager **230**–L
naître **40**–A
nappe **55**–12
navets **69**–16
navette **152**–19
navette spatiale **205**–19
naviguer sur une page Web **197**
ne pas boire d'alcool **112**–F
ne pas boire et conduire **143**–G
ne pas conduire ni manœuvrer
    des équipements lourds **112**–E
ne pas fumer **114**–G
ne pas jeter des ordures **219**–L
ne pas ouvrir la porte à des
    étrangers **143**–F

ne pas pouvoir respirer **116**–N
ne pas prendre avec des produits
    laitiers **112**–D
ne pas s'engager **154**–2
ne soyez pas en retard **174**–E
négocier un prix **157**–D
neigeux **13**–12
Neptune **205**–8
nerveux (nerveuse) **42**–10
NETTOYAGE COLLECTIF **148–149**
nettoyage de la piscine **184**–21
nettoyant à four **61**–3
nettoyant à vitres **61**–14
nettoyer **76**–A
nettoyer la maison **39**–O
nettoyer le filtre à air **101**–D
nettoyer le filtre à charpie **101**–D
nettoyer le four **60**–C
nettoyer les débris **147**–M
nettoyer votre bureau **10**–I
nettoyer…les dents **119**–A
nettoyeur **128**–2
neuf **16**
neutron **195**–32
neuvième **16**
neveu **34**–19
nez **104**–6
nid **209**–12
nièce **34**–18
niveau **180**–29
Noël **22**–18
noeud papillon **89**–16
noir **24**–13
noix **73**–36
noix de coco **68**–24
nom **4**–1
nom de famille **4**–4
NOMBRES **16**
nombres cardinaux **16**
nombres entiers **192**
nombres impairs **192**–3
nombres ordinaux **16**
nombres pairs **192**–4
nommer l'illustration **9**–V
nord **155**–1
Nord du Canada **201**–1
nord-ouest du Pacifique **201**–14
note en bas de page **190**–10
notes **10**–4
notes autoadhésives **183**–39
nourrir **36**–C, **177**–D
nourrir les plantes **176**–D
nouvel an **22**–9
nouvel emploi **172**–3
nouvelle lune **205**–9
Nouvelle-Angleterre **201**–11
novembre **21**–35

noyau **194**–7, **195**–29

nuageux **13**–10

nuit **18**–20

numérateur **192**–5

numéro d'accès **14**–16

numéro d'appartement **4**–6

numéro d'ordonnance **112**–5

numéro de compte d'épargne **132**–11

numéro de compte de chèque **132**–14

numéro de permis de conduire **136**–11

numéro de Sécurité Sociale **4**–15

numéro de téléphone **4**–11, **15**–30

numéro de téléphone cellulaire **4**–12

numéro UGS **27**–5

nylon **99**–21

objectif **194**–16

objets de valeur **132**–8

obscurci par le brouillard
   de pollution **13**–14

observatoire **205**–21

observer **195**–C

obstétricien(ne) **120**–2

obtenir de bonnes notes **10**–H

obtenir de la monnaie **26**–A

obtenir la carte grise du véhicule
   auprès du vendeur **157**–E

obtenir sa citoyenneté **40**–G

obtenir un diplôme **40**–D

obtenir un permis
   d'apprentissage **137**–F

obtenir un prêt **49**–J

obtenir une carte de
   bibliothèque **133**–A

obtenir votre permis **137**–I

OBTENTION D'UN DIPLÔME **206**–**207**

océan **204**–6, **225**–1

octobre **21**–34

oculaire **194**–14

oculiste **120**–7

odomètre **159**–28

œil **105**–11, **106**

œillet **211**–20

oeufs **66**–7

œufs brouillés **76**–7

œufs durs **76**–8

œufs pochés **76**–9

œufs sur le plat **76**–10

œufs tournés **76**–11

officiel **229**–6

offrir quelque chose **12**–D

oie **214**–13

oignons **69**–19

oignons verts **69**–20

oiseau **208**–4

oiseau-mouche **214**–10

OISEAUX, INSECTES ET
   ARACHNIDES **214**

ombre **225**–13

ombre à paupières **109**–35

omelette **76**–12

omoplate **107**–28

once de fromage **75**–11

once liquide de lait **75**–1

oncle **34**–8

oncologue **120**–5

ongle **106**–18

onglet **197**–7

onguent **113**–24

onguent antibactérien **117**–11

Ontario **201**–4

onze **16**

onzième **16**

opéra **223**–11

opérateur (opératrice) de
   machine **168**–37

opérations mathématiques **192**

opératrice de machine à coudre **98**–14

ophtalmologiste **120**–7

ophtalmologue **120**–7

opinion **44**–3

opossum **216**–4

opticien **130**–9

optométriste **115**–6

orage **13**–16

orange **24**–4

oranges **68**–5

orang-outan **217**–39

orchidée **211**–19

ordinateur **7**–15, **183**–17

ordinateur de bureau **196**

ordinateur portable **196**–16

ORDINATEURS **196**

oreille **105**–12

oreille percée **32**–17

oreiller **58**–11

oreillons **111**–7

organiser des documents **171**–L

organiser vos idées **191**–G

organiseur **183**–49

organismes **194**–1

orgue **238**–20

orignal **216**–1

orme **210**–16

ornement **239**–15

ornithorynque **217**–46

orteil **94**–23, **105**–10

orthodontie **119**

orthodontiste **119**–5

os **107**–33

otarie **213**–33

ouest **155**–2

ouïes **212**–2

ouragan **145**–14

ourlet **100**–8

ours **216**–11

ours en peluche **37**–23

oursin **212**–21

OUTILS ET FOURNITURES POUR LE
   BÂTIMENT **180**–**181**

ouvre-boîte **78**–1, **146**–8

ouvre-boîte électrique **54**–14

ouvrez votre livre **6**–G

ouvrier (ouvrière) agricole **177**–8

ouvrier (ouvrière) du bâtiment **178**–1

ouvrier (ouvrière) engagé(e) **177**–20

ouvrier imprudent **179**–1

ouvrier prudent **179**–2

ouvrir un compte **132**

pack de six **74**–9

pack de six boissons gazeuses **74**–21

paille **79**–18

pain **67**–11, **74**–22

pain à l'ail **81**–28

pain blanc **71**–18

pain de blé **71**–19

pain de froment **71**–18

pain de seigle **71**–20

pain de viande **81**–31

pains **74**–10

paire de ciseaux **100**–16

palais de justice **125**–13

palais des congrès **127**–24

pallette **175**–13

palmes **225**–7

palmier **210**–14

palourdes **71**–15

pamplemousse **68**–6

pancréas **107**–45

panda **217**–41

panier **56**–3

panier à linge **57**–1

panier à vaisselle **54**–5

panier de lessive **101**–2

panier de provisions **73**–9

panneau d'autoroute **154**–17

PANNEAUX DE SIGNALISATION **154**

pansement adhésif **117**–5

pantalon capri **88**–8

pantalon corsair **88**–8

pantalon de survêtement **89**–23

pantalons **87**–12

pantalons de sécurité **93**–22

pantalons de travail **92**–5

pantalons larges **97**–30

pantalons serrés **97**–29

panthère **217**–40

pantoufles **91**–26

paon **214**–14

papayes **68**–20

papier à en-tête **183**–42

papier aluminium **72**–23

papier de bricolage **232**–12

papier de verre **181**–56

papier hygiénique **57**–19, **146**–13

papier peint **59**–8

papillon **214**–19

papillon de nuit **214**–21

paquet de biscuits **74**–20

paquets **74**–8

paragraphe **190**–3

parallélogramme **193**–33

parapluie **90**–17

parasites intestinaux **111**–13

parasol de plage **225**–14

parc d'attraction **223**–10

parc de stationnement **124**–1

PARC ET LE TERRAIN DE JEUX **224**

parcmètre **129**–25

parcomètre **129**–25

PARCS NATIONAUX DES
   ÉTATS-UNIS **220**–**221**

pardessus **90**–2

pare-brise **158**–1

pare-chocs **158**–8

parenthèses **190**–19

parents **44**–6

parfum **108**–6

parka **90**–9

parler à des amis **173**–A

parler au téléphone **15**–C

parler de votre expérience **174**–L

parler une langue étrangère **170**–N

parlez au professeur **6**

paroi cellulaire **194**–5

partager un livre **8**–M

participer à un programme de
   surveillance de quartier **143**–L

participer en classe **10**–B

parties d'une fleur **211**

partir **160**–J

PARTIR EN VOYAGE **162**–**163**

passage à niveau **154**–14

passage de la sécurité **160**

passage pour écoliers **154**–15

passage pour piétons **128**–15

passager **150**–2, **152**–3, **161**–15

passages pour piétons **154**–13

passeport **41**–10

passer **230**–G

passer au contrôle de sécurité **160**–D

passer au micro-ondes pendant
   5 minutes **77**–T

passer en jugement **141**–D

passer l'aspirateur sur le tapis **60**–H

passer l'examen de citoyenneté **140**–I

passer le coin en courant **153**–H

passer le contrôle technique **157**–J

passer le premier permis de conduire **137**
Passer Main **155**–E
passer sous le pont **153**–A
passer sur le pont **153**–B
passer un appel d'urgence **15**
passer un appel téléphonique **15**
passer un examen **10**
passer un examen écrit **137**–E
PASSE-TEMPS ET JEUX **232–233**
passoire **78**–17
pastèques **68**–18
pastilles pour la gorge **113**–30
pastrami **71**–23
patates douces **69**–18
pâte dentifrice **109**–23
pâtes **67**–12
patient(e) **118**–6, **121**–18
patinage artistique **227**–5
patinage avec patins à roues alignées **228**–10
patinage sur glace **227**–4
patiner **230**–U
patins à glace **231**–9
patins à roues alignées **231**–10
patio **53**–16
patron **164**–4
patte **216**–20
pattes **33**–7
paume **106**–15
paupière **106**–10
pause **235**–E
pavé (steak) de flétan **71**–6
payer en espèces **27**–A
payer l'addition **82**–I
payer le premier et le dernier mois de loyer **48**–E
payer les frais de dossier **137**–D
payer les impôts **140**–B
payer **27**–G
payer une amende (de retard) **133**–E
paysage **162**–2
PBX **182**–13
peau **107**–31
pêche **226**–4
pêches **68**–10
pêcheur commercial **167**–17
pédale d'accélérateur **159**–46
pédale de frein **159**–45
pédiatre **120**–4
peigne **33**–21, **108**–13
peigner…les cheveux **108**–G
peindre **49**–P, **178**–A, **233**–E
peintre en bâtiment **168**–46
peinture **181**–25
peinture à l'huile **233**–19
peinture acrylique **232**–10

peler les carottes **77**–K
pelle **176**–7, **178**–22
pelle rétrocaveuse **178**–8
pellicule **235**–22
pelote à épingles **100**–13
pelouse **53**–26
péninsule **204**–7
péninsule du Yucatan **201**–19
penser au sujet **191**–E
percer une dent **119**–D
perceuse électrique **180**–8
perche (eau douce) **212**–6
percussion **238**
père **34**–4
père célibataire **35**–23
périmètre **193**–43
période coloniale **198**
périodiques **133**–4
perles **95**–34, **99**–32
permis de conduire **40**–4, **136**–9
peroxyde d'hydrogène **117**–9
perruche **215**–15
persil **69**–28
personne âgée **30**–5
personnel de l'hôpital **120**
personnel soignant **120**
perte de l'ouïe **115**–2
pèse-lettre **135**–8, **183**–27
pèse-personne **57**–27
peser les aliments **75**–B
pétales **211**–8
petit **96**–2
petit enfant **31**–6
petit(e) **32**–6
petite annonce **48**–2
petite branche **210**–1
petite cuiller (cuillère) **83**–31
petite culotte **91**–14
petite main **23**–1
petite ville **52**–3
pétition **148**–5
petits pains **74**–11, **80**–17
pétoncle **212**–19
pétoncles **71**–12
pétrole **218**–6
phare **158**–7
PHARMACIE **112–113**
pharmacie **128**–4
pharmacien **112**–1
pharmacienne **112**–1
phlébotomiste **121**–29
phoque **213**–34
photo **136**–4
photo drôle **206**–2
photo sérieuse **206**–3
photocopieuse **183**–23
photographe **206**–1

photos **58**–3
photosynthèse **194**–10
phrase **190**–2
physicien **195**–33
physiothérapeute **115**–12
physiothérapie **115**–11
physique **195**
pi **193**–46
piano **238**–14
pic **214**–8
pics **233**–30
pièce de théâtre **223**–8
pièces **26**, **175**–5
pièces d'une machine à coudre **98**
PIÈCES D'UNE VOITURE **158–159**
pied **104**–8
pied presseur **98**–19
pierre **208**–6
piéton **128**–14
pieuvre **212**–9
pigeon **214**–15
piles **146**–15
pilons **70**–23
pilote **161**–11
piloter un avion **170**–F
pilule **113**–21
piments **69**–29
pin **210**–9
pince à cheveux **108**–19
pince à creusets **195**–44
pince à dénuder **181**–42
pince à linge **101**–10
pinceau **181**–22, **233**–20
pinces **78**–23, **180**–7
pinces à cheveux **108**–21
pinces de platine **194**–21
pincettes **117**–4
pingouin **214**–11
ping-pong **228**–14
pinte de yaourt glacé **75**–3
pioche **178**–21
piquant **216**–23
pique-niquer **224**–D
piqure d'insecte **110**–11
piscine **51**–22, **184**–22
piste **5**–21
piste cyclable **224**–3
pistolet **142**–13
pistolet à peinture **181**–21
pizza **79**–10
placard **58**–5
placoplâtre **178**–19
plage **204**–10
PLAGE **225**
plaine côtière du Golfe **201**–16
plaines **204**–19
plan d'étage **186**–4

planche à découper **54**–27
planche à repasser **101**–14
planche de surf **225**–16
plancher **46**–6
plancher en bois **58**–21
PLANIFICATION DE CARRIÈRE **172**
planifier une carrière **172**
planifier une entrevue d'emploi **173**–I
planifier une réunion **171**–J
plante d'intérieur **56**–4, **211**–27
planter **177**–A
planter un arbre **176**–E, **219**–N
plantes **208**–5, **210**
plaque à aiguille **98**–18
plaque d'immatriculation **136**–12, **158**–12
plaque de rue **129**–26
plaque dentaire **119**–12
plat **55**–20
plateau **55**–17
plateau à desserts **83**–10
plateau mexicain **201**–15
plate-bande **53**–20
plate-forme de chargement **175**–15
platine **194**–17
plâtre **113**–20
pleine lune **205**–12
pleurer **206**–B
plier le linge **101**–F
plombage **119**–8
plombier **63**–20
plonge **83**–13
plongée en apnée **227**–11
plongée sous-marine **227**–12
plonger **230**–K
plongeur **83**–14, **185**–2
pluie acide **218**–13
plume **214**–4
plumeau **61**–1
pluvieux **13**–11
pneu **158**–5
poche **100**–7, **217**–50
poche de glace **117**–13
pochette **89**–19
pochette matelassée **183**–40
podium **206**–5
poêle à frire **78**–5
poêlon **54**–24
poids **32**, **75**
POIDS ET MESURES **75**
poignée de porte **53**–12
poignées **78**–29
poignet **106**–14
poinsettia **211**–24
point **190**–11
point d'exclamation **190**–13
point d'extrémité **193**–21

point d'interrogation **190**–12

point de départ **162**–1

point décimal **17**–7

point virgule **190**–18

pointeur **197**–12

pointeuse **165**–7

points d'intérêt **220**–1

points de suture **117**–15

poires **68**–4

pois **69**–21, **96**–21

poisson **66**–1, **71**, **209**–14

poisson frais **71**–16

poisson grillé **81**–29

poisson plat **212**–15

poisson rouge **215**–16

poisson surgelé **71**–17

poisson-chat **71**–2

poisson-épée **71**–5, **212**–10

poitrine **104**–4, **107**–25

poitrines **70**–19

poivrons **69**–7

policier (policière) **141**–1, **168**–48

polir les meubles **60**–E

pollution **218**

pollution de l'air **218**–11

pollution de l'eau **218**–14

pollution par les pesticides **218**–16

polo **92**–14

pomme de terre au four **81**–25

pommeau de douche **57**–13

pommes **68**–1

pommes de terre **69**–17

pommes de terre rissolées **80**–3

pompier **144**–9, **167**–26

pompiste **162**–3

ponceuse électrique **180**–11

poncho **90**–19

ponctuation **190**

pop **237**–25

porc **70**

porc-épic **216**–10

porche avant **53**

port USB **196**–7

portail **53**–9

porte **46**–3

porte brosses à dents **57**–24

porte d'embarquement **161**–8

porte d'entrée **53**–11

porte de garage **53**–7

porte moustiquaire **53**–15

porte savon **57**–3

porte tambour **184**–2

porte-téléphone cellulaire **94**–15

porte vitrée coulissante **53**–18

porte-bébé **37**–17

portefeuille **94**–13

porte-jarretelles **91**–16

porte-journaux **56**–23

porte-monnaie **94**–14

porter **36**–A

porter le plateau **82**–H

porter les livres **11**–F

porte-serviettes **57**–15

porteur **160**–1

portier **184**–1

poser des briques **178**–B

poser des questions **174**–M

poser une question **8**–K

posez le crayon **6**–J

POSTE **134–135**

poste **125**–11

poste de débutant **172**–1

poste de pilotage **161**–10

poste de police **124**–6

poste de secours **225**–21

poste de travail modulaire **182**–7

poster la carte **135**–D

postérieur **107**–30

postier (postière) **169**–49

postier(ère) **135**–7

pot **37**–12

pot à crème **55**–15

poubelle **53**–24

pouce **106**–16

pouce [po] **17**–15

poudre de bain **108**–4

poudre pour bébés **37**–14

poudre pour le visage **109**–41

poule **215**–8

poulet **66**–3, **70**–16

poulet cru **70**–24

poulet cuit **70**–25

poulet frit **76**–1

poulet rôti **81**–22

poulpe **212**–9

poumon **107**–39

poupée **59**–21

poupées en papier **233**–28

poussette **37**–18, **37**–20

pousser la balançoire **224**–B

poussette **37**–18, **37**–20

poutre en I **178**–3

poutrelle **178**–3

pouvoir exécutif **138**

pouvoir judiciaire **138**

pouvoir législatif **138**, **139**–23

pré **204**–20

préciser son nom aux services

publics **49**–O

préfecture (service des cartes

grises) **124**–4

PRÉFECTURE (SERVICE DES

CARTES GRISES) **136–137**

prélever…du sang **118**–F

premier **16**

premier congrès continental **198**–6

premier ministre **199**–7

premier président **198**–11

PREMIERS SOINS **117**

premiers soins **117**

prendre avec de la nourriture ou

du lait **112**–A

prendre des leçons de code de

la route **137**–B

prendre des leçons de conduite **137**–G

prendre des notes **10**–C, **171**–K

prendre des radios **119**–B

prendre l'autobus pour aller

à l'école **38**–H

prendre la commande **82**–E

prendre possession **49**–K

prendre sa retraite **41**–O

prendre soin d'enfants **170**–P

prendre un avion **160**

prendre un bain **108**–B

prendre un livre **133**–C

prendre un médicament **114**–D

prendre un message **171**–Q

prendre une douche **38**–C, **108**–A

prendre une feuille de papier **9**–Y

prendre une heure avant de

manger **112**–B

prendre une photo **206**–A

prendre…la température **118**–B

prenez le crayon **6**–I

prenez place **6**–F

prénom **4**–2

PRÉPARATION ET SALUBRITÉ DES

ALIMENTS **76–77**

préparer la voiture **162**–A

préparer le déjeuner **38**–F

préparer le dîner **39**–Q

préparer une trousse d'urgence en

cas de catastrophe **146**–B

préposé **5**–13, **182**–2

préposé à l'expédition **175**–14

préposé à la préparation

alimentaire **185**–4

préposé au classement **182**–10

préposé au comptoir **79**–17

préposé aux billets **160**–3

préposé aux commandes **175**–10

préposé du service des cartes

grises **136**–3

préposé(e) aux soins **120**–16

PRÉPOSITIONS **25**

PRÉPOSITIONS INDIQUANT LE

MOUVEMENT **153**

prescription **112**–2

présent **240**–3

présentation **182**–6

présenter un ami **3**–I

présentoir **98**–16

président **138**–8, **199**–5

président de la Court Suprême **138**–13

presse-ail **78**–11

pressing **128**–2

pression **99**–26

pression artérielle élevée **111**–14

prêter de l'argent **26**–C

preuves **141**–9

printemps **21**–37

prise **58**–28

prise d'alimentation **159**–42

prise téléphonique **142**–3

prisme **195**–35

prisonnier **141**–15

prix **27**–7

prix courant **27**–2

prix réduit **27**–3

problème compliqué **23**–24

problème de mot **192**–11

problème difficile **23**–24

problème mathématique **192**

problème simple **23**–23

problèmes d'habillement **97**

problèmes de vue **115**–1

problèmes dentaires **119**

PROBLÈMES ET RÉPARATIONS

DOMESTIQUES **62–63**

PROCÉDURES D'URGENCE **146–147**

procédures médicales **118**

procès équitable **140**–5

processus d'écriture **191**

procureur **141**–10

producteur (productrice) **177**–13

produit **192**–9

produit adoucissant **101**–6

produit assouplissant **101**–6

produit insectifuge **226**–23

produits de boulangerie **73**

produits de pâtisserie **73**

produits laitiers **72**

produits surgelés **72**

professeur **5**–8

profondeur **17**–18

programme sur la nature **236**–7

programmer des ordinateurs **170**–I

projecteur LCD **6**–6, **235**–29

promener un chien **129**–F

promotion **172**–4

prononcer une sentence **141**–F

propriétaire **51**–27

propriétaire de l'usine **175**–1

propriétaire de magasin **166**–11

protège-oreilles **90**–13, **179**–16

protège-tibia **231**–13

protéger votre sac ou votre
porte-monnaie **143**–D

proton **195**–31

provinces des Prairies **201**–3

provinces maritimes **201**–6

pruneaux **68**–26

prunes **68**–13

psychiatre **120**–8

puces **63**–25

pull à col échancré **96**–10

pull à col en v **96**–8

pull à col rond **96**–7

pull à col roulé **96**–9

pull-over **28**–2, **87**–14

pull-over blanc est devant le
pull-over noir **25**–7

pull-over gris est sous le pull-over
orange **25**–11

pull-over noir est derrière le
pull-over blanc **25**–8

pull-over orange est sur le
pull-over gris **25**–9

pull-over turquoise est dans
la boîte **25**–6

pull-over vert est entre les
pull-overs roses **25**–12

pull-over violet est à côté du
pull-over gris **25**–10

pull-overs bleus sont en desous
des pull-overs rouges **25**–5

pull-overs jaunes sont sur la
gauche **25**–1

pull-overs marrons sont sur la
droite **25**–3

pull-overs rouges sont au-dessus des
pull-overs bleus **25**–4

pull-overs violets sont au milieu **25**–2

pulvérisation nasale **113**–32

puma **216**–2

punaises de lit **63**–24

pupitre **6**–7

purée de pommes de terre **81**–23

purificateur d'air **113**–14

puzzle **59**–17

pyjama **91**–24

pyjama-couverture **91**–27

pyramide **193**–39

quai **152**–7

quarante **16**

quarantième **16**

quart **17**–4

quart de lune **205**–11

quart de tasse de sucre brun **75**–8

quatorze **16**

quatorzième **16**

quatre **16**

quatre-vingt dixième **16**

quatre-vingt-dix (nonante) **16**

quatre-vingtième **16**

quatre-vingts (octante) **16**

quatrième **16**

Québec **201**–5

queue **73**–11, **216**–22

quilles **222**–4, **228**–3

quincaillerie **148**–4

quinze **16**

quinzième **16**

quitter le travail **38**–N

quotidiennement **20**–21

quotient **192**–10

R&B **237**–28

rabot **181**–57

raccords **181**–18

raccourcir le pantalon **100**–B, **100**–D

raccrocher **15**–D

racine **210**–5

racines **211**–3

raclette **61**–15

racquetball **228**–12

radiateur **158**–19

radio **159**–37

radioactivité **218**–15

radiocassette et lecteur de CD **234**–1

radiologue **120**–6

radio-réveil **102**–6

radis **69**–4

rafting **226**–2

raie **33**–4, **212**–11

rail de sécurité **59**–10

raisins **68**–3

raisins secs **68**–25

ralentir **154**–9

rallonge (électrique) **181**–14

rallonger le pantaloon **100**–A

ramasse-poussière **61**–17

ramasser les livres **11**–E

rame de métro **152**–6

ramure **216**–16

ranch **52**–10

randonnée **226**–7

randonnées avec sac à dos **226**–6

ranger les bagages à main **160**–G

ranger les jouets **60**–G

rangez vos livres **9**–Z

râpe **78**–2

râper le fromage **77**–G

raquette de tennis **231**–2

rasoir **109**–27

rasoir électrique **109**–26

rassemblement paisible **140**–1

rat **215**–17

râteau **176**–8

ratisser (les feuilles) **176**–C

raton laveur **216**–13

rats **63**–27

rayé **96**–20

rayon **72**–6, **193**–35

rayon de la bijouterie **95**–8

rayon des chaussures **95**–7

rayon des fruits et légumes **72**–2

raz-de-marée **145**–17

RCR (réanimation
cardio-respiratoire) **117**–17

réception **182**–15, **184**–12

réceptionniste **118**–2, **164**–5, **169**–51,
182–14, **184**–11

recevoir des commentaires **191**–K

recevoir la carte **135**–F

recevoir une contravention **162**–C

réchaud de camping **226**–16

RECHERCHE D'EMPLOI **173**

RECHERCHE D'UN LOGEMENT **48–49**

rechercher le mot **8**–A

RÉCIPIENTS ET EMBALLAGE **74**

récolter **177**–B

récoltes **177**

réconforter **36**–I

recruteur **172**–14

rectangle **193**–29

reçu **27**–6

récupérer vos bagages **160**–L

récurrer l'évier **60**–K

recycler **219**–C

recycler les journaux **60**–B

rédaction **190**–4

rédiger une version finale **191**–L

rédiger une version préliminaire **191**–H

réduire la quantité de déchets **219**–A

réécrire **191**–J

réfrigérateur **54**–9

refuser une invitation **12**–J

regarder **102**–B

regarder dans les yeux **174**–J

regarder la télévision **39**–X

regarder les annonces de
voitures **157**–A

reggae **237**–31

régime de bananes **68**–29

régions des États-Unis **201**

régions du Canada **201**

régions du Mexique **201**

règle **17**–13

réglementations de sécurité **164**–6

régler le thermostat **219**–J

régler les problèmes de santé **115**

règles **64**–7

règles d'écriture **190**

rein **107**–43

relevé de compte **132**–16

remarié(e) **35**–24

rembobiner **235**–C

rembourser l'argent **26**–D

remercier l'intervieweur **174**–N

remercier quelqu'un **12**–E

remettre les lettres dans l'ordre **9**–W

remettre les livres **11**–G

remorque **156**–17

remplacer les essuie-glaces **157**–K

remplir l'espace blanc **9**–O

remplir la laveuse **101**–C

remplir le lave-linge **101**–C

remplir le réservoir d'essence **157**–G

remplir une demande d'emploi **173**–J

remplir un formulaire **4**

remuer **77**–O

renard **216**–15

RENCONTRER ET SALUER **2–3**

rencontrer les voisins **49**–R

rencontrer un agent immobilier **49**–G

rendez-vous **22**–4, **118**–1

rendre **110**–E

rendre l'examen **10**–O

rendre la rédaction **191**–M

rendre un livre **133**–D

RENSEIGNEMENTS PERSONNELS **4**

réparateur **62**–10

réparateur d'appareils
électroménagers **166**–4

réparateur de matériel
électronique **167**–24

réparer des appareils ménagers **170**–J

réparer les robinets qui fuient **219**–F

repasser les vêtements **101**–G

répondeur **14**–17

répondre **135**–H

répondre à une question **8**–L

représentant du service à la
clientèle **167**–20

représentant élu **139**–32

reptiles **213**

repu **42**–6

requin **212**–4

réserve **185**–5

réservoir d'essence **158**–10

résidences universitaires **52**–8

résoudre des problèmes
mathématiques **170**–M

respecter les lois **140**–C

respiration artificielle **117**–16

responsabilités **140**

responsable **165**–8

responsable des admissions **120**–14

restaurant **125**–14

RESTAURANT **82–83**

restaurant minute **128**–10

RESTAURANT MINUTE **79**

RESTAURATION RAPIDE **79**
rester à l'écart des fenêtres **147**–I
rester à l'écoute **15**–H
rester au lit **114**–B
rester calme **147**–E
rester en forme **114**–E
résultat **10**–3
résultats des élections **139**–31
retirer **109**–Q
retirer de l'argent **132**–F
retirer votre carte **132**–G
retouches **100**
retour de bouteilles consignées **73**–16
retourner **27**–H
retourner en classe **11**–M
rétroprojecteur **7**–16
rétroviseur **159**–35
rétroviseur extérieur **158**–3
RÉUNION DES LOCATAIRES **64–65**
RÉUNION FAMILIALE **44–45**
RÉUSSIR À L'ÉCOLE **10**
réussir l'examen de conduite **137**–H
réussir un examen **10**–E
réutiliser les sacs à provisions **219**–B
réveil **58**–24
revenir à la maison **39**–R
REVENIR DU MARCHÉ **66–67**
réverbère **148**–3
revers **100**–9
réviser **191**–J
rhinocéros **217**–28
rhume **111**–1
rideau de douche **57**–14
rideaux **58**–7
rimmel **109**–39
rince-bouche **109**–25
rincer…les cheveux **108**–F
rire **44**–A
risques d'accident et matériaux
    dangereux **179**
rivage **204**–12
rivière **155**–10, **204**–3
riz **67**–10, **81**–30, **177**–1
robe **86**–3
robe de chambre **91**–29
robe de cocktail **89**–20
robe de grossesse **88**–5
robe de nuit **91**–25
robe du soir **89**–18
robe maternité **88**–5
robinet **57**–8
robinet coule **63**–17
robinet de fermeture du gaz **146**–4
robot culinaire **54**–26
rock **237**–23
roman **133**–16
rondelle **180**–37

rondelles d'oignon **79**–4
rongeurs **215**
rosbif **71**–21
rose **24**–7, **211**–15
rôti **70**–1
rôti de bœuf **71**–21
rôtissoire **78**–13
roue de secours **158**–23
rouge **24**–1
rouge à lèvres **109**–38
rouge-gorge **214**–16
rougeole **111**–5
rouleau (à peinture) **181**–23
rouleau à pâtisserie **78**–30
rouleau d'essuie-tout **74**–23
rouleaux **33**–19
ruban **99**–30
ruban à masquer **181**–53
ruban adhésif en toile **181**–49
ruban adhésif transparent **183**–30
ruban correcteur **183**–37
ruban d'emballage **183**–32
ruban isolant **181**–43
rue **150**–5, **155**–8
ruelle **51**–24
RUES EN VILLE **126–127**
s'assurer de bien comprendre **12**–N
s'endormir **39**–Z
s'engager sur l'autoroute **153**–I
s'enregistrer électroniquement **160**–A
s'entraîner **230**–N
s'étirer **230**–M
s'étouffer **116**–L
s'excuser **12**–F
s'habiller **38**–D
s'habiller de manière adéquate **174**–B
s'incliner **3**–H
s'inscrire au Service sélectif **140**–D
sable **225**–23
sabots **216**–17
sac **161**–18
sac à bandoulière **94**–17
sac à dos **94**–18, **226**–15
sac à main **87**–9
sac à provisions **67**–13
sac de couchage **226**–12
sac de farine **74**–19
sac de laitue **69**–31
sac pour bébé **37**–16
sacoches **94**–2
sacs **74**–7
sacs à main **94**–2
sacs à ordures **61**–24
sacs d'aspirateur **61**–12
sacs de stockage en plastique **72**–25
saigner **116**–M
saigner du nez **110**–17

saisir au clavier **196**
saisir des données **171**–B
saisir le code PIN **132**–E
saisir le NIP **132**–E
saisons **21**
salade **80**–15
salade d'épinards **80**–13
salade de chou **80**–18
salade de fruits **80**–21
salade de pâtes **80**–20
salade de pommes de terre **80**–19
salade du chef **80**–14
saladier **54**–28, **55**–21
salaires **165**–12
salamandre **212**–27
salami **71**–24
salière et poivrière **55**–13
SALLE À MANGER **55**
salle à manger **82**–1
salle d'attente **182**–16
salle d'audience **141**–7
salle d'opération **121**
salle de bain **46**–4
SALLE DE BAIN **57**
salle de banquet **185**–14
salle de classe **5**–7
SALLE DE CLASSE **6–7**
salle de conférence **182**–4
salle de danse **184**–26
salle de réunion **184**–25
salle des ordinateurs **5**–15
salon **47**–12
SALON **56**
salon de coiffure **131**–18
salon de coiffure pour hommes **129**–19
salopette **88**–6
salubrité des aliments **76**
saluer l'appelant **171**–M
saluer l'intervieweur **174**–H
saluer les gens **3**–G
samedi **20**–14
sandales **88**–9
sandwich au fromage grillé **80**–10
sandwich au poulet **79**–5
sandwich club **80**–12
sans issue **154**–6
sans sucre **122**–7
satellite **205**–20
Saturne **205**–6
saucisses **70**–12, **80**–2
saule **210**–13
saumon entier **71**–3
sauter **230**–I
sauterelle **214**–24
savon **57**–4, **108**–3
saxophone **238**–5
scanner **183**–20

scanner un document **171**–H
scarabée **214**–18
scie à main **180**–4
scie à métaux **180**–5
scie circulaire **180**–9
scie sauteuse **180**–10
science **189**–11
SCIENCE **194–195**
science-fiction **237**–18
score **229**–1
scorpion **214**–30
se brosser…les dents **109**–J
se brûler **116**–H
se cacher **240**–D
se casser un os **116**–P
se conduire mal **44**–B
se connecter et envoyer un courriel **197**
se couper…les ongles **109**–N
se détendre **39**–U
se faire porter malade **186**–A
se faire vacciner **114**–I
se fiancer **41**–J
se gargariser **109**–L
se lever **38**–B
se marier **41**–K
se mettre à l'abri **147**–J
se mettre du vernis…à ongles **109**–O
se noyer **116**–I
se passer la soie dentaire sur…
    les dents **109**–K
se pencher **230**–O
se perdre **162**–B
se préparer pour une entrevue **174**–A
se présenter **2**–C
se présenter aux élections **139**–A
se présenter à une entrevue **173**–K
se présenter en cour **141**–C
se raser **109**–M
se rendre à la maison **39**–R
se rendre à une agence de
    recrutement **173**–E
se renseigner quant aux
    caractéristiques **48**–B
se réveiller **38**–A
se sentir étourdi **110**–C
seau **61**–7, **225**–8
seau à couches **37**–7
sèche-linge **50**–13, **101**–4
sécher…les cheveux **108**–H
sécheresse **145**–11
sécheuse **50**–13, **101**–4
séchoir **33**–23, **108**–18
secondes **18**–3
sections d'une rédaction **190**
SÉCURITÉ AU TRAVAIL **179**
SÉCURITÉ PUBLIQUE **143**
segment de ligne **193**–20

sein **107**–26
seize **16**
seizième **16**
sélectionner **196**–B
semaine **20**–15
semaine dernière **20**–18
semaine prochaine **20**–20
semelle **94**–21
semence **211**–1
semis **211**–4
Sénat **138**–5
sénateur **138**–6
sénateur d'État **139**–25
sénatrice **138**–6
sens **106**
sens interdit **154**–2
SENSATIONS **42–43**
SENTIMENTS **42–43**
sentir **106**–C
séparer **76**–B
sept **16**
septembre **21**–33
septième **16**
sequins **99**–33
séquoia **210**–18
seringue **118**–12
serpent à sonnettes **213**–38
serre **214**–2
serre-joints en C **180**–6
serrer des mains **3**–J
serrer la main **174**–J
serrure est cassée **62**–6
serrurier **62**–11
serveur **82**–8, **83**–9
serveur (serveuse) **169**–56, **185**–8
serveuse **83**–9
service à l'auto **128**–11
SERVICE ALIMENTAIRE **185**
service au téléphone **171**
service au volant **128**–11
service aux chambres **184**–17
SERVICE MILITAIRE ET ORGANISMES
    GOUVERNEMENTAUX **138–139**
services à la clientèle **130**–12
services publics **48**–5
serviette **55**–10, **83**–26, **88**–13
serviette de bain **57**–16
serviettes désinfectantes **61**–23
serviettes humides **146**–12
serviettes humides pour bébés **37**–15
servir **230**–P
servir des clients **170**–T
servir le repas **82**–F
set de table **55**–11
seul(e) **42**–17
sexe **4**–16
shampooing **108**–10

short **89**–25
siège arrière **159**–54
siège avant **159**–51
siège de sécurité pour
    enfant **37**–19, **159**–53
siège droit **161**–28
siège incliné **161**–27
siéger sur un jury **140**–E
signal faible **14**–12
signal puissant **14**–11
signaler les crimes à la police **143**–K
signaler les paquets suspects **143**–J
signature **4**–19
signer un contrat de location **48**–D
signez votre nom **4**
silencieux **158**–16
SIMILAIRES MAIS DIFFÉRENTES **28–29**
singe **217**–26
sirop contre la toux **113**–29
six **16**
sixième **16**
skateboard (planche à roulettes) **224**–7
ski alpin **227**–1
ski de randonnée **227**–3
ski nautique **227**–7
skier **230**–V
skis **231**–24
slip **91**–13
smoking **89**–17
socle **194**–20
socquettes **91**–11
sœur **34**–5
sofa **56**–18
soft-ball **229**–10
soie **98**–5
soie dentaire **109**–24
SOIGNEZ-VOUS **114–115**
SOINS DENTAIRES **119**
SOINS MÉDICAUX **118**
soir **18**–19
soixante **16**
soixante-dix (septante) **16**
soixante-dixième **16**
soixantième **16**
soja **177**–3
sol glissant **179**–6
soldat **169**–58
solde **132**–17
soleil **209**–8
solides géométriques **193**
solution **192**–14
somme **192**–7
sommet de montagne **204**–14
sommier **58**–19
sonnette **51**–31, **53**–14
sortie de secours **51**–25, **161**–14
sortir de l'autoroute **153**–J

sortir de la salle **11**–O
sortir les ordures **60**–Q
souci **211**–13
soucoupe **83**–25
soudeur (soudeuse) **169**–63
souffler **240**–C
souffleuse à feuilles **176**–2
soul **237**–28
soulever les livres **11**–E
souliers de ville **95**–29
souliers lacés **95**–29
souligner le mot **9**–S
soumettre une demande **48**–C
soupe **72**–18, **80**–16
soupe de poulet facile à préparer **77**
source lumineuse **194**–19
sources d'énergie **218**
sourcil **106**–9
sourd(e) **32**–12
sourire **2**–D
souris **63**–28, **196**–15, **215**–18
sous chef **185**–6
sous le capot **158**
sous-exposé **235**–35
sous-sol **47**–13
soustraire **192**–B
SOUS-VÊTEMENTS ET VÊTEMENTS
    DE NUIT **91**
sous-vêtements pour femmes **91**
sous-vêtements pour hommes **91**
sous-vêtements unisexes **91**
soutien-gorge **91**–20
soyez à l'heure **174**–F
spaghetti **81**–26
sparadrap stérile **117**–7
spatule **78**–19
spécialistes médicaux **120**
sphère **193**–42
SPORTS D'ÉQUIPE **229**
SPORTS D'HIVER ET NAUTIQUES **227**
SPORTS INDIVIDUELS **228**
stade **126**–1
stage **172**–6
stand **122**–3
station d'accueil **234**–3
station de métro **151**–11, **152**
station de taxis **152**–18
station service **125**–10
station spatiale **205**–18
stationnement **124**–1
stationnement interdit **154**–11
stationnement pour personnes
    handicapées **128**–6, **154**–12
stationner la voiture **129**–E
steak **70**–2, **81**–24
stéthoscope **118**–10
stop **154**–1

store (à lamelles) **58**–8
stress **115**–4
stuc **178**–15
styles **96**
stylo **7**–22
subir un choc électrique **116**–F
succédané de sucre **79**–20
sucette **37**–24
sucre **73**–30
sucreries **84**–8
sucrier **55**–14
sud **155**–3, **201**–13
sud-est **201**–13
sud-ouest **201**–12
suite **184**–16
suivre les conseils du médecin **114**–J
suivre les instructions **9**, **147**–F
sumac à feuille de chêne **210**–24
sumac lustré **210**–23
sumac vénéneux **210**–25
supermarché **127**–18
supprimer **196**–C
sur le campus **5**
surdose de drogues **116**–K
surexposé **235**–34
surf des neiges **231**–23
surfeur **225**–15
surpris(e) **43**–30
suspendre les vêtements **101**–H
suspens **237**–20
svelte **32**–9
sweatshirt **89**–22
sweatshirt à capuche **89**–22
symbole **155**–5
SYMPTÔMES ET BLESSURES **110**
synagogue **127**–16
syntonisateur **234**–13
système d'înjection de
    carburant **158**–17
SYSTÈME JURIDIQUE **141**
système solaire et les planètes **205**
système téléphonique
    automatisé **14**–23
table à langer **59**–1
table basse **56**–19
table d'examen **118**–7
table d'extrémité **56**–14
table d'opération **121**–40
table de billard **50**–15
table de chevet **121**–21
table de nuit **58**–23
table de pique-nique **224**–8
table de salle à manger **55**–9
table de salon **56**–19
table pliante **102**–4
tableau **6**–1, **56**–9
tableau blanc **6**–3

tableau d'affichage **7**–14
tableau d'information **131**–24
tableau de bord **159**
tableau périodique **195**–26
tablette **54**–2, **161**–21
tablier **92**–11, **93**–30
TÂCHES MÉNAGÈRES **60**
taco **79**–8
taie d'oreiller **58**–14
taille **32**
taille unique **96**–6
taille-bordures **176**–12
taille-crayon **7**–23
taille-crayons électrique **183**–26
tailler les bordures **176**–B
tailles **96**
tailleur **100**–3
talon **94**–22, **106**–24
talon de chèque de paye **165**–11
talons aiguille **89**–21, **95**–25, **97**–32
talons hauts **89**–21, **95**–25, **97**–32
talons plats **97**–31
tamanoir **217**–24
tambourin **238**–17
tamia **215**–20
tamis **78**–22
tampon **183**–47
tampon encreur **183**–46
tampons à récurer en laine d'acier **61**–5
tante **34**–7
taper **170**–R, **196**–A
taper l'objet **197**–D
taper le message **197**–E
taper une lettre **171**–A
taper votre mot de passe **197**–A
tapis **56**–24, **58**–22
tapis de bain **57**–28
tapis de caoutchouc **57**–5
tapis roulant **175**–9
tard **19**–24
tarif **152**–2
tarte **81**–35
tas de compost **53**–25
tasse **83**–24
tasse à thé **55**–6
tasse d'huile **75**–2
tasse de farine **75**–10
tatou **216**–8
tatouage **32**–18
taxe de vente **27**–8
taxi **150**–3
TB (tuberculose) **111**–15
technicien d'urgence médicale **121**–32
technicien informatique **167**–19, **182**–12
teindre les cheveux **33**–D
teinture pour bois **181**–24
teinturerie **128**–2

télé (téléviseur) **56**–6
télé à grand écran **50**–14
télé réalité **236**–6
télécommande universelle **234**–9
télécopieur **183**–21
TÉLÉPHONE **14**–15
téléphone cellulaire **14**–8
téléphone intelligent **15**–27
téléphone public **15**–25, **129**–23
téléphone sans fil **15**–24
téléphoniste **14**–21
télescope **205**–23
télé-vendeur (vendeuse) **169**–60
téléviseur portable **234**–8
télévision à écran plat **234**–7
témoin **141**–11
température **13**, **110**–8
tempête de grêle **13**–21
tempête de neige **13**–23
tempête de poussière **13**–19
tennis **228**–15
tennis de table **228**–14
tensiomètre **118**–9
tente **226**–10
tentures **56**–16
tenue chirurgicale **93**–38
tenue d'hôpital **93**–31
termes historiques **199**
termites **63**–22
terrain **5**–2
terrain de base-ball **224**–1
terrain de basket **229**–7
terrain de jeux **50**–3
terrasse **240**–2
Terre **205**–3
terreau **208**–2
tête **104**–1
tête de laitue **69**–32
tête de lit **58**–10
tétine **37**–2
thamnophis **213**–39
thé **81**–39
thé glacé **79**–12
théâtre **127**–23
théière **54**–17, **55**–16
thérapeute **115**–14
thérapeute occupationnel **168**–45
thérapie verbale **115**–13
thermomètre **118**–11
thon **71**–7, **72**–19, **212**–8
tibia **106**–21
tiers **17**–3
tiges **211**–9
tigre **217**–37
timbre **134**–23
tique **214**–27
tir à l'arc **228**–1

tirer des conclusions **195**–E
tirer le wagonnet **224**
tiroir **54**–23, **58**–2
tisane **81**–40
titre **133**–7, **133**–14, **190**–5
toasts **80**–4
toge **206**–8
toile **233**–17
toile de peintre **181**–54
toilettes **5**–9
toit **46**–1
toit coule **62**–3
tôle à biscuits **78**–27
tomates **69**–6
tomber **116**–O
tomber amoureux **40**–H
tomber en panne **162**–D
tomber en panne d'essence **162**–E
tondeuse à gazon **176**–6
tondre le gazon **176**–A
toque de chef **93**–28
tornade **145**–15
tortue **213**–43
tortue terrestre **213**–42
tôt **19**–22
total **27**–9
touche dièse **14**–7
touche étoile **14**–6
toucher **106**–E
toupie **180**–12
tour **127**–13, **196**–3
tourelle porte-objectif **194**–15
tourne-disque **234**–12
tourner à droite seulement **154**–7
tourner à droite sur Pine **155**–B
tourner à gauche sur Oak **155**–C
tournesol **211**–10
tournevis **180**–30
tournevis Philips **180**–31
tourniquet **152**–8
tousser **110**–A
tracteur **177**–9
traducteur (traductrice) **168**–35
traduire le mot **8**–C
train **150**–7
traire **177**–C
trait d'union **190**–20
traiteur **185**–16
trajet **155**
transcrire des notes **171**–C
transférer l'appel **171**–O
transfert **152**–5
transmission automatique **159**
transmission manuelle **159**
TRANSPORT PUBLIC **152**
travail avec un partenaire **8**
travailler **38**–K

travailler avec vos camarades
    de classe **8**
travailler en groupe **8**–I
travailler seul **10**–J
travailleur (travailleuse) **175**–3
travaux routiers **154**–16
traverser en dehors des passages
    pour piétons **128**–C
traverser la rue **128**–A
traverser la rue en courant **153**–G
traverser le tunnel **153**–K
trèfles **233**–32
treize **16**
treize colonies **198**–1
treizième **16**
tremblement de terre **144**–5
trench-coat **90**–21
trente **16**
trentième **16**
trépied **235**–25
très grand **96**–5
très grand lit à deux places **184**–15
très petit **96**–1
tresses africaines **33**–14
triangle **193**–32
tribunal **125**–13
tricot **88**–3, **91**–1
tricot de corps **91**–2
tricoter **233**–F
tricycle **224**–12
trier la lessive **101**–A
trigonométrie **192**–18
tripes **70**–8
triste **43**–19
triton **212**–26
trois **16**
trois fois par semaine **20**–24
troisième **16**
trombone **183**–31, **238**–10
trompe **217**–47
trompette **238**–11
tronc **210**–4
trottoir **53**–2, **129**–24
trousse de premiers
    soins **117**–1, **146**–18
trouver des idées **191**–F
trouver des réponses **8**–H
trouver des solutions **8**–H
trouver un abri **147**–H
trouver un emploi **40**–F
truelle **176**–10, **178**–13
truite **71**–1
t-shirt **86**–4
t-shirt propre **101**–16
t-shirt sale **101**–15
tsunami **145**–17
tuba **238**–12

tube de colle **232**–11
tube de dentifrice **74**–24
tubes **74**–12
tuile **178**–11
tulipe **211**–11
turbulence **161**–22
turquoise **24**–9
tuyau **181**–17
tuyau d'échappement **158**–15
tuyaux sont gelés **63**–16
types de film **237**
types de formation professionnelle **172**
types de matériaux **98**, **99**
types de mathématiques **192**
types de médicaments **113**
types de musique **237**
types de problèmes de santé **115**
types d'émissions télévisées **236**
un **16**
un dollar **26**–7
un milliard **16**
un million **16**
une fois par semaine **20**–22
une heure **18**–6
une heure cinq **18**–7
une heure dix **18**–8
une heure et demie **18**–11
une heure et quart **18**–9
une heure quarante **18**–12
une heure quarante-cinq **18**–13
une heure quinze **18**–9
une heure trente **18**–11
une heure vingt **18**–10
une pièce d'un dollar **26**–6
uni (couleur) **96**–19
uniforme **88**–10, **231**–16
unité centrale **196**–4
UNIVERS **205**
université **188**–7
Uranus **205**–7
URGENCES ET DÉSASTRES
  NATURELS **144–145**
URGENCES MÉDICALES **116**
usager de la bibliothèque **133**–3
usine **126**–3
USINE **175**
usine de vêtements **98**
USTENSILES DE CUISINE **78**
utiliser des ampoules
  écoénergétiques **219**–H
utiliser la ponctuation **190**–C
utiliser une caisse enregistreuse **170**–S
utiliser une carte de crédit **27**–B
utiliser une carte de débit **27**–C
utiliser une carte-cadeau **27**–E
vacances **22**–6
vache **215**–1

vague **225**–17
vague de chaleur **13**–13
vallée **204**–18
vandalisme **142**–1
vapeurs toxiques **179**–3
variable **192**–12
varicelle **111**–6
vase **55**–23
véhicule de camping **156**–10
véhicule utilitaire sport **156**–7
veilleuse **37**–27
veine **107**–37
vélo **129**–22, **151**–15
velours **99**–10
velours côtelé **99**–11
vendeur **94**–3
vendeur ambulant **129**–29
vendeur au détail **169**–53
vendeurs **84**–7
vendre des voitures **170**–K
vendredi **20**–13
VENTE-DÉBARRAS **102–103**
venteux **13**–18
ventilateur **55**–19
Vénus **205**–2
ver **212**–23
VERBES SE RAPPORTANT À DES
  SPORTS **230**
verdict **141**–14
verger **177**–10
vérifier l'eau, le gaz et
  l'électricité **147**–N
vérifier l'huile **157**–H
vérifier l'orthographe **197**–F
vérifier la prononciation **8**–D
vérifier les messages **171**–R
vérifier les sites d'emploi sur
  Internet **173**–D
vérifier son courriel **39**–W
vérifier son travail **10**–L
vérifier…la pression artérielle **118**–A
vérifier…le pouls **122**–A
vernis à ongles **109**–33
verre à eau **83**–22
verre à vin **83**–23
verre plein **23**–9
verre vide **23**–10
verres de contact **115**–8
verrou **51**–34
verrouillage des portes **159**–25
verrouiller vos portes **143**–E
verser la sauce à la cuiller **77**–F
verser l'eau **82**–C
vert **24**–5
vertébrés **194**–12
vésicule biliaire **107**–44
vessie **107**–46

veste **89**–14, **90**–8
veste de chef **93**–29
veste de cuir **90**–4
veste en duvet **90**–16
veste épaisse **97**–27
veste légère **97**–28
veston **89**–14
vêtements chauds **146**–6
vêtements de nuit **91**
vêtements de soirée **89**
vêtements de sport **89**
VÊTEMENTS DE TOUS LES JOURS **86–87**
vêtements de travail **88**
VÊTEMENTS DE TRAVAIL **92–93**
vêtements décontractés **88**
VÊTEMENTS DÉCONTRACTÉS, DE
  TRAVAIL ET DE SOIRÉE **88–89**
VÊTEMENTS SAISONNIERS **90**
vêtements usagés **102**–2
vétérinaire **169**–62
viande **66**–2
VIANDES ET VOLAILLES **70**
vice-président **138**–9
victime **142**–10
vide-ordures **51**–26
vider la poubelle **60**–L
vider la sécheuse **101**–E
vider le sèche-linge **101**–E
vigne **210**–22
vignette **136**–13
vignoble **177**–16
VIH (virus de l'immunodéficience
  humaine) **111**–17
vilain chien **23**–18
village **52**–3
ville **4**–7, **52**–1
vingt **16**
vingt dollars **26**–10
vingt et un **16**
vingt et unième **16**
vingt-cinq **16**
vingt-deux **16**
vingtième **16**
vingt-quatre **16**
vingt-trois **16**
violence des gangs **142**–4
violet **24**–8
violette **211**–23
violon **238**–6
violoncelle **238**–7
virgule **190**–14
vis à bois **180**–33
vis à métaux **180**–32
visage **106**
visière de sécurité **179**–12
visite chez le dentiste **119**

visiter des maisons **49**–H
vitamines **113**–17
vitre **178**–16
vitre est brisée **62**–5
vitrine **94**–5
vivre aux États-Unis pendant
  5 ans **140**–H
voie à sens unique **154**–3
voie de sortie **146**–3
voie ferrée **152**–14
voiles sèche-linge **101**–5
voilier **225**–3
voir **106**–A
voiture **150**–1
voiture de sport **156**–4
voiture hybride **156**–3
voiture urbaine **152**–20
voiture 2 portes **156**–2
voiture 4 portes **156**–1
VOITURES ET CAMIONS **156**
vol à l'étalage **142**–8
vol d'identité **142**–9
vol et agression **142**–11
vol retardé **161**–30
volaille **70**
volant **159**–26
volant de lit **58**–17
volley-ball **229**–14
vomir **110**–E
voter **140**–A
voyager **41**–P
vue laide **23**–22
vue magnifique **23**–21
water-polo **229**–15
webcaméra **196**–12
western **237**–15
xylophone **238**–15
yaourt **72**–22
yoga **122**–4
yogourt **72**–22
zèbre **217**–33
zéro **16**
zone d'embarquement **161**–9
zone de fouilles **160**–4
zone de jeu **130**–11
zone de test **136**–2
zone rurale **52**–4
zone urbaine **52**–1
zoom **235**–23

Research Bibliography

The authors and publisher wish to acknowledge the contribution of the following educators for their research on vocabulary development, which has helped inform the principals underlying OPD.

Burt, M., J. K. Peyton, and R. Adams. *Reading and Adult English Language Learners: A Review of the Research.* Washington, D.C.: Center for Applied Linguistics, 2003.

Coady, J. "Research on ESL/EFL Vocabulary Acquisition: Putting it in Context." In *Second Language Reading and Vocabulary Learning*, edited by T. Huckin, M. Haynes, and J. Coady. Norwood, NJ: Ablex, 1993.

de la Fuente, M. J. "Negotiation and Oral Acquisition of L2 Vocabulary: The Roles of Input and Output in the Receptive and Productive Acquisition of Words." *Studies in Second Language Acquisition* 24 (2002): 81–112.

DeCarrico, J. "Vocabulary learning and teaching." In *Teaching English as a Second or Foreign Language,* edited by M. Celcia-Murcia. 3rd ed. Boston: Heinle & Heinle, 2001.

Ellis, R. *The Study of Second Language Acquisition.* Oxford: Oxford University Press, 1994.

Folse, K. *Vocabulary Myths: Applying Second Language Research to Classroom Teaching.* Ann Arbor, MI: University of Michigan Press, 2004.

Gairns, R. and S. Redman. *Working with Words: A Guide to Teaching and Learning Vocabulary.* Cambridge: Cambridge University Press, 1986.

Gass, S. M. and M.J.A. Torres. "Attention When?: An Investigation Of The Ordering Effect Of Input And Interaction." *Studies in Second Language Acquisition* 27 (Mar 2005): 1–31.

Henriksen, Birgit. "Three Dimensions of Vocabulary Development." *Studies in Second Language Acquisition* 21 (1999): 303–317.

Koprowski, Mark. "Investigating the Usefulness of Lexical Phrases in Contemporary Coursebooks." *Oxford ELT Journal* 59(4) (2005): 322–32.

McCrostie, James. "Examining Learner Vocabulary Notebooks." *Oxford ELT Journal* 61 (July 2007): 246–55.

Nation, P. *Learning Vocabulary in Another Language.* Cambridge: Cambridge University Press, 2001.

National Center for ESL Literacy Education Staff. *Adult English Language Instruction in the 21ˢᵗ Century.* Washington, D.C.: Center for Applied Linguistics, 2003.

National Reading Panel. *Teaching Children to Read: An Evidenced-Based Assessment of the Scientific Research Literature on Reading and its Implications on Reading Instruction.* 2000. http://www.nationalreadingpanel.org/Publications/summary.htm/.

Newton, J. "Options for Vocabulary Learning Through Communication Tasks." *Oxford ELT Journal* 55(1) (2001): 30–37.

Prince, P. "Second Language Vocabulary Learning: The Role of Context Versus Translations as a Function of Proficiency." *Modern Language Journal* 80(4) (1996): 478-93.

Savage, K. L., ed. *Teacher Training Through Video - ESL Techniques: Early Production.* White Plains, NY: Longman Publishing Group, 1992.

Schmitt, N. *Vocabulary in Language Teaching.* Cambridge: Cambridge University Press, 2000.

Smith, C. B. *Vocabulary Instruction and Reading Comprehension.* Bloomington, IN: ERIC Clearinghouse on Reading English and Communication, 1997.

Wood, K. and J. Josefina Tinajero. "Using Pictures to Teach Content to Second Language Learners." *Middle School Journal* 33 (2002): 47–51.